# An Eyewitness History of

# SLAVERY IN AMERICA

## From Colonial Times to the Civil War

Dorothy Schneider
and
Carl J. Schneider

An imprint of Facts On File, Inc.

*For Elizabeth Knappman*

**An Eyewitness History of Slavery in America**



Checkmark Books
An imprint of Facts On File, Inc.
132 West 31st Street
New York NY 10001

**Library of Congress Cataloging-in-Publication Data**
Schneider, Dorothy.
Slavery in America: from colonial times to the Civil War/Dorothy Schneider and Carl J. Schneider.
p. cm.—(Eyewitness history series)
Includes bibliographical references and index.
ISBN 0-8160-3863-5 (acid-free paper) (hardcover) — ISBN 0-8160-4403-1 (acid-free paper) (pbk).
1. Slavery—United States—History. I. Schneider, Carl J. II. Title.
III. Series.
E441.S36 2000
973'.0496—dc21 99-054779

Checkmark Books are available at special discounts when purchased in bulk quantities for businesses, associations, institutions or sales promotions. Please call our Special Sales Department in New York at (212) 967-8800 or (800) 322-8755.

You can find Facts On File on the World Wide Web at
http://www.factsonfile.com

Text design by Joan M. Toro

Jacket design by Cathy Rincon

## Note on Photos

Many of the illustrations and photographs used in this book are old, historical images. The quality of the prints is not always up to modern standards, as in many cases the originals are from glass negatives or the originals are damaged. The content of the illustrations, however, made their inclusion important despite problems in reproduction.

Printed in the United States of America.

VB FOF 10 9 8 7 6 5 4 3
(pbk) 10 9 8 7 6 5 4 3 2

This book is printed on acid-free paper.

# CONTENTS

# PREFACE

This book sets forth eyewitness accounts of the birth, tragic life, and death of slavery in North America during the time of that "peculiar institution." Clippings from contemporary newspapers, documents, diaries, letters, speeches, and memoirs give readers a sense of the era, as if they were hearing anecdotes, reading newspapers, debating the pros and cons of what to do about the problems slavery generated, and being bewildered by conflicting arguments and evidence.

What motivated the actions described in the record? Did a master free a slave because of humanitarian impulses or to avoid supporting her when she could no longer earn her keep? Did he insist on selling his slaves in family lots for the sake of their happiness or to sell off weaker slaves to maximize profit? Did a state actually enforce the laws it passed? Did it tax the slave trade to hinder the traffic, get revenue from it, shut out Africans for fear of insurrections, prevent the depreciation of the value of slaves, or to encourage the immigration of white workers? Was a slave's narrative of his suffering and flight altered when he dictated it to a white "editor"? Was a mistress's entry in her diary of a wish to get rid of all her husband's slaves a statement of principle, or was she only having a bad day?

Eyewitness accounts of history are like flashes of lightning on a landscape—what you see is brilliantly illuminated but lacks context. To provide a sense of the whole, we give you overviews in the chronologies, and historical backgrounds in the chapter introductions. The lengthy excerpts from documents in appendix A flesh out the eyewitness accounts and offer insight into the attitudes of the time. They are especially instructive about what people took for granted and how little they questioned the morality of slavery. The biographies in appendix B more fully describe the participants. The glossary in appendix C defines terms specific to slavery.

As a whole, the book lays before the reader the complexities and extent of slavery and the wide differences in the ways people experienced and reacted to this terrible institution—an institution so evil, so corrupting, and so opposed to human happiness and dignity that no kindness or goodwill within it could ease the trauma it inflicted or lessen the damage that continues to plague our society.

# ACKNOWLEDGMENTS

Along the way, many people have helped us. Mary Attridge procured innumerable books for us through interlibrary loan. The staff of the Library of Congress Photographic Division steered us through their impressive collection, and we owe gratitude also to the librarians at the Schomburg Center and other sections of the New York Public Library system. We thank the libraries of Connecticut College and Wesleyan University for use of their scholarly journals and government publications. Prof. Robert Forbes of Yale and Adam Rothman of Columbia lent us their expertise on sources. Anne Penniman generously allowed us to quote from her family letters. Frances Cloud Taylor helped us understand the workings of the Underground Railroad in southern Pennsylvania; we are most grateful to her artist husband, Tom Taylor, for permission to use his pictures. Wanda Castner, Sam Connor, Jean Pieretti, Richard Tietjen, and Kay Tucker called our attention to materials we might otherwise have missed. We particularly thank our agent, Elizabeth Knappman, who originally conceived of the book, and our editor, Nicole Bowen, who is always a joy to work with.

# 1

# The West Coast of Africa 1441–1866

## The Historical Context

### *Slavery in Africa*

Africans knew slavery long before Europeans sailed to their shores. They enslaved their enemies and their criminals. Sometimes they enslaved debtors. Like all other peoples in the long history of slavery, Africans enslaved outsiders—members of other tribes, or erring members of their own tribes.

Slavery became an integral part of Africa's economic organization. According to slave trader Theodore Canot, "The financial genius of Africa, instead of devising bank-notes or the precious metals as a circulating medium, has from time immemorial declared that a human creature—the true representative and embodiment of labour, is the most valuable article on earth."[1] The slave system was both entrenched and widespread. No one will ever know how many Africans owned how many slaves in the early days, but scholars speculate that in the late 19th century, a majority of Africans were either slaves or the descendants of slaves.[2]

For several reasons, however, most slaves in Africa did not experience anything like the horrors that beset Africans shipped to Europe and the New World as slaves. Why not? Most important, African slaves and their masters shared the same race. Their masters might consider them inferiors—but not by birth, only in that they had been outwitted or overpowered. Second, enslavement did not mean entering a completely alien world. Most slaves and captors looked much alike, spoke similar languages, practiced similar ceremonies, ate similar food, and had similar traditions and customs. Third, many slaves in Africa were criminals or prisoners of war—though sometimes a tribe raided its neighbors to take slaves, and sometimes kidnappers stole children from other tribes to enslave them. Fourth, slaves often lived and worked under conditions quite like those of their captors, though they lacked status in the tribe.

For many slavery was simply a matter of degree. African societies were organized into kinship groups headed by leaders to whom members owed respect and labor. Many slaves were simply more dependent and of lower class than other tribespeople.[3] What mattered was not freedom, but belonging, and slavery offered a new belonging, assimilation into a new group—albeit at first in a lowly position. A slave might be educated along with the free members of the tribe. When a male slave married, he might move away from his master's compound, work his own fields in exchange for fixed dues, accumulate property, and even take another wife. Eventually he could expect manumission and kinship within the tribe. Concubines were freed when they bore children, and their children along with them.

About 1755 Gustavus Vassa reminisced about slavery in his boyhood home in Guinea: "Those prisoners which were not sold or redeemed, we kept as slaves; but how different was their condition from that of the slaves in the West Indies! With us, they do no more work than other members of the same community, even their master; their food, clothing, and lodging were nearly the same as theirs (except that they were not permitted to eat with those who were free-born); and there was scarce any other difference between them, than a superior degree of importance which the head of a family possesses in our state, and that authority which, as such, he exercises over every part of his household. Some of these slaves have even slaves under them as their own property, and for their own use."[4]

Not every African-owned slave was so gently treated. Slave experiences differed from time to time, from place to place, and, of course, from master to master. Different tribes employed slaves in different ways. Some used them as human sacrifices. Tribes who forced them to work gold mines or hunt elephants for ivory inflicted hardships unknown to those of tribes who existed on agriculture. Tribes who owned just a few might assimilate them in one to three generations. Among the larger tribes, where slaves lived farther from their masters, the process might take longer.

Slavery by its very nature invited corruption. A desire for more slaves could cause a war or prompt kidnappings. The system might tempt a tribesman to enslave his unwanted wife or his enemy within the tribe.

From the 15th to the 19th centuries, as the slave trade with Europeans (and eventually Americans) burgeoned, the system of African slavery increased in scope and brutality. "Kings used imports to buy captives . . ., and the goods allowed monarchs to build up larger retinues of slave retainers, more isolated and more dependent" than slaves had formerly been.[5] As their numbers increased, the slaves were more removed from their masters. Hope for assimilation into the new tribes faded. Slaves were often sold and had to begin again and again as helpless aliens in new communities, which expected harder work. Africans sold their own slaves to white traders.[6] African slaveowners, no longer thinking in terms of assimilation into the tribe, were apt to treat slaves more severely and exploit them more.

As the African economy changed, slaveowners employed their slaves in newly developed occupations. Slaves labored not only on plantations and in mines but also as porters for merchants; as company boatmen; and as staff for administrative, military, and commercial establishments. Arabs sent them on expeditions to the African interior to obtain ivory, from which only a few returned. Reporter Henry Morton Stanley wrote about long lines of half-starved slaves, bound with chains that would have restrained an elephant, on marches that would last for months. Those who lagged behind were killed, he said, and estimated that every pound of ivory cost the life of a man, woman or child in Africa. Missionary David Livingstone estimated that not more than one in five slaves who started to the coast reached their destination, not more than one in nine on some routes.[7]

## *Europeans Command the Slave Trade*

By the time Europeans arrived, Africans were long accustomed to foreign invasions for slaves. As Henrietta Buckmaster writes, "The progenitors of the first American slaves were those who had fought against the battering tides of Romans, Persians, Byzantines, and at last with their empires weakened, had seen their civilization slowly collapse before the Moslems who brought religion and slave traders from the East, and the Christians who brought religion and slave traders from the West."[8]

So it came as nothing out of the ordinary when, in the mid-15th century, the Portuguese began transporting slaves out of Africa. Other European nations soon competed in the profitable enterprise, with the Dutch and the English successively dominating it. At first the Europeans raided unarmed family groups or undefended villages, until they realized that it was easier to bargain for slaves and gold with Africans in villages near the west coast. Soon they began planting small settlements, defended by forts, at intervals along that coast, usually near the mouth of a river or on an island. These *slave factories* they manned with *factors*—agents—who negotiated with the Africans, encouraging them to organize slave-hunting expeditions.

Beginning in 1636 Americans too sent ships to Africa, at first to transport slaves to the British colonies in North America but later more often on a triangular voyage. They sailed from, say, Rhode Island to Africa with a cargo of rum to trade for slaves; on the next leg, the Middle Passage, they carried slaves to the Caribbean islands and South America; finally, they returned home with molasses, with which to make more rum. American traders were never major players, even in their busiest years (from 1783 to 1807), carrying no more than a sixth of the slaves transported. Nonetheless, between 1725 and 1807 more than nine hundred vessels left Rhode Island ports (whence most American slaving voyages began) for the west coast of Africa, carrying away more than 105,000 slaves.[9]

The enterprise was dangerous and economically risky but, if it succeeded, lucrative. The explorations of the 15th, 16th, and 17th centuries were opening up huge new parts of the world. To European and later American ears, these areas cried out for labor to develop and exploit their riches. Africa itself discouraged development: Its fragmentation into tiny tribes made it difficult to conquer; its terrain and climate were hazardous, a "graveyard for white men"; and it already produced in plenty what Europeans wanted—gold, ivory, and spices. But the Caribbean islands and the vast continents of South and North America could be developed only with thousands, millions, of laborers.

As slaves the Indians of the Americas ultimately proved unsatisfactory to the Europeans. Also, with their familiarity with the countryside, they were capable of frequent escapes. In contrast, Africans were adapted by birth to subtropical weather that often killed and always disheartened European laborers. Many whites thought them divinely created for just such a purpose.

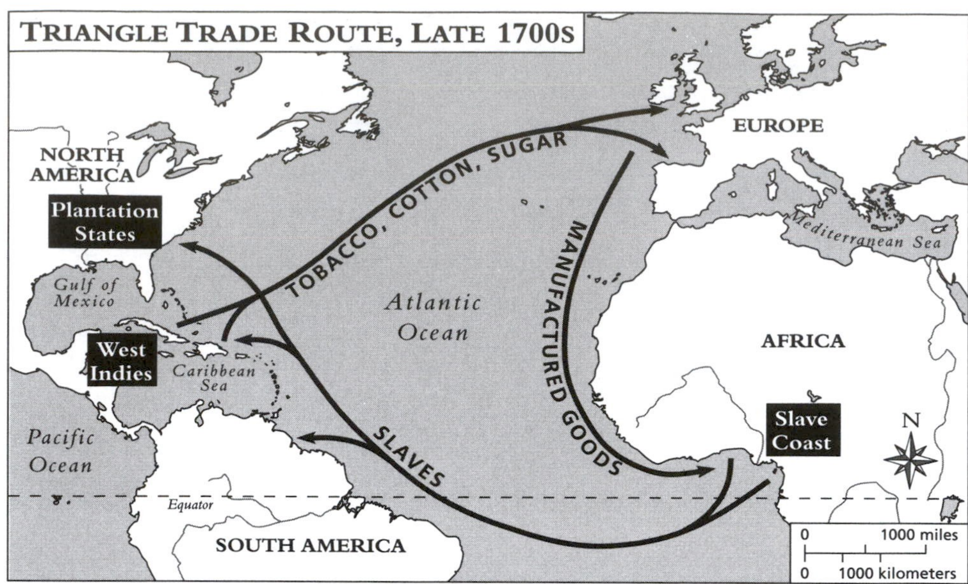


In one variation of the triangle trade route, ships carried tobacco, cotton, or sugar from America to Europe, where they were traded for manufactured goods. These goods were then taken to Africa and traded for slaves. On the Middle Passage, the slaves were brought to South America, the Caribbean, and the plantation states. (© *Facts On File, Inc.)*

Few whites thought of slavery as a moral issue. What history they knew of ancient Greece and Rome taught them that slavery had long been commonplace, ordinary, the way things were. Europeans too dwelt in societies organized into hierarchies, in which the rich and powerful exercised harsh control over the workers whose labor supported their lives of privilege and luxury. Greed, racial prejudice, and the conviction that Africans lived in ignorance and misery combined to justify—or excuse—making them slaves.

Then too, Christians were determined to convert the world to Christianity, with or without the consent of the "converted." Churchmen from the pope down gave slavery license, sometimes representing it as a crusade against pagans. God, they said, intended for some men to rule over other people, and slavery offered an opportunity to convert thousands. So church fathers approved mass baptisms of slaves just before they embarked on the ships that would take them forever from their homelands.

If anyone questioned slavery, answers lay ready to hand. What with all the slaves that Africans owned, traders could persuade themselves that they were merely moving Africans from one master to another. They argued that the slave trade disposed of Africa's criminals and that without it Africans would slay their prisoners of war. Once on the plantations of the New World, they said, slaves would live better than in Africa, for masters would take good care of their property.[10]

So the trade flourished, and nations competed for it. Portuguese, Dutch, and English rulers tried to shut out even their own subjects from the trade, bestowing rights to it on favored relatives and merchants. The Portuguese, the Dutch West India Company, and the British Royal African Company in turn maintained on the African coast the slave factories from which most slave ship captains bought their slaves.

## *Africans in the Slave Trade*

Over the centuries, the slave trade grew increasingly sophisticated, commercializing the African economy. By 1788 slave ship's doctor Alexander Falconbridge reported, "The slaves are bought by the black traders at fairs, which are held for that purpose, at the distance of upwards of two hundred miles from the sea coast; and these fairs are said to be supplied from an interior part of the country. Many negroes . . . have asserted that they have travelled during the revolution of several moons [months] . . . before they have reached the places where they were purchased by the black traders. At these fairs, which are held at uncertain periods, but generally every six weeks, several thousands are frequently exposed to sale who had been collected from all parts of the country for a very considerable distance round."[11]

Free Africans as a group by no means objected. Enslavement did not offend their moral sense. As far as the record shows, though nobody wanted to *be* enslaved, only a few Africans protested against the slave trade. A good many Africans engaged in the commerce, especially the most powerful leaders. The shrewdest of their followers also profited in the flourishing new economy. European goods created new markets with eager buyers.

These goods dazzled many Africans. Slaver John Barbot in 1746 described their uses: "The broad linen serves to adorn themselves, and their dead men's sepulchers within; they also make clouts [patches] thereof. The narrow cloth to press palm-oil; in old sheets they wrap themselves at night from head to foot. The copper basins to wash and shave, the Scotch pans serve in lieu of butcher's tubs, when they kill hogs or sheep; from the iron bars the smiths forge out all their weapons and country and household tools and utensils. Of friezes and perpetuanas [cloth] they make girts [belts] four fingers broad, to wear about the waist, and hang their sword, dagger, knife, and purse of money or gold, which they commonly thrust between the girdle and their body. They break Venice coral into four or five parts, which afterwards they mould into any form, on whetstones, and make strings or necklaces, which yield a considerable profit. . . . Muskets, firelocks, and cutlaces they use in war. Brandy is most commonly spent at their feasts. . . . With tallow they anoint their bodies from head to toe, and even use it to shave their beards, instead of soap.[12]

The trade not only commercialized the economy and changed the everyday life of Africans but also corrupted them. Allegedly, African kings sold wives with whom they were angry; African parents sold children whom they could not feed; and desperate Africans sold themselves. Barbot told of a son who defeated his royal father's efforts to sell him by first selling his father—only to be met on his return home by fellow tribesmen who took his profits and sold *him*.[13]

To meet the demands of the market for more slaves, traders stirred up wars among tribes. Tribal kings began to look for excuses to attack. Kidnapping turned into a business. As Zachary Macaulay wrote in his journal in 1793, "If a child, for instance, is devoured by one of these animals [leopards], the [local African] King, glad of an opportunity, immediately brings a palaver against [accuses] the people of the town to which the child belongs. It avails them nothing to protest their innocence or to give assurance of their total ignorance of what became of the child. They are found guilty of making away with the child, on which the whole town, men, women and children are condemned to slavery."[14]

Soon enough, Africans learned the ways of sharp trading. The Europeans cheated them, and they cheated the Europeans. As John Newton wrote, "Not an article that is capable of diminution or adulteration, is delivered genuine, or entire [by the European traders to the Africans]. The spirits are lowered [diluted] by water. False heads are put into the kegs that contain the gun powder; so that, though the keg appears large there is not more powder in it, than in a much smaller one. The linen and cotton cloths are opened, and two or three yards, according to the length of the piece, cut off, not from the end, but out of the middle, where it is not readily noticed. The natives are cheated, in the number, weight, measure, or quality of what they purchase, in every possible way; and by habit and emulation, a marvellous dexterity is acquired in these practices. And thus the natives, in their turn, in proportion to their commerce with the Europeans, and (I am sorry to add) particularly with the English, become jealous, insidious, and revengeful."[16]

The Africans learned fast. African kings demanded gifts and the payment of customs—at a fee always subject to negotiation. They changed their minds about agreements that Europeans regarded as firm contracts. They plucked gray hairs from slaves' heads and beards to make them look younger and greased their bodies to make them appear healthy. They dallied in producing slaves, causing delays of weeks or even months and thereby driving up the price. Kings and courtiers traded on their own accounts, insisting that their own slaves be bought first, regardless of quality. At the factories, African employees cheated and stole from the foreign captains.

Even a tribal chieftain could see only what was happening in his own small sphere. How was he to evaluate the enormous impact of the trade on the culture and economy of the continent? Only a few highly placed Africans came to deplore the effects of slavery—the change to a market economy, the tribal wars stimulated by the demand for more slaves, and the forcible removal of so many people. Most African kings, their visions restricted to the horizons of their own small tribes, simply went with the flow, profiting as best they could from the growing commerce. European goods opened up new opportunities for upward mobility for other Africans, too.

## *Europeans in the Slave Trade*

Far more lethal than its inhabitants, the continent of Africa itself took its revenge on the white intruders. They had undertaken to invade an alien environment. Against its hardships and diseases their guns offered no protection. Factors who had to live in Africa almost all died from one tropical illness or another, after a few years usually passed in drunkenness and disgust. They might enjoy their black mistresses, whom it cost almost nothing to maintain and whom they could dismiss at will, but in most ways their lives were miserable. They lived in factories built among stinking swamps, attacked by mosquitoes that robbed them of sleep unless they drugged themselves with opium or liquor. Their employers suspected them of cheating and trading for their own profit and charged them sky-high prices for supplies. Sometimes companies enforced an almost military discipline among their factors, fining, imprisoning, even flogging them.

For obvious reasons, competent agents were hard to find. "Lament you may [about our poor bookkeeping] without you send over people fitting to doe it," one factor wrote the Royal African Company, "for what by sickness & mortallity in this damn'd cursed country we have hardly any People that are able to put penn to paper that understand anything."[17] But William Bosman thought the rapid turnover a good thing: "[I]f men lived here as long as in Europe, 'twould be less worth while to come hither, and a man would be obliged to wait too long before he got a good post, without which nobody will easily return rich from Guinea. . . . [T]he money we get here is indeed hardly enough acquired: if you consider we stake our best pledge, that is our lives, in order to [get] it."[18]

The factories were vulnerable to attack. The Europeans had to depend heavily on the goodwill of African kings and their own abilities to persuade Africans that their presence was a good thing. As agent Thomas Thurloe wrote to the Royal African Company in 1679, "[A] factor once settled ashoare is absolutely under the command of the king of the country where he lives, and liable for the least displeasure to loose all the goods he hath in his possession with danger also of his life. Besides in case of mortallity it is very difficult to recover of the negroes any thing that was in the hands of the deceased."[19] Occasionally a European going about his business in the slave trade was seized and held for ransom or as hostage by an African king, or simply enslaved.

The slaver captains who sailed to Africa found themselves adrift in an alien world, in which only the most astute and lucky flourished. They did not know the territory, they did not know the languages, and they did not know the culture. Their job was to buy slaves and get out as cheaply and as quickly as possible. Time was of the essence, for the sake of their own health and that of the slaves, on whom their profits depended. Sometimes their ships could not sail home because so many of the crews had died.

Everyone and everything seemed to conspire to delay the slavers. When they sailed up the rivers to capture, entice, or buy slaves, tribesmen attacked, burned, and sank them. In 1759, the *Gazette and Country Journal* of South Carolina reported, "[A sloop commanded by Captain Ingledieu, while] slaving up the River *Gambia,* was attacked by a number of Natives, about the 27th of *February* last, and made a good Defence; but the Captain finding himself desperately wounded, and likely to be overcome, rather than fall into the Hands of such merciless Wretches, when about 80 Negroes had boarded his Vessel, discharged a Pistol into his Magazine, and blew her up." Though some captains continued to venture inland, others decided that they might be better off to pay higher prices to the established factors on the coast.

The slaver captain had to depend on Africans at every turn. When he arrived with his trading goods, he did not dare leave them unguarded on the beach. He had to hire an African "captain of the sand" to watch over them until he could hire other Africans to transport them inside the fort. When he bought slaves, he had to employ a "captain of the slaves" to get them to the beach. Then he had to house them somewhere until he could complete his cargo. He learned that if he loaded immediately the slaves he first bought, he ran the risk of having them jump overboard. If he kept them in chains, too many of them inconveniently sickened and died. So he arranged to send his early purchases to barracoons (holding pens) in the forts, to be guarded and fed by Africans under a "captain of the trunk." If he did not find enough slaves for sale on the coast, he might have to entrust trading goods to Africans who would make excursions inland to buy slaves for him. When he finally completed his purchases of slaves and the supplies to maintain them and his crew on the way home, he had to hire canoes manned by Africans to transport them all to his ship. He had to negotiate prices and rely on local judgment as to when the tides and weather permitted loading. Even if these "canoo-men" upset their rafts and lost his goods, the captain dared not reproach them, for fear of reprisals.

Meanwhile, his employers at home were pressuring him to buy only choice slaves, from preferred areas. Some especially wanted Africans from the Gold Coast (modern Ghana) and Whydah (modern Ouidah, in Benin), reputedly hard workers in their own countries and able to endure even the hardships of sugar plantations. Slave buyers in the Caribbean islands and South America wanted male slaves 15 to 25 years old. In North America, particularly as the 18th century progressed, purchasers also wanted women of childbearing age. The owners set their captains no easy task, for much of the time they had to take what slaves they could get.

The competition for slaves made the task so much the harder, complained a Rhode Island slaver in 1736 at a spot where seven ships carrying rum to barter for slaves lay at anchor: "We are ready to devour one another, for our case is desperate. . . . I have got on board sixty-one slaves and upwards of thirty ounces of gold, and have got thirteen or fourteen hogsheads of rum yet

Most of the Africans who were captured and enslaved came from the West African coastal region that stretches from modern Senegal in the north to Angola in the south. *(© Facts On File, Inc.)*

left on board, the trade is so very dull it is actually enough to make a man crazy."[20]. The dishonest dealings of one slave captain might bring the wrath of Africans down on others, cutting off the supply of slaves altogether.

The trading companies also struggled to fight off competition. The Portuguese, having established some influence with the Africans through their missionaries, tried to stop the Africans from selling slaves to the English and Dutch on the grounds that these "heretics"—Protestants—would not provide the slaves with a good Roman Catholic environment. All the nationalities involved tried to force or cajole African kings into giving them exclusive trade rights. Thus the agent recorded in the journal of Fort William in Whydah: "*Oct. 10, 1717* . . . Sent Bank and Fettera [junior factors?] to Dedoon to open a correspondence [negotiations] with that King for Trade, that I may have all his Slaves. Such as are Good for my Self and the rest to sell for him to Shipps. But withall they are to stipulate it so that he may [not] demand more for his Slaves than the common price nor ask better Goods than the Capt'ns at Town give. What Advantages I propose to him is that if I have any Goods better than another which none else shall happen to have, he may take them all unto his hands and by that means be able to command them at what price he pleases. . . . I sent him a wickered Bottle [of] Sperits."[21]

Just as the companies tried to control the source of supply, so they did with the market. For years they vied for the *asiento,* by which the king of Spain awarded the exclusive privilege of selling slaves to the Spanish-controlled islands in the New World. Once it was attained, there followed complaints from the Spanish buyers: the numbers of slaves shipped were inadequate to the needs of the plantations, and the slaves themselves were unsatisfactory, sickly, weakened by their long voyage—and overpriced. The companies countered with accusations of bad faith by the Spanish after the slaves reached their ports and complained that they were not even making a profit. Besides, they said, the Spanish had not paid the agreed-upon price.

The companies constantly sought trade advantages, as in 1686 when the British Royal African Company complained to the British government that the Dutch had bought up all the *perpetuanas,* a hard-wearing fabric then much in demand among the Africans. But they also went beyond mere complaints. In 1784 the British African Committee ordered the governor at Cape Coast Castle, "[Do not] suffer the Americans or any foreign ships to trade on that part of the coast under your command on any account whatsoever . . . and if any such attempt should be made . . . you are to fire on such ships and use every other means in your power to force them off the coast."[22]

When at the end of the 17th century the Royal African Company was finally forced to offer its facilities to other English traders, its leaders repeatedly grieved that these independent traders were not paying the company fees high enough to cover their expenses and that in their ignorance of trading they were driving up the prices of slaves. Besides, the company said, these boorish new traders misbehaved: "The [Royal African] Company further complain that the Natives grow insolent, and are encouraged by other Traders to insult the Companys Forts, and bring them out of Difficultys on purpose to obtein Bribes, to compose Differences of their own creating. . . . [T]his they say appears by Letters from their Factors, and particularly that one of the Separate Traders, having made a bargain for some Negroes carryed them to Barbadoes without paying for the same, but that the Company in order to secure the Peace and a friendly correspondence with the Negroe kings, sent to Barbadoes and bought the said Negroes and returned them to the king from whome they were so taken."[23]

The path to profitability never did run smooth.

## *As for the Slaves . . .*

Slaves brought from inland had endured not only the shock of capture but also the dreadful experience of coffles (slave processions), in which they traveled sometimes for hundreds of miles over periods of six months or more, enduring poor food, cold, and new diseases. Large numbers of the old and very young died on the trail, and all were weakened. Whether they walked or traveled downriver in canoes, they suffered and sickened. In 1789, trader William James testified before a British Privy Council committee: "Twenty or Thirty Canoes, sometimes more and sometimes less, come down at a Time. In each Canoe may be Twenty or Thirty Slaves. The Arms of some of them are tied behind their Backs with Twigs, Canes, Grass Rope, or other Ligaments of the Country; and if they happen to be stronger than common, they are pinioned above the Knee also. In this Situation they are thrown into the Bottom of the Canoe, where they lie in great Pain, and often almost covered with Water."[24] Slaves provided by the Foola tribe were invariably infested with worms, reported Dr. Thomas Winterbottom: "This probably arises from the very scanty and wretched diet which they are fed in the *path,* as they term the journey [from

A coffle from the interior to the coast *(Library of Congress)*

Branding slaves after purchase (*Blake,* History of Slavery and the Slave Trade)

the place of capture to the coast], and which, from the distance they are brought inland, often lasts for many weeks, at the same time that their strength is further reduced by the heavy loads they are obliged to carry."[25]

In the barracoons on the coast, thousands more died as a result of bad food, impure water, and disregard for sanitation. "[I]t was common lore that . . . slavers simply disposed of the sick or the slow or any other sort of disabled captive whose handicap threatened to spoil the value of others. Since everyone knew that delays in the ports of embarkation would bring on epidemics among slaves penned up in cramped barracoons for long periods of time, it became the practice to kill the first slaves to show symptoms of diseases feared to be contagious. Slavers simply could not release infected slaves alive, for fear of spreading contagion even more widely and to avoid loosing freedmen capable of inciting revolts. Instead, they murdered a few in order to save the costs of mortality among the remainder."[26] The bodies of the dead, partially burned or thrown out to be eaten by hyenas, surrounded the barracoons.

Some authorities argue that the causes of slave mortality at sea lay not so much in conditions on the Middle Passage as in the slaves' state of health when they were loaded onto the ships. Slaves coming aboard were already weakened by the natural catastrophes of drought, famine, and epidemics; by the rough treatment imposed by their captors; by the delays in loading; or by the unfavorable seasons for shipping, all of which were part of the whole haphazard system.

Dazed by capture, the coffle, and the barracoons, these men, women, and children were thrust into ugly, strange, inhumanly crowded environments, far from home. Few understood the languages of their oppressors. Worse still, they often could not understand one another, so many different tribes did they represent, and so far from home had they been driven. The branding to which the traders subjected them (to prevent the substitution of inferior slaves) further humiliated people used to signifying status by tattooing their skins. Many of them had never seen an ocean or a large ship.

What had happened to their familiar world? What was to become of them?

## *Outlawing the International Slave Trade*

In the 18th century, new ideas about the rights of individuals inspired the American and French revolutions and lowered the level of comfort with slavery among Europeans and Americans. Throughout the slave-trade era, a few voices had been raised against it. In the early 17th century, for instance, Englishman Richard Jobson had replied to an African trader who offered him slaves, "I made answer we were a people, who did not deal in any such commodities, neither did we buy or sell one another, or any that had our owne shapes; he [the African trader] seemed to marvel much at it, and told me it was the only merchandise they carried down into the country, where they fetch all their salt, and that they were sold there to white men who earnestly desired them."[27] Now such words began to prick the consciences of the many.

In 1807 both England and the United States outlawed the international slave trade. Over the next decades other nations followed suit. England at once began to enforce the ban on the high seas. Constrained by space and its greater dependence on commerce than on agriculture, Britain had never relied much on slaves for its home labor force, although thousands had labored, suffered, and died on its New World plantations. Now the rapidly growing Industrial Revolution offered more profits than the slave trade. As British slave trader James Jones wrote to the president of the Board of Trade in 1788, "[The slave trade] is a very uncertain and precarious trade, and if there is not a probable prospect of considerable Profit no Man of Property who hath any Knowledge of it would embark or continue in it. . . . It is a lottery, in which some men have made large fortunes, chiefly by being their own insurers, while others follow the example of a few lucky adventurers and lose money by it."[28]

In the United States, the situation was more complex, with sharp divisions between northern commercial and southern agricultural interests. But it was clearly inconsistent to argue passionately for the liberties of white American men on the grounds of human equality and inalienable rights, and at the same time to enslave blacks. Moreover, the United States, unlike other slaveholding nations, had discovered the advantages of relying on natural increase for its supply of slaves. Encouraged or enforced reproduction among black women provided cheaper and better slaves than importation of slaves weakened by conditions in Africa and on the Middle Passage, and who had to be taught the ways of plantation life. During the American Revolution, the North American colonies had suspended the slave trade, and all had gone well. Besides, the prohibition on the importation of new slaves increased the value of those already there. All in all, the country could get along without an international slave trade.

However, not everyone in the country agreed. Sporadic efforts to legalize the international trade again were made until 1865. Many American ships and entrepreneurs participated in an extensive illegal trade throughout that period. Certainly the insecure young nation had little interest in spending money to suppress it; for the most part, the United States made only token efforts to enforce the ban.

Slave ships of several nations—notoriously the Portuguese—continued to smuggle slaves, concocting ruses to defy England's powerful navy. Ships of other nations often flew an American flag because the United States did not allow other nations to board its vessels. Slavers often carried several flags, shifting them according to those of their pursuers.

Even when the British or American navy captured slave ships, their owners and captains were seldom convicted. No one knows the size of this illegal trade, but it evidently was substantial. For whatever the evidence of a pirate and smuggler is worth, slaver captain Richard Drake wrote, "Out of seventy-two thousand slaves received and transshipped from Rio Basso, in five years, we lost only eight thousand and this included deaths by accidental drowning, suicides, and a smallpox epidemic in 1811, when our barracoons were crowded and when we shipped 30,000 blacks to Brazil and the West Indies."[29] Even when a slaver was convicted, American judges often imposed light sentences. Of six captains and owners tried under the slave-trade acts in 1839, for instance, one escaped while free on bail, two forfeited bail, two were acquitted, and one's case was discontinued.

But throughout the Western world, antislavery sentiment was strengthening, and the demand for slaves was decreasing. In their homeland, Africans were confused and often dismayed by the ending of the slave trade. As Malcolm Cowley commented, "Slavery was their economic system and their justice. Their work was performed by slaves; their wealth was established by slaves; their gunpowder, rum, and cotton were purchased by slaves. At law, slavery was almost the only punishment for crime."[30] King Holiday of Bonny considered the ending of the trade a blow to African culture: "[Our] country fash [custom is to have] too much wife and too much child. God made we black and we no sabby book [can't read], and we no havy head for make ship for send we bad mans for more country [to send our rogues to another country], and we law is, 'spose some of we child go bad and we no can sell 'em [if slave-trading stops], we father must kill dem own child; and 'spose trade be done we force kill too much child the same way."[31]

All in all, scholars estimate, Africa exported some 11,698,000 people to the New World during the Atlantic slave trade. Some 7 percent of these came to what is now the United States.[32]

## Chronicle of Events

**1441**
For the first time, Europeans (Portuguese) carry slaves from Africa to European markets.

**1448**
By this date, Portugal has established a regular trade in slaves between Africa and the Iberian Peninsula.

**1452**
Pope Nicholas V gives King Alfonso general powers to conquer and enslave pagans (non-Christians).

**1481**
Portugal makes the Guinea trade a monopoly of the ruling house.

**1482**
Portugal establishes the trading post El Mina (Elmina) on the Gold Coast of Africa.

**1494**
The Treaty of Tordesillas, approved by the pope, gives Portugal a trading monopoly in Africa, Asia, and Brazil and Spain a monopoly in the rest of the New World.

**1502**
Ovando's instructions as governor of Hispaniola allow him to transport black slaves born in Spain or Portugal ("slaves born in the power of Christians"). Later in the year, Ovando requests that no more slaves be sent to Hispaniola, because they encourage the Indians to revolt. Queen Isabella of Spain so orders.

**1505**
The flow of slaves into Hispaniola resumes after the death of Queen Isabella of Spain.

**1506**
Ovando, governor of Hispaniola, is ordered to expel all Berber and pagan slaves.

**1510**
Regular slave traffic from Spain to Hispaniola begins, after King Ferdinand of Spain orders 250 "Christian" blacks sent out.

**1513**
King Ferdinand of Spain begins to sell licenses to import blacks.

**1518**
King Charles grants to Lorenzo de Gomenot, governor of Bresa, the right to ship 4,000 blacks to Hispaniola.

**1526**
Lucas Vásquez de Ayllón, a Spanish explorer, tries to establish a settlement in the region of North America that later becomes the Carolinas; he brings in slaves who escape and live with the Indians.

**1538**
Henry Eynger and William Sailler are licensed to carry 4,000 blacks to the Indies in four years, during which they will hold a monopoly. But the Council of the Indies soon annuls the contract, because they deliver "inferior" blacks.

**1552**
Fernando Ochoa is granted a seven-year monopoly under which to deliver 23,000 slaves to Hispaniola, but the contract is never fulfilled and is eventually annulled.

**1554**
M. Gainsh takes five Africans to England.

**1562**
Englishman Sir John Hawkins begins his first slave-trading voyage to Africa.

**1564**
Sir John Hawkins begins his second slave-trading voyage to Africa.

**1567**
Sir John Hawkins begins his third slave-trading voyage to Africa.

**1580**
The crowns of Portugal and Spain are united, with Portugal supplying slaves for the Spanish empire in the New World.

**1592**
The Dutch end the two-century-old Portuguese monopoly of trade in Africa.

**1595**
Spaniard Gomez Reynal receives the first *asiento* (the privilege of supplying slaves to Spain's colonies) from Spain to deliver 38,250 slaves to Hispaniola in nine years, at the rate of 4,250 annually, of whom 3,500 must be landed alive; the slaves must be fresh from Africa, including no mulattoes, mestizos, Turks, or Moors.

**1600**
On Reynal's death, the *asiento* is transferred to Portuguese Juan Rodrigues Coutinho and extended to 1609.

**1611**
The Dutch build Fort Nassau at Mouri, on the Gold Coast.

**1618**
James I of England creates the Company of Adventurers of London to trade in Africa.

**1621**
The Dutch establish the Dutch West India Company, which secures a monopoly of African trade and the right to develop the Dutch possessions in the New World, thus gaining control over the source of slaves and the market for them.

**1631**
The English establish their first important African settlement on the Gold Coast, at Kormantin.

**1633**
The French grant a Rouen company a monopoly of trade between Cape Verde and the Gambia.

**1636**
Massachusetts shipbuilders launch the slaver *Desire*—and the American slave trade begins.

**1637**
The Dutch take El Mina, the strongest Portuguese fortification on the African coast.

**1640**
With the revolt of Portugal, Philip IV of Spain forbids all commerce with Portugal, including the slave trade.

Diagram of a slave factory on the West Coast of Africa (*Library of Congress*)

The introduction of sugarcane into English and later into French islands in the Caribbean increases the demand for black slaves.

**1641–1648**
The Portuguese and the Dutch engage in war in Angola.

**1642**
Louis XIII of France authorizes the entry of France into the slave trade, "for the good of their [the slaves'] souls."

**1645**
Two Bostonians sail for Guinea to trade for blacks. On their return, they are arrested; the General Court directs that the blacks be returned to Africa.

**1657**
England's East India Company receives a new charter.

**1659**
Virginia encourages the international slave trade by reducing import duties for merchants who bring black slaves into the colony.

**1663**
The Company of Royal Adventurers in England is chartered to trade with Africa.

**1664–1667**
The English and the Dutch battle in West Africa.

**1664**
The French become established in northwest Africa, particularly in Senegal. They form the Compagnie des Indes Occidentales to trade in Africa from Cape Verde to the Cape of Good Hope.

**1666**
The French begin to grant licenses to trade in Africa to private traders.

**1672–1678**
The French and the Dutch fight in West Africa.

**1672**
Charles II of England charters the Royal African Company, giving it a monopoly to trade in British territories in Africa.

The French form the Compagnie du Senegal, abandoning the Compagnie des Indes Occidentales. The new company soon fails, as do subsequent monopolistic companies.

**1688**
England's Glorious Revolution nullifies all charters, forcing the Royal African Company to struggle for legal sanction of its monopoly on African trade.

**1689**
The British parliament issues a new charter to the Royal African Company, without a monopoly, and grants permission for all Englishmen, including those resident in America, to trade with Africa.

The Royal African Company contracts to supply the Spanish West Indies with slaves.

**1698**
The British throw open trade in West Africa to all subjects of the Crown.

**1703**
Massachusetts imposes a duty of four pounds upon every black imported.

**1713**
England gains the *asiento,* the privilege of supplying 4,800 slaves a year for 30 years to Spain's American colonies.

**1752**
The British dissolve the Royal African Company.

**1775–1783**
The American Revolution drastically cuts the international slave trade.

**1807–1808**
England and the United States prohibit the international slave trade, but the trade continues to operate illegally, despite the vigorous efforts of the Royal Navy to stop it.

**1811**
In Africa, slave trading begins to shift northward.

**1844**
British commissioners in Sierra Leone inform the British foreign secretary that they "believe that the

slave trade is increasing, and that it is conducted perhaps more systematically than it has ever been hitherto . . . notwithstanding the stringent methods adopted by the British Commodore with the powerful force under his command" to stop it.

**1845**
Cornelius E. Driscoll boasts in a Rio de Janeiro bar that in New York City for a thousand dollars he can get any man off a charge of slave smuggling.

**1858**
Thomas Savage, U.S. vice-consul in Cuba, reports that his efforts to stop the use of the American flag for slave trading have aroused hostility.

**1860**
Richard Drake publishes *Revelations of a Slave Smuggler.*

## EYEWITNESS TESTIMONY

### *Enslavement: Capture*

*Slaves.* Those sold by the Blacks are for the most part prisoners of war, taken either in fight, or pursuit, or in the incursions they make into their enemies territories; others stolen away by their own countrymen; and some there are, who will sell their own children, kindred, or neighbors. . . .

The kings are so absolute, that upon any slight pretence of offences committed by their subjects, they order them to be sold for slaves, without regard to rank, or possession. . . .

Abundance of little Blacks of both sexes are also stolen away by their neighbours, when found abroad on the roads, or in the woods; or else in the Cougans, or corn-fields, at the time of the year, when their parents keep them there all day, to scare away the devouring small birds, that come to feed on the millet. . . .

In times of dearth and famine, abundance of those people will sell themselves, for a maintenance, and to prevent starving. . . .

*Slave trader John Barbot's description of Guinea, in Donnan,* Slave Trade Documents *1:284–85.*

In February, 1730, Job's father hearing of an English ship at Gambia River, sent him with two servants to attend him, to sell two Negroes, and to buy paper, and some other necessaries; but desired him not to venture over the river, because the country of Mandingoes, who are enemies to the people of Fanta lies on the other side. . . . [Job disobeyed.] He crossed the River Gambia, and disposed of his Negroes for some cows. As he was returning home, he stopped for some refreshment at the house of an old acquaintance; and the weather being hot, he hung up his arms in the house, while he refreshed himself. . . . [A] company of the Mandingoes, who live upon plunder, passing by at that time, and observing him unarmed, rushed in . . . at a back door, and pinioned Job, before he could get to his arms, together with his interpreter, who is a slave in Maryland still. They then shaved their heads and beards, which Job and his man resented as the highest indignity; tho' the Mandingoes meant no more by it, than to make them appear like slaves taken in war. On the 27th of February, 1730, they carried them to Captain Pike at Gambia, who purchased them. . . .

*Bluett,* Life of Job, *in* Africa Remembered, *39–41.*

When a trader wants slaves, he applies to a chief for them, and tempts him with his wares. . . . Accordingly, he falls on his neighbours, and a desperate battle ensues. If he prevails, and takes prisoners, he gratifies his avarice by selling them; but, if his party be vanquished, and he falls into the hands of the enemy, he is put to death: for, as he has been known to foment their quarrels, it is thought dangerous to let him survive. . . . I was once a witness to a battle in our common. . . . There were many women as well as men on both sides; among others my mother was there, and armed with a broad sword. After fighting for a considerable time with great fury, and many had been killed, our people obtained the victory. . . . The spoils were divided according to the merit of the warriors. Those prisoners which were not sold or redeemed we kept as slaves. . . .

*African Olaudah Equiano, about 1755, in* Africa Remembered, *77–78.*

On the Windward Coast another mode of procuring slaves is pursued; that is, by *boating,* a mode that is very destructive to the crews of the ships. The sailors . . . go in boats up the rivers, seeking for negroes among the villages situated on the banks of these streams. But this method is very slow and not always effectual. After being absent from the ship during a fortnight or three weeks, they sometimes return with only from eight to twelve negroes. . . .

*Ship's doctor Alexander Falconbridge,* Account of the Slave Trade (1788), *in Dow,* Slave Ships, *136.*

[A] captain of a Liverpool ship had got, as a temporary mistress, a girl from the king of Sierra Leone, and instead of returning her on shore on leaving the coast, as is usually done, he took her away with him. Of this the king complained to Sir George Young very heavily, calling this action *panyaring* [kidnapping] by the whites.

*Testimony before a committee of the British House of Commons, 1790, in Blake,* Slavery and the Slave Trade, *112.*

Granny Judith said that in Africa they had very few pretty things, and that they had no red colors in

European traders haggling with dealers (*Library of Congress*)

cloth, in fact they had no cloth at all. Some strangers with pale faces come one day and drapped [dropped] a small piece of red flannel down on the ground. All the black folks grabbed for it. Then a larger piece was drapped a little further on, and on until the river was reached. Then a large piece was drapped in the river and on the other side. They was led on, each one trying to git a piece as it was drapped. Finally, when the ship was reached, they drapped large pieces on the plank and up into the ship till they got as many blacks on board as they wanted. Then the gate was chained up, and they could not get back. That is the way Granny Judith say they got her to America.

*Ex-slave Richard Jones, in* Lay My Burden Down, *57.*

I was born in Africa, several hundred miles up the Gambia river. . . .

For some years [before 1821], war had been carried on in my Eyo Country, which was always attended with much devastation and bloodshed; the women, such men as had surrendered or were caught, with the children, were taken captives. The enemies who carried on these wars were principally the Oyo Mahomedans, with whom my country abounds—with the Foulahs, and such foreign slaves as had escaped . . . , joined together, making a formidable force of about 20,000, who annoyed the whole country. They had no other employment but selling slaves to the Spaniards and Portuguese on the coast.

. . . [A] rumour was spread in the town that the enemies had approached with intentions of hostility. It was not long after that when they had almost surrounded the town to prevent any escape of the inhabitants; the town being rudely fortified with a wooden fence, about four miles in circumference, containing about 12,000 inhabitants, which would produce 3,000 fighting men. . . . [T]he enemies entered the town, after about three or four hours' resistance. Here a most sorrowful imaginable scene was to be witnessed—women, some with three, four, or six children clinging to their arms, with the infants on their backs, and such luggage as they could carry on their heads, running as fast as they could through prickly shrubs, which, hooking their . . . loads, drew them from the heads of the bearers. . . . While they were endeavouring to disentangle themselves from the ropy shrubs, they were overtaken and caught by the enemies with a noose or loop thrown over the neck of every individual, to be led in the manner of goats tied together, under the drove of one man. In many cases a family was violently divided between three or four enemies, who each led his away, to see one another no more. Your humble servant was thus caught—with his mother, two sisters (one an infant about ten months old), and a cousin.

*Samuel Crowther, Anglican bishop of West Africa, describing events of 1821, letter of February 22, 1837, in* Africa Remembered, *299–301.*

## *Enslavement: The Path to the Coast*

All those slaves the Portuguese cause to be bought, by their *Pombeiros,* a hundred and fifty or two hundred leagues up the country, whence they bring them down to the seacoasts. . . .

These slaves, called *Pombeiros,* have other slaves under them, sometimes a hundred, or a hundred and fifty, who carry the commodities [trading goods] on their heads up into the country.

Sometimes these *Pombeiros* stay out a whole year, and then bring back with them four, five and six hundred new slaves. Some of the faithfullest remain often there, sending what slaves they buy to their masters, who return them other commodities to trade with anew.

*James Barbot,* A Voyage to New Calabar, *1699, quoted in Rawley,* Transatlantic Slave Trade, *35.*

[S]ome slaves are also brought to these Blacks, from very remote inland countries, by way of trade, and sold for things of very inconsiderable value; but these slaves are generally poor and weak, by reason of the barbarous usage they have had in traveling so far, being continually beaten, and almost famish'd; so inhuman are the Blacks to one another. . . .

*Slave trader John Barbot's description of Guinea, in Donnan,* Slave Trade Documents *1:284–85.*

Here they [our kidnappers] tied our hands, and continued to carry us as far as they could, till night came on. . . .

[I traveled far and was sold several times; sometimes I had hopes of being adopted.] From the time I left my own nation, I always found somebody that understood me till I came to the sea coast. The languages of different nations did not totally differ, nor were they so copious as those of the Europeans, particularly the English. They were therefore, easily learned; and, while I was journeying thus through Africa, I acquired two or three different tongues . . . I never met with any ill treatment, or saw any offered to their slaves, except tying them, when necessary, to keep them from running away. . . .

. . . At last I came to the banks of a large river. . . . I had never before seen any water larger than a pond or a rivulet; and my surprise was mingled with no small fear when I was put into one of these canoes, and we began to paddle and move along the river. We continued going on thus till night, and when we came to land, and made fires on the banks, each family by themselves; some dragged their canoes on shore, others stayed and cooked in theirs, and laid in them all night. . . . [A]t the end of six or seven months after I had been kidnapped, I arrived at the sea coast. . . .

*Gustavus Vassa, describing events of 1756, in* Great Slave Narratives, *21–26.*

In the march, a scouting party was detached from the main army. To the leader of this party I was made waiter, having to carry his gun, etc. . . . The distance they had now brought me was about four hundred miles. All the march I had very hard tasks imposed on me, which I must perform on pain of punishment. I was obliged to carry on my head a large flat stone used for grinding our corn, weighing . . . as much as twenty-five pounds; besides victuals, mat and cooking utensils. . . . Though I was pretty large and stout of my age, yet these burdens were very grievous to me, being only six years and a half old.

*Venture,* Life and Adventures *(1798), 8–10.*

### *Enslavement: The Barracoons*

As the slaves come down to Fida from the inland country, they are put into a booth, or prison, built for that purpose, near the beach, all of them together; and when the Europeans are to receive them, they are brought out into a large plain, where the surgeons examine every part of every one of them, to the smallest member, men and women being all stark naked. Such as are allowed good and sound, are set on one side, and the others by themselves; which slaves so rejected are there called Mackrons, being above thirty five years of age, or defective in their limbs, eyes or teeth; or grown grey, or that have the venereal disease, or any other imperfection. These being so set aside, each of the others, which have passed as good, is marked on the breast, with a red-hot iron, imprinting the mark of the French, English, or Dutch companies, that so each nation may distinguish their own, and to prevent their being chang'd by the natives for worse, as they are apt to do. In this particular, care is taken that the women, as tenderest, be not burnt too hard.

The branded slaves, after this, are returned to their former booth. . . . There they continue sometimes ten or fifteen days, till the sea is still enough to send them aboard; for very often it continues too boisterous for so long a time. . . . Before they enter the canoes, or come out of the booth, their former Black masters strip them of every rag they have, without distinction of men or women; to supply which, in orderly ships, each of them as they come aboard is allowed a piece of canvas, to wrap around their waist. . . .

*Slave trader John Barbot's description of Guinea, in Donnan,* Slave Trade Documents *1:293.*

The traders frequently beat the negroes which are objected to by the captains and use them with great severity. It matters not whether they are refused on account of age, illness, deformity or for any other reason. At New Calabar, in particular, the traders have frequently been known to put them to death. Instances have happened at that place, when negroes have been objected to, that the traders have dropped their canoes under the stern of the vessel and instantly beheaded them in sight of the captain.

*Ship's doctor Alexander Falconbridge,* Account of the Slave Trade *(1788), in Dow,* Slave Ships, *141.*

[In the barracoon] our slaves had two meals a day, one in the morning consisting of boiled yams and the other in the afternoon of boiled horse-beans and slabber sauce poured over each. This sauce was made of chunks of old Irish beef and rotten salt fish stewed to rags and well seasoned with cayenne pepper. The negroes were so fond of it that they would pick out the little bits and share them out; but they didn't like the horse-beans.

The brandy that we brought out for trade was very good but the darkies thought it was not hot enough and didn't bite—as they called it; therefore, out of every puncheon we pumped out a third of the brandy, put in half a bucketful of cayenne pepper, then filled it up with water and in a few days it was hot enough for Old Nick, himself, and when they came to taste it, thinking that it was from another cask, they would say, "Ah, he bite."

*Mariner William Richardson, in Dow,* Slave Ships, *13.*

### *The Slaving Establishment in Africa: European Factors and Factories*

[1672] Account of the Limits and Trade of the Royal African Company. . . . they took Cabo-Corso Castle from the Dutch, which is now their chief port and place of trade, with 100 English, besides slaves, and the residence of their Agent-General, who furnishes thence all their under-factories with goods, and receives from them gold, elephants' teeth and slaves. Near Cabo-Corso is the great Dutch castle called the Mina; and more leewardly the company have another factory at Acra for gold. Their next factory is at Ardra for slaves only, which are there very plentiful; next follows Benin with a factory where they procure great quantities of cotton cloths to sell at Cabo-Corso and on the gold Coast; then more leewardly lies the Bite, whither many ships are sent to trade at New and Old Calabar for slaves and teeth, which are there to be had in great plenty, and also in the rivers Cameroons and Gaboons which are near, but no factories, those places being very unhealthy.

*Donnan,* Slave Trade Documents *1:192–93.*

[The Dutch Castle of El Mina, a fort that protects trading rights,] is justly famous for beauty and strength, having no equal on all the coasts of Guinea. . . . The general's lodgings are above in the castle, the ascent to which is up to a large white and black stone staircase, defended at the top by two small brass guns, and four pattareroes, of the same metal, bearing upon the Place of Arms; and a *corps de garde* pretty large, next to which is a great hall of small arms of several sorts, as an arsenal; through which and by a by-passage you enter a fine long gallery, all wainscotted, at each end of which are large glass windows, and through it is the way to the general's lodgings, consisting of several good chambers and offices along the ramparts.

*French description of 1682, in Pope-Hennessy,* Sins of the Fathers, *73.*

Our factory . . . stands low near the marshes, which renders it a very unhealthy place to live in; the white men the African Company send there, seldom returning to tell their tale; 'tis compass'd round with a mud wall, about six foot high, and on the south-side is the gate; within is a large yard, a mud thatch'd house, where the factor lives, with the white men; also a storehouse, a trunk for slaves, and a place where they bury their dead white men, call'd, very improperly, the hog-yard; there is also a good forge and some other small houses: To the east are two small flankers of mud, with a few popular-guns and harquebusses, which serve more to terrify the poor ignorant negroes than to do any execution. . . .

The factory is about 200 yards in circumference, and a most wretched place to live in, by reason of the swamps adjacent, whence proceed noisome stinks. . . . This factory, feared as 'tis, proved very beneficial to us, by housing our goods which came ashore late, and could not arrive at the king's town where I kept my warehouse, ere it was dark, when they would be very incident [vulnerable] to be pilfer'd by the negro porters which carry them, at which they are most exquisite [skilled]; for in the day-time they would steal the cowries [shells used as money], altho' our white men that attended the goods from the marine watched them, they having instruments like wedges, made on purpose to force asunder the staves of the barrels, that contain'd the cowries, whereby the shells dropt out; and when any of our seamen . . . came near . . . , they would take out their machine, and the staves would insensibly close again, so that no hole did appear, having always their wives and children running by them to carry off the plunder; which with all our threats and complaints made to the king, we could not prevent, tho' we often beat them cruelly. . . .

*Capt. Thomas Phillips, journal of the 1693 voyage of the* Hannibal, *in Dow,* Slave Ships, *58–60.*

We find you are sensible how much wee have suffered in our trade by Ned Barter's promoting his own private interest before our common good, his dealing with & giving encouragement to other traders, which gives us good assurance you will not only use all endeavours to seize his person & estate in order to make satisfaction for the murther he has committed and the damage he has done, but will be very carefull that none of our servants under your care shall practise the like for the future.

*Royal African Company, 1702, to Cape Coast, in Davies,* Royal African Company, *280–81.*

The factory consists of merchants, factors, writers, miners, artificers and soldiers; and excepting the first rank, who are the Council for managing affairs, are all of them together a company of white negroes, who are entirely resigned to the Governor's commands, according to the strictest rules of discipline and subjection; are punished (garrison fashion) on several defaults, with mulcts [fines], confinement, the dungeon, drubbing or the wooden horse; and for enduring this, they have each of them a salary sufficient to buy canky [fermented corn], palm-oil and a little fish to keep them from starving. . . . When a man is too sober to run in debt, there are arts of mismanagement or loss of goods under his care, to be charged or wanting. Thus they are all liable to be mulcted for drunkenness, swearing, neglects and lying out of the Castle, even for not going to church (such is their piety); and thus by various arbitrary methods their service is secured *durante bene placito* [at the pleasure of the company].

*Ship's surgeon John Atkins,* Voyage to Guinea, *1737, quoted in Pope-Hennessy,* Sins of the Fathers, *162–63.*

[We conclude] that a private trade, directly tending to Monopoly, hath been set up and established by the Governors and Chiefs of the Forts in *Africa;* and that this private Trade, so injurious to the Interests of the Public, hath been carried on by them in Conjunction with Persons at Home, some One or more of whom have at the same Time been Members of the

Committee [the Company of Merchants Trading to Africa] above Mentioned.

*The British Board of Trade to the House of Commons, 1777, in Coughtry,* Notorious Triangle, *127.*

## *The Slaving Establishment in Africa: Africans and the Slave Trade*

[Your merchants] are taking every day our natives, sons of the land and sons of our noblemen and vassals and our relatives . . . *it is our will that in these kingdoms there should not be any trade of slaves.* . . .

*Congo chief Afonso I, 1526, letter to the king of Portugal, in Rawley,* Transatlantic Slave Trade, *29.*

The [African] gold mines were seven in number. . . . The kings have slaves whom they put in the mines and to whom they gave wives, and the wives they [the slaves] take with them; and they bear and rear children in these mines. The kings, also, furnish them with food and drink.

*16th-century Portuguese traveler, in Reynolds,* African Slavery, *8.*

[At Whydah the] queen is about fifty years old, as black as jet, but very corpulent. . . . She received us very kindly, and made her attendants dance after their manner before us. She was very free of her kisses to Mr. Buckerige, whom she seemed much to esteem. . . . We presented her with an anchor of brandy each, and some hands of tobacco, which she received with abundance of thanks and satisfaction, and so bid her good night. She was so extremely civil before we parted, to offer each of us a bed-fellow of her young maids of honour while we continued there, but we modestly declined. . . .

*Capt. Thomas Phillips, journal of the 1693 voyage of the* Hannibal, *in Dow,* Slave Ships, *56.*

. . . Pepprell, the king's brother, made us a discourse, as from the king, importing, He was sorry we would not accept of his proposals; that it was not his fault, he having a great esteem and regard for the Whites. . . . That what he so earnestly insisted on thirteen bars for male, and ten for female slaves, came from the country people holding up the price of slaves at their inland markets, seeing so many large ships resort to Bandy for them. . . .

We had again a long discourse with the king, and Pepprell his brother, concerning the rates of our goods and his customs. This Pepprell being a sharp blade, and a mighty talking black, perpetually making sly objections against something or other, and teazing us for this or that dassy, or present, as well as for drams, etc. it were to be wish'd, that such a one as he were out of the way, to facilitate trade.

We fill'd them with drams of brandy and bowls of punch till night, at such a rate, that they all, being about fourteen with the king, had such loud clamorous tattling and discourses among themselves, as were hardly to be endured.

Thus, with much patience, all our matters were adjusted indifferently, after their way, who are not very scrupulous to find excuses or objections, for not keeping literally to any verbal contract; for they have not the art of reading and writing, and therefore we are forced to stand to their agreement, which often is no longer than they think fit to hold it themselves. . . .

*John Barbot,* A Voyage to New Calabar, *1699, in Donnan,* Slave Trade Documents *1:430–34.*

The king of Almammy had, in the year 1787,. . . enacted a law, that no slave whatever should be marched through his territories. At this time, several French vessels lay at anchor in the Senegal, waiting for slaves. The route of the black traders in consequence of this edict of the king, was stopped, and the slaves carried to other parts. The French . . . remonstrated with the king. He was, however, very unpropitious to their representations, for he returned the presents that had been sent him by the Senegal company . . .; declaring, at the same time, that all the riches of that company should not divert him from his design. In this situation of affairs, the French were obliged to have recourse to . . . the Moors . . . , [who] set off in parties to surprise the unoffending negroes, and to carry among them all the calamities of War.

*C. B. Waldstrom, in Donnan,* Slave Trade Documents *2:600.*

[A black trader at Bonny] informed me that only one ship had been there for three years during that period [the American Revolution]. . . . Upon further inquiring of my black acquaintance what was the consequence of this decay of their trade, he shrugged up his shoulders and answered, *"Only making us traders poorer and obliging us to work for our maintenance."* One of these black merchants being informed that a particular set of people, called Quakers, were for abolishing the trade, he said *it was a very bad thing, as they should then be reduced to the same state they were in during the war, when, through poverty, they were obliged to dig the ground and plant yams. . . .*

*Alexander Falconbridge,* Account of the Slave Trade *(1788), in Dow,* Slave Ships, *136.*

There is a famous Smart—named Gumbu Smart. Historically, they say he was born in a northern province, the Bombali district, and lived from 1750 to 1820. He was captured when he was a young boy. The story goes that he had killed a brother of his, and he ran away from his village, where he was then caught by slave bounty hunters. He was sold to the factors at Bunce island. . . . [Because the white factors thought him intelligent,] Smart was sent out with goods to purchase slaves. And because he realized what he was doing, he bought a lot of his countrymen, the Loko people, and he kept them and he built up a formidable force. He got enough power to control an area of the country around the town of Rokon.

*Smart's descendant Peter Karefa-Smart, in Ball,* Slaves, *422–23.*

## *The Slaving Establishment in Africa: Europeans and Americans in the Slave Trade*

*The voyage made by M. John Hawkins Esquire, and afterward knight,. . . begun in An. Dom. 1564.*

. . . In this place [near Cape Verde and the mouth of the Sierra Leone River] the two shippes riding, the two Barkes, with their boates, went into an Island of the Sapies, called La Formio, to see if they could take any of them, and there landed to the number of 80 in armour, and espying certaine made to them, but they fled in such order into the woods, that it booted them not to follow: so going on their way forward till they came to a river, while they could not passe over, they espied on the other side two men, who with their bowes and arrowes shot terribly at them. Whereupon we discharged certaine harquebuzes to them againe, but the ignorant people . . . knewe not the danger thereof: but used a marveilous crying in their flight with leaping and turning their tayles, that it was most strange to see, and gave us great pleasure to beholde them. At the last, one being hurt with a harquebuz upon the thigh, looked upon his wound and wist [knew] not howe it came, because hee could not see the pellet. Here master Hawkins perceiving no good to be done amongst them, because we could not finde their townes, and also not knowing how to goe into Rio Grande, for want of a Pilote, . . . and finding so many sholes, feared with our great ships to goe in, and therefore departed. . . .

*Hakluyt,* Principal Navigations, *in Donnan,* Slave Trade Documents *1:47–57.*

[The slave trade is] indeed the best Traffick the Kingdom [of Great Britain] hath, as it doth occasionally give so vast an Employment to our People both by Sea and Land. . . . [The African trade is] a Trade of the most Advantage to this kingdom of any we drive, and as it were all profit. . . . [The African and West Indian trades are] the most profitable of any we drive, and [I] do joyn them together because of their dependence on each other.

*John Cary, 1695, quoted in Rawley,* Transatlantic Slave Trade, *173–74.*

And first having monopolized all the Coast of Africa . . . Which vast Tract of Coast is lockt up from none but the Subjects of England, but, in a manner, free to all strangers, as French, Dutch, Portuguese, Danes, and Hamburghers. . . .

. . . [T]he Royal Company . . . oppress their Fellow-Subjects, by taking their Ships, imprisoning and starving their Seamen, illegally condemning the said Shipps and Goods without any Jury, and converting the said Ships and Goods to their own use.

To this, add the Injuries committed upon those persons which miserably fall under their power, as the breaking open their Chests, and rifling their Writings, concealing and hiding their Books of Accompts. . . . If after such Cruelties they escape with their Lives to return home, which few do, by reason of the barbarous usage of their persons by the Agents of the Company aforesaid, who have often declared, That they will shew more mercy to a Turk, than to an Interloper, as they term those of the King's Subjects which Trade upon the Coast of Africa without their Licence. . . .

*Anonymous 1690 pamphlet of complaints against the Royal African Company, in Donnan,* Slave Trade Documents *1:377–380.*

Health inspection of slaves before boarding *(Blake,* History of Slavery and the Slave Trade)

It is scarce possible to conceive what a Number of English Vessels this Permission [the end of the Royal African Company's monopoly in 1698] brought to the [Gambia] and what Confusion it occasioned in the Trade. Each Captain out-bidding the other to get the sooner loaded, the Price of Negros at Jilfray rose to forty Bars a head; so that the Mercadores or Mandingo Merchants would no longer sell their Slaves either at Barakonda, or Guioches, to the French or England Company for the usual Price of fifteen or seventeen Bars, but chose to come down the River, tempted by the great Profits made, which sufficiently compensated their Trouble. By this Means the Servants of the French and English Companies were forced to sit idle, and wait patiently to see the Issue of this ruinous Commerce. Between January and June, 1698, these separate Traders exported no fewer than three thousand six hundred Slaves, by which Means they overstocked the Country with more Goods than they could consume in some Years.

*Astley,* Voyages and Travels, *2:78, in Donnan,* Slave Trade Documents *1:429–30, n 3.*

The Prussian general receiv'd us at his fort very civilly, but told us, he had no occasion for any of our goods; the trade being every where on that coast, at a stand, as well by reason of the vast number of interlopers and other trading ships, as for the wars among the natives, and especially that which the English and Dutch had occasion'd on account of a black king the English had murder'd. . . .

*John Barbot,* A Voyage to New Calabar, *1699, in Donnan,* Slave Trade Documents *1:430.*

Liverpool, 14 April, 1762.

Capn Ambrose Lace,

Sir.—You being Master of the ship *Marquis of Granby,* . . . ready to sail for Africa, America, and back to Liverpoole, the Cargoe we have shipd on Board . . . we consign you for sale, For which you are to have the usual Commission of 4 in 104 on the Gross Sales, and your Doctor, Mr. Lawson, 12d. per Head on all the slaves sold, and we give you these our orders. . . . We . . . Recommend your keeping a good Look out that you may be Prepaird against an attack, and should you be Fortunate enough to take any vessell or vessells From the enemy, we recommend your sending them Home or to Cork . . . , and on your arrival at Old Callebar if one or more ships be there you will observe to make an agreement with the Master or Masters so as not to advance the Price on each other. . . . [P]ray mind to be very Choice in your Slaves. Buy no Distemperd or old Ones, But such as will answer at the Place of Sale and stand the Passage. . . . The Privilege we allow you is as Follows: yourself ten Slaves, your first mate Two, and your Doctor Two, which is all we allow except two or three Hundred wt of screveloes amongst your Officers, but no Teeth [ivory].

*Instructions from the ship's owners, in Dow,* Slave Ships, *93–95.*

[Captain Saltonstall of the Boston slaver *Commerce* in trying to persuade the Fantes to break their exclusive trade treaty with the English] used every argument to inflame the minds of the Blacks, and instill into them that spirit of Republican freedom and independence, which they [the Americans] through rebellion have established for themselves.

*Gov. Morgue of Cape Coast Castle, 1783, in Coughtry,* Notorious Triangle, *115.*

On the arrival of the ships at Bonny and New Calabar, it is customary for them to . . . begin to build what they denominate a *house.* . . . . The design of this house is to secure those on board from the heat of the sun . . . and from the wind and rain . . . , [but] The slight texture of the mats admits both the wind and the rain, . . . [and] increases the heat of the ship to a very pernicious degree, especially between decks. The increased warmth occasioned by this means, together with the smoke produced from the green mangrove (the usual firewood) which, for want of a current of air to carry it off, collects and infects every part of the ship, render a vessel during its stay here very unhealthy. The smoke also, by its acrimonious quality, often produces inflammations in the eyes which terminates sometime in the loss of sight.

Another purpose for which these temporary houses are erected is to prevent the purchased negroes from leaping overboard.

*Ship's doctor Alexander Falconbridge,* Account of the Slave Trade *(1788), in Dow,* Slave Ships, *133–34.*

This trip we cast anchor in a small river not far from the American colony of Liberia and our captain took me ashore with his first mate and a dozen of the crew, all of us well armed and sober. We had several breakers of rum with us, as a "dash" [present] for the negro chief, King Boatswain, a half-Christian black, and spent the day feasting in his village. When night came he summoned several hundred of his warriors and we sallied out against a tribe of blacks called Queahs. We came upon them while all were asleep and burnt their bamboo huts and made a general slaughter. The men and women were massacred and the boys and girls driven to the river where they were soon transferred to the *Gloria*'s bowels.

The next day Captain Ruiz invited king Boatswain to a big banquet on board the brig. The old fellow was sick but his son came with over two hundred of his principal men. We had abundance of rum and tobacco, the former, thanks to my medical skill, heavily drugged with laudanum. Before night we had every darkey under hatches and were off with a flying jib. Our entire cargo cost no more than the "dash" given to the savage chief.

*Richard Drake,* Revelations of a Slave Smuggler *(1860), in Dow,* Slave Ships, *242–43.*

## *The Slaving Establishment in Africa: Christendom in the Slave Trade*

[We ask] that leave be given to them to bring over heathen negroes, of the kind of which we have already experience. . . . Your Highness may believe that if this is permitted it will be very advantageous for the future of the settlers of these islands, and for the royal revenue; as also for the Indians your vassals, who will be cared for and eased in their work, and can better cultivate their souls' welfare, and will increase in numbers.

*Petition from the Jeronimite Fathers to the King of Spain, about 1518, in Donnan,* Slave Trade Documents *1:15–16. They sought an exception to the king's edict that only Christian slaves could be shipped.*

Almost everybody is convinced that the conversion of these barbarians is not to be achieved through love, but only after they have been subdued by force of arms and become vassals of Our Lord the King [of Portugal].

*Jesuit missionary writing from Angola, 1575, in* Portuguese Seaborne Empire, *101.*

Your Reverence writes me that you would like to know whether the negroes who are sent to your parts have been legally captured. . . . I think your Reverence should have no scruples on this point, because this is a matter which has been questioned by the Board of Conscience in Lisbon. . . . Nor did the bishops who were in Sao Thome, Cape Verde, and here in Loando—all learned and virtuous men—find fault with it. We have been here ourselves for forty years and there have been [among us] very learned Fathers; . . . never did they consider this trade as illicit. . . . [S]ince the traders who bring those negroes [to Brazil] bring them in good faith, those inhabitants can very well buy from such traders without any scruple. . . . Therefore, we here are the ones who could have greater scruple, for we buy these negroes from other negroes and from people who perhaps have stolen them. . . . [T]here are always a few who have been captured illegally because they were stolen or because the rulers of the land order them to be sold for offenses so slight that they do not deserve captivity, but . . . to lose so many souls as sail from here—out of whom many are saved—because some, impossible to recognize, have been captured illegally does not seem to be doing much service to God, for these are few and those who find salvation are many and legally captured.

*Jesuit Brother Luis Brandaon, letter from Angola, March 12, 1610, in Donnan,* Slave Trade Documents *1:123–24.*

At the same time the Most Reverend Cardinal Cibo writ us a letter in the name of the sacred college [of cardinals], complaining that the pernicious and abominable abuse of selling slaves was yet continued among us, and requiring us to use our power to remedy the said abuse; which, notwithstanding, we saw little hopes of accomplishing, by reason that the trade of this country lay wholly in slaves and ivory.

*Italian Father Jerom Merolla da Sorrento, describing his stay in the Congo, in Donnan,* Slave Trade Documents *1:319–20.*

# 2

# The Middle Passage 1500–1866

## The Historical Context

### *Preparations for the Middle Passage*

The slaving captains who sailed to Africa from Europe or America usually set out, as we have noted, on a triangular voyage. On the first leg, they traveled from their home ports to Africa with goods to trade for slaves. On the second leg, the dreaded Middle Passage, they carried the slaves they had purchased or captured from Africa to the slave marts of the New World. On the third leg, they transported sugar, tobacco, or other agricultural products from the Caribbean islands or colonies in South or North America back to their home ports. Danger threatened throughout the voyage but especially on the Middle Passage, where other ships might attack in the hopes of capturing the cargo of slaves, the slaves might rebel, or illness might sweep the ship.

The Middle Passage would take at best six weeks, usually much longer. Before it could begin, unless the captain had managed to buy a full load of slaves and supplies at one place, the slaver would have to sail along the coast of Africa, touching at several ports, to bargain for more. For example, the log of the Dutch ship *St. Jan,* cruising along the Slave Coast in 1659, shows the captain's indecision and frustration: "*Sunday.* Again resolved to proceed on our voyage, as there also but little food was to be had for the slaves in consequence of the great rains which fell every day, and because many of the slaves were suffering from the bloody flux in consequence of the bad provisions we were supplied with at El Mina, amongst which were many barrels of groats [grain], wholly unfit for use."[1] In the end, the *St. Jan* set out on the Middle Passage with insufficient supplies, only to have its water supply drain away through leaks in its barrels—leaks that no one could fix, the ship's cooper having died.

A captain probably carried with him the instructions of the owners of his ship, spelling out how to handle the slaves, specifying his bonus for keeping mortality among them low, and stating whether he was to be allowed to ship some slaves for his own profit. One way or another he (and probably his ship's surgeon) had a personal stake in getting as many slaves as possible to market in the New World, a stake in the form either of a bonus ("head money") for each slave delivered or in profits to be anticipated from selling the slaves he carried on his own account. To increase these profits, the captain might give his own slaves the best food and accommodations and have the ship's carpenter or cooper teach them a trade, to add to their value. He might even steal a few extra slaves, by reporting that they had died on the voyage and then selling them himself. Suspecting that they might be cheated in such ways, owners instituted all sorts of regulations, like requiring death certificates signed by two or three people on the ship for each slave lost. But, thousands of miles away from their ships, how were they to enforce their rules? In this corrupt trade, the owners had to hire as honest a captain as they could and hope for the best.

At his home port, the captain picked up a crew one way or another. Service on slavers had a bad reputation among sailors, so he might have to resort to trickery or impressment to fill out his crew. In 1808, historian Thomas Clarkson described English public houses where, "the young mariner, if a stranger to the port, and unacquainted with the nature of the Slave Trade, was sure to be picked up. The novelty of the voyages, the superiority of the wages in this over any other trades, and the privileges of various kinds, were set before him. Gulled in this manner he was frequently enticed to the boat, which was waiting to carry him away. If these prospects did not attract him, he was plied with liquor till he became intoxicated, when a bargain was made over him between the landlord and the mate. . . . Seamen also were boarded in these houses, who, when the slave-ships were going out, but at no other time, were encouraged to spend more than they had money to pay for; and to these . . . but one alternative was given, namely a slave-vessel, or gaol."[2] A crew thus recruited was a sullen, angry lot, whose brutishness the experiences on a slaving ship hardened into cruelty and sadism.

The captain usually had on board a surgeon (that is, a doctor), on whom he had to depend to separate healthy slaves from weak or infected ones before embarking them in Africa and to preserve the health of the slaves loaded. At best, the captain was leaning on a broken stick. If medical knowledge in general was severely limited—and it was—knowledge of tropical diseases hardly existed. Physicians had little to guide them, beyond their own observations and what they could glean from those more experienced. To make matters worse, physicians also avoided service on slavers. The ship's surgeon had probably signed on only because he could not make a living elsewhere or because he faced personal problems. "Abundance of these poor Creatures [slaves] are lost on Board Ships to the great prejudice of the Owners and Scandal of the Surgeon, merely thro' the Surgeon's Ignorance," wrote Dr. T. Aubrey in 1729, "because he knows not what they are afflicted with, but supposing it to be a Fever, bleeds and purges, or vomits them, and so casts them into an incurable *Diarrhoea,* and in a few Days they become a Feast for some hungry Shark."[3]

Officers and crew of the ship almost certainly fell sick in the pestilential climate of Africa. Through the 17th century, perhaps as many as 60 percent of them died, and few replacements were available—certainly none for the surgeon. Then the captain, supposing he had survived, had to face the daunting dangers of the Middle Passage: storms, insufficient water and food, epidemics, misconduct and mutinies among his crew, slave revolts and suicides, and attacks from pirates and ships of other nations, to whom he might lose his crew and his cargo, if not his vessel itself. The slave ships sailed in a miasma of fear and distrust.

## *Boarding the Slaves*

As for the slaves arriving at the coast from the interior of Africa, many had never before looked upon an ocean or a ship. Exhausted and terrified by the shock of capture; the long, forced march from inland; the trip downriver chained and crammed into canoes; and imprisonment for weeks or months in the barracoon, they were taken aboard vessels for which their languages might have no word. They were under the harsh control of white men—a phenomenon that they might be experiencing for the first time. Who could blame them if they took the Europeans for devils?

Rumors and questions flew among these frightened people—at least among those who could understand one another. Who were these creatures with white skins and long hair? Was the white man's country this hollow place, the ship? Did it move, and if so, how? The enslaved Gustavus Vassa (Olaudah Equiano) remembered his own experiences in about 1756: "I asked how the vessel could go? They told me they could not tell; but that there was cloth put upon the masts by the help of the ropes I saw, and then the vessel went on; and the white men had some spell or magic they put in the water when they liked, in order to stop the vessel. I was exceedingly amazed at this account, and really thought they [the white men] were spirits. I therefore wished much to be from amongst them, for I expected they would sacrifice me."

What did the white men want them for? Were the whites going to eat them, or grind their bones for gunpowder? Even when told that the white men wanted him only to work for them, Equiano said, "Still I feared I should be put to death, the white people looked and acted, as I thought, in so savage a manner; for I had never seen among any people such instances of brutal cruelty; and this not only shown toward us blacks, but also to some of the whites themselves. One white man in particular I saw, when we were permitted to be on deck, flogged so unmercifully with a large rope near the foremast, that he died in consequence of it."

Thrust into a series of alien environments, stunned by the loss of control over their own lives and bodies, the captive Africans had lost also all standards by which they could reasonably judge probabilities.

They knew for certain only that they were being removed farther and farther from their homes. Many of them believed that if they could die near Africa their spirits could return to the places and people they loved. So, of course, they were willing to take almost any risk while they remained in sight of land, certainly including rising against their captors or jumping overboard. Olaudah Equiano testified, "[A]lthough not being used to the water, I naturally feared that element the first time I saw it, yet, nevertheless, could I have got over the nettings [put up to prevent suicides], I would have jumped over the side, but I could not; and besides, the crew used to watch us very closely who were not chained down to the decks, lest we should leap into the water; and I have seen some of these poor African prisoners most severely cut, for attempting to do so."[4]

Boarding itself was terrifying. Taken directly from their voyage downriver in African canoes or removed from the barracoons where they had been held, the slaves were lined up on the beaches and subjected to a series of demeaning experiences. The ship's surgeon inspected them, looking in their mouths and private parts, trying to weed out the weak and old, and to permit on board no one with a venereal or other infectious disease. In the early days the slaves were baptized as Christians with holy water contained in the "hog-troughs" from which they would eat on the ship. The mass ceremony must have bewildered them. Theoretically they had all been instructed enough to understand what was going on, but the instruction was conducted in a "common" African language that they may or may not have understood. Afterward, they were flung to the ground and branded with hot irons—in the early days on the breast, later on the shoulder. Africans stripped them, claiming their clothing for their own use, leaving them nude. The heads of both men and women slaves might be shaved, and they were scrubbed down with sand. Then African "Canoomen" loaded them into their crafts for the trip through the surf to the ships lying at anchor.

## *Life on Board*

The slaves now faced the physical horrors of the voyage. As long as the ship was within sight of shore, they were chained or closely confined to keep them from jumping overboard. Once out of sight of land, the men were kept in chains below decks during the night but brought on deck in daytime in fair weather, at least for meals and an exercise period. The women and children, judged less likely to rebel successfully, enjoyed more freedom.

How much space was allowed each slave below decks depended partly on national practice and partly on the greed of the ship's owners and master. They were always crowded, whether they traveled standing, sitting, or lying down. Seated, one slave might have to sit between the legs of another. Lying down, he might not have space enough to turn over. The height of the space between decks often did not allow him to stand erect, perhaps not even to sit up. Slaver John Barbot reported on Portuguese practice about 1700: "[I]t is pitiful to see how they croud those poor wretches, six hundred and fifty or seven hundred in a ship, the men standing in the hold ty'd to stakes, the women between decks, and those that are with child in the great cabin, and the children in the steeridge. . . ."[5]

Usually each man was shackled either to another man (whose language he might or might not understand) or to a group of men by a long chain that ran through rings on their arms and was attached at either end to fittings on the bulkhead. That meant that, unable to reach the tubs and buckets used as toilets, they were forced to relieve themselves where they lay, sat or stood. Since almost everyone was seasick and had diarrhea, or "the bloody flux," these lodgings stank unbearably. Candles would not burn in the fetid air.

Experienced captains advised novices to wash these spaces down frequently. The Portuguese provided mats that at least kept the slaves off the damp decks, but these soon became soaked from the decks, the sweat of the slaves, and the rain that came in through the scuttles. The mats were changed every two or three weeks. Bad weather and high seas often forced the sailors to cover

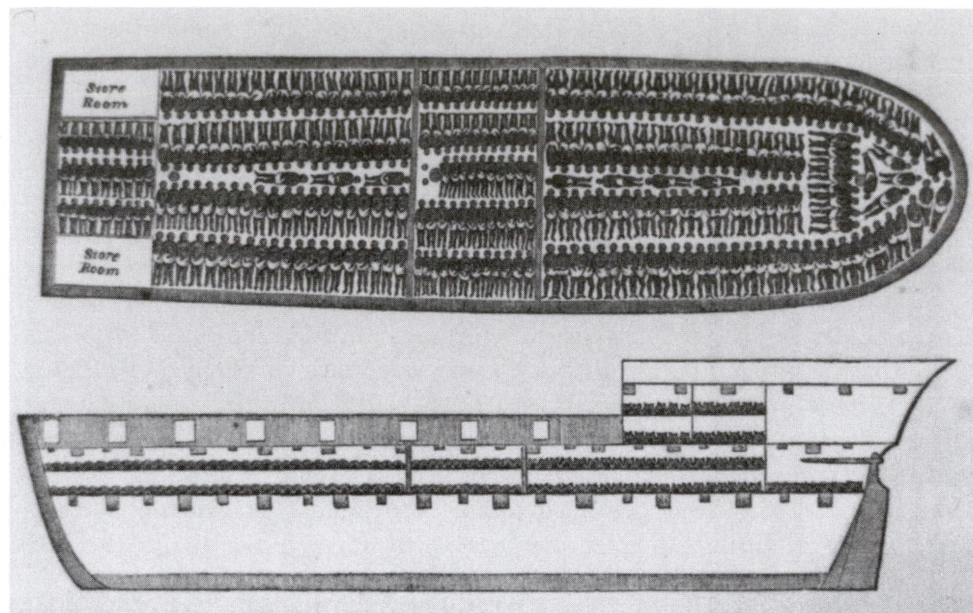


Diagram of the hold of a slaver (*Blake,* History of Slavery and the Slave Trade)

the barred portholes and gratings designed to give the slaves a bit of air; with the heat from packed bodies, the temperature soared.

In daytime, the slaves were taken up on deck to be fed and exercised—forcibly, if necessary—under the watchful eyes, guns, and whips of the crew and the African trusties brought along to guard them (about such individuals, more below). They exercised, willy-nilly, by dancing. Sometimes a sailor played a fiddle or bagpipes for them to dance to. But even on deck, the men might spend most of the day in irons, on a long chain locked to ringbolts fixed in the deck, fifty or sixty of them fastened to one chain.

Many slaves were too depressed to want to eat, or they might not like the food offered. Captain and crew tried to make them eat, by thrashing them—even babies—or forcing food down their throats with a specially designed *speculum orum,* holding hot coals on a shovel near their lips to make them open their mouths, pouring hot lead on them, or breaking their teeth. "I was soon put down under the decks, and there I received such a salutation in my nostrils as I had never experienced in my life; so that, with the loathsomeness of the stench, and crying together, I became so sick and low that I was not able to eat, nor had I the least desire to taste anything," Equiano remembered. "Two of the white men offered me eatables; and, on my refusing to eat, one of them held me fast by the hands, and laid me across, I think, the windlass, and tied my feet, while the other flogged me severely."[6]

But if supplies ran low, slaves might be given little to eat. "Numberless quarrels take place among them [the slaves] during their meals; more especially when they are put upon short allowance, which frequently happens if the passage . . . proves of unusual length," wrote Alexander Falconbridge. "In this case, the weak are obliged to be content with a very scanty portion. Their allowance of water is about half a pint each at every meal."[7]

Some captains tried to prevent sexual intercourse between the whites and the slaves. Others regarded seduction and rape as natural benefits for sailors and officers on slaving ships. As slave trader John Newton remarked in the 1750s,

"Where resistance or refusal would be utterly in vain, even the solicitation of consent is seldom thought of."[8] So, many a sailor simply forced himself on a slave women. Others relied on seduction, and often a slave woman would go ashore with a broken heart, and perhaps pregnant, her sailor lover having abandoned her to her fate.

On the Middle Passage, the slaves of course succumbed to seasickness, a condition inevitable in the bad air and rank smells of the holds in which they were confined at night and in storms. More dangerous were the illnesses brought on by their exposure to infection from European diseases little known in Africa. When one slave sickened, he or she inevitably infected the others. Epidemics of smallpox raged among them, as well as of unidentified fevers. Skin ailments made the slaves itch unbearably and produced terrible sores and abscesses on their bodies. Ophthalmia blinded them, temporarily or permanently. Record after record talks about the flux, a particularly violent form of diarrhea, in which the patients involuntarily discharged blood and mucus.

No wonder that even those who lived were in dreadful condition when they landed—"crippled, covered with mange, losing their hair, emaciated in frame, suffering from fevers and dysenteries, often barely alive."[9]

The better ship's surgeons tried to cope, setting up infirmaries on board or even persuading the captain to stop at some island when an epidemic threatened. But in the face of most illnesses, they were helpless. "Almost the only means by which the surgeon can render himself useful to the slaves," wrote ship's doctor Alexander Falconbridge in 1788, "is by seeing that their food is properly cooked and distributed among them. It is true, when they arrive near the markets . . ., care is taken to polish them for sale by an application of the lunar caustic to such as are afflicted with the yaws. This, however, affords but a temporary relief."[10]

Now and then a captain and crew, panicked by sickness aboard and fearful that their profits were vanishing before their eyes, would resort to murder to retrieve them. "The insurer takes upon him the risk of the loss, capture, and death of slaves, or any other unavoidable accident to them; but natural death is always understood to be expected: by natural death is meant, not only when it happens by disease or sickness, but also when the captive destroys himself through despair, which often happens: but when slaves were killed, or thrown into the sea in order to quell an insurrection on their part, then the insurers must answer."[11] So the slave traders might choose to thrust the cost on the insurance company by throwing the weak but still breathing slaves to the sharks.

The more humane or more intelligent slavers tried to ease the terrible shipboard conditions as much as they could, if only to increase their profits. Observing that "the fewer in number [the slaves on board,] the better accommodations and better feed and care they will have taken of them and the healthier they will arrive at market," Rhode Islanders designed their ships smaller to carry fewer slaves and sail faster.[12] As slavers grew more experienced, they learned the importance of better ventilation, better sanitation, vaccination against smallpox, lime juice to protect against scurvy, and food that the Africans liked. Some captains hired African healers who could understand the captives' languages, both to keep them calm and to spy out budding mutinies.[13] These trusties tried to reassure the slaves by telling them where they were going and what was wanted of them—at least quelling their fears of being eaten.

Throwing slaves overboard—for illness? rebellion? insurance? *(Library of Congress)*

## *Slave Rebellions on Board*

Deep depression among the slaves led many to attempt suicide, either individually or in groups. Ships' logs tell of their pathetic wailing as they mourned for homes and families. Despite all efforts to force them to eat, some starved themselves. Some went mad. Thousands more in effect died of broken hearts, too weakened by all they had suffered, the hopelessness of their plight, and grief to survive the hardships of the voyage.

Desperation drove those of different temperament to rebellion. The odds against them were long. What chance had they, after all, with so many of them chained for so much of the time, closely confined and vigilantly watched by ruthless, armed seamen, being themselves without weapons and having no knowledge of navigation and little of geography, uncertain even what moved the ship? If the mutiny succeeded, how were they to sail the ships, how were they to navigate, and where was home? As English sailor William Richardson commented, with remarkable detachment, "I could not but admire the courage of a fine young black who, though his partner in irons lay dead at his feet, would not surrender but fought with his billet of wood until a pistol ball finished his existence. The others fought as well as they could, but what could they do against fire-arms?"[14]

Bewilderment about their fates compounded the slaves' desperation. John Atkins observed in 1721, "When we are slaved and out at Sea, it is commonly imagined, the Negroes Ignorance of Navigation, will always be a Safeguard; yet, as many of them think themselves bought to eat, and more, that Death will send them into their own Country, there has not been wanting Examples of rising and killing a Ship's Company."[15]

Women slaves—less closely watched, less likely to be chained, and freer to move around the ship—joined the men in conspiring to mutiny. "[P]utt not too much confidence in the Women nor Children lest they happen to be Instrumental to your being surprised which might be fatall," warned Samuel Waldo, owner of the slaver *Africa,* in his 1734 instructions to the ship's captain.[16]

The slaves improvised weapons by breaking their shackles, seizing the troughs from which they ate, or stealing tools from the ship's carpenter. Occasionally an unwary crew member would give a slave a knife. One cargo of slaves, discovering an old anchor, possessed themselves of a hammer and broke it up for weapons. In another instance, the slaves "laid on him [the captain] and beat out his Brains with the little Tubs, out of which they eat their boiled Rice. . . . "[17] More observant slaves tried first to seize the ship's store of arms and ammunition.

Now and then, most likely if they were still near the shore, the slaves won and escaped. "We have an account from Guinea, by Way of Antigua," reported the *Boston News Letter* of September 25, 1729, "that the *Clare* Galley, Capt. Murrell, having completed her Number of Negroes had taken her Departure From the Coast of Guinea for South Carolina; but was not got 10 Leagues on her Way, before the Negroes rose and making themselves Masters of the Gunpowder and Fire Arms, the Captain and Ship Crew took to their Long Boat, and got shore near Cape Coast Castle. The Negroes run the Ship on Shore within a few Leagues of the said Castle, and made their Escape."[18] Most notable were the successful *Amistad* mutineers, who demanded that the surviving officers sail toward the rising sun, for they believed that they had come from the east. The officers complied by day but at night steered to the north, so as to land in Connecticut. There, with the support of abolitionists and after prolonged court suits, the slaves eventually managed to extricate themselves and return to Africa.

But most mutinies failed: the slavers' guns were almost always too powerful for the mutineers' improvised weapons. Sometimes everyone lost, as when in 1735 slaves on the British ship *Dolphin* "overpowered the crew, broke into the powder room, and finally in the course of their effort for freedom blew up both themselves and the crew."[19]

Most commonly the slavers won Pyrrhic victories, suffering losses among the crew or damage to the ship they could ill afford and almost certainly the loss of slaves, on whom their profits depended. In the 1727 mutiny aboard the English slaver *Ferrers,* "all the grown Negroes on board . . . run to the forepart of the Ship in a body, and endeavored to force the Barricadeo on the Quarter-Deck, not regarding the Musquets or Half Pikes, that were presented to their Breasts by the white Men, through the loop-Holes. So that at last the chief Mate was obliged to order one of the Quarter-deck Guns laden with Partridge-Shot, to be fired amongst them; which occasioned a terrible destruction: For there were near eighty Negroes killed and drowned, many jumping overboard when the Gun was fired. This indeed put an end to the Mutiny, but most of the Slaves that remained alive grew so sullen, that several of them were starved to death, obstinately refusing to take any Sustenance."[20]

In defending against slave uprisings captains were often handicapped by lack of manpower, because of the frequent illnesses and deaths among their sailors. In the uprising of 1704 on the *Eagle Galley,* which carried four hundred slaves, not more than ten seamen capable of service were on board, another dozen having left in the boats to find wood and water on a nearby island. Fortunately for the crew, only some twenty slaves actively participated in the rebellion.

Probably the most effective step a captain could take to prevent quarrels and rebellion was to hire Africans who understood something of what was going on to supervise the slaves. On the voyage of the *Hannibal* in 1693–94, Capt. Thomas Phillips noted: "[W]e have some 30 or 40 Gold Coast negroes, which we buy, and are procur'd us there by our factors, to make guardians and overseers of the Whidaw negroes, and sleep among them to keep them from quarreling, and in order, as well as to give us notice, if they can discover any caballing or plotting among them, which trust they will discharge with great diligence; they also take care to make the negroes scrape the decks where they lodge every morning very clean, to eschew any distempers that may engender from filth and nastiness. When we constitute a guardian, we give him a cat of nine tails as a badge of his office, which he is not a little proud of, and will exercise with great authority."[21]

But often the best efforts of the captain could not prevent a mutiny. Eighteenth-century captain William Snelgrave prided himself on his humane treatment of slaves. Through an interpreter he would tell the adults among them that they had been bought to till the soil. He instructed them in how to behave on board. If any white man abused them, he said, they should complain to the interpreter, who would inform him, and he would deal justly with the offenders; if they made disturbances or attacked the white men, however, they would be severely punished. To the captain's bewilderment, the slaves would rebel anyway. Seldom did it occur to any white man to ask himself what he might have done in their circumstances.

Scholars have discovered fairly detailed accounts of 55 mutinies on slavers from 1699 to 1845, plus references to more than a hundred others. Slaves may have mutinied on some 10 percent of the voyages.[22]

## *Slave Mortality Rates*

All in all, the miracle is that so many slaves survived the voyages, which lasted from five or six weeks to several months. In their debilitated state, they could so easily have died. An accounting of the *James* in 1675 assigns all sorts of reasons for the deaths of the slaves it had carried: convulsions, fevers, consumption, worms, and refusal to eat. One woman "Miscarryed and the Child dead within her and Rotten and dyed 2 days after delivery." Another, "Being very fond of her Child Carrying her up and downe, wore her to nothing by which means fell into a feavour and dyed."[23]

Mortality rates on slavers on some disastrous early voyages ran to more than 50 percent, but they gradually fell, thanks in part to increased speed and in part to somewhat better care of the slaves. "In all, total slave mortality at sea dropped irregularly from something like 25 to 30 percent early in the eighteenth century to 10 to 15 percent by the end of the eighteenth century and finally to 5 to 10 percent by the 1820s."[24] Most modern scholars believe that conditions on a ship had less to do with mortality rates at sea than did the length of the voyage, the region of Africa from which individual slaves came, their health before embarkation, the length of the trip from the interior and of detention at the barracoons before sailing, and the demand for slaves.[25]

Still, and even under the best conditions, the Middle Passage remained hazardous for all on the ship, especially for the slaves. Only the whites' concern for profits protected the slaves, and when push came to shove, the whites simply abandoned the blacks to whatever terrible fate threatened. Take once again the *St. Jan,* which on March 4, 1659, sailed from the Gold Coast of Africa, to spend months cruising along the Slave Coast trying to buy slaves and supplies. Ultimately it ran out of both bread and water; fifty-nine male slaves, forty-seven women, and four children died thereby. On November 1, the *St. Jan* was lost on the Reef of Rocus, "and all hands immediately took to the boat, as there was no prospect of saving the slaves, for we must abandon the ship in consequence of the heavy surf." On November 4, the crew arrived at Curaçao, where "the Hon'ble Governor Beck ordered two sloops to take the slaves off the wreck, one of which sloops with eighty four slaves on board, was captured by a privateer."[26]

## Navigation and Defense

Whatever problems he had to handle on board during the Middle Passage, the slaver captain also had to make the quickest possible passage across the Atlantic, taking into consideration distance, the likelihood of bad weather or of being becalmed, and the hazard of attacks from other ships. Every day he cut from the Middle Passage contributed to profits—not to mention that conditions aboard the slavers were so disagreeable even for the ship's officers as to encourage all possible speed.

Storms at sea frequently spelled not merely discomfort but disaster for the ships, their crews, and their human cargoes. "Suddenly the weather closes in, and the seas rise so high and so strongly that the ships must obey the waves, sailing at the mercy of the winds without true course or control," wrote Brazilian Sebastiao Xavier Botelho in 1840. "It is then that the din from the slaves, bound to one another, becomes horrible. . . . The tempo of the storm increases, and with it the danger. A portion of the food provisions is heaved overboard, and also other objects, to save the cargo and the crew. Many slaves break legs and arms; others die of suffocation. One ship or another will break apart from the fury of the storm, and sink. Another drifts on, dismasted, its rigging ruined by the will of the ocean, unable to heed the helm, on the verge of capsizing."[27]

The significant variations in the times recorded for the voyage across the Atlantic suggest how much depended on the captain's skills. John Barbot commented in 1700, "[T]he great mortality, which so often happens in slave-ships, proceeds as well from taking in too many, as from want of knowing how to manage them aboard, and how to order the course at sea so nicely [precisely], as not to overshoot their ports in America, as some bound to Cayenne with slaves, have done; attributing the tediousness of their passage, and their other mistakes, to wrong causes, as being becalm'd about the line [equator], etc.[,] which only proceeded from their not observing the regular course, or not making due observations of land when they approach'd the American continent; or of the force and strength of the current of the Amazons. Others have been faulty in not putting their ships into due order before they left the Guinea coast."[28]

The captain also had to keep an eye out for pirates and the vessels of other nations, any of which might attack his ship to steal the slaves and the ship. The records show many such attacks. Successfully maneuvering sailing ships on the high seas under battle conditions required both art and luck. Some owners insured against risks "of the Seas, Men of War, Fires, Enemies, Pirates, Rovers, Thieves, Jettisons, Letters of Mart, and Counter Mart, Surprizals, Takings at Sea, Arrests, Restraints and Detainment of all Kings, Princes, and people of what Nation, Condition or Quality soever."[29] Others took their chances.

To some degree, of course, the success of a voyage depended on the design and soundness of the ship. Capt. William Sherwood wrote in 1790, "I think the construction [of a slave ship] is more material [to the health of slaves] than the tonnage; in a long narrow ship the air circulates more freely: a short quarter deck, no top-gallant forecastle, no gangway, and a very low waist, are Circumstances of greater advantage than a mere extension of tonnage."[30] Sheathing the ship's bottom with copper increased its speed.

Recent scholarship places the total number of slaving trips to the New World between 1527 and 1866 at 27,233. Almost 12 million slaves were embarked from Africa, and about one and a half million died on the Middle Passage. [31]

## Chronicle of Events

**1684**
Portugal enacts a measure regulating the slave-carrying capacity of a ship and setting the quantity of provisions that must be carried.

**1731**
On the ship of slave trader Capt. George Scott of Rhode Island, slaves mutiny and kill members of the crew.

**1732**
Slaves in his cargo kill Capt. John Major of Portsmouth, New Hampshire, and all his crew and seize the schooner and cargo.

**1747**
Slaves on board the ship of Captain Beers of Rhode Island rise and kill most of the crew.

**1761**
Captain Nichols of Boston loses forty of his slaves by insurrection but saves his ship.

**1770**
Increased prices for slaves in Brazil result in somewhat better conditions on slave ships.

The Portuguese governor's order imposes new standards of hygiene on slave ships out of Luanda (in modern Angola).

**1785**
The Portuguese empire makes it more difficult for slavers to evade legal restrictions on loading and requirements for carrying a certain amount of provisions for slaves.

**1788**
England imposes official restrictions on slave ships—limiting the number of slaves to be carried, outlawing insurance on cargoes of slaves except for fire and the perils of the sea, requiring the employment of trained surgeons, and offering premiums to surgeons and captains if the mortality rate of a Middle Passage is no more than 3 percent.

**1790**
The use of fruits and vegetables to combat scurvy on slave ships begins to spread.

**1799**
England changes the requirements for slave ships, specifying the height between decks rather than tonnage, thus further reducing capacity.

**1800–1830**
The *bergantim* emerges as the main type of slaving vessel, with more hold space for provisions than other slave ships.

**1802**
Denmark abolishes the slave trade.

**1807**
Great Britain and the United States prohibit the international slave trade.

**1808**
The British undertake to stop all maritime trading in slaves from West Africa.

The introduction of copper-sheathed hulls marginally lowers the average sailing times of slave ships.

**1810**
Increased freight charges for shippers and higher fees to agents on commission in Africa ease the economic pressures that had caused inadequate provisioning of slave ships.

Trained physicians begin to influence policy on slaving in Africa and Brazil.

**1813**
Sweden abolishes the slave trade.

**1814**
The Netherlands abolishes the slave trade.

**1820**
Vaccination against smallpox comes into wider use in the slave trade.

Spain abolishes the slave trade.

**1830**
The legal international slave trade ends.

**1835**
The British parliament authorizes the Royal Navy to capture slave ships flying the Portuguese flag as though they were British.

Death of the *Amistad* captain *(Library of Congress)*

**1839**

*July:* African captives, led by Joseph Cinqué, rebel aboard the Spanish slaver *Amistad*.

*August 26:* Lieutenant Gedney, U.S. Navy, captures the *Amistad* and takes it to New London, Connecticut, where its African captives are imprisoned.

**1841**

The British parliament authorizes British admiralty courts to adjudicate cases of slave vessels operating contrary to an Anglo-Brazilian treaty of 1826.

## EYEWITNESS TESTIMONY

### *Embarking and Provisioning*

To the greater glory of God and the Virgin Mary, with the help of God, we are undertaking to go from Vannes, where we were outfitted, to the coast of Guinea in the ship[.] The Diligent, belonging to the brothers Billy and Mr. LaCroix, and from thence to Martinique to sell our blacks and make our return to Vannes.

*Lt. Robert Durand, 1731,* Hartford Courant, *September 21, 1998.*

I was carried on board. I was immediately handled, and tossed up to see if I were sound, by some of the crew; and I was now persuaded that I had gotten into a world of bad spirits, and that they were going to kill me. Their [white] complexions, too, differing so much from ours, their long hair, and the language they spoke . . . united to confirm me in this belief. . . . When I looked round the ship too, and saw a large furnace of copper boiling, and a multitude of black people of every description chained together, every one of their countenances expressing dejection and sorrow, I no longer doubted of my fate; and, quite overpowered with horror and anguish, I fell motionless on the deck and fainted. When I recovered a little, I found some black people about me, who I believed were some of those who had brought me on board, and had been receiving their pay; they talked to me in order to cheer me, but all in vain. I asked them if we were not to be eaten by those white men with horrible looks, red faces, and long hair.

*Gustavus Vassa (Olaudah Equiano), experiences of about 1756, in* Great Slave Narratives, *27.*

[We desire you to go to New Calabar, and there barter your cargo] for good healthy young negroes and ivory, and . . . not to buy any old slaves or children but good healthy young men and women, . . . and when you are half-slaved don't stay too long if there is a possibility of getting off for the risk of sickness and mortality then become great. . . .

[L]et no candle be made use of in drawing spirits or to go near the powder. . . . We recommend you to treat the negroes with as much lenity as [as leniently as] safety will admit and suffer none of your officers or people to abuse them under any pretence whatever, be sure you see their victuals well dressed and given them in due season. . . . We recommend you to make fires frequently in the negroes' rooms as we think it healthy and you have iron kettles on board for that purpose. We recommend mutton broth in fluxes [sicknesses], so that you'll endeavour to purchase as many sheep and goats to bring off the coast for that purpose as you conveniently can.

*Instructions to Capt. George Merrick of the* Africa, *from John Chilcott & Company, 1774, in Pope-Hennessy,* Sins of the Fathers, *109.*

### *The Slaves: Living Conditions at Sea—Food and Drink*

Their chief diet is call'd dabbadabb, being Indian corn ground as small as oat-meal, in iron mills, which we carry for that purpose; and after mix'd with water, and boil'd well in a large copper furnace, till 'tis as thick as a pudding, about a peckful of which in vessels, call'd crews, is allow'd to 10 men, with a little salt, malagetta, and palm oil, to relish; they are divided into messes [eating groups] of ten each, for the easier and better order in serving them: Three days a week they have horse-beans boil'd for their dinner and supper, great quantities of which the African company do send aboard us for that purpose; these beans the negroes extremely love and desire, beating their breast, eating them, and crying Pram! Pram! which is Very good! they are indeed the best diet for them, having a binding quality, and consequently good to prevent the flux, which is the inveterate distemper that most affects them, and ruins our voyages by their mortality.

*Capt. Thomas Phillips, journal of a voyage of the* Hannibal, *1693–1694, in Donnan,* Slave Trade Documents *1:406.*

We frequently bought from the natives considerable quantities of dried shrimps to make broth; and a very excellent dish they made, when mixed with flour and palm oil and seasoned with pepper and salt. Both whites and blacks were fond of this mess [food]. In addition to yams we gave them for a change, fine shelled beans and rice cooked together, and this was served up to each individual with a plentiful proportion of the soup. On other days their soup was mixed with peeled yams, cut up thin and boiled, with a proportion of pounded biscuit. For the sick we provided strong soups and middle messes, prepared from mutton, goats' flesh, fowls, etc., to which were added sago and lilipees, the whole mixed with port wine and sugar. . . . [The slaves'] personal comfort was also carefully studied. On their coming on deck, about eight o'clock in the morning, water was provided to wash their hands and faces, a mixture of lime juice to cleanse their mouths, towels to wipe with and chew sticks to clean their teeth. These were generally pieces of young branches of the common lime or of the citron of sweet lime tree. . . . They are used about the thickness of a quill and the end being chewed, the white, fine fibre of the wood soon forms a brush with which the teeth may be effectually cleaned by rubbing them up and down. These sticks impart an agreeable flavor to the mouth and are sold in little bundles, for a mere trifle, in the public markets of the West Indies. A draw of brandy bitters was given to each of the men and clean spoons being served out, they breakfasted about nine o'clock. About eleven, if the day were fine, they washed their bodies all over, and after wiping themselves dry, were allowed to use palm oil, their favorite cosmetic. Pipes and tobacco were then supplied to the men and beads and other articles were distributed among the women to amuse them, after which they were permitted to dance and run about on deck to keep them in good spirits. A middle mess of bread and cocoa-nuts was given them about mid-day. The third meal was served out about three o'clock and after everything was cleaned out and arranged below, they were generally sent down about four or five o'clock in the evening.

*Memoirs of Capt. H. Crow, 1830, in Dow,* Slave Ships, *184–85.*

## *The Slaves: Living Conditions at Sea—Lodging*

If it be in large ships carrying five or six hundred slaves, the deck in such ships ought to be at least five and a half or six foot high,. . . for the greater height it has, the more airy and convenient it is for such a considerable number of human creatures; and consequently far the more healthy for them. . . . We build a sort of half-decks along the sides with deals and spars . . . , that half-deck extending no farther than the sides of our scuttles and so the slaves lie in two rows, one above the other, and as close together as they can be crouded. . . .

We are very nice [careful] in keeping the places where the slaves lie clean and neat, appointing some of the ship's crew to do that office constantly, and several of the slaves themselves to be assistant to them in that employment; and thrice a week we perfume betwixt decks with a quantity of good vinegar in pails, and red-hot iron bullets in them, to expel the bad air, after the place has been well wash'd and scrubb'd with brooms: after which, the deck is clean'd with cold vinegar. . . .

*John Barbot's voyage to the Congo, 1700, in Donnan,* Slave Trade Documents *1:459, 465.*

The stench of the hold while we were on the coast was so intolerably loathsome, that it was dangerous to remain there for any time. . . . [N]ow that the whole ship's cargo were confined together, it became absolutely pestilential. The closeness of the place, and the heat of the climate, added to the number in the ship, which was so crowded that each had scarcely room to turn himself, almost suffocated us. This produced copious perspirations, so that the air soon became unfit for respiration, from a variety of loathsome smells, and brought on a sickness among the slaves, of which many died. . . . This wretched situation was again aggravated by the galling of the chains, now become insupportable, and the filth of the necessary tubs [toilets], into which the children often fell, and were almost suffocated. . . .

*Gustavus Vassa (Olaudah Equiano), experiences of about 1756, in* Great Slave Narratives, *30.*

In each of the apartments are placed three or four large buckets, of a conical form, nearly two feet in diameter at the bottom and only one foot at the top and in depth about twenty-eight inches, to which, when necessary, the negroes have recourse. It often happens that those . . . at a distance from the buckets, in endeavoring to get to them, tumble over their companions. . . . These accidents, although unavoidable, are productive of continual quarrels. . . . In this situation, unable to proceed and prevented from getting to the tubs, they desist from the attempt; and as the necessities of nature are not to be resisted, they

The hold of the slaver *Gloria* (*Library of Congress*)

ease themselves as they lie. This becomes a fresh source of broils and disturbances. . . . The nuisance . . . is not unfrequently increased by the tubs being much too small for the purpose intended and their being usually emptied but once every day.

*Ship's doctor Alexander Falconbridge,* Account of the Slave Trade *(1788), in Dow,* Slave Ships, *142–43.*

## The Slaves: Living Conditions at Sea—Exercise

If they [the slaves] go about it [dancing for exercise] reluctantly, or do not move with agility, they are flogged; a person standing by them all the time with a cat-o'-nine-tails in his hand for that purpose. Their music, upon these occasions, consists of a drum . . . [T]he poor wretches are frequently compelled to sing also; but when they do so, their songs are generally, as may naturally be expected, melancholy lamentations of their exile from their native land.

*Ship's doctor Alexander Falconbridge,* Account of the Slave Trade *(1788), in Pope-Hennessy,* Sins of the Fathers, *4 n.*

## The Slaves: Living Conditions at Sea—Sickness

But our greatest care of all is to buy none that are pox'd, lest they should infect the rest aboard; for tho' we separate the men and women aboard by partitions and bulk-heads, to prevent quarrels and wranglings among them, yet do what we can they will come together, and that distemper which they call the yaws, is very common here, and discovers itself by almost the same symptoms as the . . . clap does with us; therefore our surgeon is forced to examine the privities of both men and women with the nicest scrutiny, which is a great slavery, but what can't be omitted.

*Capt. Thomas Phillips, journal of the 1693 voyage of the* Hannibal, *in Dow,* Slave Ships, *61.*

The distemper which my men as well as the blacks mostly die of, was the white flux, which was so violent and inveterate, that no medicine would in the least check it. . . . I cannot imagine what should cause it in them so suddenly, they being free from it till about a week after we left the island of St. Thomas.

And next to the malignity of the climate, I can attribute it to nothing else but the unpurg'd black sugar, and raw unwholesome rum they bought there, of which they drank in punch to great excess, and which it was not in my power to hinder. . . .

*Capt. Thomas Phillips, journal of a voyage of the* Hannibal, *1693–1694, in Dow,* Slave Ships, *67.*

As for the sick and wounded . . . our surgeons, in their daily visits betwixt decks, finding any indisposed, caus'd them to be carried to the Lazaretto [sick bay], under the fore-castle. . . . Being out of the croud, the surgeons had more conveniency and time to administer proper remedies; which they cannot do leisurely between decks, because of the great heat . . . , which is sometimes so excessive, that the surgeons would faint away, and the candles would not burn; besides, that in such a croud of brutish people, there are always some very apt to annoy and hurt others, and all in general so greedy, that they will snatch from the sick slaves the fresh meat or liquor that is given them. . . .

*John Barbot's voyage to the Congo, 1700, in Donnan,* Slave Trade Documents *1:459f.*

The ship *Zong* . . . sailed from . . . the coast of Africa, the 6th September, 1781 . . . and on the 27th November following she fell in with [Jamaica]; but . . . the master, either through ignorance or a sinister intention, ran the ship to leeward, alleging that he mistook Jamaica for Hispaniola. . . .

The sickness and mortality on board the *Zong* . . . was not occasioned by the want of water . . . : yet [on November 29th] . . . before there was any present or real want of water, "the master of the ship called together a few of the officers, and told them . . . that, if the slaves died a natural death, it would be the loss of the owners of the ship; but if they were thrown alive into the sea, it would be the loss of the underwriters": and, to palliate the inhuman proposal, he . . . pretended that "it would not be so cruel to throw the poor sick wretches . . . into the sea, as to suffer them to linger out a few days under the disorders with which they were afflicted. . . ." [T]he same evening . . . [he] picked, or caused to be picked out, from the cargo of the same ship, one hundred and thirty-three slaves, all or most of whom were sick or weak, and not likely to live; and ordered the crew by turns to throw them into the sea; which most inhuman order was cruelly complied with . . . [F]ifty-four persons were actually thrown overboard alive on the 29th of November; and . . . forty-two more were also thrown overboard on the 1st December.

*1783 account, in Donnan,* Slave Trade Documents *2:554–56.*

The same day the Smallpox declared itself on the ship we immediately began innoculating [sic] the slaves and such of the officers and sailors as had not gone through the operation before. . . . [We then landed on an uninhabited island, where we constructed shelters for the diseased slaves and fed them turtle soup.] In twenty-nine days they were all perfectly cleansed of smallpox.

*Capt. Samuel Chase to his Newport, Rhode Island, shipowners, December 1797, in Coughtry,* Notorious Triangle, *149.*

## *The Slaves: Living Conditions at Sea—Abuse*

The Reader may be curious to know their [the mutinous slaves'] punishment:. . . Captain Harding weighing the Stoutness and Worth of the two Slaves, did as in other Countries they do by Rogues of Dignity, whip and scarify them only; while three others, Abettors, but not Actors, nor of Strength for it, he sentenced to cruel Deaths; making them first eat the Heart and Liver of one of the killed [whites]. . . . The woman he hoisted up by the Thumbs, whipp'd and slashed her with Knives, before the other Slaves till she died.

*Ship's doctor's report of mutiny on the English slaver* Robert, *1721, in Harding,* River, *13.*

[T]he enormities committed in an African ship, though equally flagrant, are little known *here* and are considered *there,* only as a matter of course. When the women and girls are taken on board a ship, naked, trembling, terrified, perhaps almost exhausted with cold, fatigue, and hunger, they are often exposed to the wanton rudeness of white savages. The poor creatures cannot understand the language they hear, but the looks and manner of the speakers are sufficiently intelligible. In imagination, the prey is divided, upon the spot, and only reserved till opportunity offers.

*John Newton,* Journal of a Slave Trader, *1750–1754, quoted in Reynolds,* African Slavery, *50–51.*

In the afternoon while we were off the deck, William Cooney seduced a woman slave down into the room and lay with her brutelike in view of the whole quarter deck, for which I put him in irons. I hope this has been the first affair of the kind on board and I am determined to keep them quiet if possible. If anything happens to the woman I shall impute it to him, for she was big with child. Her number is 83.

*John Newton,* Journal of a Slave Trader, *1750–1754, quoted in Pope-Hennessy,* Sins of the Fathers, *100.*

The [nine-month-old] child took sulk and would not eat. . . . [T]he captain took the child up in his hand, and flogged it with the cat [o'-nine-tails]. . . . [T]he child had swelled feet; the captain desired the cook to put on some water to heat to see if he could abate the swelling, and it was done. He then ordered the child's feet to be put into the water, and the cook putting his finger into the water, said, "Sir, it is too hot." The captain said, "Damn it, never mind it, put the feet in," and so doing the skin and nails came off, and he got some sweet oil and clothes and wrapped round the feet in order to take the fire out of them; and I myself bathed the feet with oil, and wrapped cloths around; and laying the child on the quarter deck in the afternoon at mess time, I gave the child some victuals, but it would not eat; the captain took the child up again, and flogged it, and said, "Damn you, I will make you eat," and so he continued in that way for four or five days at mess time, when the child would not eat, and flogged it, and he tied a log of mango, eighteen or twenty inches long, and about twelve or thirteen pound weight, to the child by a string round its neck. The last time he took the child up and flogged it, and let it drop out of his hands, "Damn you (says he) I will make you eat, or I will be the death of you"; and in three quarters of an hour after that the child died. He would not suffer any of the people that were on the quarter deck to heave the child overboard, but he called the mother of the child to heave it overboard. She was not willing to do so, and I think he flogged her; but I am sure that he beat her in some way for refusing to throw the child overboard; at the last he made her take the child up, and she took it in her hand, and went to the ship's side, holding her head on one side, because she would not see the child go out of her hand, and she dropped the child overboard. She seemed to be very sorry, and cried for several hours.

*Isaac Parker, testimony before the Commons Select Committee, 1764, in Anstey,* Atlantic Slave Trade, *33.*

## *The Slaves: Living Conditions at Sea—Depression and Suicides*

The negroes are so wilful and loth to leave their own country, that they have often leap'd out of the canoos, boat and ship, into the sea, and kept under water till they were drowned, to avoid being taken up and saved by our boats. . . . We have likewise seen divers [several] of them eaten by the sharks, of which a prodigious number kept about the ships in this place, and I have been told will follow here hence to Barbadoes, for the dead negroes that are thrown over-board in the passage. . . . We had about 12 negroes did wilfully drown themselves, and others starv'd themselves to death, for 'tis their belief that when they die they return home to their own country and friends again. . . .

*Thomas Phillips, journal of the 1693 voyage of the* Hannibal, *in Dow,* Slave Ships, *62–63.*

[My officers urged me to] cut off the legs and arms of the most wilful [slaves] to terrify the rest, [but I refused] to entertain the least thought of it, much less put in practice such barbarity and cruelty to poor creatures, who, excepting their want of Christianity and true religion (their misfortune more than fault) are as much the works of God's hands, and no doubt as dear to him as ourselves; nor can I imagine why they should be despised for their colour, being what they cannot help, and the effect of the climate it has pleased God to appoint them. I can't think there is any intrinsic value in one colour more than another, nor that white is better than black, only we think so because we are so, and are prone to judge favourably in our own case, as well as the blacks, who in odium of the colour, say, the devil is white and so paint him.

*Thomas Phillips, journal of the 1693–1694 voyage of the* Hannibal, *in Pope-Hennessy,* Sins of the Fathers, *99.*

It frequently happens that the negroes on being purchased by Europeans, become raving mad and many of them die in that state, particularly the women. One day at Bonny, I saw a middle-aged, stout woman, who had been brought down from a fair the preceding day, chained to the post of a black trader's door, in a state of furious insanity. On board the ship was a young negro woman chained to the deck, who had lost her senses soon after she was purchased and taken on board. In a former voyage we were obliged to confine a female negro of about twenty-three years of age, on her becoming a lunatic. She was afterwards sold during one of her lucid intervals.

*Ship's doctor Alexander Falconbridge,* Account of the Slave Trade *(1788), in Dow,* Slave Ships, *150–51.*

The slaves in the night were often heard making a howling melancholy kind of noise, sometimes expressive of extreme anguish. I repeatedly ordered the woman, who had been my interpreter in the latter part of the voyage, to inquire into the particular causes of this very melancholy noise. [She answered that it was because the slaves had dreamed they were back in their own country, only to wake to the reality of the slave ship.]

*Ship's surgeon Thomas Trotter, testifying before the Select Committee of the House of Commons, 1789–1791, in Pope-Hennessy,* Sins of the Fathers, *193.*

## *The Slaves: Living Condition at Sea—Rebellions*

When our slaves are aboard we shackle the men two and two, while we lie in port, and in sight of their own country, for 'tis then they attempt to make their escape, and mutiny; to prevent which we always keep centinels [sentinels] upon the hatchways, and have a chest full of small arms, ready loaden and prim'd, constantly lying at hand upon the quarter-deck, together with some granada shells; and two of our quarter-deck guns, pointing on the deck thence, and two more out of the steerage.

*Slaver captain, 1693, in Harding,* River, *10.*

We are sometimes sufficiently plagued with a parcel [group] of slaves, which come from a far in-land country, who very innocently persuade one another, that we buy them only to fatten and afterwards eat them as a delicacy.

When we are so unhappy as to be pestered with many of this sort, they resolve and agree together (and bring over the rest of their party) to run away from the ship, kill the Europeans, and set the vessel a-shore: by which means they design to free themselves from being our food.

*Dutchman William Bosman, description of the coast of Guinea, 1701, in Donnan,* Slave Trade Documents *1:443.*

On the first day of January [1701], Casseneuve's journal takes notice of their sailing out of Cabinde bay, . . . in order to proceed to Jamaica,. . . himself, the super-cargo, Mr. Barbot, the captain, and the first mate, with several of their men being sick, and having buried here and at sea, six of their crew and the third mate . . .: which gave an opportunity to the slaves aboard to revolt on the fifth. . . .

About one in the afternoon, after dinner, we according to custom caused them, one by one, to go down between decks, to have each his pint of water; most of them were yet above deck, many of them provided with knives, which we had indiscreetly given them two or three days before, as not suspecting the least attempt of this nature from them; others had pieces of iron they had torn off our forecastle door. . . . [T]hey had also broken off the shackles from several of their companions feet, which served them, as well as billets they had provided themselves with, and all other things they could lay hands on, which they imagin'd might be of use for their enterprize. Thus arm'd, they fell in crouds and parcels [groups] on our men, upon the deck unawares, and stabb'd one of the stoutest of us all, who receiv'd fourteen or fifteen wounds of their knives, and so expir'd. Next they assaulted our boatswain, and cut one of his legs so round the bone, that he could not move, the nerves being cut through; others cut our cook's throat to the [wind]pipe, and others wounded three of the sailors, and threw one of them overboard in that condition, from the fore-castle into the sea; who, however, by good providence, got hold of the bowline of the fore-sail, and sav'd himself, along the lower wale of the quarter-deck, where, (says Casseneuve;) we stood in arms, firing on the revolted slaves, of whom we kill'd some, and wounded many; which so terrify'd the rest, that they gave way, dispersing themselves some one way and some another between decks, and under the fore-castle; and many of the most mutinous, leapt over board, and drown'd themselves in the ocean with much resolution, shewing no manner of concern for life.

Thus we lost twenty seven or twenty eight slaves, either kill'd by us, or drown'd. . . .

*James Barbot's voyage to the Congo River, in Dow,* Slave Ships, *83–84.*

The story told by the Mendians [of the *Amistad* rebellion] is as follows: They belong to six different tribes living near each other in Africa, and yet can well understand each other's dialect. They are not related and met for the first time at the Slave Factory at Lomboko, near the mouth of the Gallinas river. They had been previously kidnapped singly, and hurried down to the coast, by the Spaniards or the natives who had been instigated by them. At Lomboko they were put on board the Portuguese ship Tecora, in chains, with several hundreds of other Africans, and taken to Havana. Here they were landed and kept in a Baracoon (an oblong enclosure without a roof) for ten days, when Ruiz purchased them, forty-nine in number. Montez also purchased the boy Ka-li and three girls, who were brought from Africa in another ship. The whole fifty-three were put on board the Spanish coaster Amistad, which cleared for Principe, about 300 miles distant, where Ruiz and Montez lived. On the passage the Mendians had dealt out to them a very small quantity of food and drink. When they took any water without leave, and at other times, they were severely scourged by order of their masters. The cook told them that on arriving at Principe they were to be killed and eaten. The Mendians took counsel, and resolved on attempting to recover their liberty. They contrived to rid themselves of their chains—armed themselves with case-knives—killed the cook—attacked the captain, who slew two of the Africans and wounded others—and achieved a victory. Two sailors took to the boat and escaped. Cinqué took command. Ruiz and Montez were put in irons, and had dealt out to them the same quantity of food and water that they had dealt out to the Africans. This continued for two days only, when their irons were removed, and they were treated very well. When the water became short, Cinqué refused it to himself and his comrades, supplying the children and the Spaniards with a small quantity daily!

Two were killed in the rencontre [fight], seven died on board the Amistad, eight died at New Haven, one was drowned at Farmington, and thirty-five survive.

Philanthropist, *December 29, 1841, in* Slave Testimony, *201–02.*

Joseph Cinqué, leader of the successful mutiny on the *Amistad* *(Library of Congress)*

### *Captains and Crews: Recruitment and Duties*

[T]he Compa. [company] not having of late had any good satisfaction of the purchasing and disposing of our Negroes doe order that all Negroes as they are brought aboard shall be taken Notice off and Numbered by the Master, the Mates, and Boatswaine, Chirurgeon [doctor], and Carpenter, or soe many of them as shall be aboard, and dayly entered into the bookes signed by our Sub: Gov'r: or Dep'ty Gov'r: and that the said Officers doe signe the bookes as often as any Negroes come aboard, and that all said Negroes brought aboard be Expressed in bills of Lading to be signed by the Comander and witnessed by some of the said officers before they weigh anchor and one or more bills of lading to be left with our Factors ashoare if there be any, or with the next ship that is to follow to be sent to us. And that the Negroes be mustered within 14 days after setting saile and soe from 14 days to 14 days all the voyage until their arrival and that every Muster be entered into the said booke by the said Officers[.] And if any Mortality shall happen amongst your Negroes in yo'r Voyage wee require for our satisfaction that you send or bring home a Certificate under yo'r Mates and Chirurgeons hands testefying the time of the death of such as shall happen to dye, for Wee shall allow none but what are soe certifyed to be dead.

*Instructions from the Royal African Company to Captain Robert Barrett, October 25, 1687, in Donnan,* Slave Trade Documents *1:361–62.*

[The crews for our ships] are for the most part supplied with the refuse and dregs of the nation. The prisons and glass houses furnish us with large quotas of boys impatient of their parent or masters, or already ruined by some untimely vice and for the most part devoid of all good principles.

*John Newton,* Journal of a Slave Trader, *1750–1754, quoted in Reynolds,* African Slavery, *30.*

It was not until after we had done with cruising off the Azores Islands [in 1860] and had taken our departure for other parts, that our [the crew's] suspicions were aroused that the whaling business was merely a blind. The first evidence came to light after the crew had been set to work breaking out the hold, and it appeared in the shape of huge quantities of rice, hardtack, salt beef, pork, etc., in quantities large enough to feed a regiment for a long time. . . .

For weeks the sham of whaling was carried on. . . .

The crew generally seemed to be well pleased at the new phase the voyage had taken and were anxious for the time to come when the ship would be well filled with "blackfish" oil, as they termed the negroes.

*Sailor Edward Manning,* Six Months on a Slaver, *in Dow,* Slave Ships, *282–83.*

## *Captain and Crews: Dangers and Difficulties*

Thursday the 23d. From noon yesterday we had but faint small breezes of wind until three in the evening, at which time the ship that stood after us was got within random gun-shot of us, appearing a fine long snug frigate; so that now we no longer doubted but she was an enemy, therefore letting fly my colours, we fir'd a shot athwart his fore foot; upon which he shew'd an Engllish ensign; but for all his cheat we knew what he was. . . . [At] four . . . being within carbine shot of us, he run out his lower tier of guns . . . and struck his false colours, and hoisted the French white sheet. I . . . order'd all my men to their guns, . . . and expected his broad-side, which when within pistol-shot, he gave us, and his volley of small shot. We return'd his civility very heartily with ours; after which he shot ahead of us, and brought to, and fell along our larboard side, and gave us his other broad-side, as we did him; then each of us loaded and fired as fast as we could, until ten o'clock at night, when his foretop mast came by the board [fell]; then he fell astern of us . . . and took his leave of us. . . . I was extremely glad that by God's assistance we defended the ship, though she was most miserably shatter'd and torn in her mast and rigging. . . .

*Thomas Phillips, journal of the 1693 voyage of the* Hannibal, *in Dow,* Slave Ships, *36–37.*

[The 1806 insurance policy for the slaver *Rambler,* out of Rhode Island, covered risks] of the Seas, Men of War, Fires, Enemies, Pirates, Rovers, Thieves, Jettisons, Letters of Mart, and Counter Mart [Letters of Marque, that is, license to capture the merchant shipping of an enemy nation], Surprizals, Takings at Sea, Arrests, Restraints and Detainment of all Kings, Princes, and people of what Nation, Condition or Quality soever . . . Risque of Captures at Sea by American Cruisers and insurrection of Slaves but not of Common Mortality.

*Coughtry,* Notorious Triangle, *98–99.*

## *Captains and Crews: Profit and Loss*

With this praye [prey—three hundred Negroes] hee [Capt. John Hawkins] sayled over the Ocean sea unto the Island of Hispaniola, and arrived first at the port of Isabella: and there hee had reasonable utterance [disposal of goods by sale or barter] of his English commodities, as also of some part of his Negros, trusting the Spaniards no further, then that by his owne strength he was able still to master them. From the port of Isabella he went to Puerto de Plata, where he made like sale . . . ; from thence also hee sayled to Monte Christi another port on the North side of Hispaniola, and the last place of his touching, where he had peaceable traffique, and made vent of [sold] the whole number of his Negros: for which he received in those 3. places by way of exchange such quantitie of merchandise, that hee did not onely lade his owne 3. shippes with hides, ginger, sugars, and some quantities of pearles, but he fraighted also two other hulkes with hides and the like commodities, which hee sent into Spaine. . . . And so with prosperous successe and much gaine . . ., he came home, and arrived in the moneth of September 1563.

*Richard Hakluyt,* Principal Navigations, *in Donnan,* Slave Trade Documents *1:44–47.*

It also concerns the adventurers [entrepreneurs] in Guinea voyages for slaves, not to allow the commanders, supercargo [agent in charge of cargo] or officers, the liberty of taking aboard any slaves for their own particular account, as is too often practised among European traders, thinking to save something in their salaries by the month: for experience has shown, that the captain's slaves never die, since there are not ten masters in fifty who scruple to make good their own out of the cargo; or at least such licence-slaves are sure to have the best accommodations aboard, and the greatest plenty of subsistance out of the ship's stock: and very often those who were allow'd to carry but two slaves, have had ten or twelve, and those the best of the cargo, subsisted out of the general provisions of the ship, and train'd up aboard, to be carpenters, coopers, and cooks, so as to sell for double the price of other slaves. . . .

*James Bardot's voyage to the Congo, 1700, in Donnan,* Slave Trade Documents *1:465.*

If any of the slaves die, the surgeon loses [on] his head money [usually one shilling for each slave sold], and the Captain [on] his commission; if the slaves are brought in bad order to market, they average low, and the officers' privilege slaves [bought for the officers' own profit], which are generally paid them on an average with the cargo, are of less value to them.

*Parliamentary Accounts and Papers, 1790, in Anstey,* Atlantic Slave Trade, *34.*

## *The Illegal International Slave Trade after 1807*

[After the Spaniards had bought me from an African,] I was put on board with a great many others, until the vessel was quite full. When we got clear of the mouth of the river we saw an English man of

Capture of a pirate slaver after the ban on the international slave trade (*Library of Congress*)

war brig, commanded by Capt. Hagan. The Spaniards prepared to fight, but the shot of [the] man of war [was] too much for them. Three of the Spaniards were killed, and several wounded, and a shot cut the mast in two, when she was taken. Captain Hagan took the slaves out of irons, when all very glad and danced too much.

Captain Hagan took us to Sierra Leone, where we were made free.

*WILLIAM THOMAS x his mark.* Anti-Slavery Reporter, *February 8, 1843, in* Slave Testimony, *226.*

For some time the American ship *Nightingale* of Boston, Francis Bowen, master, has been watched on this coast under the suspicion of being engaged in the slave trade. . . . A few days ago observing her at anchor at Kabenda, I came in and boarded her and was induced to believe she was then preparing to receive slaves. Under this impression the ship was got under way and went some distance off but with the intention of returning under the cover of the night; which was done and at 10 P.M. we anchored and sent two boats under Lieutenant Guthrie to surprise her and it was found that she had 961 slaves on board and was expecting more. Lieut. Guthrie took possession of her as a prize. . . .

*Taylor of the U.S. sloop of war* Saratoga, *describing the capture of the* Nightingale, *April 21, 1861, in Dow,* Slave Ships, *275.*

# 3

# Americans in the Slave Trade 1526–1865

## THE HISTORICAL CONTEXT

### *The Introduction of Slavery*

Rudimentary records show that even in the 16th century when the continent was still largely wilderness, black slaves were brought to North America at intervals. In 1526, a Spaniard from Hispaniola tried to set up a colony in what is now North Carolina. He failed, and the hundred-odd slaves he had brought along escaped, presumably taking refuge with Indians. Two years later, a slave survived a shipwreck in a part of New Spain now in Texas. In 1538, Estevanico de Dorante (also known as Esteban), the slave of a Spaniard, guided a party of explorers searching for gold. Zuni Indians killed him.

Africans arrived in North American British colonies almost as soon as European settlers did. In 1619, Dutch traders brought ashore near Jamestown in Virginia some 19 blacks whom they had seized from a captured Spanish slave ship. Settlers eagerly sought their labor. Probably they hired the blacks as indentured servants, bound to work for a fixed term of years, rather than as slaves for life. At that time, English law considered baptized Christians exempt from slavery, and the Spanish usually baptized slaves in Africa before embarking them. Little else is known about their lives, though at least one for a time enjoyed freedom and property. Others certainly came in the early days as indentured servants, but by 1660 the Virginia labor force included blacks in bondage for life.[1]

In all the English colonies, north and south, slavery got off to a slow start in the 17th century but increased rapidly in the 18th century, as the colonists recognized the need for a large labor force to develop the new continent. They looked first to the Indians, then to Africans, who were already laboring as slaves in vast numbers elsewhere in the New World.

The European governments of almost all of the colonies encouraged slavery. In the Dutch empire of New Netherlands, African slavery was the primary labor system. When New Netherlands fell to Britain in 1664, creating New York and New Jersey, the articles of capitulation recognized slavery as a legal institution. In prerevolutionary South Carolina, land policies under "headright" granted families 50 acres per settler. Slaves were counted in calculating their masters' entitlement to land. By the eve of the American Revolution, slavery was legal in all of the original colonies.

Over time, slavery moved south. White immigrants, many of them indentured servants who worked for an agreed-upon time and thereby earned their freedom, provided ample labor in the North; as their numbers swelled, northern colonial governments passed laws shutting out blacks from some occupations. But the heat, the swamps, and the low wages of the South did not appeal to free laborers. Settlers of the Deep South who came from slaveholding territories looked on slavery as a way of life. So it was that slavery gradually died out on the northern Atlantic coast, with its poor, rocky soil and small farms, but flourished in the South, where planters needed many hands to clear, drain, and cultivate the fertile lands along the coast. With the invention of the cotton gin and the boom in the international demand for southern cotton, planters turned to the Southwest for new, fertile land and to slavery to supply the workers for this labor-intensive crop. Even in 1790, more than 600,000 of the 697,624 slaves in what has become the continental United States lived in southern states. By 1830 the North had only 3,568 slaves, two-thirds of them in New Jersey, while the Old South had 2,005,457.[2]

In 1725 the North American British colonies held about 75,000 slaves. In the United States, what with the international slave trade; the acquisition of territories from France, Spain, and Mexico; and natural increase by birth, this number grew to 700,000 by 1790, a million and a half in 1820, more than 3 million in 1850, and nearly 4 million in 1860.[3]

## *The International Slave Trade*

From the earliest years of settlement, Americans, especially New Englanders, participated in the profitable international slave trade, building and outfitting ships and transporting slaves. After 1664, with the encouragement of New York's royal proprietor, the duke of York (whose wealth was invested in slaving), Americans began to import slaves solely for sale. International traders landed most of the slaves below the Mason-Dixon Line—perhaps sailing up and down the tidal rivers and exchanging slaves for tobacco at plantation wharves; perhaps delivering their cargoes to commission merchants, who sold them by auction on the York Peninsula of Virginia, at Yorktown, West Point, Hampton, and Bermuda Hundred.

As the early slaveholders became experienced, they began to look for slaves from particular African tribes. Koromantees, including the Fanti and the Ashanti, were said to be "remarkable for their extraordinary strength and symmetry, their distinguished appearance and proud bearing. They were blacker and taller and handsomer than their fellow slaves; vigorous, muscular and agile, intelligent, fierce, ruthless in war, fanatically attached to the idea of liberty, and strangers to fear."[4] On the other hand, natives of Guinea were more experienced in growing rice. Congo blacks were supposed to be placid; Ibos sensitive and despondent, apt to commit suicide.

American owners often shunned slaves imported from the Caribbean, preferring those who came directly from Africa. As William Beverly wrote to John Fairchild in 1743, "[P]eople are Cautious of buying such negroes as can talk English from yr [your] Island [Barbados] (such use they fancy are great rogues which was ye [the] Case of yr Negros wch [which] you ordd [ordered] Ford to sell for you). Yet they make no scruple to buy New Negs [Negroes from Africa]."[5]

In 1807, the U.S. Congress joined a European movement aimed at closing down the international slave trade—partly because the country was overstocked with slaves, partly because by then many people thought slavery wrong. Several colonies, such as Virginia in 1769, had long since agreed not to import slaves from Africa; several states, including Rhode Island, Massachusetts, and Connecticut, which collectively owned most of the American slave ships, had forbidden their citizens to engage in the trade. But many ignored the laws, and some experts estimate that even after the federal ban, 10,000 to 20,000 African slaves were imported illegally every year.[6] It proved next to impossible to stop ships from landing slaves in Georgia and Louisiana or to stop immigration from Mexico and Cuba. Nor did the U.S. government try very hard. In 1820, the collector of customs at Mobile, Alabama, reported, "From the Chandalier Islands to the Perdido river [a distance of more than a hundred miles] including the coast, and numerous other islands, we have only a small boat, with four men and an inspector, to oppose the whole confederacy of smugglers and pirates." In 1817 the governor of Georgia estimated that 20,000 slaves were smuggled into that state from Florida each year.[7]

From time to time, diehards tried to make the international trade legal again. In the late 1850s, for instance, some southerners argued for its restoration to encourage more people to own slaves so that they would support secession. But popular opinion, fueled by fear of insurrection and eagerness to preserve the value of the slaves already in the United States, opposed such a move. Even immediately before the Civil War, a Georgia secessionist asked, "Suppose we re-open the African slave trade, what would be the result? Why, we would soon be drowned in a black pool; we would be literally overwhelmed with a black population."[8]

## *Breeding Supplants Importing Slaves*

As in other slaveholding regions, in the early years almost all slaves brought into North America were men, being better suited to heavy labor. That the misery of the new slaves would be aggravated by the absence of women mattered little—though occasionally a few women were purchased "to keep [the male slaves] at home and to make them Regular."[9]

Gradually however, American slaveholders realized that they could acquire slaves more easily through breeding than buying. Slaves born in North America were not weakened by the shock of capture, the hardships of the African coffle and barracoon, and the horrors of the Middle Passage. They were born into the American slave world, not abruptly introduced into an alien environment. They had to be supported during infancy and early childhood, but no purchase price had to be paid for them.

So in the first half of the 18th century, American slaveholders began buying women in numbers equal to those of men. The gender ratio of imported slaves evened out. Nowhere else did this phenomenon occur: reliance on "natural increase" for the supply of slaves was unique to the North American colonies and later the United States.

Gradually, agriculture in the Upper South faltered as the soil wore out. Slave owners recognized that they could profit by exporting slaves to regions of the country with a growing need for labor—the Deep South and the Southwest. By the 1790s, Virginia, Maryland, and Delaware were exporting more slaves than they imported. From 1820 to 1860, the interregional movement of slaves—from North to South and especially to the Southwest—averaged each year some 20,000 slaves, partly through planter migrations but mostly through trading. "For slave children living in the Upper South in 1820, the cumulative chance of being 'sold South' by 1860 might have been something like 30 percent. . . . In the exporting states it would have been quite rare [for a slave] to have survived into middle age without being sold locally or interregionally."[10]

Henry Clay remarked to the Kentucky Colonization Society in 1829, "Nowhere in the farming portion of the United States would slave labor be generally employed, if the proprietor were not tempted to raise slaves by the high price of the Southern market, which keeps it up in his own."[11] Also, as a Virginia judge noted in 1848, "The scantiness of net profit from slave labor has become proverbial, and . . . nothing is more common than actual loss, or a benefit merely in the slow increase of capital from propagation."[12]

Slave-breeding farms never existed in these states or elsewhere—if for no other reason than that it took too long to rear a baby to an age of productive and profitable labor. But slave owners North and South did all they could to encourage, entice, or force slave women to have babies early and often. Some masters even promised slave women freedom if they bore a certain number of babies. Women slaves thus did double duty, laboring in the fields and creating new capital for their masters in the form of babies. As a former slave remarked, "A white man start out wid a few womenfolk slaves, soon him have a plantation full of little niggers runnin' 'round in deir shirt tales and a kickin' up deir heels, whilst deir mammies was in de field a hoeing and geeing at the plow handles, workin' lak a man."[13]

Georgian John C. Reed's grandfather advised him, "John, get as many young breeding-women as you can. Hire them out where they will not be abused, and after a while you can collect them on a good plantation of your own. The increase of your negroes will make you rich."[14]

## *The Domestic Slave Trade*

Thus the domestic slave trade—the trade within and among the colonies—was well developed by the end of the 18th century. For the slaves this trade meant insecurity about the future, little permanence, and all too often separation from family and friends.

In the South, slaveholders increasingly regarded their slaves as their major capital—even more so than their land. Few plantation owners or farmers worried about depleting their holdings; with so much new land available, they simply exhausted their soil and moved west. Their slaves, however, were a renewable resource, fresh supplies always available. They were also mobile, capable of moving on. What was more, they were a cash crop.

If worst came to worst, or if an owner had too many slaves, they could be sold. As Alabama attorney Henry Watson Jr. complained in 1834, "[M]ost owners sought to acquire all they could afford—sometimes more. [My neighbors] all run in debt—invariably, never pay cash, and all always one year behind hand. They wait for a sale of their crops. The roads are bad, the prices low, they cannot pay. They all wait to be sued. A suit is brought—no defense is made—an execution is taken out and is paid with all the costs and they even think it a good bargain. The rate of interest allowed is but 8 pr. cent. So much is this below the real value that a man will let his debts go unpaid, pay interest and costs and buy negroes for making cotton or land and think it even then profitable and will be much obliged to his plaintiff if he will wait for the due course of law and not personally fall out with him. [To requests for payment] his answer is "you must wait, I *can't* pay you, I *must* buy a *negro,* it is out of the question, I have the money but I *must* buy a *negro.*"[15]

Slave ownership conferred not only wealth but also prestige and status. Even the two-thirds or so of white southerners who did not own slaves had a stake in the slave system, for it supported the myth of white superiority.

Though some slave owners boasted of never selling the family slaves, others became addicted to the trade. They mortgaged their land and the slaves they already owned to buy more—to the point that in 1840 Missourians hesitated to buy slaves from Mississippi or Alabama for fear that they were already mortgaged.

Slave traders and slave owners gambled on the future prices of slaves. As Frederick Olmsted pointed out, "The supply of hands [laborers] is limited. It does not increase in the ratio of the increase of the cotton demand. If cotton should double in price next year, or become worth its weight in gold, the number of negroes in the United States would not increase four per cent. unless the African slave-trade were re-established. Now step into a dealer's 'jail' in Memphis, Montgomery, Vicksburg, or New Orleans, and you will hear the mezzano [muezzin, auctioneer] of the cotton lottery crying . . . 'If you have got the right sile [soil] and the right sort of overseer, buy [this slave], and put your trust in Providence! He's just as good for [producing] ten bales [of cotton] as I am for a julep at eleven o'clock.' And this is just as true as that any named horse is sure to win the Derby. And so the price of good labourers is constantly gambled up to a point, where, if they produce ten bales to the hand, the purchaser will be as fortunate as he who draws the high prize of the lottery; where, if they produce seven bales to the hand, he will still be in luck; where, if rot, or worm, or floods, or untimely rains or frosts occur, reducing the crop to one or two bales to the hand, as is often the case, the purchaser will have drawn a blank."[16]

The gambling fever fed on itself. By 1860, however, some professional traders were backing off, in the face of mounting abolitionist feeling in the North. In 1859, trader Philip Thomas wrote to a colleague, "I am firmly of the opinion that times are growing worse and worse as fast as the moments flee and the sooner we get out of [slave trading] the better."[17] Slaves overhearing their owners' comments on the approach of war wondered why people still wanted to buy more slaves. Nonetheless on January 17, 1860, the Milledgeville, Georgia, *Federal Union* reported, "There is a perfect fever raging in Georgia now on the subject of buying negroes. Several sales which have come under our eye within a month past afford an unmistakable symptom of the prevalence of a disease in the public mind on this subject. . . . Men are borrowing money at exorbitant rates of interest to buy negroes at exorbitant prices. . . . [Slaves are 25 percent higher,] with cotton at ten and one-half cents than they were two or three years ago, when it was worth fifteen or sixteen cents. Men are demented upon the subject."[18]

From time to time and for one reason or another, slave states tried to limit the domestic traffic in slaves, forbidding their importation into the state for sale—though citizens were left free to import as many as they wished for their own use. In 1855, Judge H. L. Benning of the Georgia Supreme Court speculated on that state's motives: "The main reason . . . was, I think, a fear that this traffic, if permitted, would in the end, empty the more northerly of the slave states of their slaves, and thus convert those states from friends and allies into enemies and assailants. The chief reason was, I think, not at all to promote abolition in this State, but to prevent abolition in other States. Another reason was, no doubt, a disposition to keep the proportion of the free population to the slave from being materially changed. And avarice probably had some degree of influence—the avarice of slaveholders already in the state, the value of whose slaves would be diminished as the supply from abroad [outside the state] should be increased."[19]

In any case, slave traders continually flouted these laws. Often, they simply went across the border to a neighboring state to execute the necessary papers. If to protect itself against receiving troublemakers a state demanded certificates of good character for slaves on sale, traders soon reduced the requirement to a travesty. Thus, slave trader Bacon Tait in 1832 advised a friend to take along a certificate for slaves he was planning to sell in Mississippi: "[Y]ou can put as many negroes as you please in *one certificate*. The usual way as I understand of obtaining these certificates is to get two freeholders to go along and look at your negroes. You then tell them the name of each negro—the freeholders then say that they know the negroes and give the certificates accordingly."[20]

## *Domestic Slave Traders*

After the end of the legal international trade in 1808, domestic slave traders grew ever more sophisticated and professional. Smelling profit, they foraged through the Upper and Deep South for slaves they could buy and resell. Traders in Maryland and Virginia often pretended to be planters buying slaves for their own use or to be agents purchasing families for some unnamed planter. Though some worked only on commission, typically they bought slaves outright. They paid cash—which appealed to the planters, who were almost always short of cash in their credit-based economy.[21] Sometimes the traders protected their investments by vaccinating and insuring the slaves.

They bought roughly equal numbers of males and females—though they paid less for women (except for the light-skinned "fancy girls" destined to become concubines or prostitutes). They preferred younger slaves, concentrating most heavily on those 15 to 25. Sometimes they asked for certificates of good conduct with their purchases, but they were not above palming off persistent runaways and rebels on unsuspecting new owners. Only rarely did they buy, or have the opportunity to buy, complete nuclear families; slaves were usually on the market either for the convenience of the master or because of the demand for a

The Charleston slave market (*Crowe,* With Thackeray in America)

particular kind of slave. "Trading . . . accounted from the 1810s or 1820s onward for at least 60 percent of the overall interregional movement; and those sales occurred, not because of crippling debt or the death of owners, but overwhelmingly for speculative reasons. In the antebellum South, the slaveowning class was generally willing, simply for reasons of financial advantage, to separate black families. The scale of those separations was such that one out of every five marriages of Upper South slaves would have been prematurely terminated by the trade; if other interventions by masters are added, the proportion rises to about one in three. Furthermore, the trade would have separated about one in three of the exporting region's slave children (under fourteen years) from their parents; again local sales and other actions by masters would have raised this proportion to about one in two. And, with very intensive rates of importation into Lower South states throughout the antebellum period, the impact on the importing states was similarly profound."[22] Occasionally an owner would specify that a slave was not to be sold out of the state or that members of a family group were not to be separated—though, of course, slave traders preferred to buy without such restrictions and did not always honor them.

Everyone professed to scorn slave traders, those dealers in human flesh. But they not only flourished financially but often enjoyed high social position and were elected to public office. In fact, they performed a necessary function in the slave-based economy, and many who professed contempt for them nonetheless bought from and sold to them or loaned them money to carry on their business. As Angelina Grimké cogently remarked, "There is no difference in *principle,* in Christian ethics, between the despised slave dealer (who makes his fortune by trading in the bodies and souls of men, women and children) and the Christian who buys slaves from, or sells slaves to him; indeed, if slaves were not wanted by the respectable, the wealthy, and the religious in a community, there would be no slaves in that community and of course no slave-dealers."[23]

The slave traders had no trouble finding willing sellers and willing buyers. As profits soared, speculation in slaves increased. Most sales were not forced: only 4

A slave trader's coffle setting out
(*Library of Congress*)

or 5 percent were occasioned by the death or debt of masters. Sales multiplied in good times, with the demand for more labor.[24] In this respect, the slave trade did not differ from any other type of business: profit drove it.

## *The Coffles*

The traders moved the slaves they bought south and west, shipping them down the coast, transporting them by train, or more often driving them in coffles on forced marches, sometimes in chains and irons. (Other slaves traveled in coffles with their owners to new homes.)

These sad processions usually began with a false show of gaiety, motivated either by fear of the lash wielded by the trader or his black drivers or by a little rum measured out to the slaves. The slaves knew all too well that they were leaving friends and family behind. Sometimes traders simply gave slave babies too heavy for their mothers to carry to anyone who would take them. On the journey itself most of the slaves walked the weary miles, only the toddlers riding in the wagons. They walked day after day, in good weather or bad, cold or heat. "We have got along very well," reported one Thomas Burton, who supervised a coffle that set out from North Carolina to Mississippi in December 1845. "So far all well and able to eat a good allowance, with the exception of colds. J. D. Long and myself has very severe colds. We are worse off than any of the negroes. . . . We have travelled 20 miles per day since we left you. We are now 150 miles from home. We have had a severe time for travelling today. . . . [It] has been raining and freesing all day but slow and we have drove some 22 or 3 miles. . . ."[25] At night, they bivouacked where they could. On the journey some traders abused the bodies of the younger slave women for their own pleasure or made them available to other whites. The journey ended with the slave jail, the slave auction or salesroom, and an unknown future with a new master.

## *Slave Auctions and Sales*

The slave traders were abetted by the owners of "nigger jails," who "fixed up" the slaves to look more attractive to purchasers; by brokers or commission merchants, who took on the task of selling slaves for owners who did not wish to dirty their own hands; and by auctioneers.

The slave jails served a triple function—as places to confine and punish slaves who had angered their masters, as temporary stopping places for masters traveling with their slaves, and as holding pens for slaves waiting to be sold. Slaves held there for sale were better fed than the others, so as to fatten them in order to raise their purchase prices. Even so, former slave Sella Martin remembered, "[My mother] was sickened to the heart by the systematic falsehoods which the trader made the slaves tell to those who came to purchase them; by the vice which was inseparable from crowding men and women together, and by the terrible cruelty which the trader practised upon those who would not give up their virtue and their honour at his bidding."[26] Some slave jails offered slaves directly for inspection and sale.

Slaves were also sold at various other places: on the wharves where ships had landed them, in courthouse yards, in marketplaces, or in the offices of brokers who purchased or received slaves for sale on commission. Slave traders schemed to get the highest possible prices, hiding defects and advanced age as much as they could. They learned that planters preferred to buy slaves in the spring, when they could immediately put them to work on the new crop, rather than having first to carry them over the winter; also, they found that it was bet-

A holding pen for slaves (*National Archives*)

ter to offer a large lot for sale, because the big sale would attract more buyers, who might bid each other up. In all these situations, prospective buyers thought themselves entitled to inspect the slaves for defects, handling them freely and demanding that the slaves move on command to demonstrate their strength and health. Usually an auctioneer ran the sale, pushing the bidding as high as he could.

## *Private Sales*

Some owners bypassed the traders by advertising their own slaves for sale, asking interested persons to apply to a printer, editor, or owner of the slave jail or to inspect the slaves on the owner's premises.[27] Now and then a master sent a slave around to find a purchaser, carrying a note signed by the owner attesting to his or her health, good temper, and skills. "The bearer, Mary Jane, and her two

Auction house in New Orleans (*Library of Congress*)

daughters, are for sale," wrote an owner in Washington, D.C. "They are sold for no earthly fault whatever. She is one of the most ladylike and trustworthy servants I ever knew. She is a first rate parlour servant; can arrange and set out a dinner or party supper with as much taste as the most of white ladies. She is a pretty good mantua maker; can cut out and make vests and pantaloons and roundabouts and joseys for little boys in a first-rate manner. Her daughters' ages are eleven and thirteen years, brought up exclusively as house servants. The eldest can sew neatly, both can knit stockings, and all are accustomed to all kinds of house work. They would not be sold to speculators or traders for any price whatever."[28]

In these private sales, it was easier for an owner to show some concern for the slave's wishes—not to leave the neighborhood or not to be parted from family. A country owner might yield to a slave's yearning to live in the city. Or, on the other hand, the owner might show the indifference to the slaves' feeling manifested in an advertisement in the *New Orleans Bee:* "NEGROES FOR SALE.—A negro woman, 24 years of age, and her two children, one eight and the other three years old. Said negroes will be sold SEPARATELY or together, *as desired*. The woman is a good seamstress. She will be sold low for cash, or EXCHANGED FOR GROCERIES."[29]

## *Kidnapping and Slave Stealing*

Because slaves were valuable property, both owners and traders faced the hazard of slave stealing. For instance, the Murrell gang, which operated in the Southwest in the early 1830s, would conspire with a slave, promising him a reward (perhaps his freedom) if he would run off with them, let himself be sold, and then escape to rejoin them; sometimes the gang repeated the process until the slave threatened to expose them, at which point they murdered him.[30]

But if slave owners and slave traders risked losing their property, free blacks risked much worse—losing their liberty. Being kidnapped and sold into slavery was a real and present danger for free blacks in both free and slave states. It could happen to children, adults, or whole families. In 1846, the Raleigh, North Carolina, *Star* reported the "taking off of a little son of a poor blind free negro . . . under such circumstances as to justify the suspicion that he was stolen to enslave him."[31]Former slave J. W. Lindsay remarked in an 1863 interview, "There are speculators there who are all the time speculating in human flesh & blood,—buying up men, women & children and if they find out that there are any free families who are not much noticed by the inhabitants, they will go in the dead hour of the night & kidnap them, take them off 25 or 30 miles, put them into a slave pen, & that is the last of them. . . ."[32]

Since southern courts did not allow blacks to testify against whites, and since the word of a white was almost always taken against that of a black, kidnappers' victims were hard put to prove their right to freedom. In December of 1851, for instance, Marylander Thomas McCreary snatched 16-year-old Elizabeth Parker, who lived just over the Pennsylvania line, and sold her in New Orleans for $1900. Two weeks later, he stole her younger sister, Rachel, fighting off the Millers, her employers, with a knife. Mr. Miller and a rescue party pursued them to Baltimore, had Rachel transferred from a slave pen to prison, and petitioned for her freedom; on the way home Miller was poisoned. The aroused citizens of Chester County, Pennsylvania, finally succeeded in getting both Parker girls back to their homes, after an 1853 trial in Maryland in which 49 white witnesses came from Pennsylvania to testify.[33]

The records show that many alleged victims of kidnappers, mostly black but some white, served in slavery for years, making effort after vain effort to regain their freedom. Even those few who succeeded could gain no recompense for their sufferings and losses.

## *Slave Participation in the Slave Trade*

One way and another, slaves sometimes managed to influence their own sales. The men who ran slave jails recognized this and threatened slaves who did not cooperate with them. As former slave Washington Taylor remembered, "Pussuns [being inspected in the slave pens] had ter be on dere p's an' q's an' showin' off so as to sell well when some one come ter buy 'em, an' ef yo' didn't put on dat pleasin' look, yo'd pay fer it when de pussuns went out o' de ya'd. An' ef dey sol' yo' on trial an' yo' was brought back, yo' 'd be 'mos' killed."[34] Owners also recognized that the attitude of the slave could make a difference. In 1833, one master advertised in the Cambridge, Maryland, *Chronicle:* "I will sell one or more or all of three Negro men, to persons in the county that they will consent to live with. . . ."[35] Other sellers used rewards, like North Carolinian speculator Obadiah Fields, who said, "It was understood that I should give the negroes a present if they would try to get homes and not do anything against the interest of their sales, and to Isaac I gave $3; to Dick $2; to Fan $1; to Isabel $2; Dick and Isaac a hat each at 1 = $2."[36]

At an auction a slave might hang his head and shuffle listlessly before a buyer who looked mean or put his best foot forward when a kind-looking buyer approached. Sometimes slaves on the auction block would boast of their own abilities simply out of pride in bringing a high price. Now and then a slave succeeded in blocking a sale completely—like Lucy, who was being sold away from her child. Her owner finally wrote to the auctioneer to whom he had entrusted her, "I fear you cannot sell Lucy, in her low spirited situation for more than four hundred and twenty five dollars, which sum I am not disposed to take. Therefore if you cannot get four hundred and fifty dollars twenty four hours after the receipt of this be so kind as to send her [back]."[37] Slaves even cut off their own hands to prevent their sale.

A slave might write to a former mistress asking to be brought back. Another might find possible buyers for herself and ask to be sold in order not to be parted from husband or child. Or a slave might seek out a buyer who would allow him to hire his own time and eventually buy himself. At least one slave begged a Moravian church to buy him, "for he wanted to find salvation, and feared to be lost."[38]

## *Buying Freedom and Manumission*

Although slaves had to have extraordinary intelligence, determination, and luck to make it work, a surprising number actually bought themselves. Legally, slaves could own nothing, but in fact some earned a little money for themselves. Plantation owners often permitted their slaves to farm small plots and sell their produce or make baskets or brooms for sale; in gray-market transactions, slaves sold "moonshine" and stolen goods.

A more likely way for slaves to accumulate money, however, arose from the practice of "hiring out," by which owners who did not for a period need the services of a slave leased their labor to someone else. It occurred to some slaves that they might, with their masters' assent, hire their own time. That is, a slave would promise to support himself and pay his owner a profit out of the wages he earned by running his own business or working for another employer. Frederick Douglass, for instance, while still a slave in Baltimore, hired his own time and went to work in a shipyard, eventually saving up the funds that he used in his escape. Other slaves managed to save enough to buy their own freedom.

Buying oneself was always a risky business, because owners often failed to keep their promises. A slave and his owner might agree on a purchase price and the slave make regular payments toward it, perhaps even pay off the whole amount, but if the master denied that the payments had been made or otherwise defaulted on the agreement, the slave could do little. Courts often held to the letter of the law rather than the actualities of the slave economy, refusing to enforce the bargains on the grounds that a slave, as property, could not make a contract.

All the same, numbers of slaves not only bought themselves but went on to buy other members of their families in order to set them free. Former slave Jerry Moore told the story of his father, who had belonged to "a old bachelor named Moore, in Alabama. Moore freed all his niggers 'fore 'mancipation except three. They was to pay a debt, and my father was Moore's choice man and was one of the three. He bought hisself. He had saved up some money, and when they went to sell him he bid $800. The auctioneer cries round to git a raise, but wouldn't nobody bid on my father 'cause he was one of Moore's 'free niggers.' My father done say after the war he could have buyed hisself for $1.50."[39]

Some free blacks, both women and men, devoted their energies and earnings to buying slaves to liberate them. In 1831 in Petersburg, Virginia, John Updike manumitted a slave, whom he described as "lately purchased by me from Shadrach Brander, so that the said Rheuben Rhenlds shall be and remain free from this time henceforth forever."[40]

Here and there a master, convinced that slaveholding was wrong, decided to free his slaves. Difficulties lay in his path. His conscience might trouble him. "You know, my dear Son," wrote Henry Laurens, "I abhor Slavery. I am not the man who enslaved them. . . . [N]evertheless I am devising means for manumitting many of them and for cutting off the entail of Slavery. . . . [But] what will my Children say if I deprive them of so much Estate?"[41]

Other masters genuinely worried about what would happen to their slaves once freed. Could they manage on their own, support themselves, save up against sickness and old age? After all, free blacks faced a hostile environment, filled with racial prejudice. Even in free states they were shut out of many occupations, and their civil rights were rigorously limited. Some free states would not admit them at all. How would they survive? What kind of fresh start did their former masters owe them? In about 1816, William Sumner of Tennessee worried about just such problems; he proposed to take 40 slaves to Indiana to give them a fresh start there. "I think," he wrote, "that after a man has had the use of slaves and their ancestors, twenty or thirty years, it is unjust and inhuman to set them free, unprovided with a home, &c. &c."[42] Yet for cash-poor planters costs like these could be formidable.

Further, slave states frequently limited the power of masters to manumit. Because they feared the presence of a large free black population, some states absolutely forbade the practice. Others required the assent of the legislature to each individual manumission. If they did permit manumission, most slave states required that the freed blacks leave the state within a short time. In the 1850s, Louisiana and Tennessee ordered that freed slaves be sent out of the United States.

Out of the difficulties of manumission developed an unofficial status of semi-freedom. Especially in the 1840s and 1850s, a number of slaves attained quasi freedom. That is, they lived as independently as possible, though they remained legally enslaved—a position that some whites assured them was better than freedom, since it still brought them their masters' support. In fact, of course, it depended on the favor of the master; if he changed his mind or died, it ended.

A good many masters chose to wait until they died to free their slaves. All too often they drew their wills improperly or failed to foresee events. What if, for instance, the will freed a slave but did not provide a bond that he would never become dependent on the state for support? Was the manumission valid? Sometimes the court did rule for the slave—as in the case of Dolly Mullin, whose master in 1821 had left her a tract of land but had neglected to free her. The court nonetheless gave her both freedom and the land, on the grounds that slaves could not own land and therefore her master must have intended to free her. One master in 1801 executed a deed freeing his slave Catin, "with the qualification and condition, . . . that she shall hold and enjoy freedom, . . . immediately after my death. But during my life she is to remain in my service and power. . . ." Between 1801 and her master's death, Catin had children; when he died she was indeed freed, but her children remained slaves, because they had been born to a slave mother.[43]

Relatives of owners often contested wills that manumitted; they demanded ownership of the slaves for themselves or simply lied to the illiterate slaves and denied them their freedom. The British traveler Eyre Crowe told a pathetic story "of a lax white trader, who, besides his legitimate offspring, left a second family of dusky-coloured children. Not knowing, what was a fact, that he was insolvent, he left them free by his will. The creditors, not to be baulked, sold these little mulattoes as slaves, to be sent down South."[44] One wary master, well aware of the difficulties, in his will freed his black daughter and left her half his estate, taking the precaution of bribing his sister into cooperation by leaving the other half to her, *if she arranged for the boarding and education of his daughter as the will provided.*[45]

Despite all this, some manumissions did occur, most often freeing a master's child or a slave who had long rendered faithful service. In the year 1860, when slaves numbered almost 4 million, some 3,000 of them were manumitted.[46]

Because of the clash of the laws of free states with those of slave states, some slaves were able to claim involuntary manumission. They argued, that is, that if their master had taken them into a free state, he had by the laws of that state freed them. Since the laws of the various free states differed one from another, involuntary manumission could easily occur. In Ohio, for instance, any master who made certain purchases that could be interpreted as showing intention to settle in the state thereby freed any slaves traveling with him—but it took a knowledgeable slave or friend of a slave to prove it. How many slaves were so freed no one knows, but state supreme courts rendered decisions in only 575 such cases during the entire slaveholding era, in 57 percent of which the slave won his freedom.[47]

## Chronicle of Events

**1526**
Lucas Vásquez de Ayllón, a Spanish official from Hispaniola, attempts to establish a colony in North America, landing two hundred Spaniards and one hundred black slaves near what is now Cape Fear, in North Carolina.

**1528**
A shipwrecked slave arrives in Texas (part of New Spain).

**1538**
Estevanico de Dorantes, a black slave of a Spanish master, guides a party sent by the Conquistadores to find the golden cities of Cibola in New Spain, only to be killed by Zuni Indians.

**1619**
*August:* The first African blacks in the British North American colonies are brought ashore at Jamestown, Virginia, from a "Dutch man of Warr." They apparently serve as indentured servants for a term of years.

**1626**
The Dutch West India Company imports 11 black male slaves into New Netherlands.

**1629**
In the charter of the New Netherlands, the Dutch West India Company promises "to supply the colonists with as many Blacks as they conveniently can."

**1636**
The first American slave vessel, the *Desire,* is built and launched at Marblehead, Massachusetts.

**1638**
*December 10:* At Salem, Massachusetts, Capt. W. Pierce exchanges a group of captive Pequot Indian warriors for "salt, cotton, tobacco, and Negroes."

**1641**
A Virginia court in *re Negro John Punch* sentences three runaway servants, adding one year to the indentures of the two white men but sentencing the black to lifetime service.

The first blacks land at Jamestown in 1619 (*Library of Congress*)

Massachusetts sanctions slavery for captives taken in "just" wars, strangers sold into slavery, and individuals required by the colonial authorities to be sold into servitude.

A Virginia court allows John Graweere, a "negro servant," to purchase his child from the owner of the child's mother, in order to raise the child as a Christian.

**1642**
Blacks captured by the Dutch from the Spanish try to claim their freedom in New Amsterdam but are sold into slavery.

**1644**
The Dutch Bureau of Accounts suggests to the West India Company that it allow the colonists to import into New Netherlands as many blacks as they can pay cash for.

**1645**
Virginian A. Vanga emancipates a number of slaves in his will.

**1646**
Francis Potts sells a black woman and child to Stephen Carlton, "to the use of him forever."

**1659**
A Virginia law reduces taxes on exporting tobacco whenever slaves are traded for tobacco.

**1661**
A treaty between the Dutch and the English provides for the delivery of 2,000–3,000 hogsheads of tobacco annually in return for slaves and merchandise.

**1662**
A Virginia law sets a tax on "all negroes, male and female being imported."

**1664**
At the fall of New Netherlands to the British, creating New York and New Jersey, the articles of capitulation recognize slavery as a legal institution.

**1678**
Boston merchants sell blacks in Virginia as slaves or indentured servants.

**1682**
A law decrees that "all servants brought into Virginia, by sea or land, not being Christians, whether negroes, Moors, mulattoes, or Indians . . . and all Indians, which shall hereafter be sold by neighboring Indians, or any other trafficking with us, as slaves, shall be slaves to all intents and purposes."

**1691**
Virginia prohibits freeing a black or mulatto without also providing for her or his transportation out of the state within six months.

**1695**
Maryland levies a duty of ten shillings on imported blacks. Several other colonies soon follow suit.

**1699**
Virginia sets a tax of 20 shillings for every slave imported.

**1702**
Queen Anne directs that the Royal African Company take care that New York have "a constant and sufficient supply of merchantable Negroes, at moderate rates."

**1703**
Massachusetts requires masters manumitting slaves to post a bond so that freed slaves will not become public charges.

**1706**
Louisiana settlers send a request to France that they be allowed to trade American Indian slaves in the West Indies for black slaves, at the rate of three Indians for two blacks.

**1715**
Maryland enacts a law providing that all slaves imported into the province, and their descendants, shall be slaves during their natural lives.

**1719**
The first shipment of African slaves lands in Louisiana—about five hundred "well-made and healthy negroes" between eight and thirty years old, including some "who know how to cultivate rice."

**1723**
Virginia passes an act to limit the importation of slaves.

**1730–1750**
The gender ratio of male and female slaves evens out, as more women are imported.

Slaveholders begin to set an economic value on women slaves' child bearing.

**1732**
James Oglethorpe and other officials forbid the importation of slaves into Georgia.

**1734**
Virginia again sets a tax on importing slaves.

A law is drafted, to take effect in 1735, prohibiting slavery in Georgia. It will be widely disregarded.

**1735**
The first major petition for legal slavery in Georgia is sent to London.

**1749**
Over the opposition of the Scots of New Inverness, Georgia, trustees permit the importation of black slaves.

**1767**
Members of the Virginia House of Burgesses, meeting as a private body, boycott the British slave trade, resolving "[t]hat they will not import any Slaves or purchase any imported, after the First day of *November* next, until the said Acts of Parliament [the Townshend Acts] are repealed." Similar boycotts are soon adopted in South Carolina, Georgia, and North Carolina.

**1770**
King George III instructs the governor of Virginia "upon pain of the highest displeasure, to assent to no law by which the importation of slaves should be in any respect prohibited or obstructed."

**1772**
The Virginia House of Burgesses tells George III that "the importation of slaves into the colonies from the coast of Africa hath long been considered a trade of great inhumanity, and under its present encouragement, we have too much reason to fear will endanger the very existence of your Majesty's American dominions."

**1774**
The First Continental Congress suspends trade with Great Britain, providing that Americans will not import slaves or buy slaves imported after December 1, "after which time, we will wholly discontinue the slave trade."

Connecticut forbids anyone to bring slaves into the Colony "to be disposed of, left, or sold."

The outbreak of open hostilities with England shuts down the international American slave trade until the end of the American Revolution.

*August:* The Provincial Convention in North Carolina resolves "[t]hat we will not import any slave or slaves, or purchase any slave or slaves imported or brought into the Province by others . . . after the first day of November next."

**1776**
The Second Continental Congress votes "[t]hat no slaves be imported into any of the thirteen United Colonies."

**1778**
Virginia abolishes the importation of blacks into the state.

**1779**
Rhode Island forbids residents to purchase slaves for removal from the state or to remove them from the state without their consent.

**1782**
Virginia encourages private manumissions by removing earlier restrictions; most southern colonies soon follow suit.

**1785**
New York prohibits the importation of slaves and passes manumission acts, stating that masters freeing slaves need no longer post two hundred pounds' security to prevent their becoming dependent on the community.

**1787**
The Northwest Ordinance provides that "there shall be neither slavery nor involuntary servitude in the said territory [the Northwest Territory] otherwise than in punishment of crimes."

South Carolina closes its overseas and domestic slave trade.

Delaware passes legislation to regulate slave trading to other states, especially the trade in kidnapped free blacks.

North Carolina lays a prohibitive duty on slaves imported from Africa.

Rhode Island prohibits its residents from participating in the slave trade—without much effect.

**1788**
Connecticut and Massachusetts prohibit their residents from participating in the slave trade.

South Carolina decides to permit the continuation of its domestic slave trade.

**1789**
Maryland refuses the request of a group of Quakers to prohibit the exportation of slaves.

**1791**
Massachusetts courts find the brigantine *Hope,* John Stanton, master, guilty of violating the statute against participation in the international slave trade.

**1792**
Inhabitants of Beaufort, South Carolina, petition against the practice of northerners who "have for a number of years past been in the habit of shipping to these Southern States, slaves, who are scandalously infamous and incorrigible."

**1794**
Congress prohibits the slave trade between the United States and any foreign place or country.

**1798**
Georgia prohibits the international slave trade.

**1799–1804**
The federal government prosecutes a series of cases against Rhode Island slave traders, with limited success.

**1800**
Congress places restrictions on the international slave trade, forbidding citizens and residents any interest in vessels engaged in carrying slaves from one foreign place to another.

**1803**
South Carolina bans the importation of slaves from the French West Indies, for fear they may instigate a rebellion.

South Carolina opens a port for the importation of slaves from Africa.

**1804**
The United States forbids the importation of blacks from foreign territory into the Louisiana Purchase after October 1.

**1806**
Virginia requires that manumitted slaves leave the state within 12 months.

**1807–1808**
The United States prohibits the importation of slaves, on penalty of fine, imprisonment, and loss of ships and cargoes; captured smuggled slaves are to be disposed of according to state law.

**1816**
Mexican revolutionary Manuel Herrera creates a government at Galveston, which begins smuggling slaves into Louisiana.

**1817**
Jean Lafitte begins capturing Spanish slave ships and selling them in Galveston, whence slaves are smuggled into the United States.

Georgia officially bans the slave trade.

**1819**
Virginia and North Carolina remove restraints on interstate slave trade.

Congress passes an anti–slave trade act, providing that Africans illegally taken from Africa and recaptured by the U.S. government be returned to the coast of Africa, there to be looked after by U.S. agents. The act prompts President James Monroe to send out agents to selected African territories for this purpose.

The United States sends a squadron to the coast of Africa to suppress the slave trade illegally carried on by American vessels.

**1820**
The United States forces Jean Lafitte out of slave trading.

**1826**
Pennsylvania passes a personal liberty or antikidnapping law, penalizing anyone who shall "take or carry away from the State any negro with the intention of selling him as a slave, or of detaining or causing to be detained such negro as a slave for life."

**1827**
Tennessee officially bans the slave trade.

*September 15:* The Texas congress decrees that state records of slaves be kept and that a tenth of the slaves belonging to any estate passed along by inheritance be freed.

*November:* The Texas congress provides that slaves may be sold from one owner to another.

**1832**
Alabama removes restraints on the interstate slave trade.

**1833**
Kentucky forbids residents (except immigrants) to buy and import slaves even for their own use, unless those slaves are acquired "by will, descent, distribution, or marriage, or gift in consideration of marriage."

**1834**
Louisiana removes restraints on the interstate slave trade.

**1835**
The *Enterprise,* en route between Alexandria, Virginia, and Charleston, South Carolina, with about 75 slaves, is driven by a storm to Bermuda, where the slaves are freed.

Spain and Great Britain sign a treaty giving British cruisers authority to seize Spanish vessels suspected of carrying slaves.

**1836**
The provisional government of Texas makes it unlawful "for any free negro or mulatto to come within the limits of Texas"; violators are to be sold at auction.

**1840**
Slaves stage a successful mutiny on the *Amistad,* which lands in an American port.

**1841**
Slaves aboard the *Creole,* en route from Virginia to Louisiana, mutiny under the leadership of Madison Washington and take the ship to Nassau.

The U.S. Supreme Court declares the Africans of the *Amistad* free men.

**1842**
The Ashburton Treaty with Great Britain requires the United States to keep near the coast of Africa a naval force adequate to suppress the slave trade.

**1843**
Commodore Matthew Perry is sent to the African coast with four vessels to suppress the slave trade, but slavers often evade this force.

**1846**
Mississippi removes restraints on the interstate slave trade.

**1848**
South Carolina removes restraints on the interstate slave trade.

**1849**
Kentucky removes restraints on the interstate slave trade.

Young black men in the Charleston open-air slave market (*Crowe,* With Thackeray in America)

**1850**
Maryland removes restraints on the interstate slave trade.

**1855**
Tennessee and Georgia remove restraints on the interstate slave trade.

**1858**
*December:* The slaver *Wanderer* illegally lands about 420 African slaves near Brunswick, Georgia.

**1859**
The secretary of the navy reports the capture of 11 slave ships by U.S. warships.

**1860**
Manumissions reportedly number some 3,000.

*July:* The slaver Clotilde illegally delivers 103 slaves into Mobile Bay, whence they are transshipped up the Alabama River.

**1861**
Texas, now a member of the Confederacy, absolutely prohibits manumission.

## EYEWITNESS TESTIMONY

### *Breeding for Profit*

And I Shd. [should] Be obliged to Yr. Excellency, for advising those who may be concerned for me, in such Encrease of Negroes, not so much to Consult my most Immediate Profit, as to render the Negroes I now have happy and contented, wch [which] I know they cannot be without having each a Wife. . . . [T]ho the Women will not work all together so well as ye [the] Men, Yet Amends will be sufficiently made in a very few years by the Great Encrease of Children who may easily [be] traind up and become faithfully attached to the Glebe and to their Master.

*The earl of Egmont, 1769, in Littlefield,* Rice and Slaves, *65.*

The exportation [of slaves from Virginia to other southern states] has averaged 8,500 for the last twenty years. . . . It is a practice, and an increasing practice in parts of Virginia, to rear slaves for market. How can an honorable mind, a patriot, and a lover of his country, bear to see this ancient dominion . . . converted into one grand menagerie where men are to be reared for market like oxen for the shambles[?]

*Thomas Jefferson Randolph to the Virginia House of Delegates, January 21, 1832, in Bancroft,* Slave Trading, *69–70.*

Massa, he bring some more women to see me. He wouldn't let me have jus' one woman. I have 'bout fifteen and I don't know how many children. Some over a hunerd, I's sho'.

*Ex-slave Elige Davison, in Tadman,* Speculators and Slaves, *123.*

### *Buying Oneself*

[Ellen] having been found to be a remarkably steady and industrious woman . . . the extraordinary character of the said petitioner and her husband induced her master about two years ago when she was likely to be separated from her husband, in consequence of the removal of her master . . . to encourage her in her endeavouring to raise money by subscription to purchase herself and her . . . child. The master subscribed a considerable sum for this purpose and many of your petitioners also subscribed. By this means and by her own indefatigable efforts and industry she has raised money sufficient for the purchase of herself and her child Ellen.

*Petition to the state of Virginia, 1815, in Johnston,* Race Relations, 7.

My uncles paid fifteen hundred dollars apiece for themselves. They bought themselves three times. They got cheated out of their freedom in the first instance, and were put in jail at one time, and were going to be sold down South, right away; but parties who were well acquainted with us, and knew we had made desperate struggles for our freedom, came forward and advanced the money, and took us out of jail, and put us on a footing so that we could go ahead and earn money to pay the debt. . . . My uncles bought me and my mother, as well as themselves. . . . I had a grandfather who had long been free, and when the boys grew up, he would take them and learn them a trade, and keep them out of the hands of the traders. . . .

*Gutman,* Black Family, *203–4.*

### *Coffles*

The next morning but one we started with this negro trader upon that dreaded and despairing journey [from North Carolina] to the cotton fields of Georgia. . . . A long row of men chained two-and-two together, called the "coffle," and numbering about thirty persons, was the first to march forth from the "pen"; then came the quiet slaves—that is, those who were tame in spirit and degraded; then came the unmarried women, or those without children; after these came the children who were able to walk; and following them came mothers with their infants and young children in their arms.

This "gang" of slaves was arranged in travelling order, all being on foot except the children that were too young to walk and too old to be carried in arms. These latter were put into a waggon. But mothers with infants had to carry them in their arms; and their blood often stained the whip when, from exhaustion, they lagged behind. When the order was given to march, it was always on such occasions accompanied by the command, which the slaves were made to understand before they left the "pen," to "strike up lively," which means that they must begin a song.

[T]he negroes, who have very little hope of ever seeing those again who are dearer to them than life, and who are weeping and wailing over the separation, often turn the song thus demanded into a farewell dirge.

*Sella Martin in* Slave Testimony, *704–5.*

In the afternoon, before one of these gangs was sent off, a very dark woman was brought [in] with quite a light-colored baby. One of the traders asked the owner, likewise a trader, what he was going to do with that brat. "D—d if I know", was the reply. "I'm bothered to know what to do with it."—"We can't take it in the wagons and have it squalling all the way!"—"Here," said the owner to an inhabitant of Platte City, who just then came in with a boy for sale, "don't you want this thing? You may have it for twenty-five dollars. D—n it," he continued, snatching the babe from its mother's arms by the shoulder and hefting it, "it weighs twenty-five pounds! Will you take it?"—"Yes."—"Take it now."—And the child was carried off amid the heart-rending shrieks and pleadings of the agonized mother.

*John Doy, in Bancroft,* Slave Trading, *137, n. 38.*

[The trader] has [in his coffle] about 16 fellows, seven boys, the balance women and girls, except one child. . . . He has 12 fellows in the chain all of which jumping Jinny [the trader's wife] drives before her. She carries up the rear armed and equipped in a style which reduces it to a certainty that if life lasts you will see her in Montgomery.

*Letter to Isaac Jarratt, March 3, 1834, in Tadman,* Speculators and Slave, *76.*

## *Domestic Slave Trade*

[Wanted:] One hundred Negroes, from 20 to 30 years old, for which a good price will be given. They are to be sent out of state, therefore we shall not be particular respecting the character of any of them—Hearty and well made is all that is necessary.

*1787 advertisement by Moses Austin in Richmond, Virginia, in Tadman,* Speculators and Slaves, *15.*

[In 1799 a shortage of $10,000 in the Georgia treasury led to the discovery that a Mr. Sims, a member of the legislature, had "borrowed" the money and commissioned one Speers to buy slaves in Virginia.] Speers accordingly went and purchased a considerable number of negroes; and on his way returning to this state the negroes rose and cut the throat of Speers and another man who accompanied him. The slaves fled, and about ten of them, I think, were killed. In consequence of this misfortune Mr. Sims was rendered unable to raise the money at the time the legislature met.

*Charleston, South Carolina,* City Gazette, *December 21, 1799, in Phillips,* American Negro Slavery, *189.*

I took your Negroe George some time ago home, thinking I might be the better able to Sell him: who after beening [being] with me a night behaved himself in such an Insolent manner I immediately remanded [him] back to the Gaol [jail]. About a Week since [ago] I put him up at Public Sale at Christopher

Selling a slave woman by the pound (*Library of Congress*)

Witman's Tavern, where there was a Number of Persons who inclined to Purchase him. But he protested publicly that he would not be sold, and if Any one should purchase him he wou'd be the Death of him and Words to the like purpose which deter'd the people from biding [bidding].

*Trader George Nagel, in Wax, "Negro Resistance," 14.*

The enterprising and go-ahead Colonel Jennings has got a raffle under way now . . . [The prizes are] the celebrated trotting horse "Star," buggy and harness . . . [and a] stout mulatto girl "Sarah," aged about twenty years, general house servant.

*The New Orleans* True Delta, *in Bancroft,* Slave Trading, *328.*

Dear Sir. The demand brisk for likely Negroes

| | |
|---|---|
| Extra No. 1 men | $1500 |
| No. 1 " | $14–1475 |
| Extra No. 1 fieldgirls | $13–1350 |
| No. 1 " | $12–1275 |
| Likely ploughboys 17 and 18 | $12–1350 |
| " " 15 and 16 | $1050–1175 |
| " " 12 to 14 | $850–1050 |
| Likely girls 14 and 15 | $1000–1150 |
| " " 12 and 13 | $850–1000 |
| Girls 10 and 11 | $700–825 |
| No. 1 woman and child | $1250–1350 |

Families rather dull [not in demand] and hard to sell
Yours respectfully, Dickinson, Hill & Company

*Circular, December 20, 1858, in Tadman,* Speculators and Slave, *61.*

## Fancy Girls

[In 1710 a pastor denounced Louisianians for] maintain[ing] scandalous concubinages with young Indian women, driven by their proclivity for the extremes of licentiousness. They have bought them under the pretext of keeping them as servants, but actually to seduce them, as they in fact have done.

*Usner, "American Indians," 107.*

[In 1854 in Lexington, Kentucky, I visited] a negro jail—a very large brick building with all the conveniences of comfortable life, including hospital. 'Tis a place where negroes are kept for sale. Outer doors and windows all protected with iron grates, but inside the appointments are not only comfortable, but in many respects luxurious. Many of the rooms are well carpeted and furnished, and very neat, and the inmates whilst here are treated with great indulgence and humanity, but I confess it impressed me with the idea of decorating the ox for the sacrifice. In several of the rooms I found very handsome mulatto women, of fine persons and easy genteel manners, sitting at their needle work awaiting a purchaser. The proprietor made them get up and turn around to show to advantage their finely developed and graceful forms.

*Kentuckian Orville H. Browning, describing slave women to be sold as "fancy girls," in Bancroft,* Slave Trading, *130–31.*

## Kidnapping

In many cases [in Delaware], whole families of free colored people have been attacked in the night, beaten *nearly* to death with clubs, gagged and bound, and dragged into distant and hopeless captivity, leaving no traces behind, except the blood from their wounds. . . . . . . A monster in human shape, was detected in the city of Philadelphia, pursuing the occupation of courting and marrying mulatto women, and selling them as slaves. . . . They have lately invented a method of attaining their object, through the instrumentality of the laws:—Having selected a suitable free colored person,. . . the kidnapper employs a confederate, to ascertain the distinguishing marks of his body; he then claims and obtains him as a slave, before a magistrate, by describing those marks, and proving the truth of his assertions, by his well-instructed accomplice.

*Philadelphian Dr. Torrey, 1817, in Child,* Appeal, *34–35.*

A colored man and a fugitive slave [in New Bedford, Massachusetts,] were on unfriendly terms. The former was heard to threaten the latter with informing his master of his whereabouts. Straightway a meeting was called among the colored people under the stereotyped notice, "Business of importance!" The betrayer was invited to attend. The people came at the appointed hour, and organized the meeting by appointing a very religious old gentleman as president, who, I believe, made a prayer, after which he addressed the meeting as follows: "*Friends, we have got him here, and I would recommend that you young men just take him outside the door, and*

Kidnapping (*Library of Congress*)

*kill him!*" With this, a number of them bolted at him; but they were intercepted by some more timid than themselves, and the betrayer escaped their vengeance, and has not been seen in New Bedford since.

*Frederick Douglass, reminiscing about his experiences of 1835–1836, in* Narrative, *117.*

The nigger stealers done stole me and my mammy outen the Choctaw Nation, up in the Indian Territory, when I was 'bout three years old. Brother Knox, Sis Hannah, and my mammy and her two stepchildren was down on the river washing. The nigger stealers driv up in a big carriage, and mammy just thought nothing, 'cause the ford was near there and people going on the road stopped to water the horses and rest awhile in the shade. Bimeby [by and by], a man coaxes the two biggest children to the carriage and give them some kind of candy. Other children sees this and goes, too. Two other men was walking round smoking and getting closer to mammy all the time. When he can, the man in the carriage got the two big stepchildren in with him, and me and Sis climb in too, to see how come. Then the man holler, "Git the old one and let's git from here." With that the two big men grab Mammy, and she fought and screeched and bit and cry, but they hit her on the head with something and drug her in and throwed her on the floor. The big children began to fight for Mammy, but one of the men hit 'em hard, and off they driv, with the horses under whip. . . . Down in Louisian' us was put on what they call the block and sold to the highest bidder. My mammy and her three children brung $3,000 flat. The stepchildren was sold to somebody else.

*Spence Johnson, born free about 1859, in* Lay Me Down, *157.*

## *Manumission*

YANIMEROW IN THE RIVER GAMBIA Jan: 27th: [1735/6]

*Sir,* This is to acquaint you of my safe arrival at and return here from Bonda being conducted safe and used with great civility all the way, which was owing to the respect and regard all the natives in every part have for the Company and by being conducted by one white man only which was the Governors nephew on the Companys behalf which made no little noise and was of much service to me, one of my wives had got another husband in my room and the other gave me over, my father died soon after my misfortune of being seized and sold for a slave, but my children are all well. . . .

*Job Ben Solomon, letter, in* Slave Testimony, *5. Solomon was freed from slavery through the offices of Gov. James Oglethorpe of Georgia.*

A Negro slave named Kitt, owned by Hinchia Mabry . . . has rendered meritorious service in making the first information against several counterfeiters, and is hereby emancipated and his owner ordered paid 1,000 pounds out of the public treasury.

*1779 Act of Virginia legislature, in Higginbotham,* In the Matter of Color, *49.*

From a full conviction that slavery is an evil of great magnitude and no less repugnant to the Divine command of doing to others as we would they should do unto us [and] that it is inconsistent with the true interest and prosperity of my country, I did confirm freedom to all the Negroes that by law, I had property in by a Deed of Emancipation bearing date the first of the 8th month, 1782, duely acknowledged and admitted to record in the Clerk's office of Henrico County, . . . but as it is still necessary that those who are ancient and incapable of getting a living (being over forty-five years of age at the time of emancipation) should be supported, I now desire and direct it to be done and that the young ones may have learning sufficient to enable them to transact the common affairs of life for that purpose I have had a Schoolhouse put on my land called Gravely hills tract containing by estimation 350 acres the use and profits whereof I give for that purpose forever, or so long as the Monthly Meeting of Friends in this County may think it necessary for the benefit of the children and descendants of those who have been emancipated by me, or other black children whom they may think proper to admit; reserving only to my heirs hereafter named the priviledge of cutting timber occasionally for building. . . .

*Will of Robert Pleasants, 1800, in* Journal of Negro History *2 (1917):329–30.*

No Northern man began the world with more enthusiasm against slavery than I did. For forty years and upwards, I have felt the greatest desire to see Maryland become a free State, and the strongest conviction that she could become so. . . . No slave State adjacent to a free State can continue so. . . .

I have emancipated seven of my slaves. They have done pretty well, and six of them, now alive, are supporting themselves comfortably and creditably. Yet I cannot but see that this is all they are doing now; and, when age and infirmity come upon them, they will probably suffer. It is to be observed, also, that these were selected individuals, who were, with two exceptions, brought up with a view to their being so disposed of, and were made to undergo a probation of a few years in favorable situations, and, when emancipated, were far better fitted for the duties and trials of their new condition than the general mass of slaves. Yet I am still a slaveholder, and could not, without the greatest inhumanity, be otherwise. I own, for instance, an old slave, who has done no work for me for years. I pay his board and other expenses, and cannot believe that I sin in doing so. The laws of Maryland contain provisions of various kinds, under which slaves, in certain circumstances, are entitled to petition the courts for their freedom. As a lawyer, I always undertook these cases with peculiar zeal, and have been thus instrumental in liberating several large families and many individuals. I cannot remember more than two instances, out of this large number, in which it did not appear that the freedom I so earnestly sought for them was their ruin.

*Francis Scott Key, 1838 letter to Benjamin Tappan, in Fox,* American Colonization Society, *17–18.*

BROOKLYN, N.Y., Nov. 23, 1842.

SAMUEL MARTIN, a man of color, and the oldest resident of Port Gibson, Mississippi, emancipated six of his slaves in 1844, bringing them to Cincinnati where he believed they would have a better opportunity to start life anew. These were two mulatto women with their four quadroon children, the color of whom well illustrated the moral condition of that State, in that each child had a different father and they retained few marks of their partial African descent. Mr. Martin was himself a slave until 1829. He purchased his freedom for a large sum most of which he earned by taking time from sleep for work. Thereafter he acquired considerable property. He was not a slave holder in the southern sense of that word. His purpose was to purchase his fellowmen in bondage that he might give them an opportunity to become free.

Cincinnati Morning Herald, *June 1, 1844, quoted in* Journal of African History *3 (1918):91.*

## *Migrations*

Mississippi is ruined. Her rich men are poor and her poor men are beggars. . . . The people are running their Negroes to Texas and Alabama and leaving their real estate and perishable property to be sold. So great is the [economic] panic and so dreadful the distress that there are a great many farms prepared to receive crops, and some of them actually planted, and yet deserted. . . .

North Carolingian, *1840, in Buckmaster,* Let My People Go, *101.*

*On the Emigrant Road into Texas:. . .* We overtook, several times in the course of each day, the slow emigrant trains, for which this road, though less frequented than years ago, is still [in the 1850s] a chief thoroughfare. . . . Several families were frequently moving together, coming from the same district, or chance met and joined, for company, on the long road from Alabama, Georgia, or the Carolinas. . . . As you get by, the white mother and babies, and the tall, frequently ill-humoured master, on horseback, or walking with his gun, urging up the black driver and his oxen. As a scout ahead, is a brother, or an intelligent slave, with the best gun, on the look-out for a deer or a turkey. . . . They travel ten or fifteen miles a day, stopping wherever night overtakes them. The masters are plainly dressed, often in homespun, keeping their eyes about them, noticing the soil, sometimes making a remark on the crops by the roadside; but generally dogged, surly, and silent. The women are silent too, frequently walking, to relieve the teams; and weary, haggard, mud be-draggled, forlorn, and disconsolate, yet hopeful and careful. The negroes, mud-incrusted, wrapped in old blankets or gunny-bags, suffering from cold, plod on, aimless, hopeless, thoughtless, more indifferent, apparently, than the oxen, to all about them.

*Olmsted,* Cotton Kingdom, *284–86.*

## *Sales of Slaves*

EXECUTORS' SALE.—Agreeable to an order of the Court of Wilkinson County, will be sold on the first Tuesday of April next, before the Court-House door in the town of Irwington, ONE NEGRO GIRL, about *two years old,* named Rachel, belonging to the estate of William Chambers, deceased. Sold for the benefit of the *heirs* and CREDITORS of said estate.

Samuel Bell,
Jesse Peacock. *Executors.*

*Advertisement in the* Milledgeville Journal, *December 26, 1837, quoted in Goodell,* Slave Code, *66.*

[The slaves] were dressed in every possible variety of uncouth and fantastic garb, in every style and of every imaginable color; the texture of the garments was in all cases coarse, most of the men being clothed in the rough cloth that is made expressly for the slaves. . . . The women, true to the feminine instinct, had made, in almost every case, some attempt at finery. All wore gorgeous turbans, generally manufactured in an instant out of a gay-colored handkerchief by a sudden and graceful twist of the fingers; though there was occasionally a more elaborate turban, a turban complex and mysterious, got up with care, and ornamented with a few beads or bright bits of ribbon. Their dresses were mostly coarse stuff, though there were some gaudy calicos; a few had ear-rings, and one possessed the treasure of a string of yellow and blue beads. The little children were always better and more carefully dressed than the older ones, the parental pride coming out in the shape of a yellow cap pointed like a mitre, or a jacket with a strip of red broadcloth round the bottom. The children were of all sizes, the youngest being fifteen days old. . . .

The negroes were examined with as little consideration as if they had been brutes indeed; the buyers pulling their mouths open to see their teeth, pinching their limbs to find how muscular they were, walking them up and down to detect any signs of lameness, making them stoop and bend in different ways that they might be certain there was no concealed rupture or wound; and in addition to all this treatment, asking them scores of questions relative to their qualifications and accomplishments. All these humiliations were submitted to without a murmur, and in some instances with good-natured cheerfulness—where the slave liked the appearance of the proposed buyer, and fancied that he might prove a kind "Mas'r."

Slaves waiting for buyers in a slave trader's shop (*Crowe,* With Thackeray in America)

The auctioneer . . . is a rollicking old boy, with an eye ever to the look-out, and that never lets a bidding nod escape him; a hearty word for every bidder who cares for it, and plenty of jokes to let off when the business gets a little slack. Mr. Walsh has a florid complexion,. . . possibly not more so than is natural in a whiskey country. Not only is his face red, but his skin has been taken off in spots by blisters of some sort, giving him a peely look; so that, taking his face all in all, the peeliness and the redness combined, he looks much as if he had been boiled in the same pot with a red cabbage.

*Report by "Doesticks" (Mortimer Thompson) of a sale in Savannah, in the* New York Daily Tribune, *March 9, 1859.*

Pierce Butler has gone to Georgia to be present at the sale of his Negroes. It is highly honorable to him that he did all he could to prevent the sale, offering to make any personal sacrifice to avoid it. But it cannot be avoided, and by the sale he will be able to keep Butler Place & have a fortune of 2 or 300,000 dollars, after paying his debts. . . . It is a dreadful affair, however, selling these hereditary Negroes. There are 900 of them belonging to the estate, a little community who have lived for generations on the plantation, among whom, therefore, all sorts of relations of blood & friendship are established. Butler's half, 450, to be sold at public auction & scattered over the South. Families will not be separated, that is to say, husbands & wives, parents & young children. But brothers & sisters of mature age, parents & children of mature age, all other relations & the ties of home & long association will be violently severed. It will be a hard thing for Butler to witness and it is a monstrous thing to do.

*Sidney George Fisher, diary entry for February 17, 1859, in* A Philadelphia Experience, *317.*

I saw slaves sold. I can see that old block now. My cousin Eliza was a pretty girl, really good-looking.

Her master was her father. When the girls in the big house had beaus coming to see 'em, they'd ask, "Who is that pretty gal?" So they decided to git rid of her right away. The day they sold her will always be remembered. They stripped her to be bid off and looked at. I wasn't allowed to stand in the crowd. I was laying down under a big bush. The man that bought Eliza was from New York. The Negroes had made up 'nough money to buy her off theyself, but they wouldn't let that happen. There was a man bidding for her who was a Swedelander. He always bid for the good-looking colored gals and bought 'em for his own use. He ask the man from New York, 'What you gonna do with her when you git her?" The man from New York said, "None of your damn business, but you ain't got money 'nough to buy her." When the man from New York had done bought her, he said, "Eliza, you are free from now on." She left and went to New York with him. Mama and Eliza both cried when she was being showed off, and Master told 'em to shut up before he knocked their brains out.

*Ex-slave Doc Daniel Dowdy, in* Lay My Burden Down, *155.*

## *Separation of Families*

I have . . . heard you have lost some of your Small Negroes by death, do when you write inform me which of them are dead. I have to inform you that I have had one child since I last Saw you, his Name is Joshua, you will please to tell my Sister Clary not to Let my poor children Suffer & tell her she must also write & inform me how she & my children are. . . . Mr. Miller is now on the brink of death, & is about to sell 40 of his Negroes and it is likely [my husband] Joshua may be one. I wish to Stay with Him as long as possible as you must know its very bad to part man & wife. I should be glad to no [know] what sort of a life Clary leads. . . . be pleased to inform me how my little daughter Judith is & if she is now injoying health. I have no more at present only my best wishes to all my friends & relations and Except my warmest Love & friendship for your Self. . . .

*Letter of November 30, 1807, from Virginia slave Gooley to her former owner, who had moved to Kentucky, taking some of Gooley's children and other relatives with her, in Gutman,* Black Family, *184.*

Dear Husband I write you a letter to let you know my distress my master has sold albert to a trader on Monday court day and the other child is for sale also and I want you to let [me] hear from you very soon before next cort if you can I don't know when don't want you to wait till Christmas I want you to tell dr Hamelton and your master if either will buy me they can attend to it know [now] and then I can go afterwards I don't want a trader to get me they asked me if I had got any person to buy me and I told them no they took me in the court house too they never put me up a man buy the name of brady bought albert and is gone I don't know where they say he lives in Scottesville my things is in several places some is in staunton and if I should be sold I don't know what will become of them I don't expect to meet with the luck to get that way till I am quite heartsick nothing more I am and ever will be your kind wife

*Maria Perkins of Charlottesville, 1852 letter to Richard Perkins, in Gutman,* Black Family, *35.*

It would certainly have been harsh to separate these four boys, and sever ties which bind even slaves together. True, it must be done, if the executor discovers that the interest of the estate requires it; for he is not to indulge his charities at the expense of others.

*Chief Justice Ruffin of North Carolina, in* Judicial Cases *2:59.*

[The slaves] said that "when your child dies you know where it is, but when he is sold away, you never know what may happen to him."

*Northern traveler, 1866, in Gutman,* Black Family, *193.*

## *Slave Jails*

I may as well describe here the order of the daily proceedings, as during the whole time I remained in the pen [in New Orleans], they were, one day with the other, pretty much the same. . . .

As may be imagined, the slaves are bought from all parts, are of all sorts, sizes, and ages, and arrive at various states of fatigue and condition; but they soon improve in their looks, as they are regularly fed and have plenty to eat. As soon as we were roused in the morning, there was a general washing, and combing, and shaving, pulling out of grey hairs, and dying the hair of those who were too grey to be plucked without making them bald. When this was over—and it was no light business—we used to breakfast, getting bread and bacon, and coffee, of which a sufficiency was given us, that we might plump up and become sleek. Bob [a mulatto assistant of the trader] would then proceed to instruct us on how to show ourselves off, and afterwards form us into companies, according to size; those who were nearly the same height and make being put into separate lots; the men, the women, and the children of both sexes, being divided off alike. In consequence of this arrangement, the various members of a family were of necessity separated, and would often see the last of each other in that dreadful showroom. . . .

The buying commenced at about ten in the morning, and lasted till one, during which time we were obliged to be sitting about in our respective companies ready for inspection. At one we used to go to dinner, our usual food being a repetition of the morning meal, varied with vegetables, and a little fruit sometimes. After dinner we were compelled to walk, and dance, and kick about in the yard, for exercise; and Bob, who had a fiddle, used to play up jigs for us to dance to. If we did not dance to his fiddle, we used to have to do so to his whip, so no wonder we used our legs handsomely, though the music was none of the best. When our exercises were over, we used to be "sized out" again, ready for the afternoon sale, which commenced at three, and ended at six. This over, we had tea, and were then free to do what we liked in the pen, until Bob rang us off to bed at ten.

*Ex-slave John Brown, in Tadman,* Speculator and Slaves, *98–99.*

[At Lumpkin's Jail] I entered a large open court. Against one of the posts sat a good natured fat man, with his chair tipped back. It was Mr. Lumpkin. I duly introduced myself as from New York, remarking that I had read what the Abolitionists had to say, and that I had come to Richmond [Virginia] to see for myself. Mr. Lumpkin received me courteously and showed me over his jail. On one side of the open court was a large tank for washing, or lavatory. Opposite was a long, two-story brick house, the lower part fitted up for men and the second story for women. The place, in fact, was a kind of hotel or boardinghouse for negro-traders and their slaves. I was invited to dine at a large table with perhaps twenty traders, who gave me almost no attention, and there was little conversation. They were probably strangers to one another.

*Otis Bigelow, describing a visit in the 1850s, in Bancroft,* Slave Trading, *102–3.*

The Sugar House of Charleston [South Carolina] is a building created for the purpose of punishing and selling slaves in. I visited it. It is simply a prison with a treadmill, a work yard, putrid privies, whipping posts and a *brine barrel* attached. There are, I think, three corridors. Many of the cells are perfectly dark. They are all very small. . . .

If a planter arrives in the city with a lot of slaves for sale, he repairs to the Sugar House and places them in custody, and there they are kept until disposed of, as usual—"by auction for cash to the highest bidder."

If any slaveholder, from any or from no cause, desires to punish his human property, but is too sensitive, or what is far more probable, too lazy to inflict the chastisement himself—he takes *it* (the man, woman, or child), to the Sugar House, and simply orders *how* he desires it to be punished; and, without any trial—without any questions asked or explanations given, the command is implicitly obeyed by the officers of the institution. A small sum is paid for the board of the incarcerated.

If any colored person is found out of doors after ten o'clock at night, without a ticket of leave from its owner, the unfortunate wanderer is taken to the Sugar House and kept there till morning; when, if the master pays one dollar fine, the slave is liberated; but, if he refuses to do so, the prisoner is tied hand and foot and lashed before he or she is set at liberty.

*Redpath,* Roving Editor, *60.*

## Slave Traders

Mr. Whitehead [a former slave trader] is a gentleman of great intelligence, high minded and honorable. He possesses fine business qualities, an energetic character, persevering and laborious habits and great moral worth.

*Memorandum from members of the Virginia legislature to President James Polk, late 1840s, in Tadman,* Speculators and Slaves, *197.*

[T]he most utterly detestable of all southern Yankees is the Negro Trader—Speculator he delights to call himself in late years. . . . [He stands] pre-eminent in villainy and a greedy love of filthy lucre. . . . The natural result of their calling seems to be to corrupt; for they have usually to deal with the most refractory and brutal of the slave population, since good and honest slaves are rarely permitted to fall into the unscrupulous clutches of the speculator. . . . [Of his stock] nearly nine-tenths [are] vicious ones sold for crimes or misdemeanors, or otherwise diseased ones sold because of their worthlessness as property. These he purchases at about half what healthy and honest slaves would cost him; but he sells them as both honest and healthy, mark you.

*Southerner David Hundley, 1860, quoted in Tadman,* Speculators and Slave, *183.*

[T]hey was 258 niggers out of them nigger yards in Memphis [Tennessee] what gits on that boat. They puts the niggers upstairs and goes down the river far as Vicksburg [Mississippi], that was the place, and then us gits offen the boat and gits on the train 'gain and that time we goes to New Orleans.

They has three big trader yard in New Orleans. . . . We hears some of 'em say there's gwine to throw a long war, and us all think what they buy us for if we's gwine to be sot free. . . .

They have big sandbars and planks fix round the nigger yards, and they have watchmans to keep them from running 'way in de swamp. Some of the niggers they have just picked up on the road, they steals them. They calls them "wagon boy" and "wagon gal." . . . . You sees, if they could steal the niggers and sell 'em for the good money, them traders could make plenty money that way.

*Ex-slave Betty Simmons, in* Lay My Burden Down, *158.*

[His master, having recaptured Louis Talbert, who had not only escaped twice but also led many other slaves to freedom, dared not put him to work among his other slaves but sold him to a trader, from whom he again escaped.] The slavetrader was much enraged when he discovered his loss and blamed the captain of the [Mississippi River] boat for having his yawl [with which Talbert made his escape] where it was so easy of access. When they arrived at Memphis, he sued the captain for the price of his slave, contending that the captain was responsible for the loss of his property. The trader lost the suit and had the costs to pay, then the captain sued him for the detention of the boat, and gained the suit, and the trader had to pay seven hundred dollars. Then the captain sued him for the value of the yawl which his slave had carried off and got judgment against him, which it is said cost him seven hundred dollars more.

*Coffin,* Reminiscences, *156.*

### *Voluntary Enslavement*

Your petitioner respectfully shews unto your worships, that she is desirous of becoming a slave, and for that purpose has selected John Clark for her master, and now makes this public declaration of the same and asks the court that a record may be made of the same according to law, and that she may become the slave and property of said John Clark for life. She further states that this request is made by her of her own free will and accord without any force or compulsion from any one; and she asks that all necessary and proper orders and decrees may be made in the premises, to fully carry out the law in such cases made and provided—that she is now about twenty-eight years old—copper color—weighs about 125 pounds —stout.

*Janet Wright's petition, approved August 24, 1861, by the Court of Pleas and Quarter Sessions for Guilford County, North Carolina, in Franklin, "Enslavement of Free Negroes," 423. This action may not have been legal, since Wright later applied unsuccessfully to the state legislature for voluntary enslavement.*

# 4

# Slave Life
1619–1865

## The Historical Context

"The Southern States are an aggregate . . . of communities, not of individuals," wrote John C. Calhoun. "Every plantation is a little community, with the master at its head." That master exercised absolute power over his slaves. Although the law forbade him to kill them *intentionally,* the isolation of the plantation and the legal inability of blacks to testify against whites effectively gave the master the power of life and death.

Slaves born in Africa who came to North America exchanged the temporary chaos and suffering of the Middle Passage for the confusion and hardship of life in a strange land. They did not know where they were. Few if any of the people around them understood what they said, and they understood little or none of what they heard. They were surrounded by strange objects, whose uses they could not imagine. Almost always the slave traders and slave owners who received them treated them as savages to be subdued, workers whose power had to be harnessed, and sources of profit—not as human beings. The slaves had been stripped of their status, their names, their families and friends, and their customs and culture. They were surrounded by fear, distrust, and sometimes hatred. No wonder it was commonplace for newly arrived slaves to try to run away or sink into a deep, sometimes suicidal depression. They stood naked to misery, not knowing what would happen to them.

Slaves who had been born in North America—almost all of them, that is, as time went on—still had a struggle to survive in subjection. Their families could offer them only limited protection against hunger, cold, and separation and almost none against the cruelties of whites and the ever-harsher laws constructed to control blacks.

Ninety-five percent of the slaves lived in rural places, usually raising cotton, sugar, tobacco, and rice.[1] The size of the master's farm or plantation affected every aspect of a slave's life. How closely did the slave live and work with the master and mistress? Would the slave be put to a specialized task or have to combine farm and housework? Would the slave's spouse live on the same plantation or "abroad"? Was the farm or plantation large enough to support a slave community? Would the slave be isolated from other blacks? In the 1850s, most of the 400,000 or so slaveholders owned 10 or fewer slaves—usually only one or two. But the typical slave lived in a community of some 40 slaves—only about a quarter of them in communities as large as 50.[2] The *proportion* of white families owning slaves decreased during the

Pictures drawn from life of slave children and wharf hands (*Crowe,* With Thackeray in America)

antebellum era, from 36 percent in 1830 to 31 percent in 1850 and 26 percent in 1860.[3]

The relatively few slaves in cities usually lived under somewhat better conditions and more independently than country slaves. "A city slave," wrote Frederick Douglass, "is almost a freeman, compared with a slave on the plantation. He is much better fed and clothed, and enjoys privileges altogether unknown to the slave on the plantation. There is a vestige of decency, a sense of shame, that does much to curb and check those outbreaks of atrocious cruelty so commonly enacted upon the plantation. He is a desperate slaveholder, who will shock the humanity of his non-slaveholding neighbors with the cries of his lacerated slave. Few are willing to incur the odium attaching to the reputation of being a cruel master; and above all things, they would not be known as not giving a slave enough to eat. There are, however, some painful exceptions to this rule."[4]

## *Slave Life: Food, Shelter, and Clothing*

Slave owners had to regard blacks as their inferiors—how else could they go on calling themselves Christians and professing democracy? Accordingly, they felt called upon to house, clothe, and feed their slaves only sufficiently to enable them to work. An 1846 statement of Louisiana planters of the usual expenses of a sugar plantation shows an annual income of $3,650, with these expenditures:[5]

| | |
|---|---|
| Household and family expenses | $1,000 |
| Overseer's salary | 400 |
| Food and clothing for 15 working hands [slaves] at $30 | 450 |
| Food and clothing for 15 old negroes and [slave] children | 250 |
| 1-1/2 per cent on capital invested . . . , to keep it in repair | 600 |

How well or badly the slaves lived varied with the wealth or poverty of their owner, his generosity or miserliness, and his understanding of his own economic interests.

On the larger plantations, the overseer typically distributed the slaves' food to heads of families or to unmarried adults once a week, perhaps on Saturday nights—or perhaps in midweek, to prevent them from selling it for whiskey on Sunday. Every night the slaves took the next day's portion to a cookhouse, where a cook prepared two of their daily meals. The slaves ate where they could, near their work, from troughs or gourds, with spoons, shells, or their bare hands. Slave wives and mothers, after a day's hard labor in the fields, might cook their families' evening meal in their cabins: "a bit of bacon fried, often with eggs, corn-bread baked in the spider [frying pan] after the bacon, to absorb the fat, and perhaps some sweet potatoes roasted in the ashes."[6] Diets consisting mainly of rice, fatback, cornmeal, and salt pork rendered slaves vulnerable to blindness, sore eyes, skin irritations, rickets, toothaches, pellagra, beriberi, and scurvy. In 1850 in Louisiana, the life expectancy of a black male at birth was 29 years, of a black female 34 years.[7]

Industrious slaves, if the master permitted, might supplement their diets with vegetables grown on their own small plots, berries picked in the woods, or animals they hunted. Some "stole" from masters; many slaves reasoned that they were entitled to the fruits of their own labor, and others were driven by hunger. Some masters and overseers used food to control the slaves, awarding an extra pound of meat weekly to slaves who had done their work and caused no trouble, or passing out extra rice to those who had picked a given amount of cotton. House slaves could feast on scraps from their master's table—but often they were allowed no time for meals and had to eat in what spare moments they could snatch.

If they were not required to sleep in the bedroom (or just outside its door) of a member of the master's family, or left to find rest where they could, slaves lived in cabins—two families to each cabin. These varied from solid, brick structures to the more common plank or log huts, the chinks stuffed perhaps with rags, moss, or red mud. The cabins were usually dark and drafty. Fanny Kemble (a British actress who had married a planter) described those on her husband's plantations as "filthy and wretched in the extreme. . . . Firewood and shavings lay littered about the floors, while the half-naked children were cowering round two or three smouldering cinders. The moss with which the chinks and crannies of their ill-protecting dwelling might have been stuffed was trailing in dirt and dust upon the ground, while the back door of the huts, opening upon a most unsightly ditch, was left wide open for the fowls and ducks, which they are allowed to raise, to travel in and out, increasing the filth of the cabin by what they brought and left in every direction."[8] Slave women were often simply too exhausted after working all day in the fields, or too heavily tasked by their mistresses with weaving in the evenings, to keep their dwellings tidy—though some owners set apart three days a year for house-cleaning.

Slave owners furnished slaves every year with either clothes or the material to make them. Pierce Butler, for example, handed out to each slave two pairs of shoes and a few yards of flannel and of another material called "plains," a stiff, heavy, dark gray or blue woolen cloth, rather like carpet. Such materials were intolerable in the hot summers, so the slaves often worked nearly naked—scrambling for cover when a stranger approached. Because no replacements were available if children tore or wore out their clothes—if indeed they received any—many of them also went naked. On some plantations, slave women wove all the materials for clothing and household linens.

## *Slave Life: Medical Care, Child Care, Care of the Aged*

What with the sanitary conditions, the slaves' poor diet, their miserable working situations (particularly on the rice plantations), and their exposure to the weather, they often fell ill. Besides the usual fevers, diseases of malnutrition, and the almost universal rheumatism, they suffered from leprosy, pleurisy, lockjaw, venereal diseases, tuberculosis, and pneumonia. Epidemics of cholera and yellow fever were frequent. Hard labor too late in pregnancy or while nursing and inadequate care during childbirth left women who survived debilitated.

Given the state of medical knowledge in the days of slavery, it probably did not make much difference whether or not a slave owner hired a doctor to look after ailing slaves. Dr. Samuel A. Cartwright of the University of Louisiana wrote of a "disease" he called "Dysaesthesia Aetheiopica, or Hebetude of Mind and obtuse Sensibility of Body," which, he said caused slaves to "break, waste, and destroy everything they handle—abuse horses and cattle—tear, burn, or rend their own clothing, and, paying no attention to the rights of property, steal others to replace what they have destroyed. They wander about at night, and keep in a half-nodding state by day. They slight their work—cut up corn, cane, cotton, and tobacco, when hoeing it, as if for pure mischief. They raise disturbances with their overseers, and among their fellow-servants, without cause or motive, and seem to be insensible to pain when subjected to punishment." He also believed he could cure the "disease" of running away, which he called *Drapetomania*.[9]

Many masters trusted more to their own medical treatments, based on experience and observation. "I never have employed Doctors to my Negroes," wrote Pierce Butler, ". . . because they seldom feel for Negroes as they ought to, and therefore are light on their prescriptions. . . . If the complaint is a fever and in the summer, let a vomit [emetic], unless to pregnant women, be given, after that some gruel, the next day if the fever continues let 12 ounces of blood be taken and a purge given of 5 grains Calomel and ten of Jallop[;] if that should not operate in three hours, let the doce [dose] be repeated till it operates 4 or 5 times, then let them have gruel, or fowl broth. If the fever continues a second bleeding must take place and after it plenty of tea or gruel, when the fever is checked let them drink plenty of decoction of wild cherry bark. In winter bleed, purge and sweat freely with snake root for fevers."[10] At the first hint of cholera, many owners would move their entire households to the woods, correctly "supposing there might be some local cause for the diseases."[11] Other owners handed over the care of the sick to older slave women, who used folk remedies, such as fence-grass tea to avert fever and elder twigs and dogwood berries for chills.

Plantations of any size usually cared during the day for babies and toddlers, a necessary provision when all slave mothers worked throughout the daylight hours and the early deaths of slave mothers left many babies motherless. On the better-run plantations, the mistress herself would oversee the care of these children or an experienced slave mother would be given their charge. All too often, however, care was left to slave girls seven or eight years old. One advocate of putting slaves to work in the fields at age five argued that they would be better employed there than in the nursery, for they often caused severe injuries and even death among infants. His charge was probably true. One ex-slave reminisced about how she detested taking care of children: "I'd drop 'em, leave 'em, pinch 'em, quit walking 'em and rocking 'em. I got tired of 'em all the time."[12]

As they aged, slaves lost value for their owners. If they had skills, slaves too old to sell could still be hired out to other employers, at a rate that brought in more money than if they had been sold and the profits invested. But field hands without such skills eventually could no longer do field work, and they then became heavy burdens on the master, for no return. All too often, conscienceless masters simply turned them away, to survive as best they could on the charity of other slaves. Sojourner Truth told about the death of her father while she was still a slave in New York State. She was not permitted to care for him or even to visit him. After several makeshift arrangements, in his last days he was left alone. "Yet, lone, blind, and helpless as he was, James for a time lived on. One day, an aged colored woman, named Soan, called at his shanty, and James besought her, in the most moving manner, even with tears, to tarry awhile and wash and mend him up, so that he might once more be decent and comfortable; for he was suffering dreadfully with the filth and vermin that had collected upon him. Soan was herself an emancipated slave, old and weak, with no one to care for her; and she lacked the courage to undertake a job of such seeming magnitude. . . . And shortly after her visit, this faithful slave, this deserted wreck of humanity, was found on his miserable pallet, frozen and stiff in death."[13]

## *Marriage and Maternity*

Slaves could not enter into legal marriages, for they could make no valid contracts. But could they be married in the eyes of God? Churches waffled. Some white clergymen presided at slave marriages, but they usually omitted from the ceremony the phrases "until death do us part" and "let no man put asunder," for they knew that the master might sell husband away from wife or wife from husband. In 1835 the Savannah River Baptist Association of Ministers ruled, "Such separation among persons situated as our slaves are, is civilly, a separation by death. . . . The slaves are not free agents, and a dissolution by death is not more entirely without their consent and beyond their control than by such separation."[14]

Some masters tried to regulate slave marriages and divorces, providing gifts for first-time marriages and penalizing divorces. At least one overseer arbitrarily "divorced" couples who had minor spats, whether or not they wished it. Sometimes masters simply arranged newly arrived slaves in two lines, gestured to the men to pick the wives they wanted, and unceremoniously declared, "All right, you're married." Other masters told male slaves to move in with women whom they thought ready for childbearing. Still others let the slaves initiate marriages but reserved the right to approve them. For favored slaves, masters might even provide formal marriage ceremonies in their own houses.

Some left marriages up to the slave community, which might exercise some judgment about whether or not a wedding should take place—in a way sanctioning the wedding. Caroline Johnson Harris remembered that where she lived the slaves did not have to ask the master: "Just go to Aunt Sue an' tell her you want to git mated. She tells us to think 'bout it hard fo' two days, 'cause marryin' was sacred in the eyes of Jesus. Arter two days Mose an' me went back an' says we done thought 'bout it and still want to git married. Den she called all de slaves arter tasks to pray for de union dat God was gonna make. Pray we stay together an' have lots of chillun an' none of 'em git sol' away from de parents. Den she lay a broomstick 'cross de sill of de house we gonna live in an jine our hands together. Fo' we step over it she ast us once mo' if we was sho' we wanted to git married. 'Course we say yes. Den she say, 'In de eyes of Jesus step in to de Holy land of mat-de-money.' When we step 'cross de broomstick, we was married. Was bad luck to tech de broomstick. Fo'ks always stepped high 'cause dey didn't want to have a spell cast on 'em—Aunt Sue used to say whichever one teched de stick was gonna die fust." Other slave communities arranged marriages more or less formally, with a ceremony performed by a black preacher, or with marriage "by the blanket": "We comes together in the same cabin; and she brings her blanket and lay it down beside mine; and we gets married that a-way."[15]

Slaves often married slaves on neighboring plantations. "Saturday nights," a former slave reminisced, "the roads were . . . filled with [slave] men on their way to the 'wife house' [the plantation or farm of a different owner], each pedestrian or horseman bearing in his bag his soiled clothes and all the good things he could collect during the week for the delectation of the household."[16] Of course, as another ex-slave said, "If a man married abroad it meant that he wouldn't see his wife only about once a week."[17] Some of these "abroad" marriages were bigamous. "[Hector] told me," wrote Fanny Kemble, the wife of his owner, "that a great number of the men on all the different plantations had *wives* on the neighboring estates as well as on that to which they properly belonged. 'Oh, but,' said I, 'Hector, you know that cannot be; a man has but one lawful wife.' Hector knew this, he said, and yet seemed puzzled himself, and rather puzzled me to account for the fact, that this extensive practice of bigamy was perfectly well known to the masters and overseers, and never in any way found fault with or interfered with. Perhaps this promiscuous mode of keeping up the slave population finds favor with the owners of creatures who are valued in the market at so much per head."[18]

Whatever the form of the wedding, marriages that could be ended by the whim of a master enjoyed no security. A master might order an already-married man to take another wife or surrender his wife to himself for the night. In either case, the slave could not effectively protest. Slave Molly told Fanny Kemble that Tony "was not her *real* husband. . . . [H]er real husband had been sold from the estate for repeated attempts to run away. . . . [S]he did not know whither or to whom her *real* husband had been sold; but in the meantime Mr. K . . . had provided her with . . . Tony, by whom she had had nine children, six of whom were dead; she, too, had miscarried twice."[19]

Their marriages denied slaves their traditional roles as husband and wife. The slave husband could not support his family, for he could own nothing; he could not even protect his wife and children against beatings and rape. The wife, exhausted by her labor, was hard put to cook, clean, and care for her family. Slave men were emasculated—sometimes literally, castrated by way of punishment. Women were unsexed: sexual advances from slaveholders, separation of mothers and children, physical brutality, and assignment of "men's work" all destroyed the female slave's identity as a woman.

Under such circumstances, what was a slave man or woman to think of marriage? How seriously were they to take it? Yet slaves fell in love, experiencing anguish when they were separated from their spouses, and slave communities managed to preserve a standard of monogamy—though, of course, it was not always met. Insofar as they could, these communities also held to the standard of fidelity within a marriage. Many slave couples lived together in a trial period before marriage. Some black communities did not consider it wrong for a woman to have a child before she married; others thought she ought to find a husband before the child was born.[20]

Masters obviously had an interest in slave women's bearing babies early and often. Owners were frequently ambivalent in their treatment of pregnant and nursing women—pulled one way by their desire for healthy babies and another by their eagerness to get as much work as possible out of the mothers. Some masters took pregnant women off field labor in about the fifth month of pregnancy, placing them in special work gangs with lighter tasks. James H. Hammond's manual for plantation operations required that no plowing or lifting be required of them, instructed that the plantation midwife attend deliveries, allowed the mothers to "lie up" for a confinement of one month, and gave them extra allowances of sugar, coffee, rice, and flour. Babies were to be furnished with layettes of pieces of cloth and rags. During the 12-month period of suckling, the manual said, nursing mothers should not have to leave their homes until sunrise, and their work must always lie within half a mile of the "children's house," where the babies were tended. Mothers were to go there for a forty-five-minute period three times a day until the babies were eight months old, then twice a day until the twelfth month, and once a day during the twelfth month. Only about three-fifths as much work was to be expected of nursing mothers as of other slaves.[21]

Practice did not always meet these requirements. "Mother said she knowed she could not go home [from the field] and suckle dat child and git back in 15 minutes [as the overseer ordered]," said Celia Robinson, "so she would go somewhere an' sit down an' pray de child would die."[22] Pregnancy and nursing sometimes failed to protect slave mothers against brutal beatings.

Infant mortality before 1865 ran high among whites as well as blacks, but Fanny Kemble's survey of its incidence among the slaves on her husband's plantation still horrifies: "The practice of sending women to labor in the fields in the third week after their confinement is a specific for causing . . . infirmity. . . . *Fanny* has had six children; all dead but one. . . . *Nanny* has had three children; two of them are dead. . . . *Leah,* Caesar's wife, has had six children; three are dead. *Sophy* . . . has had ten children; five of them are dead. . . . *Sally,* Scipio's wife, has had two miscarriages and three children born, one of whom is dead. . . . *Charlotte,* Renty's wife, has had two miscarriages, and was with child again. . . . [*Die*] had had sixteen children, fourteen of whom were dead; she had had four miscarriages: one had been caused with falling down with a very heavy burden on her head, and one from having her arms strained up to be lashed."[23]

All slave mothers faced the heartbreaking knowledge that their babies, whether mulatto, black, or mostly white, were born into lifelong slavery. Since the status of the baby was that of its mother, many a child who looked white—and whose father and grandfathers had been white—was treated as black and a slave.

Slave mothers could not count on watching their children grow up, even if the children survived. Masters who resided in a city might send new slave babies back to their plantations as soon as they were weaned but keep the slave mothers in the city to tend their own children, "because they do not want the time of the mother taken up with attendance upon *her own children,* it being too valuable to the mistress. As a *favor* she is sometimes permitted to go to see them once a year."[24] Frederick Douglass could remember seeing his field-hand mother only four or five times in his life, each time very briefly and at night, when after her day's work she walked the twelve miles from the plantation where she was hired out, knowing that she had to walk twelve miles back again before sunrise and another day of labor. She died when he was seven; he was not allowed to see her during her illness or attend her funeral.

Such treatment explains the bitter recollections of Jennie Hill: "How well I remember how I would sit in my room with the little ones on my lap and the tears would roll down my cheeks as I would ponder the right and wrong of bringing them into the world. What was I bringing them into the world for? To be slaves and go from morning to night. They couldn't be educated and maybe they couldn't even live with their families. They would just be slaves. All that time I wasn't even living with my husband. He belonged to another man. He had to stay on his farm and I on mine. That wasn't living—that was slavery."[25]

Sometimes emotions like these, or a desire for revenge on a white man who had impregnated her against her will, moved a slave mother to action. Rumor had it that slave women knew how to abort unwanted babies. Records exist of "barren" slave women who bore babies after emancipation, but no one knows for sure how often slave women deliberately aborted. Between 1790 and 1860, smothering was reported as responsible for the deaths of some 60,000 slave infants, but these figures are unreliable. Not only are they probably wrong in themselves, but many of these deaths may have resulted from sudden infant death syndrome or poor prenatal or postnatal care rather than infanticide.[26]

## *White-Black Sexual Relations*

The atmosphere of the plantation was laden with sexuality, tinged with the lure of the forbidden. State and church alike banned black-white relationships. The press deplored them as encouraging "insolence" from black women. Nonetheless these relationships were commonplace throughout the history of slavery—particularly between white men and black women. In many ways this was inevitable, for blacks and whites lived intimately. It was also fed by the myth of the passionate sexuality of black women, a myth propagated by white men ever since the early days of the African slave trade. In the patriarchal slave states, men idealized white women, turning to slaves for physical satisfaction. Slave owners and their sons frequently fathered the babies of their slaves, in casual couplings or long-term relationships. White men bought beautiful slaves to serve as concubines. Overseers harassed and raped the black women over whom they exercised power. Some white hosts offered their male guests black women to sleep with. Perverted sexuality often prompted the terrible beatings inflicted on slave women.

As traveler William Blane commented in 1824, "Indeed in the Southern States, the ladies would be very angry, and turn anyone out of society, who kept a white woman for his mistress; but would not scruple even to marry him, if he had a colored one, and a whole family of children by her."[27] One family eager for a marriage between a young man in his twenties and a much younger girl arranged for him to maintain a black mistress until his fiancée reached marriageable age. Rumors flew. In 1828, Sarah Haysworth Gayle wrote in her diary of a neighbor: "His children and his son's children are their slaves, and probably, nay I think I heard, that his *child* and his *grand-child* have one mother."[28] Fanny Kemble observed tartly, "[I]t seems, indeed, as if marriage (and not concubinage) was the horrible enormity which cannot be tolerated, and against which, moreover, it has been deemed expedient to enact laws. Now it appears very evident that there is no law in the white man's nature which prevents him from making a colored woman the mother of his children, but there *is* a law on his statute books forbidding him to make her his wife."[29]

This social phenomenon became such a problem that fathers often sent their sons north to school. As one southern merchant told landscape architect Frederick Law Olmsted, "I tried to get my brother to send them [his sons] North with me to school. I told him he might as well have them educated in a brothel at once, as in the way they were growing up."[30]

Sexual relations between white women and black men were rare, but now and then white men had occasion to divorce their wives for sleeping with black men. "I believe the only cause of Lewis ———'s wife quitting him and taking up with this slave," testified a witness in an 1824 Virginia divorce case, "was that the slave was much younger and a more likely man than ———. There being a great difference in the age of Lewis ——— and his wife."[31]

## *The Powers That Be: Masters and Mistresses*

The slave economy twisted all it touched. It damaged the white people who lived in it as surely as it did the blacks. It allowed, even expected, whites to discipline and punish and sell away from their families black people with whom they had lived all their lives. It taught young white sons and daughters contempt for the black mammies who had raised them and for the black children with whom they had played. It shut out the slave states from the development of industry, roads, schools, and other services and conveniences proceeding so rapidly in the North.

The relative power of white men over white women and free blacks, and their absolute power over their slaves, inevitably corrupted them. Aside from his conscience and his own economic interest, the only restraint on the slave owner's conduct was community opinion—and that was weak in an agricultural economy where most slaves lived on remote plantations and farms and racism was rampant. As Frederick Law Olmsted wrote, "Suppose you are my neighbour; if you maltreat your negroes, and tell me of it, or I see it, am I going to prefer charges against you to the magistrates? I might possibly get you punished according to law; but if I did, or did not, I should have you, and your family and friends, far and near, for my mortal enemies."[32]

The white master typically based his behavior on patriarchal attitudes, by which he was the overlord of his wife, his children, and his servants, his lightest word to be obeyed by all. His ultimate means of control over his slaves—physical force—encouraged him to indulge his tempers and passions, and hardened him to cruelty. In Thomas Jefferson's words, "The whole commerce between master and slave is a perpetual exercise of the most boisterous passions; the most unrelenting despotism on the one part, and degrading submission on the other. . . . [T]he parent storms; the child looks on, catches the lineaments of wrath, puts on the same airs in the circle of smaller slaves, gives a loose tongue to the worst of passions, and, thus nursed, educated, and daily exercised in tyranny, cannot but be stamped with odious peculiarities. The man must be a prodigy who can retain his manners and morals undepraved by such circumstances."[33]

Masters varied, of course. Some lived close to their slaves and were familiar with every aspect of their lives and work. Others resided in distant cities, leaving the management of the plantation and the supervision of the slaves to overseers. Some owners were jovial and genial, others mean-spirited and vindictive. A consensus among both whites and slaves held "adopted" or "Yankee" slaveholders—those not born to the practice—to be among the worst. Black slaveholders—what few existed—were also rated low, whether because of the inferior status of all blacks or because of their particular characters. Most blacks who bought slaves did so to free them, but a few, having managed to accumulate considerable property, used their slaves to work their land or to assist them in their trades or businesses.

The slave owner typically thought of his wife as morally pure and mentally inferior. She shared none of the growing independence of women in the free states. Whatever property she had owned, including slaves, became her husband's when she married. If she married a small farmer, she might well have to labor in the fields alongside him and his slaves. If she married a plantation owner, she usually came to the heavy responsibilities of running a large household without much preparation. She had not been trained to it, for she had been taught to think physical labor and household tasks beneath her. The richer her husband, the more numerous his slaves, the more time she had to devote to caring for them—planning and checking on their work, providing them with clothes, supervising the care of their children. Forbidden to travel without a chaperone (or at all), isolated on her husband's plantation, she suffered loneliness, especially for the company of other white women.

As her slaves well knew, a mistress's authority derived from her husband. Plantation mistress Mary Hamilton Campbell told how her husband's slave Eliza spoke to her of *"our master."*[34] The plantation overseer might ignore or defy the mistress's orders. Her husband might refuse to back her decisions, and she might be reduced to coaxing and wheedling to persuade him to right what she perceived as injustices inflicted on his slaves. "I had a long and painful conversation with Mr. [my husband] upon the subject of the flogging which had been inflicted on the wretched Teresa," Fanny Kemble wrote. "These discussions are terrible: they throw me into perfect agonies of distress for the slaves, whose position is utterly hopeless; for myself, whose intervention in their behalf sometimes seems to me worse than useless; for Mr., whose share in this horrible system fills me by turns with indignation and pity."[35]

Some plantation mistresses genuinely loved certain of their slaves—particularly their house servants—and did their best to make their lives a little more bearable. Others lived at sword's point with the people who served them. One slave owner's wife went into the kitchen at the end of every meal and spat in the leftovers to keep the slaves from eating them. Another put out her cook's eye with a fork for serving underdone potatoes.

Many a slave owner's wife was humiliated by the daily presence of her husband's black mistress(es); her children and theirs played together and often looked much alike. In 1824, a woman sought a divorce shortly after her wedding; her husband had just told her "that he had two mulatto children who were more comely and handsome than any she would ever have and that he would bring the [slave] mother and her children home. . . . In a few more days this negro woman and two mulatto children were brought upon the plantation. They were received by her husband with much interest and shew of affection. He now again acknowledged the children openly, and admitted the eldest to every act of familiar intercourse of which its age was capable. He would take it upon his knee, and instructed it to abuse your unhappy applicant and place her under the most positive and threatening injunction not to correct it—

declaring his strong attachment for the mother and stating that the two children were his and that he meant to do more for them, upon principle, than for his lawful children."[36]

## *The Powers That Be: Punishment*

The slave system was founded on and sustained by brute force—physical punishment. Both masters and mistresses themselves could beat their slaves or order them beaten by overseers, black drivers, or men employed for that purpose in slave jails. These slaves were the intimates of their owners, yet, as Elizabeth Fox-Genovese writes, "Mistresses whipped slave women with whom they might have shared beds, whose children they might have delivered or who might have delivered theirs, whose children they might have suckled and who frequently suckled theirs."[37]

The power of the state sanctioned these beatings and other even more severe punishments. Only rarely could slaves find protection in the justice system. The laws of slave states solidly backed the absolute authority of owners. Laws grew harsher as the numbers of slaves increased and white fears rose. They denied the slave freedom of movement; if he ventured off his owner's property without a written pass, any white person or patrollers hired to catch him out could stop him. He had no right of *habeas corpus,* for he did not own his own body. He could not testify against a white person. Except on the frontier, where fear of Indians sometimes outran fear of blacks, the law forbade him to carry a gun. He usually was legally forbidden to buy and sell goods without his owner's specific permission. He could not go to church or be baptized unless his master approved. Only lack of enforcement of the local slave code, the conflicting laws of the free states, or abolitionist defiance of fugitive slave laws could help him.

The punishments inflicted on slaves testify to the worst side of human nature. They ranged from the commonplace beatings with lashes designed to hurt, to horrifyingly inventive tortures. They were often tinged with perverted sexuality and sadism. For proof of their excesses historians do not need the writings of abolitionists, who focused on them with a kind of sick fascination. The testimony of former slaves, the diaries of southern women, southern newspapers, and public records teem with accounts of these unspeakable cruelties.

## *African-American Culture: Status, Self-Respect, and Community*

Influence goes both ways. No two groups can live together without compromises and without changing one another. Slaves resisted—sometimes directly, more often subtly. They used their skills in everything from cooking to growing cotton to making iron to protect themselves and expand their independence within the system. They asserted their freedom by finding ways to exercise choice. They reclaimed their own identities, their own cultures. They clung to remnants of their African memories and customs. "[S]laves established families, created churches, selected community leaders, and carved out a small realm of independent economic activity. An elaborate network of kinship—with its own pattern of courtship, rites of marriage, parental responsibilities, and kin obligations—linked slaves together. . . . In addition to preachers, slaves chose other leaders from their own ranks. Often these were drivers or artisans, but sometimes men and women of no special status in the owners' view."[38]

Individual slaves found ways, sometimes pathetic, of protecting their own self-respect, many of these depended on whites. Blacks bragged of having been born in North America and boasted about the status of their owners. Black drivers laying out work for other slaves, and "mammies" presiding over kitchens and nurseries proudly exercised the minor powers delegated to them by their owners. But others dominated by sheer force of personality.

Slaves invested one another with dignity, as when they taught their children to address the aged as "aunt" and "uncle"—a practice picked up by some whites. Despite the heavy odds against them, many slaves established and maintained stable families. Within the black community, slaves cared for each other, covered for each other, and supported each other in times of trouble. A runaway hiding in nearby woods could count on his friends for food from their own meager rations. By song, drums, or grapevine, slaves passed on to their friends and relations on other farms and plantations the news garnered on their masters' errands or at their masters' tables.

Some slaves gained influence by expertise—whether in reading, arithmetic, voodoo, or herbal medicine. They exercised their talents in music to earn freedom from field labor. They made themselves indispensable by their skills.

Humiliated, deprived of identity, forced to work endless hours, and tortured, slaves nonetheless somehow maintained a culture and community of their own.

## *African-American Culture: Literacy, Folklore, and Religion*

Slave owners insisted on the inferiority of Africans and the benefits to be gained by living in a superior (white) civilization. Yet they denied their slaves access to much of that civilization by making it a crime to teach slaves to read. Some learned anyway. Henry Bibb started by tracing out the letters from his passes, though he did not know what they symbolized. Frederick Douglass bribed white children to teach him a little at a time. Those who learned taught others. Slaves risked beatings to attend schools operated by whites like Levi Coffin—until slave owners closed down the schools. But, of course, most slaves remained illiterate: as her husband's slave Israel told Fanny Kemble when she asked him why he had never tried to learn, "Missis, what for me learn to read? me have no prospect!"[39]

Christianity was not denied to the slaves as consistently as was education. Some masters thought it—or the form of it offered slaves—helpful in keeping them in line. White ministers preached to them obedience and humility. Former slave Lunsford Lane would remember that "on Sabbath there was one sermon preached expressly for the colored people, which it was generally my privilege to hear. I became quite familiar with the texts: 'Servants be obedient to your masters'—'not with eye service as men pleasers'—'He that knoweth his master's will and doeth it not, shall be beaten with many stripes,' and others of this class: for they formed the basis of most of these public instructions to us. The first commandment impressed upon our minds was to obey our masters, and the second was like unto it, namely, to do as much work when they or the overseers were not watching us as when they were."[40]

A slave holiday in Petersburg, Virginia (*Crowe*, With Thackeray in America)

Masters might allow slaves to attend white churches—in a separate section—or black churches, or permit a black preacher to conduct services on the plantation, or have slaves attend family prayers. Other masters, though, forbade them the consolations of Christianity, even threatening beatings if the slaves prayed.

John Thompson, an early 19th-century slave, was probably accurate in observing that "most worshipped outside a church in . . . the 'invisible institution.'"[41] The slaves' version of Christianity spread from plantation to plantation. Slaves secretly sang or prayed in their cabins, covering their heads with pots so that the sound would not be heard, or they attended their own services in the woods.

Thus just as blacks developed their own form of the English language, they developed their own form of Christianity, using bits and pieces of African culture and adapting Christianity to their own situation. On this basis they changed its theology and created their own ways of worshipping. "The antebellum Negro was not converted to God. He converted God unto himself."[42] Dutch factor William Bosman commented in 1705 that Africans believed in one omnipotent and omnipresent God, but, they said, He must be approached through their idol-gods to whom He had committed the government of the world.[43] Union army chaplain W. G. Kiphant noted the slaves' emphasis on "the deliverance of the children of Israel. Moses is their *ideal* of all that is high, and noble, and perfect, in man. I think they have been accustomed to regard Christ not so much in the light of a *spiritual* Deliverer, as that of a second Moses who would eventually lead *them* out of their prisonhouse of bondage."[44]

Blacks' spirituals, "shouts," and physical modes of worship influenced white Christians, particularly through common attendance at camp meetings. In 1819, Methodist John Watson complained that at these religious gatherings, "in the *blacks'* quarters, the coloured people get together, and sing for hours together, short scraps of disjointed affirmations, pledges, or prayers, lengthened out with long repetitious *choruses*. These are all sung in the merry chorus-manner of the southern harvest field, or husking-frolic method, of the slave blacks; and also very greatly like the Indian dances. With every word so sung, they have a sinking of one or other leg of the body alternately; producing an audible sound of the feet at every step, and as manifest as the steps of actual negro dancing in Virginia &c. [I]f some, in the meantime sit, they strike the sounds alternately on each thigh. . . . [T]he evil is only occasionally condemned and the example has already visibly affected the religious manners of some whites. From this cause, I have known in some camp meetings from 50 to 60 people crowd into one tent, after the public devotions had closed, and there continue the whole night, singing tune after tune, . . . scarce one of which were in our hymn books. Some of these from their nature, (having very long repetition choruses and short scraps of matter) are actually composed as sung and are almost endless."[45]

Meanwhile, remnants of African conjuring and witchcraft survived alongside Christianity. Many a slave went to the plantation magician for a powder to make his owner merciful, for a love potion, or even for a ritual to make himself invulnerable in an insurrection. As ex-slave William Adams put it, "There are lots of folks, and educated ones, too, what says we-uns believes in superstition. Well, it's 'cause they don't understand. 'Member the lord, in some of His ways, can be mysterious. The Bible says so. There am some things the Lord wants all folks to know, some things just the chosen few to know, and some things no one should

A slave ball in Charleston, South Carolina (*Crowe,* With Thackeray in America)

know. Now, just 'cause you don't know 'bout some of the Lord's laws, 'tain't superstition if some other person understands and believes in such."[46]

African-American folklore told stories that explained natural phenomena and passed along folk wisdom: "Tain't no use o' sp'ilin de Sat'day night by countin' de time to Monday mornin.'"[47] It also portrayed slaves as outwitting their masters, often allegorically through animal stories. Former slave Cecelia Chappel told about "a partridge and a fox who killed a beef and skinned it. The fox (the master) managed to get all the beef except the liver, by saying that his wife needed it for soup. They agreed to eat the liver, so as soon as the partridge (the slave) had cooked it, he ate his portion quickly and then feigned sickness, whereupon the fox concluded that the beef was poisoned and gave it all back to the partridge."[48]

Hard physical work preempted the time and energy of the slaves. Some masters gave them Saturdays off, and almost all allowed them free Sundays—little enough time for looking after the tasks of daily life and the hunting, fishing, gardening, and berrying with which they might supplement their diets. But some of them stole time on Sundays for wrestling, running races, strumming a banjo, singing, dancing, playing marbles, telling stories, fiddling, drinking, gambling, or visiting. A planter got big tasks like cornshucking done by inviting all the slaves in the neighborhood to work in his barn in return for whiskey and a meal. The slaves' most important holidays came just before harvesting and at Christmas, when celebrations might go on for six days, with much feasting and drinking at the owner's expense and perhaps dances and athletic contests.

## CHRONICLE OF EVENTS

**1630**
A Virginia court sentences Hugh Davis to a whipping for having intercourse with a black woman.

**1639**
Virginia enacts a law requiring that all men except blacks secure arms and ammunition or be subject to fine.

**1640**
Virginia court sentences Robert Sweat to public penance for having gotten a "negro woman" with child; it sentences her to whipping.

**1654**
A Virginia court recognizes the right of blacks to hold slaves, by denying John Casor's suit for freedom from his black master, Anthony Johnson.

**1660**
The king of England orders the Council for Foreign Plantations to consider how people purchased "from other parts" as servants or slaves may be converted to Christianity.

**1662**
Virginia enacts a law declaring that slave offspring inherit the status of the mother.

Virginia and Maryland prohibit intermarriage between blacks and whites.

**1667**
Virginia rules that Christian baptism "does not alter the condition of the person as to his bondage or freedom."

**1674**
New York provides that "no Negro slave who becomes a Christian after he has been bought shall be set at liberty."

**1680**
Virginia enacts a statute ruling that "no Negro or slave" may carry arms, on pain of 20 lashes; no black may lift up his hand against any "Christian," on pain of 30 lashes; if any black runs away and resists recapture, he may be killed.

**1684**
The New York assembly prohibits slaves from selling goods.

**1691**
A Virginia statute banishes any white man or woman intermarrying with a black, mulatto, or Indian and fines any English woman having a child out of wedlock by a black, the child to be bound out until age 30 (in 1765, this was reduced to 21 for males and 18 for females).

**1702**
New York passes "An Act for Regulating Slaves," prohibiting meetings of more than three slaves, trading by slaves, testimony by slaves except in cases of slave conspiracy, and self-protection by slaves against whites; authorizing masters to punish slaves at will; and creating the office of Common Whipper for slaves.

**1704**
The South Carolina legislature grants ministers of the gospel the right to hold "all such negroes as shall be given and allotted to the several parishes by the Society . . . for the Propagation of the Gospel in Foreign Parts, or by any other charitably disposed persons."

**1705**
The Virginia "slave code" defines the status of slaves, ruling that all non-Christian servants brought into the colony (that is, most Indians and blacks) are slaves, even if they later are converted to Christianity; that "all Negro, mulatto, and Indian slaves within this dominion shall be held to be real estate"; that any master who kills a slave while "correcting" her or him shall be acquitted of blame; that no black, mulatto, or Indian, bond or free, may ever lift his hand against any white person; and that no slave has the right to bear arms or to move about without written permission from the master.

Virginia law provides that a minister marrying a black man and a white woman shall pay a fine of ten thousand pounds of tobacco.

**1706**
New Jersey becomes the first North American colony to pass a castration law for slaves who *attempt* rape.

**1708**
A New York act makes it a capital crime for a black, Indian, or slave to kill any "of her Majesties Leige People *not* being Negroes Mulattoes or Slaves within this Colony."

**1710**
A New York law forbids black, Indian, and mulatto slaves to appear in the streets at night without a lantern with a lighted candle in it.

**1712**
A New York statute makes it a crime for a black, Indian, or other slave "wilfully [to] murder any Negro, Indian or mulatto slave within this colony."

A New York law forbids any freed black, Indian, or mulatto slave to own real estate.

New York provides that "no Negro, Indian or mulatto, that shall hereafter be made free, shall enjoy, hold or possess" property within the colony.

**1730**
The decision in the Virginia case *Tucker* v. *Sweney* allows executors to treat slave children born after the master's death as "Horses or Cattle."

**1740**
South Carolina passes a comprehensive "Negro Act," proscribing slaves from "freedom of movement, freedom of assembly, freedom to raise food, to earn money, [and] to learn to read English," and restricting them to low-quality, inexpensive clothing.

**1751**
George II repeals the Virginia act of 1705 making slaves real estate.

**1769**
A Virginia statute authorizes the castration of any slave who attempts to rape a white woman.

**1773**
Slave M. Palmer of Silver Bluff, South Carolina, establishes the first black church in America with a group of slaves and free blacks.

**1775**
Virginia slaveholder William Pitman beats and stomps a slave boy to death and incurs the penalties of the law.

**1785**
Virginia law declares that "every person, who has one-fourth or more of Negro blood shall be deemed a mulatto, and the word negro in any section of this or any other statute, shall be construed to mean mulatto as well as negro."

**1788**
The New York legislature passes the first new, comprehensive slave code since 1730, stipulating that every presently enslaved person be a slave for life.

**1790**
Congress confines the privilege of naturalization to free whites.

**1800**
South Carolina forbids blacks to hold religious meetings at night and subjects to fines nonresident plantation owners who have no white overseers.

**1801**
Congress decrees that the laws of Virginia and Maryland will continue in force within the District of

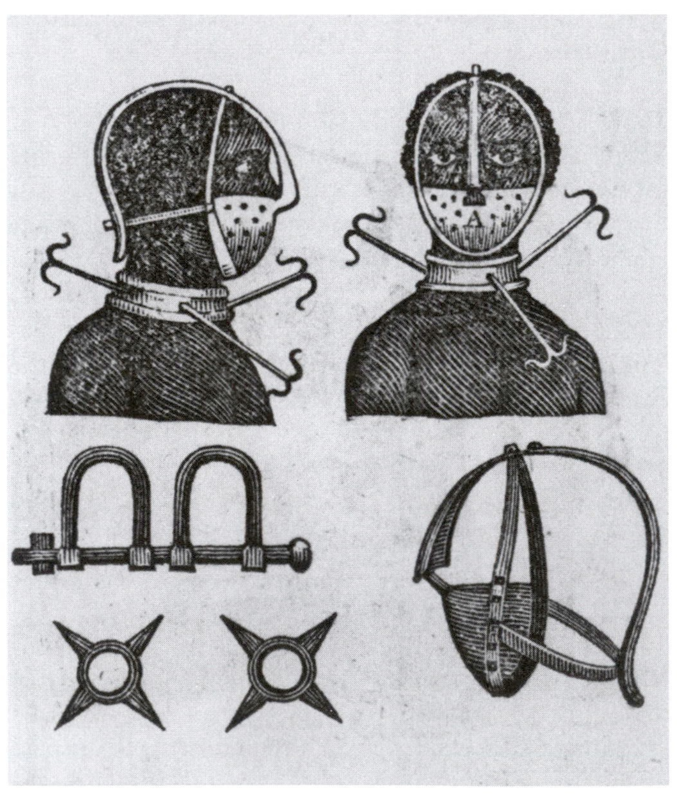

Display of instruments of torture used on slaves (*Library of Congress*)

Columbia, thus establishing there a slave code enforced by federal authority.

**1804**
Ohio writes its first black laws, patterned after southern slave codes, to deter slaves from escaping into Ohio from Virginia and Kentucky.

**1805**
Virginia statute declares it lawful for a master to allow slaves to accompany his family to religious worship conducted by a white man.

**1809**
New York recognizes black marriages, even between slaves, and makes the law retroactive to give legitimacy to all children of slaves.

**1813**
New York extends jury trial to slaves.

**1816**
Southern slaveholders begin settling in Texas.

**1820s and 1830s**
The Christian clergy mount efforts to see that slaves are instructed in religion, to propagandize masters on their duties, to provide catechisms for slaves, and to send missionaries to slaves.

**1823**
Episcopalian priest Frederick Dalche urges religious instruction for slaves to teach respect for their masters.

**1829**
The decision in the North Carolina case of *State* v. *Mann* asserts that the purpose of the legal system is to convince each slave that he has no will of his own and that "[t]he power of the master must be absolute to render the submission of the slave perfect."

**1831**
Virginia passes a law by which any slave who attends a meeting where a free colored person preaches may be whipped not more than 39 lashes, and any slave who listens to any white preacher at night may receive the same punishment.

North Carolina passes a law by which any colored person, free or slave, teaching a slave to read or write, or providing him with any book or pamphlet, may be punished by imprisonment or whipping.

**1836**
The Dixwell Avenue Congregational Church of New Haven, Connecticut—the first black Congregational church—calls as its pastor ex-slave Rev. James W. C. Pennington, D.D., of the University of Heidelberg.

**1837**
The Connecticut Supreme Court frees a slave held "temporarily" in Connecticut for about two years.

Texas makes insurrection, poisoning, rape of a white female, assault on a white with intent to kill, maiming a white person, arson, murder, and burglary punishable by death if committed by a slave.

**1840**
Texas law criminalizes unauthorized trading (buying and selling goods) with slaves.

Texas forbids slaves to carry deadly weapons without written permission of their owners.

**1841**
Ex-slave James W. C. Pennington writes *The Origin and History of the Colored People.*

Ex-slave Frederick Douglass begins speaking against slavery and racial prejudice.

Texas gives all Texans the lawful right and responsibility to apprehend runaway slaves and take them before a local justice of the peace, to be returned to their owners or jailed and later sold at auction.

**1846**
The Texas legislature creates a formal slave-patrol system.

**1849**
Forty Alabama men compete in an essay contest, run by the Baptist State Convention, on "The Duties of Christian Masters."

James W. C. Pennington publishes his slave narrative, *The Fugitive Blacksmith.*

**1850**
*The Narrative of Sojourner Truth* is published.

**1852**
Texas law permits slave owners to collect indemnities for any slave convicted and executed for committing a capital offense.

**1853**
Ex-slave William Wells Brown publishes *Clotel,* the first novel written by a black.

**1857**
In *Dred Scott* v. *Sanford,* the United States Supreme Court rules that a slave, an ex-slave, or a descendant of slaves cannot be a citizen of the United States and that Congress cannot prohibit slavery in the territories.

**1859**
Jermain Wesley Loguen publishes his fugitive slave narrative.

New Mexico enacts a slave code for its slaveless society.

Arkansas passes a law enslaving all free blacks in the state by January 1, 1860.

**1862**
"Refugeeing"—taking slaves to Texas to keep them away from the advancing Union forces—becomes common.

## Eyewitness Testimony

### *Arriving from Africa*

We were landed up a river a good way from the sea, about Virginia county, where we saw few or none of our native Africans, and not one soul who could talk to me. I was a few weeks weeding grass and gathering stones in a plantation. . . . [T]he gentleman, to whom I suppose the estate belonged, being unwell, I was one day sent for to his dwellinghouse to fan him. . . . I had a fan put in my hand, to fan the gentleman while he slept, and so I did indeed with great fear. While he was fast asleep I indulged myself a great deal in looking about the room, which appeared to me very fine and curious. The first object that engaged my attention was a watch which hung from the chimney, and was going. I was quite surprised at the noise it made, and was afraid it would tell the gentleman anything I might do amiss; and when I immediately after observed a picture hanging in the room, which appeared constantly to look at me, I was still more affrighted. . . .

*Gustavus Vassa on his experiences about 1756, in* Great Slave Narratives, *34–35.*

[When receiving a new group of slaves, the owners would] arrange the men in one row and the women in another and make signs to them to choose each man a wife and would read the marriage service to them and thus save time by settling their matrimonial affairs. The young people of the family would select names from novels they had read and other sources, and sew these names into the clothes of each.

*Emmaline Eve, in Fox-Genovese,* Plantation Household, *135.*

### *Necessities: Food*

I rec'd a letter from Valley a few days ago which has made me very uneasy. He says my Negroes are starving, they have been without a grain of corn for two weeks & living entirely on Fish & Oysters. I cannot expect you to know how my mind is hurt by this information, and the inattention of Mr. Wayne [overseer] to whom I had written to purchase corn and draw on either my Factors [agents] in Charleston, or myself to pay for it, yet he has let my Negroes suffer, and my work stand.

*Major Pierce Butler, 1794 letter, in Bell,* Major Butler's Legacy, *131.*

We [slave children] were not regularly allowanced. Our food was coarse corn meal boiled. . . . It was put into a large wooden tray or trough, and set down upon the ground. The children were then called, like so many pigs, and like so many pigs they would come and devour the mush; some with oyster-shells, others with pieces of shingle, some with naked hands, and none with spoons. . . . There were four slaves of us in the kitchen—my sister Eliza, my aunt Priscilla, Henny, and myself; and we were allowed less than a half of a bushel of corn-meal per week, and very little else, either in the shape of meat or vegetables. It was not enough for us to subsist upon. We were therefore reduced to the wretched necessity of living at the expense of our neighbors. This we did by begging and stealing, whichever came handy in the time of need, the one being considered as legitimate as the other.

*Douglass,* Narrative, *33, 44, 65–66.*

I have seen pa go out at night with a big sack and come back with it full. He'd bring sweet potatoes, watermelons, chickens and turkeys. . . . Where he went I cannot say, but he brought the booty home. The floor of our cabin was covered with planks. Pa had raised up two planks, and dug a hole. This was our storehouse.

*Former slave, in Webber,* Deep Like the Rivers, *170.*

### *Necessities: Clothing*

Their yearly clothing consisted of two coarse linen shirts, one pair of linen trousers, like the shirts, one jacket, one pair of trousers for winter, made of coarse negro cloth, one pair of stockings, and one pair of shoes; the whole of which could not have cost more than seven dollars. . . . The children unable to work in the field had neither shoes, stockings, jackets, nor trousers, given to them; their clothing consisted of two coarse linen shirts per year. When they [the clothing articles] failed them, they went naked until the next allowance-day. Children from seven to ten years old, of both sexes, almost naked might be seen at all seasons of the year.

*Douglass,* Narrative, *28.*

[For religious services and parties the slave] gals come out in the starch dresses. . . . They took their hair down outen the strings. . . . De gals charmed us wid honeysuckle and rose petals hid in dere bosoms. . . . Dey dried chennyberries and painted dem and wo' em on a string around dere necks. . . . [C]ourting gals . . . tried to do just like the young white missus would do.

*Gus Feaster, in White,* Ar'n't I a Woman? *143–44.*

[I]jes had two dresses. De best one was made of plain, white muslin. . . . [I] got walnut bark to color it brown. . . . [I] allus had to wash it on Saturday, 'cause we all had to go to church on Sunday. . . . [I made my walking dress] jes like old Miss taught me . . . with a cord 'round de bottom, a cord as big as my little finger, so's I couldn't tear it, cause I went over fences like a deer.

*Sarah Waggoner, in Fox-Genovese,* Plantation Households*, 183.*

Slave cabins (*Library of Congress*)

## *Necessities: Shelter*

Among Isabella's [Sojourner Truth's] earliest recollections was the removal of her master, Charles Ardinburgh, into his new house, which he had built for a hotel, soon after the decease of his father. A cellar, under this hotel, was assigned to his slaves, as their sleeping apartment,—all the slaves he possessed, of both sexes, sleeping (as is quite common in a state of slavery) in the same room . . . its only lights consisting of a few panes of glass, through which she thinks the sun never shone, but with thrice reflected rays; and the space between the loose boards of the floor, and the uneven earth below, was often filled with mud and water, the uncomfortable splashings of which were as annoying as its noxious vapors must have been chilling and fatal to health. . . . [S]he wonders not at the rheumatisms, and fever-sores, and palsies, that distorted the limbs and racked the bodies of those fellow-slaves in after-life.

*Sojourner Truth's report of her early life as a slave in New York state, in* Narrative*, 4–13.*

These cabins consist of one room, about twelve feet by fifteen, with a couple of closets smaller and closer than the staterooms of a ship, divided off from the main room and each other by rough wooden partitions, in which the inhabitants sleep. They have almost all of them a rude bedstead, with the gray moss of the forests for mattress, and filthy, pestilential-looking blankets for covering. Two families (sometimes eight and ten in number) reside in one of these huts, which are mere wooden frames pinned, as it were, to the earth by a brick chimney outside, whose enormous aperture within pours down a flood of air, but little counteracted by the miserable spark of fire, which hardly sends an attenuated thread of lingering smoke up its huge throat. A wide ditch runs immediately at the back of these dwellings, which is filled and emptied daily by the tide. Attached to each hovel is a small scrap of ground for a garden, which, however, is for the most part untended and uncultivated.

*Kemble,* Journal, *67–68.*

## *Medical Care*

I am impelled by feelings of humanity to call upon you . . . in behalf of a poor sufferer. . . . She is the property of on[e] Posten in whose service she was burnt almost to death before Easter, & has ever since remained in the most shocking situation, she is now loathsome to every beholder, without a change of clothing, or one single necessary of life, or comfort. Can you not compel the savage creature who owns her to do something for her?

*Concerned citizen, letter to the mayor of Alexandria, Virginia, 1813, in Owens,* Property, *48.*

The infirmary is a large two-story building, terminating the broad orange-planted space between the two rows of houses which form the first settlement; it is built of whitewashed wood, and contains four large-sized rooms. . . . But [only] half the casements, of which there were six, were glazed, and these were obscured with dirt, almost as much as the other windowless ones were darkened by the dingy shutters, which the shivering inmates had fastened to in order to protect themselves from the cold. In the enormous chimney glimmered the powerless embers of a few sticks of wood, round which, however, as many of the sick women as could approach were cowering, some on wooden settles, most of them on the ground, excluding those who were too ill to rise; and these last poor wretches lay prostrate on the floor, without bed, mattress, or pillow, buried in tattered and filthy blankets, which, huddled round them as they lay strewed about, left hardly space to move upon the floor. . . . I left this refuge for Mr.'s [my husband's] sick dependents with my clothes covered with dust, and full of vermin. . . .

*Kemble,* Journal, *70–73.*

Yesterday morning [Sina] lost an infant. The doctor was with us all day, and when he left just before sunset he did not express any special fears about her situation. I had been with her until two o'clock, and went over after the doctor left. After tea your sister and myself were engaged giving out Negro cloth. Your father rode over at nine o'clock and said he saw no change except a profuse perspiration. She was perfectly sensible, but drowsy from the influence of opiates, and her pulse numbered 100. He returned to the house but a short time when he was summoned back; and she died at ten o'clock without a struggle. . . .

Eve left four children, and [Sina] leaves five. Nine motherless ones now to care for!

*Plantation mistress Mary Jones, November 20, 1856, in* Children of Pride, *265.*

[My] mother was a kind of doctor too. [She] would ride horseback all over the place an' see how they was gettin' along. She'd make a tea out o' herbs for them who had fever an' sometimes she gave them water from slippery elms.

*R. S. Taylor, in Fox-Genovese,* Plantation Households, *171.*

'Twa'n't no used to send fo' a docta, no'm, 'cause dey didn't have no medicine. My grandmother got out in de woods and got 'erbs. She made sage bam [balm]. One thing I remember, she would take co'n shucks—de butt end of de shucks—and boil 'em and make tea. 'Twould breck de chills and fever. De Lo'd fixed a way. We used roots for medicine too.

*Goodson, "Medical-Botanical Contributions," in* Black Women in American History *2:480.*

## *Slave Life: Care for the Aged*

[M]y poor old grandmother . . . had served my old master faithfully from youth to old age. She had been the source of all his wealth; she had peopled his plantation with slaves; she had become a great grandmother in his service. She had rocked him in infancy, attended him in childhood, served him through life, and at his death wiped from his icy brow the cold death-sweat, and closed his eyes forever. She was nevertheless left a slave—a slave for life—a slave in the hands of strangers; and in their hands she saw her children, her grandchildren, and her great-grandchildren, divided, like so many sheep, without being gratified with the small privilege of a single word, as to their or her own destiny. . . . [H]er present owners finding she was of but little value . . . took her to the woods, built her a little hut, put up a little mud-chimney, and then made her welcome to the privilege of supporting herself there in perfect loneliness; thus virtually turning her out to die!

*Douglass,* Narrative, *61–62.*

He is a quiet orderly old Man, not able to do much Work and therefore is never drove to Labour, but suffer'd to go his own way. I observe he makes larger Crops of Rice and Corn for himself than most able Young Negroes, which I believe is greatly owing to their Aid for they all Respect and Love him. . . . I shall order proper Care to be taken of him, if his Life shall happen to surpass his Strength for Labour . . . and continue to make the same Annual Allowance during all the Time that he is able to perform any Work.

*Plantation owner Henry Laurens, 1755(?), in Littlefield,* Rice and Slaves, *71.*

### *Slave Life: Maternity*

When her fourth baby was born and was about two months old, she just studied all the time about how she would have to give it up, and one day she said, "I just decided I'm not going to let Old Master sell this baby; he just ain't going to do it." She got up and give it something out of a bottle, and pretty soon it was dead."

*Lou Smith in* American Slave *6:302.*

Pappy was a driver under de overseer, but mammy say dat she stay at de little nursery cabin and look after all de little babies. Dey had a cabin fixed up with homemade cradles and things where dey put all de babies. Der mammies would come in from de field about ten o'clock to nurse 'em and den later in de day, my mammy would feed de youngest on pot-likker and de older ones on greens and pot-licker. Dey had skimmed milk and mush, too, and all of 'em stayed as fat as butter balls, me among 'em.

*Ex-slave Callie Williams,* American Slave*, Alabama.*

### *Slave Life: Marriage*

One general principle prevails in all the States . . . and that is, that *a slave cannot make a contract, not even the contract of matrimony.*

*Wheeler, Law of Slavery, quoted by Goodell,* Slave Code, *93.*

After I been at he place 'bout a year, de massa come to me and say, "You gwine live with Rufus in dat cabin over yonder. Go fix it for livin'." I's 'bout sixteen year old and has no larnin', and I's jus' igno'mus chile. I's thought dat him mean for me to tend de cabin for Rufus and some other niggers. . . .

[After I had two children by Rufus, I quit him.] I never marries 'cause one 'sperience am 'nough for this nigger. After what I done for de massa, I's never wants no truck with any man. De lawd forgive dis cullud woman, but he have to 'scuse me and look for some others for to 'plenish [replenishl de earth.

*Ex-slave Rose William, in Gutman,* Black Family, *84–85.*

I laks Essex mighty well, an' I'll be sorry ter see him go—I'll be sorry too fer lil Robert not to have no daddy, but I can't go! . . . I knows . . . dat it's mighty easy ter git a good husband, an' mighty hard ter git a good mistis.

*Fannie, explaining why she refused to be sold with her first husband, in Eppes,* Negro, *56–57.*

Send me some of the children's hair in a separate paper with their names on the paper. Will you please git married, as long as I am married. My dear, you know the Lord knows both of our hearts. You know it never was our wishes to be separated from each other, and it never was our fault. Oh, I can see you so plain, at any-time. I had rather anything to had happened to me most than ever to have been parted from you and the children. As I am, I do not know which I love best, you or Anna. If I was to die, today or tomorrow, I do not think I would die satisfied till you tell me you will try and marry some good, smart man that will take care of you and the children, and do it because you love me; and not because I think more of the wife I have got than I do of you.

The woman is not born that feels as near to me as you do. You feel this day like myself. Tell them they must remember they have a good father and one that cares for them and one that thinks about them every day—My very heart did ache when reading your very kind and interesting letter. Laura I do not think I have change any at all since I saw you last.—I think of you and my children every day of my life.

*Ex-slave Spicer, post–Civil War letter to his wife, Laura, who with their children had been sold away from him before the war, in Gutman,* Black Family, *6–7.*

### *Slave Life: White-Black Sexual Relations*

His [Benjamin Banneker's] maternal grandmother, Molly Welsh, a native of England, . . . came to Maryland—, with a ship load of emigrants, and, to defray the expense of the voyage was sold to a master with whom she served an apprenticeship of seven years. After her term of service had expired, she bought a small farm—, and purchased as laborers, two Negro slaves, from a ship which lay in Chesapeake Bay. They proved valuable servants. One of them, said to have been the son of an African king, a man of industry, integrity, fine disposition, and dignified manners, she liberated from slavery and afterwards married.

*Martha E. Tyson, 1854, quoted in Johnston,* Race Relations, *189.*

[Captain Davis'] most visible Foible, was keeping a Mulatto Servant (or Slave) who in Reality was his Mistress. . . . [H]e suffered almost every Thing to pass through her Hands, having such Confidence in her, that she had the Custody of all his Cash, as well as Books. . . . [A]ll Persons who had any Business with Captain Davis, were expected not to treat her with Contempt.

*William Stephens, 1739, in Higginbotham,* In the Matter of Color, *231.*

I had often heard of the beauty of quadroons. . . . They . . . have the appearance of being virtuous: but they are generally prostitutes and kept mistresses. Young men and single men of wealth have each a quadroon for his exclusive use. They are furnished with a Chamber and a sitting room and servants, and the comforts and elegancies of life. It generally costs from $1,500 to $2,000 a year to keep a quadroon. I am informed that the quadroon is faithful to a proverb in these arrangements. Married men in this City [New Orleans] are frequently in the habit of keeping quadroons.

*Davidson, Diary (1836), 348, in Clinton,* Plantation Mistress, *212.*

[Ephraim Christopher, now in his 80s, has been] living in the same house with the slave Maria [a woman of 37 years], and living with her as his mistress. Her 13 children were all mulattos. . . . He had been selling one [of the children] almost every year.

*South Carolina court record, 1854, in Tadman,* Speculators and Slave, *127.*

A negro has been arrested for a rape on a respectable white lady. We expect he has been hung up a tree [lynched] before this.

*Austin, Texas,* State Gazette, *1860, in Campbell,* Empire, *105.*

### Slave Culture: Folklore

I knows why that boll weevil done come. . . . Away back yonder a spider live in the country, 'specially in the bottom. He live on the cotton leaves and stalks, but he don't hurt it. These spiders kept the insects eat up. They don't plow deep then, and plants cotton in February, so it made 'fore the insects git bad.

Then they gits to plowing deep, and it am colder 'cause the trees all cut, and they plows up all the spiders and the cold kill them. They plants later, and there ain't no spiders left to eat up the boll weevil.

*Ex-slave Caroline Matthews, in* Lay My Burden Down, *13.*

Every time I think of slavery and if it done the race any good, I think of the story of the coon and dog who met. The coon said to the dog, "Why is it you're so fat and I am so poor, and we is both animals?" The dog said: "I lay round Master's house and let him kick me and he gives me a piece of bread right on." Said the coon to the dog: "Better, then, that I stay poor." Them's my sentiment. I'm like the coon, I don't believe in 'buse.

*Ex-slave Stephen McCray, in* Lay My Burden Down, *14.*

### Slave Culture: Funerals

When a slave dies, the master gives the rest day, of their [the slaves'] own choosing, to celebrate the funeral. This, perhaps a month after the corpse is interred, is a jovial day with them; they sing and dance and drink the dead to his new home, which some believe to be in old Guinea.

*Henry C. Knight, 1824 letter, in Blassingame,* Slave Community, *37.*

Negro graves were always decorated with the last article used by the departed, and broken pitchers and broken bits of colored glass were considered even more appropriate than the white shells from the beach nearby. Sometimes they carved rude wooden figures like images of idols, and sometimes a patchwork quilt was laid upon the grave.

*Mrs. Telfair Hodgson, reporting on her father's Georgia plantation in the 1850s, in Blassingame,* Slave Community, *37.*

### Slave Culture: Literacy

I was never so surprised in my whole life as when [on the Middle Passage] I saw the book talk to my master. . . . When nobody saw me, I open'd it and put my ear down close upon it, in great hope that it would say something to me.

*Slave Olauda Equiano in Lambert, "'I Saw the Book Talk,'" 191.*

"Now," said he, "if you teach that nigger (speaking of myself) how to read, there would be no keeping him. It would forever unfit him to be a slave. He would at once become unmanageable, and of no value to his master. As to himself, it could do him no good, but a great deal of harm. It would make him discontented and unhappy." These words sank deep into my heart. . . . I now understood . . . the white man's power to enslave the black man. . . . From that moment, I understood the pathway from slavery to freedom.

*Douglass,* Narrative, *50.*

Judge Scalaway . . . addressed her as follows: "Margaret Douglass, stand up. You are guilty of one of the vilest crimes that ever disgraced society; and the jury have found you so. You have taught a slave girl to read in the Bible. . . . The Court, in your case, do not feel for you one solitary ray of sympathy, and they will inflict on you the utmost penalty of the law. In any other civilized country you would have paid the forfeit of your crime with your life, and the Court have only to regret that such is not the law in this country. The sentence for your offence is, that you be imprisoned one month in the county jail, and that you pay the costs of this prosecution."

*Ex-slaves William and Ellen Craft,* Running, *in* Great Slave Narratives, *288–89.*

## *Slave Culture: Music*

My ole Mistiss promise me,
W'en she died she'd set me free.
She lived so long dat 'er head got bal'.
an' she give out 'n de notion a-dyin' at all.
Ole Massar lakwise promise me,
W'en he died, he'd set me free.
But ole Massar go an' make his will
Fer to leave me a-plowin' ole Beck still.
Yes, my ole Massar promise me;
But "his papers" didn' set me free.
A dose of pizen he'ped 'im along.
May di Devil preach 'is funer'l song.

*In Webber,* Deep Like the Rivers, *76.*

Dey tried to make 'em [the slaves] stop singin' and prayin' durin' de war, 'case all dey'd ask for was to be sot free, but de slaves would get in de cabins and turn a big wash pot upside down and sing into dat, and de noise couldn't get out.

*Ex-slave Callie Williams,* American Slave, *Alabama.*

I'd jump up dar and den and holler and shout and sing and pat, and dey would all cotch de words and I'd sing it to some old shout song I'd heard 'em sing from Africa, and dey'd all take it up and keep at it, and keep a-addin' to it, and den it would be a spiritual.

*Former slave, in Blassingame,* Slave Community, *27–28.*

## *Slave Culture: Recreation*

The days between Christmas and New Year's day are allowed as holidays; and, accordingly, we were not required to perform any labor, more than to feed and take care of the stock. This time we regarded as our own, by the grace of our masters; and we therefore used or abused it nearly as we pleased. Those of us who had families at a distance, were generally allowed to spend the whole six days in their society. This time, however, was spent in various ways. The staid, sober, thinking, and industrious ones of our number would employ themselves in making corn-brooms, mats, horse-collars, and baskets; and another class of us would spend the time in hunting opossums, hares, and coons. But by far the larger part engaged in such sports and merriments as playing ball, wrestling, running foot-races, fiddling, dancing, and drinking whisky; and this latter mode of spending the time was by far the most agreeable to the feelings of our masters. . . .

[The slaveholders'] object seems to be, to disgust their slaves with freedom, by plunging them into the lowest depths of dissipation. . . . One plan is, to make bets on their slaves, as to who can drink the most whisky without getting drunk. . . .

*Douglass,* Narrative, *83–85.*

Before him [the banjo player] stood two athletic blacks, with open mouth and pearl white teeth, clapping "Juber" to the notes of the banjo; the fourth black man held in his right hand a jugy gourd of persimmon beer, and in his left, a dipper or water gourd, to serve the company. . . . The rest of the company, male and female, were dancers, except a little squat wench, who held the torch light.

*Visitor's report of a persimmon beer celebration in slave quarters, in Owens,* Property, *146.*

## *Slave Culture: Religion*

**Q:** Who is duty bound to give to Servants comfortable clothing, wholesome and abundant food?
**A:** The master.
**Q:** Who is duty bound to instruct Servants in a knowledge of the Holy Scriptures, and to give them every opportunity and encouragement to seek their soul's salvation?
**A:** The master.
**Q:** Who is the Master of us all in Heaven?
**A:** God.
**Q:** Does God show favour to the Master more than to the Servant, and just because he is a Master?
**A:** No.
**Q:** What are the Servants to count their Masters worthy of?
**A:** All honour.
**Q:** How are they to try to please their Masters?
**A:** Please them well in all things, not answering again.
**Q:** Is it right for a Servant when commanded to do anything to be sullen and slow, and answering his Master again?
**A:** No.
**Q:** But suppose the Master is hard to please, and threatens and punishes more than he ought, what is the Servant to do?
**A:** Do his best to please him.

*The Rev. Charles Colcock Jones,* Catechism *(1837), 127–30.*

After the praise meeting is over, there usually follows the very singular and impressive performance of the "Shout," or religious dance of the negroes. Three or four, standing still, clapping their hands and beating time with their feet, commence singing in unison one of the peculiar shout melodies, while the others walk round in a ring, in single file, joining also in the song. Soon those in the ring leave off their singing, the others keeping it up the while with increased vigor, and strike into the shout step, observing most accurate time with the music. This step is something halfway between a shuffle and a dance, as difficult for an uninitiated person to describe as to imitate. At the end of each stanza of the song the dancers stop short with a slight stamp on the last note, and then, putting the other foot forward, proceed through the next verse. . . . The shout is a simple outburst and manifestation of religious fervor—a "rejoicing in the Lord"—making a "joyful noise unto the God" of their salvation.

*H. G. Spaulding, 1863, in Blassingame,* Slave Community, *65–66.*

One of his [John Watson's] slaves was a preacher, and a favourite among them. He sometimes went to plantations twenty miles away—even further—on a Sunday, to preach a funeral sermon, making journeys of fifty miles a day on foot. . . . He was the most rascally negro, the worst liar, thief, and adulterer on his place. Indeed, when he was preaching, he always made a strong point of his own sinfulness, and would weep and bellow about it like a bull of Bashan, till he got a whole camp meeting into convulsions.

*Olmsted,* Cotton Kingdom, *375.*

[W]hile in North Carolina, I heard of two recent occasions, in which public religious services had been interrupted, and the preachers—very estimable coloured men—publicly whipped.

*Olmsted,* Cotton Kingdom, *175–76.*

After I had paid [the conjurer] his charge, he told me to go to the cowpen after night, and get some fresh cow manure, and mix it with red pepper and white people's hair, all to be put in a pot over the fire, and scorched until it could be ground up into snuff. I was then to sprinkle it about my master's bedroom, in his hat and boots, and it would prevent him from ever abusing me in any way. After I got it all ready prepared, the smallest pinch of it scattered over the room was enough to make a horse sneeze from the strength of it; but it did no good. . . . It was my job to make a fire in my master's chamber, night and morning. Whenever I could get a chance, I sprinkled a little of this dust about the linen of the bed. . . . This was to act upon them as what is called a kind of love powder, to change their sentiments of anger, to those of love toward me. But this all proved to be vain imagination.

*Ex-slave Henry Bibb,* Narrative, *71.*

"Dey didn't 'low us to go to church, neither. Sometimes us slip off an' hav a little prayer meetin' by usse'ves in a old house wid a dirt flo'. Dey' git happy an' shout an' couldn't nobody hyar 'em, caze dey didn't make no fuss on de dirt flo', an' one stan' in de do' an' watch. Some folks put dey head in de wash pot to pray [so that the sound would not be heard], an' pray easy, an' sombody be watchin' for de overseer. Us git whupped for ev'ything iffen hit was public knowed.

*Ex-slave George Young,* American Slave, *Alabama.*

## *Slave Culture: Self-Respect and Status*

In complimenting a woman called Joan upon the tidy condition of her house, she answered, with that cruel humility that is so bad an element in their [slaves'] character: "Missis no 'spect to find colored folks' house clean as white folks'." The mode in which they have learned to accept the idea of their own degradation and unalterable inferiority is the most serious impediment that I see in the way of their progress, since assuredly "self-love is not so vile a sin as self-neglecting." In the same way yesterday, Abraham the cook, in speaking of his brother's theft at the rice island, said "it was a shame even for a colored man to do such things."

*Kemble,* Journal *(1839), 298.*

When Colonel Lloyd's slaves met the slaves of Jacob Jepson, they seldom parted without a quarrel about their masters; Colonel Lloyd's slaves contending that he was the richest, and Mr. Jepson's slaves that he was the smartest, and most of a man. Colonel Lloyd's slaves would boast his ability to buy and sell Jacob Jepson. Mr. Jepson's slaves would boast his ability to whip Colonel Lloyd. These quarrels would almost always end in a fight between the parties, and those that whipped were supposed to have gained the point at issue. They seemed to think that the greatness of their masters was transferable to themselves. It was considered as being bad enough to be a slave; but to be a poor man's slave was deemed a disgrace indeed.

*Douglass,* Narrative, *36–37.*

## *The Powers That Be: Masters*

The haughty and imperious part of a man develops rapidly on one of these lonely sugar plantations, where the owner rarely meets with any except his slaves and minions.

*Rutherford B. Hayes, in Campbell,* Empire, *201.*

[T]he children of slaveholders are universally inferior to themselves, mentally, morally, physically, as well as pecuniarily. . . . The young master not being able to own as many slaves as his father, usually works what he has more severely, and being more liable to embarrassment, the slaves' liability to be sold at an early day is much greater. For the same reason, slaves have a deep interest, generally, in the marriage of a young mistress. Very generally the daughters of slaveholders marry inferior men;

A slave owner's vision of slave life. The caption reads: *"God bless you massa! you feed and clothe us. When we are sick you nurse us and when too old to work, you provide for us!" "These poor creatures are a sacred legacy from my ancestors and while a dollar is left me, nothing shall be spared to increase their comfort and happiness."* (*Library of Congress*)

men who seek to better their own condition by a wealthy connection. . . . Sometimes these are the sons of already broken-down slaveholders. In other cases they are adventurers from the North who remove to the South, and who readily become the most cruel masters.

*Ex-slave James W. C. Pennington, Fugitive Blacksmith (1849), in* Great Slave Narratives, *258–59.*

During the three hours, or more, in which I was in company with the proprietor [of a Virginia farm], I do not think ten consecutive minutes passed uninterrupted by some of the slaves requiring his personal direction or assistance. He was even obliged, three times, to leave the dinner-table.

"You see," said he, smiling, as he came in the last time, "a farmer's life, in this country, is no sinecure. . . . I only wish your philanthropists would contrive some satisfactory plan to relieve us of it; the trouble and the responsibility of properly taking care of our negroes, you may judge, from what you see yourself here, is anything but enviable."

*Olmsted,* Cotton Kingdom, *42.*

This exceptional condition [of the master's family living relatively well on a Virginia farm] . . . is maintained at an enormous expense, not only of money, but of nerve, time, temper, if not of humanity, or the world's judgment of humanity. There is much inherited wealth, a cotton plantation or two in Mississippi and a few slips of paper in a broker's office in Wall Street, that account for the comfort of this Virginia farmer. . . . And after all he has no road on which he can drive his fine horses; his physician supposes the use of chloric ether, as an anaesthetic agent, to be a novel and interesting subject of after-dinner eloquence; he has no church within twenty miles, but one of logs, attendance on which is sure to bring on an attack of neuralgia with his wife, and where only an ignorant ranter of a different faith from his own preaches at irregular intervals; there is no school which he is willing that his children should attend; his daily papers come weekly, and he sees no books except such as he has especially ordered from Norton or Stevens.

*Olmsted,* Cotton Kingdom, *86.*

[In Louisiana a slave] said . . . that there were many free negroes all about this region. Some were very rich. He pointed out to me three plantations, within twenty miles, owned by coloured men. These bought black folks, he said, and had servants of their own. They were very bad masters, very hard and cruel—hadn't any feeling. "You might think, master, dat dey would be good to dar own nation; but dey is not. I will tell you de truth, massa; I know I'se got to answer; and it's a fact, dey is very bad masters, sar. I'd rather be a servant to any man in de world, dan to a brack man. If I was sold to a brack man, I'd drown myself. I would dat—I'd drown myself! dough I shouldn't like to do dat nudder; but I wouldn't be sold to a coloured master for anyting."

*Olmsted,* Cotton Kingdom, *262.*

## *The Powers That Be: Mistresses*

[W]oman . . . has but one right and that is the right to protection. The right to protection involves the obligation to obey. A husband, lord and master . . . nature designed for every woman.

*George Fitzhugh,* Sociology for the South, *214.*

*Go* inter de *house,* Miss Carrie! Yer ain't no manner er use heah only ter git yer face red wid de heat. I'll have dinner like yer wants it. Jes' read yer book an' res' easy til I sen's it ter de dining room.

*Caroline Merrick's slave cook, in Fox-Genovese,* Plantation Household, *142.*

The overseer has driven off many of the most valuable negroes. . . . I can no longer leave the Miserable creatures prey to the worst part of mankind without endeavouring to mitigate as far as it is in my power, the pangs of their cruel situation.

*Fanny Bland Tucker, 1787 letter to her husband, in Clinton,* Plantation Mistress, *191.*

I despise myself for suffering my temper to rise at the provocations offered by the servants. I would be willing to spend the rest of my life at the north, where I never should see the face of another negro. . . . Indulgence has ruined them. . . . I believe my servants are going to craze me. . . .

*Sarah Haynsworth Gayle, diary, 1827, July 21, 1828, and July 6, 1835, in Fox-Genovese,* Plantation Household, *22–23.*

I would be glad if you could ride down [to our plantation] and see after little matters for me before it gets too warm. When Patience gets through house-cleaning, etc., with Flora, I want her to go to Arcadia [another family plantation] and pick all the geese carefully (also those at Montevideo) and have the feathers put into bags and sunned regularly. We want Gilbert to shear the sheep at both places now at once, and then Patience and Flora must pick and wash the wool until it is free from all grease or smell of any kind, and then have it all carded up ready to be made into mattresses. . . . And when Niger goes to the Island, they must take care of the poultry. Do charge them about the cats and Jet. . . . Tell Flora she must weed around all the flowers in the garden; I am afraid to trust the old man. . . . Cato can find employment for Miley and Kate. . . . I hope you have a *comfortable house* for your servant [slave] Lucy. You must not forget her welfare, for she is an excellent woman, and I think will be faithful to you.

*Mary Jones giving instructions to her newly married daughter for care of the family plantations in her absence, May 22, 1857, in* Children of Pride, *318–19.*

An abolitionist vision of a mistress whipping a slave woman (*Library of Congress*)

Miller McKim . . . told me . . . that some of the worst cases were those of concubines, mulattoes, who suffered from the jealousy of the wives of their masters. He mentioned two beautiful mulatto girls whose statements of barbarous cruelty were so shocking that he could not believe them and had their persons examined by a lady of his party, who found on their lacerated backs full confirmation of their dismal story. The parties whose names he mentioned were ladies of some of the best families.

*Fisher, diary entry of August 31, 1863,* Philadelphia Perspectives, *459.*

I wonder if it be a sin to think slavery a curse to any land. . . . God forgive us, but ours is a *monstrous* system and wrong and iniquity. Perhaps the rest of the world is as bad—this *only* I see.

*Journal entry, March 18, 1861, in* Mary Chesnut's Civil War, *29.*

## *The Powers That Be: Punishments by Civil Authority*

[When slaves are executed] the Planters suffer little or nothing by it, for the Province is obliged to pay the full value they judge them worth to the Owner. . . .

*John M. Brickell,* Natural History of North Carolina *(1737), quoted in Kay and Cary,* Slavery in North Carolina, *87.*

In it [the Work House of Charleston, South Carolina] there were about forty individuals of both sexes. In the basement, there is an apparatus upon which the negroes, by order of the police, or at the request of their masters, are flogged. The latter can have nineteen lashes inflicted on them according to the existing law. The machine consists of a sort of crane, on which a cord with two nooses runs over pullies; the nooses are made fast to the hands of the slave and drawn up, while the feet are bound tight to a plank. The body is stretched out as much as possible, and thus the miserable creature receives the exact number of lashes as counted off! . . .

A tread-mill has been erected in a back building. . . . Two treadmills [are] in operation. Each employs twelve prisoners. . . . Six tread at once upon each wheel, while six rest upon a bench placed behind the wheel. Every half minute the left hand man steps off the treadwheel, while the five others move to the left to fill up the vacant place; at the same time the right hand man sitting on the bench, steps on the wheel, and begins his movement. . . . Thus, even three minutes sitting, allows the unhappy being no repose. The signal for changing is given by a small bell attached to the wheel. The prisoners are compelled to labour eight hours a day in this manner. Order is preserved by a person, who, armed with a cowhide, stands by the wheel.

*Traveller Karl Bernhard, Duke of Saxe-Weimar, 1825–26, in Ball,* Slaves, *305–6.*

Heard a man at the tavern [in Middletown, Delaware] describe minutely a scene he had lately witnessed at St. Louis, the burning of a *Negro alive* for killing a sheriff. . . . Was surprised and shocked to find all present thought the punishment a just one & not too severe for a Negro!

*Fisher, diary entry for April 12, 1856,* Philadelphia Perspectives, *256.*

## *The Powers That Be: Punishments by Private Citizens*

I perceived . . . something resembling a cage, suspended to the limbs of a tree, all the branches of which appeared covered with large birds of prey, fluttering about and anxiously endeavouring to perch on the cage. . . . I perceived a Negro, suspended in the cage and left there to expire! . . . [T]he birds had already picked out his eyes; his cheekbones were bare; his arms had been attacked in several places; and his body seemed covered with a multitude of wounds. From the edges of the hollow sockets and from the lacerations with which he was disfigured, the blood slowly dropped and tinged the ground beneath. No sooner were the birds flown than swarms of insects covered the whole body of this unfortunate wretch, eager to feed on his mangled flesh and to drink his blood.

*Letter published 1782, in De Crèvecoeur,* Letters from an American Farmer, *178.*

The wife of Mr. Giles Hicks, living but a short distance from where I used to live, murdered my wife's cousin, a young girl between fifteen and sixteen years of age . . . She had been set that night to mind Mrs. Hicks's baby, and during the night she fell asleep, and the baby cried. She, having lost her rest for several nights previous, did not hear the crying. They were both in the room with Mrs. Hicks. Mrs. Hicks, finding the girl slow to move, jumped from her bed, seized an oak stick of wood by the fireplace, and with it broke the girl's nose and breastbone, and thus ended her life . . . There was a warrant issued for her arrest, but it was never served . . . It was a common saying, even among little white boys, that it was worth a half-cent to kill a "nigger," and a half-cent to bury one.

*Douglass,* Narrative, *41–42.*

She then described to me that they were fastened up by their wrists to a beam or a branch of a tree, their feet barely touching the ground, so as to allow them no purchase for resistance or evasion of the lash, their clothes turned over their heads, and their backs scored with a leather thong, either by the driver himself, or, if he pleases to inflict their punishment by deputy, any of the men he may choose to summon to the office; it might be father, brother, husband, or lover, if the overseer so ordered it.

*Kemble,* Journal *(1839), 215.*

When they wanted to whip severely, they put the head and hands in stocks in a stooping posture.

The last two years I was in Tennessee, I saw nine persons at different times, made fast to four stakes, and whipped with a leather strap from their neck to their heels and on the bottoms of their feet, raising blisters: then the blisters broken with a platted whip, the overseer standing off and fetching hard blows.

*William A. Hall, in* A North-Side View *in* Four Fugitive Slave Narratives, *220–21.*

I's seen po' niggers 'mos' tore up by dogs and whupped 'tell dey bled w'en day did'n do lak de white folks say.

*Ex-slave Charity Anderson,* American Slave, *Alabama.*

[Forman] is a Georgian, a slaveholder and a warm advocate of slavery . . . He admitted that . . . he had himself known instances of slaves being whipped to death, and of their being tied before a fire for the purpose of torture. But he added that persons guilty of such barbarities were always hated & despised by the community, and generally murdered by the slaves. "And what do you do with the slaves who kill such masters?" said I. "Oh, of course," he answered, "we are obliged to put them to death."

*Fisher, diary entry of December 26, 1852,* Philadelphia Perspective, *244.*

Finally my father let his sister take me and raise me with her children. She was good to me, but before he let her have me he willed I must wear a bell till I was twenty-one year old, strapped round my shoulders with the bell 'bout three feet from my head in a steel frame. That was for punishment for being born into the world a son of a white man and my mammy, a Negro slave. I wears this frame with the bell where I couldnt reach the clapper, day and night. I never knowed what it was to lay down in bed and get a good night's sleep till I was 'bout seventeen year old, when my father died and my missy took the bell offen me.

*Ex-slave J. W. Terrill, in* Lay My Burden Down, *166.*

# 5

# Slave Work
## 1619–1865

## The Historical Context

Slaves newly arrived in the American colonies or the United States found only one familiar element—agriculture. Most came from agrarian economies in some ways similar to that of the American South. In Africa, some of them had grown rice, a major crop in the South. Until the end of the Civil War, southern agriculture, like that of Africa, depended primarily upon manual labor rather than on machines. So the slaves understood the field labor to which most of them were assigned, though probably in the small African villages they had worked more independently. The gender division of work might also have differed.

On the smaller southern farms, where the owner possessed or hired the use of only one or two slaves, they worked alongside him, and quite possibly his wife and children, in the fields. Additionally, they probably had to labor at household tasks. Ex-slave Mary Lindsay remembered how hard that kind of living was: "I have to git up at three o'clock sometimes so I have time to water the hosses and slop the hogs and feed the chickens and milk the cows, and then git back to the house and git the breakfast."[1]

### *House Servants*

The larger the farm or plantation, the more specialized the work assigned. On the larger plantations, some slaves toiled only in their master's house. On the largest, the kitchen staff might include a presiding cook, her assistants, and numerous servers to transport the food from the kitchen—separate from the main house—and wait at table. "My job," reminisced Mammy Charity Anderson, "was lookin' atter de corner table whar nothin' but de desserts set."[2]

Several slaves might be assigned to the tasks of looking after the master's white children—though many families preferred white women as chief nurses. "Mrs. B favored me with the congratulations I have heard so many times on the subject of my having a white nurserymaid for my children," wrote Fanny

Kemble. "Of course, she went into the old subject of the utter incompetency of Negro women to discharge such an office faithfully; but, in spite of her multiplied examples of their utter inefficiency, I believe the discussion ended by simply our both agreeing that ignorant Negro girls of twelve years old are not as capable or as trustworthy as well-trained white women of thirty."[3] But on many a plantation, black women did indeed raise white children, caring for them every moment of the day and night.

House servants also cleaned; did the huge washings and ironings required by 19th-century styles; spun, wove, and sewed; and acted as maids and valets. Some slaves preferred this work, partly because they escaped the hard physical labor of the fields and partly because it bestowed special privileges and status on them. They picked up information as they waited at table, overheard conversations, and went on errands off the property. Carriage drivers, trusted slaves carefully chosen for reliability and skill with equipage, got to leave the plantation frequently as they drove white men on business errands or white ladies shopping and visiting. Similarly, midwives often worked off their home plantations. Black "mammies" sometimes parleyed their authority over white children into power within the household generally, acting as surrogate mistresses and mothers.[4] The "mammy," John Cocke noted in his diary in 1863, "of course lives as well as the Mistress of the House & Mother of the children under her care. . . . She too like the foreman of the plantation, has her perquisites of office—and the privileges of bestowing small benefits upon her children & [all] the family and its visitors calling her Aunt—as Uncle is universally bestowed upon the Male House Servants."[5]

Cooks proudly carried the keys to the pantry, the symbol of household authority. Specialized skills also gave slaves a bit of leverage with their masters. One Henry Watson found himself in a dilemma about his cook Ellen, who tried his patience, but, as he remarked, "It is very difficult to get a negro who understands good cooking. If they do then ten to one they have some bad habits or bad temper & are not fit to be about. . . . Yet at times I think I can never be as well-suited—Ellen is a good *milker,* a negro rarely is. She makes *good bread,* few can do it, or do do it. She makes Excellent *coffee.* . . ."[6]

Other slaves detested household assignments because they came continually under the eye of master and mistress; they might even have to sleep in bedchambers or just outside their doors. Such intimacy might make for affection between master or mistress and slave—or, like all close living, it might rankle.

## *Artisans and Other Skilled Workers*

Large plantations also afforded opportunities for outside slaves to specialize. W. E. B. Du Bois justly remarked, "There was one thing that the white South feared more than Negro dishonesty, ignorance, and incompetency, and that was Negro honesty, knowledge, and efficiency." Yet determined as masters might be to keep slaves ignorant and dependent, their own comfort and convenience and their own economic interests argued for teaching slaves more skills. The slave who could read, write, and calculate could better secure his master's profits when he took a load of cotton to be sold or a load of corn to be milled. Owners who wished to live with a modicum of comfort and ease on their isolated plantations needed slaves with special skills.

The richest owners might send a slave lad to England to learn landscape gardening, just as they sent their cooks abroad to learn French cuisine. Slightly less affluent masters apprenticed promising slave youngsters to neighboring artisans for training as carpenters, coopers, blacksmiths, and shoemakers. Other slaves learned their crafts on their own plantations from their seniors or from skilled white workers. Blacks found their way about the forests and picked up survival skills from their fellow Indian slaves. Some of those who ran their masters' boats on the coast and the inland rivers became expert pilots. In his travels through the South, Frederick Law Olmsted ran across a slave who in his youth "had been employed, for some years, as a waiter, but, at his own request, was eventually allowed to learn the blacksmith's trade, in the plantation shop. Showing ingenuity and talent, he was afterwards employed to make and repair the plantation cotton-gins. Finally, his owner took him to a steam-engine builder, and paid $500 to have him instructed as a machinist. After he had become a skilful workman, he obtained employment as an engineer. . . ."[7]

Women slaves were usually confined to the domestic arts. Even so, some of them were prized for their deftness in dressing hair, making hats and shawls, spinning, weaving, tailoring, or cooking.

With slave artisans, a plantation could produce almost everything needed for daily consumption. When a slave acquired a reputation for expertise in, say, blacksmithing, neighbors might order their tools from him, to the profit of his owner. "Of my working Negroes," Maj. Pierce Butler informed a prospective buyer of his plantation in 1809, "I keep from 40 to 50 male slaves out of the field, to wit, about 14 house carpenters, 2 mechanics, 6 ship carpenters, 12 to 15 Ditchers, 4 Tanners, Curriers and Shoemakers. I turn my own leather, make my own shoes and those of my Neighbors—my own harness, etc. 4 Blacksmiths, three masons, 2 brick makers, two painters who are also sailmakers. . . ."[8]

The more adroit of these artisans sometimes progressed to inventing. Former slave John Parker told how he had invented a "clod smasher, which was a very important farm implement of that period with so much new land to break up." He made a model and showed it to the white superintendent—who stole both the model and the idea.[9] The Mississippi master of a slave who invented a "double plow" tried to get it patented, but the U.S. attorney general refused on the ground that "a machine invented by a slave, though it be new and useful, cannot, in the present state of the law, be patented," adding that even "if such a patent were issued to the master, it would not protect him in courts against persons who might infringe it."[10]

## *Field Hands*

The great majority of slaves did field work, where day after day they dug ditches to drain the fields, patched eroded land, built fences, plowed, planted, hoed weeds, and picked and harvested. The strongest men and women were put to digging ditches, cutting trees, hauling logs with leather straps attached to their shoulders, and building and repairing roads and railroads. They began at sunrise or shortly before and labored on with a couple of breaks for meals until sundown. By common practice, slaves had part of Saturday and all Sunday off to cultivate their garden patches, maintain their cabins, amuse themselves, or rest; harsh masters, however, worked their slaves seven days a week, and far beyond the usual 12–14 hours daily that most required.

This dull, backbreaking labor sapped their strength, aged them prematurely, and shortened their lives. Fanny Kemble wrote of "Engineer Ned's" plea that his wife be placed on lighter tasks: "[S]he had to work in the rice fields, and was 'most broke in two' with labor, and exposure, and hard work while with child, and hard work just directly after childbearing; he said she could hardly crawl, and he urged me very much to speak a kind word for her to massa. She was almost all the time in the hospital, and he thought she could not live long."[11]

On the larger farms and plantations, field workers were typically placed in gangs, depending on strength and in some cases on gender. At about six, children were set to work running errands, gathering wood, looking after babies and toddlers, or toting seed. Children just beginning field work, usually at about age 10 or 12, old women, nursing mothers, and women in the last months of pregnancy made up the trash gangs, clearing debris off roadsides, raking stubble, pulling weeds, doing light hoeing, and picking cotton.

Healthy women who were not pregnant were considered three-quarter hands, pregnant women half-hands. Some plantations put women in separate gangs—to which they occasionally assigned men as punishment, forcing them to do "women's work," like washing. Yet on other plantations women, particularly

Picking cotton (*Library of Congress*)

Testing tobacco. The sign reads: "In General Pierce We Put Our Manly Trust." (*Crowe,* With Thackeray in America)

after they reached the menopause, were put to the hardest tasks. "I split rails like a man," ex-slave Sally Brown remembered. "I used a huge glut [a wedge] made out's wood, and a iron wedge drove into the wood with a maul, and this would split the wood."[12] At night, women still had cooking and housework to do, besides stints of spinning and quilting set by their mistresses.

The papers of a Louisiana plantation described its field hands' annual cycle of hard labor. In January and February, for instance, mule teams hauled manure, and the hands racked it up; other hands shelled and shucked corn, hauled fence rails, put up fences, and cleared corn stalks by plowing them under or burning them. The manager of one plantation noted that on a February day, "Four hands chopped down willows in the bottoms. Others were chopping weeds, hauling cottonseed, and cleaning out the ditch in the bottom of No. 8 field. While Allen, one of the few skilled slaves, was repairing harrows and sharpening ploughs, twenty-four hands were rolling logs, picking up chunks and brush in the deadening, stopping up washings [erosion] and making a levee in the bottoms of No. 2. Several cleaned the gutters on the gin, while five sickly hands were picking wool."[13]

On many plantations, slaves worked by the *gang* system—that is, for a specific time each day. Under such a system, with no prospect but another hard day's labor on the morrow, how were slaves to be motivated? Some, perhaps, would respond to praise; most could be moved to work by the lash. But left unsupervised, as they inevitably must be for much of the time on large plantations, what was to keep them at it? Even if an overseer was riding horseback up and down the rows, slaves might slack off when he was at the other end of their rows.

In fact, masters and the overseers and slave drivers they designated as supervisors had a lot of trouble getting work done. Out of their sight, slaves slowed down or stopped their work. Slaves broke or lost tools. Frederick Olmsted, who traveled extensively throughout the slave South, believed that slave labor on most farms and plantations was egregiously inefficient. In desperation, some slave owners and supervisors resorted to some kind of reward—perhaps extra

Taking cotton to market (*Blake,* History of Slavery and the Slave Trade)

food, or tobacco, or even money. "[T]o git mutch ditching done," wrote overseer Roswell King, "I must give them rum."[14]

Especially in South Carolina and Georgia, owners used the more efficient system of *task labor,* allotting slaves specific tasks to be accomplished on any one day, after which their time was their own. "For instance, in making drains in light, clean meadow land, each man or woman of the full hands is required to dig one thousand cubic feet; in swamp-land that is being prepared for rice culture, where there are not many stumps, the task for a ditcher is five hundred feet: while in a very strong cypress swamp, only two hundred feet is required; in hoeing rice, a certain number of rows, equal to one-half or two-thirds of an acre, according to the condition of the land; in sowing rice (strewing in drills), two acres; in reaping rice (if it stands well), three-quarters of an acre; or, sometimes a gang will be required to reap, tie in sheaves, and carry to the stack-yard the produce of a certain area. . . . Hoeing cotton, corn or potatoes; one half to one acre. Threshing: five to six hundred sheaves. In ploughing rice land (light, clean, mellow soil) with a yoke of oxen, one acre a day, including the ground lost in and near the drains—the oxen being changed at noon. A cooper, also, for instance, is required to make barrels at the rate of eighteen a week. . . . These are the tasks for first-class able-bodied men; they are lessened by one quarter for three-quarter hands. . . . "[15] Slaves who knew they could finish their tasks early if they hurried had a reason to work quickly.

## *Supervisors*

Some masters lived on their plantations or moved with the seasons from one of their plantations to another. Others chose to live elsewhere: Pierce Butler avowed that "my principal object is to be saved the necessity of ever going to see my Estate."[16] In either case, they might delegate the supervision of the slaves to one among the slaves or, more rarely, to a white "overseer."[17] With an absentee landlord, the overseer bore heavy responsibilities. Ideally, he would plan the farm work, decide when to plant and when to harvest, closely superintend the slaves, clothe them, distribute their food, look after their health and well-being, and discipline them. (Masters did not want their slaves—their capital—crippled or sick, but they did want the best possible profit.) The overseer's wife assisted him. She was charged with supervising the household servants.

Overseers seldom thought their lot a happy one. "If there ever was or ever will be a calling in life as mean and contemptible as that of an overseer," one of them complained, "I would be right down glad to know what it is, and where to be found. . . . If there be . . . a favorable crop, the *master* makes a splendid crop; if any circumstances be unpropitious and an inferior crop is made, it is the overseer's fault, and if he flogs [the slaves] to keep them at home, or locked up . . . he is a brute and a tyrant. If no meat is made, the overseer *would* plant too much cotton. . . . If hogs are taken good care of the overseer is wasting corn, and 'the most careless and thriftless creature alive.' If he does not 'turn out' [waken and set to work] hands in time, he is *lazy;* if he 'rousts' them out as your dad and mine had to do, why he is a brute." Another wailed, "If I donte please every negro on the place they run away rite strate."[18]

Overseeing was not a job for an educated man. It carried little prestige. Many overseers exploited their power over the slaves, raping and torturing them cruelly. Frederick Douglass wrote of one who shot a disobedient slave in cold blood.[19] Some stole from their employers. Overseers of such a kind earned the Simon Legree* reputation often associated with the position.

To the slaves, the overseer was usually a natural enemy. On occasion they bore tales about him to the master, who, wary that the overseer might cheat him, was likely to listen to the slaves' complaints. "The negroes have great spite and hatred towards them [overseers] and frequently fight them, when the overseer pretends [dares] to whip them," complained Elijah Fletcher. "The negroes think as meanly of the poor white people, as the rich white people do themselves and think anybody that is so poor as to be an overseer mean [lowly] enough."[20]

Because he could not be everywhere on the plantation at all times, the overseer might delegate part of his authority to black slave drivers—also called variously *foremen, overlookers, leading men, headmen, bosses, whipping bosses, crew leaders, overdrivers, underdrivers,* and *straw bosses.* Masters might use such drivers as stewards in place of a white overseer. A few of them acquired astonishing power and status. Olmsted tells of one whom his owner called a "watchman": "He carried by a strap at his waist, a very large number of keys, and had charge of all the stores of provisions, tools, and materials of the plantations, as well as of all their produce, before it was shipped to market. He weighed and measured out all the rations of the slaves and the cattle; superintended the mechanics, and made and repaired, as was necessary, all the machinery, including the steam-engine [that ran the rice mill]. In all these departments, his authority was superior to that of the overseer. The overseer received his private allowance of

* An overseer who has Tom flogged to death in Harriet Beecher Stowe's novel *Uncle Tom's Cabin.*

family provisions from him, as did also the head-servant at the mansion, who was his brother. His responsibility was much greater than that of the overseer; and Mr. X. said he would trust him with much more than he would any overseer he had ever known."[21]

A driver usually lived in the first house in the yard. Every morning he awakened the other slaves with a blast on a conch shell or by ringing a bell. As instructed by the overseer or owner, he assigned tasks to the workers in his charge and checked their work. In many ways slave drivers resembled army sergeants. They were, so to speak, non-commissioned officers, providing liaison between superiors and slaves, whites and blacks. They belonged to the ranks of slaves, but they had the power and responsibility of authority over the others, and they were responsible for their welfare—even to the point of distributing their food. Their powers of punishment were usually limited to a given number of strokes of the lash. They could sometimes also act as ombudsmen for the other slaves, intervening if they thought the tasks assigned too heavy. Inevitably, some of them swaggered about and abused their fellows; other drivers protected the slaves they supervised, only pretending to whip them.

Almost all slave drivers were male. Now and then, however, the records show a slave forewoman in charge of the slave women, the adolescents, and the old people on the plantation. A South Carolina planter liked to appoint women as temporary overseers to cover each hill of corn and make sure that it was properly sown.[22]

## *Breeders*

Of all the kinds of work that slaves performed, probably the most valuable to their owners, and the worst compensated, was reproduction. In an economy where an owner's most valuable property was his slaves, women of childbearing age were a double asset. In them the owner had a win-win investment: they could do both productive and reproductive work.

In 1858, the magazine *Southern Cultivator* published an article on the economics of breeding: "I own a woman who cost me $400 when a girl, in 1827. Admit she made me nothing—only worth her victuals and clothing. She now has three children, worth over $3000 and have been field hands say three years; in that time making enough to pay their expenses before they were half hands, and then I have the profit of all half hands. She has only three boys and a girl out of a dozen [pregnancies]: yet, with all her bad management, she has paid me ten per cent. interest, for her work was to be an average good, and I would not this night touch $700 for her. Her oldest boy is worth $1250 cash and I can get it."[23]

Slave owners read magazine articles on the best conditions for breeding and talked about the capabilities of particular women for that task. Masters were obsessed with the potential for increasing their capital. They forced male slaves to take more than one wife and to stand at stud. They pressured slave women to have babies by reminding the women whom they gave permission to marry, "Don't forget to bring me a little one or two for next year." They threatened barren women with being sold away. They assigned easier work to pregnant women and nursing mothers. They rewarded prolific women with money, dresses, occasionally even emancipation if they bore a certain number of children. One owner gave every woman with six children alive at one time every Saturday off. Pauli Murray writes of attempts to hire out her beautiful great-grandmother to breed her.[24]

## *Town and City and Institutional Slaves*

The small minority of slaves who lived in towns or cities—less than 6 percent—frequently worked as body or household servants.[25] But the male slaves also worked in shipyards, brickyards, cotton presses, and warehouses. They assisted masters who were tailors and saddlemakers. They were employed as butchers, waiters, barbers, painters, masons, bricklayers, and glaziers. Some kept taverns. As a rule, they had better working conditions than field hands.

Institutions, such as churches, might also buy slaves, usually to hire out to other employers. Southern factories and mines relied heavily on slave labor, either from slaves they owned or slaves hired out from other masters. The Manchester and Wilmington Railroad, running along what James Redpath called "the most desolate looking country in the Union," owned most of its hands. "The railroad hands sleep in miserable shanties along the line," Redpath reported. "Their bed is an inclined pine board—nothing better, softer, or warmer, as I can testify from my personal experience. Their covering is a blanket. The fireplaces in these cabins are often so clumsily constructed that all the heat ascends the chimney. . . . [T]he temperature of the cabin, at this season of the year (November), is bitterly cold and uncomfortable. . . . Of course, as the negroes are not released from their work until sunset, and as, after coming to their cabins, they have to cook their ash-cakes or mush, or dumplings, these huts are by no means remarkable for their cleanly appearance. Poor fellows! In that God-forsaken section of the earth they seldom see a woman from Christmas to Christmas."[26]

In 1856, the governor of Tennessee advocated that the state buy slaves to build a canal on Muscle Shoals, picturing it as an idyllic arrangement (from the point of view of the state): "In this way the work would only cost the interest on the money invested [in the slaves], the loss sustained on the property by death or casualty, the subsistence of the hands, and the charges of superintendence—the work would be accomplished without any difficulty in its details, and with just reference to its durability and usefulness. With the effective hands, it might be convenient to purchase a suitable number of women to cook, wash, and perhaps perform the lighter parts of the work, and this would be perfectly consistent with the humanity of purchasing men with their wives, whenever such opportunities of purchase might offer. . . . At suitable places along the canal, the hands might cultivate . . . the vegetables which would be proper to promote their comfort, and the preservation of their health. . . . This corps of pioneers [construction workers] . . . might afterwards be employed on Railroads, Turnpike roads, improving the navigation of our rivers, and opening other canals where the public good might require."[27]

## *Hiring Out*

Particularly in the later years of slavery, many urban slaves were engaged in the practice of "hiring out"—used also to a lesser extent in the countryside.

Masters usually hired out slaves whose labor they did not immediately need, renting out their labor for a specific period of time in return for a fixed amount of money. But in some cases, masters bought slaves with the intent of hiring them out. A German farmer near Natchez owned four slave men, whom he hired out as porters or servants in town, while he employed a white man to work with him on his farm. "To explain the economy of this arrangement, he said that one of his men [slaves] earned in Natchez $30 a month clear of all expenses, and the others much more than he could ever make their labour worth to him. A negro of moderate intelligence would hire, as a house-servant, for $200 a year and his board, which was worth $8 a month; whereas he hired this white fellow, who was strong and able, for $10 a month."[28]

Other masters used hiring out as a means of training their slaves. They might, like Frederick Douglass's master, hire them to a farmer notorious for "breaking" defiant slaves, or they might hire them to craftsmen.[29] "The slave-holders in that state [Maryland] often hire the children of their slaves out to non-slaveholders, not only because they save themselves the expense of taking care of them, but in this way they get among their slaves useful trades," wrote James Pennington. "They put a bright slave boy with a tradesman, until he gets such a knowledge of the trade as to be able to do his own work, and then he takes him home."[30]

If a slave developed an unusual talent, like playing a musical instrument or jigging, his master might hire him out as an entertainer. One planter in 1856 advertised the services of a kind of slave combo led by "Robin," who had taught himself to play the fiddle, using bows of twigs on horses' hairs strung across pieces of wood, and had taught his three brothers to play as well. His master had then hired a teacher to polish their musical skills.[31] Another made money by betting on the ability of his slave to outdance all challengers.

Some scholars think that slaves were hired out five or six times as often as they were sold.[32] So many slaves were hired out and so diverse were the occupations for which they were hired, that annual days were set aside for arrangements to be made. The practice also spun off subsidiary businesses. In some cities, agencies sprang up to hire out as servants or factory hands slaves whom their owners sent into town for that purpose.[33]

Of course hiring out had its problems. Slaves hired out acquired some degree of independence. If they were dissatisfied with their working or living conditions, they might complain to their masters; the owners, wanting their slaves kept healthy, might then threaten to end the contract, or at least not renew it the next year unless the situation improved. One ironworks superintendent reported gloomily, "Our [slave] hands are here today wanting flour, coffee & tobacco. I have for the past month been putting them off—I am afraid they will leave in a body & throw us behind. . . . We by all means should have something to satisfy them if we wish to keep them."[34] What was more, the use of task work by some industries gave slaves a degree of control over their own time and labor. In certain lumber camps, for example, slaves on the task-work system actually subcontracted with runaway slaves hiding in the forest to do their jobs for them. These hired-out slaves paid the runaways with part of the bonus they received for producing shingles over and above their stint—not to mention their profits from the sale of the fur from animals they hunted in the woods in their spare time.[35]

Employers who hired slaves were expected to return them at the end of the contract in good condition. "Whoever hired a negro gives on the spot a bond for the amount, to be paid at the end of term, even should the hired negro fall sick or run off in the meantime," wrote traveler Johann Schoepf in the early 1780s. "The hirer must also pay the negro's head tax, feed him and clothe him. Hence a negro is capital put out at a very high interest, but because of elopement and death very unstable."[36] If an employer who had hired a slave called a doctor for him, who was to pay—the master or the hirer? If a hirer shot and wounded a slave attempting to run away, was he liable for the damage to her? What if a slave were killed doing dangerous work that the hirer had set him to?

Lawsuits were brought asking that hirers recompense owners for the loss of or damage to slaves. For instance, one master won the full price of his slave, who had run away and been hired to unload a ship; its owners were held responsible for the slave's drowning.[37] Hirers ran another risk, too, as Olmsted pointed out: "But a more serious loss frequently arises, when the slave, thinking he is worked too hard, or being angered by punishment or unkind treatment, 'getting the sulks,' takes to 'the swamp,' and comes back when he has a mind to. Often this will not be till the year is up for which he is engaged, when he will return to his owner, who glad to find his property safe, and that it has not died in the swamp, or gone to Canada, forgets to punish him, and immediately sends him for another year to a new master."[38]

When a hiring-out arrangement proved satisfactory all around, it might be renewed year after year. Enterprising slaves sought out people to hire them whom they thought desirable as masters. Some persuaded their owners to let them hire out their own time, assuming financial responsibility for their own keep and, in addition, agreeing to pay their owners either a percentage of their wages or a fixed amount weekly, monthly, or annually.

Residents of the slave states argued about whether or not this practice was wise. "Recent events demonstrate the fact that the employment of free negroes, mulattoes, and . . . slaves who hire their own time, on board of steamboats on the western waters, is a cause of serious loss and danger to the slave states and slave owners," wrote the editor of the St. Louis *Daily Evening Gazette* on August 18, 1841. "These have the opportunity of constant communication with slaves of Missouri, Kentucky and the other southern States, and have also very frequent communication with the free negroes and abolitionists of Illinois, Indiana, Ohio, and Pennsylvania. This communication renders the slaves restless and induces them to run away, and furnishes them a means of escape. . . . The negro hands on board the steamboats can frequently conceal runaway negroes . . . without the consent of the captain."[39] Attorney Charles Colcock Jones lamented the increased freedom of the hired-out slave: "There are, you may say, hundreds of Negroes in this city [Savannah] who go about from house to house—some carpenters, some house servants, etc.—who never see their masters except at pay day, live out of their yards, hire themselves without written permit, etc."[40]

But slave owners also feared the likely reactions of white workers, who could vote. What if they opposed the slave system, seeing slaves as competitors for jobs? "Drive out negro mechanics and all sorts of operatives from our Cities, and who must take their place[?]" asked industrialist C. G. Memminger. "The same men who make the cry in the Northern Cities against the tyranny of Capital—and there as here would drive all before them . . . who interfere with them—and would soon raise hue and cry against the Negro, and be hot Abolitionists—and every one of those men would have a vote."[41]

The whole debate over slaves' hiring their own time got tangled up with the issue of whether whites or blacks were better workers. "Take I say again and again one of my most faith[ful] servants [slaves] give him some encouragement or fourth part of what you must give to a white lad [and] take my word for it you'll find him ten times better than any you can hire," wrote David Ross of the Oxford Iron Works. "[H]e will labour day by day[,] he has ten time[s] more experience and [is] a much honester man, he will receive your instructions with patience and humility & if a reprimand becomes necessary he will receive it without putting out your eyes."[42]

The hiring-out system triumphed, simply because it worked too well to be abandoned. On the frontier, the practice met the need for diversification of labor. Widows and orphans who inherited slaves could avoid the problems of managing them by hiring them out. Small farmers who could not scrape together the price of a slave might rent one. A horse owner might rent an expert jockey for a particular race. A plantation mistress in need of new dishes might briefly hire an expert potter. Most important of all, hiring out paid masters well.

After all, owners could hire out skilled slaves, even aged ones, for more than double a good rate of interest on what they would bring in a sale.[43] "While employers of hired, rented, or leased slaves paid owners annual fees ranging from $80 to $100, payments made by self-hired slaves averaged from $150 to over $200 annually, in the thirty-year period before the Civil War." Prices for renting slaves fluctuated with the prices of buying them, "but generally slave owners could expect a return of 10 to 20 percent of the local value of a male slave per year."[44] A prospective buyer might rent a slave for a year to test him. Mines and factories rented slaves as employees. During the Civil War, the Confederacy hired slaves as hospital nurses

## *Slaves as Entrepreneurs*

No matter how many laws forbade them to own anything, slaves could not be kept out of the money economy. In 1859, Robert F. W. Allston, noting that during a two-year absence his slaves had taken possession of his hogs, so that he had few to sell, decided to experiment with letting them raise the hogs for him, giving every slave who headed a family the privilege of keeping one hog, provided that every fall the slave should bring the overseer two young hogs fit for killing during the next winter. For the smaller of the two, the slave was to be paid at the rate of $5 per hundred pounds. The rest of the litter(s) belonged to the slave, though he could not sell them off the plantation.[45] Alabama planter William Jemmison set up his slaves as sharecroppers.[46]

Without such incentives, slaves grew expert in dodging work, feigning illness, running away to hide in the woods for a while, and goldbricking.

A barber shop in Richmond, Virginia (*Crowe,* With Thackeray in America)

Other owners resorted to offering prizes, sometimes including money, for the fastest cotton picking. Thrifty slaves sometimes arranged with their masters to sell off unneeded rations of cornmeal for the slaves' profit. Industrious slaves grew their own cotton and garden produce, raised poultry, collected moss, wove baskets, carved trays, and manufactured brooms for sale.

Slave entrepreneurs moved from hiring out their own time to setting up their own businesses. They turned particularly to occupations where close supervision was impractical or to occupations that southern white laborers scorned, like the food and personal services industries, but slaves also worked as carpenters, coopers, wheelwrights, painters, masons, bricklayers, teamsters, draymen, liverymen, and boatmen. Unskilled slaves became peddlers and hawkers. Others set up groceries and secondhand clothing shops and truck farms. Women did laundry, catered, and sold their services as midwives and nurses. Elizabeth Keckley, who bought her own freedom with the profits of her dressmaking business in St. Louis, went on to become dressmaker to Mary Todd Lincoln. A few blacks not only bought their own freedom and that of their families but also acquired land and slaves to till it.

In conducting any business, the slave entrepreneur faced enormous difficulties. The law was always on the side of the whites with whom the slave dealt. They could take advantage of the slave at will. If he deposited money in

Market women (*Crowe,* With Thackeray in America)

a bank, the bank might refuse to return it—after all, the law said that slaves could not own property. "I have been cheated by a rich slaveholder out of half a bushel of corn in buying half a barrel," wrote David West. "I knew it and he knew it; but he knew I would not dare say anything about it,—the law was such that he could have me whipped, if I were to contradict him."[47]

## Chronicle of Events

**1492**
Columbus discovers the West Indies, opening markets for slaves to work in the mines.

**1643**
The introduction of sugar planting into the West Indies creates a demand for slaves.

**1665**
The "Duke of York laws" promote slave labor in the British North American colonies, discourage the presence of white indentured servants, and grant port and warehouse privileges to ships in international slaving.

**1694**
The introduction of rice culture into Carolina leads to the rapid importation of slaves.

**1711**
A market house is established in New York City as the central location for the hiring of all slaves.

**1780**
Ex-slave Dr. James Derham, born 1757, practices medicine in New Orleans.

**1793**
Eli Whitney patents the cotton gin, thereby increasing the market value of slaves by making cotton production more profitable and swelling the demand for cheap labor.

Artist's conception of the first cotton gin (*Library of Congress*)

**1810**
Congress denies blacks the right to work as mail carriers.

**1813**
Congress restricts employment on American ships to citizens of the United States and "persons of color, natives of the United States."

**1821**
The South Carolina legislature requires that black crew members of any ship coming into port must be arrested and held in jail while their ship lies in harbor.

**1829**
The poems of slave George Moses Horton are published to raise money for his freedom and transportation to Liberia; the plan fails.

**1846**
Texas passes a law (widely violated) forbidding slaves to hire their own time for more than one day a week, except during Christmas holidays.

**1853**
The Marshall Mechanics Association is formed in Texas to prevent "as far as possible, mechanical labor by slaves, from coming in competition with that of white men."

**1856**
Congress denies blacks preemption rights on public lands.

**1859**
An outcry arises in the South for renewal of the slave trade to meet labor demands and produce more cotton.

White workers in Charleston, South Carolina, petition the legislature for relief from competition with blacks, whether slave or free.

"Cotton Is King" (*Crowe,* With Thackeray in America)

**1865**
Free Negro Martin A. Delaney is commissioned a field officer in the U.S. Army.

Congress charters the Freedman's Bank, an interstate bank.

Shipyard caulkers in Baltimore strike to prevent yards from hiring black caulkers.

## Eyewitness Testimony

### *The Workers: Artisans and Other Skilled Workmen*

Master Hugh . . . took me into the ship-yard of which he was foreman, in the employment of Mr. Walter Price. There I was immediately set to calking, and very soon learned the art of using my mallet and irons. In the course of one year . . . I was able to command the highest wages given to the most experienced calkers. I was now of some importance to my master. I was bringing him from six to seven dollars per week.

*Ex-slave Frederick Douglass,* Narrative, *103.*

You must know then that many of my servants [slaves] at Oxford have double trades, some of them treble, most of my Blacksmiths are also potters, and part of them go into the pot houses when the furnace is in blast. . . .

*Ironworks owner David Ross, letter of July 25, 1813, in Lewis,* Coal, Iron, and Slaves, *28.*

[On a trip to New Orleans about 1830] We were all bound to take our turn at the helm, sometimes under direction of the captain, and sometimes on our own responsibility, as he could not be always awake. . . . [A]s I was the only negro in the boat, I was compelled to stand at least three turns at the helm to any other person's one; so that . . . I learned the art of steering and managing the boat far better than the rest. I watched the manoeuvres necessary to shoot by a "sawyer" [tangle of dead trees], to land on a bank, avoid a snag, or a steamboat, in the rapid current of the Mississippi, till I could do it as well as the captain.

*Henson,* Autobiography, *50–51.*

My father . . . liberated all the children he had by my mother, and one other slave woman, with one exception—that was a daughter whom he had educated and put to the milliner's trade. After she had learned the trade, he went to the place where she was, with money to establish her in business. But he found she had two children by a white man. This so enraged him, that he carried her and her two children back to his farm, and put her to work in the field, and there, he said, she was to die.

*Mrs. Henry Gowens, in* Four Fugitive Slave Narratives, *100.*

I sought to distinguish myself in the finer branches of the business [blacksmithing] by invention and finish; I frequently tried my hand at making guns and pistols, putting blades in pen knives, making fancy hammers, hatchets, sword-cases, &c., &c. . . .

*James W. C. Pennington,* Fugitive Blacksmith, *1850, in Owens,* Property, *180.*

Henry Fort . . . had been stoker for the engineer and Tuesday morning [after the white employees who had been running the mill went off to fight for the Confederacy] he came to the Master and asked permission to fire up—"Henry," said the Master, "it will be no use to fire up without an engineer." "No sir, I kno's dat but I ben a'studyin' an' a'studyin' on dat ingin' a long time—an I kin run her jis' as well as John Cardy—an' Marse Ned, me an' Mac an' Peter kin run dat whole cuncern if you will keep de books an' will let us pick out de helpers we wants." The Master was surprised and pleased, but also somewhat doubtful. "Do you think you boys can do it?" "Yes Marse Ned we sho' kin—jis' as I sed I kin run de ingin' same as John Cardy—Peter is run de saw fur Wheeler when you didn't know nuthin' erbout it—an' Mac is jis' as good a miller as yer wants ter see."

*Reminiscences of a slaveholder's daughter, Eppes,* Negro, *108.*

Rev. Emperor Williams was . . . a master mason, and from 1846 to 1858 was the trusted foreman of his owner. . . . His master had a difficult piece of cornice work on the corner of Perdido and Carondelet Streets. None of the white men could put it up. Williams said he could, and his master replied that if he did he should have his freedom. He took the plans of the difficult piece of work, laid them on the floor of his cabin, and studied them all night until he got every part perfectly in his mind. The next day he took his gang of men and accomplished his difficult work.

*W. D. Goodman interview, in* Slave Testimony, *621.*

*Tom* has been doing very well thus far; has made eight pair of shoes for the children, besides mending, and over a dozen lasts of various sizes, all of which display quite a genius in design and execution. I will make him for the present complete the tanning and make up some shoes for the needy ones here. He is certainly a smart boy, and learned well in Mount Vernon.

*Plantation mistress Mary Jones, October 7, 1863, in* Children of Pride, *1110.*

## The Workers: Breeders

Planters oblige [slave women who do not bear children after a year or two of cohabitation with their husbands] to take a second, third, fourth, fifth or more Husbands or Bedfellows; a fruitful woman amongst them being very much valued by the Planters, and numerous Issue esteemed the greatest riches in the Country.

*John Brickell,* Natural History of North Carolina, *in Oakes,* Ruling Race, *26.*

Mr. Covey was a poor man; he was just commencing in life; he was only able to buy one slave; . . . he bought her, as he said, for a *breeder.* . . . She was a large able-bodied woman, about twenty years old. She had already given birth to one child, which proved her to be just what he wanted. After buying her, he hired a married man of Mr. Samuel Harrison, to live with him one year; and him he used to fasten up with her every night!

*Ex-slave Frederick Douglass, describing events of the early 1830s,* Narrative, *74–75.*

Women with six children alive at any one time are allowed all Saturday to themselves.

*Bassett,* Southern Plantation Overseer, *32.*

[Master was] mighty careful about raisin' healthy nigger families and used us strong, healthy young bucks to stand the healthy nigger gals. When I was young they took care not to strain me and I was as handsome as a speckled pup and was in demand for breedin'.

*Ex-slave Jeptha Choice, in Tadman,* Speculators and Slaves, *123.*

## The Workers: Drivers

[When a pregnant woman fainted in the field], de driver said dat she was puttin' on an' dat she ort ter be beat. De master said dat she can be beat but don't ter hurt de baby. . . . [The driver put the woman into a hold in the ground] 'bout ter her arm pits, den he kivers her up an' straps her han's over her haid, [and took] de long bull whup an' he cuts long gashes all over her shoulders an' raised arms, den he walks off an' leaves her dar fer a hour in de hot sun. . . . De flies an' de gnats day worry her, an' de sun hurts too an' she cries a little, den de driver comes out wid a pan full of vinegar, salt an' red pepper an' he washes de gashes. De 'oman faints an' he digs her up, but in a few minutes she am stone dead.

*Analiza Foster's mother, in Fox-Genovese,* Plantation Households, *190.*

[N]early all the drivers I have seen are tall and strong men—but a great deal of judgment, requiring greater capacity of mind than the ordinary slave is often supposed to be possessed of, is certainly needed in them. A good driver is very valuable and usually holds office for life. His authority is not limited to the direction of labour in the field, but extends to the general deportment of the negroes. He is made to do the duties of policeman, and even of police magistrate. It is his duty, for instance, on Mr. X's estate [a flourishing rice plantation in Georgia], to keep order in the settlement; and, if two persons, men or women, are fighting, it is his duty to immediately separate them, and then to "whip them both". . . .

Having generally had long experience on the plantation, the advice of the drivers is commonly taken in nearly all the administration, and frequently they are, *de facto,* the managers. Orders on important points of the plantation economy, I have heard given by the proprietor directly to them, without the overseer's being consulted or informed of them; and it is often left with them to decide when and how long to flow the rice-grounds—the proprietor and overseer deferring to their more experienced judgment. Where the drivers are discreet, experienced, and trusty, the overseer is frequently employed merely as a matter of form, to comply with the laws requiring the superintendence or presence of a white man among every body of slaves; and his duty is rather to inspect and report than to govern. Mr. X . . . has sometimes left his plantation in care of one of the drivers for a considerable length of time, after having discharged an overseer. . . .

*Olmsted,* Cotton Kingdom, *193–94.*

## The Workers: Factory Operators, Miners, and Lumbermen

[People in North Carolina] make money almost from nothing. [Slaves do most of the work, and] the profit arising is so much greater because no establishment is necessary beyond the working hands themselves. [Each working hand] what with these [making tar, pitch, and turpentine] and other uses made of the forest, should bring in to his master one to two hundred pounds current a year.

*Johann Schoepf, report of his travels in the early 1780s, in Kay and Cary,* Slavery in North Carolina, *44.*

[I recommend to the owner of an ironworks] as soon as he Can conveniently do it to get Young Negro Lads to put under the Smith Carpenters Founders Finers & Fillers as also to get a certain number of able Slaves to fill the Furnace Stock the Bridge Raise Ore & Cart and burn the same. Wood Cutters may for some Time be hired here. There should be Two master Colliers one at the Furnaces another at the Forge with a Suitable Number of Slaves or Serv[an]ts under Each who might Coal in the Summer and Cut wood in the winter.

*Charles Carroll, 1753 "Proposals," in Lewis,* Coal, Iron, and Slaves, *25.*

The employ of the plantation negroes is not by any means so fatiguing, and laborious, as those employed here; they [plantation negroes] can generally find conveniency to Skulk [shirk], more or less at their respective jobbing about a plantation; a thing intirely out of the question here where every negroe is under the eye of the superintendant. . . . Added to this the work is of the most fatiguing kind; digging, Shoveling & wheeling dirt, tumbling large pieces of the Rock, where every muscle of the body must be strained, boring holes, and driving wedges, & fellows [pieces in wheels to which the spokes are attached?] & Tongs with heavy Sledges; indeed the handling of the bits, sledges, crowbars, drills, Fellows & tongues &c is heavy work of itself, and requires a constant exertion of muscular power. . . .

*Robert Leckie to the commissioner of public buildings, marble quarries [near Washington, D.C.], May 16, 1817, quoted in Starobin,* Industrial Slavery, *35.*

The weather here [in Mississippi] is very warm, too warm for our hands to work all the day without killing them up—the exercise of walking a little, makes the sweat roll off from any one in large drops. . . . All our negroes [14 male and nine female slaves who came from North Carolina] seem to be dissatisfied here. Such Shantees as they have will not do in the winter—the Mosquitoes torment them almost to death in the night time—the meat they use is very salty and a little spoiled.

*Agent Joseph Hicks to railroad contractor Samuel Smith Downey, July 1836, quoted in Starobin,* Industrial Slavery, *67.*

As you approach near the [Chowan River, in North Carolina,] fishery beach, the hum and song indicate business and good humor . . . [You are] hearing the merry songs and pithy original jests and sayings of the workmen and attendants—seeing the two fine large boats loaded down with the sein [seine] rowing out to the middle of the river more than three miles wide to shoot it, that is, to drop it out into the river. First—the two boats row off in company and astern of each other, the leading boat, bow foremost, the hinder stern foremost, for the sein is astern. When they have gone out far enough, they separate, one boat going down, the other up the river, as far as they design, dropping out the sein as they separate and so continue until they reach shore on their return. Then while the sein is drawn up by mules and horses, the sein hallers sleep, eat, or otherwise amuse themselves until the sein comes ashore—then all hands—if it is discovered it is a large hall [haul], the excitement, motions, and preparations are thrilling. . . . Now the shelters are crowded with the processors, the cutters &c. . . . They halled all night as they do in a big run of fish.

*W. D. Valentine diary, 1840, quoted in Starobin,* Industrial Slavery, *27.*

In each of them [three southern cotton factories] are employed from 80 to 100 persons, and about an equal number of white and black. In one of them, the blacks are the property of the mill-owner, but in the other two they are the slaves of planters, hired out at monthly wages to work in the factory. There is no difficulty among them on account of colour, the white girls working in the same room and at the same loom with the black girls; and boys of each colour, as well as men and women, working together without apparent repugnance or objection.

*Britisher James Silk Buckingham,* Slave States *(1842), quoted in Starobin,* Industrial Slavery, *141.*

The immense profits which have and still continue to reward well directed industry in the gold mines of California, exceed those which have ever flowed from mere labor, inexhaustible in extent and indefinite in duration. Had this wide field for investment been open to the slave labor of the Southern States, wages would have risen, and consequently the value of slaves at home would have been greatly enhanced.

*Mississippi governor John A. Quitman, 1850, bemoaning the admission of California to the Union as a free state, in Starobin,* Industrial Slavery, *218.*

I would respectfully urge on the board the propriety of purchasing a sufficient number of young men and boys . . . to keep . . . the canal in repair; for the following reasons: 1st because of the difficulty, trouble, and expense to the company of hiring them even at exorbitant rates[;]. . . 2ndly because of the great savings to the company as an economical measure.

*"James River and Kanawah Canal Report," Virginia Board of Public Works Report, 1854, quoted in Starobin,* Industrial Slavery, *29.*

The great feature of success is the number and sort of hands we shall use the machinery [in the cotton mill] with. These we have already selected out, and have them training; they run thus: one old man sixty five years old at the "gin and lap"; one man (maimed, forefinger off) at "cards"; one old man sixty years old at "drawing"; one boy ten and one girl twelve years old at "speeders"; three boys seven to nine, and three girls and boys, ten years old, "spinning"; six women and girls to the reels; but one good field hand, and she a girl but fourteen years old—17 all told.

*DeBow's Review (1858), quoted in Starobin,* Industrial Slavery, *167.*

My owner hired me to the contractors for building the railroad between Charleston and Savannah and I was employed in the construction of the road both at my trade of blacksmithing and in getting out and laying the ties.

*Interview with Solomon Bradley, 1863, American Freedmen's Inquiry Commission, in* Slave Testimony, *371.*

## *The Workers: Field Hands*

[Isabella, later known as Sojourner Truth], became more ambitious than ever to please [her master]; and he stimulated her ambition by . . . boasting of her to his friends, telling them that "*that* wench . . . is better to me than a *man*—for she will do a good family's washing in the night, and be ready in the morning to go into the field, where she will do as much at raking and binding as my best hands.". . .

When Isabella went to the field to work, she used to put her infant in a basket, tying a rope to each handle, and suspending the basket to a branch of a tree, set another small child to swing it. It was thus secure from reptiles and was easily administered to, and even lulled to sleep, by a child too young for other labors. . . .

*Sojourner Truth's life as a slave, in* Narrative, *20–21, 25.*

[Rice-growing was] the most unhealthy work in which the slaves were employed, and in spite of every care, . . . they sank under it in great numbers. The causes of this dreadful mortality, are the constant moisture and heat of the atmosphere, together with the alternate floodings and drying of the fields, on which the negroes are perpetually at work, often ankle deep in mud, with their bare heads exposed to the fierce rays of the sun.

*Captain Basil Hall, in Bell,* Major Butler's Legacy, *127.*

After I got to be some size, my owner hired me out to some poor people that lived in the country. I was

Gathering sugarcane (*Blake,* History of Slavery and the Slave Trade)

only about six years old, but I think he got about three dollars per month for me. They hired me to nurse, but I had to nurse, cook, work in the fields, chop wood, bring water, wash, iron, and in general just do everything. . . .

Every morning I was up at five o'clock. I slept in the room with the white folks. I made a pallet in the corner every night, and in the morning I took it up. After dressing myself, I made the fires, went and milked two cows, drove them to the pastures, and came back and brought water from the spring for the house. Then I cleaned up, helped with breakfast, and got ready to go to the field to work. . . .

In the field my boss used to take two rows and give me one, and I had to be at the end with my one row when he finished his two.

*Ex-slave,* God Struck Me Dead, *116–17.*

[S]ome thirty men and women were at work, repairing the road. The women were in majority, and were engaged at exactly the same labour as the men: driving the carts, loading them with dirt, and dumping them upon the road; cutting down trees, and drawing wood by hand, to lay cross the miry places; hoeing, and shovelling. They were dressed in coarse gray gowns, generally very much burned, and very dirty; which, for greater convenience of working in the mud, were reefed up with a cord drawn tightly around the body, a little above the hips—the spare amount of skirt bagging out between this and the waist-proper. On their legs were loose leggins, or pieces of blanket or bagging wrapped about, and lashed with thongs; and they wore very heavy shoes. Most of them had handkerchiefs, only, tied around their heads; some wore men's caps, or old slouched hats, and several were bareheaded.

*Olmsted,* Cotton Kingdom, 161–62.

I never knowed what it was to rest. I just work all de time from mornin' till late at night. I had to do everythin' dey was to do on de outside. Work in de field, chop wood, hoe corn, till sometimes I feels like my back surely break. . . .

In de summer we had to work outdoors, in de winter in de house. I had to card and spin till ten o'clock. Never get much rest, had to get up at four de next mornin' and start again.

*North Carolina ex-slave Sarah Gudger, in Hymowitz and Weissman,* History of Women in America, 43.

A tobacco plantation (*Library of Congress*)

The field negroes, as a class, are coarse, filthy, brutal, and lascivious; liars, parasites, hypocrites, and thieves; without self-respect, religious aspirations, or the nobler traits which characterize humanity. . . . Morally, they are on a level with the whites around them. The slaveholder steals their labor, rights and children; they steal his chickens, hogs and vegetables. . . . The laws forbidding the acquisition of knowledge, and the fact that slavery and intelligence are incompatible, keep them, as nearly as possible, as ignorant and degraded as the quadrupeds of the fields.

*Redpath,* Roving Editor, 222.

## *The Workers: House Servants*

[My mother] just raised the whole kaboodle of them together [her mistress's children and her own. I] was born about the same time as the baby Jennie. They say I nursed on one breast while that white child, Jennie, pulled away at the other!

*Ex-slave Mattie Logan, in Fox-Genovese,* Plantation Household, *151–52.*

I could not bring my baby [on a visit] without assistance. She is a great deal fonder of her *Mammy* than she is of me. She nurses her and it would be a great trial to go without her.

*Laura S. Tibbetts, in Fox-Genovese,* Plantation Household, *162.*

[I] learnt to spin, knit an' weave, [and I] helped wid de washing an' toted loads o' water . . . to de long wash troughs [hewn-out logs, set on racks]. We had to rub de clothes by hand, some beat 'em on blocks wid hickory battling sticks. . . . Deir wuz a heap o' ironing to be done. De white folks wore lots of white ruffled up, full things dat had to be starched and ironed.

*Julia Stubbs, in Fox-Genovese,* Plantation Households, *178.*

Betsy, recalcitrant maid of the Williamses, is sold to a telegraphy man. She is handsome as a mulatto ever gets to be. And clever in every kind of work. My [maid] Molly thinks her mistress very lucky in getting rid of her. She was a dangerous inmate. But she will be a good cook, a good chamber maid, a good dairy maid, a beautiful clear starcher (and the most thoroughly good-for-nothing woman I know) to her new owners, if she chooses.

*Diary entry, May 29, 1862,* Mary Chesnut's Civil War, *350.*

But, thank de Lawd, I had good white folks and dey sho' did trus' me, too. I had charge of all de keys to de house, and I waited on de Missis' and de chillun. I laid out all de clo'se on Sat'dy night, and den Sunday mawnin's I'd pick up all de dirty things. Dey did'n' have a thing to do.

*Ex-slave Charity Anderson,* American Slave, *Alabama.*

A driver accompanying his mistress on her shopping expedition (*Crowe,* With Thackeray in America)

## *The Workers: Overseers, Managers, and Stewards*

I have allmost constantly found Nigroes tell Truth enough of distant overseers & I am now told that Moore has sold every grain of his own Corn yet Suds [feeds?] his own horse three times a day out of mine, that he has now seven Hoggs raised in my Estate that the Nigroes can't get a drop of Milk tho' there is a plenty even to spare Old Buidine & his [Moore's] Pigs every day. . . . I remember all the Bacon I laid in for Mill Wrights, Carpenters &c was also expended. . . .

*Planter James Mercer, December 5, 1778, in Mullin,* Flight and Rebellion, *31.*

As for old Betty, she is free already. She does as she pleases, and you feed and cloth her. As for Jacob he certainly is a most deserving Negro. If you liberated Jacob, what will Bram say? He has earned you more than Ten thousand Dollars. I know of no people more Jealous of their rights and privileges than Negroes—be assured if you begin you will create a great Murmur among the people. Jacob is very useful as head carpenter—his health is bad and I dont allow him to do anything but lay off work, as he has a large family of fine Children on the Estate. I think it would be better for to restrict one hundred dollars to be paid him yearly as long as he was useful would be much better for him, for freedom would force him to work hard for a living, which would soon kill him. As for Molley, you are no stranger to her long wish for freedom (when in Phila). I have no doubt she would have gone off with the British if her husband and children was with her, yet she is certainly a very deserving Woman and I wish the eve of her days comfortable, but I cannot (believe) freedom would be any blessing to her. As for Abraham, he and many more are very deserving Negroes. Abram is truly a faithful, sober honest negro I believe, and if you wish to do something for him send for him to Philada. Let him serve you seven years, he is the one that can git a good living free, and the only one in four that you mentioned. Be assured you have not 50 negroes but what it would be a curse to free them.

*Overseer Roswell King objecting to his employer's proposal to free four slaves, in Bell,* Major Butler's Legacy, *141.*

In the management of slaves, the temper and disposition of each negro should be particularly consulted. Some require spurring up, some coaxing, some flattering, and others nothing but good words. When an overseer first goes upon a plantation to live, he should study their dispositions well, before he exerts too much rigor. Many a noble spirit has been broken down by injudicious management, and many a lazy cunning fellow has escaped, and put his work on the shoulders of the industrious. Give me a high spirited and even a high tempered negro, full of pride, for easy and comfortable management. Your slow sulky negro although he may have an even temper, is *the devil* to manage.

The negro women are all harder to manage than the men. The only way to get along with them is by kind words and flattery. If you want to cure a sloven, give her something nice occasionally to wear, and praise her up to skies whenever she has on any thing tolerably decent.

*Southern Agriculturalist (July 1834), quoted in Blassingame,* Slave Community, *151–52.*

[The overseer, Mr. Austin] Gore, was proud, ambitious, and persevering. He was artful, cruel, and obdurate. He was just the man for such a place, and it was just the place for such a man. . . . He was just proud enough to demand the most debasing homage of the slave, and quite servile enough to crouch, himself, at the feet of the master. He was ambitious enough to be contented with nothing short of the highest rank of overseers, and persevering enough to reach the height of his ambition. He was cruel enough to inflict the severest punishment, artful enough to descend to the lowest trickery, and obdurate enough to be insensible to the voice of a reproving conscience. . . .

Overseers will sometimes indulge in a witty word, even with the slaves; not so with Mr. Gore. He spoke but to command, and commanded but to be obeyed; he dealt sparingly with his words, and bountifully with his whip, never using the former where the latter would answer as well. . . . He was, in a word, a man of the most inflexible firmness and stone-like coolness. I was made overseer. The management was pretty much left to me. . . .

I was harder on the servants than [my master] wanted I should be.

*Dan Josiah Lockhart, in* Four Fugitive Slave Narratives, *38–39.*

No wonder, then, that the overseer desires to have entire control of the plantation. . . . *presses everything at the end of the lash; pays no attention to the sick, except to keep them in the field as long as possible; and drives them out again at the first moment, and forces sucklers and breeders to their utmost. He has no other interest than to make a big cotton crop.*

Southern Agriculturalist, *quoted in Olmsted,* Cotton Kingdom, *440.*

[The overseer tried to whip my mother and] she knocked him down and tore his face up . . . [He told the master] that he went down in the field to whip the hands and that he just thought he would hit Lucy a few licks to show the slaves that he was impartial. The master replied, "Well, if that is the best you can do with her, damned if you won't just have to take it."

*Leonard Franklin, in Fox-Genovese,* Plantation Households, *187–88.*

Now my heart is nearly broke. I have lost poor *Leven,* one of the most faithful black men [that] ever lived. [H]e was truth and honesty, and without a fault that I ever discovered. He has overseed the plantation nearly three years, and [has] done much better than any white man [had] ever done here. . . .

*Louisiana planter, in Fogel and Engerman,* Time on the Cross, *77.*

## *Work Practices: Hiring Out*

I have formerly advertis'd all Persons not to employ my Negro Man *Lancaster* in white washing or any other kind of Work whatever, but to little purpose; since he constantly earns Money (which he loses either by *Gaming* or spends among the little *Punch-Houses*) altho' he has been *run away* for this Month past: I do therefore once more peremptorily forbid all Persons from employing the said *Lancaster* in any Manner whatever.

*Notice in the* South-Carolina Gazette, *October 24, 1741, in Wax, "The Great Risque," 146.*

*To be Hired as a wet Nurse,* A HEALTHY YOUNG NEGRO WOMAN, With a good breast of milk and no child. Enquire at No. 106, King-street.

*Charleston, South Carolina* Royal Gazette, *May 1, 1782, in Bancroft,* Slave Trading, *155, n. 27.*

Decr' 3, 1837 Campbill County, Va.

Mrs. Elizabeth Brown) You Sent us word that you wanted us your Servants [slaves] to come out to Kentucky this fall past and since that has wrote that we must not come untill next fall and as we all was very anxious to come we are very sorry of the disappointment . . . I myself am verry sorry and is in hopes that you will send after us all next Spring if you Please and if you cant Send for all Pray be so good as to Send for me and my Son Harrison I have to work for $11 per month and as I am getting old it is rather more than I can make and clothe myself. . . . I have had the misfortune Since you left here to loose my wife and daughter and if you dont send for me verry quick I shall be compelled to get me another wife If you should not send for me next Spring be so good as send what is the least money you will take for me by the month. . . . If you please madam. Nothing more at Present but remain your good old Servant Matthew Watts

Slave Testimony, *27.*

Tell Howell I cannot agree for Betty to be hired to Matilda [a free negro]; her [Matilda's] character is too bad. I know her of old, she is a drunkard, and is said to be bad in every respect. I should object to her [Betty's] being hired to any colored person no matter what their character was, and if she cannot get into a respectable family I had rather she came home and if she can't work out put her to spinning and weaving. Her relatives here beg she may not be hired to Matilda. She would not be worth a cent at the end of the year.

*Georgian Mrs. S. R. Cobb, letter of January 9, 1843, in* American Slavery, *12.*

The negro hiring days have come, the most woeful of the year! So housekeepers think who do not own their own servants; and even his class is but a little better off than the rest, for all darkeydom must have holiday this week, and while their masters and mistresses are making fires and cooking victuals or attending to other menial duties the negroes are promenading the streets decked out in their finest clothes. . . .

I was rather amused at the efforts of a market gardener to hire a young woman as a domestic servant. The price her owner put upon her services was not objected to by him, but they could not agree about other terms. The grand obstacle was that she would not consent to work in the garden, even when she had nothing else to do. After taking an hour's walk in another part of town I again met the two at the old bargain. Stepping towards them, I now learned that she was pleading for other privileges—her friends and favourites must be allowed to visit her. At length she agreed to go and visit her proposed home and see how things looked.

Atlantic Intelligencer, *January 5, 1859, in Phillips,* American Negro Slavery, *407–8.*

## *Work Practices: Slave Entrepreneurship*

[Their small plots provide slaves with a] sufficient quantity of Tobacco for their own use, a part of which they may sell, and likewise on Sundays, they gather Snake-root, otherwise it would be excessive dear if the Christians were to gather it; with this and the Tobacco they buy Hats, and other Necessaries for themselves, as Linen, Bracelets, Ribbons, and several other Toys for their Wives and Mistresses.

*John Brickell, before 1740, in Kay and Cary,* Slavery in North Carolina, *37–38.*

After toiling all day for my mistress, I used to sleep three or four hours, and then get up and work for myself the remainder of the night. I made collars for horses, out of plaited husks. I could weave one in about eight hours; and I generally took time enough from my sleep to make two collars in the course of a week. I sold them for fifty cents each. One summer, I tried to take two or three hours from my sleep every night; but I found that I grew weak, and I was obliged to sleep more. With my first money I bought a pig. The next year I earned for myself about thirteen dollars; and the next about thirty. There was a good deal of wild land in the neighborhood that belonged to Congress. I used to go out with my hoe, and dig up little patches, which I planted with corn, and got up in the night to tend it. My hogs were fattened with this corn. . . . Besides this, I used to raise small patches of tobacco, and sell it to buy more corn for my pigs. In this way I worked for five years, at the end of which time, after taking out my losses, I found that I had earned one hundred and sixty dollars. With this money I hired my own time for two years. . . . At the end of the two years, I had earned three hundred dollars, besides feeding and clothing myself. I now bought my time for eighteen months longer, and went two hundred and fifty miles west, nearly into Texas, where I could make more money.

*James L. Bradley, quoted in* Slave Testimony, *688.*

The laborers [at Graham's coal pits] are permitted to do extra work for their own gain, and . . . do earn money in that manner. I even saw afterwards where they had opened two (not very deep,) shafts to the coal, for their own private working—though their proceedings had been stopped, and certainly should not have been permitted to be commenced, on so distinct and independent a footing.

*Edmund Ruffin,* Farmer's Register, *August 1, 1837, in Lewis,* Coal, Iron, and Slaves, *120.*

A restaurant waiter (*Crowe,* With Thackeray in America)

[My grandmother] was much praised for her cooking; and her nice crackers became so famous in the neighborhood that many people were desirous of obtaining them. In consequence of numerous requests of this kind, she asked permission of her mistress to bake crackers at night, after all the household work was done; and she obtained leave to do it, provided she would clothe herself and her children from the profits. . . . She had laid up three hundred dollars, which her mistress one day begged as a loan, promising to pay her soon. . . . [N]o promise or writing given to a slave is legally binding. . . .

*Jacobs,* Slave Girl, *12–13.*

A slave woman selling peanuts (*Crowe,* With Thackeray in America)

## *Work Practices: Task Labor*

[The] Dayly Task for a Negro Wood Cutter is a Cord, some can cut more but I never knew more than a Cord Required, if they Cut more, it is usual to pay them for it.

*James Millis, North Carolina ironworks superintendent, 1777, in Kay and Cary,* Slavery in North Carolina, *37.*

The ordinary plantation task is easily accomplished, during the winter months in 8 to 9 hours and in summer my people seldom exceed 10 hours labor *per day.* Whenever the daily task is finished the balance of the day is appropriated to their own purposes. In severe freezing weather no task is exacted, and such work is selected as can be done with least exposure. During heavy rains and in thunder showers, my people are always dismissed and allowed to go home. The task is allotted to each slave in proportion to his age and physical ability. Thus they are considered 1/4, 1/2, 3/4, or full task hands. . . . Men and women are all engaged together in the planting, cultivation and harvesting of the Crop, but in the preparation [*sic*] of the Rice Lands, as ditching, embanking etc. the *men* alone are engaged with the spade. It is customary (*and never objected to*) for the more active and industrious hands to assist those who are slower and more tardy in finishing their daily task.

*James R. Sparkman, March 10, 1858, in* South Carolina Rice Plantation, *346.*

## *Work Laws*

The negro act of South Carolina contains the following language: "Whereas many owners of slaves, and *others,* who have the care, management, and overseeing of slaves, *do confine them so closely to hard labor, that they have not sufficient time for natural rest;* be it therefore enacted, that if any owner of slaves, or others having the care, &c., shall put such slaves to labor more than *fifteen* hours in twenty-four, from the twenty-fifth of March to the twenty-fifth of September; or more than *fourteen* hours in twenty-four hours, from the twenty-fifth of September to the twenty-fifth of March, any such person shall forfeit a sum of money. . . ."

*Child,* Appeal, *43.*

Preparing cotton for processing (*Library of Congress*)

# 6

# Runaways
## 1619–1865

## THE HISTORICAL CONTEXT

### *Escaping*

From the beginning of slavery in North America, slave owners had a hard time holding onto their slaves. If those slaves were Indians, they knew the terrain, knew how to live in the forest, and had friends nearby; they escaped successfully at a rate discouraging to their owners. Many more problems confronted African slaves, but they too fled. Their desperation may be measured by the report of one slave that he ran away so that his master would "sell me running"—that is, sell the chance of owning him to a new master if he could catch the fugitive, for, said the slave, he didn't much care whose hands he fell into as long as he could get away from his present master.

Most African runaways were short term. Slave owners came to accept as a fact of life the periodic absence in nearby woods and swamps of slaves who ran away to avoid punishment or a heavy work assignment, to join their "abroad" spouses (living on another plantation), or just to take a break from slavery's dreadful monotony. So ordinary were these departures that one mistress who knew her missing slave was about to deliver a baby went out into the woods to visit her and carried the infant back to the plantation.

Some runaways stayed out for long periods. For instance, a young house servant struck her mistress and fled to escape the beating promised when the master came home. Her husband hid her in a cave. He eventually finished the cave with pine logs, made furniture for it, and installed a stove with a pipe running out into the swamp (to hide the source of the smoke). There she lived for seven years, during which time she bore three children with only her husband to attend her. Other slaves gave them food. As another slave told the story, "It was freedom 'fore she come out of that cave for good."[1]

Fugitives were a different matter: they ran to escape bondage completely. Escape was hardest for newly imported African slaves, who did not speak

English and had no idea where they were or in what direction to move. But even slaves born in this country usually knew little about geography and climate, let alone free and slave territories, beyond their own immediate area. Only gradually did word get around that for most of them the best advice was to "follow the North Star."

Although blacks began to flee northward before 1800, information about Canada did not circulate much before the War of 1812. When it did, masters did their best to suppress and distort it: no one could long survive there, they said, with such poor soil and such a cold climate—particularly not people with African blood. But truth will out: slaves hired out by Virginia and Kentucky masters to Ohio farmers lived near enough Canada to hear rumors, and they passed them on to slaves back in the border states. Slaves sold farther south carried the word with them. Later, escaped fugitives returning to rescue their families, the few white abolitionists who went south to encourage escapes, and sometimes even casual travelers dared to inform slaves about ways and means, as well as destinations.

Even armed with such information, slaves faced long odds. Most successful escapes were second, third, even sixth tries. Henry Bibb, sold to speculators after his sixth attempt, finally won his freedom by accepting their offer to give him a percentage of the proceeds and directions to Canada if he would cooperate in getting himself sold for a high price.

Slaves pondering escape had to overcome the natural fear of leaving familiar territory and beloved family and friends. As a North Carolina slave told James Redpath, "[I don't run away because if I were caught] I might be sold away from [my family], which I won't be, if I don't try to run away—leastways till I'm old."[2]

They had also to weigh the risks of going through country where most whites and some blacks were against them, and of the terrible punishments inflicted on captured fugitives.

Almost all slave masters were both determined to defend the slave system and personally insulted by "desertion." Almost all of them thought of a captured fugitive as almost totally useless thereafter, indeed dangerous to have around, because he might encourage discontent and inspire other slaves to escape. Instead of shrugging and concluding that they were better off without such troublemakers, however, masters were determined to get vengeance, to keep slaves from getting away with escape. Commonly, they imposed a brutal whipping followed by hanging, or a beating and a sale south.

No wonder that fugitives often fought desperately to keep from being recaptured. Frederick Olmsted tells of a black man arrested on suspicion of being a runaway, whose captors put him in a skiff and told him to row them to shore. Instead, he seized a hatchet and assaulted one of them. In the scuffle they both fell overboard. The suspected fugitive was rescued and put ashore, his captors going to fetch arms and a pack of "negro dogs" with which to pursue him. Eventually they found him standing at bay on a large raft, armed with a club and a pistol, threatening death to any man who approached. They shot him, and he fell into the water. They attempted rescue, but he preferred to drown, battling against them even as he sank.

What strikes the reader now is the utter inability of most slave owners to empathize with the condition of the runaways, to wonder what misery drove slaves to such risks. Instead, even the most intelligent of masters focused on what the escape had done to themselves. "Our negroes run away, which troubles us to catch them, and our servants vex us, which troubles us to whip them," complained David Bush of Louisiana.[3] George Washington wrote, "The running off of my cook has been a most inconvenient thing to this family, and what rendered it more disagreeable is that I had resolved never to become the master of another slave by purchase. But this resolution I fear I must break."[4]

## *Escaping: Who Ran?*

In the face of all this, slaves still fled. Which of them? Fewer escaped from the Deep South than from Maryland, Virginia, Kentucky, or Missouri, all closer to free territory. Often the most privileged slaves escaped, their expectations apparently raised by their favored positions. Most successful fugitives were robust young males. The fugitive traveled fastest who traveled alone; taking along the family multiplied the risks. Infants and young children could not walk the long distances required, could not go for long periods without food and drink, and were given to crying at inconvenient moments.

Male slaves, more apt to be sent on off-plantation errands and be hired out, more likely to visit their "abroad" wives than vice versa, knew the local territory better than the women. They were a more common sight on the roads than women slaves and so were less likely to be stopped. Whereas mothers and small children were usually sold as "families," fathers were more often sold singly and had less to keep them in their unfamiliar new homes.

When women did decamp, they more often played truant than became genuine fugitives. At the ages of most fugitives, from 16 to 35, most slave women were bearing, nursing, and caring for babies and small children, whom they could neither endure to leave nor hope to take with them. During those years, too, as pregnant and nursing mothers they received the best care of their lives, as their masters eased demands in order to protect the lives and health of the new slave babies. Slave owners of course were well aware of this obstacle. Slave owner's wife Fanny Kemble overheard a conversation about the dangers of taking slaves into the northern states, where they might try to claim their freedom or be set free by abolitionists—but there was a sure preventive: "Oh, stuff and nonsense; I take care, when my wife goes North with the children, to send Lucy with her; *her children are down here, and I defy all the abolitionists in creation to get her to stay North.*"[5]

## *Escaping: How Many?*

No one knows how many slaves actually escaped, let alone how many tried, or how many more took to nearby woods for a time. Benjamin Drew, who interviewed fugitives in Canada, estimated about 30,000 there in 1855, but the figure was and is widely disputed. Estimates of how many had escaped to the North by the time of the Civil War range, almost meaninglessly, from 25,000 to 100,000.[6]

## *Escaping: Where?*

Up until 1850 and the passage of the harsh Fugitive Slave Law, fugitives made new lives for themselves in the northern free states and territories. After that year, many of them, as well as newly fleeing slaves, found more security in Canada. While the Spanish held Florida, fugitives from the Deep South accepted their invitation to freedom. Some Indian tribes, particularly in Florida, gave fugitives refuge, either in a relatively benign form of slavery or as tribal members. In the early 18th century, slaves escaping from South Carolina fled to the Creek Indians of Georgia. Mexico provided shelter and freedom to other fugitives, especially those from Texas. A few made their escape down the Mississippi River to New Orleans and its oceangoing vessels.

## *Escaping: When and How?*

Many fugitives took advantage of free time on weekends and during the Christmas holidays to escape. They also favored the months when the corn was high enough in the fields to conceal them.

They devised all sorts of ruses. Traveling on foot, they took to water and used pepper to throw dogs off their trails. The bolder stole horses and money to help them on their way. Some stowed away on boats, where often they got help from black sailors. Some could and did pass for white. Others waited for the trail to cool by hiding for weeks, months, even years in kitchens or attics before they took flight. They adopted disguises, women posing as men, or occasionally the other way round. Ellen Crafts escaped with her husband by posing as his white master. Some daring men had themselves packed in boxes to be shipped north—at least one foresighted fugitive bringing along a fan. Fugitives obtained passes by paying poor whites to forge them or through acquaintance with a slave who could write.

Occasionally, fugitives were able, by threatening suicide, to scare off would-be captors, who dared not make themselves liable to the master for the loss of his slave property.

## *Escaping: What Became of Them?*

Though they were a self-selected, persistent, venturesome group, fugitives who had escaped still faced all sorts of problems. Only a small proportion of them could read and write. Few indeed had any money. Most of them had left behind all that was familiar and loved. They mourned for and worried about their still-enslaved families and friends. As one successful fugitive wrote back home, "I wish to tell All that wantes to know how I made my escape that I made it in the knight when the Moon was gon away and thar was no eyes To see but god and it was threw him that I am know gitting along and ples to say to my Farther and to my fartherinlaw that I feel happy in my ascape untill I thinkes about my Wife and I hope that you bouth will talk to her and tell Her to be not dischomfiered for I thinks that I shall see you agin. Tell him to tell her if she is not sole [sold] at Chrismous she mus let me know how she and the childrens are agatting along and dear farther ples to see her and see If thar is anney way for me to Send a man to by her. . . . all I wantes is En opportunity to send a man to by her."[7]

In the havens they sought out, either in the free states and territories or in foreign countries, the fugitives faced among most of the populace—even among abolitionists—both racial prejudice and an assumption of the inferiority of black people. Workmen resented the competition of the fugitives for jobs. In the free states, the fugitives lived in constant danger of being kidnapped or of being dragged back into slavery under the fugitive slave laws. Through no fault of their own, security eluded them.

Yet, even putting aside blacks of such extraordinary gifts as Frederick Douglass and Harriet Tubman, some of the fugitives succeeded in establishing themselves through sheer determination and wit. The highly skilled among them, of course, had a better chance than the rest, but the records occasionally show touching stories of black women who by washing clothes educated their families and bought their own homes. In the major cities of the North, some black communities protected their own members and helped new arrivals.

### *Helping the Fugitives: "Negro Stealing"*

Although many pursued the slaves so mercilessly, fortunate fugitives found help along the way. The slave states called people who aided the fugitives "Negro stealers." Of course, slaveholders detested them. As a white Alabaman wrote, "Some time last march a white man by the name of Miller appeared in the nabourhood and abducted the above negroes, was caught at vincanes, Indi. With said negroes and was thare convicted of steling and remanded back to Ala. to Abide the penalty of the law and on his return met his Just reward by getting drowned at the mouth of cumberland River on the Ohio in attempting to make his escape."[8]

William Still, a successful runaway, who aided the escapes of many others (*Seibert,* Underground Railroad)

Some of the "Negro stealers" were white southerners born and bred. Most of these apparently worked for profit. Slave Aaron Sidles and one Timothy Guard, a white man, conspired for Sidles's freedom and Guard's profit. Sidles would run away, forcing the trader who owned him to "sell him running" at a reduced price. Guard would buy Sidles, permit him to go into business for himself, guarantee to collect debts owed him, and eventually let him buy himself for $1600. Guard was as good as his word, and Sidles, working as steward on a steamboat, paid him off in about seven years.[9] Deals like these presented many hazards to slaves, though. The Murrell gang, operating in the Southwest in the 1830s, specialized in "helping" blacks to escape on condition that they would then allow themselves to be sold. The gang promised then to help them in real escapes, but in actuality they continued to resell them; if the slaves threatened exposure, they murdered them.

But some southern "Negro stealers" worked from conscience, or a liking for adventure, or both. John Fairfax so operated for some 12 years, now and then serving jail sentences but completing one daring rescue after another until he was finally cruelly imprisoned and his health broken. He was said to have "stolen"—liberated—all the slaves of both his father and his uncle, among many others. His friends in the Underground Railroad anxiously awaited word from him as he adventured through the South, posing as a proslavery advocate. He always went armed, armed the fugitives he was helping, and wanted no slave with him who was not willing to fight for his freedom.

Of the "Negro stealers" from the North, by far the bravest were themselves successful fugitives. Ex-slaves like Harriet Tubman and Josiah Henson, who had ended their own bondage by flight, left safety to rescue not only their families but slaves whom they did not even know. With a price on their heads, they went back into deadly danger time after time. Although most Northerners, even abolitionists, had too much respect for the law of property to approve of abducting slaves, a handful of whites, prominent among them Laura Haviland and Canadian Dr. Alexander Ross, ventured into the slave states to encourage and abet escapes.

## *Helping the Fugitives: The Underground Railroad*

The thousands of abolitionists and other humanitarians who constituted the Underground Railroad seldom risked their lives, but they did stand to lose their status in the community, their property, and even their freedom. These workers on the Underground Railroad came from all walks of life, young and old, women and men; many were ministers and many Quakers. Their neighbors called them *niggerites, amalgamationists,* and *nigger-thieves* and accused them of using the labor of the fugitives they sheltered and then hurrying them off without paying them. Sometimes their churches expelled them. Their neighbors spied on them, and slave hunters and their sympathizers threatened and terrorized them. Their work demanded conviction, courage, and willingness to sacrifice property and reputation.

Levi Coffin, often called the "president" of the Underground Railroad, always insisted that the network began in the South. No doubt its elements arose of themselves, as responses to fugitives' appeals for shelter or food. Arnold Cragston remembered how when still a slave he had gone to another plantation courting, and an old woman there asked him to row a pretty girl across the river. He had refused out of fright, but then he saw the girl—a *very* pretty girl. The trip across the river terrified him; "It took me a long time to get over my scared feeling, but I finally did, and I soon found myself going back across the river, with two and three people, and sometimes a whole boatload. I got so I used to make three and four trips a month."[10]

In the free states, the Underground Railroad usually originated among free blacks, who opened their homes to the fugitives, aided them with money and clothes, and when possible passed them on to other friends. In time whites joined the network. In the 1830s and 1840s, the federal government opened up new cotton fields by driving the Indians from the Gulf states. Consequently the demand for slaves increased, more slaves fled lest they be sold south, anti-slavery sentiment grew, and the Underground Railroad became nationwide. It was probably busiest in the 1850s and early 1860s when the incursions of Union troops into the South drastically altered circumstances. About 1850 the Underground Railroad began to send fugitives by real railroads as well as by the wagons, buggies, sleighs, and boats it had always used.

Most active in states such as Ohio, which was separated only by a river from the slave state of Kentucky and was linked by Lake Erie to Canada, the Underground Railroad also had many "conductors" and "station masters" in Pennsylvania and the New England states. Only a few of its operators—Coffin, the Rev. Samuel J. May, Frederick Douglass, and Harriet Tubman—knew more than five or six other people in it.

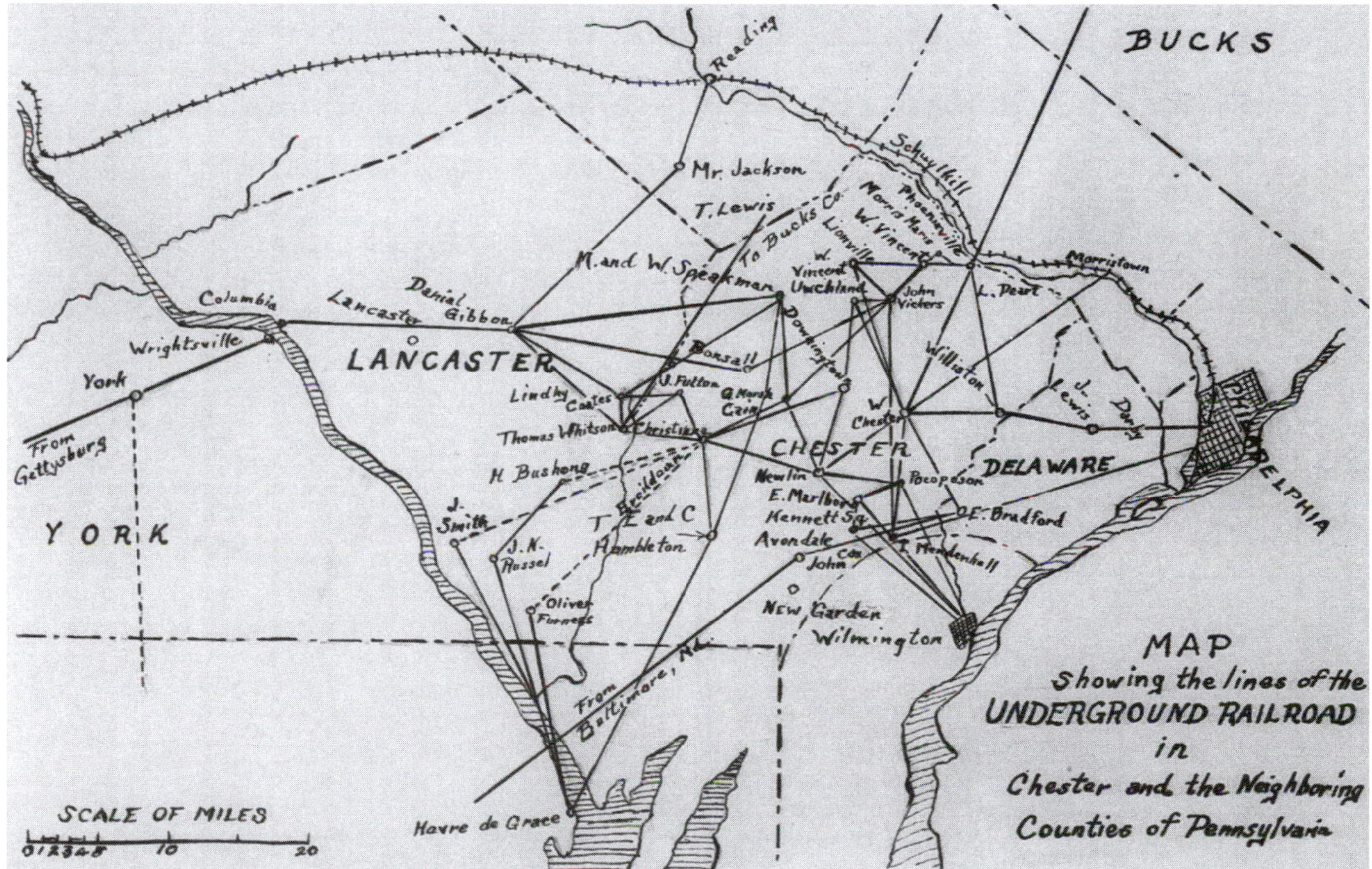


A map showing the lines of the Underground Railroad in Chester and neighboring countries of Pennsylvania (*Courtesy of the artist, Thomas B. Taylor*)

The Cox Home, a station on the Underground Railroad, Chester County, Pennsylvania (*Courtesy of the artist, Thomas B. Taylor*)

Everyone connected with the Underground Railroad had stories of narrow escapes and hairbreadth rescues. Laura Haviland told about an abolitionist woman preparing food for the journey of the fugitive Zack when her husband came in saying that their house had been surrounded by nine slave hunters. "Wife, what shall we do?" "Let them search the two lower rooms first, and while you go with them you tell Zack to slip into my room while you are with them, and I'll see to him." Working quickly, she rolled up her feather bed, drew the straw mattress to the front of the bed frame, ordered Zack to jump in, threw back the feather bed, and herself lay down on the front side. After a thorough search of the clothespress, the wardrobe, and under the bed, the slave hunters withdrew in frustration.

Coffin's *Reminiscences* is packed with one such tale after another, no doubt polished to a high gloss by frequent retelling. A stiff-backed Quaker of conscience and nerves of steel, he nevertheless injected an antic humor into the whole desperate undertaking. At one point, he concocted a plan to get a bit of his own back from certain slave hunters. He knew that they believed he and his wife were still sheltering a young fugitive—whom in fact they had already sent on and who had arrived safely in Canada. Coffin mischievously hired a free black woman who resembled the fugitive in build and general appearance and set her to work in his house. After she had been there about a week, he organized an "escape" for her, in an obvious disguise, in the hope that the marshal would give chase, the driver of the escape vehicle would manage to be captured, and ultimately Coffin could have the marshal and his posse arrested for kidnapping a free black woman.

## *Deterring Runaways: Laws to Restrict Mobility*

As the slavery period wore on, slave owners tried to alay their fears of losing slaves by ever-harsher laws restricting their mobility, chiefly by curfews and passes. Some of these restrictions extended to free blacks, whom whites always suspected of inspiring and aiding slave escapes. North and South Carolina, Georgia, Florida, Alabama, Louisiana, and Texas all had laws requiring that free black sailors should be jailed while their vessels were in port, at the expense of their employers.

## *Deterring Runaways: Patrols*

In the slave states, patrollers watched the roads for slaves who did not have passes permitting them to leave their masters' property. Theoretically, whites took turns at patrolling, working in rotation for two or three weeks. But many planters disliked the job, avoiding it for themselves and their sons by paying fines or hiring someone in their places. Some communities simply hired patrollers, who were apt to be poor, uneducated, and conscienceless. Some of these men looked forward to patrolling as a way to get out with the boys, as a break from the dull routines of the farm, or a chance to pick up a little money—not only from wages and rewards but also from bribes exacted from the slaves.

The system never worked well. In the cities, the patrollers were often called to other tasks, like keeping order among whites. In the countryside they usually rode on Sundays and nights, but not regularly—generally to deal with depredations by runaways, suspicious fires, and unusual gatherings of slaves. Slaves bargained with them for liquor and favors, hid runaways from them, and strung grapevines and ropes across roads to knock unwary patrollers from their horses.

## *Deterring Runaways: "Negro Hunters"*

Far more wide-ranging than the local patrollers were the "Negro hunters," who operated either on their own, as entrepreneurs looking to collect rewards for returning fugitives, or as agents of slave holders trying to retrieve fugitives from afar. Some of them were ne'er-do-well northerners who preferred tracking down human beings to working at regular jobs. For operations close to home, most southern "Negro hunters" had packs of dogs trained to trace, tree, and attack black fugitives. The more disreputable of these slave hunters—and as

An artist's conception of the methods used by patrollers and bounty hunters to capture fugitives (*Library of Congress*)

a class they did not stand high in public repute—descended to kidnapping free blacks (and, it was whispered, even whites) and selling them into slavery or to encouraging slaves to escape in order to catch them and collect the rewards for their capture.

## *Deterring Runaways: The Fugitive Slave Laws*

Of all the deterrents against running away, the most controversial and virulent were the various fugitive slave laws. From the earliest days of slavery in America, slave owners had tried to get agreements among the colonies or states for the return of fugitives. In 1643, the several colonies of the New England Confederation had made such a pact with one another. Throughout the colonial era, public sentiment continued to support such a policy.

The American Revolution forced some reevaluation; nevertheless, the 1787 ordinance for the government of the Northwest Territory provided that "any person escaping into the same, from whom labor or service is lawfully claimed

"What's Sauce for the Goose Is Sauce for the Gander." (*Library of Congress*)

in any one of the original states, such fugitive may be lawfully reclaimed and conveyed to the person claiming his or her labor or service aforesaid." Southerners forced into the Constitution a similar provision (Article 4, Section 2): "No person held to Service or Labour in one State, under the Laws thereof, escaping into another, shall, in Consequence of any Law or Regulation therein, be discharged from such Service or Labour, but shall be delivered up on Claim of the Party to whom such Service or Labour may be due." Still dissatisfied, southerners then fought through the Congress the Fugitive Slave Law of 1793, empowering slave owners and their agents to seize or arrest an alleged fugitive, take her or him before a federal judge or local magistrate, and obtain a warrant to remove the fugitive. This law's notorious omission of protections for falsely accused "fugitives" opened the way to kidnappings.

But to pass a law is not to enforce it. As during the early 19th century antislavery sentiment grew, slave escapes multiplied, and free states more often refused to obey fugitive slave laws. Some of them even passed "personal liberty laws" that obstructed their operation and tried to protect free blacks from

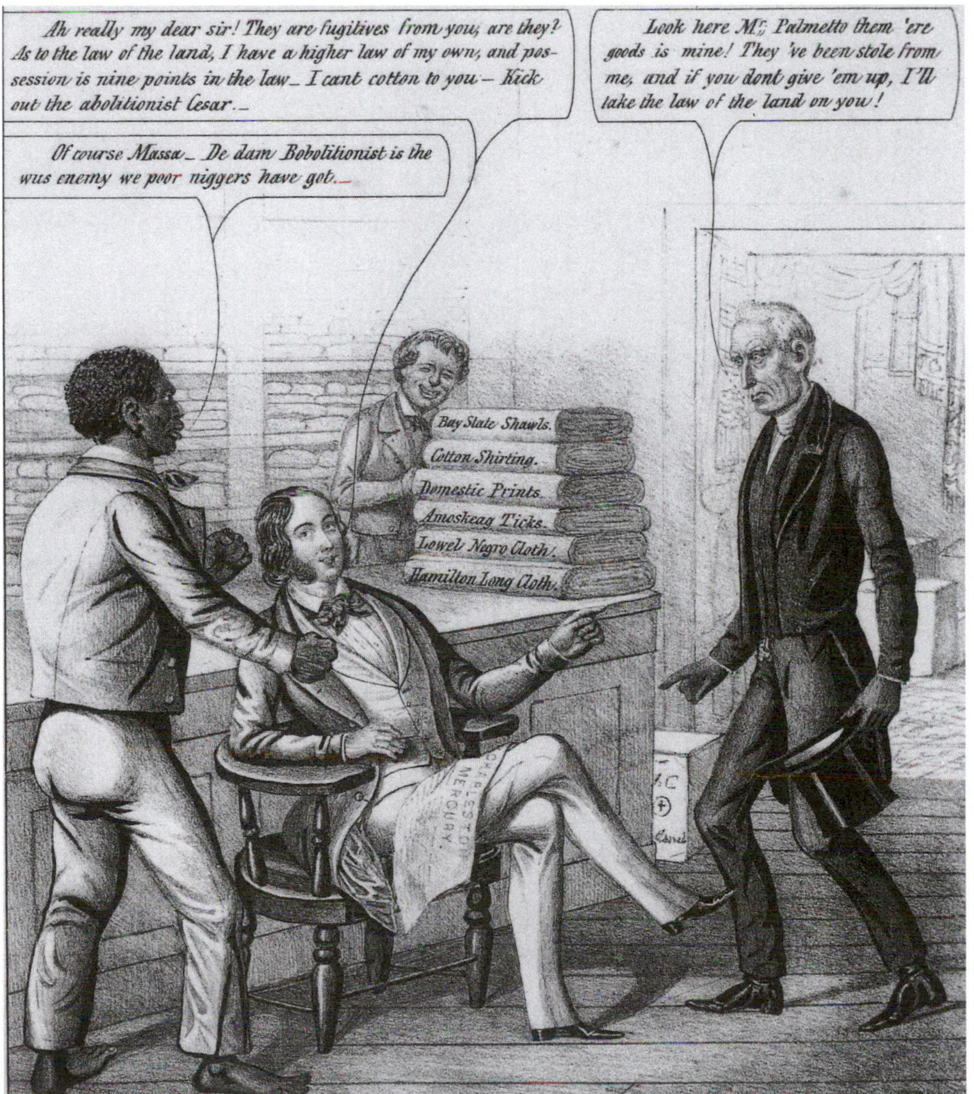

enslavement by false allegations or mistaken identity. These states did, after all, have responsibilities to their own free black populations—and, truth to tell, sometimes they used these personal liberty laws to protect real fugitives.

Because of the contradictions among the laws of the various states and between state and federal laws, the situation of the accused fugitive in the state courts was chancy. In 1816, for instance, a Pennsylvania court ruled in *Commonwealth* v. *Halloway* that Pennsylvania birth guaranteed freedom to the daughter of a slave mother who had fled from her Maryland master before she became pregnant. "Whatever may have been our ideas of the rights of slave holders in our sister states," said the court, "we cannot deny that it was competent to the legislature to enact a law ascertaining the freedom of the issue of slaves born after the passing of the act within this state." But in 1823, a Massachusetts court held in *Commonwealth* v. *Griffith* that his Virginia owner's agent was justified in arresting the fugitive Randolph, a resident and property owner of New Bedford. Here the court decreed that the agent was protected by federal law, even though under Massachusetts law Randolph owed service to no one. For, said the court, the Constitution is "a compact by which all are bound," and "we there entered into an agreement that slaves should be considered as property."

Federal courts upheld the traditional fugitive slave policy, most famously in *Prigg* v. *Pennsylvania.* In this 1842 case, the Supreme Court of the United States ruled that "the owner of a slave is clothed with entire authority in every State in the Union, to seize and recapture his slave, whenever he can do it without any breach of the peace, or any illegal violence;" it proclaimed the responsibility of the federal government "to enforce all the rights and duties growing out of [the fugitive slave clause] in the constitution." The Court also denied that the individual states had any authority to legislate the treatment of fugitive slaves. The Court went on to declare that all state judges and officials ought to enforce the federal law *but that the federal government could not force them to do so.* Abolitionists immediately seized on this part of the ruling to argue that the Court had released states from any obligation to assist in the return of fugitive slaves, and they persuaded more free states to pass personal liberty laws.

In *Jones* v. *Van Zandt* in 1847, the Supreme Court again harshly enforced the Fugitive Slave Law of 1793. Van Zandt, a conductor in the Underground Railroad, was sued for damages for offering fugitives a ride in his wagon. The defense pled that he had had no means of knowing that these persons were escaped slaves; being in Ohio, where no slavery existed, he had naturally assumed all persons to be free. The defense attorneys also attacked the law itself, arguing that the federal government lacked power to support slavery, that slavery was incompatible with the Declaration of Independence and contrary to natural right, that the law violated the Bill of Rights, and that Congress was not empowered to enforce the fugitive slave clause of the Constitution. Van Zandt lost. The Court ruled that the law was constitutional and that a judge was bound to uphold it regardless of whether he agreed with it morally.

Differences continued to sharpen between the slave and free states over the treatment of fugitive slaves, heightening the emotions of both slaveholders and abolitionists. Slaveholders accused the free states of failing to honor their obligations as members of the Union and of luring away their slaves. Abolitionists accused slave states of trying to force their assistance in the operation of a system that they deemed immoral. Feelings rose higher and higher, and the struggle over slavery began to test whether the Union could endure half free and half slave.

In 1850, the South pushed through Congress an even harsher and more punitive law, more invasive of the rights claimed by free states. The Fugitive Slave Law of 1850 specifically required all marshals and deputy marshals to carry out its provisions—that is, to arrest and keep safe fugitives—under personal penalty of large fines and liability to damages in civil suits, and *to assist slaveholders in removing their slaves.* It "commanded" citizens to aid and assist the execution of the law. It ordered local courts to issue to slaveholders (properly attested by their home states) certificates empowering them to use force and restraint to remove fugitives. It forbade either interference with this process or any other help to fugitives, under penalty of imprisonment, heavy fines, and civil damages. It prohibited local courts from considering the testimony of alleged fugitives or affording them trial by jury. The law was a slaveholder's dream and an abolitionist's nightmare, an invitation to open confrontation. The invitation was accepted.

## *Confrontation*

The Fugitive Slave Law of 1850 was simultaneously cause and result. Almost inevitably, given the South's strength in Congress, it was produced by the divisions in lifestyle, beliefs, and economic interests that slavery had created between the North and the South. In turn, it wrought havoc, widening differences and tripling the distrust and dislike between the two parts of the country. The free states defied the law in two ways—officially, by actions of the state and local governments, and unofficially, often illegally, by the actions of private citizens.

For some years, as noted, the free states had responded to fugitive slave laws and the kidnapping of their black people with personal liberty laws. In drafting these, the states usually maneuvered to take advantage of loopholes in the federal laws without directly contradicting their letter. Personal liberty laws barred state officers from enforcing federal fugitive slave laws and required them to defend fugitives; prohibited the use of state-owned buildings to detain fugitives; and offered alleged fugitives the protections of due process, habeas corpus, and trial by jury. After 1850, personal liberty laws multiplied.

Private citizens immediately responded to the 1850 federal fugitive slave legislation with defiant words and deeds. "To law framed of such iniquity I owe no allegiance," the Rev. Theodore Parker of Boston preached. "Humanity, Christianity, manhood revolts against it. . . . For myself I say it solemnly, I will shelter, I will help, and I will defend the fugitive with all my humble means and power. I will act with any body of decent and serious men, as the head, or the foot, or the hand, in any mode not involving the use of deadly weapons, to nullify and defeat the operation of this law."[11]

"Owen Lovejoy lives at Princeton, Illinois, three-quarters of a mile east of the village, and he aids every fugitive that comes to his door and asks it," proclaimed that congressman in 1859. "Thou invisible demon of slavery, dost thou think to cross my humble threshold, and forbid me to give bread to the hungry and shelter to the homeless! I bid you defiance in the name of my God!" All over the North, attempts to rescue arrested fugitives resulted in riots.

Officials, theoretically governed by both federal and state laws, were placed in an unenviable situation. Pity those of Troy, New York, who in 1859 arrested one Charles Nalle at the request of his master (who was also Nalle's white half-brother). According to one version, Harriet Tubman, who was visiting Troy, rushed to the office of the U.S. commissioner who was holding Nalle prisoner. A crowd had already gathered there and had become so excited that the officials dared not take Nalle down to a waiting wagon. Tubman added to the disorder by sending little boys to cry "Fire!" The officers tried to clear the stairs, but there stood Tubman, the revered "Moses" of her people, in the way.

Whatever Tubman's role, efforts by the officers to take Nalle down through the crowd resulted in "pulling, hauling, mauling, and shouting"; pistols were drawn, and chisels were used as weapons. Rescuers seized Nalle and put him in a skiff, to be ferried across the river to West Troy. But there, still manacled, he was again arrested; four hundred persons again rushed to the rescue, attacking the barricaded office where he was being held. According to a newspaper account, "Soon a stone flew against the door—then another—and bang, bang! went off a couple of pistols but the officers who fired them took good care to aim pretty high. The assailants were forced to retreat for a moment. 'They've got pistols,' said one. 'Who cares?' was the reply; 'they can only kill a dozen of us—come on.' More stones and more pistol-shots ensued. At last the door was pulled open by an immense negro, and in a moment he was felled by a hatchet in the hands of Deputy-Sheriff Morrison; but the body of the fallen man blocked up the door so that it could not be shut, and a friend of the prisoner pulled him out."[13] Nalle ultimately found a safe haven in Canada.

But another mob was unable to rescue from jail the fugitive slave and Baptist preacher Anthony Burns. Hired out by his owner, he had stowed away on a vessel bound from Richmond to Boston, where his owner had tracked him down and had him arrested on a false charge of theft. After the failed rescue attempt, in which a policeman was killed, federal troops, the state militia, and the Boston police were called out to restore order. They faced some 50,000 infuriated Massachusetts residents. Nonetheless, the federal government returned Burns to Virginia, at an estimated cost of $100,000.

Often during these confrontations, peaceably inclined abolitionists tried to resolve matters by offering to purchase the fugitive, only to have their offers refused. So it was with Charles Nalle, with Anthony Burns, and also with Shadrach, a fugitive arrested in Massachusetts in 1851 by federal officers and held in the federal courthouse because the state refused the use of any of its buildings. He was ultimately rescued by a crowd of blacks, who sent him to Canada. Rejections of their offers of money hardened the conviction of many abolitionists that only force could end the abuses of slavery.

Some nine hundred fugitive slaves were returned to their owners between 1850 and 1861, many of them without resistance, especially along the Ohio River and the Mason-Dixon Line. But according to southern estimates, they represented no more than a tenth of the slaves who escaped during those years. The fugitive slave laws did little to protect the property of slaveholders and much to propel the nation into war.

## Chronicle of Events

### 1660

Virginia provides that any English servant who runs away with blacks who are servants for life (and therefore cannot be punished by having the term of their servitude extended) shall himself serve extended time to compensate for the blacks' absence.

### 1687

Eleven slaves flee by boat to Spanish Florida, asking for Roman Catholic baptism and claiming that their former owners will not allow them to learn Roman Catholic doctrine. The Spaniards refuse to return them but pay their former masters for them. (See 1731.)

### 1699

A Spanish royal decree promises protection "to all Negro deserters from the English who [flee] to St. Augustine and [become] Catholics."

### 1717

New York passes legislation prohibiting slaves from running away.

### 1730

The Spanish decide that slaves who flee from Carolina to Florida will be sold and the proceeds given to their former masters. (See 1731.)

### 1731

The Spanish decide that slaves who flee from Carolina to Florida will be neither returned nor paid for.

### 1733

A Spanish decree welcomes English slaves to Florida, with the result that many march there in groups from South Carolina.

The governor of South Carolina offers £20 alive and £10 dead for "Several Run away Negroes who are near the Congerees, & have robbed several of the Inhabitants thereabouts."

### 1738

*March:* Spanish Florida grants freedom and land to runaway slaves and proclaims that all runaways who come in the future will be free, encouraging them to "unite themselves to our arms" in the coming war against the English.

*June 10:* The freed runaway slaves promise that "they [will] always be the most cruel enemies of the English."

*November 21:* When 23 runaway slaves arrive in St. Augustine, the governor announces that he will establish them at a well-fortified settlement at Mosa at the mouth of the St. Johns River.

### 1739

*September:* Slaves sack and burn the armory at Stono, South Carolina, then march toward a Spanish Florida fort manned by a black militia company. On the way they enlist more fugitives, gather arms, kill whites, and stir expectations of freedom. The rebellion is crushed by the state militia.

*December:* South Carolina militia is called out to pursue a group of fugitive slaves committing robberies around Dorchester.

### 1740

*May–July:* In the "Inglorious Expedition," Georgia and Carolina troops attempt to invade Florida in retaliation for "the Protection our deserted Slaves have met with" there.

### 1763–1783

Florida, under (temporary) British rule, no longer functions as a haven for fugitive slaves.

### 1776

The Company of Negroes, free Black Loyalists (including fugitive slaves) who have fought on the British side, are evacuated from Boston to Halifax, Nova Scotia.

### 1779

The British commander in chief issues the Phillipsburg Proclamation, offering freedom to every slave who deserts to the British forces.

### 1783

The British leaving New York issue General Birch certificates (so named for a British general) guaranteeing freedom and permission to go to Nova Scotia, or wherever else they choose, to slaves who claim refugee status under the Phillipsburg sanction of 1779.

**1787**
The Northwest Territory Ordinance requires residents of that territory to return fugitive slaves from other American territories and states.

The Constitution of the United States includes a fugitive slave clause.

**1791**
The British parliament charters the Sierra Leone Company to establish a government of the colony of ex-slaves there and to trade with the colony and its hinterland. Black Loyalists in Nova Scotia are invited to settle in Sierra Leone.

**1792**
Eleven hundred freed slaves who had migrated to Nova Scotia after the American Revolution found Freetown, Sierra Leone, in West Africa.

**1793**
The Fugitive Slave Law of 1793 makes the aiding of fugitive slaves a penal offense punishable by a fine of 500 dollars.

**1804**
The Underground Railroad is "incorporated" (though still not named) when General Thomas Boude of Columbia, Pennsylvania, shelters a slave and refuses the demands of her owner to carry her off; the townspeople's sympathies are further roused by the arrival of 56 slaves manumitted by their Virginia owner but claimed by his heirs.

**1814**
In the War of 1812, British vice admiral Alexander Cochrane invites American slaves to take refuge with British forces.

**1819**
The United States annexes East Florida, which has been a refuge for runaway slaves.

**1829**
Mexico abolishes slavery and welcomes fugitives from the United States.

**1830–1840**
The removal of the Indians from the Gulf states and the consequent opening of new cotton fields motivates many slaves to flee for fear of being sold south.

Isaac Hopper, credited with using Underground Railroad methods as early as 1787 (*Library of Congress*)

**1831**
The Underground Railroad receives its name.

**1836**
Texas slaveholders complain about slaves escaping to Mexico.

Texas law provides punishments for harboring runaway bondsmen.

Philadelphians organize a society called the Underground Railroad, in actuality a branch of the much larger informal network.

**1837**
A group of fugitive slaves kills a Texas sheriff and escapes into Mexico.

**1844**
Twenty-five mounted and armed slaves leave Bastrop, Texas, for Mexico; seven or eight apparently make good their escape.

**1845**
*July:* Seventy-five Maryland slaves arm and begin to march toward Pennsylvania; some are killed, and 31 are recaptured.

**1847**
Sam Houston asks Pres. James Polk to initiate action on a measure to require the extradition of runaway slaves from Mexico.

**1848**
In Kentucky a white college student leads 75 slaves toward the Ohio River; after two battles all the slaves are killed or recaptured.

Residents of a small Michigan town defy slave catchers by escorting a fugitive family out of town.

Black women in Cincinnati, armed with washboards and rolling pins, prevent the recapture of fugitives who have just crossed the Ohio River.

Seventy to 80 slaves attempt to escape from Washington, D.C., on the schooner *Pearl,* only to be captured.

**1849–1850**
Seminole Indian chief Wild Cat immigrates to Coahila, Mexico, with 150–800 Indians and fugitive blacks.

**1850**
The new fugitive slave law strengthens the property rights of slaveholders and endangers blacks living in free states. The federal government rigorously enforces it, but states react by passing personal liberty laws.

Many blacks leave for Canada, including 200 armed Pittsburgh waiters vowing to die before being taken back into slavery.

Several hundred blacks rout Creek Indians and escape to Mexico.

Thirty Missouri slaves arm themselves and march toward freedom, but they surrender when surrounded by heavily armed whites.

**1851**
In Boston, Shadrach, seized by slave catchers and brought into court, is rescued. Eight blacks and whites are indicted, but the jury does not convict.

In Syracuse, New York, the fugitive Jerry is rescued from a police station. Eighteen are indicted, but the jury does not convict.

In Christiana, Pennsylvania, armed blacks under the leadership of William Parker, in a pitched battle to prevent the recapture of four fugitive slaves, kill Maryland slave owner Edward Gorsuch.

John Brown forms the black League of Gileadites in Springfield, Massachusetts, to resist the Fugitive Slave Law of 1850.

Philadelphians form the General Vigilance Committee to resist the Fugitive Slave Law of 1850.

Ellen Craft, who in 1848 escaped while disguised as a young planter, with her husband as her valet (*Seibert,* Underground Railroad)

**1854**
Despite strong opposition from Massachusetts citizens, the federal government returns fugitive Anthony Burns to his Virginia master, at a cost of $100,000.

**1856**
In Colorado City, Texas, a large group (perhaps four hundred) of free and hired-out Negroes, assisted by Mexicans, devise a plan for slaves to rise and fight their way to Mexico.

**1857**
The Mexican government again rebuffs U.S. overtures for a treaty providing for the return of fugitive slaves.

**1858**
A Texas law stipulates that anyone returning a runaway from a nonslave area will receive one-third of the value of the slave from the state treasury.

Allegedly, black leaders George De Baptiste and William Lambert organize in Detroit a secret society (African-American Mysteries? Order of the Men of Oppression? Order of Emigration?) to assist fugitives.

A biracial group from Oberlin, Ohio, rescues fugitive John Price and sends him to Canada.

**1862**
In Corinth, Mississippi, blacks in a contraband camp organize a cohesive community for work, education, and worship. In 1863 the federal military demands that it be dismantled.

## Eyewitness Testimony

### *Escaping*

Whereas many persons of this Colony [Connecticut] doe for their necessary use purchase negroe seruants, and often times the sayd seruants run away to the great wronge, damage and disapoyntment of their masters and owners, for prevention of which for the future, as much as may be, it is ordered by this Court that Whateuer negroe or negroes shall hereafter, at any time, be fownd wandring out of the towne bownds or place to which they doe belong, without a ticket or pass from the authority, or their masters or owners, shall be stopt and secured by any of the inhabitants, or such as shall meet with them, and brought before the next authority to be examined and returned to their owners, who shall sattisfy for the charge if any be. . . .

*1690, in Williams,* History of the Negro Race *1:253–54.*

Whereas many times negroes, mulattoes, and other slaves unlawfully absent themselves from their masters and mistresses service, and lie hid and lurk in obscure places killing hoggs and committing other injuries to the inhabitants . . . *Be it enacted* . . . their majesties justices of the peace of the country [where such Negroes are hiding out] . . . are hereby impowered and commanded to issue out their warrants directed to the sherrife . . . to apprehend such negroes, mulattoes, and other slaves, which said sherriffe is hereby likewise required upon all such occasions to raise such and soe many forces from time to time as he shall think convenient and necessary for the effectual apprehending . . . [and] it shall and may be lawfull . . . to kill and destroy such negroes . . . slaves by gunn or any otherwise whatsoever.

*Provided* that where any negroe or mulattoe slave or slaves shall be killed . . . the owner . . . shall be paid . . . four thousand pounds of tobacco by the publique.

*Virginia act, 1691, Finkelman,* Law of Freedom, *18.*

[The fugitive is] sensible and artful, speaks quick, and sometimes stutters a little; HE MAY POSSIBLY HAVE A TICKET THAT I GAVE HIM TWO DAYS BEFORE HE WENT AWAY, DATED THE 6TH OF APRIL, MENTIONING HE WAS IN QUEST OF A RUNAWAY, AS I DID NOT MENTION WHEN HE WAS TO RETURN, HE MAY ENDEAVOUR TO PASS BY THAT.

*Advertisement in* South Carolina Gazette, *May 1, 1786, quoted in Blassingame,* Slave Community, *115.*

[I]n the evening of the 19th December 1815, . . . a black woman, destined for transportation to Georgia with a coffle, which was about to start, attempted to escape, by jumping out of the window of the garret of a three story brick tavern in F. street, about day-break in the morning. . . . [A doctor] was called to visit her immediately after her fall, and found, besides her arms

". . . But I did not want to go, and I jump'd out of the window."

An abolitionist's conception of a slave trying to escape her captors (*Torrey,* American Slave Trade)

being broken, that the lower part of the spine was badly shattered, so that it was doubtful whether she would ever be capable of walking again, if she should survive. . . .

. . . Asking her what was the cause of her doing such a frantic act as that, she replied, "They brought me away with two of my children, and wouldn't let me see my husband—they didn't sell my husband, and I didn't want to go;—l was so confused and 'istracted, that I didn't know hardly what I was about—but I didn't want to go, and I jumped out of the window;—but I am sorry now that I did it;—they have carried my children off with 'em to Carolina."

*Torrey,* American Slave-Trade, *67–69.*

The chief practical difficulty . . . was connected with the youngest two of the children. They were of three and two years respectively, and of course would have to be carried. . . . Sometime previously I had directed her [my wife] to make me a large knapsack of two-cloth, large enough to hold them both, and arranged with strong straps to go round my shoulders. . . . I resolved to start on the night of the following Saturday. Sunday was a holiday; on Monday and Tuesday I was to be away on farms distant from the house; thus several days would elapse before I should be missed. . . .

It was a dark, moonless night, when we got into the little skiff, in which I had induced a fellow-slave to set us across the river. . . . In the middle of the stream the good fellow said to me, "It will be the end of me if this is ever found out; but you won't be brought back alive, Sie, will you?" "Not if I can help it;" I replied; and I thought of the pistols and knife I had bought some time before of a poor white. . . . For a fortnight we pressed steadily on, keeping to the road during the night, hiding whenever a chance vehicle or horseman was heard, and during the day burying ourselves in the woods. Our provisions were rapidly giving out. Two days before reaching Cincinnati they were utterly exhausted. All night long the children cried with hunger, and my poor wife loaded me with reproaches for bringing them into such misery. . . . But now something must be done; it was necessary to run the risk of exposure by daylight upon the road. . . .[At the first house] I asked if he would sell me a little bread and meat. He was a surly fellow. "No, I have nothing for niggers!" At the next, I succeeded no better, at first. The man of the house met me in the same style; but his wife, hearing our conversation, said to her husband, "How can you treat any human being so? If a dog was hungry I would give him something to eat.". . . She asked me to come in, loaded a plate with venison and bread, and, when I laid it into my handkerchief, and put a quarter of a dollar on the table, she quietly took it up and put it in my handkerchief, with an additional quantity of venison. . . .

[That night they reached Cincinnati, where members of the underground railroad provided rest and shelter and sent them thirty miles by wagon. After that they walked, traveling by night and resting by day, almost starving when their road cut through a wilderness. But they came upon an Indian village, where the Indians fed them, gave them a wigwam in which to rest, and guided them on their way. In Sandusky, Ohio, Henson found work loading a ship, and a sympathetic captain, who agreed to take the Henson family to Buffalo.] The next evening we reached Buffalo, but it was too late to cross the river that night. "You see those trees," said the noble-hearted captain, next morning, pointing to a group in the distance; "they grow on free soil, and as soon as your feet touch that, you're a *mon*.". . . "Here, Green," said he to a ferryman, "What will you take this man and his family over for—he's got no money?" "Three shillings." He then took a dollar out of his pocket and gave it to me. . . .

It was the 28th of October, 1830, in the morning, when my feet first touched the Canada shore.

*Autobiography of the Rev. Josiah Henson, in* Four Fugitive Slave Narratives, *60–69 passim.*

[In 1845 in Maryland on a road there appeared] a group of slaves numbering about seventy-five men . . . in marching order headed for the free state of Pennsylvania. One of the slaves had a gun, another a pistol, and the rest carried scythe blades, swords and clubs. They went six abreast headed by a powerful negro fellow, sword in hand.

*In Harding,* River, *113–14.*

Early yesterday morning a negro drayman carried to the office of Adams & Company's Express, two large square boxes addressed to "Williamson, No.———, Buttonwood Street, Philadelphia." On being interrogated as to whence they came, the negro showed some confusion. Still the boxes were placed on the

Express wagon and transported to the cars. As the driver of the wagon turned one of the boxes over rather roughly, he heard a sort of grunt, which proceeded from it. Suspicion was aroused, the boxes opened, and each one found to contain a stout negro, carefully folded up, with a small quantity of bread and a bladder of water, and one of them with a fan—a useful article in his warm situation.

*New Orleans,* Daily Delta, *May 7, 1849, quoted in* American Slavery, *17.*

The Dismal Swamps [in the Carolinas] are noted places of refuge for runaway negroes. They were formerly peopled in this way much more than at present. . . .[C]hildren were born, bred, lived, and died here. Joseph Church [a slave owned by a church] told me [in 1853] he had seen skeletons, and had helped to bury bodies recently dead. There were people in the swamps still, he thought, that were the children of runaways, and who had been runaways themselves "all their lives.". . .

[Nowadays] They cannot obtain the means of supporting life without coming often either to the outskirts to steal from the plantations, or to the neighbourhood of the camps of the lumbermen. They depend much upon the charity or the wages given them by the latter. The poorer white men, owning small tracts of the swamps, will sometimes employ them, and the negroes frequently. In the hands of either they are liable to be betrayed to the negro-hunters. . . .

*Olmsted,* Cotton Kingdom, *121.*

I have known runaways to lodge in the kitchen of a gentleman in town for months at a time, without ever being discovered and supported entirely by his own servants; there is scarcely a runaway in any neighborhood but a portion of the servants know about it and assist in supporting him.

*Virginia overseer, in Cole, "Militant Black Women," in* Black Women in American History, *266.*

I lived in that dismal little hole, almost deprived of light and air, and with no space to move my limbs, for nearly seven years [after I had hidden from my master]. . . .[M]y body still suffers from the effects of that long imprisonment, to say nothing of my soul. . . . Countless were the nights that I sat late at the little loophole scarcely large enough to give me a glimpse of one twinkling star. . . .Season after season, year after year, I peeped at my children's faces, and heard their sweet voices, with a heart yearning all the while to say, "Your mother is here." Sometimes it appeared to me as if ages had rolled away since I entered upon that gloomy, monotonous existence. At times, I was stupefied and listless; at other times I became very impatient. . . .

*Jacobs,* Slave Girl, *224–25.*

The trader . . . sold the chance of me to [Timothy] Guard for $1,000. The conditions were, if Guard ever saw me in the United States, he was to pay the money. He saw me the next night, for I went in. I had a previous understanding with Guard, that if he bought me, I was to have a chance to buy myself. He gave me a paper signed before witnesses, that I was to be free, when I paid him $1,600. He also gave me papers stating that I was allowed to trade for myself: if I would not pay, he would, and if any one would not pay me, he would compel them. I went to work as steward of a steamboat [on the Mississippi]. At first, I got $35 a month, which raised till I got $100 a month. I paid off Guard between six and seven years after. . . .

*Aaron Sidles,* A North-Side View, *in* Four Fugitive Slave Narratives, *190.*

I hope you will remember me now just the same as you did when I was there with you because my mind are with you night and day the Love that I bear for you in my breast is greater than I thought it was if I had thought I had so much Love for you I dont think I ever Left being I have escape and has fled into a land of freedom I can but stop and look over my past Life and say what a fool I was for staying in bondage as Long My dear wife I dont want you to get married before you send me some letters because I never shall get married until I see you again My mind dont deceive and it appears to me as if I shall see you again.

*Samuel Washington Johnson, in Gutman,* Black Family, *266–67.*

## *Helping the Fugitives: "Negro Stealing"*

Divers evil and ill-disposed persons have hitherto attempted to steal away negroes or other slaves, by specious pretence of promising them freedom in another country, against which pernicious practice no punishment suitable hath been yet provided.

*South Carolina legislature, 1712, in Higginbotham,* In the Matter of Color, *187.*

[John] Fairfield, [a southern abolitionist], . . . would go South into the neighborhood where the slaves were whom he intended to conduct away and, under an assumed name and a false pretence of business, engage boarding, perhaps at the house of the master whose stock of valuable property he intended to decrease. He would proclaim himself to be a Virginian and profess to be strongly pro-slavery in his sentiments, thus lulling the suspicions of the slaveholders while he established a secret understanding with the slaves—gaining their confidence and making arrangements for their escape. Then he would suddenly disappear from the neighborhood and several slaves would be missing at the same time. . . .

Fairfield was several times betrayed and arrested in the South and put in prison, but being a Free Mason, high in the Order, he managed to get out of prison without being tried. . . .

. . . At one time I was told of one of Fairfield's adventures up the Kanawha River, near Charleston, Virginia. Several colored people in Ohio, who had relatives in slavery at and near the salt works, importuned Fairfield to bring them away. . . . Taking two free colored men with him whom he claimed as his slaves, he went to the salt works on the Kanawha and professing to be from Louisville, Kentucky, said that he had come to engage in the salt trade. He contracted for the building of two boats and for salt with which to load them when finished. These arrangements afforded time for his colored men to become acquainted with the slaves he wished to rescue, gain their confidence, and mature the plans for their escape.

Some of the slaves were good boatmen, as also were Fairfield's men, and it was planned that when the first boat was finished, one of the slaves and one of Fairfield's men should get into it on Saturday night and float down the river a short distance and to a point agreed upon and take in a company of slaves, both men and women. They were then to take advantage of the high water and swift current of the Kanawha, and make all possible speed to the Ohio River. . . .

When Fairfield learned that one of his boats and one of his men were gone, he affected to be much enraged and accused his other man of having some knowledge of the affair, and threatened him with severe punishment. The man denied having any part in the plot, but Fairfield professed to doubt him and said that he should watch him closely.

. . . Fairfield remained at the salt works to await the completion of his other boat and to watch his other negro servant, of whom he professed to be very distrustful. In a few days the boat was completed and the next Saturday night it disappeared, together with Fairfield's negro man and ten or twelve slaves. Fairfield was now ruined! both his boats and both his slaves were gone; and the loss of his property made him almost frantic. He started in hot pursuit, accompanied by several men. . . . When they reached the Ohio River they found the boat tied to the bank on the Ohio side, but the fugitives were gone.

The pursuers ferried across the river and, according to Fairfield's suggestion, divided company and took different routes, with the understanding that they were all to meet at a point designated. But Fairfield never met them and was never seen at the salt works afterward. . . .

*Coffin,* Reminiscences, *275–79 passim.*

To me, it [the publication of *Uncle Tom's Cabin*] was a command. A deep and settled conviction impressed me that it was my duty to help the oppressed to freedom. . . .

I was initiated into a knowledge of the relief societies, and the methods adopted to circulate information among the slaves of the South; the routes to be taken by the slaves, after reaching the so-called free states; and the relief posts, where shelter and aid for transportation could be obtained. . . .

On my arrival in Richmond [in 1857], . . . I spent a few weeks in quietly determining upon the best plans to adopt. Having finally decided upon my course, I invited a number of the most intelligent, active and reliable slaves to meet me at the house of a colored preacher, on a Sunday evening. On the night appointed for this meeting, forty-two slaves came to hear what prospect there was for an escape from bondage. . . . I explained to them my . . . purpose in visiting the slave states, the various routes from Virginia to Ohio and Pennsylvania, and the names of friends in border towns who would help them on to Canada. I requested them to circulate this information discreetly among all upon whom they could rely. . . . I requested as many as were ready to accept my offer, to come to the same house on the following Sunday evening, prepared to take the "Underground Railroad" to Canada.

On the evening appointed nine stout, intelligent young men declared their determination to gain their freedom, or die in the attempt. To each I gave a few dollars in money, a pocket compass, knife, pistol, and as much cold meat and bread as each could carry with ease. . . . I learned, many months after, that they all had arrived safely in from slavery; all of whom I had the privilege of forwarding to Canada by the Underground Railroad.

*Canadian Alexander Ross,* Recollections, *3, 5, 10–12.*

[John Mason, a fugitive slave] was willing to risk the forfeiture of his own freedom, that he might, peradventure, secure the liberty of some. He commenced the perilous business of going into the State from whence he had escaped and especially into his old neighborhood, decoying off his brethren to Canada. . . . This slave brought to my house in nineteen months 265 human beings whom he had been instrumental in redeeming from slavery; all of whom I had the privilege of forwarding to Canada by the Underground Railroad. . . . He kept no record as to the number he had assisted in this way. I have only been able, from conversations with him on the subject, to ascertain about 1,300, whom he delivered to abolitionists to be forwarded to Canada. Poor man! He was finally captured and sold.

*Black missionary Rev. W. M. Mitchell, in Siebert,* Underground Railroad, *184.*

## *Helping the Fugitives: The Underground Railroad*

Soon after we located at Newport [Indiana], I found that we were on a line of the U.G.R.R. [Underground Railroad]. Fugitives often passed through that place, and generally stopped among the . . . families of free colored people, mostly from North Carolina, who were the descendants of slaves who had been liberated by Friends many years before. . . . I learned that the fugitive slaves who took refuge with these people were often pursued and captured. . . . [I] inquired of some of the Friends in our village why they did not take them in and secrete them, when they were pursued, and then aid them on their way to Canada? I found that they were afraid of the penalty of the law. . . .

In the winter of 1826–27, fugitives began to come to our house. . . .

Many of my pro-slavery customers left me for a time, my sales were diminished, and for a while my business prospects were discouraging, yet my faith was not shaken, nor [did] my efforts for the slaves lessen. New customers soon came in. . . . My trade increased and I enlarged my business. I was blessed in all my efforts and succeeded beyond my expectations. The Underground Railroad business increased as time advanced, and it was attended with heavy expenses, which I could not have borne had not my affairs been prosperous. . . . We had different routes for sending the fugitives to depots, ten, fifteen, or twenty miles distant, and when we heard of slave-hunters having passed on one road, we forwarded our passengers by another. . . .

[T]hree principal lines from the South converged at my house. . . . The roads were always in running order, the connections were good, the conductors active and zealous, and there was no lack of passengers. . . . We knew not what night or what hour of the night we would be roused from slumber by a gentle rap at the door. That was the signal announcing the arrival of a train of the Underground Railroad, for the locomotive did not whistle, nor make any unnecessary noise. . . .

[Slave-hunters] often threatened to kill me and at various times offered a reward for my head. I often received anonymous letters warning me that my store, porkhouse, and dwelling would be burned to the ground, and one letter, mailed in Kentucky, informed me that a body of armed men were then on their way to Newport to destroy the town. . . .

*Coffin,* Reminiscences, *70, 72–73, 76.*

In the year 1831, a fugitive named Tice Davids came over the line and lived just back of Sandusky. . . .

When he was running away, his master, a Kentuckian, was in close pursuit and pressing him so hard that when the Ohio River was reached he had no alternative but to jump in and swim across. It took his master some time to secure a skiff, in which he and his aid followed the swimming fugitive, keeping him in sight until he had landed. Once on shore, however, the master could not find him. . . . [A]fter a long . . . search the disappointed slave-master went into Ripley, and when inquired of as to what had become of his slave, said . . . he thought "the nigger

Harriet Tubman, the "Moses" who guided escaped slaves to freedom (*Siebert,* Underground Railroad)

must have gone off on an underground road." . . . [T]his incident gave the name to the line. First the "Underground Road," afterwards "Underground Railroad."

*Smedley,* Underground Railroad, *34, 35.*

The abolition incendiaries are undermining, not only our domestic institutions, but the very foundations of our capital. Our citizens will recollect that the boy, Jim, who was arrested while lurking about the Capitol in August, would disclose nothing until he was subjected to torture by screwing his fingers in a blacksmith's vice, when he acknowledged that he was to have been sent North by railroads. . . . Nothing more could be got from him until they gave the screw another turn, when he said, *"the railroad went underground all the way to Boston."*

*Washington, D. C., newspaper, October 1839, in Buckmaster,* Let My People Go, *108–9.*

The way was so toilsome over the rugged mountain passes, that often the *men* who followed [Harriet Tubman] would give out, and foot-sore, and bleeding, they would drop on the ground, groaning that they could not take another step. They would lie there and die, or if strength came back, they would return on their steps, and seek their old homes again. Then the revolver carried by this bold and daring pioneer, would come out, while pointing it at their heads she would say, "Dead niggers tell no tales; you go on or die!" And by this heroic treatment she compelled them to drag their weary limbs along on their northward journey. . . .

*Sarah Bradford, describing Tubman's methods in leading slaves to freedom, in* Harriet, *39.*

LOW MOOR, May 6, 1859

Mr. C. B. C.,

*Dear Sir:*—By to-morrow evening's mail, you will receive two volumes of the "Irrepressible Conflict" bound in black. After perusal, please forward, and oblige,

Yours truly,
G. W. W.

*Coded letter announcing the arrival of two fugitives, in Siebert,* Underground Railroad, *58.*

Lawrence [Kansas] *April 4th,* 1859

Mr. F. B. Sanbourn

Dear Sir . . . Lawrence has been . . . known and cursed by all slave holders in and out of Mo. for being an abolition town. . . .

. . . In the last four years . . . nearly three hundred fugitives hav[e] passed through and received assistance from the abolitionists here at Lawrence. Thus you see we have been continually strained to meet the heavy demands that were almost daily made upon us to carry on this (not very) *gradual emancipation.* . . . Many of the most zealous in the cause of humanity complained (as they had good cause to) that this heavy (and continually increasing) tax was interfering with their business to such a degree that they could not stand it longer. . . . This was about the state of affairs last Christmas when as you are aware the slaves have a few days holiday. Many of them chose this occasion to make a visit to Lawrence and during the week some twenty four came to our town, five or six of the number brought means to assist them on their journey. These were sent on, but the remainder must be kept until money could be raised to send them on. $150 was the am't necessary to send them to a place of safety. Under the circumstances it necessarily took some time to raise that am't. . . . Lawrence like most all towns has her bad men pimps and worst of all a few democrats, all of whom will do *anything* for money. Somewhere in the ranks of the intimate friends to the cause these traitors to God and humanity found a judas who for thirty pieces of silver did betray our cause. . . . Every thing goes to prove that the capture of [Dr.] Day's party was the work of a traitor. . . . We would like . . . that you plead our cause with those of our friends who are disposed to censure us and convince them we are still worthy and in great need of their respect and cooperation. . . . [H]eavy expenses of the trial of Dr Day and son . . . has been principally borne by the society here and has amounted to near $300. . . . We have some eight or ten fugitives now on hand who cannot be sent off until we get an addition to our financial department.

*Col. J. Bowles to Mr. F. B. Sanborn of Concord, Massachusetts, in Siebert,* Underground Railroad, *347–50.*

[To hide fugitives] I built an addition to my house in which I had a room with its partition in pannels. One pannel could be raised about a half inch and then slid back, so as to permit a man to enter the room. When the pannel was in place it appeared like its fellows. . . . In the abutment of Zanesville bridge on the Putnam side there was a place of concealment prepared.

*Eli F. Brown, in Siebert,* Underground Railroad, *64.*

## *Deterring Runaways: Patrols*

Sir:

According to the law I have appointed Paterrolers [patrollers] to Kech our Negroes in order & to serch all Disorderly houses after night & unlawful Meetings & where they find a large quantity of Negroes assembled at night to take them up and cary them before a justice which has been done but we have a set of disorderly People who calls themselves Methodists and are joined by some of those who call themselves Baptists, who make it a rule two or three times a week to meet after dark & call in all the Negroes they can gather & a few whites & free mulattoes who pretend under the cloak of Religion to meet at a School house where no one lives & there they pretent to preach & pray with a sett of the greatest Roges of Negroes in this County & they never break up Till about two or three o'clock in the morning & those Negroes who stays with them goes through the neighborhood and steels everything they can lay there hands on. . . . & I have ordered the Peterrolers to go to such unlawfull meetings & to take up all the Negroes that they should find at such places which they have done & the masters of the Negroes has approved of this plan very much, but these people who are determined to encorige or [our] Negroes to wrong & the other day they sent to the Capt. of the Paterrolers that on Friday night they wood have a Meeting & if they came there and offered to toch a Negro That they wood protect the Negroes & if they said a word would beat them [the patrollers]. . . .

*Letter from Holt Richardson to the governor of Virginia, September 5, 1789, in Johnston,* Race Relations, *97–98.*

I have known the slaves to stretch clothes lines across the street, high enough to let the horse pass, but not the rider: then the boys would run, and the patrols in full chase would be thrown off by running against the lines. The patrols are poor white men, who live by plundering and stealing, getting rewards for runaways, and setting up little shops on the public roads. They will take whatever the slaves steal, paying in money, whiskey, or whatever the slaves want. They take pigs, sheep, wheat, corn,—any thing that's raised they encourage the slaves to steal: these they take to market next day. It's all speculation—all a matter of self interest, and when the slaves run away, these same traders catch them if they can, to get the reward. If the slave threatens to expose his traffic, he does not care—for the slave's word is good for nothing—it would not be taken. There are frequent quarrels between the slaves and the poor white men.

*Francis Henderson, in Drew,* Refugee, *157.*

## *Deterring Runaways: "Negro Hunters"*

Two or three days since, a gentleman of this parish, in *hunting runaway negroes,* came upon a camp of them in the swamp, arrested two of them, but the third made fight; and upon being *shot in the shoulder,* fled to a sluice, where the *dogs succeeded in drowning him.*

*The St. Francisville (La.)* Chronicle, *February 1, 1839, in Dumond,* Antislavery, *15.*

No particular breed of dogs is needed for hunting negroes: blood-hounds, foxhounds, bull-dogs, and curs were used. . . . They are shut up when puppies, and never allowed to see a negro except while training to catch him. A negro is made to run from them, and they are encouraged to follow him until he gets into a tree, when meat is given them. Afterwards they learn to follow any particular negro by scent, and then a shoe or a piece of clothing is taken off a negro, and they learn to find by scent who it belongs to, and to tree him, etc. . . .

When the hunters take a negro who has not a pass, or "free papers," and they don't know whose slave he is, they confine him in jail, and advertise him. If no one claims him within a year he is sold to the highest bidder, at a public sale, and this sale gives title in law against any subsequent claimant.

*Olmsted,* Cotton Kingdom, *122.*

## *Deterring Runaways: The Fugitive Slave Laws*

If any servant runn away from his master into any other of these confederated Jurisdiccons, That in such case vpon the Certyficate of one Majistrate in the Jurisdiccon out of which the said servant fled, or upon other due proofs, the said servant shall be deliuered either to his Master or any other that pursues and brings such Certificate or proofe.

*Articles of Confederation of the New England Confederation, 1643, in Siebert,* Underground Railroad, *19.*

We have obtained a right [in the U.S. Constitution] to recover our slaves, in whatever part of America they may take refuge, which is a right we have not had before. In short, considering the circumstances, we have made the best terms for the security of this species of property it was in our power to make. We would have made better if we could; but, on the whole, I do not think them bad.

*Pinckney of South Carolina, 1788, in Siebert,* Underground Railroad, *294.*

There was a man came to Hartford [Connecticut] from Savannah. . . . He brought a slave girl with him to care for the smaller children. . . . All went on well for about two years. . . . One day when I was at work in the store, a gentleman came where I was; he asked if this was deacon mars. I said "Yes, sir." He said Mr. Bullock was about to send Nancy to Savannah, "and we want to make a strike for her liberty, and we want some man to sign a petition for a writ of habeas corpus to bring Mr. Bullock before Judge Williams; they tell me that you are the man to sign the petition." . . . The court said it was the first case of the kind ever tried in the State of Connecticut. . . .

At the time appointed all were in attendance to hear from Judge Williams. The judge said that slavery was tolerated in some of the States, but it was not now in this State; we all liked to be free. This girl would like to be free; he said she should be free,—the law of the State made her free, when brought here by her master. . . .

*Ex-slave James Mars,* Life, *55–56, describing an experience in the 1820s (?).*

[T]he master . . . a stranger, must go into a free state, seize his slave without form or process of law, and unaccompanied by a single civil officer, must carry that slave, in the face of a fanatical and infuriated population, perhaps from the centre of extremists of the state, a distance of two or three hundred miles to the place where the judge may happen to reside. . . . [Even when the master gains a favorable judgment,] there is no provision in that law [the Fugitive Slave Law of 1793] by which the judgment can be enforced. . . .

*General Assembly of Virginia, 1849–1850, in Campbell,* The Slave Catchers, *8.*

[In consequence of the Fugitive Slave Law of 1850] people held indignant meetings, and organized committees of vigilance whose duty was to prevent a fugitive from being arrested, if possible, or to furnish legal aid, and raise every obstacle to his rendition. The vigilance committees were also the employees of the U. G. R. R. and effectively disposed of many a *casus belli* [cause of dispute] by transferring the disputed chattel to Canada.

*Abolitionist Rev. Theodore Parker of Boston, in Siebert,* Underground Railroad, *71.*

And Rev. Dr. Dewey, whom we accounted one of the ablest expounders and most eloquent defenders of our Unitarian faith,—Dr. Dewey was reported to have said at two different times, in public lectures or speeches during the fall of 1850 and the winter of

1851, that "he would send his *mother* into slavery, rather than endanger the Union, by resisting this law [the Fugitive Slave Law of 1850] enacted by the constituted government of the nation." He has often denied that he spoke thus of his "maternal relative," and therefore I allow that he was misunderstood. But he has repeatedly acknowledged that he did say, "I would consent that my own brother, my own son, should go, *ten times rather* would I go myself into slavery, than that this Union should be sacrificed."

*May,* Recollections, *367.*

Shall we resist Oppression? Shall we defend our Liberties? Shall we be FREEMEN or SLAVES? . . . Should any one attempt to execute [the] provisions [of the Fugitive Slave Law of 1850] on any one of us, either by invading our home or arresting us in the street, we will treat such an one as assaulting our persons with intent to kill, and, God being our helper, will use such means as will repel the aggressor and defend our lives and liberty.

*New York City blacks,* National Anti-Slavery Standard, *October 10, 1850, in Pease and Pease,* Fugitive Slave Law, *15.*

If any man approaches [my] house in search of a slave—I care not who he may be, whether constable, or sheriff, magistrate or even judge of the Supreme Court—nay let it be President Millard Fillmore surrounded by his cabinet and his bodyguard, with the Declaration of Independence waving above his head as his banner, and the constitution of his country upon his breast as his shield—if he crosses the threshold of my door, and I do not lay him a lifeless corpse at my feet, I hope the grave may refuse my body a resting place, a righteous heaven my spirit a home.

*Black abolitionist Martin Delany, in Harding,* River, *159.*

I know that . . . colored men, men of my complexion . . . cannot expect . . . any mercy from the laws, from the constitution, or from the courts of the country. . . . I stand here to say that if, for doing what I did . . . I am to go in jail six months and pay a fine of a thousand dollars, according to the Fugitive Slave law . . . I . . . say that I will do all I can for any man thus seized and held, though the inevitable penalty . . . hangs over me.

*Charles Langston of Ohio, 1858, jailed for aiding a fugitive, in Harding,* River, *210.*

In nineteen cases out of twenty where a fugitive slave enters Illinois, he is arrested and returned without any judicial process whatever. Those portions of the State which border on the Kentucky and Missouri lines are in harmony with their neighbors on the other side, and a fugitive slave is returned as regularly as a stolen horse.

*Sen. Stephen A. Douglas, in Campbell,* The Slave Catchers, *112.*

# 7

# Canada, Other Refuges, and the Colonization/ Emigration Movement 1501–1865

## The Historical Context

### *Slavery in Canada*

Throughout most of its history, Canada has put up with a great deal of pother from its neighbor to the south, a good bit of which sprang from that neighbor's ugly and awkward dealings with slavery.

Why did Canada itself not institutionalize slavery? After all, some form of slavery, whether among the native Indians or imported by Europeans, probably existed as early in Canada as in the rest of North America. Early on, though, climate, geography, economics, religion, and politics combined to stunt its growth and to let it die a natural and relatively painless death.

In New France, French policy fairly consistently called for an economy based on furs and fish—an economy that would not threaten the industries of the mother country. Neither trapping nor fishing required a large labor force, so neither created a demand for slaves. Now and then someone in New France, whether an official sent out from France or a local inhabitant, pled for slaves wherewith to promote shipbuilding or mining, but France regularly dismissed these pleas in short order.

The dominant Roman Catholic church condoned slavery—monks and nuns owned slaves—but also insisted on the slave's possession of an immortal soul and the virtue of pleasing God by freeing slaves. Most slaves were baptized into Christianity, often with the master as godfather. With its inheritance of Roman law, France regarded slavery as a temporary plight, not as a condition based on natural inferiority. Most slaves in New France, whether Indians (*panis*) or blacks, lived in or near Montreal, rather than in the isolated countryside. Most worked as domestics, a few in each household, living closely with their masters and mistresses. In such intimate circumstances, slaves and owners sometimes intermarried, white men usually marrying *panis* and white women usually marrying black slaves.

Canadian Dr. Alexander Ross, famous for his daring invasions of the American South to help slaves escape (*Siebert,* Underground Railroad)

All these factors tended to mitigate slavery in New France. Slaves there were sold publicly, often alongside livestock. But slave trading was limited and almost entirely domestic. The number of slaves in New France probably never exceeded 4,000, with Indian slaves significantly outnumbering blacks. In 1759, of the 3,604 slaves recorded, only 1,132 were black.[1]

If slavery was seldom questioned in New France, neither was it defended. It just was, but only the slaves cared very much, nobody needed slaves very much, nobody was profiting from slaves very much, and nobody was gaining status from owning slaves. Eventually slavery dwindled, though it still existed when in 1763 the British took over the colony, and the Treaty of Paris of that date recognized it.

In the rest of what is now Canada slavery existed only incidentally among some of the Indian tribes and among settlers who brought slaves with them. The northern climate did not call for large gangs to work the land, and indentured servants met the need for laborers at least as well as slaves would have. It was expensive to maintain slaves throughout the long, cold winters. Particularly after 1787, when the American Northwest Territory was declared legally free of slavery, it was difficult to hang on to slaves: they could so easily flee south, and the Canadian courts were apt to rule against masters in favor of fugitives. The very hardships of the Canadian terrain and climate gave prestige to manual work more quickly than in the American South. Over the years, Canadians came to think of slavery as an *American* phenomenon, to be deplored rather than adopted.

Sadly, the early demise of slavery in Canada did not end prejudice against non-whites, which to the contrary mounted through the years with successive increases in the black population.

## *The First Wave: The Loyalist Blacks of the American Revolution*

From the time of the American Revolution, the black population in Canada grew almost entirely because American blacks sought freedom there. Providing and sustaining a refuge for these fugitives was no easy task.

Invariably, whether slaves fled to Canada individually or were transported there in mass migrations, resettlement proved much more difficult than anyone had anticipated. On the whole, Canadian governments set an admirable record in dealing with refugees, trying persistently to help them, however slowly and inefficiently. Individually, white Canadians reacted to the blacks in much the ways of humans anywhere and at any time: some generously, some indifferently, some jealously, and some with the cruelties of racial prejudice.

When in the 1770s American colonists loyal to the king of England (known as Tories in the thirteen colonies, Loyalists elsewhere), realized that American patriots were going to defy the British government, they began moving to Canada, taking their slaves with them. The numbers of these Loyalists were significant—perhaps as many as 30,000, 10 percent of them black.[2] They usually settled in Quebec or in land east of Montreal. Over the years many of them manumitted their slaves—or simply abandoned responsibility for them. The work these slaves had formerly done did not exist in their new homes, and their owners now found it expensive to feed, shelter, and clothe them. With the Tories, though, came an increase in the domestic slave trade. Quebec's black population also increased in 1777, when Vermont outlawed slavery and many owners sold their slaves into Quebec. But in the Revolutionary period, most blacks immigrated into Nova Scotia.

Throughout the history of American slavery, wartime gave slaves opportunities to seek refuge with the enemy. So it was with wars between the Indians and the white settlers, the American Revolution, the War of 1812, and the Civil War. Sometimes, blacks fleeing to their masters' enemies found the freedom they sought, sometimes not, for some of those enemies regarded the slaves as spoils of war, to be sold for individual profit. Moreover, Englishmen who promised the slaves freedom in the heat of battle usually had no firm plan about what to do with them afterward. Sometimes, they genuinely wanted to help the slaves, but more often they were focused on depriving the Americans of labor and valuable property. During the Revolution and the War of 1812, the English might use the defecting slaves' labor to their own advantage or even enlist them to fight against their former masters—but what was to be done with them later?

Indians who took black captives in wars or raids might sell them back to white Americans or adopt them into their tribes. But for the British during the

American Revolution and the War of 1812, the usual solution was to remove them to another location. Among the locations considered, Canada always featured prominently.

At the end of the American Revolution, but before the Treaty of Paris, Sir Guy Carleton, commander in chief of British troops in North America, guaranteed the freedom of all slaves who sought asylum behind British lines and formally claimed British protection. Carleton tried to handle the disposition of these blacks fairly, promising to recompense their owners and to offer the former slaves a choice of places in which to settle—the West Indies, Florida (temporarily), or Canada. On what basis were these newly freed slaves, many of them former field hands, to choose? Most opted for Jamaica or St. Augustine, but many could find no work there and later had to be transferred elsewhere. Ultimately, a good many of them landed in Nova Scotia—by about 1783 the province probably contained about 3,000 free blacks, of whom 1,336 were men, 914 women, and 750 children.[3] Carleton had not stopped to get the consent of the authorities in Nova Scotia, leaving them to cope as best they could with this influx of immigrants, most of whom through no fault of their own were indigent, unskilled, illiterate, and without experience in living independently.

The authorities of Nova Scotia tried to deal with the situation, conscious that the British had made promises to the blacks, some of whom, indeed, had fought for England. The Nova Scotians got their neighbors in New Brunswick to take in some; they kept some at work for a while repairing military barracks. To many they gave grants of land, seeds, and rations to sustain them until their first crops were harvested.

But everything went wrong. Most of the black immigrants had little if any experience in farming on their own, certainly not in the thin soil and endless winters of Canada. They felt, sometimes with reason, that the authorities were not dealing with them fairly. Unable to read or do accounts, they fell prey to the scams of opportunistic whites. Too many of them lived in near peonage, sharecropping for their neighbors, miserably clothed, housed, and fed, and repeatedly having to be rescued from starvation. In these circumstances, they could not rally to build a self-sustaining community. Only here and there did a black clergyman provide the leadership to stimulate the cooperation necessary to lift the community by its own efforts.

## *Sierra Leone, a Refuge from a Refuge*

Into this misery hope came in 1791, in the form of an offer to emigrate once again, this time to Sierra Leone in West Africa. The idea originated in England, where a 1772 court decision effectively ending slavery precipitated the question of what was to become of the blacks there, now free. The answer—establish in Africa the black colony of Sierra Leone. The answer made more sense at the end of the 18th century than it would later, for many of the new freedmen had actually been born in Africa.

The colony was founded in 1791. That year, black leader Thomas Peters arrived in England with a petition from 102 Nova Scotian and 100 New Brunswick black families complaining of their wrongs and asking "to procure . . . some establishment where [they] may attain a competent settlement for themselves and be enabled by their industrious exertions to become useful subjects to His Majesty." Sierra Leone seemed the obvious solution.

Peters certainly thought so. When the Sierra Leone Company, formed by a group of British abolitionists, offered to transport to the new colony free blacks with good character references, pay off their debts, and give each adult male 20 acres of land there, Peters enthusiastically began recruiting in Canada—too enthusiastically. Things got off to a bad start; both Peters and his English coworker exceeded their authority, propagandizing rather than trying to select only blacks genuinely dissatisfied with their lot in Canada, and promising that the future landholders would have to pay neither rent nor taxes, though the Sierra Leone Company had made no such guarantee.

Black clergy in Canada supported the project, and in short order the recruiters signed up nearly a thousand blacks. They gathered around Halifax, camping out in the December weather, while the representatives of the Sierra Leone Company scrambled for supplies and ships. On January 10, 1792, 15 ships carrying people and supplies set out on the six-week voyage to Sierra Leone.

It is hard to overestimate the problems confronting the Sierra Leone Company and the new settlers in the infant colony. The settlers must have spent many a despairing night asking themselves why they had ever moved. Provisions arrived late and spoiled. A fever that assailed them on the ships turned into an epidemic on shore, and about a hundred settlers died. So did many of the doctors and storekeepers sent to help them. Materials arrived in the wrong order, equipment for growing cotton before building supplies. Storms destroyed their huts. Quarrels broke out. When land was finally allotted in November, the promised 20 acres dwindled to four. Understandably, when the company tried to collect rents, the settlers rebelled.

One way and another, though, they muddled along. They had come hoping to give their children better opportunities. So most of them stuck it out, clinging together, calling themselves "the Nova Scotians," holding themselves aloof from later immigrants, and furnishing much of the energy and many of the skills on which Sierra Leone depended. This clannishness was encouraged by the strikingly different background of the next group of immigrants to the colony.

## *The Second Wave: The Jamaican Maroons*

Meanwhile, in 1796, Nova Scotia had once again been called upon to deal with another group of black refugees—the Jamaican Maroons. They came from a colony of escaped slaves who for a century had been hiding in the Jamaican interior, constantly reinforced by slaves newly escaped from plantations. They had raided white settlements and intermittently engaged in wars. The last of these wars, begun in 1795, had ended with a negotiated settlement by which the Maroons (possibly from a corruption of the Spanish *cimarron,* meaning "wild" or "untamed") surrendered on condition that they could stay on their own land; the British government of Jamaica had broken faith and deported 556 of them to Nova Scotia. The much-tried Nova Scotia authorities again had not been consulted but nonetheless welcomed them, setting them to work for the military as laborers, finding land for them, appointing officers among them, and giving these longtime warriors uniforms.

All this did not sit well with many Nova Scotians, who found the Maroons' plural wives, their bizarre burial customs, and their swaggering about in military garb offensive. Nor did the Maroons take to Nova Scotia. They hated the climate and complained (often with reason) about the commissioners who supervised their work. The governor, trying to keep the peace, persuaded the Maroons to stay another year on condition that he forward to England their petitions for removal. In 1799, the British offered to pay the costs for transporting these Maroons to Sierra Leone, settling them, and educating them, if the Sierra Leone Company would accept them. In the fall, the British dispatched a ship to pick up the Maroons, with orders to the provincial authorities to deport the lot of them. By that time, the ship was frozen in the ice of the St. Lawrence, and Nova Scotia had to pay for the Maroons' support for another winter. It finally sailed on August 3, 1800. At least 25 of the Maroons died during the voyage, and the rest came near to mutiny.

Clearly they arrived in Sierra Leone in no happy mood. Equally clearly, the "Nova Scotian" residents of Sierra Leone were not happy to see these independent, tough rowdies, as clannish as themselves. For years thereafter the two groups kept apart, doing different work and belonging to different classes.

## *The Third Wave: The War of 1812—The "Refugee Negroes"*

In the War of 1812, American slaves again sought refuge behind British lines. They were well received; the British even entertained hopes of stirring up a slave rebellion.[4] In 1813, the first group was shipped to Nova Scotia—as before, without consultation with the authorities there. Once landed, these former slaves were sent off to the interior to find work. As these "Refugee Negroes" continued to arrive in growing numbers, Nova Scotia did its best to cope, even while questioning the wisdom of such mass immigrations.

The numbers of Refugee Negroes increased in 1814, when British vice admiral Sir Alexander Cochrane invited slaves to come to British warships and military posts. Anyone who did, he promised, would "meet with all encouragement" as a free settler. (Of course, he had not asked Nova Scotia or other possible British refuges about this; the man was trying to win a war and had little time for political niceties.) England later agreed to pay U.S. slave owners more than $1.2 million in compensation for 3,601 slaves who accepted Cochrane's invitation.[5]

Nova Scotia authorities improvised. They sent some who were both penniless and ill to the poor house. There smallpox killed many; vaccination temporarily halted the epidemic, but it broke out again on Melville Island, where new arrivals were kept. The government settled some of the refugees around Halifax, but land there was becoming scarce, and questions were being raised about concentrating the new inhabitants in one place. Nonetheless, most of the refugees arriving in 1814 and early 1815 were established as settlers and were given seeds, agricultural tools, and provisions for two years. Officials theorized that in winter they could work as woodsmen in the forests, cutting lumber for houses and firewood.

By the summer of 1815, the authorities had evolved a more efficient reception method for the Refugee Negroes at Melville Island, under the direction of the chief customs officer. He was empowered to give them the same rations as had been distributed to American prisoners of war in the recent conflict, open a hospital for them, and vaccinate them. He moved them on as fast as he could, presumably in accordance with governmental policy, which now preferred dispersing them among the white population rather than concentrating them in one place. He also discouraged the separation of families, by refusing rations to absent heads of families, for many fathers were leaving their wives and children to look for work in Halifax. In June of 1816, Nova Scotia was able to close down the operation at Melville Island.

Reception and resettlement had cost the province dearly, but what was too much for its taxpayers was not enough for a successful resettlement for the Refugee Negroes. Once again, as for the blacks who had escaped during the American Revolution, and for similar reasons, conditions worsened.

The land distribution did not work. The blacks were disappointed at not receiving outright grants of land, whereas Nova Scotia hesitated to give title to parcels until the occupants had proved that they could make good use of them. The blacks thought the plots too small and the land sterile. Crops failed. They lacked sufficient skill in fishing to earn their livings that way. The closer they moved to a welfare situation, the more the government's efforts went wrong, with relief fraud and refusal of rations to the homeless.

Every now and then, someone came up with a scheme to help. For instance, the surveyor general enthused over a plan for a settlement where a gang of 30 pioneer blacks would put up two houses a day, the next arrivals would clear the fields around the houses, and everybody would plant crops in the spring. The anticipated outcome was an instant flourishing community. In the event, more people arrived than had been expected. Too little land was cleared to feed them. The ground remained frozen until June. The shacks, built of green wood, fell apart. The potatoes froze, because the storage huts for them had been constructed without floors or cellars, and the common land was soon denuded of fuel.

The Council of Nova Scotia, thoroughly weary after this four-year-long nightmare, told the refugees on April 30, 1817, that after the first of June the government would stop handing out rations except to the aged and infirm, gave single men two weeks to find work, promised those who had cleared land more seed potatoes and tools, offered transportation to any refugees who wanted to return to the United States, and pledged to conduct a survey to see who would like to go to Trinidad.

Trinidad was willing, even eager, to receive refugee blacks. But those in Nova Scotia, by this time mistrustful of governmental offers, suspected reenslavement. Ninety-five did accept the offer, and they apparently got along reasonably well in Trinidad. But being illiterate, like most of the friends they had left behind in Nova Scotia, they could not communicate their satisfaction, and their silence was interpreted as a sure sign that they had been reenslaved.

With such effort, why did things go so terribly wrong for the Refugee Negroes? Most of them had been field hands in Maryland and Virginia; they had not learned to live side by side with whites, and not all of them had even had their own garden plots, where they might learn something about farming independently. Earlier refugees, mostly Anglicans and Wesleyans, had fitted more easily into the religious environment, but most of the Refugee Negroes were Baptists, an affiliation that Nova Scotian leaders associated with ignorance. Also, the former slaves had hard luck in their timing. They arrived at a time of especially severe winters and plentiful cheap, white labor. In their inexperience, some of them thought that freedom promised no work and no responsibility. As conditions worsened, instead of cooperating, they stole from each other and quarreled among themselves. The shiftless, poverty-stricken ways of life into which they drifted and the growing racial prejudices of their new white neighbors fed on each other.

Ultimately, most of the Refugee Negroes became permanent wards of the state. Seemingly unassimilable—with the exception of a community in Hammond's Plains—they remained an identifiable group within Nova Scotia until the end of the 19th century.

The five hundred Refugee Negroes in New Brunswick fared no better, possibly worse. A settlement at Loch Lomond failed, acquiring a reputation among whites as a source of trouble. Nearby Loyalist blacks tried to help, but the Refugee Negroes hesitated to cooperate with them because of religious differences. White missionaries and philanthropists succeeded no better. These Refugee Negroes refused the province's offer to resettle them in smaller groups elsewhere. They worked at menial jobs in the cities rather then entering the more stable and better-paying trades of farming, fishing, and lumbering—from which they were in any case blocked by the refusal of master workmen to train them, for fear of possible quarrels among black and white apprentices. So most took jobs as stable boys or hotel servants. Others went to live with Indians.

## *The Fourth Wave: Fugitive Slaves (1815–1861)*

As the number of slaves in the United States grew, as white fears of blacks swelled, and as the laws restricting the actions of slaves tightened, American slaves dreamed of the freedom they might find "under the British lion" in Canada. One by one or in small groups, but in increasing numbers, they "followed the North Star" to a new life in a new land. By the late 1820s, fugitive slaves were arriving in Canada in substantial numbers—which continued to grow right up to the Civil War, eventually constituting the largest group of black immigrants.

Most of those who entered Canada up until 1850 were self-selected, people with the courage and enterprise to flee into the unknown and intelligent enough to make their way through multifarious dangers. Many of them before they went to Canada had lived for a time in northern states, where they had had time to adjust to independent life in a predominantly white community. Ultimately they *chose* Canada. After 1850, when the harsh federal Fugitive Slave Law made it well-nigh impossible for black fugitives to live securely in the free American states and endangered even blacks born free, a more heterogeneous lot of blacks fled to Canada.

Like most refugees, these fugitives were driven by mixed motives, mostly negative. Above all they wanted to escape the miseries and cruelties of their lives as slaves. Like most refugees, they entertained unrealistic hopes for the land to which they fled, envisioning it as a promised land where they would be equal not only before the law but also within the society, where they would be free not only from slavery but also from racial prejudice.

Up until the 1830s, white Canadians did on the whole receive them well. But with the fugitives' increasing numbers, their welcome faded. In the pattern of racial prejudice everywhere, white Canadians began to fear mass migrations.

Fugitives Mr. and Mrs. Samuel Harper (*Siebert,* Underground Railroad)

They transmuted dislike of the actions of individual erring blacks into contempt for all blacks. After the frontier closed and with the arrival of Irish immigrants, Canada needed black labor less. Disputes with the United States over the extradition of fugitive slaves dismayed some, who feared that blacks might prove disloyal to Canada in any conflict with the United States—though in fact blacks were consistently loyal to the British government, sometimes serving in provincial militias.

On the other hand, anti-Americanism led some white Canadians to sympathize with black fugitives. But some Canadians, believing that the United

States had always wanted to annex Canada (news to most Americans), thought that the presence of blacks might make Canada less desirable to it.

If Canadians were ambivalent about the migration of blacks into Canada, so were the blacks. Many of them remained expatriate Americans rather than Canadians. They went to Canada less because they wanted to live there than because they could no longer live in the United States. In 1830, for instance, well-established blacks were forced out of Cincinnati by Ohio's threat to enforce harsh laws against them. More dramatically, the Fugitive Slave Law of 1850 pushed out of northern American cities blacks who had planned to live out their days there. So it was that during the Civil War many Canadian blacks went south to join the Union army and never returned. When the Civil War ended slavery in the United States, thousands of blacks then living in Canada returned to the States, including some of those who had served in the Canadian military, voted there, and acquired property there.

Canadian officialdom acquitted itself most impressively in its refusal to return fugitive slaves to their American masters, despite strong pressures from the U.S. government. This stance was not always easy to maintain. Sometimes fugitive slaves had committed serious crimes, including theft and murder. But Canadian justices consistently maintained that since slavery did not exist in Canada, escaping from slavery certainly did not constitute a crime in Canadian courts, *and neither did an act necessary to its success.* In 1842, the Webster-Ashburton Treaty between Canada and the United States similarly protected fugitives.

## *A Ripple (1859)*

Very late in the history of American slavery, the city of Vancouver offered sanctuary to a small number of free blacks who had been living in California. About 1850, that constitutionally free state had begun restricting blacks, first disqualifying them from giving evidence against white men, then toying with laws that would have permitted newly arrived slaveholders to continue to hold slaves, then returning a fugitive slave to his owner. The blacks of San Francisco, reading the handwriting on the wall, in the spring of 1858 investigated the possibility of emigration to British Columbia, and in April of that year 35 of them sailed. Later that year, perhaps another four hundred families followed.

They were potential citizens that any country not dead set against all blacks would welcome—literate, skilled, intelligent, prosperous, and determined not to segregate themselves. Once arrived, instead of participating in the gold rush then going on in the province, many of them bought property in Vancouver, property that appreciated rapidly.

These blacks were protected in part by their small numbers. But their very success aroused jealousy, and by 1862 racially discriminatory remarks were already appearing in the press.

## *Organized Black Communities*

Beginning in 1830, private efforts organized black communities in Canada, partly to ease the transition to independent life and work there, and partly to afford individuals mutual insurance. To some degree, white philanthropy supported all of them. Some blacks disapproved, arguing that the very existence of these communities implied that blacks could not make their own way without the help of whites. For example, beginning in 1854 the black True Band Societies were formed to protest the practice of begging support for black communities among whites and to advocate black autonomy, self-help, and responsibility. A freeborn black American, Mary Ann Shadd Cary, editor of the *Provincial Freeman* (a newspaper devoted to the interests of blacks in Canada), denounced the Refugee Home Society as a "begging scheme."

None of these organized black communities lasted long. Good intentions led to disastrous outcomes. The starry-eyed white reformers in charge of some of them lacked management skills, or integrity, or both. The communities were torn by strife, jealousy, and distrust.

Dawn, in Canada West (as Ontario and the unsettled lands to its west were known from 1841 to 1867), exemplified the problem. About 1836 a group of Oberlin students, with the support of the American Anti-Slavery Society and other American philanthropists began a series of schools within growing black communities. This British-American Institute eventually sponsored 15 schools for the "Education Mental Moral and physical of the Colored inhabitants of Canada not excluding white persons and Indians."

The Dawn community grew around the first of these manual-labor schools, of which not only the pupils but also the board were integrated. For a while it flourished, reaching a population of some 500 black settlers, who owned some 1,500 acres; it had its own saw and grist mills, brickyard, and ropewalk. Josiah Henson, a famous and prosperous fugitive slave, contributed much to both its short-lived success and its downfall. Divisions among the blacks, bad management, and religious sectarianism had by 1854 buried it in a quagmire of quarrels and lawsuits.

Ironically enough, Elgin (also in Canada West), in some ways the most successful of these communities, was the creation of a slaveholder from Louisiana, who organized and ran it with benevolent paternalism. An intelligent and dedicated man, William King founded Elgin in 1849 with his own freed slaves. He lived there and managed it himself, welcoming churches of all denominations, founding schools so good that they attracted white children from the surrounding countryside, training black teachers who went out to teach in white schools, protecting the civil rights of the black inhabitants, and teaching them to vote in their own interest. Nonetheless, many of them went off to fight in the Civil War, and after the war others sold their property and returned to the United States. Elgin closed in 1873.

Of blacks in Canada in 1862, abolitionist Samuel Gridley Howe commented, "Taken as a whole, the colonists have cost to somebody a great deal of money and a great deal of effort; and they have not succeeded as well as many who have been thrown entirely upon their own resources."[6]

All in all, though Canada was no Utopia for blacks, and although many blacks left it when they could, it afforded thousands—perhaps as many as 40,000 in Canada West alone—physical safety, the protection of law, and political equality.[7] The promise of Sir John Colborne, the lieutenant governor of Upper Canada, to the Cincinnati blacks was kept insofar as the government was concerned: "Tell the Republicans on your side of the line that we do not know men by their color. If you come to us, you will be entitled to all the privileges of the rest of his Majesty's subjects." In the words of Lewis Richardson, once a slave owned by Henry Clay, "[O]n British soil . . . the Government knows me as a man."[8] At great expense, that government tried to help African Americans when the United States was making their lives a misery. The United States remains in debt to Canada for the haven it provided to so many Americans.

## *Other Refuges for Fugitives*

Although over the years Canada sheltered many more fugitives from American slavery than did any place else, other areas also provided havens. Where a slave fled depended a great deal on his or her location and knowledge. Most runaways stayed close to home, hiding in the woods or in maroon colonies. Although until 1850, many former slaves lived in the northern free states, surprisingly few made new homes in the vast free territories owned by the United States—perhaps because most simply did not know of their existence.

As we have seen, while Spain held Florida, it openly invited American slaves to freedom there. Slaves accepted, fleeing individually or trying to march there in groups. Often those who made it wound up living among the Seminole, in the mild form of slavery common among them or as members of the tribe.

When it had the power, Mexico afforded a haven to Indians and African-American slaves. Its efforts were countered by the vigorous actions of Sam Houston and other Texans to protect the institution of slavery in Texas throughout its history as part of Mexico, as an independent country, as an American state, and as a member of the Confederacy.

## *The Colonization/Emigration Movements*

From the Revolutionary War period up until the 1830s, many people in the United States, North and South, agreed that slavery did not belong in a country founded on liberty. Even though many of the founding fathers held slaves and had excluded from the body politic women, blacks, and Indians, the contradictions between slavery and the country's professed ideals were uncomfortable.

Many slaveholders declared their willingness to free their slaves—*if only they could think of what to do with them.* Perhaps the freed slaves could be put to work on roads and other public works. Was it fair simply to liberate them and leave them to their own devices? What would happen to white people, particularly in states where blacks outnumbered whites?

For a good many white people for a good many years, right up to the Civil War, the answer was colonization: to ship free blacks off somewhere, preferably somewhere far away.

But where, precisely? Colonizationists suggested several possible locations. Haiti was near at hand, with a black government (after Toussaint Louverture brought a series of rebellions to a successful conclusion). Trinidad had indicated its interest in welcoming black settlers. Could they go to Jamaica or Panama? Surely somewhere to the west, in the vast stretches of unsettled North America, land for free blacks could be found. What about Canada? Better still, Central and South America stretched southward, with a tropical climate presumably congenial to blacks. But Africa was the most popular choice. In a sense, one suspects, Americans were trying to undo what they had done in removing slaves from their homeland. Then, too, they pointed to the example of British abolitionists in founding Sierra Leone.

The idea of establishing remote black colonies appealed to white people of different persuasions about slavery. Moderate antislavery advocates saw it as a way of encouraging slaveholders to free their slaves. Few thought that *immediate* emancipation could be achieved or would work; colonization at least would afford a start toward *gradual* emancipation. In any case, the individual slave freed and sent to a new colony would be better off. It was a peaceable process that would make few waves. The plan also relieved fears of invading slaveholders' rights to hold property. Churchmen argued that the presence of Christianized African Americans among them might help to convert neighboring Africans and discourage the slave trade in the vicinity.

Southern states eager to rid themselves of free blacks supported colonization. Every slave insurrection inspired fresh enthusiasm. Defenders of slavery argued that colonization would at once appease antislavery forces and raise the value of slaves by decreasing the black population. Whites who worried about a black majority in the southern states openly argued that through colonization they could ship off enough blacks to hold down their numbers while allowing the proportion of whites to rise by "natural increase." Colonization spoke also to those who, like Abraham Lincoln, believed that blacks and whites were better off living apart.

But white antislavery forces split on the issue. Many abolitionists regarded colonization as a ploy to protect slavery and weaken their own movement. William Lloyd Garrison fought passionately against it, arguing that to remove black people, those best suited to cultivate the plantations, would be suicidal for the country. Others asserted that it would never work: slaveholders were not about to free their slaves and send them to West Africa.

What of the people most concerned? Many black leaders opposed colonization, particularly in the early years of the 19th century. They tended to be successful people who saw no reason why African Americans should be driven from what had by now become their native land. They still entertained hopes for emancipation, equality, and integration.

Other blacks—*emigrationists*—advocated the establishment of separate black communities, some insisting on a location in North America, some choosing other sites. They doubted that the United States would soon emancipate slaves, let alone offer blacks political and social equality and integration. As the years dragged by, with proslavery forces gaining ground in such measures as the Fugitive Slave Act of 1850, the battles over free and slave territories in the West, and especially the *Dred Scott* decision (see Appendix A), even some of the African Americans who had originally opposed colonization (such as Frederick Douglass) came to see emigration as the only hope for their people. The radical black leader Martin Delany insisted that "Central and South America are evidently the ultimate destination and future home of the colored race on this continent. . . . Go we must, and go we will, as there is no alternative. . . . To remain here in North America, and be crushed to the earth in vassalage and degradation, we never will."[9]

Over the years, private individuals and groups experimented with colonies of former slaves in various locations. For instance, British abolitionist Frances Wright, who had proposed that Congress use public lands for slave labor and employ the profits to buy the slaves' freedom, in the 1820s founded a 640-acre community named Nashoba in Tennessee—a well-intentioned but ill-conceived, ill-located, and ill-managed scheme that soon foundered.

The American Colonization Society, organized in 1817, immediately set about its avowed task of shipping free blacks to Liberia, in West Africa. The society had its work cut out for it. It had at once to try to meet the objections of its opponents and yet not offend its own heterogeneous members, some of whom opposed slavery categorically and others of whom owned slaves. It had to organize and provide for the management of a new colony in hostile surroundings—an undertaking that had defeated many another group. It had to populate that colony, raising the funds to transport the emigrants and support them there until they could fend for themselves. Fugitive slaves, who of their own free will and against enormous odds, fled to Canada did not always like it there. What was to be the response of the blacks who theoretically went to Liberia voluntarily but in actuality had been confronted by their owners with the choice between remaining slaves or going to a colony of which they knew almost nothing?

In the end, of course, colonization did not work. As a solution to the overwhelming problem of slavery it had never had any validity. It did not and could not begin to address the basic evils of that terrible institution or repair the damage done to the four million black people trapped in it in 1860. In this respect, colonization was a mere placebo.

Its supporters argued that the colonization effort diminished the international slave trade. It did, they said, encourage manumission. It did serve free blacks.

The idea survived. Many, including Abraham Lincoln, advocated colonization during the Civil War. Some slave owners freed their slaves and paid for a fresh start for them as free citizens of Liberia. Other masters who wanted to free their slaves could not afford the money to ship them off and furnish them with supplies for several months. The American Colonization Society could not begin to raise enough money to meet the demand, even with some support from the federal government. Altogether the society managed to send off only some 11,000 emigrants—over more than 40 years.[10]

The African Americans who reached Liberia encountered all the problems of pioneers in a new country, and more. Some emigrants did moderately well there. Others did not, wishing themselves back in the United States. The little colony was set down in unfriendly territory, subject to attack from neighboring tribes. Until today, it has had a troubled history. Liberia survives, but it has never flourished.

## Chronicle of Events

**1501**
Portuguese explorer Gaspar Côrte-Real enslaves 50 Indian men and women in Labrador or Newfoundland.

**1607**
The lieutenant governor of Acadia (New France) tries to enslave Indians to run his gristmill.

**1628**
David Kirke brings a slave boy (later Olivier le Jeune) to Quebec.

**1629**
Kirke sells his slave—the first sale of a slave in New France.

**1670**
*Panis* (Indian slaves) are reported in Montreal; Indians on the northwest coast also are keeping slaves of their own.

**1687**
The governor of New France seizes 40 Iroquois, whom he has invited to a peace conference, and ships them to France as slaves.

**1689**
The attorney general of New France sends a memorandum to Louis XIV arguing that slavery would be profitable. Louis assents to slavery in New France, but his assent is virtually nullified by the outbreak of King William's War.

**1701**
Louis XIV again authorizes slavery in New France.

**1704**
New France's reversion to a fur-based economy ends the need for many slaves.

**1705**
The New York legislature passes an "Act to prevent the running away of Negro slaves out of the City and County of Albany to the French at Canada."

**1709**
The intendant of New France ordains that "all the *panis and Negroes who have been purchased and who will be purchased, shall be the property of those who have purchased them* and will be their *slaves.*"

**1716**
The intendant of New France pleads for the slave trade, to provide labor for agriculture, fishing, lumbering, shipbuilding, and mining.

**1720**
The intendant of New France asks the king of France to send African slaves to work in the hemp market; he forwards a memorial in which the inhabitants of New France undertake to buy 101 Africans from French slavers.

**1736**
The intendant of New France provides a uniform means of manumission, involving a notary's certificate and registration with the royal registry office.

**1745**
The king of France decrees that slaves from enemy colonies who flee into French territory may be sold, the proceeds belonging to the king.

**1752**
In Halifax, Joshua Mauger, victualler to the navy, advertises several black slaves for sale.

**1763**
Slavery is specifically protected by the Treaty of Paris between Britain and France, in which France cedes its mainland North American empire east of the Mississippi to Great Britain.

The British military governor of Quebec writes to a friend in New York asking for four slaves.

**1764**
In a treaty with the superintendent of Indian affairs for New York, several Huron agree to return all "negro's, Panis or other slaves . . . who are British property" and to turn over any slaves who may subsequently seek refuge with them. The treaty introduces English law to Quebec, depriving slaves of legal protections.

**1772**
In Great Britain, Lord Mansfield holds in *Somerset* v. *Stewart* that slavery cannot exist in England in the absence of specific legislation providing for it.

**1773**
Dr. Samuel Hopkins of Rhode Island corresponds with Rev. Ezra Stiles about the possibility of sending a few blacks to a colony on the coast of Guinea.

**1774**
With the Quebec Act, Britain restores French civil law to Quebec while retaining the English criminal code. The act also extends the boundaries of Quebec to the Ohio River, bringing under its aegis those few slaves living in the old Northwest.

**1780**
A number of slaves captured in Kentucky are brought into Quebec and sold, although at least 10 of them apparently belonged to a Loyalist.

Near Detroit, Indians continue to seize blacks for themselves.

**1781**
A legislative act of Isle St. Jean (later Prince Edward Island) declares that baptism of slaves does not exempt them from bondage.

**1783**
In England, Granville Sharp proposes an African colony for impoverished freed slaves.

Loyalist (Tory) migration brings the first major influx of blacks to the maritime Canadian colonies, as masters bring their slaves with them and former slaves who had fought for the British or sought protection behind British lines embark for Nova Scotia. As a result, black slaves almost supplant Indian slaves, even in Quebec.

**1786**
In England, Henry Smeathman publishes a *Plan of a Settlement to be Made near Sierra Leone.*

*December:* About 350 impoverished former American slaves and 60 white women sail from Plymouth, England, for Sierra Leone, with the assistance of the [London] Committee for the Relief of the Black Poor.

**1788**
Nova Scotia clergyman James MacGregor publishes an open *Letter to a Clergyman Urging Him to Set Free a Black Girl He Held in Slavery.*

**1789**
An African tribal leader, King Jimmy, burns Granville town in the African settlement of Liberated Africans to the ground.

**1790**
Through an Imperial act, Britain permits free importation into Canada of all "Negroes, household furniture, utensils of husbandry or cloathing," though furniture, utensils, and clothing were not to exceed the value of £50 for every white and £2 for every black slave.

**1791**
French civil law is applied to Lower Canada (modern Quebec), English civil law to Upper Canada, and English criminal law in both.

In Great Britain, Thomas Clarkson, Granville Sharp, and William Wilberforce form the Sierra Leone Company to administer the African colony of Liberated Africans.

Thomas Peters, a former black pioneer in the American Revolution, arrives in England with a petition on behalf of 102 Nova Scotia and a hundred New Brunswick black families, asking for "some establishment where [they] may attain a competent settlement for themselves and be enabled by their industrious exertions to become useful subjects to his Majesty."

**1792**
Eleven hundred freed slaves who migrated to Nova Scotia after the American Revolution establish Freetown, Sierra Leone, in West Africa.

**1793–1803**
Canadian abolitionists triumph over slavery, mostly by judicial decisions.

**1793**
The legislature of Upper Canada, with the king's assent, provides for the gradual abolition of slavery, forbidding the importation of slaves and the enslavement of anyone thereafter but setting no present slaves free; children born to these slaves are to be freed at age 25.

**1794**
Colonists rebel against the Sierra Leone Company, but peace is restored.

**1796**
A band of more than 550 non-Christian, warlike Jamaican Maroons is deported to Nova Scotia.

**1798**
The chief justice of Lower Canada, James Monk, frees two slaves, incidentally remarking that slavery does not exist in that province and that he will so rule henceforth.

**1800**
Pres. Thomas Jefferson and Gov. James Monroe of Virginia fail in an effort to inaugurate the colonization of blacks.

The Court of King's Bench of Lower Canada frees a slave on the ground that the Imperial Act of 1797 abolished all legislation relating to slavery in the province; the decision renders slavery virtually untenable in the province.

*July:* Nova Scotia black immigrants to Sierra Leone rebel against the Sierra Leone Company, believing that it has broken its promises about land; their rebellion is eventually quelled by the newly arrived Jamaican Maroons.

*August 3:* 551 Jamaican Maroons are deported from Nova Scotia to Sierra Leone.

*September 30:* Jamaican Maroons arrive in Sierra Leone.

**1801**
President Jefferson corresponds with British authorities about the incorporation of the free blacks of the United States into the Sierra Leone colony.

**1808**
Paul Cuffe, a black Quaker mariner living in Massachusetts, pioneers the idea of voluntary colonization.

**1811**
Black ship's captain Paul Cuffe sails the *Traveller* from Massachusetts to Sierra Leone, where he founds the Friendly Society for the emigration of free blacks from America.

**1813–1816**
The "Refugee Negroes," some 2,000 former American slaves who have sought refuge with the British in the War of 1812, are transported to Nova Scotia.

**1814**
*April:* In the War of 1812, British vice admiral Sir Alexander Cochrane promises American slaves who come to a British ship or military post a choice of military service or free transportation to a British possession in North America or the West Indies, where they can be free settlers.

**1815**
Captain Paul Cuffe at his own expense transports from the United States to Sierra Leone 38 persons of color.

**1817**
The American Colonization Society is organized.

*April 30:* The Council of Nova Scotia warns the Black Refugees of gradual withdrawal of support, offering any who wish it the opportunity to return to the United States and ordering a survey to see whether any wish to go to Trinidad.

**1820s and 1830s**
Black labor is used in Canada to fell trees, build roads, cut railroad ties, and introduce tobacco culture.

**1820**
The first effort of American colonizationists to settle a colony of black Americans in Africa fails because of the climate.

**1821**
American colonizationists set out to settle another colony of black Americans in Africa, eventually purchasing land at Cape Montserado and calling their colony Liberia.

Ninety-five Refugee Negroes sail from Nova Scotia to relocate in Trinidad.

**1823**
*January 4:* Mexico enacts the Imperial Colonization Law: "There shall not be permitted, after the promulgation of this law, either purchase or sale of slaves that may be introduced into the empire. The children of such slaves, who are born within the empire, shall be free at fourteen years of age."

*February:* The Mexican Imperial Colonization law is annulled; Stephen F. Austin is allowed to continue to colonize Texas with slaveholders.

**1825**
The assembly of Prince Edward Island repeals the Act of 1781, with intent to abolish slavery.

The *African Repository and Colonial Journal,* an instrument of the American Colonization Society, begins publication.

**1826**
Secretary of State Henry Clay requests extradition of American fugitive slaves from Canada; the British government refuses.

**1827**
The American Colonization Society petitions Congress for assistance, saying the society lacks both funds and the authority to govern a distant colony.

**1828**
Congress asks the president to reopen negotiations with the British government for the return of fugitive slaves from Canada. The British government refuses.

**1829**
The administrator of Lower Canada refuses a U.S. request for extradition of a fugitive slave and of a man who had helped him escape.

Cincinnati, with a black population of at least 2,250, enforces Ohio laws of 1804 and 1807, in effect banishing blacks who have entered the state without a certificate of freedom and without a bond of five hundred dollars guaranteeing good behavior and support and signed by two white men. Cincinnati whites riot against its blacks.

Cincinnati's blacks form a society to seek a place to relocate.

**1830**
In the spring, a large group of blacks leaves Cincinnati and founds the town of Wilberforce in Ontario; the cooperative experiment fails by 1836.

*September 20–24:* In the United States, the National Negro Convention, taking a stand against colonization, organizes the American Society of Free Persons of Color, for Improving Their Condition in the United States; for Purchasing Lands; and for the Establishing of a Settlement in Upper Canada.

**1833**
Upper Canada provides for the capture and extradition of "Fugitive offenders from Foreign Countries," leaving the governor in council free not to deliver a person if he deems it unwise.

James Birney, exemplifying a shift in public opinion, renounces colonization in a *Letter on Colonization.*

**1834**
Slavery is legally abolished in all British colonies.

The Nova Scotia Assembly passes "An Act to prevent the Clandestine landing of Liberated Slaves," in order to prevent an anticipated inundation of former slaves. This act is disallowed as discriminatory in 1836.

**1835**
Texans protest against a project for settling free blacks from the United States in Texas, then forming a provisional government.

**1837**
Blacks at Niagara in Canada violently defend Solomon Mosely, whose extradition is sought for the theft of a horse when he fled.

British authorities advise that fugitives should not be surrendered to extradition without evidence of a criminal act that "would warrant the apprehension of the accused Party, if the alleged offence had been committed in Canada."

In Upper Canada, an antislavery society is formed in Toronto but does not survive the decade.

**1840s**
As the Irish begin to immigrate in large numbers and frontiers dwindle, Canadians need black labor less.

**1842**
Canada for the first time grants extradition of a fugitive slave, Nelson Hacket, who while escaping had stolen items not necessary for his escape.

The black cooperative community of Dawn, built around a manual-arts school known as the British-American Institute, is founded in Canada West.

Joseph Jenkins Roberts (1809–1876), a black man, becomes the first president of Liberia.

The Webster-Ashburton Treaty between the United States and Canada exempts extradition for desertion, mutiny, and revolt on board ship and protects the principle that no extradition will be granted unless for an action that would be considered an offense under Canadian law.

**1847**
Liberia issues its Declaration of Independence.

**1849**
The Canadian government enacts a new extradition law. No fugitive slave is ever surrendered to the United States under this law or the Webster-Ashburton Treaty.

Former slaveholder William King founds the black colony of Elgin in Canada West with his 15 freed slaves as its nucleus.

**1850**
By this time Nova Scotia and Canada West, the two major centers of black settlement, have established separate schools for blacks.

The last segregated military Colored Corps in Canada West is disbanded.

**1851**
An experimental black colony is launched; it is known successively as the Sandwich Mission, the Fugitives' Union Society, and the Refugee Home Society, under the last of which it soon is destroyed by factionalism.

*February 26:* The Anti-Slavery Society of Canada is organized "to aid in the extinction of Slavery all over the world" by any lawful and practical means.

*September:* The North American Colored Convention meets in Toronto and approves killing pursuers in self-defense.

**1852**
The Fugitives' Union Society merges with the Refugee Home Society.

*July:* The American Continental and West Indian League is organized in Canada West to promote settlement throughout the New World.

**1853**
The National Emigration Convention of Colored People begins to investigate "intertropical" sites, especially Haiti, the Niger valley, and Central America, as refuges for blacks.

**1858**
Black physician Martin R. Delany organizes the Niger Valley Exploring Party, instructed by its sponsors to gather scientific information, not to encourage emigration.

*April:* The first black settlers arrive in Victoria, on Vancouver Island, British Columbia.

**1859**
Naturalist Robert Campbell of the Niger Valley Exploring Party issues a circular in London promising that if its report is favorable, a number of blacks who wish to grow cotton there may emigrate from Canada and the free states.

Members of the Niger Valley Exploring Party sign a treaty with the Alake of Abeokuta providing that North American blacks will settle on any unoccupied land "in common with the Egba people." The Civil War defeats their plans.

Haiti appoints James Redpath as its emigration agent in British North America and the free states of the United States.

**1861**
James Redpath, as emigration agent for Haiti, offers blacks free passage to Haiti and allotments from the public domain.

*May:* A group of 111 blacks, including some from Canada West, sail from New Haven for Haiti.

*August:* Another 113 people, including the white wives of some Canadian blacks in the May group, sail from Canada for Haiti.

*December:* Redpath announces that he will henceforth send blacks not to Haiti but to Jamaica, but Haiti continues to encourage agricultural settlement.

**1868**
The communal experiment of Dawn having failed after years of quarrels and turmoil, the British-American Institute closes.

**1873**
Elgin closes down, many of its inhabitants never having returned after fighting in the Civil War and others having sold their property and returned to the United States.

## EYEWITNESS TESTIMONY

### *Slavery in Canada*

[W]ithout Servants nothing can be done. . . . [I hope] by setting a good Example [to improve agriculture.] Black Slaves are Certainly the only people to be depended upon, but . . . they should be born in one or other of our Northern Colonies, [as] the Winters here will not agree, with a Native of the Torrid Zone.

*British military governor of Quebec, 1763 letter, in Winks,* Blacks in Canada, *26.*

### *Canada as a Refuge: The Black Loyalists of the American Revolution*

Great Riot today. The disbanded soldiers have risen against the Free negroes to drive them out of Town [Shelburne, Nova Scotia], because they labour cheaper than they—the soldiers. [27 July] Riot continues. The soldiers force the free negroes to quit the town—pulled down about 20 of their houses.

*Benjamin Marston, July 26 and 27, 1784, in Walker,* Black Loyalists, *48.*

There are a great number of Black People both in this Town and in Birch town who are in the most distressing Circumstances.

Many of them have been relieved by us, otherwise it is highly probable that some of them, during this inclement Season, must have perished—But as the number of White People, whom we have constantly to supply, are very considerable it is not in our power to afford the Blacks that assistance which their pressing Necessities loudly call for—

And as it is evident they become more and more burthensome every year [we ask that you] free this Infant Settlement from a Burden which it is by no means in a Capacity to bear.

*Shelburne, Nova Scotia, Overseers of the Poor, February 1789, in Walker,* Black Loyalists, *54.*

Some Part of the said Black People [Loyalists] are earnestly desirous of obtaining their due Allotment of Land and remaining in America [Nova Scotia] but others are ready and willing to go wherever the Wisdom of Government may think proper to provide for them as free Subjects of the British Empire.

*Thomas Peters's Petition to the British Cabinet, 1790, in Walker,* Black Loyalists, *95.*

### *Canada as a Refuge: The Cincinnati Blacks (1829–1830)*

[T]he law of 1804, known as the Ohio black law, was revived in that State, and enforced. By this law, every colored man was to give bonds in $500 not to become a town charge, and to find bonds also for his heirs. No one could employ a colored man or colored woman to do any kind of labor, under penalty of $100. There were then about 3,000 colored people there—by this law they were thrown out of employment. I was then clearing $600 a year, and refused to give bonds. The Colored people had a meeting, and talked about a court of appeals to test the law. Some talked of going to Texas,—we knew not what to do. . . . I spoke to them of Canada, and we formed a Colonization Society, of which I was President. I wrote for the Board to Sir John Colborne, at Little York, now Toronto, to know if we could find in Canada an asylum for ourselves, our wives, and children. . . . He wrote us . . . that so long as we remained true and loyal subjects, we should have every privilege extended to us that was enjoyed by any of his majesty's subjects, no distinction being made on account of color. . . . Mr. Hammonds, our friend, editor of a daily paper in Cincinnati, published the letter at my request. . . . Two or three of us, including myself, were sent for by the city government, next day. The reason was, as Mr. Hotchkiss said, that I, as one of the leading spirits, was doing a great deal of mischief; for every one that I took off to Canada was a sword drawn against the United States. . . . He said they were taking steps to have the law repealed, and wished me to stay any action about sending people to Canada. . . .

I paid no attention to what he told me, and sent three wagon loads out to Sandusky next day. In three or four weeks I and my family left—came to Sandusky—thence I took a boat, the "Gov. Cass," and went to Little York, where I entered into a contract with the Canada Company, for a township of land, agreeing to pay $6,000 a year, for ten years. It was the township of Biddulph. The black law had now become inoperative in Cincinnati, and the colored people wrote me, that they could now walk without being pushed off the side-walks, were well used, and were living in clover. Of 2,700 who were to have come, only 460 came out. They settled promiscuously [in different places] in the province, buying land here and there, and getting work. Only five or six families of them settled in Biddulph. Three weeks after they settled, fifteen families from Boston, Mass., met them there, and settled there, where they remain. We only paid for 1,220 acres, which was divided, from 25 to 50 acres to a family. Numbers, who came afterward, had to leave for other places. These families in Biddulph are now independent. Their lands now will sell at forty to fifty dollars an acre; it cost one dollar and fifty cents. I settled in Toronto, where I could have some means of making myself useful for them among the white people, and where my trade was good.

*J. C. Brown, in Drew,* Refugee, *244–47.*

## *Canada as a Refuge: The Negro Refugees (1812–1817)*

The slaves continue to come off [to my ship] by every opportunity and I have now upward of 120 men, women and children on board, I shall send about 50 of them to Bermuda in the [ship] Conflict. . . . There is no doubt but the blacks of Virginia and Maryland would cheerfully take up arms and join us against the Americans.

*British captain Robert Barnie to Admiral Warren, November 14, 1813, in Grant, "Black Immigrants into Nova Scotia," 264.*

[The interests of Nova Scotia are not being served by bringing in] a separate and marked class of people, unfitted by Nature to this Climate, or to an association with the rest of His Majesty's Colonists.

*Assembly of Nova Scotia to its lieutenant governor, 1815, in Winks,* Blacks in Canada, *116.*

Permit me to state plainly that little hope can be entertained of settling these [Refugee Negroes] so as to provide for their families and wants, they must be supported for many years. Slaves by habit & education, no longer working under the dread of the lash, their idea of freedom is Idleness and they are altogether incapable of industry. [They should either be restored to their masters in the United States or be sent to Sierra Leone.] [E]ither of these plans I believe would be agreeable to the greater part of them; but to the West Indies they will not go.

*(Governor of Nova Scotia to the Colonial Office, 1817, in Winks,* Blacks in Canada, *122.*

[The farms established for the Refugee Negroes are too small, and the land is] Sterile and unproductive, [so that it is impossible for] any persons to support families on them. . . . No class of Settlers, let their habits be ever so industrious could possibly maintain their families on lots of the same size and quality, without being reduced to suffering and perhaps to starvation. [So far the refugees have supported themselves] by marketing charcoal, staves, shingles and such other lumber as their limited quantity of land enabled them to produce, [but the lumber is now exhausted].

*Neighbors of the Preston, Nova Scotia, blacks, June 8, 1838, in Walker,* Black Loyalists, *391.*

## *Canada as a Refuge: The Fugitive Slaves (1815–1861)*

My father and myself went to the Queen's Bush [in Canada] in 1846. We went four and a half miles beyond the other farms, to Canestogo, where he cleared up and had a farm; for years scarcely any white people came in, but fugitive slaves came in, in great numbers, and cleared the land. Before it was surveyed, there were as many as fifty families. It was surveyed two years after we went there. The colored people might have held their lands still, but they were afraid they would not be able to pay when pay-day [the due date] came. Under these circumstances, many of them sold out cheap. They now consider that they were overreached—for many who bought out the colored people have not yet paid for the land, and some of the first settlers yet remain, who have not yet been required to pay all up. . . .

*William Jackson, in Drew,* Refugee, *189–90.*

[F]or years after I came here, my mind was continually reverting to my native land. For some ten years, I was in hopes that something might happen, whereby I might safely return to my old home in New Jersey. I watched the newspapers and they told the story. I found that there would be a risk in going back. . . . I then made up my mind that salt and potatoes in Canada, were better than pound-cake and chickens in a state of suspense and anxiety in the United States. . . .

*Rev. Alexander Hemsley, in Drew,* Refugee, *39.*

I was earnestly solicited . . . to open a school in a new settlement of fugitives, eight miles back of Windsor, where the Refugee Association had purchased government land, on long and easy terms, for fugitive slaves.

They had erected a frame house for school and meeting purposes. The settlers had built for themselves small log-houses, and cleared from one to five acres each on their heavily timbered land, and raised corn, potatoes, and other garden vegetables. A few had put in two and three acres of wheat, and were doing well for their first year.

In the Autumn of 1852 I opened school. . . .

The unbounded confidence they placed in me was surprising; for they often brought their business papers for me to examine, to see whether they were right. One man brought me a note, as the employer could not pay him for his work in money. He said it was a note for groceries; but the grocer refused to take it, and said it was not good. I told him there was neither date nor name to it. I wrote the man a letter, asking him to rectify the mistake, which he did; but he gave his employee credit for only half the days he had worked. They [the fugitive slaves] were . . . often deceived and cheated in many ways, because of their extreme ignorance.

*Haviland,* A Woman's Life-Work, *192, 194.*

A True Band is composed of colored persons of both sexes, associated for their own improvement. Its objects are manifold: mainly these:—the members are to take a general interest in each other's welfare; to pursue such plans and objects as may be for their mutual advantage; to improve all schools, and to induce their race to send their children into the schools; to break down all prejudice; to bring all churches as far as possible into one body, and not let minor differences divide them; to prevent litigation by referring all disputes among themselves to a committee; to stop the begging system entirely; (that is, going to the United States, and there by representing that the fugitives are starving and suffering, raising large sums of money, of which the fugitives never receive the benefit,—misrepresenting the character of the fugitives for industry, and underrating the advance of the country, which supplies abundant work for all at fair wages;) to raise such funds among themselves as may be necessary for the poor, the sick, and the destitute fugitive newly arrived; and to prepare themselves ultimately to bear their due weight of political power.

*Drew,* Refugee, *236.*

[I]t is fortunate for some conscience-stricken slaveholders, that Canada affords a refuge for a certain class of their household victims—their slave-wives, or slave-children, or both. If it be a crime to assist slaves in reaching a land of freedom, it is not a crime of which those terrible fellows, the northern abolitionists, alone are guilty. Slaveholders may pour contempt on the names and the deeds of northern philanthropists: but these have no slanderous epithets to hurl back upon the southerner, who snatches his children and the mother of his children from the threatening hammer of the auctioneer, and hurriedly and tearfully starts them for the North with the parting injunction, "Stop not short of Canada!"

*Drew,* Refugee, *322–23.*

[In the course of escaping in 1853, the fugitive William Anderson killed the man who tried to capture him, a "crime" for which he was arrested in Toronto in 1860. When the United States tried to extradict him, Canadian Governor-General Lord Elgin wrote me that] in case of a demand for William Anderson, he should require the case to be tried in their British court; and if twelve freeholders should testify that he had been a man of integrity since his arrival in their dominion, it should clear him.

*Laura S. Haviland,* Woman's Work, *207–8.*

I have had very bad luck since I have been here [Canada]. I was sick for six or eight months after I got here. My wife came out three months after. She was taken sick, and there were three weeks that I couldn't go out, but had to stay there and just turn her over in bed. I have buried three children since I have been here, and have had six children in all. The poorest day I ever see out here, I would rather be here than be with the best slaveholder that lives in the South, and I have seen slaves out there that were better treated than they can treat themselves here.

*William Cornish, 1863 interview, American Freedmen's Inquiry Commission, in* Slave Testimony, *426.*

I have travelled a good deal in the Province, and have found the prejudice greater than in the States. The political influence of the colored people now has quite a tendency to moderate the prejudice. Electioneering time, they come here for me, and I must go around and stump the county with them. The lawyers come for me with a horse and buggy, and I must go out with them, and fare just as they do. But when the election is over, they speak, of course, when we meet, but nothing more. . . . I think the root of the prejudice is to be found in the fact that the colored people came in here very rapidly, & the whites got the impression that the colored people would become a majority in the Western county. The reason that the colored people have not got along better is that they came here poor, and ignorant, and with no trades to help them along.

*Horace H. Hawkins, 1863 interview, American Freedmen's Inquiry Commission, in* Slave Testimony, *443–44.*

## *Organized Black Communities*

We [in the Wilberforce colony] have erected for our accommodations comfortable log buildings, and have a portion of our land in a state of cultivation; our crops at present continue to smile upon the labor of our hands; we shall raise the present year nearly enough to supply the present number of settlers. The people are industrious, and well pleased with their present location; and it is believed that none of them could be hired to go back to the states. Two religious societies have been organized. A sabbath school . . . is in successful operation . . . [and a] day school for the instruction of the children . . . and a temperance society has been formed consisting of about thirty in number.

*Austin Steward and Benjamin Paul to* The Liberator, *January 26, 1833, in Baily, "Antebellum Colonization," 436.*

I was not the only one who had escaped from the States, and had settled on the first spot in Canada which they had reached. [About 1835] Several hundreds of coloured persons were . . . generally working for hire upon the lands of others, and had not yet dreamed of becoming independent proprietors themselves. . . . Mr. Riseley [my employer] . . . permitted me to call meetings at his house of those who were known to be amongst the most intelligent and successful of our class. . . . [I]t was agreed, among the ten or twelve of us who assembled at them, that we would invest our earnings in land, and undertake the task . . . of settling upon wild lands, which we could call our own, and where every tree which we felled, and every bushel of corn we raised, would be for ourselves; in other words, where we could secure all the profits of our own labour. . . .

[Mr. James C. Fuller, an English Quaker,] came back with fifteen hundred dollars which had been subscribed [in England] for our benefit. . . . [I]t was thought expedient to call a convention of delegates from every settlement of blacks that was within reach; that all might see that the ultimate decision [about the money] was sanctioned by the disinterested votes of those who were thought by their companions best able to judge what would meet the wants of the community. . . . [I]t was held in June, 1838.

I urged the appropriation of the money to the establishment of a manual-labour school, at which our children could gain those elements of knowledge which are usually taught in a grammar-school. I urged that the boys should be taught, in addition, the practice of some mechanical art, and the girls should be instructed in . . . domestic arts . . .; and that such an establishment . . . would gradually enable us to become independent of the white man for our intellectual progress, as we could be for our physical prosperity. It was the more necessary, as in many districts, owing to the insurmountable prejudices of the inhabitants, the children of the blacks were not allowed to share the advantages of the common school. . . . [W]e could find no place more suitable than that upon which I had had my eye for three or four years, for a permanent settlement, in the town of Dawn. . . .

[The white man sent from England about 1853 to run the manual-training school at Dawn] soon began to buy the most expensive cattle in the market, at fancy prices, and without any reference to the fact that he had not sufficient fodder to feed them. . . . He also bought expensive farming utensils to work the farm scientifically, and then pulled down the school-buildings, as they were too primitive to suit his magnificent ideas, and he promised to erect more substantial and commodious buildings. . . .

He supported his family and his brother-in-law's family from the farm that belonged to our coloured people. . . . The fifth, sixth, seventh, eighth, and ninth year passed, and we had no school. . . . [I said to him,] "If you really do not intend to build us a school, you ought to leave the farm, and let us manage for ourselves."

With some excitement he said, "Pay me what I have expended during the many years I have tried to make this place meet its expenses, and I will go at once. . . ."

[After a law suit of some seven years] the important case was decided in our favour. Then the Court of Chancery appointed a new board of trustees, granted a bill to incorporate the institution as the Wilberforce University, also the power to sell the land, with a stipulation that the University should be erected on a plot of ground in the same county. The town of Chatham, Canada, was selected, and for four years the school has been *self-sustaining,* and has been attended by many pupils.

*Henson, on the Dawn community,* Autobiography, *76–77, 90–91, 121–23.*

The [Elgin] settlement at Buxton was first projected by the Rev. Wm. King in 1849. Mr. King was formerly a slaveholder in Louisiana, but . . . he manumitted his own slaves, about fourteen in number, (for whom he had been offered nine thousand dollars,) and brought them with him to Canada, where he settled them on farms or on lands recently purchased of the government. . . .

The land is divided into farms of fifty acres each, and so situated that a road runs past each man's farm. The houses are set thirty-three feet from this road, facing streets, so that the whole settlement, when cleared up and opened, will present a uniform appearance. The land is sold to the settlers at $2.50 per acre, the government price, and is paid in ten equal annual instalments, with interest at the rate of 6 per cent. But although ten years were allowed to the settlers to pay for their farms, a number have taken out their deeds already; and there is no doubt that before the ten years shall have expired, each settler will have his deed in possession: for which he will be indebted to his own exertions—since the settlers receive no money, no grants of land, no farming implements,—nothing but protection and advice. . . .

*Drew,* Refugee, *291–92.*

## *Colonization/Emigration Projects*

[We] respectfully suggest to that august body [the American Colonization Society] of talent and learning, and worth, that . . . they are pursuing the direct road to perpetuate slavery with all its unchristian concomitants, in this boasted land of freedom. . . . Many of our fathers and some of us have fought and bled for the liberty, Independence and peace which you now enjoy; and surely it would be ungenerous and unfeeling in you to deny us a humble and quiet grave in that country which gave us birth.

*National Convention of Colored Men, Philadelphia, 1831, in Carroll,* Slave Insurrections, *171.*

Mr. Randolph said, "He thought it necessary, being himself a slaveholder, to show that so far from being in the *smallest degree* connected with the abolition of slavery, the proposed [Colonization] Society *would prove one of the greatest securities to enable the master to keep in possession his own property.*" . . .

Thus in an Address delivered March, 1833, we are told, "It ought never to be forgotten that the slave-trade between Africa and America, had its origin in a compassionate endeavor to relieve, by the substitution of negro labor, the toils endured by native Indians. . . ."

A writer in the Kentucky Luminary, speaking of colonization, uses the following argument: "None are obliged to follow our example; and those who do not, *will find the value of their negroes increased by the departure of ours.*" . . .

An Education Society has been formed in connection with the Colonization Society, and their complaint is principally that they cannot find proper subjects for instruction. . . .

[The Education Society] pledge themselves to educate no colored persons unless they are solemnly bound to *quit the country.*

*Abolitionist Lydia Child,* Appeal, *123–37 passim.*

Our design [in founding the American Colonization Society] was, by providing an asylum on the coast of Africa, and furnishing the necessary facilities for removal to the people of colour, to induce the voluntary emigration of that portion of them already free, and to throw open to individuals and the States a wider door for voluntary and legal emancipation. The operation, we were aware, must be—and, for the interests of our country, ought to be gradual. But we entertained a hope, founded on our knowledge of the interests as well as the feelings of the South, that this operation, properly conducted, would, *in the end,* remove from our country every vestige of domestic slavery, without a single violation of individual wishes or individual rights.

*Virginian William H. Fitzhugh, 1826, in Fox,* American Colonization Society, *48.*

The great obstacles alleged [against colonization] . . . are . . . :

1. The expense of the scheme. . . .
2. [T]he difficulties attendant on colonization under the most favourable circumstances; the fearful expense of nursing an infant colony into vigor; and the very great time that must elapse before it can have attained sufficient maturity to bear an annual access of 60,000 to its numbers.
3. The habits of the negro render it doubtful whether a successful colony of that race can ever . . . be effected. . . .
4. Will the South consent to relinquish her slaves? . . .
5. [T]he tendency of the natural increase to swell with the increase of the deportation.

The South Vindicated *(1836), 147–48.*

We regard your assembly as the sovereign representatives of the colored people of the United States and the Canadian provinces. You have the supreme right to legislate for their interest, and adopt measures for their advancement. . . . And if other associations have been formed with the same or similar objects, it is to be hoped . . . that they will immediately rank under the banners that you will unfurl at Toronto.

*Vermont delegates' message, written by black emigrationist James T. Holly, to the North American Convention of Colored Men, Toronto, 1851, in Harding,* River, *168. Holly proposed that the convention set up a Canadian-based North American Union of blacks—in effect a black government-in-exile.*

I believe it to be the destiny of the negro, to develop a higher order of civilization and Christianity than the world has yet seen. I also consider it a part of his "manifest destiny" to possess all the tropical regions of this continent, with the adjacent islands. . . . [There the black race could] exercise its proper influence in moulding the destiny, and shaping the policy of the American continent.

*Black poet-journalist and barber J.M. Whitfield, in Harding,* River *185.*

The American colonization movement, as now systematized and conducted, is, in our opinion, simply an American humane farce. At present the slaves are increasing in this country at the rate of nearly one hundred thousand per annum; within the last twelve years, as will appear below, the American Colonization Society has sent to Liberia less than five thousand negroes.

| | |
|---|---|
| In 1847 | 39 |
| In 1848 | 213 |
| In 1849 | 474 |
| In 1850 | 590 |
| In 1851 | 279 |
| In 1852 | 568 |
| In 1853 | 583 |
| In 1854 | 783 |
| In 1855 | 207 |
| In 1856 | 544 |
| In 1857 | 370 |
| In 1858 | 163 |
| Total | 4,813 |

The average of this total is a fraction over four hundred and one, which may be said to be the number of negroes annually colonized by the society; while the yearly increase of slaves . . . is little less than one hundred thousand? Fiddlesticks for such colonization.

*North Carolinian Hinton Rowan Helper, in* Impending Crisis *(1860), 87–88.*

You and we are different races. Whether it is right or wrong I need not discuss, but this physical difference is a great disadvantage to us both, as I think your race suffer very greatly, many of them by living among us, while ours suffer from your presence. In a word we suffer on each side. If this be admitted, it affords a reason at least why we should be separated.

*Abraham Lincoln advocating colonization to a group of African Americans, August 1862, in Franklin,* The Emancipation Proclamation, *33.*

Sir, we were born here and here we choose to remain. . . . Don't advise me to leave, and don't add insult to injury by telling me it's for my own good. Of that I am to be the judge. It is in vain you talk to me about "two races" and their "mutual antagonism." In the matter of rights, there is but one race, and that is the *human* race. . . . Sir, this is our country as much as it is yours, and we will not leave it.

*African-American abolitionist Robert Purvis, public letter to Sen. S. C. Pomeroy,* New York Tribune, *September 20, 1862, in McPherson,* The Negro's Civil War, *97–98.*

The finest specimens of manhood I have ever gazed upon in my life are half-breed Indians crossed with negroes. It is a fact . . that while amalgamation with the white man deteriorates both races, the amalgamation of the Indian and the black man advances both races. . . . I should like to see these eighty thousand square miles [of the Indian Territory] . . opened up to the Indian and to the black man, and let them amalgamate and build up a race that will be an improvement upon both.

*U.S. senator Jim Lane during Reconstruction, quoted in Porter,* Negro on the American Frontier, *75.*

Captain Paul Cuffe, who enabled the emigration of slaves to Sierra Leone (*Library of Congress*)

## *Africa as a Refuge: Sierra Leone*

A larger body of settlers is wanted [in the Sierra Leone colony of former American slaves] to oppose the treachery of the natives, instigated by the *English slave dealers* in the neighbouring factories.

*Granville Sharp, 1788, in Walker,* Black Loyalists, *105.*

The people of the colony [Sierra Leone] are very fond of spiritous liquors, and many of them are retailers and dealers in that article. It appears to me there is not so much industry as would be but for them [liquors]. They are very fond of having a number of servants about them. The industry on their farms are too much neglected. Their young men are too fond of leaving the colony and become seamen for other people. I have thought if commerce could be introduced in the colony, it might have this good tendency of keeping the young men at home, and in some future day qualify them to become managers of themselves. And when they become thus qualified to carry on commerce, I see no reason why they may not become a nation to be numbered among the historians' nations of the world. . . .

I think of keeping open a small intercourse between America and Sierra Leone in hopes through that channel some families may find their way to Sierra Leone.

*Paul Cuffe to William Allen, April 22, 1811, in Pease, "American's Impressions," 39–40.*

## *Africa as a Refuge: Liberia*

I had directions from Mr. McClain to see all of the passioners [passengers] on board by three o'clock which I did, so after I saw all on board Me and Mr. McClain came ashore again when he advise me when I Got to Monrovia [the capital of Liberia] to set me out some coffee trees which I has not done as yet being I has not had the opportunity, when we arrived to the Jolucal mountin we did not meat the Bovner [an official?], he was in the States, but I will make it my Business to do so as soon as he coms. I has not been up the River as yet, but I has been inform that the land up thir is very good, but I am in hopes when I Goes up that I will make a living which it is my desires, for I believe an industrious person can live here. . . . [T]h[e]y is some as smart people as I would wish to be in company with and some bad enough to pay for it since of them has been ashore th[e]y has been stealing but I am in hopes that I shall never be guilty of that th[e]y is some of them sily enough to say they wish themself Back and there is a great many a going to school, I am included in the number, but I has Regret very much that I refuse when I was there. . . .

*Abram Blackford, letter of September 9, 1844, from Liberia to his former owner, in* Slave Testimony, *61–62.*

[Free black men who had migrated North] found themselves so depressed and despised and crowded out of employment, and so much less respected than they had been in Charleston, that they could not endure it, but returned to their old homes. . . . [Thereafter, however, they concluded] that in this country they can never possess those rights and privileges which will make them men [and sailed for Liberia].

African Repository and Colonial Journal *(1847), quoted by Johnson and Roark,* Black Masters, *218.*

We have been here eight months, and we have all been very sick, with the fever, but I am happy to be able to say that we are still alive and enjoying as good health, as we might expect. For four or five months after we arrived in Africa, my children looked better than I think I ever saw them; they were so fond of palm oil and rice, and eat so much of it, that they fattened very fast. Myself and Rosabella also, enjoyed very good health for four or five months of our residence in Liberia. . . . When I arrived in Baltimore, preparatory to sailing, I had, with what you gave me, a little over one hundred dollars, but after paying board for two weeks, and buying some things necessary for house keeping and paying off all my accounts for moving, and getting a few things to the amount of $10, I found that when I got on board of Ship, I had only $33 left. When I arrived, I spent two months at Monrovia, which is a very expensive place to live in, having to pay for your wood and water. I found *this* would never do for me, so I got the favor of the agent to allow me a room, up the St. Pauls' river. . . . I went to work to cut down my lot and clear a spot for a house, not knowing at that time how I should go about it, having no means. Many persons however advised me to go to *shoemaking*. . . . I took their advice, and when the six months were out. I had a house of my own to live in. It is 22 by 13 feet and though very rough, yet it is very comfortable. I have found my trade to be very valuable to me indeed. . . . The greatest drawback, is the want of *leather.*

The only farmers here who are making anything for sale, are those who come to this country with money. Farming is more difficult now than it has been, as all the land on the St. Paul's river has been bought and the emigrants now, have to go back in the forest, some two, three and four miles, and whatever they may plant, is destroyed by the wild hog, the wild cow and many other wild animals. We hope, however, that the time will soon come, when persons will venture to settle a little back from the river, and beasts of burden will be brought into use. . . .

*Letter of William C. Burke of August 20, 1854, from Liberia, to his former owners, Col. and Mrs. Robert E. Lee, in* Slave Testimony, *100–1.*

[H]is employer suggested to [a slave who worked for many years as a lumberman] that he might *buy* his freedom, and he immediately determined to do so. . . . [U]pon collecting the various sums that he had loaned to white people in the vicinity, he was found to have several hundred dollars more than was necessary. With the surplus, he paid for his passage to Liberia, and bought a handsome outfit.

*Olmsted,* Cotton Kingdom, *116.*

I want to know exactly whether if I go [to Liberia] at the expense of the State of Virginia, I shall be able to return when I please, as I shall probably wish to return to bring my wife and children. My Misstress died the 1st day of last Decr and left me free to go to Liberia. . . . The provisions of the will were that if I did not leave the country in a year I was to be sold. I have a wife and four children. I have not been able to get these as they belong to a lady here, but hope to return for them. . . .

*William James Henry, 1855 letter from Lynchburg, Virginia, in* Blacks in Bondage, *162.*

That Emily Hooper, a negro and a citizen of the republic of Liberia, be and she is hereby permitted voluntarily to return into a state of slavery as a slave of her former owner, Miss Sallie Mallett of Chapel Hill. . . .

*A bill enacted February 1859 by the North Carolina legislature providing for the reenslavement of a free black, in Franklin, "The Enslavement of Free Negroes," 415.*

## *Other Refuges*

[Capt. Davis was quoted as saying] that no less than nineteen Negro slaves which he had in Carolina, run away from him lately all at once, under that strong Temptation of the Spaniards . . . which he said he found verified; for he saw all his said Negroes now at St. Augustine, who laughed at him.

*December 18, 1738, in Porter,* Negro on the American Frontier, *162–63.*

"But negro property isn't very secure there [in a section of Louisiana], I'm told. How is't? Know?"

"Not at all secure, sir; if it is disposed to go, it will go: the only way you could keep it would be to make it always contented to remain. The road would always be open to Mexico, it would go when it liked."

"So I hear. Only way is, to have young ones there and keep their mothers here, eh? Negroes have such attachments, you know. Don't you think that would fix 'em, eh? No? No, I suppose not. If they got mad at anything, they'd forget their mothers, eh? Yes, I suppose they would. Can't depend on niggers. But I reckon they'd come back. Only be worse off in Mexico—eh?"

"Nothing but—"

"Being free, eh? Get tired of that, I should think. Nobody to take care of them. No, I suppose not. Learn to take care of themselves."

*Olmsted,* Cotton Kingdom, *413.*

Fourteen Negro slaves [from Texas] with their families came to me this day and I sent them free to Victoria.

*Mexican general Jose Urrea, April 3, 1836, in Campbell,* Empire, *44.*

We have often wondered why some bold and enterprizing men in our state do not club together and go into Mexico and bring away the large Number of fine likely runaways known to be not far over the line, forming a pretty respectable African colony.

*San Antonio* Herald *1855, in Campbell,* Empire, *63–64.*

We caught him [the fugitive slave] once, but he got away. . . . I had my six shooter handy. . . . [E]very barrel missed fire . . shot at him three times with rifles, but he'd got too far off. . . . My dog got close to him once, but he had a dog himself, and just as my dog got within about a yard of him, his dog turned and fit [fought] my dog. . . . We run him close, though, I tell you. Run him out of his coat, and his boots, and a pistol. . . . He got into them bayous, and kept swimming from one side to another. If he's got across the river . . the Mexicans'd take care of him.

*Texan's 1855 report, Olmsted,* Journey through Texas, *256–57, quoted in Tyler, "Fugitive Slaves in Mexico," 1.*

# 8

# Rebels
## 1526–1865

### THE HISTORICAL CONTEXT

Slavery infected North America with hatred, fury, and rebellion. It turned friendly Indians into enemies. Slaves brought from Africa might flee or fight; they might in despair commit suicide. Their new owners tried to subdue these impulses by sheer physical force—manacles and the lash. These might—or might not—suppress the behavior, but the desire for freedom persisted in slaves born on this continent. Their rage and despair sprang from their enslavement and the near impossibility of freeing themselves.

Many slaveholders blamed discontent among the slaves not on their enslaved condition but on "outside agitators"—Yankees in general, abolitionists in particular, and certain religious denominations, notably Quakers and Methodists. "We are exposed to still greater perils by the swarm of missionaries white and black that are perpetually visiting us," wrote Edwin C. Holland in 1822, "who, with the sacred volume of God in one hand, breathing peace to the whole family of man, scatter at the same time with the other the firebrands of discord and destruction, and secretly disperse among our Negroes, the seeds of discontent and sedition. It is an acknowledged fact, that some of those religious itinerants, those apostolic vagabonds, after receiving charities from the philanthropy and open-hearted generosity of our people, have by means of Tracts, and other methods of instruction all professedly religious in their church, excited among our Negroes such a spirit of dissatisfaction and revolt, as has in the end brought down upon them, the vengeance of offended humanity. And given to the gallows and to exile the deluded instigators of a most diabolical unholy Insurrection."[1]

Rumors flew about the unholy schemes of abolitionists. "[T]here is a great excitement in this country on the account of Negro rebellion," wrote Benjamin Bowman in 1860. "[A]bolition Emissarys ar going through this country instigating Negros to Burne the towns and kill there Masters[.] [T]here has all ready been some 12 or fourteen towns burnt[.] Dallasville is burnt entirely up and many others towns that I could name[.] [T]he people of

Dallasville have sustained over a half Million of losses[.] [T]hey caught one of the ablitionst last Weake and hung him up to a limb without jug [judge] or jury tho they had proof sufficient to justify there course[.] [I]t is Dangros for a Stranger to travel through this Country at this time in Dallas county they ar Whipping about thirty Negros pr Day[.] [T]he Negros ar Confessing all about the plot[.] [T]hey say that the Abolisionists have promised them there freedom if they would burne all the towns Down in the State[.] [A]llso they was to breake out on the Sixth Day of August when the men was all gon to the Election than kill all the Wimmin and Children that they could[.] [A]ll the likely young ladies they Was to save for Wives for themselves[.] [T]hose Secret Emmisaries promised them that they would be her with an army from Kanses about the time the Negros was to breake out[.] [T]his they have proof of from hundreds of Negros, What will be the result of the strife God only knows[.]"[2]

True enough, in the latter half of the 18th century and into the 19th, antislavery sentiments prompted a few in the South and more in the North to help slaves as best they could. Free blacks in the North organized to help fugitives and create a refuge for them in Canada, and to found black schools and churches. Black and white abolitionists together maintained the Underground Railroad. Abolitionists not only propagandized endlessly in the North but also tried to reach white southern ears and consciences, or even to get their materials to the few slaves who had learned to read. With rare exceptions, such as David Walker, however, abolitionists black or white rarely tried to stir slaves to insurrection. Very occasionally, a free black in the South fomented and led an uprising.

In 1818 southerners took to court the Rev. Mr. Jacob Gruber, a Methodist minister, on a charge of intent to incite insurrection. His attorney freely admitted the abolitionist hopes of the Methodists, but, he said, they planned to achieve these by peaceable means. Gruber's arguments against slavery in his sermons, said the attorney, were "directed exclusively to the whites. . . . He could not have designed . . to influence the conduct of the slaves, but was obviously, and clearly, seeking to reform the hearts of the masters."[3]

Slaves with hopes of escape or insurrection might seize on whatever helpful information or hope for help they could pick up from what they heard in sermons or covertly read or gleaned from their masters' conversations. But probably the echoes of the successful Haitian slave revolution in 1791, led by Toussaint L'Ouverture, stirred them far more, giving them far more hope and inspiration to try to gain their own freedom.

## *The Laws of Slavery*

Early on, slaves tried to sue for freedom in the courts, and some succeeded. But as the institution of slavery was formalized, and as in the 1830s more and more civil rights were taken away, that legal approach was denied them.

New state laws declared them property in all respects save one: they could be punished if they broke the law. As property, they could not sue, they could not have a trial by jury, they could not testify against a white, and they would be judged by slaveholders, on the grounds that these would best protect the property interests of the owners of the accused slaves, "by infusing into the trial, that temperate and impartial feeling, which would probably exist in persons owning the same sort of property."[4]

The law did not even effectively protect slaves against the violence of their owners. True enough, their owners were not supposed to kill them, but the law recognized many mitigating circumstances for even this act. In the unlikely case that a homicide charge was brought against a master in the death of a slave, the accused might defend himself by alleging that the slave had provoked him or that the slave had been conspiring to rebel. For instance, a North Carolina law of 1774 designated the willful and malicious killing of a slave as murder and set the penalty of a year's imprisonment for a first offense and death for a second. However, this law exempted the homicide of "any Slave in the Act of Resistance to his lawful Owner or Master, or to any Slave dying under moderate correction."[5]

Protection for slaves from the violence of persons other than their owners was enacted mainly to keep masters from having their property harmed. On the whole, the law left slaves terrifyingly vulnerable. It was not until 1860 that the Mississippi legislature made it a crime for a *black* man to rape a black female under ten years old.[6] The law did not recognize rape of a slave woman by a white man. Though in the course of the 19th century some states granted slaves more safeguards, for the most part they were outside the law unless they themselves violated it.

A slave found guilty of a crime presented a problem, for he could not be punished in the same way as a white. He could not be fined, for he owned no property. If the state imprisoned or executed or deported him, it would be depriving his master of his services. Courts usually resorted to beatings as punishment or, in extreme cases, executed the slave and reimbursed his master for his value. A slave found guilty, wrote R. R. Cobb in 1858, "can be reached only through his body, and hence in cases not capital, whipping is the only punishment which can be inflicted. In the case of manslaughter, some of the States prescribe branding on the cheek as an additional punishment, more particularly with a view to protect distant and innocent purchasers from negroes who have been guilty of homicide. The extremes, death and whipping, being the only available punishments, it becomes necessary, in forming a slave code, to throw all offences under the one or the other. Hence, many offences are, from public policy, necessarily made capital, which, when committed by a white person, are not."[7]

A white might commit with impunity an action labeled as a crime when committed by a black. Moreover, the mitigating circumstances that would reduce the punishment for a crime committed by a white would not help the accused slave. Slaves were supposed to bear humbly and obediently insults and injuries that would excuse retaliation in a white. "[T]he same provocation which will so reduce the offence in a citizen, will not in a slave. A legal provocation for a slave, is such as, having due regard to the relative condition of the white man and the slave, and the obligation of the latter to conform his instinct and his passions to his condition of inferiority, would provoke a well-disposed slave into a violent passion. Hence, the mere fact of an engagement, on a sudden heat of passion, would not of itself form such a provocation."[8]

In short, the courts held, "Masters and slaves cannot be governed by the same common system of laws: so different are their positions, rights, and duties."[9]

## *Suicide and Self-Mutilation*

Some slaves turned their rage at their condition and at their masters against themselves, at the same time depriving their masters of the property they constituted. In the early days of slavery, many were prompted to suicide by the belief that in death they would return to Africa. Slaves in despair wounded themselves, suffocated themselves by drawing in their tongues to close off the passage of air, took poison, or drowned themselves. One 16-year-old, deciding that "she'd as leave be dead as to take the beatings her master gave her, . . . went into the woods and eat some poison oak. She died, too."[10]

Fear of being sold prompted some to mutilate themselves rather than leave their families and friends. Former slave Lewis Clarke in 1846 told of a carpenter named Ennis whose master bargained with a slave trader to carry him downriver: "He took a broadaxe and cut one hand off; then contrived to lift the axe, with his arm pressing it to his body, and let it fall upon the other, cutting off the ends of the fingers."[11]

## *Rebellions by Individual Slaves*

More commonly, slaves rebelled. Usually, of course, they just flared up for a moment, refused to obey, or ran away to the woods or swamps for a while. However, thousands of slaves resisted violently. In self-defense or revenge, or maddened by cruelty and frustration, they recklessly ignored the enormous odds against them. They fought off beatings. They burned their masters' buildings, damaged their crops, and killed their livestock. They assaulted whites, robbed them, and poisoned them.

Everyday irritations chafed slaves into disobedience and defiance. A slave who had endured many beatings might refuse to take another—like Frederick Douglass, who fought the master to whom he had been hired out: "We were at it for nearly two hours. Covey at length let me go, puffing and blowing at a great rate, saying that if I had not resisted, he would not have whipped me half so much. The truth was, that he had not whipped me at all. . . . [H]e had drawn no blood from me, but I had from him."[12]

Another slave might brood on his wrongs until he exploded into fury, and suddenly a tool became a weapon. Abram first assaulted his master with a hoe, then picked up a stone, which, he said, "I hurl'd at his head face, &c. again and again, until I thought he was certainly dead."[13] The slave Battiste terrorized a whole neighborhood in Alabama: "[V]arious citizens of Mobile frequently complained to the police that they lived in terror . . . of said slave, and were afraid to leave their houses. . . . [I]t was difficult for police officers to find him, and difficult to arrest him when found; . . . he had gone greased, in order to facilitate his escape, and wore his clothes without buttons, in such a manner that he could, and did readily divest himself when seized."[14]

Women sometimes reacted with equal violence. Mary Armstrong recalled her vengeance on her mistress: "[I picked] up a rock 'bout as big as half your fist and hits her right in the eye and busted the eyeball, and tells her that's for whippin' my baby sister to death. You could hear her holler for five miles."[15] Jinny testified in court that her fellow slave Creasy had broken her plow handle and as she set off to get it fixed her mistress struck her, "whereupon Creasy seized her, and her mistress called Sall; upon which Sall came up and struck her mistress upon the forehead and knocked her down and gave her several blows with the axe and killed her.[16] Celia, bought as a concubine by her widowed Missouri owner, killed him and burned his body in her fireplace.[17]

Now and then a slave's rebellion forced the owner into respectful wariness. After his battle royal, Frederick Douglass was never again beaten. Plantation mistress Susanna Warfield acknowledged in her diary that a particular slave "exercises dominion over me—or tries to do it—one would have thought to see her in the fury she was in yesterday that I was the Servant, she the mistress."[18] Or the owner might decide to sell the slave. Alternatively, as one slave who had beaten her mistress with her fists, knocking her through the panels of a door, reminisced, "The master . . . told me that as my mistress and I got along so badly, if I would take my child and go to New Jersey, and stay there, he would give me my freedom; I told him I would go. It was late at night; he wrote me a pass, gave it to me, and early the next morning I set out for New Jersey."[19]

## *Ruses and Deceptions*

Other slaves reacted less directly, more subtly, getting a bit of their own back whenever they thought they could do so without being detected. Most commonly, of course, they feigned sickness—women perhaps more often than men, because sometimes the owners were afraid to take chances with their reproductive abilities.

To protect themselves and each other, to gain some control over their lives, slaves lied. They covered their real emotions with a show of feelings more acceptable to their owners. They wept copiously even as they secretly rejoiced at the death of a cruel master.

Jim, who escaped to Canada, went back to the plantation for his family, "confessing" to his master, "I thought I wanted to be free, massa, so I run away and went to Canada. But I had a hard time there, and soon got tired of taking care of myself. I thought I would rather live with massa again and be a good servant. I found that Canada was no place for niggers; it's too cold, and we can't make any money there. Mean white folks cheat poor niggers out of their wages when they hire them. I soon got sick of being free and wished I was back on the old plantation. And those people called abolitionists, that I met with on the way, are a mean set of rascals. They pretend to help the niggers but they cheat them all they can. They get all the work out of a nigger they can and never pay him for it. I tell you, massa, they are mean folks. . . . Well, old massa seemed mightily pleased with my lies. He spoke pleasant to me, and said: 'Jim, I hope you will make a good missionary among our people and the neighbors.'" Jim did indeed do missionary work, but hardly of the expected kind. A few months later he led a group of 14 slaves across the Ohio River and onto the Underground Railroad.[20]

## *Insurrections: White Fears*

Oddly enough, the records show relatively little fear among slaveholders of rebellions of individual slaves, at least up until the Civil War. Time and time again, however, they reveal southern whites' deep-seated dread of the group revolts known as "insurrections." Presumably they felt that they had less to worry about from their own slaves than from those of others. "I am afraid of the lawless Yankee soldiers," Betty Herdon Maury wrote in her diary in April 1862, "but that is nothing to my fear of the negroes if they should rise against us."[21]

Fanny Kemble, newly arrived in the South, was struck by the miasma of fear: "[A] most ominous tolling of bells and beating of drums . . on the first evening of my arrival in Charleston, made me almost fancy myself in one of the old fortified frontier towns of the Continent, where the tocsin is sounded, and the evening drum beaten, and the guard set as regularly every night as if an invasion were expected. In Charleston, however, it is not the dread of foreign invasion, but of domestic insurrection, which occasions these nightly precautions. . . . [O]f course, it is very necessary where a large class of persons exists in the very bosom of a community whose interests are known to be at variance and incompatible with those of its other members. And no doubt these daily and nightly precautions are but trifling drawbacks upon the manifold blessings of slavery . . .; still, I should prefer going to sleep without the apprehension of my servants' cutting my throat in my bed, even to having a guard provided to prevent their doing so."[22]

After the Stono Rebellion of 1739 in South Carolina, white fear mounted to such a point that several farmers abandoned their homes. A century later, in 1836, plantation owner Iveson Brookes wrote to his wife, "The substance of [my dream] is that in some twenty or thirty years a division of the Northern & Southern States will be produced by the Abolitionists and then a war will issue between the Yankees & slave-holders—that the Army of Yankees will be at once joined by the N[egroe]s who will shew more savage cruelty than the blood thirsty Indians—and that Southerners with gratitude for having escaped alive will gladly leave their splendid houses & farms to be occupied by . . . those who once served them.—This all looks so plausible that I have been made to conclude that all who act with judicious foresight should within two years sell every [?] of a negro & land & vest the money in Western lands—so as to have a home and valuable possessions to flee to in time of danger."[23]

So strongly did whites fear slave insurrections that scholars still differ as to whether certain fancied conspiracies to rebel actually occurred. It was so easy to explain away a series of fires, say, by assuming that they had been set by slaves plotting to kill whites. Thus in New York City in 1712, for instance, there may or may not have been an insurrection. After several buildings burned, shaky evidence convicted some 25 African Americans, slave and free, of a plan to burn the town, destroy all its whites, and obtain their freedom, a plot in which they allegedly sealed their oath of secrecy by sucking each other's blood and rubbing conjurer's powder on their bodies to make them invincible. The convicted were burned alive, hanged, chained and starved, or broken on the wheel.

## *Insurrections: Their Nature*

Nevertheless, groups of slaves did rebel. In 1774, Abigail Adams wrote to her husband, "There has been in town a conspiracy of the negroes. At present it is kept pretty private, and was discovered by one who endeavored to dissuade them from it. . . . I wish most sincerely there was not a slave in the province; it always appeared a most iniquitous scheme to me to fight ourselves for what we are daily robbing and plundering from those who have as good a right to freedom as we have."[24]

In the early days, both slave men and women participated in these revolts. After a revolt in Louisiana in the early 1770s, for instance, one Mariana received a hundred lashes and lost her ears, though her punishment was lighter than that handed out to her male coconspirators. But even the earliest slave revolts were primarily male. Women were more apt to rebel individually, than collectively.[25]

Revolts could occur anywhere—in town, on a plantation, even in a coffle. In 1829 in Kentucky, "a white driver," by the name of Gordon, who had purchased in Maryland about sixty negroes, was taking them, assisted by an associate named Allen, and the wagoner who conveyed the baggage, to the Mississippi. The men were handcuffed and chained together. . . . It appears that, by means of a file the negroes, unobserved, had succeeded in separating the irons which bound their hands, in such a way as to be able to throw them off at any moment. About 8 o'clock in the morning, while proceeding on the state road leading from Greenup to Vanceburg, two of them dropped their shackles and commenced a fight, when the wagoner rushed in with his whip to compel them to desist. At this moment, every negro was found to be perfectly at liberty." The slaves overcame the men in charge, killing two, pillaged the wagon, stole $2,400, and 16 of them took to the woods. "The neighbourhood was immediately rallied, and a hot pursuit given—which, we understand, has resulted in the capture of the whole gang and the recovery of the greatest part of the money. Seven of the negro men and one woman, it is said were engaged in the murders, and will be brought to trial at the next court in Greensburg."[26]

More often than not, slave revolts were unplanned. A master or overseer who inflicted an unusually severe beating, violated a tacit agreement about the length of work hours, or suddenly withdrew privileges might find himself with a revolt on his hands. For hunger, a burning sense of injustice, or just the last straw could arouse not only individual but also group rebellions. This sort of local uprising was aimed at getting even, securing privileges, or restoring the accustomed order of things that the master or overseer had transgressed.

More rarely, slaves rebelled with the intention of escaping from or even overthrowing the slavery system. As a rule, these slaves planned to withdraw into self-governing, independent communities of fugitives, known as maroons. Less realistically, a small number dreamed of reversing the power structure, with blacks claiming the power then commanded by whites. We all dream of glory, and slaves did too. Though we must always allow for the possibility that white reports reflected more of abolitionist hopes or slaveowner fears than of reality, rumors abounded of the ambitions of black rebels. The *Liberator* reported in 1856 that a Tennessee slave woman had been told "that the negroes all intended rising on the day of the election, and that their plan was to take advantage of the absence of the white men on that day, and while they were all from home at the polls voting, to kill all the women and children, get all the money and arms, and waylay the men on their return home from the election and murder them; then make for the railroad cars, take them and go to Memphis, where they could find arms and friends from up the river to carry them off to the Free States if they did not succeed in taking this country."[27] In 1835, reports circulated that blacks then rising on the Brazos River in Texas had in their plans "divided all the cotton farms and they intended to ship the cotton to New Orleans and make the white men serve them in turn."[28]

Obviously, revolts were more likely on large plantations than on small farms. The more distant the master-slave relationship, the more probable a revolt. Slaves imported from Africa were more prone to rebel than those born into American slavery. So were slaves who lived where blacks heavily outnumbered whites. Islamic culture among the slaves more encouraged revolt than Christianity, especially because it divided slaves from owners. Geography too influenced rebellions, as when slaves saw a possibility of sustaining a maroon community in mountain fastnesses or forests or swamps. So also, hard times could encourage slaves to rebel, seeing their masters unable to provide them with food.

Whatever the intent or the immediate cause, the slaves' chances of success were almost nil. They were up against a system backed not only by the powers of the states but also by the beliefs of the community, slaveholders or not. The whites controlled the weapons. They constructed "black codes," specifically aimed at preventing rebellion by limiting the mobility and controlling the conduct of slaves. Efficient as the slave grapevine was in communicating within and among plantations and farms, isolation made secret planning difficult. Where were the leaders to come from? Free blacks were legally constrained almost as much as slaves; slave states tried vigorously to hold their numbers down, requiring that manumitted slaves leave the state. Natural leaders among slaves were frequently coopted by being singled out for positions of privilege, such as drivers, on the plantations so that they would have more to lose by rebelling. Conspirators could not even count on the secrecy of other blacks, who might betray the plot out of fear or loyalty to a master or mistress or white child, or in hope of a reward. The possible reward of freedom could powerfully motivate a slave who overheard rebellious plans. In any case, conspirators had to risk everything on one stroke. They could not retreat and regroup—they would not survive for a second try. Almost all planned insurrections were discovered and put down before they began or were crushed very soon after.

This pattern of failure gradually decreased the number of rebellions. Rationally, a slave would be better off trying to run away. Slim as his chances were in that effort, he risked less. Or he might simply decide to make the best of his enslavement, seeking what control over his life and what privileges he might acquire within the system. Nonetheless, slave rebellions persisted into the Civil War.

## *Insurrections: Specific Uprisings*

Among the many insurrections in the history of American slavery, a few stand out.

Escape attempts sometimes blurred into rebellions, as armed slaves fled in a self-protective group. Thus it was in the Stono, South Carolina, uprising of

September 9, 1739. When the Spanish held what is now Florida they repeatedly encouraged American slaves to escape there, offering them freedom and protection. On that September Sunday, about 20 slaves, perhaps encouraged by a Spanish emissary, sacked and burned the armory, seized arms and ammunition, and raided stores for supplies and liquor, killing the storekeepers and leaving their heads on their doorsteps. They then marched toward a Spanish fort in Florida manned by black militia. Along the way, waving banners and beating drums, calling out "Freedom," they enlisted other slaves. They burned and plundered plantations, killing 20 or 30 whites. But about 10 miles from Stono, a group of white planters caught up with the blacks, their numbers now grown to 60–100, and overcame most of them, though a small group escaped, only to be subdued the next Saturday.

More careful planning preceded Gabriel's rebellion in and around Richmond, Virginia, in 1800. Gabriel Prosser was semi-literate, with some knowledge of tactics. He was a defiant slave. Caught stealing a pig, he had fought punishment, biting off the ear of the man who was trying to inflict it; while in jail for that offense, he planned an insurrection. He was also a deeply religious man who believed himself called by God to lead an uprising; he wanted to model himself on the Biblical Samson. Upon his release, he concocted his plot with other slaves under the guise of religious meetings, they planned to kill all whites except Quakers, Methodists, and the French. He appointed a weapons-maker and sent out emissaries into the countryside to enlist men.

The conspirators planned to seize the bridges and raid the local magazine for weapons, the mills for bread, and the state house treasury for money, dividing the money among them. Then they would crown Gabriel king of Virginia. They expected all blacks and maybe some poor whites to join them, not only in Virginia but across the continent. They also hoped for help from the Catawba Indians. Should they fail, however, they would retreat into the mountains. Alas for their dreams, two slaves betrayed them before they began operations, and the authorities set about arresting all the conspirators they could find, including Gabriel himself.

Twenty-odd years later, in about 1821, freeman Denmark Vesey organized an insurrection of slaves and free blacks in Charleston, South Carolina. Vesey, a mulatto, had spent two decades at sea as a slave on a slaving vessel, until in 1800, when he won a lottery. With his $1,500 prize he bought his own freedom and set himself up as a carpenter. An eccentric, a polygamist with slave wives and children, he was intelligent, ambitious, and domineering. He spent hours studying the Bible, eventually concluding that he had a religious duty to incite slaves to rebellion.

Vesey thought that he could expect aid from England and from Haiti and that all slaves would rise in his support. He planned long and carefully, over some five years. He recruited at local congregations, urging slaves to behave proudly and quoting the Bible to persuade them that acquiescence in bondage was sinful. He named as one of his lieutenants a sorcerer, a slave named Gullah Jack, who some other slaves thought could make them invulnerable. Estimates of the number of people involved in the plot run as high as 9,000.[29] But some scholars, notably Richard C. Wade, believe that "no conspiracy in fact existed, or at most that it was a vague and unformulated plan in the minds or on the tongues of a few colored townsmen. No elaborate network had been established in the countryside; no cache of arms lay hidden about the city; no date for an uprising had been set; no underground apparatus, carefully organized and secretly maintained, awaited a signal to fire Charleston and murder the whites. What did exist were strong grievances on one side and deep fears on the other."[30]

Whatever the case, too many people shared the secret for it to be safe. Two blacks reported it, the insurrection was foiled, and those convicted suffered deportation or death.

Finally, there was Nat Turner, in himself an insurrection poised to happen. From his childhood near Suffolk, Virginia, he believed himself a born prophet, "intended for some great purpose." He saw visions and heard voices, found blood on corn and hieroglyphs on leaves. An eclipse of the sun in February 1831 persuaded him, he said, that "I should arise and prepare myself, and slay my enemies with their own weapons. . . . I communicated the great work laid out for me to do, to four in whom I had the greatest confidence (Henry, Hark, Nelson, and Sam). It was intended by us to have begun the work of death on the 4th of July last. Many were the plans formed and rejected by us, and it affected my mind to such a degree that I fell sick, and the time passed without our coming to any determination how to commence—still forming new schemes and rejecting them, when the sign appeared again, which determined me not to wait longer." Thereupon the group agreed to spare no one and to "carry terror and devastation wherever we went."[31] The five and their recruits rampaged murderously through the countryside, killing some 55 whites.

Turner, like so many of his predecessors, had believed that he could raise a large black army. He could not. The militia soon overcame his band of some 60 men, capturing Turner himself a couple of weeks later.

## *Insurrections: Their Results*

Insurrections immediately resulted in harsher controls and stiffer punishments on blacks. Whites, who complained of the barbarity of insurrectionists' actions, did not hesitate to torture and kill those whom they suspected of such plots and to display their mutilated bodies. All too typical were the reactions of the citizens of Gallatin, Tennessee, in 1856: "[T]he question was, what shall be done with the four leaders now in jail? A number of voices said, *'hang them at once.'* On this a vote was taken, and one tremendous shout of 'Aye' was interrupted by only three small voices. . . . The meeting then adjourned to the jail, and though the jailor did all in his power to prevent it, the aforesaid Sam, Jack, Ellick and Dick were taken out and executed."[32]

In the long run, however, insurrections may have led to compromises and adjustments to the slave system, with an eye to keeping it working. Just as individual rebellions sometimes taught owners not to meddle with certain slaves, so group insurrections sometimes led to accommodations and concessions on the part of white society. Almost certainly they hastened the end of the African slave trade, as whites became wary of bringing in more potential insurrectionists.

On the other hand, the string of rebellions, particularly Nat Turner's, helped to defeat such organized abolitionism as had existed in the South. For a time in the second half of the 18th and the beginning of the 19th centuries, a number of southerners had agreed that slavery was morally wrong and seriously looked for a way to end it. But in the 1830s, in the wake of the insurrections, this feeling transmuted into passionate defenses of slavery as a system ordained by God, healthy for blacks and whites alike, and essential to the welfare of their states.

## *Maroon Communities*

Fugitive slaves, both men and women, sometimes found their freedom for shorter or longer time in maroon communities, or communities of "outlyers." These centered especially in the Carolinas, Virginia, Louisiana, Florida, Georgia, Mississippi, and Alabama, in semitropical, sparsely settled locations. They began early. What might be called the first was founded by the hundred or so black slaves who in 1526 rebelled against the Spanish colonizer Lucas Vásquez de Ayllón. The rebels took refuge with Indians and became the first permanent inhabitants, other than Indians, of what is now the United States.[33]

Wartime offered inviting opportunities for slaves to escape and set up maroon colonies. In 1783, William Reynolds of Charleston complained that 30 of his slaves had run away to follow the British army to Georgia and thereafter had joined up with the Creek Indians.[34] Wars also left behind bands of black soldiers who had fought against the United States. After the American Revolution, for instance, blacks who had taken the British side carried on guerrilla warfare along the Savannah River until 1783. During the War of 1812, the British built a fort for themselves and their black and Indian allies. After the war, three hundred fugitive slaves took it over, cultivating land for 50 miles round about. The fort was destroyed only after its defenders fired on an American gunboat. Survivors among them went on to fight in the Seminole wars. In the confusion of the Civil War, maroons flourished as never before, favoring locations invaded by Union troops, especially in Virginia, the Carolinas, Florida, and Louisiana.

Unsettled political and economic conditions also provided opportunities for slaves to found maroon colonies. Sometimes in these they allied themselves with poor whites and Indians.

Most "outlyers" were nomadic. Occasionally, though, a group established itself on a permanent site, preferably one easily defended. When they could, outlyers chose places near disputed borders or friendly Indian tribes. In the early 18th century, some outlyers tried to re-create African villages, choosing as a chief a slave who had been an African prince, building homes of grasses and branches, and planting crops. The most noted of the established communities was that in the Great Dismal Swamp between Virginia and North Carolina, founded before 1800. There some 2,000 fugitives and their descendants lived, more or less accepted, trading with their white neighbors on the borders of the swamp. So long did some of these colonies last that children born in them grew up to become their leaders. Some maroons never saw a white person.

Many maroons supported themselves by raiding and stealing. The insecure and difficult conditions under which they lived turned some of them into desperadoes. Their guerrilla activities, of course, aroused the inhabitants on whose property they preyed. States might respond to pleas for protection by paying Indians so much for each maroon scalp taken.

Residents also feared that the maroons would lure away their slaves or foment insurrection among them. In the early days, maroon colonies did indeed depend on slaves for support and encouraged them to desert and rebel. But their interests were not identical. Slaves sometimes went in fear of the maroons, who seized their supplies and their women. Colonial powers would sometimes allow a maroon enclave to exist in peace *if* it would capture runaway slaves and help them put down slave revolts. Similar tactics on the part of the whites eventually made maroons into enemies of the Indians, on whom they had originally relied for help.

Slavery, with all its indignities and cruelties, failed to quell the spirit of all the African Americans on whom it was inflicted. In small ways and large, daring the lash and death itself, many of them fought for at least some degree of control over their own fates. The record on slave escapes and rebellions is too murky to allow us ever to know precisely how often they occurred. But it does clearly reveal that these risings figured significantly in the history of the country during the dreadful days of slavery. One small illustration: in February 1841, Cong. Joshua Giddings complained "that Congress had appropriated $250,000 in 1821 to pay Georgia slaveholders for slaves who had fled to the Seminole tribes of Florida between 1770 and 1790; that an unused portion of this sum, amount[ing] to $141,000, was prorated to these slaveholders by special act of Congress as 'compensation for the offspring which they would have borne their masters, had they remained in servitude'; that the fugitives had intermarried with the Seminoles, and the latter could not come out of the swamps without surrendering their wives and children to slavery; that bloodhounds were imported from Cuba at a cost of $5,000 to track them down; that by order of the commanding General all Negroes, cattle and horses belonging to the Indians were the property of the army unit capturing them; that $20 each was paid to the soldiers from the United States Treasury for more than 500 of these slaves, who were turned over to claimants."[35]

## Chronicle of Events

**1526**
Black slaves of the Spanish colonizer Lucas Vásquez de Ayllón (in what is now South Carolina) rebel, fleeing to the Indians, with whom they remain as the first permanent inhabitants other than Indians of what is now the United States.

**1657**
In Hartford, Connecticut, Africans and Indians are said to have joined in an uprising and destroyed some buildings.

**1676**
In Virginia, blacks join white indentured servants, unemployed workers, and other whites in Bacon's Rebellion, a fairly long-lived political and economic movement led by an aristocrat but largely composed of disaffected whites.

**1682**
Virginia requires that church wardens must read the act of 1680 "on Negro insurrection" twice a year during divine service and forbids a master or overseer to allow a slave of another to remain on his plantation more than four hours without permission of the slave's owner.

**1687**
A slave insurrection is attempted at Northern Neck, Virginia.

**1708**
In Queen's County, New York, an Indian slave and his black wife kill their master and his family, for which they and two black accomplices are put to death.

**1710**
A plan of insurrection on foot in Surrey City, Virginia, is revealed by the slave Will, in return for his freedom.

**1712**
Violence resulting from an alleged New York City slave revolt results in the deaths of nine whites and the execution of 18 slaves. It provokes even harsher conditions for all blacks, slave or free; new restrictions permit manumission only after a master guarantees the slave's ability to be self-supporting, prohibit the harboring of any slaves, forbid slaves to carry arms or to testify against free people, and make arson by a slave a capital offense.

**1720**
In Charleston, South Carolina, slaves attack whites in their homes and on the street.

**1722**
In Virginia near the mouth of the Rappahannock river, two hundred blacks arm themselves, intending to kill whites in church, but flee upon discovery.

**1723**
When fires break out in Boston, Indian and black slaves are suspected of arson.

**1728**
In Savannah, slaves plan an insurrection but quarrel among themselves.

**1730**
Slaves in Williamsburg, Virginia, hearing a rumor that the king has ordered that all baptized persons be freed, plan to rebel.

A black insurrection arises in the plantations around New Orleans.

South Carolina slaves allegedly conspire to destroy all the whites.

A slave plunders and burns a house in Malden, Massachusetts, complaining that his master had sold him to a man whom he does not like.

**1734**
In Burlington, Pennsylvania, slaves allegedly conspire to kill every master and his sons and their draft horses, set the masters' property on fire, and secure their saddle horses for flight to the Indians.

**1738**
When 23 runaway slaves arrive in St. Augustine, the Spanish governor announces that he will establish them at a well-fortified settlement at Mosa, at the mouth of the St. Johns River.

**1739**
Slaves sack and burn the armory at Stono, South Carolina, then march toward a Florida fort manned by a black militia company. On the way they enlist more

runaways, gather arms, kill whites, and stir expectations of freedom. The colonial militia crushes the rebellion.

In South Carolina, the militia is called out to pursue a group of runaway slaves committing robberies around Dorchester.

**1740**

*May–July:* In the "Inglorious Expedition," Georgia and Carolina troops attempt to invade Florida in retaliation for "the Protection our deserted Slaves have met with" there.

*June:* 150 unarmed slaves gather near Charleston; 50 are captured and hanged.

**1740–1741**

A series of fires in New York City sets off hysterical suspicions of slave insurrection, resulting in severe punishment of 154 free and slave blacks.

**1751**

South Carolina prescribes punishment for any black who instructs another about poisons.

**1754**

Black women allegedly burn the buildings of C. Croft of Charleston, South Carolina.

**1755**

Slaves Mark and Phillis are executed for poisoning their master, Mr. John Codman of Charlestown, Massachusetts—he by hanging and she by being burned alive.

**1768**

British captain John Wilson allegedly attempts to incite Boston slaves to insurrection, assuring them that the British troops have come to secure their freedom.

**1782**

A white man, a notorious robber, gathers about 50 blacks and whites and terrorizes a community in Georgia.

**1791**

Toussaint Louverture, a former slave, leads a successful (and bloody) rebellion against French rule in Santo Domingo, eventually establishing the Republic of Haiti and abolishing slavery. In the United States, Toussaint Louverture becomes a symbol of slave rebellion.

**1793**

In Albany, New York, three blacks are executed for setting a major fire.

**1795**

The Pointe Coupee uprising in Louisiana results in the hanging of 26 slaves.

The "General of the Swamps," leader of a group of outlyers, is caught and killed.

**1796**

Fires, allegedly set by blacks, break out in Charleston, South Carolina, New York, Savannah, Baltimore, and Newark and Elizabeth, New Jersey.

**1800**

Led by visionary blacksmith Gabriel Prosser and his preacher brother Martin, slaves unsuccessfully try to march on Richmond to kill the city's white inhabitants (except the Quakers, Methodists, and French).

The Virginia legislature asks the governor to correspond with the president of the United States about purchasing lands outside the state for a penal colony to which to transport slaves involved in insurrection.

**1807**

A number of Africans brought to Charleston, South Carolina, for sale starve themselves to death in the slave pens.

**1811**

Free mulatto Charles Deslondes from Haiti leads a slave rebellion in Louisiana. One hundred eighty or more poorly armed slaves strike toward New Orleans, only to be defeated by slaveholders, free black militia, and federal troops.

**1812**

Insurrections are crushed in Virginia, Louisiana, and Kentucky.

**1813**

Insurrections are crushed in the District of Columbia, South Carolina, and Virginia.

**1814**

Insurrections are crushed in Maryland and Virginia.

**1816**
White storekeeper George Baxley leads an unsuccessful slave insurrection in Spottsylvania City, Virginia.

**1822**
Denmark Vesey, a former slave, allegedly conspires to organize a slave revolt in South Carolina. His plans are betrayed by followers, and he is executed along with 37 slaves; 30 others are sold out of the state.

**1826**
Seventy-seven slaves mutiny on a Mississippi River steamer, kill five, and escape to Indiana.

On the *Decatur,* going from Baltimore to Georgia, 29 slaves rebel, throw the captain and the mate overboard, put a white crew member in command, and order him to steer for Haiti.

Inhabitants of New Bern, Tarborough, and Hillsborough, in North Carolina, informed that 40 slaves whom they suspect of insurrectionary intention are assembled in a nearby swamp, surround it and kill all the slaves.

**1828**
Four slave artisans being carried by ship from Charleston to New Orleans commit suicide during the voyage.

**1829**
Slaves in a coffle from Maryland to the South attack their guards, killing two.

The governor of Georgia talks of a conspiracy in Georgetown, South Carolina, and of fires set by slaves in Augusta and Savannah.

**1831**
*August 22:* Nat Turner's rebellion begins in the home of his master, Joseph Travis, and spreads through Southampton County, Virginia. The killing spree is ended by a band of white men, who hang Turner and a number of his fellows.

**1835**
Texas revolts against Mexico, at least partly over the slavery issue; slaves unsuccessfully attempt an insurrection.

**1837**
Slaves plot insurrection in Alexandria, Louisiana; vigilantes hang nine.

**1841**
One hundred thirty-five slaves on the *Creole* out of Richmond rise and take the ship to Nassau, where the British authorities free them.

**1845**
Seventy-five Maryland slaves arm and begin to march toward Pennsylvania; some are killed, and 31 are recaptured.

**1849–1850**
In Philadelphia, blacks attacked by white mobs defend themselves with bricks and paving stones.

John Brown canonized. The legend reads: "Meeting the Slave-mother and her Child on the steps of Charleston jail on his way to execution. The Artist has represented Capt. Brown regarding with a look of compassion a Slave-mother and Child who obstructed the passage on his way to the Scaffold.—Capt. Brown stooped and kissed the Child—then met his fate. From the original painting by Louis Ransom." (*Library of Congress*)

**1851**
Blacks in Lancaster, Pennsylvania, riot for freedom.

**1854**
Texas forbids either blacks or whites to aid, plan, or incite a slave rebellion.

**1856**
In Colorado City, Texas, a large group (perhaps four hundred) of free and hired-out blacks, assisted by Mexicans, plan for slaves to rise and fight their way to Mexico.

One hundred fifty black men march on Dover, Tennessee, attempting to liberate the black iron workers jailed for trying to seize the mines where they work.

**1858**
John Brown proposes the organization of a biracial, armed movement to uproot slavery, moving down from northern Virginia into the Deep South to form a provisional government of black and white people in a kind of guerrilla territory within the United States, under the formal aegis of the U.S. government.

**1859**
*October 16:* John Brown leads a small biracial group attempting to capture the armory at Harpers Ferry, Virginia. His hanging makes him an abolitionist martyr.

**1860**
White authorities in Waxahachie, Texas, claim to uncover a plan for a black uprising, and a Committee of Vigilance leads a mob in lynching the supposed leaders: Sam Smith, Cato, and Patrick.

In Alabama, 25 blacks and four whites are executed for allegedly participating in a plot to take over the area.

**1861**
Forty black men are hanged in the Natchez, Mississippi, area for allegedly plotting insurrection.

Two black men and a black woman are hanged in northern Arkansas for allegedly plotting insurrection.

*December:* Sixty slaves march through New Castle, Kentucky, "singing political songs and shouting for Lincoln," and no one dares stop them.

## Eyewitness Testimony

### *Laws Governing Slaves: Enslavement*

[W]hatsoever freeborn woman shall intermarry with any slave, from and after the last day of the present assembly, shall serve the master of such slave during the life of her husband; and . . . all issue of such free woman, so married, shall be slaves as their fathers were.

*Maryland law of 1663, in Olexer,* Enslavement of the American Indian, *48.*

*And be it further enacted,* That if any slave hereafter emancipated shall remain within this commonwealth more than twelve months after his or her right to freedom shall have accrued, he or she shall forfeit all such right, and may be apprehended and sold by the overseers of the poor of any county or corporation in which he or she shall be found, for the benefit of the poor. . . .

*Virginia law, 1805, in Finkelman,* Law of Freedom, *111.*

### *Laws Governing Slaves: Slave Codes*

In order to show the true aspect of slavery among us, I will state distinct propositions, each supported by the evidence of actually existing laws:

1. Slavery is hereditary and perpetual, to the last moment of the slave's earthly existence, and to all his descendants, to the latest posterity.
2. The labor of the slave is compulsory and uncompensated; while the kind of labor, the amount of toil, and the time allowed for rest, are dictated solely by the master. . . .
3. The slave being considered a personal chattel, may be sold, or pledged, or leased, at the will of his master. . . .
4. Slaves can make no contracts, and have no legal right to any property, real or personal.
5. Neither a slave, nor free colored person, can be a witness against any white or free man, in a court of justice. . . .
6. The slave may be punished at his master's discretion—without trial. . . .
7. The slave is not allowed to resist any free man under any circumstances. . . .
8. Slaves cannot redeem themselves, or obtain a change of masters, though cruel treatment may have rendered such a change necessary for their personal safety.
9. The slave is entirely unprotected in his domestic relations.
10. The laws greatly obstruct the manumission of slaves, even where the master is willing to enfranchise them.
11. The operation of the laws tends to deprive slaves of religious instruction and consolation.
12. The whole power of the laws is exerted to keep slaves in a state of the lowest ignorance.
13. There is in this country a monstrous inequality of law and right. . . . [T]he same offences which cost a white man a few dollars only, are punished in the negro with death.

*Abolitionist Lydia Child,* Appeal *(1836), 41–42.*

The tribunal for the trial of slaves [in South Carolina] . . . is the worst system which could be devised. The consequence is, that the passions and prejudices of the neighborhood arising from a recent offense, enter into trial, and often lead to the condemnation of the innocent.

*Judge John Belton O'Neall, 1848, in Higginbotham,* In the Matter of Color, *180.*

The slave, who is but *"a chattel"* on all *other* occasions, with not one solitary attribute of personality accorded to him, becomes *"a person"* whenever he is to be *punished!* He is the only being in the universe to whom is denied all self-direction and free agency, but who is, nevertheless, held responsible for his conduct, and amenable to law. Forbidden to *read* the law, and kept as ignorant and as unenlightened as possible, he is nevertheless accounted criminal for acts which are deemed innocent in others, and punished with a severity from which all others are exempted. He is under the *control* of law, though *unprotected* by law, and can know law only as an enemy, and not as a friend.

*Goodell,* Slave Code *(1853), 309.*

### *Laws Governing Slaves: Concerning Slaves as Victims*

*Be it enacted* . . . if any slave resist his master . . . and by the extremity of the correction should chance to die, that his death shall not be accompted ffelony, but the master . . . be acquit from molestation, since it cannot be presumed that prepensed malice . . . should induce any man to destroy his owne estate.

*Virginia act, 1669, in Finkelman,* Law of Freedom, *17.*

For the prevention and restraining of inhuman severities which by evil masters or overseers, may be used towards their Christian servants, that from and after the publication hereof, if any man smite out the eye or tooth of his man servant or maid servant, or otherwise maim or disfigure them much, unless it be by mere casualty, he shall let him or her go free from his service, and shall allow such further recompense as the court of quarter sessions shall adjudge him. . . . That if any person or persons whatever in this province shall wilfully kill his Indian or negroe servant or servants he shall be punished with death.

*New Hampshire law, 1718, in Williams,* History of the Negro Race, *I:311.*

They further informed me . . . that for killing a negro, ever so wantonly, as without provocation, there could be nothing but a fine; they gave a late instance of this; that (further) to *steal* a negro was death, but to *kill him* was only fineable.

*Bostonian Josiah Quincy Jr., visiting South Carolina, 1773, in Bell,* Major Butler's Legacy, *67.*

Be it enacted . . . That the offence of Killing a Slave shall hereafter be denominated and considered homicide, and shall partake of the same degree of guilt when accompanied with the like circumstances that homicide now does at common law.

*North Carolina law, 1817, in Finkelman,* Law of Freedom, *201.*

The prisoner was put upon his trial . . . for the murder of his own female slave, a woman named Mira. The witnesses . . testified to a series of the most brutal and barbarous whippings, scourgings and privations, inflicted by the prisoner upon the deceased, from about the first of December, to the time of her death in the ensuing March, while she was in the latter stages of pregnancy, and afterwards, during the period of her confinement and recovery from a recent delivery. A physician . . called to view the body of the deceased, stated that there were five wounds on the head of the deceased, four of which appeared to have been inflicted a week or more before her death; that the fifth was a fresh wound, about one and a half inches long, and to the bone, and was, in his opinion, sufficient to have produced her death; that there were many other wounds on different parts of her body, which were sufficient independent of those on the head, to have caused death. The reasons assigned by the prisoner to those who witnessed his inhuman treatment of the deceased, were, at one time, that she stole his turnips and sold them to the worthless people in the neighborhood, and that she had attempted to burn his barn, and was disobedient and impudent to her mistress; at another, that she had attempted to burn his still house, and had put something in a pot to poison his family. There was no evidence except her own confessions, extorted by severe whippings, that the deceased was guilty of any of the crimes imputed to her; nor did it appear that she was disobedient or impertinent to her master or mistress; on the contrary, she seemed, as some of the witnesses testified, to do her best to obey the commands of her master, and that when she failed to do so, it was from absolute inability to comply with orders to which her condition and strength were unequal. . . .

[Chief Justice Ruffin:] [T]he prisoner employed himself from day to day in practising grievous tortures upon an enfeebled female. . . . He beat her with clubs, iron chains, and other deadly weapons, time after time; burnt her; inflicted stripes over and often, with scourges, which literally excoriated her whole body; forced her out to work in inclement seasons, without being duly clad; provided for her insufficient food; exacted labour beyond her strength, and wantonly beat her because she could not comply with his requisitions. These enormities, besides others too disgusting to be particularly designated, the prisoner, without his heart once relenting or softening, practised from the first of December until the latter end of the ensuing March; and he did not relax even up to the last hour of his victim's existence. . . .

*North Carolina case State* v. *Hoover, 1839, in Finkelman,* Law of Freedom, *227–29.*

## Individual Rebels: Fighting Back

[G]reat disorders, insolences and burglaries are oft times raised and committed in the night time by

Indians, negro and mulatto servants and slaves, to the disquiet and hurt of her majesty's good subjects.

*1703 Massachusetts act establishing a curfew, in Higginbotham,* In the Matter of Color, *77.*

Shall a man be deem'd a rebel that supports his own rights? It is the first law of nature, and he must be a rebel to God, to the laws of nature, and his own conscience, who will not do it.

*Rev. Isaac Skillman,* Oration upon the Beauties of Liberty, *1772, in Aptheker,* One Continual Cry, *24.*

At first the quarrel began between my wife and her mistress. I was then at work in the barn, and hearing a racket in the house, induced me to run there and see what had broken out. When I entered the house, I found my mistress in a violent passion with my wife, for what she informed me was a mere trifle. . . . I earnestly requested my wife to beg pardon of her mistress for the sake of peace, even if she had given no just occasion for offence. But whilst I was thus saying, my mistress turned the blows which she was repeating on my wife to me. I reached out my great black hand, raised it up and received the blows of the whip on it which were designed for my head. Then I immediately committed the whip to the devouring fire.

Some days after his [my master's] return, in the morning as I was putting on a log in the fireplace, not suspecting harm from any one, I received a most violent stroke on the crown of my head with a club two feet long and as large around as a chair post. This blow very badly wounded my head. . . . The first blow made me have my wits about me . . ., for as soon as he went to renew it I snatched the club out of his hands and dragged him out of the door. He then sent for his brother to come and assist him, but I presently left my master, took the club he wounded me with, carried it to a neighboring justice of the peace, and complained of my master. He finally advised me to return to my master and live contented with him till he abused me again, and then complain. . . . But before I set out for my master's, up he came and his brother Robert after me. The Justice improved this convenient opportunity to caution my master. He asked him for what he treated his slave thus hastily and unjustly, and told him what would be the consequence if he continued the same treatment towards me. After the justice had ended his discourse with my master, he and his brother set out with me for home, one before and the other behind me. . . . [T]hey both dismounted . . . and fell to beating me with great violence. I . . . immediately turned them both under me, laid one of them across the other, and stamped them both with my feet. . . .

*Venture,* Life and Adventures *(1798), 14–15.*

[Sarah is] the biggest devil that ever lived, having poisoned a stud horse and set a stable on fire, also burnt Gen. R. Williams stable and stock yard with seven horses and other property to value of $1500. She was handcuffed and got away at Ruddles Mills on her way down the river, which is the fifth time she escaped when about to be sent out of the country.

*Kentucky planter's 1822 advertisement, in Blassingame,* Slave Community, *116.*

[Sinda] passed at one time for a prophetess among her fellow slaves on the plantation, and had acquired such an ascendancy over them that, having given out . . . that the world was to come to an end at a certain time, and that not a very remote one, the belief in her assertion took such possession of the people [slaves] on the estate that they refused to work, and the rice and cotton fields were threatened with an indefinite fallow in consequence of this strike on the part of the cultivators. Mr. K[ing], who was then overseer of the property . . . acquiesced in their determination not to work; but he expressed to them his belief that Sinda was mistaken, and he warned her that if, at the appointed time, it proved so, she would be severely punished. . . . [P]oor Sinda was in the wrong. Her day of judgment came indeed, and a severe one it proved. . . . [T]he spirit of false prophecy was mercilessly scourged out of her, and the faith of her people of course reverted from her to the omnipotent lash again.

*Kemble,* Journal *(1839), 118–19.*

Then there was the unruly slave, whom no master particularly wanted for several reasons: first, he would not submit to any kind of corporal punishment; second, it was hard to determine which was the master or which the slave; third, he worked when he pleased to do so. . . . This class of slaves were usually industrious, but very impudent. There were thousands of that class, who spent their lives in their master's service doing his work undisturbed, because the master understood the slave. . . . [T]here were thousands of high-toned and high spirited slaves, who had as much self-respect as their masters, and who were industri-

An individual slave rebellion—a more frequent occurrence than an insurrection (*Library of Congress*)

ous, reliable, and truthful, and could be depended on by their masters in all cases. . . . These slaves knew their own helpless condition. . . . But . . . they did not give up in abject servility.

*Ex-slave Henry Clay Bruce, in Blassingame,* Slave Community, *215–16.*

[My mother] was a black African an' she sho' was wild an' mean. [Nobody could whip her unless she was tied up, so] sometimes my master would wait 'til de next day to git somebody to he'p tie her up, den dey'd fergit to whip 'er. [She was the cause] of my ol' masser firin' all de overseers. . . . [S]he was so mean he was afraid dey'd kill her. She'd work without no watchin' an' overseers wa'n't nothin' nohow.

*Susan Snow, in Fox-Genovese,* Plantation Households, *187.*

[Having heard a slave say] that if he ever struck her [as he had just struck another], it would be the day he or she would die, [the overseer struck her; she knocked him from his horse with her hoe and then] pounced upon him and chopped his head off. . . . [Then she] proceeded to chop and mutilate his body; that done to her satisfaction, she then killed his horse, [then] calmly went to tell the master of the murder. . . . [He said,] "You are free from this day and if the mistress wants you to do anything for her, do it if you want to."

*Ex-slave Irene Coates, in Fox-Genovese,* Plantation Households, *317.*

At this, Ma [Fannie] took the baby by its feet, one foot in each hand, and with the Baby's head swinging downward, she vowed to smash its brains out before she'd leave it. Tears were streaming down her face. . . . It was seldom that Ma cried and everyone knew that she meant every word. Ma took her baby with her.

*Fannie's daughter, describing her mother's reaction when told that she was to be sold for attacking her mistress and could not take her baby with her, in Lerner,* Black Women, *38.*

## *Individual Rebels: Ruses and Revenges*

After that I again refused to eat anything, at all; but pretended to be sick all of the time. I also told Frankee to tell my master that I was subject to such turns every spring, and I should not live through this. . . . He then again tried to make me eat . . ., often leaving victuals by my bedside at night, or order Frankee to do it. He would then inquire of her if I had eaten anything yet. She replied, no, sir, I have not seen him eat anything since last Friday noon. I had his horse to water every day; and as I went out of, or across the yard, where I knew he would see me, I would pretend to be so weak that I could scarcely go. . . . I would, however, have it understood that during all this time I did not go without victuals. . . . One morning he sent me to eat my breakfast. I went, and returned. When I came back, he asked me if I had eaten my breakfast? I told him, no, sir, I thank you, I did not wish for any. You did not, did you? Gad dam you, you are sick, are you? You may die and be damned, by Gad;—you may die and be damned;—your coffin shall not cost me a quarter of a dollar, by Gad;—you shall be buried on your face, by Gad;—you may die and be damned. . . .

I went to one Major Lewis, a free black man, and very cunning. I gave him money to go to my master and run me down, and endeavor to convince him that I was really sick, and should never be good for anything. In a few days from this, my master came down in the kitchen and says, boy get up; there, boy, (holding it out in his hand,) there is the very money I gave for you; I have got my money again, and you may go and be damned; and don't you never step into my house again; if you do, I will split your damned brains out.

*William Grimes,* Life *(1855), 82–83.*

[A Virginia planter complained of] the liability of women, especially to disorders and irregularities which cannot be detected by exterior symptoms, but which may be easily aggravated into serious complaints. . . . "They don't come to the field and you go to the quarters and ask the old nurse what's the matter and she says, 'Oh; she's not . . fit to work, sir'; and . . . you have to take her word for it that something or other is the matter with her, and you dare not set her to work; and so she will lay up till she feels like taking the air again, and plays the lady at your expense."

*Olmsted,* Seaboard Slave States, *190.*

About four years ago a negro who gave the impression of being a good subject, and even wanting to appear religious, came to see me for about a month, making me fine promises and begging me, almost on his knees to free him by buying him from a bad position. I was foolish enough to agree to this . . . and, in all of this, I was duped by a first-class knavery, either on the part of those who sold him to me well guaranteed, while he had been fraudulently brought into the state, or by the negro himself who . . . did not give me even one hundred dollars . . . and who finally by negligence or bad will on the part of Mr. Soule my lawyer, succeeded in having himself recognized as free, while it would have been so easy to prove the opposite. Hence I lost the negro, and, besides, I was condemned to pay him twelve Hundred dollars for *His work.*

*Clothile Bornet, February 14, 1846, in Owens,* Property, *220.*

[My mother] often hid us all in the woods. . . . When we wanted water, she sought for it in any hole or puddle formed by falling trees or otherwise. It was often full of tadpoles and insects. She strained it, and gave it round to each of us in the hollow of her hand. For food, she gathered berries in the woods, got potatoes, raw corn, etc. After a time, the master would send word to her to come in, promising he would not sell us.

*Ex-slave Moses Grandy, quoted in Webber,* Deep Like the Rivers, *166.*

Ole Marsa would spell out real fas' anything he don't want me to know 'bout. One day Marsa was fit to be tied, he was in setch a bad mood. Was ravin' 'bout de crops, an' taxes, an' de triflin' niggers he got to feed. "Gonna sell 'em, I swear before Christ, I gonna sell 'em," he says. Den ole Missus ask which ones he gonna sell an' tell him quick to spell it. Den he spell out G-A-B-E and R-U-F-U-S. 'Course I stood dere without battin' an eye, an' makin' believe I didn't even hear him, but I was packin' dem letters up in my haid all de time. An' soon's I finished dishes I rushed down to my father an' say 'em to him jus' like marsa say 'em. Father say quiet-like: "Gabe and Rufus," an' tol' me to go back to de house an' say I ain't been out. De next day Gabe and Rufus was gone—dey had run away. Marsa nearly died, got to cussin' an' ravin' so he took sick. Missus went to town an' tol' de sheriff, but dey never could fin' dose two slaves.

*Ex-slave, quoted in Webber,* Deep Like the Rivers, *228–29.*

[O]ld Aunt Delia, the cook who had been in the family for years and completely bossed the kitchen, came right out and said, "How many times I spit in the biscuits and peed in the coffee just to get back at them mean white folks."

*Murray,* Proud Shoes, *159–60.*

All the slaves were allowed to stop at home that day [when the master died] to see the last of him, and to lament with mistress. After all the slaves who cared to do so had seen his face, they gathered in groups around mistress to comfort her; they shed false tears, saying "Never mind, missus, massa gone home to heaven." While some were saying this, others said, "Thank God, massa gone home to hell."

*Ex-slave Jacob Stroyer, in Raboteau,* Slave Religion, *297.*

### *Individual Rebels: Suicides and Self-Mutilations*

[When the wife learned of her imminent sale, she and her husband] resolved to put an End to their lives, rather than be parted; and accordingly, at seven o'clock (the Wench being at the House of her countryman), they went up Stairs into the Garret, where the Fellow, as is supposed, cut out the Wench's Throat with a Razor, and then shot himself with a Gun prepared for the Purpose. They were both found lying upon the Bed, she with her Head cut almost off, and he with his Head shot all to Pieces.

*Boston* Evening Post, *December 8, 1746, quoted in Gutman,* Black Family, *349.*

At night [the newly arrived slaves] would begin to sing their native songs. . . . In a short while they would become so wrought up that, utterly oblivious to the danger involved, they would grasp their bundles of personal effects, swing them on their shoulders, and setting their faces towards Africa, would march down into the water [of Lake Phelps] singing as they marched till recalled to their senses only by the drowning of some of the party.

*Trotter, overseer for the rice-producing Lake Company in North Carolina, c. 1785, in Redford,* Somerset Homecoming, *132.*

When the bidding started [for a slave on the auction block] she grabbed a hatchet, laid her hand on a log and chopped it off. Then she throwed the bleeding hand right in her master's face.

*Nancy Bean, in Fox-Genovese,* Plantation Households, *329.*

He [a master] was so mean they [his slaves] got up a plot to run off and they never come in till after twelve o'clock that night. They had plotted to go and jump in the Mississippi River and drown themselves. . . . [A]fter that he quit beating and knocking on 'em, and if he got an overseer that was too mean he would turn him off. . . . They said they meant to drown, too, but they thought about their little children and come on home.

*Ex-slave,* God Struck Me Dead, *199.*

## *Group Rebellions: Insurrections*

[Virginia lacks adequate slave-control laws,] in consequence of which, negroes have run together in certain parts of the Colony, causing assemblages so dangerous as to threaten the peace of the whole community.

*Sir Edmund Andros, royal governor of Virginia, 1694, in Harding,* River, *31.*

[Suppose the slaves rebel,] will these masters and mastrisses take the sword at hand and warr against these poor slaves, licke, we are able to believe, some will not refuse to doe; or have these negers not as much right to fight for their freedom, as you have to keep them slaves?

*Germantown Quaker protest, 1688, in Aptheker,* One Continual Cry, *22*

"In the year 1712," says the Rev. D. Humphreys, "a considerable number of negroes of the Carmantee and Pappa Nations formed a plot to destroy all the English, *in order to obtain their liberty;* and kept their conspiracy so secret, that there was no suspicion of it till it came to the very execution. However, the plot was by God's Providence happily defeated. The plot was this. The negroes sat fire to a house in York city. . . . The fire alarmed the town, who from all parts ran to it; the conspirators planted themselves in several streets and lanes leading to the fire, and shot or stabbed the people as they were running to it. Some of the wounded escaped, and acquainted the Government, and presently by the firing of a great gun from the fort, the inhabitants were called under arms and pretty easily scattered the negroes; they had killed about 8 and wounded 12 more. In their flight some of them shot them, others their wives, and then themselves; some absconded a few days, and then killed themselves for fear of being taken; but a great many were taken, and 18 of them suffered death."

*Joshua Coffin,* Account of . . . Slave Insurrections, *10–11.*

[The] fires [in Boston] have been designedly and industriously kindled by some villanous and desperate negroes, or other dissolute people . . . it being vehemently suspected that they have entered into a combination to burn and destroy the town.

*Massachusetts governor, 1723, in Higginbotham,* In the Matter of Color, *76.*

[In the firing during the Stono Rebellion] One Negroe fellow [advanced upon his master. H]is Master asked him if he wanted to kill him the Negroe answered he did at the same time snapping a Pistoll at him but it mist fire and his master shot him thro' the Head about fifty of these Villains attempted to go home but were taken by the Planters who Cutt off their heads and set them up at every Mile Post they came to.

*In Porter,* Negro on the American Frontier, *168.*

[During the Stono Rebellion some slaves] shewed so much Integrity and Fidelity, that it was at that Time a Service to the Province, as well as to their Masters' Families, and saved them from the Fate of several of their unfortunate Neighbors; and bravely withstood that barbarous Attempt at the Hazard of their own Lives.

*South Carolina lieutenant governor Bull, November 1739, in Wax, "The Great Risque," 141.*

[Five slave] conspirators, after their master [Henry Ormond of Beaufort County] was abed, went up to his room and with an handkerchief attempted to strangle him, which they thought they had effected, but in a little time after they left him, he recovered, and began to stir, on hearing which they went up and told him he must die, and that before they left the room; he begged very earnestly for his life, but one of them, his house wench, told him it was in vain, that as he had no mercy on them, he could expect none himself, and immediately threw him between two feather beds, and all got on him till he was stifled to death.

Virginia Gazette, *September 6, 1770, quoted in Kay and Cary,* Slavery in North Carolina, *79.*

My brother Gabriel was the person who influenced me to join him and others in order that (as he said) we might conquer the white people and possess ourselves of their property. I enquired how we were to effect it. He said by falling upon them (the whites) in the dead of night, at which time they would be unguarded and unsuspicious. I then enquired who was at the head of the plan. He said Jack, alias Jack Bowler. I asked him if Jack Bowler knew anything about carrying on war. He replied he did not. He said a man from Carolina who was at the siege of Yorktown, and who was to meet him (Gabriel) at the Brook and to proceed on to Richmond, take, and then fortify it. This man from Carolina was to be commander and manager the first day, and then, after exercising the soldiers, the command was to be resigned to Gabriel. If Richmond was taken without the loss of many men, they were to continue for some time, but if they sustained any considerable loss they were to [head] for Hanover or York, they were not decided which, and continue at that place as long as they found they were able to defend it, but in the event of a defeat or loss at those places they were to endeavor to form a junction with some negroes which, they had understood from Mr. Gregory's overseer, were in rebellion in some quarter of the country. This information which they had gotten from the overseer, made Gabriel anxious, upon which he applied to me to make scythe-swords, which I did to the number of twelve. Every Sunday he came to Richmond to provide ammunition and to find where the military stores were deposited. Gabriel informed me in case of success, that they intended to subdue the whole of the country where slavery was permitted, but no further.

The first places Gabriel intended to attack in Richmond were, the Capitol, the Magazine, the Penitentiary, the Governor's house and his prison. The inhabitants were to be massacred, save those who begged for quarter and agreed to serve as soldiers with them. The reason I think insurrection was to be made at this particular time was, the discharge of the number of soldiers, one or two months ago, which induced Gabriel to believe the plan would be more easily executed.

Given under our hands this 15th day of September 1800.

Gervas Storrs
Joseph Selden

*Confession of Solomon, in* Blacks in Bondage, *127–28.*

I have nothing more to offer than what George Washington would have had to offer had he been taken by the British and put to trial by them. I have adventured my life in endeavoring to obtain the liberty of my countrymen, and am a willing sacrifice to their cause.

*Courtroom testimony of an anonymous black insurrectionist, 1804, in Harding,* River, *52.*

This gentleman . . . mentioned, that his servant had informed him, that A—[a witness who was promised that his name would not be divulged] had stated, that about three months ago, Rolla, belonging to Governor Bennett, had communicated to him the intelligence of the intended insurrection [Denmark Vesey's], and had asked him to join—That he remarked, in the event of their rising, they would not be without help, as the people from San Domingo and Africa would assist them in obtaining their liberty, if they only made the motion first themselves.

*J. Hamilton Jr., intendant, Charleston, August 16, 1822, in* Slave Insurrections, *9.*

On Thursday the 27th, DENMARK VESEY, a free black man, was brought before the Court for trial,

Assisted by his Counsel, G.W. Cross, Esq. . . . There is ample reason for believing, that this project was not, with him, of recent origin, for it was said, he had spoken of it for upwards of four years.

These facts of his guilt the journals of the Court will disclose—that no man can be proved to have spoken of or urged the insurrection prior to himself. All the channels of communication and intelligence are traced back to him. His house was the place appointed for the secret meetings of the conspirators, at which he was invariably a leading and influential member; animating and encouraging the timid, by the hopes of prospects of success; removing the scruples of the religious, by the grossest prostitution and perversion of the sacred oracles, and inflaming and confirming the resolute, by all the savage fascinations of blood and booty.

*J. Hamilton Jr., intendant, Charleston, August 16, 1822, in* Slave Insurrections, *16.*

The Court tried JESSE, the slave of Mr. Thomas Blackwood.

The testimony against *Jesse* was very ample. His activity and zeal . . . were fully proved. He had engaged with Vesey to go out of town on Sunday the 16th, to bring down some negroes from the country, to aid in the rising on that night; and remarked, to the witnesses, on his way to Hibbens' ferry, "if my father does not assist I will cut off his head." All the particulars in proof against him, he confirmed after receiving his sentence, by his own full and satisfactory Confession. . . .

This man excited no small sympathy, not only from the apparent sincerity of his contrition, but from the mild and unostentatious composure with which he met his fate.

*J. Hamilton Jr., intendant, Charleston, August 16, 1822, in* Slave Insurrections, *18.*

[N]o description can accurately convey . . . the impression which his [Gullah Jack Pritchard's] trial, defence and appearance made on those who witnessed the working of his cunning and rude address. Born a conjurer and a physician, in his own country (for in Angola they are matters of inheritance) he practised *these arts* in this country for fifteen years, without its being generally known among the whites. . . . It does not appear that Jack required much persuasion to induce him to join in a project, which afforded him the most ample opportunities of displaying his peculiar art, whilst it is very obvious that his willingness, to do all that Vesey might require, was in no little degree stimulated, by his bitterness and his gall against the whites. . . . If the part which he was to play in this drama, bespoke that the treacherous and vindictive artifices of war in his own country, existed in unimpaired vigour in his memory, his wildness and vehemence of gesture and the malignant glance with which he eyed the witnesses who appeared against him, all indicated the savage, who indeed had been *caught,* but not *tamed.* . . . Such was their belief in his invulnerability, that his charms and amulets were in request, and he was regarded as a man, who could *only* be harmed but by the *treachery* of his fellows.

*J. Hamilton Jr., intendant, Charleston, August 16, 1822, in* Slave Insurrections, *23–24.*

[Bacchus, allegedly a Denmark Vesey conspirator] went to the gallows, *laughing and bidding his acquaintances in the streets* "good bye"; on being hung, owing to some mismanagement in the fall of the trap, he was not thrown off, but the board canted, he slipped; yet he was so hardened that he *threw himself forward, and as he swung back he lifted his feet, so that he might not touch the board!*

*Confession, quoted in* American Slavery, *130.*

Friends and brothers, we are to commence a great work to-night! Our race is to be delivered from slavery, and God has appointed us as the men to do his bidding; and let us be worthy of our calling. I am told to slay all the whites we encounter, without regard to age or sex. We have no arms or ammunition, but we will find these in the houses of our oppressors; and, as we go on, others can join us. Remember, we do not go forth for the sake of blood and carnage; but it is necessary that, in the commencement of this revolution, all the whites we meet should die, until we have an army strong enough to carry on the war upon a Christian basis. Remember that ours is not a war for robbery, nor to satisfy our passions; it is a *struggle for freedom*. Ours must be deeds, not words. Then let's away to the scene of action.

*Nat Turner, 1831, in Williams,* History of the Negro Race, *87–88.*

I heard a loud voice in the heavens, and the Spirit instantly appeared to me and said. . . . I should arise and prepare myself, and slay my enemies with their own weapons . . for the time was fast approaching when the first should be last and the last should be first.

*Nat Turner, 1831, in Harding,* River, *75.*

THE BANDITTE. They [Nat Turner's insurrectionists] remind one of a parcel of blood-thirsty wolves rushing down from the Alps; or, rather like a former incursion of the Indians upon the white settlements. Nothing is spared; neither age nor sex respected—the helplessness of women and children pleads in vain for mercy. . . . The case of Nat. Turner warns us. No black-man ought to be permitted to turn a Preacher through the country.

Enquirer, *August 30, 1831, quoted in Williams,* History of the Negro Race, *90.*

The predictions of Mr. Randolph some years since are now becoming true; the whites are running away from the blacks, the masters from the slaves, in lower Virginia, the place of insurrection. I received an intimation from a gentleman yesterday to go to his house to advize his negroes, 8 in number, most young ones, to embark for Liberia, as he was willing to emancipate them.

*Collin H. Minge, October 1831, in Fox,* American Colonization Society, *25.*

I never did intend murder, or treason, or the destruction of property, or to excite or incite slaves to rebellion, or to make insurrection. The design on my part was to free the slaves.

*John Brown, after the incident at Harper's Ferry, in Williams,* History of the Negro Race, *222.*

The Harpers Ferry affair [John Brown's rebellion] proves to be more serious than at first it appeared to be—not in reference to the Negro population, for that had nothing to do with it; but in reference to the hostility of large numbers of men of all classes in the free states to the slaveholding states, even unto blood, and their readiness to aid and abet such attempts with counsels and money, and to employ reckless agents to carry them out. Such sparks as these, struck to produce a universal conflagration, should be stamped out immediately. Such enemies should be met and overwhelmed without quarter in a moment. A decision of this sort is demanded by our circumstances, and brings the free and the slave states to a perfect understanding on the whole subject.

*Slaveholder Rev. Charles C. Jones, November 7, 1859, in* Children of Pride, *527–28.*

## *Group Rebellions: Maroon Communities (Outlyers)*

[In the 1650s in Virginia fugitive Africans are rumored to be attempting] to form small armed groups in various sections of the colony and to harass neighboring plantations, at the same time creating bases to which others might flee.

*Harding,* River, *30.*

[I applied] for the assistance of some Notchee Indians in order to apprehend some runaway Negroes, who had sheltered themselves in the Woods, and being armed, had committed disorders. . . .

*Gov. James Glen of South Carolina, 1744, in Aptheker, "Maroons,"* Maroon Societies, *153.*

We have had most alarming times this Summer all along shore, from a sett of Barges manned mostly by our own negroes who have run off—These fellows are dangerous to an individual singled out for their vengeance whose property lay exposed—They burnt several houses.

*Virginia resident, 1781, in Aptheker,* Revolts, *207.*

The safety of our frontier I conceive requires this course [sending troops against the Indians in Georgia]. They have, I am informed, several hundred fugitive slaves from the Carolinas and Georgia at present in their Towns and unless they are checked soon they will be so strengthened by desertions from Georgia & Florida that it will be found troublesome to reduce them.

*Lt. Col. Thomas Smith, U.S. Army, July 30, 1812, in Aptheker, "Maroons,"* Maroon Societies, *155.*

[Our] slaves are become almost uncontrollable. They go and come when and where they please, and if an attempt is made to stop them they immediately fly to the woods and there continue for months and years Committing depredations on our Cattle hogs and Sheep. . . . [P]atrols are of no use on account of the danger they subject themselves to.

*Complaint of North Carolina planters, December 1830, in Aptheker,* Revolts, *289.*

A nest of runaway negroes were lately discovered in the fork of the Alabama and Tombeckbee rivers, and broken up, after a smart skirmish by a party from Mobile county. Three of the negroes were killed, several taken and a few escaped. They had two cabins and were about to build a fort. Some of them had been runaway for years, and had committed many depredations on the neighboring plantations.

*Charleston* Observer, *July 21, 1827, in* American Slavery, *15.*

This much I can say that old Hal . . . and his men [outlyers] fought like spartans, not one gave an inch of ground, but stood, was shot dead or wounded fell on the spot.

*White attacker of outlyers, 1827, in Harding,* River, *81.*

Many deserters [from the Confederate army] . . . are collected in the swamps and fastnesses of Taylor, La Fayette, Levy and other counties [in Florida], and have organized, with runaway negroes, bands for the purpose of committing depredations upon the plantations and crops of loyal citizens and running off their slaves. These depredatory bands have even threatened the cities of Tallahasee, Madison, and Marianna.

*Confederate officer John K. Jackson, quoted in Aptheker, "Maroons,"* Maroon Societies, *164–65.*

[It is] difficult to find words of description . . . of the wild and terrible consequences of the negro raids in this obscure . . . theatre of the war. . . . In the two counties of Currituck and Camden, there are said to be from five to six hundred negroes, who are not in the regular military organization of the Yankees, but who, outlawed and disowned by their masters, lead the lives of banditti, roving the country with fire and committing all sorts of horrible crimes upon the inhabitants.

This present theatre of guerrilla warfare has, at this time, a most important interest for our authorities. It is described as a rich country, . . . and one of the most important sources of meat supplies that is now accessible to our armies. . . .

*Richmond* Daily Examiner, *January 14, 1864, quoted in Aptheker, "Maroons,"* Maroon Societies, *165.*

# 9 Indians as Slaves, as Friends and Enemies of Black Slaves, and as Slaveholders 1529–1865

## The Historical Context

### *Slavery among Indians*

Slavery existed in North America long before the arrival of the European explorers and settlers. The idea of slavery did not outrage Indians any more than it outraged Europeans or Africans. In North America, as in Africa and in Europe, it was a condition of life that few questioned.

Indian tribes enslaved—sometimes for a limited period, sometimes for life—male prisoners of war whom they did not torture or kill outright. The Iroquois, for instance, usually killed their prisoners of war, but if they felt contempt for a captive, they might make him a slave, cutting off part of his foot to prevent his running away and forcing him to do "woman's work." These practices led to slave raids on neighboring tribes, particularly among the Illinois and Iroquois, as young braves vied to prove their skills as warriors by taking scalps or captives. Some Indian nations also punished crime and debt with slavery. Enslavement dishonored the slave, denying him a warrior's death or marking him as a violator of tribal rules. Before the Europeans came, most tribes refused to accept back a member who had been captured and enslaved. (Later, when they realized that such a reaction in the face of mass enslavements might prove the death of the tribe, they reversed the practice.)

Indians enslaved Indians, then, to gain honor and preserve order, not to benefit by their labor. Even those nations that practiced agriculture farmed only on a small scale, for which the women sufficed as labor. Before whites came, Indians did not buy or sell slaves, for their cultures were not built on a market economy. But a tribe might barter slaves to placate an unfriendly neighboring tribe or in exchange for its own captured members. After Europeans established a market in slaves, Indians began to seize members of other tribes as bargaining chips, neither using them as slaves nor adopting them as members of their own tribe but accumulating them as means of exchange.

Though Indian masters had complete power of life and death over their slaves, treatment of them varied widely from tribe to tribe. In many ways, slavery among Indians paralleled slavery among Africans. A few Indian nations treated their slaves harshly, even killing them on a whim, but relations between masters and slaves were generally relaxed. Seminole masters, perhaps the most liberal, demanded little more than a tribute of corn or hogs from their slaves, allowing them to live apart more or less as they pleased and to own property—even other slaves. Most Indian groups considered their slaves eligible for adoption into the tribe. They intermarried with them. Some treated slaves' children as free. Children of Creek fathers and slave mothers were brought up in practical equality with the Creek's full-blooded offspring.

## *The Enslavement of Indians by Whites*

Early European settlers of North America, like the Indians, usually took slavery for granted, though now and then they displayed a need to justify it on the grounds that as masters they were improving the lot of slaves and saving their souls by Christianizing them. But, true to the European tradition, white colonists thought of slaves also as a source of labor and profit.

When white explorers first ventured into North America, they kidnapped Indians to act as informants and interpreters, guide them through the deserts and wildernesses, and help them communicate with other Indians. When the settlers came, they faced a more complex problem. They wanted Indians for servants or for concubines, but they feared to alienate neighboring tribes, on whom they might well depend for advice, help, and safety—indeed, their very survival. If they dared not kidnap, however, they sometimes could bargain. Indians wanted the white men's goods. When they did not have war captives to trade, they might sell erring members of their own tribes for a limited time as a punishment. They might even offer themselves or their children as security for loans, with default bringing enslavement. These practices were risky for the Indians, however, for colonists sometimes broke the terms of the agreements, selling the Indians abroad or refusing to release them at the end of their terms.

As the whites came to appreciate the size of the continent and how much labor would be needed to develop it, such arrangements no longer sufficed. The record of 16th-, 17th-, and 18th-century Europeans in North America dismayingly parallels that in Africa, in that the Europeans in both cases tried to exploit the labor of the natives. In the New World, however, whites were also determined to establish permanent settlements: they were after land as well as slaves. Their ambitions soared. Why not use Indians as slaves to till and develop the vast unsettled continent, or as trading goods for black slaves? As Emanuel Downing argued in a 1645 letter to John Winthrop, "A warr with the Narraganset is verie considerable to this plantation, ffor I doubt whither yt be not synne in vs, hauing power in our hands, to suffer them to maynteyne the worship of the devill which their paw wawes [powwows?] often doe; 2lie, If vpon a Just warre the lord should deliuer them into our hands, wee might easily haue men woemen and children enough to exchange for Moores [blacks], which wilbe more gaynefull pilladge for vs then wee conceive, for I doe not see how wee can thrive vntill wee get into a stock of slaves sufficient to doe all our buisines, for our children's children will hardly see this great Continent filled with people, soe that our servants will still desire freedome to plant for them selues, and not stay but for verie great wages. And I suppose you know verie well how wee shall maynteyne 20 Moores cheaper then one Englishe servant."[1]

For such purposes and to get land, Europeans provoked wars with the Indians, sometimes directly, sometimes indirectly. As a missionary to the Mohawks commented in 1715, "The Indians have Lately done a great deale of mischief in South Carolina having cut off a great many inhabitants but as we are very well informed, it is what they [the settlers] have brought upon themselves by abus[in]g the Indians with drink and then cheat them in Trading with them and Stealing Even their Child[re]n away and carry them to other places and sell them for slaves."[2] In 1636–37, in the Pequot War, whites descended to attacks on Indian property and noncombatants to gain their ends, burning Indian villages and crops and massacring the Indians they could find. They had brought with them the custom of enslaving prisoners of war—the Mayflower Compact included just such a proviso. They seized on every excuse. In 1622, for instance, a Virginia settler declared that after the Good Friday massacre of whites, Indians might now "most justly be compelled to servitude and drudgery, and supply the roome of men that labour, whereby even the meanest of the plantation may imploy themselves more entirely in their Arts and Occupations, which are more generous whilest Savages performe their inferiour workes of digging in mynes, and the like."[3]

The colonists made slaves, too, of Indians whom they convicted as criminals for violating white laws. Thus, for example, in 1636 an Indian named Chousop of Block Island was sentenced to "bee kept as a slave for life to worke. . . ."[4] In 1646, the New England Confederation of Colonies (Massachusetts, Plymouth, Connecticut, and New Haven) feared that "it will be chargeable keeping Indians in prison, and if they should escape, they are like to prove more insolent and dangerous after." So they further extended slavery by providing that if an Indian harmed any white citizen's property, the inhabitants of the Indian's village or of any that harbored him might be seized "either to serve or to be shipped out and exchanged for negroes as the cause will justly beare."[5] Such a law encouraged whites to kidnap Indians as slaves and to raid Indian villages.

But the settlers' relations with Indians were not monolithic. They treated different tribes differently, some as enemies, some as allies. Thus in King Phillip's War (1675–76), whites and their Indian allies fought against the Wampanoag. André Penicaut's account of a 1702 expedition against the Alabama also illustrates how whites allied themselves with some Indians while attacking others: "Going up the Rivière des Alibamons [Alabama River], seventy leagues upstream on the left side he [Boisbriant] came upon six Alibamon boats, which made him believe that there must be Alibamons off hunting in the vicinity. He sent a French soldier with a Canadian to reconnoiter. . . . He quickly led his men up close to them without making any noise. At once he had us fire a volley. All the savages were killed, only women and their children being spared; they were taken away as slaves to Mobile along with their boats loaded with their game. The Mobiliens, our neighbors six leagues away and allies of the Alibamons, saw us pass with these slaves on our way back to Mobile. They came to M. de Bienville and asked him for them, begging him to kindly give them to them, as these captives were their kin. M. de Bienville granted their request. This act of generosity . . . caused the Mobiliens later on to unite with us in the wars we carried on against the Alibamons."[6] In 1715, South Carolina agreed to reward any Tuscarora who captured any of the colony's Indian enemies with the return of a Tuscarora slave. Whether allies or enemies, the Indians suffered, as war's havoc was multiplied by starvation and deaths from the diseases that the Europeans brought with them, diseases to which the Indians had no immunity.

For some time the colonies, north and south, continued to enslave Indians. For instance, in Bacon's Rebellion, which began in a conflict over how to treat with the Indians, the Virginia Assembly in 1676 in effect granted Nathaniel Bacon a slave-hunting license by "providing that any enemy Indians [whom his soldiers] caught were to be their slaves for life," and in 1677 by ordering that these soldiers should "reteyne and keepe all such Indian slaves or other Indian goods as they either have taken *or hereafter shall take*."[7] In 1685, Chief Caruee reported an incident in a dispute between the Spanish and the British for the Indian trade: "[A]bout 3 months agoe the Scotts settled at Port Royal did send Caleb Westbrooke & Aratomahan, a chieftain among them, to the Yamasses to encourage them to make warr with the Timecho Indians who are Christians and had a Spanish Fryer [friar] and a Chappell among them which they agreeing to the Scotts furnished them with 23 fyre Arms in order to distroye the sd [said] Timechos that thereupon they proceeded and burnt several Towns and in particular the said Chappell and the Fryer's house and killed fifty of the Timechoes and brought away Two and Twenty prisoners which they delivered to the Scotts as slaves."[8]

American colonists thus incited wars among Indians. In 1715, a missionary commented on such provocations: "It is certain many of the Yammousees and Creek Indians were against the war all along. But our military men were so bent upon revenge, and so desirous to enrich themselves by making all the Indians slaves that fall into yr [their] hands . . . that it is in vain to represent the cruelty and injustice of such a procedure."[9]

Even when colonial and state governments sporadically tried to prevent them, white traders encouraged Indians to raid other tribes for slaves, whom the traders then bought, often cheating the Indians in the process. The Carolina proprietors (holders of royal grants, through 1729) seem at least from time to time to have tried especially hard to prevent such raids. In 1680, they issued instructions that "[P]eace and a friendly correspondence with the Indians that are our Neighbors . . . cannot be expected long to continue without due care be taken for the equall Administration of Justice to them and to preserve them from being wronged or oppressed. . . . [T]ake special care not to suffer any Indian that is in League or friendly correspondence with us and that lives within 200 miles of us to be made slaves or sent away from the country without special directions from us."[10] But the very frequency of such messages suggests how little they were heeded. Captain Moore of North Carolina in 1760 reported a direct defiance of orders. After his soldiers had captured some Cherokees, he said, "I allowed that it was our Duty to Guard Them to prison, or some place of safe Custody till we got the approbation of the Congress Whether they should be sold Slaves or not, and the Greater part [of my men] Swore Bloodily that if they were not sold for Slaves upon the spot, they would Kill & Scalp them

Immediately. Then the 3 prisoners was sold for £242. . . . Our men was Very spirited & Eager for Action, and is Very Desirous that your Honour would order them upon a second Expedition."[11] Even orders of the French king to Louisiana colonials in 1720 failed to stop the raids.

Individual whites also kidnapped Indians whom they enslaved, just as they did blacks. In an 1862 letter to the *Liberator,* Rosa Barnwell told of her family's experience: "I was born in Charleston S.C. I was a slave for more than twenty years. My mother was of Indian descent, and a free woman, but was kidnapped by a man named Leo Edwards, and doomed to a life of servitude. She had twelve children, one of whom was sold to Texas. God alone knows her fate. Five others now sleep between the sod, while the rest are still in slavery, and I . . . have escaped to a land of freedom, through the mercy and goodness of God."[12] A Creek Indian, Susan, was betrayed by the family her mother trusted: "A blacksmith, by the name of Jeremiah Taylor, went among the Creek nation, to work for them at smithing," testified a fellow slave. "Susan's mother, a poor woman, gave her to the blacksmith's wife to raise, when she was a little girl: and she became so much attached to the family, that when they left the tribe, she went with them. She says that Mrs. Taylor always told her she would be free, when she was a woman; but before that time arrived, Mr. and Mrs. Taylor both died. Their son John sold Susan, and she has been a slave ever since."[13]

Indian slavery, like black slavery, developed at different rates and resulted in different numbers in different colonies, with more slaves in the South both Indian and black, and more indentured servants in the North. Other local conditions also modified the practice of slavery. The English colonists in Virginia enslaved fewer Indians than Carolina settlers, simply because the Virginians needed the food that nearby Indians supplied.

Hunting Indians in Florida with bloodhounds (*Library of Congress*)

Both a domestic and an international trade developed in Indian slaves. Domestically, masters felt safer if their Indian slaves came from farther away, local Indians being far too likely to escape back home. Toward the end of the 17th century, North American settlers experimented with importing Indians from Spanish colonies as slaves. Much more often, however, the North American colonists exported Indian slaves to other places in the New World. In 1520, Spaniards in Carolina tried using North American Indian slaves to work the gold mines of Hispaniola. When, in 1637, Massachusetts settlers captured slaves in the Pequot War, they distributed the females in the towns of Massachusetts and Connecticut but shipped off some of the young boys on the Salem ship *Desire,* which then brought back from the tropics a cargo of tobacco, cotton, and blacks. New England settlers sold into slavery in the West Indies thousands of Indians captured in King Philip's War (1675–76). In 1706, slave owners in Louisiana sought permission from the French king to export Indian slaves in exchange for blacks; when the king repeatedly refused, the settlers began the trade anyway.

Indian enslavement, however, contained the seeds of its own destruction. It never proved as successful as early white colonists hoped. It diminished the settlers' chances of maintaining peace and trade with the Indian nations. The Indian slaves they took into their houses or tried to use on their farms were, after all, close to home and knowledgeable about getting around in the countryside. They found escape relatively easy. Whites, in whom slavery inspired a multitude of fears, worried about alliances among Indians, indentured servants, and slaves. Since Indian slaves knew how to run away, might they not teach the blacks, who picked up Indian lore more readily than the whites? Also, true or not, the idea spread that Indians did not work as productively as blacks. The males among them, trained to hunt, fish, and fight, deemed other work proper only for women. In any case, free Indians could be hired for such low wages that it was hardly worthwhile to enslave them.

Even when Indian slaves were shipped so far from home that they could not readily escape, they proved unsatisfactory. For one thing, many Indians thrust into the mines died even faster than the African slaves they worked beside. For another, so strongly did slaveholders prefer blacks to Indians that they would accept Indian slaves only at the rate of two for one black slave. In time, some whites experienced pangs of conscience about enslaving Indians, who had welcomed them to North America and helped them to live in the New World. As white territory moved nearer to them, the powerful tribes and confederations of Appalachians ferociously discouraged Indian enslavement. It also became apparent that the numbers of Indian slaves available, whatever the machinations of the European settlers, could not meet the rapidly rising demands for more workers.

What with all these difficulties, well before 1700 whites gave up on the idea of using Indian slaves as their core work force. Indian slavery had largely ended by the 1750s, though Indians were occasionally sold in slave markets up into the 1770s, and descendants of Indians who had borne children with blacks continued to be held in slavery.

Even when Indian slavery was at its height, numbers were small. In Louisiana, for instance, in 1726 there were 229 Indian slaves but 1,540 black slaves. By the 1760s, the number of Indian slaves had declined to about 225, while the number of black slaves had grown to perhaps 5,000.[14]

## *Indians Meet Blacks*

American Indians first met individual blacks who were exploring with or on behalf of white masters. In 1529, his Spanish master took black Arab Estevanico on an expedition to Florida, where they were shipwrecked. Four black survivors of the wreck wandered for several years among the Indians of what is now Texas, first as slaves, and after 1535 as medicine men. In 1539, Estevanico, who had by then distinguished himself by his ability to learn languages, reached Spanish settlements in Mexico. There he lived in some luxury, collecting women and gems, until he was sent later that year with two friars to discover the fabled Kingdom of Quivira—carrying with him his harem and accumulated wealth. The North American Indians whom he met on that trip preferred him to the Europeans, so the friars sent him ahead to pacify them. Maybe success went to his head; at any rate the Indians of the Zuni pueblo of Cibola killed Estevanico rather than give him the women and jewels he demanded. A few years later, in 1541, blacks also accompanied Coronado in his search for the same golden cities.

Later explorers also employed blacks on their expeditions. When in 1788 the *Lady Washington,* commanded by Robert Gray, anchored on the coast of the Pacific Northwest, Indians killed his black servant Marcos Lopez with knives and arrows. However, the mulatto York, who acted as an interpreter on the Lewis and Clark expedition of 1803–6, entertained the Indians by exhibiting feats of strength and telling them that he had been a wild animal, caught and tamed by his master. York may have been a St. Louis black who had picked up some French in Missouri. Apparently he spoke bad French and worse English. The expedition managed after a fashion by having Shoshone guide Sacajawea translate the Indians' speech to her husband, French-Canadian trader Toussaint Charbonneau, who apparently translated it into French for York, who then transmitted it in English to Lewis and Clark.[15] York may even have had a smattering of Indian dialects, for the expedition also employed him to trade with the Indians for food.

The reactions of American Indians to these and later first encounters with blacks varied from fascination to outright terror. The tribes in Virginia, according to a late-18th-century report, were awed, thinking the blacks "a true breed of Devils, and therefore they called them *Manitto* for a great while: this word in their language signifies not only God but likewise the Devil."[16] In his description of his family's escape from slavery in the 19th century, Henry Bibb tells of their meeting young Indian warriors, who ran from them. Mrs. Bibb was frightened, sure that the Indians were preparing to attack the family. It turned out, however, that they had fled in fear, never having seen black people before. Their chief reassured his young men, and the tribe received the Bibbs kindly, giving them food, shelter, rest, and advice about the best way to go on.

## *Indians and Black Slaves*

Indians and blacks in North America interacted with each other in every imaginable way—except that as far as we know, blacks did not own Indian slaves. Indians were both enemies and friends of blacks. They both succored black fugitives and hunted them down. They held blacks as slaves, and Indians and blacks toiled side by side as slaves of white masters. They intermarried. Indians married their slaves. In some nations, widows chose black prisoners of war to replace Indian husbands who had died in battle. Indian slaves of whites married black slaves. Black male slaves sometimes preferred to marry free Indian women, knowing that their children would be free. On the other hand, Hugh Jones reported in 1724 that the Virginia Indians "hate, and despise the very sight of a *Negroe*. . . . Such as are born of an *Indian* and *Negroe* are called Mustees."[17]

The complexities of Indian-black relationships are illustrated by a series of questions posed among census officials in 1832: "Sir: We the commissioners engaged in taking the census of the Creek Indians, . . . beg leave to respectfully propose the following questions. . . . If an Indian have living with him as his wife a negro slave, the property either of himself or of another, is he to be considered as the head of a family in the sense contemplated in the instructions transmitted to us and to be enrolled as entitled to a reservation? . . . Is one of mixed blood of Indian and Negro, free, keeping a separate house and having a negro slave for a wife, to be ranked and enrolled in like manner as the Indian is? . . . There is a number of free black families that seem to be in every way identified with these people and the only difference is color. I have taken their number in all cases, but am I to take them as heads of families for reservations or not?"[18]

Bewildered white settlers often could not penetrate Indian attitudes toward blacks. In the early 1850s, for instance, a missionary reported, "Within the past few years the Comanches have (for what reason I could not learn) taken an inveterate dislike to the negroes, and have massacred several small parties of those who attempted to escape from the Seminoles and cross the plains for the purpose of joining Wild Cat upon the Rio Grande. Upon inquiring of them the cause of their hostility to the blacks, [they] replied that it was because they were slaves to the whites and they were sorry for them."[19]

Indians frequently befriended blacks, especially fugitive slaves. In the late 18th century, a black fugitive, Betty, encountered the Indians of Agawam, Connecticut, who sympathized with and sheltered her because they themselves had been slaves.[20] An 1834 account tells of a black fugitive who escaped from his master on the Arkansas River and wandered on the prairies until an Indian hunting party found him. He said that "after he was taken he came ten days with those Indians without anything to eat save some plumbs, berries &c but since he had been living among them they had treated him well and had given him corn mellons Buffaloe meat &c to eat—he appeared very well satisfied with his situation [they] requireing of him nothing but to grave [graze?] their horses."[21] In 1858, Edinbur Randall spoke of the underground railroad conducted by Indians on Martha's Vineyard: "I told them that I thought the sheriff was after me, whereupon the Indians told me to go into a swamp near by. I took their advice, and went into the thickest bushes about one hundred yards, and remained there some time; at length Beaulah Vanderhoof, the Indian woman who took me in to her house, came to the swamp, called me out, and put a gown, shawl, and bonnet upon me, and took me some distance to the house of her grandmother, Mrs. Peters, hid me in the garret, and then went to engage a boat to take me from the island. This aged woman, Mrs. Peters, entered into their plans for my escape, with a will: she declared that she would have a large kettle of hot water ready to scald the sheriff, or any of his under-strappers who crossed her threshold."[22]

Blacks learned wilderness survival skills from Indians, and Indians learned about whites from the blacks whom the whites had enslaved. These alliances alarmed whites. "The [black] Slaves that are now come up talk good English as well as the Cherokee Language and . . . too often tell falcities to the Indians which they are very apt to believe," warned one Colonel Chicken in 1725.[23] In 1763, during Pontiac's rebellion: "[T]he Indians are saving and caressing all the negroes they take; should it produce an insurrection, it may be attended with the most serious consequences."[24] It is hard to discern how much or how often these white fears of blacks and Indians joining together against them had any real basis. Such alliances did help individual slaves make their escapes and strengthen Indian tribes in their resistance to white incursions. The presence of the sympathetic Yamasees near St. Augustine helped to induce runaway black slaves to leave Carolina for Spanish-ruled Florida. But Indian-black cooperation did not result in the major uprisings of white imaginings.

To the contrary—why, we wonder, did the maroon communities so rarely seek Indian collaboration? Instead, they frequently became antagonists. Some Indians helped whites to conquer maroon colonies, just as occasionally maroons joined whites in overcoming Indians.[25]

Nonetheless, white fears persisted, as in a trader's 1751 deposition: "Three runaway Negroes of Mr. Gray's told the Indians, as they said that the white people were coming up to destroy them all, and that they had got some Creek Indians to assist them so to do. Which obtained belief and the more for that the old Warriour of Kewee said some Negroes had applied to him, and told him that there was in all Plantations many Negroes more than white people, and that for the Sake of Liberty they would join him."[26]

In the later days of slavery, Indian friendship for blacks now and then led to Indian advocacy for them. In 1848, for instance, the *Cherokee Advocate* reported the arrest of a Cherokee man on a charge of having sold free blacks as slaves. "At best," the editor wrote, "the situation of the colored race is an unenviable one, and he who rises up in defense of any right they may have, especially the right of freedom, against the cupidity of those who would deprive them of it by unjust means, deserves the thanks of all friends of humanity and justice among us."[27]

More generally, however, Indians accepted black slavery, siding with white masters against blacks. They quickly grasped and profited by the greater worth of capturing blacks over capturing whites, for blacks, having a market value, could always be sold, whereas white captives might or might not be ransomed. Moreover, they recaptured black fugitives for whites, in exchange either for goods or the return of Indian slaves of their own nations. Indians and blacks opposed each other in other ways, too. In the South, black slaves sometimes fought as allies and protectors of their masters against hostile Indians.

In time, Indians began to sell blacks, trading them to whites as they traded blankets and baskets. In time, some, especially the more settled and less nomadic tribes of the South, themselves adopted black slavery, though typically in a relatively mild form. During the American Revolution, British agents gave black slaves to Creek chiefs in return for their services. As whites forced Indians to emigrate westward, more of them moved below the Missouri Compromise line, where they learned from their white neighbors the status bestowed on owners of black slaves. By 1824, the Cherokee owned 1,277 black slaves; by 1861, the Choctaw and Chickasaw laid claim to 5,000 blacks.[28] During the 1820s and 1830s Indians were some of Georgia's biggest slaveholders. By 1836 some 1,200 maroons lived in Seminole towns.[29] Subsequently, Greenwood Lefore, a half-white Choctaw chief, became one of Mississippi's biggest planters, with four hundred slaves. Cherokee chief John Ross owned about a hundred slaves in 1860. By 1860, black slaves constituted 12.5 percent of the population of the Indian Territory.[30]

Black slave ownership among Indians marked their acceptance of white culture and a market economy. Some Indians allowed their black slaves to gain position and power within their nations, but Choctaw and Chickasaw worked them under codes as harsh as those adopted by whites. Among Indians, as among whites, the laws to control slaves grew more severe with the passage of time. Slave memories reflect a spectrum of treatment by Indian masters, from lenient to harsh. Of the Creek "We [slaves] all lived in good log cabins we built. We worked the farm and tended to the horses and cattle and hogs, and some of the older women worked around the owner's house, but each Negro family looked after a part of the fields and worked the crops like they belonged to us."[31] Of a Cherokee: "Young Master never whip his slaves, but if they don't mind good he sell them off sometimes. He sold one of my brothers and one sister because they kept running off."[32]

For the most part, Indians did not accept the racism that underlay white enslavement of blacks: Indians did not, that is, assume the inferiority of blacks but accepted them on their individual merits. The Seminole in particular listened to the advice of blacks and honored them as counselors, interpreters, and negotiators in their dealings with Europeans—sensibly, for the runaway slaves of whites whom the Seminole accepted as their own "slaves" had had longer and closer relationships with whites, spoke European languages better, and understood the thinking and customs of their former masters better than the Indians.

## *The Impact of Slavery on Indians*

Slavery damaged the Indians: enslavement disrupted family and tribal relations; their own adoption of the white system of black slavery altered their culture and their very character. These changes are most obvious among the Seminole, by tradition the gentlest of slaveholders. For years they lived in amity with their black slaves, mostly fugitives who had sought refuge among them. They shared many descendants. During the Seminole Wars with the United States, Indians and blacks fought side by side. Some in the U.S. military thought of the Second Seminole War as more a war with blacks than with the Indians, noting that blacks counseled the Indians never to make peace unless the terms guaranteed that blacks would not be returned to their former white masters. Indian teams of negotiators for peace included blacks not only as interpreters but also in positions of influence and power. One of them, Abraham, impressed all who saw him. "Abraham is a non-committal man, with a countenance which none can read, a person erect and active and in stature over six feet. He was a principal agent in bringing about the peace, having been a commander of the negroes during the war, and an enemy by no means to be despised. . . . Abraham made his appearance bearing a white flag on a small stick which he had cut in the woods, and walked up to the tent of General Jesup with perfect dignity and composure. He stuck the staff of his flag in the ground, made a salute or bow with his hand, without bending his body, and then waited for the advance of the General with the most complete self-possession. He has since stated that he expected to be hung, but concluded to die, if he must, like a man, but that he would make one more effort to save his people."[33]

As the U.S. government moved Indians willy-nilly off lands the whites wanted, it interfered with the relationships between Indians and their black slaves. Notoriously, this interference hopelessly damaged the relations between the Seminole and their respected black advisors. After they went west to the Indian Territory, they never again lived in harmony; disputes and distrust arose between them. Whites tried to steal some of the Seminole slaves. The Seminole began to fear the blacks and sought to disarm the very allies at whose sides they had fought.

In the Civil War, Indian tribes chose between the North and the South largely on the basis of the degree to which slavery had by then developed among them. Most Seminole, for instance, sided with the Union, but Choctaw and Chickasaw went over to the Confederates. This was not always so with their slaves, however. A slave of the Creek, Mary Gibson, a child during the Civil War, remembered how in the Indian Territory "we Negroes got word somehow that the Cherokees over back of Fort Gibson was not going to be in the war and that there were some Union people over there who would help slaves to get away. . . . Some Upper Creeks came up into the Choska bottoms talking around among the folks there about siding with the North." One morning she awoke to find that her father and all the other male slaves had disappeared. They had been smuggled into Missouri and then into Kansas, where they joined the Union army.[34]

When conscience and war finally ended black slavery among whites, the federal government forced Indians to free their slaves—with mixed success. The Seminole, Creek, and Cherokee adopted their blacks immediately, but only among the Seminole did blacks enjoy the full rights of citizenship. The Choctaw resisted adopting theirs until 1885, and the Chickasaw refused to adopt theirs at all. In any case, as with whites and their former slaves, social and political difficulties remained, and festered.

## Chronicle of Events

**1520**
Spaniards in Carolina try to secure Indians as slaves to work in the gold mines of Hispaniola.

**1529**
Perhaps the earliest contact between Indians and blacks in North America is made when an Arab, Estevanico, black slave of a Spaniard, accompanies his master on an expedition to Florida.

**1542**
In Louisiana, the French king's protection is extended to Indians, and their enslavement is forbidden.

**1618**
Colonial *Lawes Divine, Morall and Martiall,* authorizing execution of all recaptured servants who have fled to Indian settlements, are repealed.

**1620**
The first school for blacks and Indians in North America is established.

**1637**
The colonial government of Massachusetts and the Narragansett tribe divide Pequot women and children captured in war; the Narragansett apparently adopt theirs, while Massachusetts enslaves those it takes.

**1641**
Massachusetts provides for the enslavement of Indians taken in "just wars."

**1644**
Gov. Willem Kieft of New Netherlands sends two Indian prisoners as a gift to the governor of Bermuda.

**1646**
Plymouth declares it legal to seize any Indians.

The United Colonies (Massachusetts, Plymouth, Connecticut, and New Haven) resolve that if any citizen's property is harmed by an Indian, the inhabitants of his village or any that harbors him may be seized "either to serve or to be shipped out and exchanged for negroes as the cause will justly beare."

**1655**
Virginia declares that Indian children brought into the colony by friendly Indians shall not be treated as slaves but as indentured servants, to be instructed in the trades and Christianity.

**1656**
A Virginia law promises Indians that their hostages will not be used as slaves.

A Massachusetts law forbids arming blacks and Indians or permitting them to train with the colony's military companies.

**1657**
Virginia forbids masters to sell Indian children bound to them for education or instruction; these children are to be freed at twenty-five.

Virginia forbids buying Indians from Englishmen, as the English have "corrupted" [wrongly persuaded] Indians to bring them the children of other Indians "to the greate scandall of Christianitie and of the English nation."

**1659**
Rhode Island authorizes the enslavement and sale of any Indian who steals cattle or goods exceeding twenty shillings, unless restitution is made.

**1660**
The New Netherlands Council resolves to transport to Curaçao recently captured Esopus Indians, "to be employed there, or at Buenaire, with the negroes in the Company's service."

**1662**
The Virginia assembly orders the release of a Powhatan Indian wrongly enslaved, because he speaks English perfectly and desires baptism.

A Virginia law declares that "all Indian servants male or female however procured being adjudged sixteen years of age shall be . . . tythable [taxable]."

**1664**
South Carolina settlers begin slave raids against the Stono and Westo Indians.

**1667**
Virginia rules that baptism no longer will affect the slave status of either Indians or blacks.

**1670**
Virginia divides non-Christian servants into two classes: those imported by ship, who "shall be slaves for their lives"; and those, like Indians, who come by land, who "shall serve, if boys or girles, untill thirty yeares of age; if men or women twelve yeares and no longer."

Virginia forbids free blacks and Indians, though baptized, to own Christian servants.

**1671**
The South Carolina council orders open war on Indians, with captives to be sold abroad as slaves.

**1674**
In *re Indian Hoken,* a Massachusetts court orders magistrates to "cause [Hoken] to be apprehended and sold or sent to Barbadoes."

**1675**
Massachusetts colonists provoke King Philip's War, in which most of the Wampanoag are killed.

*August 4:* Colonists sell into slavery about 160 Indians captured in King Philip's War.

*October:* Colonists sell into slavery 144 Narragansett because their tribe has given sanctuary to Wampanoag old men, women, and children.

**1676**
Indians kill a "Negro Servant" belonging to Andrew Harris at Patuxet.

At Newport, Rhode Island, a bill is passed stating, "No Indian in this colony be a slave but only to pay their debts, or for their bringing up, or courtesy they have received, or to perform covenant, as if they had been countrymen not in war."

The Virginia assembly provides that enemy Indians caught by Nathaniel Bacon and his soldiers shall be their slaves for life.

**1677**
In *re Indian Popannooie,* a Massachusetts court condemns Popanooie, his wife, and children to perpetual servitude.

The Virginia assembly orders that soldiers who have captured Indians shall keep them and also any they shall take in the future.

**1679**
In Virginia an act is passed declaring that *"for the better encouragement of soldiers,"* whatever Indian prisoners are taken in a war shall be the property of the soldiers taking them.

New York abolishes Indian slavery, declaring all free except "such as have been formerly brought from the Bay of Campeachy [Compeche, Mexico] and other foreign parts."

**1680**
Morgan Godwyn writes *The Negro's and Indians Advocate,* a treatise on the duties of masters of slaves.

**1682**
The Virginia assembly makes slaves for life of all imported non-Christian (i.e., Indian or black) servants.

**1684**
Louis XIV orders the marquis de la Barre to send all Iroquois prisoners to France to serve in the royal galleys, because "these savages are strong and rebust."

**1685**
A New York vessel kidnaps four Indians near Cape Fear and carries them to New York to sell.

**1688**
Louis XIV repeats his order for Indian galley slaves.

**1689**
Louis XIV returns surviving Indian galley slaves to New France.

**1691**
Virginia passes a law repealing the acts of 1679 and 1682 that enslaved Indians, ruling that no Indian may thenceforth be made a slave.

**1694**
Carolina decrees that Indians and slaves guilty of setting adrift a boat shall for a first transgression receive 39 lashes and for a second have their ears cut off; Englishmen for the same offense will merely be fined.

**1697**
Smallpox from a slave ship spreads five hundred miles from Charlestown through the Indian tribes, by way of contaminated trade goods.

**1704**
Indians attacking the house of the Rev. John Williams at Deerfield, Massachusetts, kill his black woman-servant, Parthena, and later his black manservant.

**1705**
The death penalty is prescribed for any slave apprehended 40 miles north of Albany without a pass.

Pennsylvania passes a law forbidding the importation of Indian slaves from North Carolina.

Virginia declares "Negro, Mulatto, and Indian slaves within this dominion, to be real estate."

**1706**
Louisiana settlers request of France that they be allowed to trade Indian slaves in the West Indies for black slaves, at the rate of three Indians for two blacks.

About this time, against the orders of the French throne, Louisiana residents begin a slave trade with the West Indies, sometimes exchanging two Indian slaves for one black slave.

**1708**
A South Carolina law rewards with a gun every friendly Indian who takes prisoner or kills an enemy Indian and empowers commanding officers to buy all captive enemy Indians above 12 years of age and ship them to the West Indies as slaves.

A Connecticut law forbids trading with any Indian, mulatto, or black servant or slave without the master's approval.

**1709**
At Quebec, Jacques Raudot decrees that "all the Pawnis [Indian slaves] and Negroes, who have been brought and who shall be purchased hereafter, shall belong in full proprietorship to those who have purchased them as their slaves."

**1711**
The Tuscarora, Coree, and Pamlico Indians, exasperated by trader abuses, war on North Carolina settlers.

**1712**
In New York City, 25 Coromantee and Paw Paw blacks, joined by mestizoes captured at sea and enslaved, set fire to a house and kill 10 or 12 whites. They are routed by gunfire.

Massachusetts prohibits the importation of Indian slaves.

**1715**
Black slaves constitute part of the military force that in South Carolina meets and routs the Yamasee Indians. With the end of the Yamasee war, Indian slave-catching fields are pushed farther inland. Connecticut prohibits importing Indian slaves, because they have committed so many crimes.

**1717**
A complaint is made that New York colony slaves run away, are hidden by the Minisink, and intermarry with Indian women.

The South Carolina Indian trade is declared a government monopoly.

**1718**
The founding of New Orleans ends the struggle between the French and the Chitimachas, in which many Indians had been captured and enslaved.

**1719**
A Carolina law rules that owners are to be taxed for Indian slaves at a rate half that for black slaves.

**1720**
France orders that Indian raids on other tribes for slaves be stopped in Louisiana; to enforce this order, the crown later decrees that offending traders are to be seized and their merchandise confiscated.

**1721**
The governor of Virginia negotiates with the Iroquois for the return of runaway black slaves.

**1723**
The Iroquois deny to the governor of New York the presence of runaway slaves among them.

**1724**
Trade in Indian slaves in the Carolinas is dying, though occasional instances occur.

**1727**
A maroon camp called Natanapalle is discovered in Louisiana, leading the governor to request the termination of the Indian slave trade.

**1728**
Louis XV taxes the owners of slaves in Louisiana.

**1729**
The governor of Louisiana uses black slaves to exterminate the Choucha, though some of these slaves are recruited to the Indian side by the promise of freedom.

Blacks support the rising of the Natchez in Louisiana.

**1732**
Virginia allows blacks, Indians, and mulattoes to testify in the trials of slaves.

**1735**
Louis XV forbids in Louisiana the sale of a female slave or her child if a free colonist has fathered the child. He decrees that after a certain time both mother and child shall be free.

**1738**
Indians on patrol for Louisiana's governor capture La Fleur, a runaway black, who accuses his owners of not giving him enough food.

**1740**
The Spanish, Indians, and blacks repel Georgia general James Oglethorpe's invasion of Florida.

The South Carolina Assembly declares all blacks, Indians, mulattos, and mestizos to be slaves "unless the contrary can be made to appear," but the act effectively frees Indian slaves, because, whereas it exempts Indians in amity with the colonists, it assumes already enslaved Indians to be in amity with the colonists.

**1748**
Jean Deslandes hires an Indian to accompany 10 of his slaves on an attack against a camp of armed runaways.

**1750**
Connecticut rules that any Indian brought into the colony shall be forfeited to its treasury, unless the importer gives security to transport the Indian out within one month.

**1751**
South Carolina enjoins traders from taking slaves or free blacks into Indian territory.

South Carolina prohibits traders from employing "Indians, Negroes, or Slaves."

**1760s**
The Lower Creek of Georgia [Seminole] begin to establish settlements in Florida in which runaway black slaves take refuge.

**1760**
The South Carolina assembly decides by a margin of one vote not to arm five hundred blacks to serve against the Cherokee.

At the surrender of Montreal, the English guarantee the French colonists their right to hold their black and Indian slaves.

A North Carolina law rules that Indian prisoners of war are slaves belonging to their captors.

**1763–1783**
Florida, under British rule, no longer functions as a haven for runaway slaves, but some slaves flee to or are captured by the Seminole there, who treat them more as vassals and allies than as slaves.

**1764–65**
The Huron, Iroquois, and Delaware (Lenni Lenape) promise once again to give up any runaway slaves, but no record shows any such transaction.

**1769**
A 14-year-old black captured by the Cherokee is sentenced to death by torture but is spared thanks to the intervention of an Indian girl.

*December 7:* Gov. Alexander O'Reilly prohibits the enslavement of Indians in the Spanish colonies; the decree does not affect those already enslaved but orders masters to declare before local authorities the number of slaves held, their age, sex, tribe, and market value.

**1776**
A few Cherokee prisoners of war are still auctioned off as slaves in the Carolinas.

**1779**
Governor O'Reilly outlaws Indian slavery in Florida.

**1785**
"Negroes, Indians and Mulattoes" are "exempted" from service in the new U.S. Army.

A posse of Indians receives a reward from the New Orleans cabildo [municipal council] for killing a black highwayman.

**1790**
The Creek agree to return black slaves they have captured.

**1790–94**
A few Indian slaves in the Spanish colonies successfully bring suit against their masters for their freedom.

**1794**
The U.S. agent says that the Creek cannot return their black prisoners and suggests that instead the United States compensate their former owners.

**1797**
A New Jersey court rules that Indians may be slaves in the state.

**1800**
Indian slavery has almost ceased in Lower Canada.

**1803**
The slave York travels as manservant to William Clark on the Lewis and Clark expedition, arousing the curiosity and awe of the Indians because of his color.

**1806**
The Virginia Court of Appeals holds that it was lawful to enslave Indians only until 1691; thereafter, only Indians descended from a female enslaved lawfully before that date could be slaves.

The slave York wins his freedom at the end of the Lewis and Clark expedition.

**1812–1814**
Spanish, Indians, and blacks repel the so-called American Patriot invasion of East Florida.

**1812**
In the "Patriot" invasion of East Florida, Americans try to take land from the Indians and Spanish. In reaction, black sergeants are sent into South Carolina to instigate slave insurrections and desertions.

Some Creek form a war party under the name of "Red Stick," some blacks participate in these battles, probably as slaves of white enemies.

**1813**
*August 30:* In the Creek War, Red Sticks attack Fort Mimms in Alabama, killing almost five hundred mestizos and whites, but no blacks.

**1814**
Gen. Andrew Jackson crushes the Red Sticks, but a faction of Creek decline to accept the treaty and flee to kin in Florida.

Runaway black slaves take over a British fort, with its abandoned arms and ammunition, in Spanish territory on the Appalachicola River for their own use and that of their Indian allies; it becomes known as the "Negro Fort."

**1817**
A British agent is reported to be stirring up Seminole and blacks at the mouth of the Appalachicola River, signalling the start of the First Seminole War.

**1818**
The First Seminole War (a slave-hunting invasion of Florida) ends informally after Gen. Andrew Jackson captures Bowleg's Town on the Suwanee River; Seminole and black survivors retreat into swamps.

**1819**
When the sovereignty of Florida passes from Spain to the United States, Americans face the problem of the Seminole and their black slaves and allies.

**1820**
The Cherokee council prohibits the purchase of goods from slaves and forbids masters to allow their slaves to buy or sell liquor.

**1823**
The Seminole sign a treaty at Fort Moultrie, agreeing to return all runaway black slaves entering their territory.

**1824**
The Cherokee council grants tribe member Shoe Boots's petition for recognition of the legitimacy and citizenship of his three children by a black slave, on

condition that "Capt. Shoe Boots cease begetting any more children by his said Slave *woman*."

**1826**
The Seminole return many runaway slaves but complain that some of their own slaves have been seized by whites and that whites are selling blacks to Indians and then claiming them again.

**1827**
The Cherokee Nation grants all adult males the vote, excepting "negroes, and descendants of white and Indian men by negro women who may have been set free. . . . No person who is of negro or mulatto parentage, either by the father or mother side, shall be eligible to hold any office or trust under this government. . . ."

**1828**
The Cherokee Nation rules that "all free negroes coming into the Cherokee Nation under any pretence whatsoever, shall be viewed and treated, in every respect as intruders, and shall not be allowed to reside in the Cherokee Nation without a permit."

The Cherokee forbid the marriage of whites and Indians to slaves and make it unlawful for slaves to own property.

**1830–1840**
The removal of the Indians from the Gulf states and the consequent opening of new cotton fields motivates many slaves to flee for fear of being sold south.

**1832**
Some Seminole chiefs sign the Treaty of Payne's Landing, agreeing to move across the Mississippi into Indian Territory with the Creek, but their reluctance and that of their black allies and counselors lead to the Second Seminole War.

**1835**
*March 24:* Col. James Morgan reports that Texas blacks who wish to join the Mexicans are making overtures to Indians, apparently without result.

*December 28:* Seminole and blacks in Florida, with the help of plantation slaves, ambush U.S. soldiers on their way to reenforce Fort King, who are betrayed by their slave guide Luis Pacheco; the Second Seminole War begins.

**1836**
The Choctaw Nation exiles abolitionists.

**1837**
*January 17:* John Caesar, a Seminole black leader in the Second Seminole War, is killed after an attack on a plantation west of St. Augustine.

*March 6:* Representatives of Seminole chiefs Micanopy and Alligator sign an agreement to suspend hostilities and agree to move the entire nation west; the United States guarantees their safety on the way and allows their negroes, their *bona fide* property, to accompany them.

**1838**
Gen. Thomas Sidney Jesup promises the Seminole blacks that if they will surrender, the U.S. government will protect them against capture or kidnapping by whites and send them west as part of the Seminole nation.

**1839–1842**
The Cherokee adopt a relatively harsh slave code as well as restrictions on free blacks.

**1841**
The U.S. government decides that the 1832 Treaty of Payne's Landing has canceled all claims against the Indians for any blacks run away or captured before that treaty.

The Cherokee make the education of blacks illegal.

**1842**
More than 20 black slaves owned by Cherokee flee toward Mexican territory, fighting off pursuers until finally captured nearly three hundred miles southwest of Fort Gibson.

A Cherokee law provides that any free black who helps a slave escape shall receive a hundred lashes and be exiled.

**1843**
The Second Seminole War ends.

**1845**
A treaty between the Seminole and Creek fails to resolve questions of title to and control of Seminole blacks and causes distrust between blacks and Indians.

When General Jesup on a visit to Indian Territory sends word to blacks that he considers them free although the Seminole still claim them as slaves, the blacks stop working for the Indians. Many take refuge at Fort Gibson and help in its construction.

**1846**

A California magistrate orders the release of enslaved Indians but forbids any Indian who accepts employment to leave without written permission from the magistrate.

**1848**

*June 28:* U.S. attorney general John Y. Mason rules that of the slaves claimed by the Seminole, only those whom Alligator brought in under an agreement with General Jesup are free.

**1849**

Marcellus Duval of the Bureau of Indian Affairs asks for troops to disarm the blacks being returned to the Seminole as slaves.

Wild Cat leads a party of Seminole and Creek, accompanied by about 20 black slave families headed by Gopher John, to Cow Bayou in Texas and then in 1850 to Mexico, where they ask admission as settlers.

**1850**

About 300 Seminole and blacks leave Indian Territory, heading across Texas for Mexico, where slavery is illegal. In Mexico, they agree to guard the border in return for grants of land; others follow.

The U.S. government ends its protection of blacks who have claimed their freedom on General Jesup's promise to all blacks in the Second Seminole War who would give themselves up.

Under Jim Bowlegs, about 180 blacks leave Indian Territory for Mexico; they are pursued by Creek and white slave traders, who kill some and capture most, returning them to Seminole country.

Fifteen hundred blacks are reported to be fighting in Texas alongside Comanche resisting the encroachments of white settlers.

**1856**

Seminole chiefs seek compensation for the loss of slaves occasioned by General Jesup's promise of freedom to all blacks who would come in or persuade their Indian masters to emigrate westward.

**1865**

The U.S. government demands the abolition of slavery among the Indians and the integration of slaves into the tribes.

*March 21:* A treaty between the Seminole and the United States abolishes slavery and puts the freedmen on equal footing with the Seminole.

## EYEWITNESS TESTIMONY

### *Enmity between Indians and Blacks*

[The Indians were] worse scared than hurt, who seeing a blackamore in the top of a tree looking out for his way which he had lost, surmised he was *Abamacho,* or the devil; deeming all devils that are blacker than themselves: and being near to the plantation, they posted to the English, and entreated their aid to conjure this devil to his own place, who finding him to be a poor wandering blackamore, conducted him to his master.

*William Wood,* New England Prospect, *1634, quoted in Williams,* History of the Negro Race, *173.*

We came hither naked and poor as the Worm out of the earth, but you have everything and we that have nothing must love you and can never break the Chain of Friendship that is between us.

Here stands the Governor of Carolina whom we know. This small Rope we shew you is all we have to bind our slaves with and may be broke but you have Iron Chains for yours. We shall bind them as well as we can and deliver them to our Friends again and have no pay for it.

*Scalileskin Retagusta, speaking for the Cherokee chiefs in London before the British king, 1730, in Wood,* Black Majority, *262.*

When [the Negro slaves in North Carolina] have been guilty of these barbarous and disobedient Proceedings [mutiny or insurrection], they generally fly to the Woods, but as soon as the *Indians* have Notice from the *Christians* of their being there, they disperse them; killing some, others flying for Mercy to the *Christians* (whom they have injured) rather than fall into the others Hands, who have a natural aversion to the Blacks, and put them to death with the most exquisite Tortures, they can invent, whenever they catch them.

*John Brickell, 1737, in Porter,* Negro on the American Frontier, *105.*

Polly, a woman of color, was brought before the circuit court [in Indiana] by Lasselle, in obedience to a writ of *habeas corpus.* He stated in his return, that he held her by purchase as his slave, she being the issue of a colored woman purchased from the Indians in the territory northwest of the river Ohio. . . .

*1820, in Wheeler,* Law of Slavery, *352.*

[The slave Swann declares that] he was brought to this country when it was a frontier settlement and much infested with savages. He was then owned by a Mr. Henry Hambleton, whose family was attacked by the Indians and several of them butchered and made captive. Your petitioner is now able to prove that by his own intrepidity and valor he preserved and carried into the fort two of the small [white] children, being closely pursued by the savages and beating them off with a butcher knife. . . .

This day came Charles Hambleton before the undersigned, a Justice of the Peace for the said County, and made oath that he was one of the children then about thirteen years of age rescued by the Negro Swann then owned by his father. And his statement of the affair in his petition is substantially true only not representing in character sufficiently honorable to the petitioner. The affiant perfectly recollects that the Indians pursued the petitioner with this affiant and the other child in his care, and came frequently with tomahawks and knives drawn within ten steps of them, when the petitioner would urge the children on and turn and beat them [the Indians] back with his butcher knife till he got in the house and saved us.

*Virginia petition, December 12, 1821, in Johnston,* Race Relations, *10, text and n. 26.*

Persecution has reared its hideous head, and not only threatened but bound and whipped and tortured some poor creatures who had been in the habit of worshipping the God of Heaven with us. . . . Yesterday . . . my poor family . . . as they were assembled for worship in their usual way in my absence, with a few coloured persons, a band of savage [Creek] monsters rushed in upon them, seized the poor black people, bound them with cords & belts and such other things as were convenient to them; they were then led out one by one to a post in the yard and beat unmercifully, on which post the blood yet remains as a witness against them.

*Rev. Lee Compere, May 18, 1828, in "Red Indians, Black Slavery, and White Racism: Interracial Tensions among Slaveholding Indians," quoted in McLoughlin,* Ghost Dance, *272.*

[Nelson Jackson, one of my slaves, in 1838] was intrusted with a team and wagon for service in Florida, the place of destination being distant about nine hundred miles. [Employed in the transport service of the U.S. Army, Jackson defended two white teamsters against an attack by the Seminole, bringing one, severely wounded, and the body of the other back to camp.] I concluded to set him free not only in justice to himself but that his course through life and his reward may be referred to as an example of all men of color.

*Virginia petition, December 6, 1844, in Johnston,* Race Relations, *10–11.*

## *Indians' Enslavement of Each Other*

As to ye [the] next Reason alleadged of humanity, it is nor more nor Lesse than this, yt [that] by buying Indians of ye Savanahs you induce them through Couvetousness to your gunns, Powder and shott & other European Commodities to make war upon their neighbours, to ravish the wife from the Husband, kill the father to get ye Child & burne and Destroy ye habitations of these poore people into whose country wee are charefully [cheerfully] Reced [received]. By them, Cherished and supplyed when we were weake or at least never have done us hurt & after wee have set them on worke to do all these horrid wicked things to get slaves to see ye Dealers in Indians call it humanity to buy them and thereby keep them from being murdered. . . .

Wee are further informed, ye Westohs would have peace & sent some of their people to ye Savanahs to mediate for them but their messengers were taken & sent away to be sold, so would ye poore Winahs, but wee are informed, yt their messingers were Layed hold of & sent away also, but if there be peace with ye Westohs and Waniahs, where shall ye Savannahs get Indians to sell ye Dealers in Indians so yt wee are convinced ye sending away of Indians made ye Westoh and Winiah Wars & Continue them & will not only continue them but make other Warrs if ye Indians are suffered still to be sent away. . . .

*The Carolina proprietors, 1683, in Olexer,* Enslavement of the American Indian, *114.*

Having got information that some French-Canadians living among the Cascassias Illinois were inciting the savage nations in the environs of this settlement to make war upon one another and that the French-Canadians themselves were participating in order to get slaves that they afterwards sold to the English, MM. Dartaguet and de Bienville dispatched M. d'Eraque with six men in a boat with letters for the Reverend Jesuit Fathers and presents for the savages to induce them to make peace among themselves. When M. d'Eraque reached the Cascassias Illinois, he delivered the letters . . . and forbade the French-Canadians to engage in further warfare with the savages or to incite them to war. He then addressed the savages, urging them . . . to live at peace with other savages, and then gave them the presents. . . .

*André Penicaut's account of the 1706 situation, in Olexer,* Enslavement, *205.*

There is a Nation of INDIANS call'd the YAMASEES, who formerly liv'd under the SPANISH Government, but now live under the ENGLISH, about 80 Miles from CHARLES-TOWN. Some of these INDIANS going a-hunting, about 200 miles to the Southward, met with some SPANISH INDIANS that lived about Sancta Maria, not far from AUGUSTINE, the Seat of the SPANISH Government; and taking them prisoners, brought them Home, designing to sell them for Slaves to Barbadoes or Jamaica as was usual; but I understanding thereof, sent for their King, and ordered him to bring these INDIANS with him to CHARLES-TOWN, which accordingly he did: There were three Men and one Woman; they could speak SPANISH, and I had a JEW for an Interpreter, so upon examination I found they profess'd the Christian Religion as the papists do: upon which I thought in a most peculiar manner, they ought to be freed from Slavery; and thereupon order'd the King to carry them to Augustine, to the Spanish governour with a Letter. . . .

*Former Carolina governor John Archdale, 1707, in Olexer,* Enslavement, *125.*

## *Indian Friends and Allies of Black Slaves*

It was a runaway negro taught them [the Indians] to fortify thus [with hidden tree limbs, reeds, and canes set into the ground at an angle, so that advancing enemies would impale their legs on them], named Harry, whom Dove Williamson sold into Virginia for roguery & since fled to the Tuscaruros. . . . I never saw such subtill [subtle] contrivances for Defence.

*Col. John Barnwell of South Carolina, 1712, in Wood,* Black Majority, *129–30 n.*

Arrived at the Pallachocola Town. Two Spaniards, on[e] Negro, and four Commantle Indians. . . . The Spanyard was Shye of Comeing into the Square for Some Time but the Negro Sat in the Square in a Bould Manner. . . .

[I intend to take him since] though he has Been Taken by the Yemasees and Lived among the Spanyards Yet that dis [does] not make him free. . . .

[The Spaniards] appeared in Behalf of the negro Assuring me that he was a Good Christian [and offering to ransom him with two Indian slaves]. . . .

There being a[nother] Negro then in the Pallachocole town Belonging to Andrew Partoson of Port-Royal, I sent five White men to take him and bring him to me. They Accordingly Took the Negro and had him, but the King of the Town Cutt the Rope and threw it into the fire and the King of sd [said] Town told the White men that they had as Good Guns as they, and Could make use of them; upon which the white man Returned unto me. . . .

*Capt. Tobias Fitch, journal entries, 1725 mission to the Cherokees, in Porter,* Negro on the American Frontier, *173–75.*

There was danger of the Choctaws determining to fall upon the city [New Orleans], if it should be deprived of all its troops; and the Negroes, to free themselves from slavery, might join them, as some had done with the Natchez.

*Father Mathurin Le Petit, letter of July 12, 1730, in Olexer,* Enslavement, *221.*

The half-Breed Fellow who came down from the Cherokee Nation in Company with James Maxwell, did seduce 6 of my Negroes to run away from me into the Cherokees, from whence they might depend on their Freedom. They proceeded on their way as far as Broad River, and there three of them receded from whom I have this Account. There is many Circumstances to coroborate [*sic*] the Truth. As he is a subtil Fellow, he may have the like Influence on many Slaves in South Carolina.

*South Carolinian's account, 1751, in Perdue,* Slavery and Cherokee Society, *38.*

[The Arikaras] are much pleased with my black Servent [York]. Their women verry fond of carressing our men &c. . . . I ordered my black Servent to Dance which amused the crowd [of Mandans] verry much, and Somewhat astonished them, that So large a man should be active &c. &c.

*Capt. William Clark, journal entry 1804–6, in Porter,* Negro on the American Frontier, *13.*

[In Ohio on our escape to Canada in 1830, my family and I] discerned some persons approaching us at no great distance. . . . [T]he advance of a few paces showed me they were Indians. . . . I walked along coldly, till we came close upon them. They were bent down with their burdens, and had not raised their eyes till now; and when they did so, and saw me coming towards them, they looked at me in a frightened sort of a way for a moment, and then, setting up a peculiar howl, turned round, and ran as fast as they could. There were three or four of them, and what they were afraid of I could not imagine. . . . [W]e heard their wild and prolonged howl, as they ran, for a mile or more. My wife was alarmed, too, and thought they were merely running back to collect more of a party, and then would come and murder us; and she wanted to turn back. I told her they were numerous enough to do that, if they wanted to, without help; and that as for turning back, I had had quite too much of the road behind us, and that it would be a ridiculous thing that both parties should run away. . . . As we advanced, we could discover Indians peeping at us from behind the trees, and dodging out of sight if they thought we were looking at them. Presently we came upon their wigwams, and saw a fine-looking, stately Indian, with his arms folded, waiting for us to approach. He was, apparently, the chief; and saluting us civilly, he soon discovered that we were human beings, and spoke to his young men, . . . and made them come in and give up their foolish fears. And now curiosity seemed to prevail. Each one wanted to touch the children, who were as shy as partridges with their long life in the woods; and as they shrunk away, and uttered a little cry of alarm, the Indian would jump back too. . . . However, a little while sufficed to make them understand whither we were going, and what we needed; and then they supplied our wants, fed us bountifully, and gave us a comfortable wigwam for our night's rest. The next day we resumed our march. . . . They sent some of their young men to point out the place where we were to turn off, and parted from us with as much kindness as possible.

*Josiah Henson, describing his family's escape from slavery,* Autobiography, *66–67.*

Representation of massacres in Florida of whites by blacks and Indians, December 1835–April 1836 (*Library of Congress*)

Many [slaves] have escaped to and joined the Indians, and furnished them with much important information, and if strong measures were not taken to restrain our slaves, there is but little doubt that we should soon be assailed with a servile as well as Indian war.

*Maj. Benjamin A. Putnam, July 31, 1836, to the secretary of war, in Porter,* Negro on the American Frontier, *270.*

It seemed that after the Friars I have mentioned and the Negro [Estevanico de Dorantes, black slave of a Spanish master,] had started [on an 1838 excursion to find the seven legendary golden cities of Cibola, with Estevanico as guide], the Negro did not get on well with the Friars because he took the women that were given him and collected turquoises and got together a stock of everything. Besides, the Indians in those places through which they went got along better with the Negro because they had seen him before. . . . [Estevanico] thought he could get all the reputation and honor himself, and that if he should discover those settlements with such famous high houses, alone, he would be considered bold and courageous. . . . For three days [the Cibolans] made inquiries about him and held a council. The account which the Negro gave them of two white men who followed him, sent by a great lord, who knew about the things in the sky, and how these were coming to instruct them in divine matters, made them think that he must be a spy or a guide from some nations who wished to come to conquer them, because it seemed to them unreasonable to say that the people were white in the country from which he came and that he was sent by them, he being black.

*Soldier-chronicler Castaneda, member of the excursion, in* Black Military Experience, *12, 13, 15.*

Very few of them [the Massachusetts Indians] are of unmixed blood, the number of pure Indians is very small, say fifty or sixty, and is rapidly decreasing. The mixture of blood arises far more frequently from connection with Negroes than with white.

*Jedidiah Morse, report to the secretary of war, 1822, in Johnston,* Race Relations, *273.*

Now he [Wild Cat] come back [from Mexico] with enticing news, and want to carry his people in that nation; and the negroes, he told them if they emigrate to that country, they will all be freed by the government. This is good news to the negroes. I am told some are preparing to go.

*Chief McIntosh, September 23, 1850, in Littlefield,* Africans and Seminoles, *154.*

## *Indian Masters of Black Slaves*

My parents were slaves in New York State. My master's sons-in-law . . . came into the garden where my sister and I were playing among the currant bushes, tied their handkerchiefs over our mouths, carried us to a vessel, put us in the hold, and sailed up the river. I know not how far nor how long—it was dark there all the time. Then we came by land. I remember when we came to Genesee,—there were Indian settlements there,—Onondagas, Senecas, and Oneidas. I guess I was the first colored girl brought into Canada. The white men sold us at Niagara to old Indian Brant, the king. . . .

Brant's third wife, my mistress, was a barbarous creature. She could talk English, but she would not. She would tell me in Indian to do things, and then hit me with any thing that came to hand, because I did not understand her. I have a scar on my head from a wound she gave me with a hatchet: and this long scar over my eye, is where she cut me with a knife. The skin dropped over my eye; a white woman bound it up. . . . Brant was very angry, when he came home, at what she had done, and punished her as if she had been a child. Said he, "You know I adopted her as one of the family, and now you are trying to put all the work on her."

*Sophia Pooley, in Drew,* Refugee, *192, 194.*

When a barbarian has split the head of his slave with a hatchet, he says, "It is a dead dog—there is nothing to be done but to cast it upon the dung hill."

*Saying of Jesuit missionaries about the Iroquois, in Lauber,* Indian Slavery, *41.*

[Cherokees take their slaves on hunting trips, where they are] employ'd to carry Burdens, to get bark for the Cabins, and other Servile Work; also to go backward and forward to their Towns, to carry News to the old People, whom they leave behind them.

*John Lawson,* A New Voyage to Carolina, *1709, quoted in Perdue,* Slavery and Cherokee Society, *15.*

A white man sells us a Negro, and then turns around and claims him again, and our big father [the U.S. government] orders us to give him up.

*Seminole chief John Hicks, 1829, in Porter,* Negro on the American Frontier, *243.*

Abraham was the most noted and for a time an influential man in the [Seminole] nation. He dictated to those of his own color, who to a great degree controlled their [Seminole] masters. They were a most cruel and malignant enemy. For them to surrender would be servitude to the whites; but to retain an open warfare, secured to them plunder, liberty, and importance.

*U.S. Army officer, 1837, quoted in Porter,* Negro on the American Frontier, *62.*

The negroes exercised a wonderful control. They openly refused to follow their [Seminole] masters, if they removed to Arkansas. Many of them would have been reclaimed by the Creeks, to whom some belonged. Others would have been taken possession of by the whites, who for years had been urging their claims through the government and its agents. In Arkansas, hard labor was necessary for the means of support, while Florida assured them of every means to indulge in idleness, and enjoy an independence corresponding with their masters. In preparing for hostilities they were active, and in the prosecution blood-thirsty and cruel. It was not until the negroes capitulated, that the Seminoles ever thought of emigrating.

*U.S. Army officer in the Seminole War, quoted in Porter,* Negro on the American Frontier, *58–59.*

Most of the labor among the wealthier classes of Cherokees, Chocktaws, Chickasaws, Creeks, and Seminoles, is done by negro slaves; for they have all adopted substantially the Southern system of slavery.

*Trader Josiah Gregg, after 1838, in Perdue,* Slavery and Cherokee Society, *72.*

Comanches steal negroes sometimes from Texas and sell them to Cherokees and Creeks. The latter have been known to pay $400 and $500 for a negro.

*U.S. government investigator, 1841–42, quoted in Porter,* Negro on the American Frontier, *69.*

My pappy was a kind of a boss of the negroes that run the [river]boat, and they all belong to old Master Joe [Vann, a Cherokee]. Some had been in a big run-away and had been brung back, and wasn't so good, so he kept them on the boat all the time mostly. . . . My pappy run away one time, four or five years before I was born, mammy tell me, and at that time [in 1842] a whole lot of Cherokee slaves run off at once. They got over in Creek Country and stood off the Cherokee officers that went to git them, but pretty soon they give up and come home. Mammy says they was lot of excitement on old Master's place and all the negroes mighty scared, but he didn't sell my pappy off. He jest kept him, and he was a good negro after that. He had to work on the boat, though, and never got to come home but once in a long while.

*Ex-slave Betty Robertson, in Perdue,* Slavery and Cherokee Society, *83.*

[A surviving Vann slave] said that [in the fall of 1844] my grandfather was on the top deck [of his boat the *Lucy Walker*], entertaining the passengers at a ball and dinner and there was a good deal of drinking. They were having a race with another boat on the river and though they were a little ahead of the other boat my grandfather came down to the boiler deck drunk and he told the negro to throw another side of meat on the fire in order to get more steam so that they could gain on the other boat. The negro told him that the boat was carrying every pound of steam it could stand and Joe Vann [a Cherokee] pulled his pistol on the negro and told him that if he did not obey him he would shoot him. The negro threw the side of meat on the fire as he was ordered and then turned and ran to the stern of the boat and jumped into the river, and he had not much more than got into the water when the boilers blew up.

*Memoirs of R. P. Vann, the grandson of Joe Vann, in Perdue,* Slavery and Cherokee Society, *103.*

[My mother was a house girl for a Creek Indian family] cooking, waiting on the table, cleaning the house, spinning the yarn, knitting some of the winter clothes, taking care of the mistress girl, washing the clothes—yes she was always busy and worked mighty hard all the time [for the Indians] wouldn't hardly do nothing for themselves.

*Phoebe Banks, in Fox-Genovese,* Plantation Households, *179–80.*

One time he [Cherokee Ben Johnson] whipped a whole bunch of the men on account of a fight in the quarters, and then he took them all to Fort Smith to see a hanging. He tied them all in the wagon, and when they had seen the hanging he asked them if they was scared of them dead men hanging up there. They all said yes, of course, but my old uncle Nick was a bad negro and he said, "No, I ain't a-feared of them nor nothing else in this world," and old Master jumped on him while he was tied and beat him with a rope, and then when they got home he tied old Nick to a tree and took his shirt off and poured the cat-o-nine-tails to him until he fainted away and fell over like he was dead. I never forgot seeing all that blood all over my uncle, and if I could hate that old Indian any more I guess I would, but I hated him all I could already I reckon.

*Ex-slave Sarah Wilson, in Perdue,* Slavery and Cherokee Society, *117–18.*

## *Indian Slaves*

[Since the Indians of Florida] can never be made submissive and become Christians, [they should be] placed on ships and scattered throughout the various islands, and even on the Spanish Main, where they might be sold as His Majesty sells his vessels to the grandees in Spain.

*Interpreter Hernando de Escalante Fontanedo, 1560s or 1570s, in Lauber,* Indian Slavery, *48.*

But one Thomas Hunt, the Master of this ship . . . betrayed four and twenty of those poor salvages [savages] aboard his ship, and most dishonestly and inhumanly, for their kind usage of me and all my men, carried them with him to Malaga; and there for a little private gain, sold these silly [innocent] salvages for rials of eight; but this vile act kept him ever after from any more employment to those parts. . . .

*Capt. John Smith, 1614, in Olexer,* Enslavement, *34–35.*

Came home and found my Indian girl had liked to have knocked my Theodorah on the head by letting her fall. Whereupon I took a good walnut stick and beat the Indian to purpose till she promised to do so no more. . . .

*Peter Thatcher of Massachusetts, diary entry of about 1674, in Olexer,* Enslavement, *55.*

And it shall be lawful, and is hereby warranted, for him to make sale of such prisoners as they think meet (they being such as the law allows to be kept).

*Instructions of the governor of Massachusetts to Capt. Benjamin Church to attack Indians, January 15, 1676, in Lauber,* Indian Slavery, *142.*

[U]pon a beare information [mere accusation] of Indians . . . without ever inquiring into the truth of ye [the] thing or ever sending to ye Waniahs to let them know ye Information had been given to ye govermt yt [that] such a murder was Comited by some of their people, demanding thereupon ye persons guilty of ye fact, a warr is proclaimed against them and pore Innocent women and Children Barberously murdered taken and sent to be sold as slaves, who in all probability had been innocent of ye fact had any such been Comited.

*The Carolina proprietors, letter to the council and governor, 1683, in Olexer,* Enslavement, *115.*

[The North Carolina Indians] are not of so robust and strong Bodies as to lieft [lift] great Burdens and endure Labour and slavish Work, as the Europeans are; yet some that are Slaves, prove very good and laborious; But, of themselves, they never work as the English do, taking care for nor farther than what is absolutely necessary to support Life, In Traveling and Hunting, they are very indefatigable; because that carries a Pleasure along with the Profit. . . . Most of the Savages are much addicted to Drunkeness, a Vice they never were acquainted with, till the Christians came amongst them. . . .

*John Lawson, 1709, in Olexer,* Enslavement, *142.*

Our Traders have promoted Bloody Warrs this last Year to get slaves and one of them brought lately 100 of those poor Souls. . . . I don't know where the fault lyes but I see 30 Negroes at Church for an Indian slave, and as for our free Indians—they goe their own way and bring [up] their Children like themselves with little Conversation among us. I generaly Pceive [perceive] something Cloudy in their looks, an Argumt. [sign] I fear, of discontent. I am allso Informed yt. [that] Our Indie Allyes [the Yamasees] are grown haughty of late.

*Minister Francis LeJau, 1712, in Wood,* Black Majority, *143 n.*

[These Indian wars are God's punishment upon the slave owners.] All we can doe is, to lament in Secret those Sins, which have brought this judgement upon us. Our Military Men are so bent upon Revenge, and so desirous to enrich themselves, by making all the Indians Slaves that fall into their hands, but such as they kill . . . that it is in vain to represent to them the Cruelty and injustice of Such a procedure.

*Anglican vicar Gideon Johnston, 1715, in Ball,* Slaves, *95.*

[T]hese Indian slaves being mixed with our negroes may induce them to desert with them, as has already happened, as they may maintain relations with them which might be disastrous to the colony when there are more blacks.

*Louisiana governor Etienne Boucher de Perier, 1727, in Usner, "American Indians," 108.*

The French army re-embarked and carried the Natchez as slaves to New Orleans, where they were put in prison; but afterwards, to avoid the infection, the women and the children were disposed of on the King's plantation and elsewhere. Among these women was the Female Sun, called the Stung Arm, who then told me all she had done in order to save the French. Some time after, these slaves were embarked to St. Domingo, in order to root out the nation in the colony.

*Antoine Simon LePage du Pratz, describing actions of 1730, in Olexer,* Enslavement, *227.*

I am very glad that your excellency has given orders to have the Indian children returned, who are kept by the traders as pawns or pledges as they call it, but rather stolen from them (as the parents came at the appointed time to redeem them, but they sent them away before hand), and as they were children of our Friends and Allies, and if they are not returned next Spring, it will confirm what the French told the Six Nations (viz.): that we looked upon them as slaves or negroes, which affair gave me a great deal of trouble at that time to reconcile.

*Indian commissioner Johnson to New York governor Clinton, 1750, in Lauber,* Indian Slavery, *200–1.*

[Indian slaves] are also full of pride and resentment, and will not hesitate to kill their masters in order to gratify their revenge of a supposed injury. The girls are more docile, and assimilate much sooner into the manners of civilization.

*John Long, journal of 1768–82, in Olexer,* Enslavement, *87.*

The Indians from Stono came down in straggling parties and plundered the fruits of labor and industry. Being accustomed to the practice of killing whatever came in their way, they ranked the planters' hogs, turkeys, and geese among their game and freely preyed upon them. The planters as freely made use of their arms in defence of their property, and several Indians were killed during their depredations. This occasioned a war and the Indians poured their vengeance indescrimanately, as usual, on the innocent and guilty for the loss of their friends. Governor West found it necessary to encourage and reward such of the colonists as would take the field against them for the public defence. Accordingly a price was fixed on every Indian the settlers could take prisoner and bring to Charlestown. These captive savages were disposed of to the traders, who sent them to the West Indies and there sold them for slaves.

*Alexander Hewatt, 1779, in Olexer,* Enslavement, *103.*

Professor Dew is of opinion that the introduction of slavery among the Indians of this country, would have averted the approaching annihilation of the aboriginal race. . . . "Slavery [he says] . . . appears to be the only means that we know of, under heaven, by which the ferocity of the savage can be conquered, his wandering habits eradicated, his slothfulness—by which, in fine, his nature can be changed."

The South Vindicated *(1836), 102–3.*

I belonged to the Rev. Adam Runkin, a Presbyterian minister in Lexington, Kentucky.

My mother was of mixed blood,—white and Indian. She married my father when he was working in a bagging factory near by. After a while my father's owner moved off and took my father with him, which broke up the marriage. She was a very handsome woman. My master kept a large dairy, and she was the milk-woman. . . . A man who belonged to the [Masonic] lodge saw my mother when she was about her work. He made proposals of a base nature to her. When she would have nothing to say to him, he told her that she need not be so independent, for if money could buy her he would have her. My mother told old mistress, and begged that master might not sell her. But he did sell her. My mother had a high spirit, being part Indian. She would not consent to live with this man, as he wished; and he sent her to prison, and had her flogged, and punished in various ways, so that at last she began to have crazy turns. . . . She tried to kill herself several times, once with a knife and once by hanging. She had long, straight black hair, but after this it all turned white, like an old person's. When she had her raving turns she always talked about her children. The jailer told the owner that if he would let her go to her children, perhaps she would get quiet. . . .

At last her owner sold her, for a small sum, to a man named Lackey. While with him she had another husband and several children. After a while this husband either died or was sold, I do not remember which. The man then sold her to another person, named Bryant. My own father's owner now came and lived in the neighborhood of this man, and brought my father with him. He had had another wife and family of children where he had been living. He and my mother came together again, and finished their days together. My mother almost recovered her mind in her last days.

I never saw anything in Kentucky which made me suppose that ministers or professors of religion considered it any more wrong to separate the families of slaves by sale than to separate any domestic animals.

*Lewis Hayden, 1853 autobiographical account, in* Slave Testimony, *695–96.*

## *Indian Relations with Maroon Blacks*

In our Quarrels with the *Indians,* however proper and necessary it may be to give them Correction, it can never be our interest to extirpate them, or to force them from their Lands: their Grounds would be soon taken up by runaway *Negroes* from our Settlements, whose Numbers would daily increase and quickly become more formidable Enemies than *Indians* can ever be, as they speak our Language and would never be at a Loss for Intelligence.

*Indian policy in the colony of South Carolina, in Perdue,* Slavery and Cherokee Society, *40.*

It will be difficult to form a prudent determination, with respect to the maroon negroes, who live among the [Seminole] Indians [in Florida]. Their number is said to be upwards of three hundred. They fear being again made slaves, under the American government; and will omit nothing to increase or keep alive mistrust among the Indians, whom they in fact govern. If it should become necessary to use force with them, it is to be feared that the Indians would take their part.

*Indian agent reporting on plans to move the Seminole west after the United States acquired Florida in 1819, in Blassingame,* Slave Community, *122–23.*

[T]here are negroes enslaved in the Indian Territory: the descendants of the bravest warriors America has produced—the hunted maroons, who, for forty years, in the swamps of Florida, defied the skill and armies of the United States. They hate slavery and the race that upholds it, and are longing for an opportunity to display that hatred. Not far from this territory, in a neighboring province of Mexico, live a nation of trained negro soldiers—the far-famed Florida Indians, who, after baffling and defying the United States, and after having been treacherously enslaved by the Creeks, incited thereto by Federal officials—bravely resisted their oppressors and made an Exodus, the grandest since the days of Moses, to a land of freedom. Already have their oppressors felt their prowess; and their historian tells us—"*they will be heard from again*."

*Redpath,* Roving Editor *(1859), 250.*

# 10

# The Argument over Slavery
# 1637–1865

## The Historical Context

### *Attitudes toward Slavery Until the 1830s*

Americans did not argue much about slavery until they began to think about demanding liberty for themselves—liberty from Great Britain and its king. A few colonists, to be sure, raised their voices against slavery from the early 17th century on—especially the Quakers and the Mennonites. Conscience, as well as the dangers and threats that slavery brought to the dominant white population, pricked a few to propose antislavery legislation. In its earliest days, Georgia forbade slavery. In 1652, the Rhode Island legislature banned servitude for more than ten years or after the age of 24—but on paper only. Colonial Massachusetts courts occasionally heard cases in which slaves sued for their freedom. But by and large, colonists accepted slavery as a fact of life that worked better in some colonies than others.

By the middle of the 18th century, the natural-rights theories of John Locke began to humanize the climate of ideas in Britain and France, and consequently in America. All men, he said, are equal, possessed of rights that no one can take away from them, free to pursue "life, health, liberty, and possessions." Clearly, no one could reasonably accept Locke's theories and at the same time approve of slavery, embedded in the American economy though it was. The defiant American rebels who used Locke's ideas to justify their own revolution against Britain could not blind themselves to the contradiction between those ideas and the realities of slavery—or so one would think. On the other hand, many Christians who said that they believed in the equality of all people under God had nonetheless gone along quite comfortably enslaving blacks and Indians. Human beings had long since proved themselves quite capable of believing contradictory things at the same time and of believing one thing and practicing another.

Nonetheless, in the latter half of the 18th century sentiment against slavery rose in the American colonies. North and South alike were alarmed by the growth of the slave system. Even as the numbers of slaves continued to multiply, slaveholders themselves deplored the institution, and many others denounced it. In a desperate effort to form an American union, the founding fathers compromised on the issue. They implicitly sanctioned slavery's existence in the Constitution but empowered Congress to prohibit the importation of slaves after 1808. In the new nation, the opposition to slavery began to gain legal victories. In 1783, a Massachusetts court interpreted that state's constitution as outlawing slavery. In 1791, Vermont joined the Union as a free state. Between 1780 and 1804, Pennsylvania, Connecticut, Rhode Island, New York, and New Jersey passed gradual-emancipation statutes.

In the South too, the moral climate of the post-Revolutionary years nurtured a vigorous antislavery movement. Southern newspapers published antislavery sentiments, which also infiltrated the evangelical sects of the Upper South. Southern politicians, editors, professors, and clergy inveighed against the institution. As late as 1832, the Virginia legislature hotly debated the issue. Scores of owners freed their slaves, on condition that they would emigrate to Liberia. In the 1820s, the slave states actually had more antislavery societies than the free states, furnishing leadership for the movement throughout the country. For example, in 1826, of the hundred societies working for voluntary manumission, colonization, and betterment for slaves, 45 were in North Carolina.[1]

## *The Difficulties of Ending Slavery*

Condemning slavery as sinful and unchristian, Americans searched for a means of ridding the country of it. Any modification of the system would disrupt the South politically, economically, and socially; it would profoundly change the whole nation. French abolitionist Brissot de Warville observed that Americans "fear that if the Blacks become free they would cause trouble; on rendering them free they know not what rank to assign them in society; whether they shall establish them in separate districts or send them out of the country."[2]

Would freed slaves enjoy the benefits of citizenship—the rights to vote, bear arms, sit on juries, hold office, testify against whites in court cases? If denied, their demands for these rights might lead to a war between blacks and whites. If they were granted, could blacks live up to the responsibilities of citizenship? Could blacks and whites live together as equals? Could whites, trained to an arrogant sense of their own superiority, learn to accept blacks as political equals—let alone social equals? Where blacks outnumbered whites, might not they take their revenge by attempting to enslave whites?

Could blacks, trained to obedience and dependence, support themselves once freed? Would they work if no one forced them to? If they were to own property, where would they get it? Would freed slaves not desert the South in a mass migration northward? How could the North absorb large numbers of them in its labor force? How would the South get its work done without them? Who would compensate slave owners for the loss of most of their capital?

If the 13 original states had not been able to agree to abolish slavery when they ratified the Constitution, how could the greater number of states now in the Union agree? Could abolition be achieved piecemeal, one state at a time? Meanwhile, what would happen when slave owners moved from a slave state to a free state? Would a free state return fugitive slaves to their owners? Would not their differences put the slave states and the free states at sword's point?

The prospect of ending slavery in the United States brought the country face to face with terra incognita. For all anyone knew, such an action might precipitate chaos. History offered no similar situation on which Americans could base their actions—a move that would profoundly change the lives of so many people.

Even that well-informed, detached, and intelligent observer Alexis de Tocqueville hesitated: "I am obliged to confess that I do not consider the abolition of slavery as a means of delaying the struggle between the two races in the southern states. The Negroes might remain slaves for a long time without complaining; but as soon as they join the ranks of free men, they will soon be indignant at being deprived of almost all the rights of citizens; and being unable to become the equals of the whites, they will not be slow to show themselves their enemies. In the North there was every advantage in freeing the slaves; in that way one is rid of slavery without having anything to fear from the free Negroes. They were too few ever to claim their rights. . . .

"I confess that in considering the South I see only two alternatives for the white people living there: to free the Negroes and to mingle with them or to remain isolated from them and keep them as long as possible in slavery. Any intermediate measures seem to me likely to terminate, and that shortly, in the most horrible of civil wars, and perhaps in the extermination of one or other of the two races."[3]

While the nation discussed these questions, the numbers of slaves dwindled in the North and soared in the South: the two sections of the country were developing their economies on different bases. In the North, free industrial laborers wanted no competition from slaves. In the South, planters depended more and more on slave labor. Hearing the ever-louder protests of northern abolitionists, they felt increasingly besieged. The slave revolts led by men such as Gabriel Prosser, Denmark Vesey, and Nat Turner frightened all southerners and hardened the slave owners' determination to control and hang on to their slaves. They turned from denouncing slavery to defending it. By the mid-1830s, the southern antislavery movement had withered to almost nothing.

From that time on, as several prescient contemporary writers pointed out, the forces for and against slavery were on collision courses. In 1848, for instance, diarist George Stanley Fisher observed, "The slavery question is becoming more important & alarming every day. The South has made another move on the chessboard. From being defensive they have become aggressive. They declare openly that it is essential to their protection that they should govern the country. That soon they will be outvoted by the North & therefore at its mercy. To acquire this political preponderance, Texas was annexed and the Mexican War undertaken. . . . When the question comes to be fairly raised—which shall govern, South or North—then the Union will be in imminent danger. It is absurd to suppose that the South can succeed. Its domination is opposed to all the principles & opinions of the country expressed by none more strongly than by themselves. They are essentially an aristocracy, a collection of landed proprietors surrounded by serfs, their property in slaves is represented [as] the only sort of property that gives political power, and they are a small minority in population of the whole country. Numbers as well as wealth, civilization and power are enormously on the side of the North. On every democratic principle, therefore, the North should govern. It will govern or the Union will be severed. . . . [T]here is great reason to fear that ere long there will be a Northern party and a Southern party, and that the former, encouraged by the consciousness of strength & exasperated by conflict will not long continue to respect the 'Compromises of the Constitution,' but will attempt the entire abolition of slavery. This would be a signal for civil war."[4]

Slavery's advocates and its antagonists radicalized. Both sides expounded more and more extreme positions, with mounting fervor and conviction; their tolerance for one another evaporated.

## *Proslavery Arguments*

Defenders of slavery lined up one argument after another:

1. They attacked the character and abilities of blacks, who, they said, needed white men's oversight. "The African is incapable of self-care and sinks into lunacy under the burden of freedom," said John C. Calhoun. "It is a mercy to him to give him the guardianship and protection from mental death."[5]
2. Slaves in the United States were not only better off than free people in Africa but also better off than workingmen in England and the northern states. As slaves, they enjoyed the blessings of Christianity and the support and protection of their masters.
3. The South *needed* slave labor; indeed, American business generally depended on it, directly or indirectly. "Religion and humanity have nothing to do with this question [slavery]," a South Carolina representative to the Constitutional Convention of 1787 proclaimed bluntly. "Interest alone is the governing principle with nations."[6] In 1859, Texan Charles DeMorse was equally direct: "We want more slaves—we *need* them. We care nothing for . . . slavery as an abstraction—but we desire the practicality; the increase of our productions; the increase of the comforts and wealth of the population; and if slavery, or slave labor, or Negro Apprentice labor ministers to this, why this is what we want."[7]
4. The Bible, history, and the natural order of the universe all supported slavery. Virginia professor Thomas Drew announced, "It is as much in the order of nature that men should enslave each other as that other animals should prey upon each other."[8]
5. Neither the nation nor the individual states were entitled to interfere with slave owners' property. "The right of property exists before society," said William O. Goode in 1834. "The Legislature cannot deprive a citizen of his property in his slave. It cannot abolish slavery in a State. It could not delegate to Congress a power greater than its own."[9]
6. Slavery freed white men to cultivate their minds and concentrate on public affairs.
7. Black slavery freed white women from the servitude to which society must otherwise relegate them to get its work done and at the same time protected their virtue by providing an outlet for white men's passions in black women.

8. The welfare of society is more important than the welfare of any one person or race, so blacks ought to accept their own enslavement for the good of society. Unitarian minister Orville Dewey told slaves, "*Your right to be free is not absolute, unqualified, irrespective of all consequences.* If my espousal of your claim is likely to involve your race and mine together in disasters infinitely greater than your personal servitude, then you ought not to be free. In such a case personal rights ought to be sacrificed to the general good. You yourself ought to see this, and be willing to suffer for a while—one for many."[10]
9. Slavery may lead to abuses, but that is no reason to abandon the institution, any more than divorces are a reason to abandon the institution of marriage.
10. Southerners had not originated slavery. It had been forced upon them by England and northern traders, but they had since made of it an institution beneficial to all.

## *Abolitionist Arguments*

Abolitionists propounded arguments as diverse for their stand.

1. If we value freedom for ourselves, we should also want it for others. "Would we enjoy liberty?" asked Reverent Nathaniel Miles of Massachusetts. "Then we must grant it to others. For shame, let us either cease to enslave our fellow-men, or else let us cease to complain of those that would enslave us."[11]
2. Slavery endangers the Union. "The existence of Slavery may be viewed as one forcible cause of a final separation of the United States," warned the *Connecticut Courant* in 1796.[12]
3. Slavery does not profit the slave owner. Those who work for wages labor more productively than slaves, and their employers do not have to support them in their nonworking years of childhood and old age.
4 Slavery damages the communities in which it exists. "Slavery is ruinous to the whites; it retards improvement; roots out our industrious population; banishes the yeomanry of the country; deprives the spinner, the weaver, the smith, the shoemaker, the carpenter of employment and support," Thomas Marshall argued before the Virginia House of Delegates in 1832. "The EVIL admits of no remedy. It is increasing, and will continue to increase, *until the whole country* will be inundated by one black wave, covering its whole extent, with a few white faces, here and there, floating on its surface. The master has no capital but what is invested in human flesh; the father, instead of being richer for his sons, is at a loss how to provide for them. There is no diversity of occupations, no incentive to enterprise. Labor of every species is disreputable, because performed mostly by slaves. Our towns are stationary, our villages almost everywhere declining; and the general aspect of the country marks the curse of a wasteful, idle, reckless population, who have no interest in the soil, and care not how much it is impoverished. Public improvements are neglected, and the entire continent does not present a region for which nature has done so much and art so little."[13]
5. Slavery causes masters to sin. "[I]t is too well known," said Judge Samuel Sewall in 1700, "what Temptations Masters are under, to connive at the Fornication of their Slaves; lest they should be obliged to find them Wives,

**Illustrations of the American Anti-Slavery Almanac for 1840.**

"Our Peculiar *Domestic Institutions.*"

*Northern Hospitality—New-York nine months law.* [The Slave steps out of the Slave State, and his chains fall. A Free State, with another chain, stands ready to re-enslave him.]

*Burning of McIntosh at St. Louis, in April, 1836.*

*Showing how slavery improves the condition of the female sex.*

*The Negro Pew, or "Free" Seats for black Christians.*

*Mayor of New-York refusing a Carman's license to a colored Man.*

*Servility of the Northern States in arresting and returning fugitive Slaves.*

*Selling a Mother from her Child.*

*Hunting Slaves with dogs and guns. A Slave drowned by the dogs.*

*"Poor things, 'they can't take care of themselves.'"*

*Mothers with young Children at work in the field.*

*A Woman chained to a Girl, and a Man in irons at work in the field.*

*Branding Slaves.*

*Cutting up a Slave in Kentucky.*

*Paid.* *Unpaid.*

Abolitionist literature, 1840 (*Library of Congress*)

> or pay their Fines. . . . It is likewise most lamentable to think, how in taking Negroes out of *Africa,* and selling of them here, That which GOD has joined together, Men do boldly rend asunder: Men from their Country, Husbands from their Wives, Parents from their Children. How horrible is the Uncleanness, Mortality, if not Murder, that the Ships are guilty of that bring great Crowds of these miserable Men and Women."[14]

While abolitionists and proponents of slavery worked ever more ardently to persuade people to their way of thinking, the great majority of the population, of course, either took more moderate positions or remained indifferent to the whole issue. Most people went about their business, "going along to get along"—like young David Bush, who, having moved away from his Delaware family to Mississippi, wrote home, "Tell Pop I have not received a letter from him since I left. I expect he is angry with me for making the purchase of negroes . . ., but he must not be as it is no more for us here to purchase a servant or negro than it is for him to hire one. There is none for us to hire, and we are necessarily compelled to purchase to get our work done."[15] A good many people hoped that slavery, if left alone, would die a natural death, fading out of the South as they saw it fading out of the North—whereas, they feared, vigorous opposition might strengthen it.

Opposition to the extension of slavery, it must be understood, seldom reached to advocacy of full equality for blacks and whites. Free states and territories all too often either tried to exclude blacks completely or denied them civil rights and limited the categories of jobs open to them. Thus in 1844, the Oregon provisional government prohibited slavery and required slaveholders to remove their chattels within three years—but warned all free blacks and mulattoes to leave the territory within two years, subjecting any who remained to periodic floggings.

Many northern whites simply did not want blacks around at all, and most southern states required freed blacks to leave. Such sentiments help to explain the long life of the colonization movement, which sent blacks out of the country entirely. Pennsylvania Democrat David Wilmot based his 1846 proposal against the extension of slavery into any territory acquired by the Mexican War on a plea for "the cause and the rights of [the] white freeman [and] I would preserve to free white labor a fair country, a rich inheritance, where the sons of toil, of my own race and own color, can live without the disgrace which association with negro slavery brings upon free labor." He added privately, "By God, sir, men born and nursed of white women are not going to be ruled by men who were brought up on the milk of some damn Negro wench!"[16]

Even ardent abolitionists often questioned the abilities of blacks. They might and did argue that blacks and whites are equal under God, but those like Theodore Weld and the Grimké sisters, Sarah and Angelina, who actually practiced integration, were the exception rather than the rule. So were those Quakers who insisted that slaveholders owed their slaves not only freedom but also compensation for their labors in the past and help in getting new starts.

## *Antislavery Divisions*

The wearing struggle against slavery divided antislavery forces more than it united them on questions of ideology and strategy. Should they confine themselves to moral suasion? Should they reinforce it by political action? Need they resort to direct militant action?

The first split came early, with disagreements over women's role in the movement and in society as a whole. The refusal of the World Anti-Slavery Society in 1840 to seat women delegates from the United States motivated Elizabeth Cady Stanton and Lucretia Mott to organize the first woman's rights convention. But already in 1835–36, the Grimké sisters had broken with the tradition that women should neither allow their names to appear in print nor appear on public platforms. Their deep devotion to the cause of antislavery demanded that they write and speak out for it—a decision that troubled other antislavery advocates. Despite women's numbers and important work, particularly in the grassroots societies, many in the antislavery movement feared that endorsing women lecturers would attract opposition; the movement could not afford, they argued, to lose support by embracing other causes. Nonetheless, talented women like Abby Kelley Foster and Sallie Holley soon followed the Grimkés' example. William Lloyd Garrison backed them, to the point of taking up the cause of women's rights as well. In 1840, the American Anti-Slavery Society split over the issue into two organizations.

Garrison's refusal to compromise on gradual emancipation or anything else drove moderates from his side. His ideology finally moved him to declare that he could neither support nor cooperate with the U.S. government, since it helped to implement slavery. In 1842, he asserted that the statements on slavery in the Constitution, together with such other federal actions as the Gag Rule (the refusal of Congress to read antislavery petitions), made the American union merely "a rope of sand—a fanciful nonentity—a mere piece of parchment—'a rhetorical flourish and splendid absurdity'—and a concentration of the physical force of the nation to destroy liberty, and to uphold slavery."[17] He opted in favor of anarchy and the dissolution of the Union. His stance horrified antislavery advocates who believed in reform, not revolution, and counted on political means within the existing system to achieve their ends.

The relations between black and white antislavery workers also caused trouble. A good many emancipationists, eager as they were to free the slaves, nevertheless were infected with the prevailing racism of the time. Few whites honestly thought of blacks as their social or intellectual equals, despite the obvious abilities of the black abolitionists they worked with. Whites treated blacks in the movement as their inferiors, assuming that they needed supervision—a particularly galling attitude, for in many ways the movement owed its very existence to the courage, sacrifices, and labors of free blacks and escaped slaves. What was more, blacks understood what many whites did not: the necessity of working not just for the end of slavery but against all forms of racial injustice. Yet as Martin R. Delany complained in 1852, "We [blacks] find ourselves occupying the very same position in relation to our Anti-Slavery friends, as we do in relation to the pro-slavery part of the community—a mere secondary, underling position, in all our relations to them, and anything more than this, is not a matter of course affair—it comes not by established anti-slavery custom or right, but . . . by mere suffrance."[18]

Blacks accordingly moved toward separatism, arranging black abolitionist conventions. They also changed their thinking about strategy. In the early years, most black abolitionists had spoken out against the use of violence to change the system, at least in part because they knew all too well the odds against slave insurrections and did not want to encourage hopeless actions.

But as the years wore on, they despaired of reform. David Ruggles, for instance, in 1841 said: "We have no right to hope to be emancipated from thralldom until we honestly resolve to be free. . . . We must remember that while our fellow countrymen of the south are slaves to individuals, *we of the north are slaves to the community,* and ever will be so, until we arise, and by the help of Him who governs the destiny of nations, go forward, and like the reformed inebriates, ourselves strike for reform—individual, general and radical reform, in every ramification of society. . . . Strike for freedom, or die slaves! . . . In our cause, mere words are nothing—action is everything. Buckle on your armour, and appear at the Black Convention, remember that our cause demands of us union and agitation—agitation and action."[19] Black writer Frances Ellen Watkins called the U.S. government "the arch traitor to liberty, as shown by the Fugitive Slave Law and the Dred Scott decision."[20] Even Frederick Douglass, who for years had insisted on moderation, began to think of violence as the only effective option: "There are three millions of slaves in this land, held by the United States Government, under the sanction of the American Constitution," he said in Boston in June 1849. "[I] would welcome the news that the slaves had risen and that the sable arms which have been engaged in beautifying and adorning the South were engaged in spreading death and devastation there."[21]

The disagreements in the antislavery movement spawned several political parties. Many had lost faith in the major parties, on the grounds that their southern members would never permit them to work effectively to end slavery. Accordingly, in 1840 antislavery forces founded the Liberty Party, including in its platform a determination to end slavery in the District of Columbia, abolish the interstate slave trade, and ban the admission of any more slave states to the Union. In 1847, a group of Liberty Party adherents, Van Buren Democrats, and Whigs united as the Free Soil Party, to oppose the extension of slavery into territory won during the Mexican War. Finally in 1854, opponents of extending slavery into the territories—old-line Whigs, antislavery Democrats, and Free Soilers—founded the Republican Party. With each change, the movement expanded, thanks to its publications, agents, and grassroots auxiliary societies.

## *Strategy and Tactics*

Just as blacks began the Underground Railroad, so they pioneered the antislavery movement in the United States. Even before the American Revolution, some slaves ended their enslavement through the courts, charging their masters with restraining their liberty. In 1773, for instance, Caesar Hendrick won his freedom from Richard Greenleaf of Newburyport, Massachusetts, collecting damages and court costs.[22] To get around the difficulties of such suits, which were expensive and slow and freed only one slave at a time, blacks resorted to a kind of class action, petitions addressed not to the courts but to the legislature. For example, in 1779, 19 New Hampshire blacks petitioned the legislature asking "from what authority they [the masters] assume to dispose of our lives, freedom and property."[23] Free blacks supported such efforts. Shipyard owner and captain Paul Cuffe signed a petition in 1780 requesting that free blacks be relieved of paying taxes, since they could not vote, and another in 1781 seeking the vote for free blacks and mulattoes. Although these petitions failed to bring about immediate action, they contributed to the antislavery sentiments that eventually moved the northern legislatures and courts to abolish slavery.

The defenders of slavery, of course, had much more political clout than blacks and early on understood its importance. In their insistence that the Constitution protect the international slave trade for 20 years and guarantee the return of fugitive slaves to their owners, they built slavery into the very foundation of the new nation. Thereafter they rammed successive fugitive slave laws through Congress. They quickly grasped the potency of enlarging slave territory. They struggled to preserve their dominance in Congress, believing it necessary to protect their agriculture. Some of them saw the production of cotton—for which they believed slave labor essential—as the primary economic prop of the nation, with the rest of the nation laboring to support those who grew and processed it. In their view, cotton was king, and the representatives of the slaveholders who supervised its production must be the most powerful bloc in Washington.

The antislavery movement, though it won an occasional political victory along the way, at first depended primarily on moral suasion. Believing themselves to hold the high ground, abolitionists undertook to convert the populace North and South to their way of thinking. Slavery, they argued, was a sin, one that had to be expiated through penance and suffering.

Grassroots antislavery societies began to appear about 1775, pledged to work to end slavery and improve the condition of blacks. They tried various methods: paying masters to free slaves, guaranteeing the support of freed slaves, protecting blacks against kidnapping, buying slaves to free them, helping freed slaves find jobs, and conducting schools. Most of all they propagandized, to shape public opinion.

The American Anti-Slavery Society, founded in 1833, sent out lecturers to expound its principles. Theodore Weld, Angelina and Sarah Grimké, Frederick Douglass, and a host of others—black and white, female and male—ranged the northern countryside. It was uphill, hazardous work. All of them literally risked their lives, and the escaped slaves among them additionally risked their freedom, to spread the gospel of liberty. Many endured physical assaults and beatings. Their jobs were at least as dangerous as those of doctors in abortion clinics at the end of the 20th century. For their pains, the American Anti-Slavery Society paid them eight dollars a week and expenses. It instructed them to oppose compensated emancipation and colonization, not to argue about plans of emancipation, and to emphasize free and equal rights for slaves.

In the South and the border states, of course, those who opposed slavery ran risks at least as great. In 1858, diarist Sidney George Fisher noted, "In the [Philadelphia] *Evening Bulletin* is an article about a recent outrage committed in Kent Co. [Maryland] such as are common now in the South. A person named Bowers had excited the indignation of the neighborhood by expressing openly free soil opinions and by taking the *New York Tribune,* an abolition paper. A charge was fabricated against him, founded on the extorted testimony of Negroes, that he had been guilty of assisting slaves to escape. He was tried and acquitted by the jury. The public were not satisfied with this and a mob seized upon him on his farm and tarred and feathered him. This act excited the indignation of a portion of the people, who in return made an attack on those concerned in it. A meeting was then called at Chestertown of the 'most respectable' inhabitants, at which resolutions were passed supporting the proceedings of the mob, denouncing all opposed to slavery, all who expressed opinions against it, all even who refused openly to approve it and threatening them with a similar punishment."[24]

Abolitionists published scores of newspapers, notably William Lloyd Garrison's *Liberator* and Frederick Douglass's *Northern Star.* In these appeared many slave narratives, reports purportedly or actually written by fugitive slaves describing their enslavement and their escapes. Their editors and publishers were attacked. Bostonians dragged William Lloyd Garrison through the streets, and in Alton, Illinois, mobs several times destroyed Elijah Parish Lovejoy's press and finally shot him dead.

Antislavery propagandists also distributed reams of pamphlets, not only in the North but also in the South. Southerners tried to confiscate them, arresting travelers whom they caught with them. One group raided post offices to seize antislavery literature; the proslavery U.S. postmaster general Amos Kendall backed the raiders. While admitting that his office conferred no legal authority on him "to exclude from the mails any species of newspapers, magazines, or pamphlets," he nonetheless wrote, "By no act or direction of mine, official or private, could I be induced to aid, knowingly, in giving circulation to papers of this description [antislavery literature], directly or indirectly. We owe an obligation to the laws, but a higher one to the communities in which we live, and if the former be perverted to destroy the latter, it is patriotism to disregard them."[25]

Besides these floods of propaganda, abolitionists exerted political pressure through memorials. In 1790, for instance, Benjamin Franklin, as president of a Philadelphia antislavery society, memorialized Congress: "From a persuasion that equal liberty was originally the portion, and is still the birth-right, of all men; and influenced by the strong ties of humanity, and the principles of their institution, your memorialists conceive themselves bound to use all justifiable endeavors to loosen the bands of slavery, and promote a general enjoyment of the blessings of freedom. Under these impressions, they earnestly entreat your serious attention to the subject of slavery; that you will be pleased to countenance the restoration of liberty to those unhappy men, who alone, in this land of freedom, are degraded into perpetual bondage, and who, amidst the general joy of surrounding freemen, are groaning in servile subjection; that you will devise means for removing this inconsistency from the character of the American people; that you will promote mercy and justice towards this distressed race; and that you will step to the very verge of the power vested in you for discouraging every species of traffic in the persons of our fellow-men."[26]

Antislavery advocates also began the grassroots political maneuver of collecting thousands of signatures on petitions. When in 1836 Congress refused to read these petitions, passing the so-called Gag Rule, John Quincy Adams fought a long-drawn-out battle to protect the citizens' right of petition. In 1842 he answered a motion to censure him for having presented an antislavery petition for the dissolution of the Union by asking, "[A]m I, the representative . . . of the *free* people of the state of Massachusetts, . . .—am I to come here and be tried for high treason because I presented a petition—a *petition*—to this house, and because the fancy or imagination of the gentleman from Kentucky supposes that there was anti-slavery or the abolition of slavery in it? The gentleman charges me with subornation of perjury and of high treason, and he calls upon this house, *as a matter of mercy and grace,* not to expel me for these crimes, but to inflict upon me the severest censure they can."[27]

Some abolitionists asked themselves whether they could in conscience use the products of slave labor. Henry Blackwell expended much of the earnings of his wife, Lucy Stone, in his efforts to produce sugar from sugar beets competitively with the slave-produced sugar from cane. James Mott gave up his cotton brokerage and went into the wool business. Levi Coffin bought and sold cotton from small non-slaveholding farms in the South. The American Anti-Slavery Society invited its members "diligently and prayerfully to examine the question, whether they can innocently make an *ordinary* use, or be concerned in the traffic of the productions of slave labor?"[28]

This Free-Labor (or Free Produce) movement, however, never had much support; even the most enthusiastic abolitionists had to recognize that it was not viable. Abolitionist lecturer Abby Kelley, for example, argued that "it is right for me to use any person's property for *his own benefit*—the slave's property I can use to batter down his prison door and that of the oppressed every where to draw them from under the heels of the tramplers—In one word, it is my duty to use these things [the products of slave labor], for to abstain would

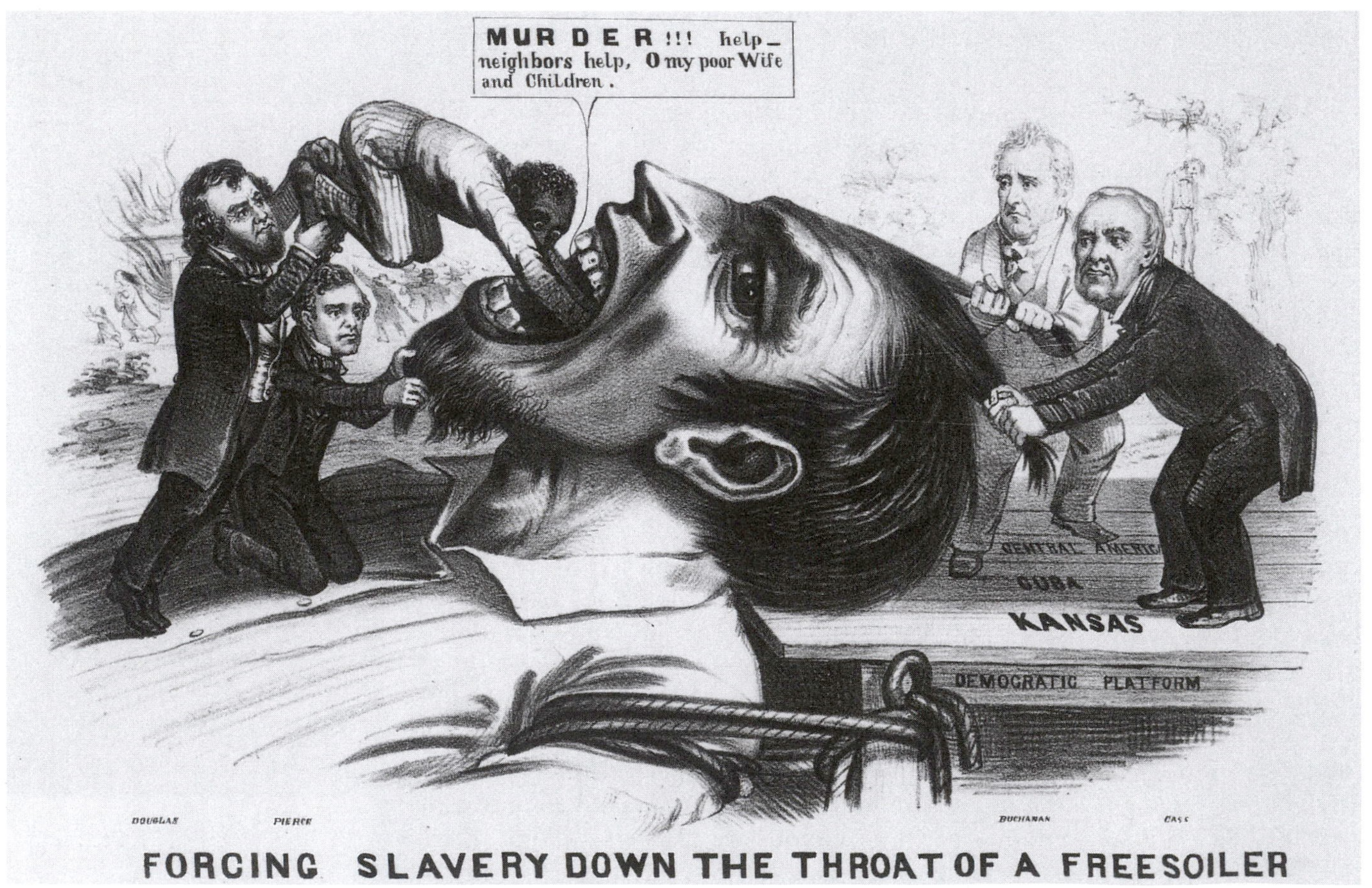


Cartoon depicting the Free Soil controversy (*Library of Congress*)

compel me to the life of a recluse [and to be unable to] plead the cause of the poor and needy."[29]

The Free Soil struggle over whether new states admitted to the Union should be free or slave was waged for years, fueled by the hope on both sides of increased political power. The Ordinance of 1787 barred slavery in the vast Northwest Territory and, by extension, in any state carved out of it. The Missouri Compromise of 1820–21 forbade slavery in the Louisiana Purchase territory north of 36 degrees and 30 minutes; it tried to preserve a balance by admitting states in pairs, one slave (Missouri) and one free (Maine). In 1845, the United States provoked war with Mexico by annexing Texas, which had long battled against Mexico, largely because Texas wanted slavery and Mexico did not. The Wilmot Proviso, introduced in the House of Representatives in 1846, would have outlawed slavery in any territory acquired in the Mexican War, but it failed to pass. In 1854, the Kansas-Nebraska Act demolished the Missouri Compromise by establishing the principle of "squatter sovereignty"—the presence or absence of slavery within a new state, that is, was to be determined by the inhabitants of that state.

Challenging the right of Congress to forbid slavery—or as they put it, to tell a man what to do with his own property—southern politicians argued that such a determination belonged to the individual states, including new states seeking admission to the Union. The Kansas-Nebraska Act brought on a no-holds-barred struggle that turned Kansas into a bloody battleground. As a congressional committee reported in 1856, "In 1854 congress passed an act establishing two new territories—Nebraska and Kansas—in this region of country, where slavery had been prohibited for more than thirty years; and instead of leaving said law against slavery in operation, or prohibiting or expressly allowing or establishing slavery, congress left the subject in said territories to be discussed, agitated and legislated on. . . .

"Thus it was promulgated to the people of this whole country that here was a clear field for competition–an open course for the race of rivalship; the goal of which was the ultimate establishment of a sovereign state; and the prize, the reward of everlasting liberty and its institutions on the one hand, or the perpetuity of slavery and its concomitants on the other. . . .

"[I]n the performance of this novel experiment, it was provided that all white men who became inhabitants in Kansas were entitled to vote without regard to their time of residence, usually provided in other territories. Nor was this right of voting confined to American citizens, but included all such aliens as . . . would declare, on oath, their intention to become citizens. Thus was the proclamation to the world to become inhabitants of Kansas, and enlist in this great enterprise, by the force of numbers, by vote, to decide for it the great question [slavery]."[30]

Abolitionist emigrant aid societies, especially in Massachusetts, recruited and armed thousands of settlers to migrate to Kansas and claim farms there. Proslavery forces in neighboring Missouri not only resolved "[t]hat we will afford protection to no abolitionist as a settler of this territory" but also encouraged raids on the abolitionist settlers. The Missourians also resolved "[t]hat we recognize the institution of slavery as already existing in this territory, and advise slaveholders to introduce their property as early as possible."[31] John Brown, always ready to pour gasoline on smoldering fires, took revenge for such practices by invading the state and murdering Kansas slaveholders. The governor of Kansas failed to keep order, and President Franklin Pierce removed him from office. When the polls finally opened to determine whether the new state should be slave or free, thousands of nonresidents from Missouri poured in and registered their proslavery votes.

By 1856, passions between slavery and antislavery forces throughout the country had reached the point that on May 22 the inflammatory oratory in the Senate chamber of antislavery senator Charles Sumner of Massachusetts provoked a physical beating from Rep. Preston S. Brooks of South Carolina. Sumner was unable to resume work for three and a half years.

By 1860, the struggle between abolitionists and the defenders of slavery had brought the United States to the brink of civil war. Slavery had almost ended in Europe, Central America, and South America. This nation, in other respects so advanced, now found itself on this score in the company of Cuba, Brazil, and portions of Asia and Africa. The slave states were isolated not only from the other states but from most of the Western world, outmoded, defensive, looking toward the past rather than the future. They clung desperately to the institution of slavery, even though in 1860 only about 400,000 of the 8,500,000 whites owned the country's 4 million slaves.[32]

## Chronicle of Events

**1637**
Roger Williams, pleading for captive Pequots, protests against "perpetuall slaverie."

**1640**
New Netherlands enacts an ordinance forbidding inhabitants to harbor or feed fugitive servants.

**1641**
The Massachusetts Body of Liberties provides that "there shall never be any bond slaverie, villinage or Captivitie amongst us unless it be lawfull Captives taken in just warres, and such strangers as willingly selle themselves or are sold to us. . . . This exempts none from servitude who shall be Judged thereto by Authoritie."

**1643**
In the Articles of Confederation, the New England Confederation of Plymouth, Massachusetts, Connecticut, and New Haven incorporate a fugitive slave law.

The colonies of New Netherlands and New Haven agree on the mutual surrender of fugitive slaves.

**1650**
Connecticut legalizes slavery.

**1652**
Rhode Island bans enslavement for more than ten years or after age 24. Despite this law, slavery survives in Rhode Island for another 150 years.

**1657**
Virginia enacts a fugitive slave law.

**1660**
The New Netherlands Council resolves to transport to Curaçao all but two or three of a group of recently captured Esopus Indians, "to be employed there, or at Buenaire . . . in the Company's service."

**1663**
Maryland legalizes slavery.

**1664**
New York and New Jersey legalize slavery.

**1666**
Maryland enacts a fugitive slave law.

**1667**
Virginia rules that baptism no longer will affect the status of slaves.

**1668**
New Jersey enacts a fugitive slave law.

**1676**
Quaker William Edmondson at Newport, Rhode Island, writes an antislavery letter of advice to Friends in America.

**1688**
Germantown Mennonites of Philadelphia issue a proclamation, written by Francis Daniel Pastorius, declaring slavery inconsistent with Christian principles.

**1691**
Virginia requires that manumitted slaves be sent out of the colony.

**1693**
George Kieth publishes *An Exhortation and Caution to Friends Concerning Buying or Keeping of Negroes.*

**1696**
The Friends' Yearly Meeting opposes the importation of slaves.

Maryland taxes the importation of black servants, slaves, and white servants.

**1700**
Samuel Sewall condemns slaveholding in *The Selling of Joseph: A Memorial.*

Pennsylvania legalizes slavery.

**1701**
John Saffin defends slaveholding in *A Brief and Candid Answer to a Late Printed Sheet, Entituled, The Selling of Joseph.*

**1702**
Slave Abda Jennings sues for his freedom in Hartford, Connecticut.

**1703**
Massachusetts requires every master who wants to liberate a slave to furnish a bond of at least £50, to indemnify the authorities should the freedman become a charge on the public.

Connecticut orders that slaves be whipped for disturbing the peace or offering to strike a white person.

Rhode Island forbids blacks and Indians to walk at night without a pass.

**1708**
Rhode Island taxes imported slaves.

**1711**
Connecticut orders that freed slaves who become indigent must be relieved by their former masters.

Pennsylvania prohibits the importation of blacks and Indians but says that "it is neither just nor convenient to set them at Liberty."

Rhode Island forbids "*clandestine* importations and exportations of passengers, or negroes, or Indian slaves."

**1714**
An emancipation plan, published anonymously, advocates sending all slaves back to Africa, except those who choose to go on serving their masters.

**1715**
Rhode Island legalizes slavery.

**1723**
Virginia abolishes manumissions.

**1728**
Rhode Island requires a master freeing a slave to give bond that the slave not become a public charge.

**1733**
Quaker Elihu Coleman of Nantucket publishes *A Testimony against That Anti-Christian Practice of MAKING SLAVES OF MEN.*

**1735**
An English law forbids the importation and use of black slaves in the colony of Georgia.

**1737**
Quakers disown Benjamin Lay for writing *All Slave Keepers That Keep the Innocent in Bondage, Apostates.*

**1740**
The South Carolina Assembly declares all blacks, Indians, mulattos, and mestizos to be slaves "unless the contrary can be made to appear," but the act effectively frees Indian slaves, because it exempts Indians in amity with the colonists and so designates enslaved Indians.

**1742**
The Society for the Propagation of the Gospel in Foreign Parts buys two young blacks to be trained as teachers in black schools in South Carolina, where the society offers black and Indian slave children a free Christian education.

**1749**
Georgia allows slavery.

**1751**
Benjamin Franklin in *Observations Concerning the Increase of Mankind* points to the evil effects of slavery upon population, industry, and the production and distribution of wealth.

**1754**
Quaker John Woolman publishes the antislavery *Considerations on Keeping of Negroes.*

**1755**
Salem instructs its representative to petition the General Court of Massachusetts to forbid the importing of slaves.

**1758**
Philadelphia Quakers cease buying and selling slaves.

**1760s**
The theory of natural rights, a spark of the American Revolution, raises questions of the morality of slavery.

**1760**
*A Narrative of the Uncommon Sufferings and Surprising Deliverance of Briton Hammon, a Negro Man,* is published in Boston.

**1762**
Anthony Benezet publishes the antislavery *A Short Account of That Part of Africa Inhabited by Negroes.*

**1764**
James Otis's *The Rights of the British Colonies Asserted and Proved* excoriates slavery.

**1765**
Massachusetts slaves begin bringing civil lawsuits for their liberty.

Worcester, Massachusetts, instructs its representative to the colonial legislature to lobby for a law against slavery.

**1766**
Boston instructs its representative to the colonial legislature to move for a law against importing and purchasing slaves.

**1767**
Members of the Virginia House of Burgesses, meeting as a private body, boycott the British slave trade, resolving "[t]hat they will not import any Slaves or purchase any imported, after the First day of *November* next, until the said [Tax] Acts of Parliament are repealed." Similar boycotts are soon adopted in South Carolina, Georgia, and North Carolina.

**1768**
Maryland Quakers cease buying and selling slaves.

**1770**
Congregational minister Samuel Hopkins of Newport, Rhode Island, begins preaching against slavery.

New England Quakers cease buying and selling slaves.

**1772**
Rev. Isaac Skillman publishes *An Oration upon the Beauties of Liberty.*

Some members of the Society of Friends are disowned (expelled) for not freeing their slaves.

In London, Lord Chief Justice Mansfield rules that slavery is not supported by English law.

The Virginia House of Burgesses tells King George III that "the importation of slaves into the colonies from the coast of Africa hath long been considered a trade of great inhumanity, and under its present encouragement, we have too much reason to fear will endanger the very existence of your Majesty's American dominions."

**1773**
*Personal Slavery Established,* published anonymously, argues that slavery is a positive good.

Benjamin Rush publishes the antislavery *An Address to the Inhabitants of the British Settlements in America, upon Slavekeeping.*

Harvard seniors Theodore Parsons and Eliphalet Pearson debate slavery.

Boston slaves petition for consideration of their "unhappy state and condition."

Massachusetts slaves petition for land for settlement.

A slave successfully sues Richard Greenleaf of Newburyport, Massachusetts, for holding him in bondage.

**1774**
The First Continental Congress suspends trade with Great Britain, providing that Americans will not import or buy slaves imported after December 1, "after which time, we will wholly discontinue the slave trade."

The Massachusetts legislature passes a bill against importing slaves, but the governor refuses to sign it.

A Massachusetts court grants freedom to slave Caleb Dodge, who has sued his master for restraining his liberty.

Connecticut and Rhode Island forbid the importation of slaves.

Virginia and North Carolina take action against importing slaves.

New York Quakers cease buying and selling slaves.

**1775–1793**
In the New Jersey supreme court, 20 of 22 freedom suits are decided in favor of slaves.

**1775**
Georgia takes action against importing slaves.

The Society for the Relief of Free Negroes Unlawfully Held in Bondage is organized. (In 1787 it becomes the Pennsylvania Society for Promoting the Abolition of Slavery and for the Relief of Free Negroes Unlawfully Held in Bondage and for Improving the Conditions of the African Race.)

**1776**
The Second Continental Congress votes "[t]hat no slaves be imported into any of the thirteen United Colonies."

Delaware prohibits the further importation of slaves from Africa.

The Society of Friends excludes all those who buy or sell a slave or refuse to emancipate their slaves.

Pastor Samuel Hopkins, in *A Dialogue, Concerning the Slavery of Africans,* urges upon the Second Continental Congress measures for immediately abolishing slavery.

Wealthy South Carolina merchant Henry Laurens, later president of the Continental Congress, writes a letter against slavery.

**1777**

The Vermont constitution prohibits slavery, gives the franchise to all males of mature age, and extends the rights of jury trial and habeas corpus to fugitives.

At New York's constitutional convention, delegates vote 36 to five to adopt an antislavery resolution.

The New York state constitution enfranchises all free propertied men, without reference to color, prior condition of servitude, or religion.

A committee of the Virginia legislature, chaired by Thomas Jefferson, proposes the gradual emancipation and exportation of slaves.

**1778**

The Articles of Confederation treats, the word *citizens* as interchangeable with the word *inhabitants,* declaring that the "free inhabitants" of each state shall be entitled to "all the privileges and immunities of free citizens in the several States."

Virginia forbids the further importation of slaves.

**1780**

The Massachusetts constitution declares that all men are free and equal by birth, in a clause later interpreted as abolishing slavery. It also enfranchises all males, regardless of race.

Pennsylvania begins gradual emancipation, freeing the children of all slaves born after November 1, 1780, at their 28th birthday.

Delaware resolves "that no person hereafter imported from Africa ought to be held in slavery under any pretense whatever."

Elizabeth Freeman of Sheffield, Massachusetts, successfully sues for her freedom; her mistress had tried to strike Freeman's sister with a red-hot poker, and Freeman had interfered and run away.

The Methodist Conference at Baltimore declares slavery "contrary to the laws of God, man, and nature."

**1781**

Decisions in *Commonwealth* v. *Jennison* and related cases effectively end slavery in Massachusetts.

**1782**

A provisional peace agreement between Great Britain and the United States stipulates that the British withdraw "without . . . carrying away any Negroes or other Property of the American Inhabitants." The British interpret this to mean that blacks with them before November 30, 1782, are free.

Virginia repeals its law confining the power of emancipation to the legislature.

**1783**

The Virginia legislature repeals a law limiting citizenship to whites and provides instead that "all free persons born within the territory of this commonwealth" shall be citizens.

Virginia emancipates slaves who served in the American army *with the permission of their masters.*

Maryland prohibits the importing of slaves from Africa.

*A Serious Address to the Rulers of America, on the Inconsistency of Their Conduct Respecting Slavery, forming a Contrast between the Encroachments of England on American Liberty and American Injustice in tolerating Slavery* is published.

**1784**

Thomas Jefferson's proposal to prohibit slavery in the whole region west of the Alleghenies fails in Congress by one vote. Jefferson comments, "Thus we see the fate of millions unborn hanging on the tongue of one man, & heaven was silent in that awful moment."

Rhode Island and Connecticut pass gradual emancipation laws.

North Carolina forbids the importation of slaves from Africa.

The Methodist Conference, at the urging of John Wesley, adopts regulations requiring slaveholding members to manumit slaves within a brief term of years, the children of such slaves to be free at birth.

**1785**
New York passes a bill for gradual emancipation but limits the legal and political rights of blacks and forbids marriage with whites.

The New York Society for Promoting the Manumission of Slaves is established—the first antislavery society organized on a public basis.

The Rhode Island Society for Abolishing the Slave Trade is organized.

**1786**
New Jersey passes manumission acts, though it does not enact effective legislation against slavery until 1804.

North Carolina declares the slave trade "of evil consequences and highly impolitic."

In England, Thomas Clarkson publishes an *Essay on the Slavery and Commerce of the Human Species, Particularly the African,* which becomes a basic handbook of the abolitionist movement.

**1787**
The U.S. Constitution institutionalizes slavery by providing that a slave will be counted as three-fifths of a person in determining representation in Congress. It gives Congress the power to tax the importation of slaves and to end the international slave trade after 1808. The Northwest Ordinance excludes slavery from the Northwest Territory (including the present-day Ohio, Indiana, Illinois, Michigan, Wisconsin, and part of Minnesota) but includes a provision for the return of fugitive slaves to their masters elsewhere.

Rhode Island prohibits its residents from participating in the slave trade—without much effect.

Virginia decrees death without benefit of clergy to anyone who knowingly sells a free person as a slave.

Blacks withdraw from St. George's Methodist Episcopal Church in Philadelphia to found the first black churches there: St. Thomas's African Episcopal Church, under Absolom Jones, and the African Methodist Episcopal Church, under Richard Allen.

"Othello" (possibly Benjamin Banneker) publishes "On Slavery," an antislavery pamphlet.

**1788**
Connecticut prohibits residents from participating in the slave trade.

After three free blacks are abducted, the Massachusetts legislature enacts a total prohibition of the slave trade.

The Delaware Society for Promoting the Abolition of Slavery and for the Relief and Protection of Free Blacks and People of Colour Unlawfully Held in Bondage is organized.

**1789**
Pennsylvanians organize an abolition society, headed by Benjamin Franklin. It appeals to the public for funds.

The Maryland Society for Promoting the Abolition of Slavery and the Relief of Free Negroes and Others Unlawfully Held in Bondage is organized.

**1790–1820**
Hot local debates on slavery are conducted in Tennessee, Kentucky, Ohio, Indiana, and Illinois, culminating in the abolition of slavery in the states north of the Ohio River and entrenching it in those to the south.

**1790**
Congress endorses the expansion of slavery into the Southwest.

The Connecticut Society for the Promotion of Freedom, and for the Relief of Persons Holden in Bondage is organized.

**1791**
A movement to refuse to buy the products of slave labor begins in England—the Free Produce movement.

Vermont is admitted to the United States, with the provision in its constitution that "no male person born in this country, or brought from over sea, ought to be bound by law to serve any person as a servant, slave, or apprentice after he arrives at the age of twenty-one years, nor female, in like manner, after she arrives at the age of twenty-one years, unless they are bound by their own consent after they arrive at such age, or are bound by law for the payment of debts, damages, fines, costs, or the like."

Kentucky is admitted to the United States. Its constitution denies the legislature the power to emancipate slaves without the owner's consent or without recompensing the owner. The constitution also forbids the legislature to pass laws prohibiting emigrants from other states from bringing their slaves with them.

Massachusetts courts find the brigantine *Hope,* John Stanton, master, guilty of violating the statute against participation in the international slave trade.

**1792**

The king of Denmark forbids his subjects to carry on the slave trade after 1802, except on the West Indies islands owned by Denmark.

The first constitution of Kentucky does not discriminate against blacks in civil rights or suffrage.

**1793**

Georgia, wary of slave insurrections, forbids importing slaves from the West Indies, the Bahamas, and Florida.

The New Jersey Society for Promoting the Abolition of Slavery is organized.

The American Convention for Promoting the Abolition of Slavery and Improving the Condition of the African Race is organized.

Quaker Warner Mifflin publishes the antislavery *A Serious Expostulation with the Members of the House of Representatives of the United States.*

**1794**

Congress prohibits carrying on the slave trade from the United States to any foreign place or country.

The French National Convention abolishes slavery in all French territories, in a law repealed by Napoleon in 1802.

An antislavery convention, with representatives from abolition societies in many states, is held in Philadelphia.

Rev. Timothy Dwight denounces slavery in *Greenfield Hill.*

Black bishops Richard Allen and Absolom Jones publish *An Address to Those Who Keep Slaves and Approve the Practice.*

**1795–1835**

The Great Awakening gives the antislavery movement impetus.

**1796**

The first constitution of Tennessee does not discriminate against blacks in civil rights or suffrage.

Methodists weaken their rules against slaveholding.

The American Convention of Delegates of the Abolition Societies calls for a boycott on products of slave labor.

St. George Tucker publishes *A Dissertation on Slavery with A Proposal for the Gradual Abolition of It, in the State of Virginia.*

**1797**

New York passes a law, to take effect July 4, 1799, stating that all children born henceforth will be free, though children born to slaves must serve until the age of 28 if male and 25 if female.

**1800**

The House of Representatives votes 85–1 to offer "no encouragement or countenance to petitions against slavery from Negroes."

Indian slavery has almost ceased in Lower Canada.

**1801**

Toussaint Louverture succeeds in gaining control of the island of Hispaniola, ensuring the liberty of slaves freed officially in 1793.

**1802**

Rev. Alexander McLeod publishes *Negro Slavery Unjustified.*

**1803**

The House of Representatives in a resolution refers to "such American seamen, citizens of the United States, as are free persons of color."

Ohio is admitted to the United States as a free state.

**1804**

Louisiana comes under the sovereignty of the United States, with the results that the slave code becomes harsher and voluntary manumission by an owner becomes difficult.

The United States forbids the importation of blacks from foreign territory into the Louisiana Purchase territory after October 1.

New Jersey provides for the gradual abolition of slavery.

Former slave trader Thomas Branigan publishes the first of his antislavery works.

**1806**

Virginia passes a law requiring all slaves emancipated after May 1, 1806, to leave the state within twelve months after being freed or to be sold.

**1807**

England and the United States prohibit the international slave trade.

Ohio prohibits blacks from settling in the state unless within 26 days they have secured a five-hundred-dollar bond ensuring their good behavior and sets a fine of a hundred dollars for harboring or concealing fugitive slaves.

Indiana enables slave owners to bring slaves into the territory.

Thomas Branigan calls on all Christians to refuse to buy the products of slave labor.

Rev. David Rice writes *Involuntary, Unmerited, Perpetual, Absolute Slavery, Examined.*

Ex-slave John Gloucester becomes the first pastor of the Negro Presbyterian Church in Philadelphia.

**1808–1832**

Local and state antislavery societies are established and function in the South.

**1809**

Ohio allows blacks with a "fair certificate of actual freedom" from a U.S. court to settle in that state.

**1813**

Argentina adopts gradual emancipation.

Congress restricts employment on American ships to citizens of the United States and "persons of color, natives of the United States."

When the Philadelphia legislature proposes excluding black immigrants, James Forten writes a series of letters in protest, under the signature, "A Man of Color."

**1814**

Colombia adopts gradual emancipation.

The Mexican congress abolishes slavery.

With the defeat of Napoleon, France promises to end the slave trade within five years but continues an illegal slave trade.

Charles Osborn organizes the Tennessee Society for Promoting the Manumission of Slaves.

**1815**

Benjamin Lundy organizes the Union Humane Society in Ohio.

**1816**

The North Carolina Manumission Society is founded.

*December 23:* The Virginia legislature requests the governor to ask the president to arrange for a territory abroad to which free American blacks may be sent.

**1817**

Indiana rules that no blacks, mulattoes, or Indians may act as witnesses except in cases against blacks, mulattoes, or Indians, or in civil cases where blacks, mulattoes, or Indians alone are parties.

Wealthy free black James Forten calls a meeting in Philadelphia to combat the idea of the inferiority of blacks.

**1818–1822**

Congress drafts bills to strengthen the Fugitive Slave Law.

**1818**

Darien, Georgia, enacts an ordinance imposing a tax of $10 for men and five dollars for women on all free "Negroes, Mullattoes, or Mustezos—persons of color." On such immigrants, a fee of $50 is to be paid in ten days, on pain of imprisonment and public sale of their persons.

A Maryland grand jury indicts Methodist elder Jacob Gruber for intent to incite mutiny and rebellion among blacks, because at a camp meeting attended by whites and slaves he has preached that slaveholding is a national sin.

**1819**

Georgia provides for the disposal of slaves illegally imported into the state, agreeing to turn them over to the Colonization Society if it will transport them to a foreign colony and reimburse the state for its expenses.

Congressman James Tallmadge Jr. of New York unsuccessfully argues that Congress should prohibit the further introduction of slavery into Missouri and emancipate all children of slaves at age 25.

Robert Walsh of Maryland defends slavery in *An Appeal from the Judgments of Great Britain Respecting the United States of America;* in *Free Remarks on the Spirit of the Constitution,* he endorses the doctrine of free soil, arguing against any extension of slavery.

Northern defenders of slavery argue that some sections of the United States should be reserved entirely for whites, with no free blacks and no black slaves.

**Early 1820s**

South Carolina produces a spate of proslavery literature.

**1820**
England begins using naval power to suppress the slave trade.

South Carolina makes it a high misdemeanor to introduce into the state any written or printed matter against slavery.

**1821**
In the Missouri Compromise, Congress admits Maine as a free state and Missouri as a slave state, and prohibits slavery in the territory of the Louisiana Purchase north of 36 degrees, 30 minutes. The compromise includes a fugitive slave provision.

U.S. attorney general William Wirt issues the opinion that "No person is included in the description of citizen of the United States who has not the full rights of a citizen in the State of his residence."

Congress receives a petition from Maryland to redress grievances caused by the underground operations of antislavery Pennsylvanians, and another from Kentucky protesting against Canada's admission of fugitive slaves.

Spanish authorities officially permit slaveholder Moses Austin to settle a colony in Texas; Austin's son Stephen arranges a distribution of land for the colonists that includes a grant of 50 (later 80) acres per slave.

Quaker Benjamin Lundy begins publication of *The Genius of Universal Emancipation.*

**1822**
New York abolishes property requirements for whites to vote but increases them for blacks.

South Carolina requires every free black over 15 to obtain a white guardian.

Antislavery Mexican authorities, newly independent from Spain, refuse to approve Austin's contract; they allow his slave-owning colonists to occupy land only provisionally.

**1823**
John Rankin publishes antislavery *Letters on American Slavery, Addressed to Mr. Thomas Rankin, Merchant at Middlebrook, Augusta County, Virginia.*

Clergyman Richard Furman publishes the proslavery *Exposition of the Views of Baptists, Relative to the Coloured Population of the United States.*

**1823**
Chile abolishes slavery.

Congress reduces funds for aiding in the suppression of the slave trade.

**1824**
Mexico decrees that "[c]ommerce and traffic in slaves proceeding from any country and under any flag whatsoever, is forever prohibited in the territory of the United Mexican States."

Sam Austin promulgates civil and criminal regulations containing a "slave code" for his colony in Texas and instructs the Mexican authorities to enforce them.

Englishwoman Elizabeth Heyrich writes *Immediate, Not Gradual Abolition.*

Rev. James Duncan publishes *A Treatise on Slavery. In Which Is Shown Forth the Evil of Slaveholding.*

**1825**
In Baltimore, Frances Wright publishes *A Plan for the Gradual Abolition of Slavery in the United States.*

A North Carolina manumission society survey finds 60 percent of the state's population to favor emancipation.

**1826**
Vermont sends a resolution to North Carolina offering to cooperate "in any measures which may be adopted by the general government for its [slavery's] abolition in the United States"—in response to which North Carolina tightens its slave-patrol and militia laws.

Pennsylvania passes a fugitive slave law.

The Massachusetts General Colored Association, dedicated to improvement of local conditions and agitation for abolition, is founded.

Episcopalian priest William Barlow urges the preaching of the acceptability of slavery to divine law.

**1827**
The people of Baltimore present a memorial to Congress asking that slaves born in the District of Columbia, after a given time and on arriving at a certain age, become free.

African Americans Samuel Cornish and John B. Russwurm found the weekly *Freedom's Journal.*

*March 11:* The Congress of Coahuila and Texas adopts a constitution stating, "From and after the promulgation of the Constitution . . . no one shall be born a slave in the state, and after six months the introduction of slaves under any pretext shall not be permitted." Colonization of Texas by slaveholders continues.

**1828**
With the approval of the authorities, slaveholding Texas settlers begin bringing in former slaves held as indentured servants, now working to pay their masters for their freedom and for the cost of moving them into Texas; children born in Texas of these "indentured servants" must serve until age 25 without pay and then on the same terms as their fathers.

**1829**
An unsuccessful attempt is made to revise the constitution of Virginia to abolish slavery.

The Female Association for Promoting the Manufacture and Use of Free Cotton is established in Philadelphia.

The Colored Female Free Produce Society of Pennsylvania is organized by the women of the Bethel African Methodist Episcopal Church.

Sarah and Angelina Grimké leave Charleston for the North to become Quakers, activist abolitionists, and champions of women's rights.

Free black New Yorker Robert Young publishes the pamphlet *The Ethiopian Manifesto.*

Free black David Walker publishes *Walker's Appeal, in Four Articles; Together with a Preamble, to the Coloured Citizens of the World, But in Particular and Very Expressly, to Those of the United States of America,* advocating self-improvement and violent revolt.

*September 15:* Mexican president Vicente Guerrero decrees all slaves forever free.

*December 2:* President Guerrero exempts Texas from the general Mexican emancipation.

**1830**
*April 6:* The Mexican president prohibits further immigration into Texas from the United States and calls for strict enforcement of rules against the further introduction of slaves.

**1831**
Bolivia emancipates slaves.

U.S. attorney general John M. Berrien pronounces South Carolina's black-seamen law (1821) constitutional.

Mississippi enacts a law saying, "It is unlawful for any slave, free Negro, or mulatto to preach the gospel upon pain of receiving thirty-nine lashes upon the naked back of the . . . preacher."

The Massachusetts Anti-Slavery Society is founded.

The Afric-American Female Society is founded in Boston.

The Colored Female Society is organized in Philadelphia.

African American Maria W. Stewart's *Religion and the Pure Principles of Morality* is published in Boston.

*January 1:* William Lloyd Garrison begins publication of *The Liberator* in Boston.

*June 6–11:* The First Annual Convention of the People of Color is held in Philadelphia.

*December:* William Lloyd Garrison organizes the New England Anti-Slavery Society (later the Massachusetts Anti-Slavery Society).

**1832**
U.S. attorney general Roger B. Taney issues an opinion that free American blacks have *no* rights under the Constitution.

The government of Coahuila and Texas decrees, "Servants and day laborers, hereafter introduced by foreign colonists, cannot be obligated by any contract to continue in the service of the latter longer than ten years."

Maria W. Stewart makes her first public address, to the Afric-American Female Intelligence Society in Boston.

Prudence Crandall establishes her school for "colored girls" in Canterbury, Connecticut.

*January 1:* William Lloyd Garrison and others organize the American Anti-Slavery Society.

*February 22:* Black women of Salem, Massachusetts, establish an antislavery society.

*July 1:* Rhode Island women establish an antislavery society.

*October 8:* Laura Haviland and Elizabeth Chandler organize the Logan Female Anti-Slavery Society in the Michigan Territory.

*December 9:* Lucretia Mott establishes the Philadelphia Female Anti-Slavery Society.

**1833–1837**
Black and white antislavery societies are integrated.

**1833**
A search agreement between London and Paris enables British cruisers to search and break up French slave ships.

The Providence Anti-Slavery Society, the New York City Anti-Slavery Society, and the Boston Female Anti-Slavery Society are organized.

Lydia Maria Child publishes *An Appeal in Favor of That Class of Americans Called Africans.*

*December 4–6:* The first American Anti-Slavery Society convention is held in Philadelphia.

*December 6:* The Kentucky Society for the Gradual Relief of the State from Slavery is organized.

**1834**

The British government abolishes slavery in all its colonies.

Legal immigration of Americans into Texas resumes.

The North Carolina Manumission Society holds its last meeting.

After a debate on slavery at Lane Theological Seminary in Cincinnati, the trustees order the students to discontinue their antislavery society and stop discussing the question; 51 students, led by Theodore Weld, withdraw (many transfer to Oberlin College) and begin intensive antislavery lecturing, under frequent mob attack.

A Colored Female Anti-Slavery Society in Middletown (Connecticut), a Colored Anti-Slavery Society in Newark (New Jersey), the Vermont State Anti-Slavery Society, and the New Hampshire State Anti-Slavery Society are organized.

The first antislavery fair raises three hundred dollars under the leadership of Lydia Maria Child.

The violence of townspeople forces Prudence Crandall to close the Canterbury Female Boarding School for the education of free black young women.

*July 10:* A New York City mob riots against blacks and antislavery activists.

*August:* The "Passover" riots of Philadelphia attack the homes of blacks, passing by those white houses with lights in the windows.

**1835**

Antiabolition riots multiply. Provoked by the murder of a white man by his black servant, a Philadelphia mob riots against blacks. William Lloyd Garrison is mobbed in Boston for his abolitionism.

The Ladies' New York City Anti-Slavery Society is established. The Female Anti-Slavery Society of Ohio is organized in Muskingum County. James Birney organizes the Kentucky Anti-Slavery Society, which is almost immediately shut down, and Theodore Weld organizes the Ohio State Anti-Slavery Society. The New York State Anti-Slavery Society is organized, amid mob violence.

*July 29:* In Charleston, South Carolina, a mob breaks into the U.S. Post Office, removes a bag of mail containing antislavery publications, and burns them; a committee then arranges to meet the mail boats, escort the mail to the post office, and remove and destroy all offensive (antislavery) publications.

*August 10:* Dr. Reuben Crandall is jailed in the District of Columbia, charged with having published papers intended to excite insurrection; he is detained there until April 1836, when after a prosecution by Francis Scott Key he is acquitted—dying soon thereafter.

*October 15:* A Louisiana committee of vigilance offers $50,000 for the capture of abolitionist Arthur Tappan.

*December 7:* Pres. Andrew Jackson asks Congress for legislation to prohibit the sending of incendiary literature through the mails into the South.

*December 19:* North Carolina formally requests other states to enact penal laws prohibiting the printing of publications that might make its slaves discontented.

*December 20:* South Carolina requests other states to suppress all abolition societies and penalize the publication of literature that might excite slaves to revolt.

**1836**

Georgia, Alabama, and Virginia ask other states to "put an end to the malignant deeds of the abolitionists."

The Supreme Judicial Court of Massachusetts frees a six-year-old slave girl whose mistress has brought her into the state on a visit.

Texas wins its independence from Mexico; the Constitution of the Republic of Texas permits slavery.

The Charleston, South Carolina, postmaster confiscates abolitionist literature.

The Methodist church, which has earlier attacked slavery, now disclaims "any right, wish, or intention to interfere with the civil and political relation between master and slave.

By this time, the Congregationalists have closed their doors to advocates of immediate abolition.

Huge numbers of antislavery petitions are generated, mostly by women.

In Boston, a black vigilance committee organizes a successful rescue of two women recaptured under the Fugitive Slave Act of 1793, precipitating the "Abolition Riot."

Theodore Weld and Henry B. Stanton recruit men and women agents for the American Anti-Slavery Society, training them to lecture and to face mob violence.

The Michigan State Anti-Slavery Society and the Rhode Island Anti-Slavery Society are organized.

Charles Ball's *Slavery in the United States* is published.

James K. Paulding defends slavery in *Slavery in the United States,* the first comprehensive criticism of abolitionism.

Sarah Grimké publishes *An Epistle to the Clergy of the Southern States.*

*January:* James G. Birney begins publication of the *Philanthropist* in Cincinnati, under threat of mob violence.

*February 2:* The Milledgeville Federal Union offers $10,000 for the kidnapping of abolitionist Amos A. Phelps.

*May 14:* The Treaties of Velasco call for the return of black slaves and indentured servants who have been captured by or taken refuge with the Mexican army.

*May 22:* In Palmyra, Missouri, American Anti-Slavery Society agent Rev. David Nelson reads from the pulpit a parishioner's offer to contribute $10,000 toward a fund for compensated emancipation; a mob assails the parishioner and drives Nelson from the state.

*May 23:* Editor Elijah P. Lovejoy of the St. Louis *Observer* reports the lynching of a black, under the headline, "Awful Murder and Savage Barbarity"; vandals damage his press; he continues publication from Alton, Illinois.

*May 26:* The U.S. House of Representatives adopts the Gag Rule, tabling antislavery petitions without reading them.

*June 8:* Princeton theological student Aaron W. Kitchell is mobbed and expelled from the state at Hillsborough, Georgia, on suspicion of talking with slaves.

Mob attacking the Charleston post office to destroy abolitionist literature (*Library of Congress*)

*July:* A mob pillages the printing press of the *Philanthropist* and attacks the black section of Cincinnati.

*August 3:* The citizens of Mount Meigs, Alabama, offer $50,000 for the capture of abolitionists Arthur Tappan and LaRoy Sunderland.

*August 6:* Congress provides a fine and imprisonment for any postmaster convicted of detaining letters, packages, pamphlets, or newspapers to prevent or delay delivery.

*September:* Angelina Grimké publishes "An Appeal to the Christian Women of the South" in the *Anti-Slavery Examiner.*

*December:* The Grimké sisters begin an antislavery speaking tour.

## 1837

The governor of New York refuses the demand of the governor of Alabama that the publishing agent of the American Anti-Slavery Society be delivered to Georgia as a fugitive from justice for the publication of antislavery literature.

A Virginia law allows slaves emancipated after 1806 to apply for permission to remain in the state.

Abolitionist Elijah Lovejoy is assassinated in Illinois for protesting the lynching of Francis McIntosh, a mulatto freeman.

The first National Anti-Slavery Society Convention is held in New York.

No southern abolition societies remain in existence.

The American Convention for Promoting the Abolition of Slavery, etc., is dissolved.

The Pennsylvania State Anti-Slavery Society and the Illinois State Anti-Slavery Society are organized.

The American Anti-Slavery Society publishes *Emancipation in the West Indies,* written by its agents James A. Thome and J. Horace Kimball.

Catharine E. Beecher publishes *An Essay on Slavery and Abolitionism, with Reference to the Duty of American Females,* arguing that slavery is a domestic concern of the South.

Angelina Grimké publishes *Letters to Catharine E. Beecher in Reply to an Essay on Slavery and Abolitionism,* as a series in *The Liberator.*

Mob attacking the stored printing press of Elijah Lovejoy (*Library of Congress*)

*An Appeal to the Women of the Nominally Free States Issued by an Anti-Slavery Convention of American Women* is published.

*March:* Angelina Grimké addresses a "promiscuous" audience (that is, of both genders) in Poughkeepsie at a meeting called by the black community.

*May 9–12:* The first Anti-Slavery Convention of American Women is held in New York.

*September:* The Tappan brothers, through the American and Foreign Anti-Slavery Society, establish the *National Era* in Washington, D.C., with Gamaliel Bailey as editor.

**1838**

The Pennsylvania Supreme Court holds that a black is not a freeman within the meaning of Pennsylvania's constitution and hence not entitled to vote.

The Presbyterian church splits into North and South, having refused to take a stand on slavery.

James G. Birney informs Congress that 225 antislavery societies existed as of May 1835; 527 in 1836; 1,006 in 1837; and an estimated 1,406 exist in 1838, with an estimated total membership of 115,000.

Reformers start the first National Female Anti-Slavery Society in New York.

The Indiana State Anti-Slavery Society is organized.

Black women of Philadelphia organize the Female Vigilant Committee to support the Underground Railroad.

Sarah Grimké publishes *Letters on the Equality of the Sexes, and the Condition of Women* as a series in the *New England Spectator.*

*February 21:* Angelina Grimké speaks to the Massachusetts legislature, representing 20,000 Massachusetts women who have signed a petition to end slavery.

*May 15–18:* During the Second Anti-Slavery Convention of American Women, a mob attacks and burns down the new Philadelphia Hall, dedicated to free speech.

*May 15:* Abby Kelley and Maria Weston Chapman begin their lecture careers, speaking at the Second Anti-Slavery Convention of American Women.

*September 6:* The American Free Produce Association is established in Philadelphia.

Free Produce store, which sold no products of slave labor, in Hamorton, Pennsylvania (*Courtesy of Frances C. Taylor*)

**1839**

The British and Foreign Anti-Slavery Society is founded in London to promote international cooperation against slavery.

New York refuses to extradite three sailors "charged with having feloniously stolen a negro slave" in Virginia.

Ohio repeals its antikidnapping law and establishes a system by which state officers superintend the arrest, trial, and delivery of fugitive slaves to their owners.

The Massachusetts Female Emancipation Society is established by antifeminist abolitionists. Anti-Garrisonians organize the Massachusetts Abolition Society. The organization of women's antislavery societies begins in Indiana.

Maria Weston Chapman publishes *Right and Wrong in Massachusetts,* attributing the split among abolitionists to a dispute over women's rights.

The Boston Female Anti-Slavery Society publishes *Liberty Bell,* an antislavery annual edited by Maria Weston Chapman.

With the assistance of the Grimké sisters, Theodore Weld publishes *American Slavery as It Is,* incorporating the testimony of slaveholders and other eyewitnesses.

*January 11:* An Evangelical Union Anti-Slavery Society is formed in New York with the intent of "purifying" the churches on the slavery question.

*May 1–3:* The Third Anti-Slavery Convention of American Women is held in Philadelphia.

*November 13:* Antislavery men favoring political action nominate James G. Birney for president and Francis J. LeMoyne for vice president of the United States.

**1840**

Russia permits factory owners to emancipate their serfs.

The American Anti-Slavery Society splits over woman's rights and political action; Garrison gains control, and his opponents break off into the American and Foreign Anti-Slavery Society.

New York black women establish the Manhattan Abolition Society.

The American Anti-Slavery Society starts the *National Anti-Slavery Standard.*

*April 1:* The National Convention of Friends of Immediate Emancipation approves the candidacy of James G. Birney and Thomas Earle for president and vice president of the United States, effectively forming the Liberty, or Human Rights, Party.

*May 12–13:* The American Anti-Slavery Society Convention is held in New York.

*June 12–23:* The World Anti-Slavery Convention, held in London, refuses to seat women delegates.

**1841**

Uruguay emancipates its slaves.

England, France, Russia, Prussia, and Austria agree to mutual search of ships on the high seas in order to suppress the slave trade.

The New York legislature repeals a law that had allowed masters passing through the state to keep slaves for up to nine months.

Ohio repeals its statute of 1839 that had established a system by which state officers cooperated in returning fugitive slaves to their owners, and it again passes its antikidnapping law of 1831.

In Cincinnati a mob pillages the printing press of the *Philanthropist* for the third time and kills and wounds blacks.

Ex-slave James C. Pennington publishes *A Text Book of the Origin and History of the Colored People.*

*May:* Lydia Maria Child becomes editor of the *National Anti-Slavery Standard.*

*May 12–13:* The Liberty Party holds its national convention in New York City, again nominating Birney for the presidency.

**1842**

The U.S. Supreme Court rules in *Prigg* v. *Pennsylvania* that the federal Fugitive Slave Law of 1793 is constitutional; that state personal liberty laws unconstitutionally levy new requirements on slaveholders wishing to recover fugitive slaves; that under the Constitution's fugitive slave clause, any slave owner can capture a fugitive slave without complying with the Fugitive Slave Law of 1793, if he can do so without a breach of the peace; and that all states ought to enforce the federal law but the federal government cannot force them to do so. Several northern states react by forbidding their officers to perform the duties imposed by the Fugitive Slave Law of 1793.

The Georgia legislature unanimously resolves that free blacks are not citizens of the United States and that Georgia will "never recognize such citizenship."

Black people of Troy, New York, meet to discuss action in the face of the Supreme Court's nullification of states' personal liberty laws.

The *New York Times* alleges that abolitionist Gerritt Smith has advised slaves to raise insurrections against their masters.

**1843**

Massachusetts, Vermont, and Ohio pass personal liberty (antikidnapping) laws.

The Black Convention is held in Buffalo, New York.

Black abolitionist Henry Highland Garnet calls on slaves to rise against their masters.

Lewis Tappan writes *An Address to the Non-Slaveholders of the South, on the Social and Political Evils of Slavery.*

**1844**

The Gag Rule, enacted annually since 1836, is defeated.

Connecticut passes a personal liberty (antikidnapping) law.

Justice Frederick Nash of North Carolina declares: "The free people of color cannot be considered as citizens in the largest sense of the term, or, if they are, they occupy such a position in society as justifies the legislature in adopting a course of policy in its acts peculiar to them."

The South Carolina legislature empowers the governor to use the militia, if necessary, to prevent the release by writ of habeas corpus of any person imprisoned under the Negro Seamen Act.

Oregon prohibits slavery and requires slaveholders to remove their chattels within three years.

**1845**

Texas enters the Union as a slave state.

The Anti-Slavery Office in Boston publishes the *Narrative of the Life of Frederick Douglass,* an escaped slave and a leader of the abolition movement.

B. S. Jones and Elizabeth H. Jones found the *Anti-Slavery Bugle* at New Lisbon, Ohio.

**1846**

Cong. David Wilmot of Pennsylvania introduces the Wilmot Proviso, prohibiting slavery in any territory acquired from Mexico. It fails in the Senate.

German settlers of Mercer County, Ohio, formally resolve to expel blacks from the county and no longer to employ or trade with blacks.

The Free Produce Association is organized by the Friends of Ohio Yearly Meeting. The Western Free Produce Association is organized in Indiana.

In St. Louis, according to later oral tradition, 12 young black men form the Knights of Tabor, undertaking to organize a liberation army called the Knights of Liberty to strike for freedom by about 1856.

**1847**

Pennsylvania passes a personal liberty (antikidnapping) law. The state also repeals the law that has allowed masters traveling through the state to keep slaves for up to six months.

The idea of "squatter sovereignty" is proposed: that the settlers of a territory, not the federal government, should decide whether a new state will be slave or free.

*The Narrative of William Wells Brown, A Fugitive Slave,* is published.

*October:* The Liberty Party holds its third national convention, nominating John P. Hale for the presidency.

*December 3:* The first issue of *North Star* appears. This antislavery weekly is edited by Frederick Douglass and Martin Delaney and published by William C. Nell.

**1848**

Slavery is abolished in all French and Danish colonies.

Rhode Island passes a personal liberty (antikidnapping) law.

The Free Soil Party is created from many antislavery groups, opposing slavery in the territories acquired by the United States in the Mexican War, and nominating Martin Van Buren for the presidency.

**1849**

A Virginia law provides that any person may emancipate any of his slaves by will or by deed, and that the children of any woman so emancipated who are born between the death of the testator or the recording of the deed and the time when her right to freedom arrives shall also be free at that time, unless the deed or will forbids it.

**1850**

Congress enacts the Missouri Compromise of 1850, admitting California as a free state, leaving it to popular sovereignty to decide free or slave status for New Mexico and Utah, prohibiting the slave trade in the District of Columbia, and passing a more stringent fugitive slave law that puts the burden of enforcement on U.S. commissioners and marshals. This law strengthens the property rights of slaveholders and endangers blacks living in free states. The federal government rigorously enforces it, and states react by passing more personal liberty laws.

The slave Shadrach is seized by his owner in Boston but is rescued and spirited away. As a result, Congress gives the president authority to use the armed forces to enforce the new fugitive slave law.

The Virginia constitution requires that any emancipated slave must leave the commonwealth within a year of emancipation and forbids the legislature to emancipate any slave or any slave's descendant.

Lucy Stone begins her service as an antislavery agent.

**1851**

Indiana takes away the right of male negroes and mulattoes to vote and excludes them from the militia.

In Syracuse, New York, Liberty Party men rescue the fugitive slave Jerry from jail and send him to Canada.

*September 11:* Whites and blacks battle in Christiana, Pennsylvania, after federal officers try to capture fugitive slaves, with the loss of four lives.

**1852**

Harriet Beecher Stowe publishes *Uncle Tom's Cabin.*

Abolitionist William Goodell publishes *Slavery and Anti-Slavery.*

**1853**

Argentina frees its slaves.

The Oregon Supreme Court rules that all blacks brought into the Oregon territory are thereby free.

Maryland enacts a law making free blacks entering the state from the North liable to sale as slaves.

Sallie Holley begins her career as an antislavery lecturer.

**1854**

Peru and Venezuela abolish slavery.

The Kansas-Nebraska Act creates the territories of Kansas and Nebraska, allows popular sovereignty to settle the slavery issue, and repeals the antislavery clause of the Missouri Compromise.

The Connecticut legislature enacts an antikidnapping law, in response to the Fugitive Slave Law of 1850.

Rhode Island extends its personal liberty law of 1848, providing, "No judge of any court of record of this State, and no justice of the peace, shall hereafter take cognizance or grant a certificate in cases" arising under the Fugitive Slave Law of 1850 "to any person who claims any other person as a fugitive slave within the jurisdiction of this state."

In Boston, 1,100 armed federal troops and officials frustrate citizens' attempts to rescue fugitive slave Anthony Burns and place him on shipboard for return to his master in Virginia.

**1855**

Michigan and Maine pass personal liberty laws opposing the Fugitive Slave Law of 1850.

Massachusetts reenacts its 1843 personal liberty law and makes it applicable to the Fugitive Slave Law of 1850.

**1856**

The Republican Party is formed on the base of the Free Soil Party.

Advocates of slavery sack and burn the town of Lawrence, Kansas.

*May 22:* Preston S. Brooks of South Carolina assaults Charles Sumner in the Senate chamber for his antislavery speech, "The Crime against Kansas."

**1857**

The U.S. Supreme Court in the *Dred Scott* decision declares that Congress has no power to limit slavery in the territories; three justices hold that a black descended from slaves has no rights as an American citizen.

Ohio and Wisconsin pass antikidnapping laws.

New Hampshire provides that no person because of descent from an African shall be disqualified from becoming a citizen of the state.

**1858**

Vermont passes an antikidnapping law and provides that no person because of descent from an African shall be disqualified from becoming a citizen of the state.

Texas entitles any person who captures a slave escaping to Mexico and delivers him to the sheriff at Austin to a reward of a third of the slave's value.

Texas prohibits "the owners of slaves from placing them in charge of farm or stock ranches, detached from the home or residence of the owner or employer."

John Brown proposes the organization of a biracial, armed guerrilla movement to uproot slavery, moving down from northern Virginia into the Deep South to form a provisional government of black and white people in a kind of guerrilla territory within the United States, under the formal aegis of the U.S. government.

Black emigrationist Martin Delaney publishes the novel *Blake,* with the theme of pan-African revolution in the Western Hemisphere.

**1859**

John Brown leads a small biracial group in capturing the federal armory at Harpers Ferry, Virginia.

**1860**

The state of New York, in *Lemmon* v. *The People,* frees slaves in transit from Virginia to Texas by coastal vessel.

Mississippi resolutions declare that northern states have (as in *Lemmon* v. *The People*) "insulted and outraged our citizens when travelling among them for pleasure, health or business, by taking their servants and liberating the same . . . and subjecting their owners to degrading and ignominious punishment."

Black emigrationist Martin Delaney goes to Canada to organize a company of black emigrants to move toward a new homeland.

**1888**

Brazil abolishes slavery, the last major slave state in the New World to do so.

## EYEWITNESS TESTIMONY

### *The Morality of Slavery: The Capabilities of Blacks*

The unhappy man, who has long been treated as a brute animal, too frequently sinks beneath the common standard of the human species. The galling chains that bind his body do also fetter his intellectual faculties, and impair the social affections of his heart. Accustomed to move like a mere machine; by the will of a master, reflection is suspended; he has not the power of choice, and reason and conscience have but little power over his conduct for he is chiefly governed by the passion of fear.

*Benjamin Franklin, calling for abolition, quoted in Kates, "Abolition, Deportation, Integration," 40–41.*

[Because of slavery] We colored people of these United States are the most degraded, and abject set of beings that ever lived since the world began. . . . It is indeed surprising that a man of such great learning, combined with such excellent natural parts [as Thomas Jefferson], should speak . . . [of the natural inferiority] of a set of men in chains. I do not know what to compare it to, unless, like putting one wild deer in an iron cage, where it will be secured, and hold another by the side of the same, then let it go, and expect the one in the cage to run as fast as the one at liberty. . . .

The whites have always been an unjust, jealous, unmerciful, avaricious and blood thirsty set of beings, always seeking after power and authority. . . . The whites want slaves, and want us for their slaves, but some of them will curse the day they ever saw us. As true as the sun ever shone in its meridian splendor, [people of] my Colour will root some of them out of the very face of the earth. They shall have enough of making slaves of, and butchering, and murdering us in the manner which they have. . . . The whites shall have enough of the blacks, yet, as true as God sits on his throne in heaven.

*Free black David Walker,* Walker's Appeal *(1829), in Dumond,* Antislavery, *115.*

The negro, constituted as he is, has such an aversion to labour, and so great a propensity for indulgence and vice, that no prospect of advantage can stimulate him. . . . Without force he will sink into lethargy, and revert to his primitive savage character, and the only feasible and effectual plan to promote his civilization is to persist in those measures which compel him to labour, inculcate morality, and tend to extirpate those vices which are inherent in the descendants of the African race.

The South Vindicated *(1836), 120.*

The negro requires government in every thing, the most minute . . . even in his meat and drink, his clothing, and hours of repose. Unless under the government of one man to prescribe rules of conduct to guide him, he will eat too much meat and not enough of bread and vegetables; he will not dress to suit the season, or kind of labor he is engaged in, nor retire to rest in due time to get sufficient sleep. . . . Nor will the women undress the children and put them regularly to bed. . . . They let their children suffer and die, or unmercifully abuse them, unless the white man or woman prescribe rules in the nursery for them to go by. . . .

The prognathous race require government also in their religious exercises, or they degenerate into fanatical saturnalia. . . .

*S. A. Cartwright, in* Cotton Is King *(1860), 727–28.*

### *The Morality of Slavery: Defenses of the Institution of Slavery*

Our Imitation of him [Abraham] in this his Moral Action [slaveholding], is as warrantable as that of [adopting] his Faith. . . . Any lawful Captives of Other Heathen nations may be made Bond men. . . . [But] Tis unlawful for Christians to Buy and Sell one another for slaves. . . . [God has ordained] some to be High and Honourable, some to be Low and Despicable; some to be Monarchs, Kings, Princes and Governours, Masters and Commanders, others to be Subjects, and to be Commanded; Servants of sundry sorts and degrees, bound to obey; yea, some to be born Slaves, and so to remain during their lives.

*Massachusetts justice John Saffin, 1701, in Tise,* Proslavery, *17.*

In Spight of all Endeavours to disguise this Point, it is clear as Light itself, that Negroes are as essentially necessary to the Cultivation of Georgia, as Axes, Hoes, or any other Utensil of Agriculture.

*Thomas Stephens, 1743, in Tise,* Proslavery, *17.*

[I should consider myself] highly favored [if I could] purchase a good number of them [slaves], in order to make their lives comfortable, and lay a foundation for breeding up their posterity in the nurture and admonition of the Lord.

*Anglican evangelist George Whitefield, ca. 1750, in Tise,* Proslavery, *21.*

[T]he nature of society . . . requires various degrees of authority and subordination; and while the universal rule of right, the happiness of the whole, allows greater degrees of Liberty to some, the same immutable law suffers it to be enjoyed only in less degrees by others. . . . [Africans are entitled to no more liberty than] concomitant circumstances being considered tends *to happiness on the whole.* . . . [A] vast inequality [exists between] different individuals of the human species, in point of qualification for the proper direction of conduct. . . . [S]ome are actually found so far to excell others both in respect to wisdom and benevolence, both in the knowledge of the principles of propriety, and a disposition to practice such principles, that the general end, happiness, would be better promoted by the exercise of authority in the former, though necessarily involving subordination of the latter, than by the enjoyment of equal Liberty in each. . . . [The Africans'] removal to America is to be esteemed a favor. . . . [Bringing them] from the state of brutality, wretchedness, and misery . . . to this land of light, humanity, and christian knowledge, is to them so great a blessing.

*Harvard senior Theodore Parsons, 1773, in Tise,* Proslavery, *30–32.*

One of the most pleasing incidents of slavery is its amelioration of the condition of the female sex. Among all savage people women are degraded into slaves, the abject drudges of their brutal lords. . . . The slave relieves the woman. Released from a condition worse than that of bondage, leisure is afforded; and with woman, in her rudest state, leisure must result in improvement. Her faculties are developed; her gentle and softening influence is seen and felt; she assumes the high station for which nature designed her; and happy in the hallowed affections of her own bosom, unwearily exerts those powers so well adapted to the task of humanizing and blessing others.

The South Vindicated *(1836), 104.*

[O]ne of the first and most essential requisites in the formation of republican character is intelligence. . . . [T]he slave-holder has, in that particular, the inestimable advantage of leisure. Relieved from the labour required for actual support, he is enabled to direct his attention to public affairs; to investigate political subjects, and exercise his privileges understandingly. This result has been fully attained at the south. . . . [N]owhere are the rights of man so fully canvassed and understood by the mass of citizens.

The South Vindicated *(1836), 110.*

Mr. May, we are not such great fools as not to know that slavery is a great evil and a great wrong. But it was consented to by the founders of the Republic. It was provided for in the Constitution of our Union. A great portion of the property of the Southerners is invested under its sanction; and the business of the North as well as of the South, has become adjusted to it.

There are millions upon millions of dollars due from the Southerners to the merchants and mechanics of this city [New York] alone, the payment of which would be jeopardized by a rupture between the North and the South. We cannot afford, sir, to let you and your associates succeed in your endeavor to overthrow slavery. It is not a matter of principle with us. It is a matter of business necessity.

*Partner in a mercantile house to Rev. Samuel J. May, 1835, in Aptheker,* One Continual Cry, *19–20.*

The poorest and humblest freeman of the South feels as sensibly, perhaps more sensibly than the wealthiest planter, the barrier which nature, as well as law, has erected between the white and black races. . . .

James H. Hammond, DeBow's Review, *June 1850, quoted in Lewis,* Coal, Iron, and Slaves, *225.*

The comparative evils of Slave Society and of Free Society, of slavery to human Masters, and of slavery to Capital are the issues which the South now presents, and which the North avoids. And she avoids them because the Abolitionists, the only assailants of Southern Slavery, have . . . asserted the entire failure of their own social system, proposed its subversion, and suggested an approximating millennium, or some system of Free Love, Communism, or Socialism, as a substitute. . . . [T]he profits which capital exacts from labor makes free laborers slaves, without the rights, privileges, or advantages of domestic slaves, and capitalists their masters, with all the advantages, and none of the burdens and obligations of the ordinary owners of slaves. . . .

*Fitzhugh,* Cannibals All *(1857), 7.*

[To argue against slavery] as a domestic institution simply because it is abused [is to be] like the socialists and free-lovers who argue against the marriage relation, because married people are always quarrelling, and running off to Indiana to be divorced. They have not the good sense to discriminate between the legitimate uses of an institution and the illegitimate abuses to which it can be subjected.

*David Hundley,* Social Relations in our Southern States, *1860, quoted in Tadman,* Speculators and Slaves, *182.*

[The] foundations [of the Confederacy] are laid, its corner-stone rests, upon the great truth, that the negro is not equal to the white man; that slavery, subordination to the superior race, is his natural and normal condition.

This, our new government, is the first, in the history of the world, based upon this great physical, philosophical, and moral truth. . . .

Many governments have been founded upon the principle of the subordination and serfdom of certain classes of the same race; such were and are in violation of the laws of nature. Our system commits no such violation of nature's laws. With us, all of the white race, however high or low, rich or poor, are equal in the eye of the law. Not so with the negro. Subordination is his place.

*Alexander H. Stephens, vice president of the Confederacy, March 21, 1861, in Durden,* Gray and the Black, *7–8.*

## *The Morality of Slavery: Sentiment against Slavery*

It seemeth to me that to sell them away as slaves is to hinder the enlargement of His kingdom. To sell souls for money seemeth to me a dangerous merchandise. If they deserve to die it is far better to be put to death under godly persons who will take religious care that means may be used that they may die penitently. To sell them away from all means of grace when Christ hath provided means of grace for them is the way for us to be active in destroying their souls, when we are highly obliged to seek their conversion and salvation.

*Puritan minister John Eliot, letter of June 13, 1675, to the Boston General Council, in Higginbotham,* In the Matter of Color, *65.*

We hear that the most part of such negers are brought hither against their will and consent, and that many of them are stolen. Now, though they are black, we cannot conceive there is more liberty to have them slaves, as it is to have other white ones. There is a saying that we should do to all men like as we will be done ourselves; making no difference of what generation, descent, or colour they are. And those who steal or rob men, and those who buy or purchase them, are they not all alike.

*Mennonites of Germantown, Pennsylvania, 1688, in Higginbotham,* In the Matter of Color, *267.*

[Slave masters] can afford to keep them with white hands [without guilt], except at some Times they chance to be besparkled with the blood of those poor Slaves, when they fall to beating them with their *twisted Hides and Horse-whips,* . . . to go with *fine powdered Perriwigs,* and great bunched *Coats;* and likewise keep their Wives idle *(Jezebel-like)* to paint *their Faces,* and *Puff,* and *powder their Hair,* and to bring up their Sons and Daughters in *Idleness* and *Wantonness,* and in all manner of *Pride* and *Prodigality,* in *decking* and *adorning* their Carkasses. . . . All, and much more, the miserable Effects produced by the Slavery of the Negroes.

*Quaker John Hepburn of New Jersey, 1714, in Locke,* Anti-Slavery, *22.*

[Preachers are] a sort of Devils, that Preach more to Hell than they do to Heaven, and so they will do forever, as long as they are suffered to reign in the worst, and Mother of all Sins, Slave-Keeping. . . . What do you think of these Things, you brave Gospel Ministers? that keep poor Slaves to Work for you to maintain you and yours in Pride, Pride and much Idleness or Laziness, and Fulness of Bread, the Sins of *Sodom. . . .*

*Quaker Benjamin Lay, 1737, in Locke,* Anti-Slavery, *26.*

Slavery is against the gospel, as well as fundamental law of England. We refused, as trustees [of the colony of Georgia], to make a law permitting such a horrid crime.

*Gen. James Oglethorpe, c. 1738, in Locke,* Anti-Slavery, *12.*

It is shocking to human Nature that any Race of Mankind, and their Posterity should be sentenced to perpetual Slavery; nor in Justice can we think otherwise than that they are thrown amongst us to be our Scourge one Day or other for our Sins; and as Freedom to them must be as dear as to us, what a Scene of Horror must it bring about.

*The Scotch of New Inverness, Georgia, to Gen. James Oglethorpe, January 3, 1739, in Locke,* Anti-Slavery, *12.*

I think that we Americans, at least in the Southern Colonies, cannot contend with a *good grace* for liberty, until we have enfranchised our slaves.

*John Laurens, in a 1776 letter, in Bell,* Major Butler's Legacy, *10.*

As much as I value a union of all the states, I would not admit the Southern States into the Union unless they agree to the discontinuance of this disgraceful trade, because it would bring weakness, and not strength, to the Union.

*George Mason at the Virginia ratifying convention, in Dumond,* Anti-Slavery, *28.*

Future inhabitants of America will inevitably be Mulattoes. . . . [T]his evil is coming upon us in a way much more disgraceful, and unnatural, than intermarriages. Fathers will have their own children for slaves, and leave them as an inheritance to their children. Men will possess their brothers and sisters as their property, leave them to their heirs, or sell them to strangers. Youth will have their grey-headed uncles and aunts for slaves, call them their property, and transfer them to others. Men will humble their own sisters, or even their aunts, to gratify their lust. An hard-hearted master will not know whether he has a blood relation, a brother or a sister, an uncle or an aunt, or a stranger from Africa, under his scourging hand.

*Rev. David Rice, 1792 speech in the Kentucky convention, in Dumond,* Anti-Slavery, *62.*

I will be as harsh as truth, and as uncompromising as justice. On this subject [slavery] I do not wish to think, speak, or write, with moderation. No! Tell a man whose house is on fire to give a moderate alarm; tell him to moderately rescue his wife from the hands of a ravisher; tell the mother to gradually extricate her babe from the fire into which it has fallen—but urge me not to use moderation in a cause like the present. I am in earnest—I will not equivocate—I will not retreat a single inch—and I will be heard!

*William Lloyd Garrison,* Liberator, *January 1831, quoted in Reynolds,* African Slavery, *89.*

I have thus, I think, clearly proved to you seven propositions, viz.: First, that slavery is contrary to the declaration of our independence. Second, that it is contrary to the first charter of human rights given to Adam, and renewed to Noah. Third, that the fact of slavery having been the subject of prophecy, furnishes *no* excuse whatever to slavedealers. Fourth, that no such system existed under the patriarchal dispensation. Fifth, that *slavery never* existed under the Jewish dispensation; but so far otherwise, that every servant was placed under the *protection of law,* and care taken not only to prevent all *involuntary* servitude, but all *voluntary perpetual* bondage. Sixth, that slavery in America reduces a *man* to a *thing,* a "chattel personal," *robs him of all* his rights as a *human being,* fetters both his mind and body, and protects the *master* in the most unnatural and unreasonable power, whilst it *throws him out* of the protection of law. Seventh, that slavery is contrary to the example and precepts of our holy and merciful Redeemer, and of his apostles.

But perhaps you will be ready to query, why appeal to *women* on this subject? We do not make the laws which perpetuate slavery. *No* legislative power is vested in *us; we* can do nothing to overthrow the system, even if we wished to do so. To this I reply, I know you do not make the laws, but I also know that *you are the wives and mothers, the sisters and daughters of those who do;* and if you really suppose *you* can do nothing to overthrow slavery; you are greatly mistaken.

*Angelina Grimké, "Appeal to the Christian Women of the South," September 1836, in Rossi,* The Feminist Papers, *296ff.*

While we know that God lives, and governs, and always will, that he is just and has declared that righteousness shall prevail, we believe, despite all corruption and caste, we shall yet be elevated with the

American people here. . . . We believe . . . that it is our duty and privilege to claim an equal place among the *American people,* to identify ourselves with American interests, and to exert all the power and influence we have, to break down the disabilities under which we labor, and look to become a happy people in this extended country.

*Charles Ray, editor of the* Colored American, *April 1840, in Harding,* River, *132.*

Our [Pilgrim Fathers were] men who had no communion with tyranny and oppression. . . . In consideration of the toils of our [black] fathers we claim the right of American citizenship. Our ancestors fought and bled for it. . . . With every fibre of our hearts entwined around our country, and with an indefeasible determination to obtain the possession of the natural and inalienable rights of American citizens, we demand redress for the wrongs we have suffered, and ask for the restoration of our birth-right privileges.

*Black abolitionist Henry Highland Garnet, 1840, in Harding,* River, *134–35.*

What, to the American slave, is your Fourth of July? I answer: a day that reveals to him, more than all other days in the year, the gross injustice and cruelty to which he is the constant victim. To him, your celebration is a sham; your boasted liberty an unholy license; your national greatness swelling vanity; your sounds of rejoicing are empty and heartless; your denunciation of tyrants brass-fronted impudence; your shouts of liberty and equality hollow mockery; your prayers and hymns, your sermons and thanksgivings, with all your religious parade and solemnity, are to Him mere bombast, fraud, deception, impiety and hypocrisy—a thin veil to cover up crimes which would disgrace a nation of savages. There is not a nation on the earth guilty of practices more shocking and bloody than are the people of the United States at this very hour.

*Frederick Douglass, "The Meaning of the Fourth of July for the Negro," Rochester, New York, 1852, quoted in Genovese,* From Rebellion to Revolution, *132.*

[T]he causes which have impeded the progress and prosperity of the South, which have dwindled our commerce and other similar pursuits, into the most contemptible insignificance; sunk a large majority of our people in galling poverty and ignorance, rendered a small minority conceited and tyrannical, and driven the rest away from their homes; entailed upon us a humiliating dependence on the Free States; disgraced us in the recesses of our own souls, and brought us under reproach in the eyes of all civilized and enlightened nations—may all be traced to one common source, and there find solution in the most hateful and horrible word, that was ever incorporated into the vocabulary of human economy—*Slavery.*

*Helper,* Impending Crisis *(1860), 12.*

The free labouring [North Carolina] farmer remarked [in 1854], that, although there were few slaves in this part of the country, he had often said to his wife that he would rather be living where there were none. He thought slavery wrong in itself, and deplorable in its effects upon the white people. . . .

He himself never owned a slave, and never would own one for his own benefit if it were given to him, "first, because it was wrong; and secondly, because he didn't think they ever did a man much good."

*Olmsted,* Cotton Kingdom, *403–4.*

## *Alternatives to Abolition: The Free Soil Controversy*

I am extremely sorry to hear the Senator from Mississippi say that he requires, first the extension of the Missouri Compromise line to the Pacific, and also that he is not satisfied with that, but requires . . . a positive provision for the admission of slavery south of that line. And now, sir, coming from a slave State, as I do, I owe it to myself, I owe it to truth, I owe it to the subject, to say that no earthly power could induce me to vote for a specific measure for the introduction of slavery where it had not before existed. . . . If the citizens of those territories choose to establish slavery, and if they come here with constitutions establishing slavery, I am for admitting them with such provisions in their constitutions; but then it will be their own work, and not ours, and their posterity will have to reproach them, and not us. . . .

*Henry Clay, 1829 speech, in Helper,* Impending Crisis, *99.*

But certain it is that the principle of interference [by the federal government] . . . should be limited to the creation of proper governments for new countries, acquired or settled, and to the necessary provision for their eventual admission into the Union; leaving, in the meantime, the people inhabiting them, to regulate their internal concerns in their own way. They are just as capable of doing so as the people of the states; and they can do so, at any rate as soon as their political independence is recognized by admission into the Union. During this temporary condition, it is hardly expedient to call into exercise a doubtful and invidious authority, which questions the intelligence of a respectable portion of our citizens, and whose limitation, whatever it may be, will be rapidly approaching its termination—an authority which would give to congress despotic power, uncontrolled by the constitution, over most important sections of our common country. For, if the relation of master and servant may be regulated or annihilated by its legislation, so may the regulation of husband and wife, of parent and child, and of any other condition which our institutions and the habits of our society recognize.

*An assertion of "squatter sovereignty," by Gen. Lewis Cass, December 24, 1847, in Blake,* Slavery and the Slave Trade, *559.*

The political influence which [the Kansas-Nebraska] Territories will give to the South, if secured, will be of the first importance to perfect its arrangements for future slavery extension—whether by divisions of the larger States and Territories, now secured to the institution, its extension into territory hitherto considered free, or the acquisition of new territory to be devoted to the system, so as to preserve the balance of power in Congress. When this is done, Kansas and Nebraska, like Kentucky and Missouri, will be of little consequence to slaveholders, compared with the cheap and constant supply of provisions they can yield. . . . White free labor, doubly productive over slave labor in grain-growing, must be multiplied within their limits, that the cost of provisions may be reduced and the extension of slavery and the growth of cotton suffer no interruption. The present efforts to plant them with slavery, are indispensable to produce sufficient excitement to fill them speedily with a free population; and if this whole movement has been a Southern scheme to cheapen provisions, and increase the ratio of the production of sugar and cotton, as it most unquestionably will do, it surpasses the statesman-like strategy which forced the people into an acquiescence in the annexation of Texas.

And should the anti-slavery voters succeed in gaining the political ascendancy in these Territories, and bring them as free States triumphantly into the Union; what can they do, but turn in, as all the rest of the Western States have done, and help to feed slaves, or those who manufacture or who sell the products of the labor of slaves.

*David Christy, in* Cotton Is King *(1860), 123–24.*

## *Alternatives to Abolition: The Free Produce Movement*

I cannot help contemplating a sugar maple-tree with a species of affection and even veneration, for I have persuaded myself to behold in it the happy means of rendering the commerce and slavery of our african [*sic*] brethren in the sugar islands as unnecessary, as it has always been inhuman and unjust.

*Dr. Benjamin Rush to Thomas Jefferson, in Locke,* Anti-Slavery, *189.*

If every bale of cotton and every piece of calico were stained with the sweat and blood which has flowed so freely in raising the raw material, who would be found ready to receive, and manufacture, and vend, and wear the fabric into which slave grown cotton has been wrought?

*Angelina Grimké, letter to Lewis Tappan, August 1841, in Dumond,* Antislavery, *350.*

[Slave-labor products] are so mixed up with the commerce, manufactures and agriculture of the world—so modified or augmented in value by the industry of other nations,—so indissolubly connected with the credit and currency of the country—that, to attempt to seek the subversion of slavery by refusing to use them, or to attach moral guilt to the consumer of them is, in our opinion, preposterous and unjust.

*William Lloyd Garrison, 1847, in Kraditor,* American Abolitionism, *218–19.*

## *The Means to Emancipation: Gradual Emancipation*

[W]e rejoice that it is in our power, to extend a portion of that freedom to others, which hath been extended to us . . . We esteem it a peculiar blessing

William Lloyd Garrison (*Holley,* A Life for Liberty)

granted to us, that we are enabled this day to add one more step to universal civilization, by removing, as much as possible, the sorrows of those, who have lived in undeserved bondage. . . .

III. *Be it enacted, and it is hereby enacted,* That all persons as well Negroes and Mulattoes as others, who shall be born within this state from and after the passing of this act, shall not be deemed and considered as servants for life, or slaves; and that all servitude for life, or slavery of children, in consequence of the slavery of their mothers, in the case of all children born within this state from and after the passing of this act as aforesaid, shall be, and hereby is, utterly taken away, extinguished, and for ever abolished.

IV. *Provided always, and be it further enacted,* That every Negro and Mulatto child, born within this state after the passing of this act as aforesaid (who would, in case this act had not been made, have been born a servant for years, or life, or a slave) shall be deemed to be, and shall be, by virtue of this act, the servant of such person, or his or her assigns, who would in such case have been entitled to the service of such child, until such child shall attain unto the age of twenty-eight years, in the manner, and on the conditions, whereon servants bound by indenture for four years are or may be retained and holden . . .

*Pennsylvania statute of 1780, in Finkelman,*
Law of Freedom, *42–43.*

## *The Means to Emancipation: Political and Judicial Action*

It is ordered by this court, and the authority thereof; that there shall never be any bond slavery, villainage or captivity amongst us, unless it be lawful captives taken in just wars, as willingly sell themselves or are sold to us, and such shall have the liberties and christian usage which the law of God established in Israel concerning such persons doth morally require; provided this exempts none from servitude, who shall be judged thereto by authority.

*Massachusetts Body of Liberties, 1641, in Williams,*
History of the Negro Race, *177.*

And forasmuch as great inconveniences may happen to this country by the setting of negroes and mulattoes free, by their either entertaining negro slaves from their masters service, or receiving stolen goods, or being grown old bringing a charge upon the country; for prevention thereof, *Be it enacted . . ., and it is hereby enacted,* That no negro or mulatto be after the end of this present session of assembly set free by any person or persons whatsoever, unless such person or persons, their heires, executors or administrators pay for the transportation of such negro or negroes out of the countrey within six moneths after such setting them free. . . .

*Virginia law, 1691, in Finkelman,*
Law of Freedom, *108.*

AN ACT for rendering the Colony of Georgia more Defencible by Prohibiting the Importation and use of Black slaves or Negroes into the same. WHEREAS Experience hath Shewn that the manner of Settling Colonys and Plantations with Black Slaves or negroes hath Obstructed the Increase of English and Christian Inhabitants therein who alone can in case of a War be relyed on for the Defence and Security of the same, and hath Exposed the Colonys so settled to the Insurrections Tumults and Rebellions of such Slaves & Negroes and in case of a Rupture with an Foreign State who should encourage and Support such Rebellions might occasion the utter Ruin and loss of such Colonys. . . .

*English law of 1735, quoted in Olexer,* Enslavement of the American Indians, *193.*

[A petition] of Felix Holbrook, and others, Negroes, praying that they may be liberated from a state of Bondage, and made Freemen of this Community; and that this Court would give and grant to them some part of the unimproved Lands belonging to the Province, for a settlement, or relieve them in such other Way as shall seem good and wise upon the Whole.

*Petition to the Massachusetts legislature, 1773, in Williams,* History of the Negro Race, *233.*

We will neither import nor purchase any slave imported after the first day of December next, after which time we will wholly discontinue the slave trade and will neither be concerned in it nor will we hire our vessels nor sell our commodities or manufactures to those who are concerned in it.

*First Continental Congress, 1774, in Harding,* River, *45.*

Therefore, no male person, born in this country, or brought from over sea, ought to be holden by law, to serve any person, as servant, slave or apprentice, after he arrives to the age of twenty-one years, nor female, in like manner, after she arrives at the age of eighteen years, unless they are bound by their own consent, after they arrive to such age, or bound by law, for the payment of debts, damages, fines, costs, or the like.

*Vermont Bill of Rights, 1777, in Locke,* Anti-Slavery, *80.*

I was involved in several causes in which negroes sued for their freedom, before the Revolution. The arguments in favour of their liberty were much the same as have been urged since . . . arising from the rights of mankind. . . . Argument might have some weight in the abolition of slavery in Massachusetts, but the real cause was the multiplication of labouring white people, who would no longer suffer the rich to employ these sable rivals so much to their injury.

*John Adams, March 21, 1795, in Higginbotham,* In the Matter of Color, *97.*

The professed object of this [Liberty] Party is to secure the rights of *colored men* in THIS country; [but] they have given no opportunity to the poor colored man to speak for him, by placing him in the legislature where he *ought* to be heard with themselves. . . . In view of this state of things, what better is this third abolition *party* for us than either of the other parties?

*Black abolitionist Thomas Van Rensselaer, 1840, in Harding,* River, *135–36.*

## *The Means to Emancipation: Threats and Military Action*

Sir, the people of the west[ern part of Virginia], I undertake to say, feel a deep, a lively, a generous sympathy for their eastern brethren. They know that the evils which now afflict them are not attributable to any fault of theirs that slavery was introduced against their will; that we are indebted for it to the commercial cupidity of that heartless [British] empire. . . . Yet we will not that you shall make our fair domain the receptacle of your mass of political filth and corruption. No, sir, before we can submit to such terms, violent convulsions must agitate this state.

*Slaveholder Charles James Faulkner, speech in the House of Delegates of Virginia, 1832, in Redpath,* Roving Editor, *99–100.*

You are not certain of heaven, because you suffer yourselves to remain in a state of slavery, where you cannot obey the commandments of the Sovereign of the universe. . . . It is your solemn and imperative duty to use every means, both moral, intellectual, and physical, that promises success [to end slavery]. . . . Promise the slave-owners renewed diligence in the cultivation of the soil, if they will render to you an equivalent for your services. . . . Point the slaveholders to the increase of happiness and prosperity in the British West Indies since the Act of Emancipation. . . . Inform them that all you desire is FREEDOM. . . . However much you and all of us may desire it, there is not much hope of redemption without the shedding of blood. . . . Brethren, arise, arise! Strike for your lives and liberties. Now is the day and the hour. Let every slave throughout the land do this, and the days of slavery are numbered. You cannot be more oppressed than you have been. . . . RATHER DIE FREEMEN THAN LIVE TO BE SLAVES.

REMEMBER THAT YOU ARE FOUR MILLION! . . . Let your motto be resistance! *Resistance!* RESISTANCE! No oppressed people have ever secured their liberty without resistance.

*Black abolitionist Henry Garnet,* Address to the Slaves of the United States, *1843, quoted in Harding,* River, *141.*

Resolved, that in the language of inspired wisdom, there shall be no peace to the wicked, and that this guilty nation shall have no peace, and that we will do all we can to agitate. *Agitate!* AGITATE!!! till our rights are restored and our brethren are redeemed from their cruel chains.

*Resolution Sponsored by Frederick Douglass at the National Convention of Colored People, 1847, in Harding,* River, *146.*

## Abolitionism

The object of this [American Anti-Slavery] Society is the entire abolition of slavery in the United States. While it admits that each State, in which slavery exists, has, by the Constitution of the United States, exclusive right to *legislate* in regard to its abolition in this State, it shall aim to convince all our fellow-citizens, by arguments addressed to their understandings and consciences, that slave-holding is a heinous crime in the sight of God, and that the duty, safety, and best interests of all concerned, require its *immediate abandonment,* without expatriation. The Society will also endeavor, in a constitutional way, to influence Congress to put an end to the domestic slave-trade, and to abolish slavery in all those portions of our common country, which come under its control, especially in the District of Columbia, and likewise to prevent the extension of it to any State that may be hereafter admitted to the Union. . . . This Society shall aim to elevate the character and condition of the people of color, by encouraging their intellectual, moral, and religious improvement, and by removing public prejudice, that thus they may, according to their intellectual and moral worth, share an equality with the whites, of civil and religious privileges; but this Society will never, in any way, countenance the oppressed in vindicating their rights by resorting to physical force.

*Constitution of the American Anti-Slavery Society, 1833, in Kraditor,* American Abolitionism, *5.*

As to the governments of this world, . . . we shall endeavor to prove, that, in their essential elements, and as at present administered, they are all Anti-Christ; that they can never, by human wisdom, be brought into conformity to the will of God; that they cannot be maintained, except by naval and military power; that all their penal enactments being a dead letter without an army to carry them into effect, are virtually written in human blood; and that the followers of Jesus should instinctively shun their stations of honor, power and emolument—at the same time "submitting to every ordinance of man, for the Lord's sake," and offering no *physical* resistance, to any of their mandates, however unjust or tyrranical.

*William Lloyd Garrison,* Liberator, *December 15, 1837, quoted in Kraditor,* American Abolitionism, *86–87.*

[V]erily some of our northern gentlemen abolitionists are as jealous of any interference [by women] in rights they have long considered as belonging to them

Abby Kelley Foster, abolitionist speaker (*Holley,* A Life for Liberty)

exclusively, as the southern slaveholder is, in the right of holding his slaves—both are to be broke up, & *human* rights alone recognized.

*Quaker James Mott, on objections raised to Abby Kelley's participation in the New England Anti-Slavery Convention, 1838, in Kraditor,* American Abolitionism, *46.*

At an anti-slavery meeting of the citizens of Sardinia and vicinity, held on November 21, 1838, a committee of respectable citizens presented a report, accompanied with affidavits in support of its declarations, stating that for more than a year past there had been an unusual degree of hatred manifested by the slave-hunters and slaveholders towards the abolitionists of Brown County [Ohio], and that rewards varying from $500 to $2,500 had been repeatedly offered by different persons for the abduction or assassination of the Rev. John B. Mahan; and rewards had also been offered for Amos Pettijohn, William A. Frazier and Dr. Isaac M. Beck, of Sardinia, the Rev. John Rankin and Dr. Alexander Campbell, of Ripley, William McCoy, of Russellville, and citizens of Adams County.

*Newspaper report in Siebert,* Underground Railway, *53.*

With [abolitionists], the rights of property are nothing; the deficiency of the powers of the General [federal] Government is nothing; the acknowledged and incontestible powers of the States are nothing; civil war, a dissolution of the Union, and the overthrow of a government in which are concentrated the fondest hopes of the civilized world, are nothing. . . . Utterly destitute of constitutional or other rightful power, living in totally distinct communities as alien to the communities in which the subject on which they would operate resides, so far as concerns political power over that subject, as if they lived in Africa or Asia, they nevertheless promulgate to the world their purpose to be to manumit forthwith, . . . and without moral preparation, three millions of negro slaves, under jurisdictions altogether separated from those under which they live. . . . Does any considerate man believe it to be possible to effect such an object without convulsion, revolution, and bloodshed?

*Henry Clay, 1839 Senate debate, in Fox,* American Colonization Society, *147.*

Abolitionists—about 5% of the voting population. Sober people, willing to see slavery abolished, but not by overthrowing the Constitution—70%. Highly respectable people who sympathize with the South—5%. The remainder—20%, who care less for principles than for spoils. Yet the abolitionists hold the balance of power from the nearly equal division of Democrats and Whigs. Hence the danger to the South should any party unite with the abolitionists.

*John Calhoun's analysis of the political strength of the North, about 1849, in Buckmaster,* Let My People Go, *172.*

These dreadful times of mobs are thought to be the last struggle of the slave-power in the North. . . . I think it was worth living a great many years to be present at the [antislavery] meeting in Tremont Temple [in Boston] last Thursday morning [in January, 1861]. . . .

Mrs. Lydia Maria Child, as full of enthusiasm as she could express by flashing eye, glowing cheek, and waving handkerchief, as she sat by the organ on the highest seat of the platform, making everybody glad by her presence; Mrs. Maria Chapman, sitting with the calm dignity of a queen, her sister and daughter beside her; T. W. Higginson, ready with brilliant eloquence of tongue or with the revolver's bullet—so it was said—to do battle for free speech that day. . . .

*Holley,* A Life for Liberty, *177–78.*

# 11

# Black Soldiers in America's Wars 1635–1865

## THE HISTORICAL CONTEXT

Black men, free and slave, have served as soldiers and sailors in American wars since colonial times, often with distinction. In the years up to the end of the Civil War, their participation in the military was never universally welcomed, often grudgingly solicited, and always controversial. Black labor (both free and slave) in support of military activity was commonplace, but white fears of armed blacks and racist doubts about their courage limited their acceptance into the military.

No historian can discriminate precisely between slaves and free blacks in military service. Records are vague, and many slaves were promised their freedom if they would fight: did they, then, fight as free men or as slaves?

### *Colonial America*

Colonial America as a rule excluded blacks from militia service and forbade them to own or use weapons. North Carolina, for example, specifically exempted slaves and free blacks from the militia service required of white males, an average of ten to twenty days a year.[1] In 1639, Virginia slaves were "excused" from owning or carrying arms; in 1705, they were barred from holding or exercising any military office, and if found in possession of a "gun, sword, club, staff, or other weapon" they were subject to 20 lashes. On the other hand, Massachusetts, for a brief period (1652–56) required "negroes" to train in the militia—though few if any actually did. Thereafter, Massachusetts barred them.[2] But militias everywhere pressed blacks, both free and slave, into military-support services—building fortifications, fixing roads, cooking, and pitching tents, thus relieving white militiamen of backbreaking labor.

Still, some black soldiers fought. The rosters of troops engaged in the French and Indian War (1754–1763) identify some as blacks and mulattoes and a few as slaves.[3] During their brief occupation of New York (1621–64), the

Dutch enlisted both free blacks and slaves in the militia; during the Indian Wars of 1641–43, they used slaves to track down fugitive Indians accused of what were later called "war crimes."

Even in the Deep South, where the outnumbered white population lived in perpetual terror of slave insurrections, exceptional circumstances occasionally prompted colonial legislatures to authorize the enlistment of slaves. Slaves could be used, they said, to defend against hostile Indians, or against the Spanish, who from their bases in Florida provided a haven for runaways, encouraged slave uprisings, and armed fugitive slaves for military service. In the face of such threats, training slaves as soldiers and mustering them into an auxiliary militia seemed to make sense. Both South Carolina and Georgia, for example, once provided by law for the enlistment of slaves in the militia. In both colonies, slave owners were obligated to provide suitable males for service. Slaves whose behavior in battle was exceptionally meritorious were to be rewarded with freedom. Masters were to be paid for the loss of their slaves' services and compensated for their injury or death, and the proportion of blacks to whites in each company was limited to one-third. In practice, however, slaves were never mustered for military service under these laws, except possibly in the 1740s, when James Oglethorpe successfully led Georgia and South Carolina troops, including some slaves, against Spanish forts to the south.[4] At least once, in the war against the Yamasee in Carolina (1715–16), the British mustered black men into temporary military service.[5]

## *The Revolutionary War*

During the Revolutionary War also, the exclusionary system broke down. Crispus Attucks, a former slave, was the first American to fall when English soldiers opened fire in the Boston Massacre. Peter Salem, also a former slave, saw action at the battle of Lexington and later attained prominence for his bravery at Bunker Hill. The militias sent in 1775 by neighboring towns and colonies to besiege Boston included free blacks and slaves. At least three black soldiers in Col. John Nixon's New Hampshire regiment were identified by the muster master as slaves "inlisted with the Consent of their Masters."[6]

In the first months of the Revolutionary War, when the Continental Congress asked that all "able-bodied men in each colony form themselves into regular companies of militia," black men volunteered, and some were accepted, despite exclusionary laws.[7] Their presence did not go unchallenged. When in 1775, the Second Continental Congress created the Continental Army with George Washington as commander in chief, questions immediately arose. Should the Continental Army recruit black soldiers? Should those black volunteers already mustered in be retained? Official policy (and practice) with respect to the recruitment of blacks ran the gamut from acceptance to exclusion, but by 1776 exclusion had become the rule.

Early in 1777, however, opposition to the enlistment of blacks confronted reality. White men, despite promises of pay raises and substantial enlistment bounties, were not volunteering in numbers sufficient to meet army requirements. Under these circumstances, recruiting officers began accepting blacks even though state laws forbade it. After 1777, black recruitment, primarily of free men, prevailed in most of the northern states.

Enlisting slaves was more complicated. Unless the slave was a fugitive, enlistment typically required the owner's permission, which depended upon either the patriotism of the master or the inducements offered by the government—or both. Rhode Island, for example, inducted two battalions of slaves, paying their owners up to two hundred pounds each for their freedom, and in 1785 it provided for the survivors' maintenance at public expense. New York in 1781 authorized the raising of two regiments of black soldiers, whose owners were given a grant of land for each slave who served.[8] As an additional inducement, and a most persuasive one, slave owners were frequently allowed to send their slaves as substitutes for their own military service.

In the southern states, proposals to enlist slaves rarely succeeded. In October 1780, the border state of Maryland did authorize the enlistment of slaves between the ages of 16 and 40. But an attempt in 1781 to raise an all-black regiment by requiring owners of six or more slaves to send one to the army failed. Maryland, however, continued to induct a few slaves. More telling was the rejection in 1781 by South Carolina and Georgia of a proposal by the Continental Congress (supported by Washington's best generals) that they recruit 3,000 slaves for their own safety and defense—this at a time when British forces threatened to overrun the entire region. Congress's proposal stipulated that the separate black battalions would be under white command and that slave owners would be compensated for each slave. The slaves themselves would receive subsistence and clothing but no pay for their service; upon discharge they would be given $50 and their freedom. South Carolina and Georgia flatly refused.

Military service at sea was another story. From the beginning of the Revolutionary War, slaves and free blacks served in the navies created first by states (beginning with Rhode Island in 1775) and then by the Continental Congress (1776). Blacks who sought service with these navies were almost always accepted, on a basis comparatively free of prejudice. Typically employed in the lowest ranks and ratings, they were sometimes rewarded for outstanding performance by promotion to higher positions and better pay—or even freedom. Caesar, a slave in the Virginia service, was set free when the legislature bought him from his master in recognition of his "gallant behavior." After his death, the legislature awarded his daughter Nancy 2,667 acres of land for her father's service in the war.[9]

In addition to the few slaves who fought as soldiers or sailors in the Revolutionary War, thousands contributed to the victory by their labor. Commonly, a state or army hired slaves, paying the owner for their services. If owners refused (because the price was not acceptable or the slave could not be spared at home), states sometimes would resort to impressment. In March 1776, for example, New York City empowered the commanding officer of each army corps in the city to call out all the black males in his district, slaves included, to work on the city's fortifications.

Slaves captured from the British military or from British sympathizers were typically considered spoils of war and put to work. Alternatively, they might be treated as private booty to be sold for the benefit of the regiment or retained as personal servants. Sometimes they would be turned over to states for disposition—hired out or sold. Some northern slaves obtained their freedom when their Tory masters fled to the British or when the state confiscated Tory estates. More often, particularly in the South, the slaves of Tories were sold, the proceeds going to the state. However procured, slaves were employed on roads and fortifications, as stevedores and teamsters, in mines and factories, in hospitals and kitchens. Slaves were particularly useful as guides and spies, because of their intimate knowledge of the territory, sometimes in this way earning their freedom at war's end. Thus the Virginia legislature awarded one James his freedom and later a pension for his service with Lafayette as a spy and courier, duly compensating his owner, William Armistead.[10]

To weaken American forces, the British offered freedom to slaves who would escape and take refuge with the king's army. When on November 7, 1775, Lord Dunmore, the British governor of Virginia, issued such an invitation, within three weeks some 300 slaves had accepted, and more followed. Fitted out with uniforms on which the words "Liberty to Slaves" were inscribed, they were officially known as Lord Dunmore's Ethiopian Regiment. The governor's black recruits saw some action, but an epidemic of smallpox killed most of them and ended the experiment.[11] Alarmed by the loss of laborers upon whom they depended to produce food and raw materials and angered by the loss of their "property," the Americans responded indignantly, warning their slaves that the British wanted only to replenish the slave stock in the West Indies and threatening that fugitives would be severely punished unless they came back in ten days.

The British repeated their coup in 1778, when Sir Henry Clinton, the commander in chief of British forces in North America, issued the Phillipsburg Proclamation, directed not just to able-bodied men but to the entire slave population. Blacks rushed to accept. One slave owner in South Carolina was appalled to discover that 15 of his slaves had disappeared in a single 24-hour period—and that was only the beginning.[12] What was more, some of the fugitives helped the British capture the plantations on which they had lived or held the white family prisoner until the British arrived.[13] Many a slave owner felt obliged to stay at home and keep an eye on his slaves, thus contributing to the manpower shortage plaguing American commanders.

No one knows how many slaves sought haven with the British. Some historians think it as many as 100,000; James Walker speaks of "tens of thousands," adding, "They swam, they hiked, they stowed away in boats and wagons, they carried each other to safety with the Redcoats. Many took advantage of the temporary presence of a British army in the neighbourhood to make a bid for freedom, others made a longer journey to British strongholds such as Charleston and Savannah. Boston King waded out to a British boat, risking a treacherous current as well as the possibility of recapture."[14]

British commanders were cautious about arming these fugitives as combat soldiers, although a black cavalry troop was formed in 1782, and some two hundred blacks participated in the defense of Savannah (1779) and Augusta (1781). Several black pioneer (engineer) corps with their own noncommissioned officers were created to work on fortifications, roads, and bridges. A few found a place in the Royal Navy as ordinary seamen. Others served as guides, inland waterway pilots, spies, and couriers. More commonly, these former slaves were employed in garrisons as servants, orderlies, cooks, and laundresses.

Not all the slaves who fell into British hands improved their condition. Those who had been seized as war booty or taken from American plantations occupied by British troops might be sold back into slavery either to a Loyalist planter (who might have lost his own slaves to the "rebels") or into the West Indies. British officers kept some as personal servants. But for the most part, the British kept their promises, shipping most of the former slaves to refuges of their choice.

Slaves who served in the Continental Army also in most cases won their freedom. Some were cruelly disappointed, like Frederick, who had served with the consent of his master, legally remaining a slave. When as a veteran he sued for 1,000 acres the state had promised each veteran, he lost—because a slave could not hold property. Another Revolutionary War soldier, Jehu Grant, was denied his pension on the grounds that he had been a fugitive when he fought for the Americans.[15]

How many blacks served in the Continental armies? Probably between 4,000 and 5,000.

## *The War of 1812*

In the War of 1812, blacks were actively involved from the outset. Even before the war, when the British man-of-war *Leopard* attacked the American frigate *Chesapeake* to search it for (alleged) deserters, three of the four sailors removed were black.[16]

The military record of slaves and free blacks in the War of 1812 resembles that of the Revolution, except that whites were even more loath to arm blacks. Many blacks tried to enlist, and some succeeded, for the start of the war found an American army of 6,000 white men facing a much larger number of British soldiers.[17] Even so, only time and the fortunes of war would drive home to the government the need for black soldiers. Civil authorities eagerly used blacks to build defenses but long hesitated to give them weapons. Even after the British occupation of Washington in 1814 alerted Philadelphia to the danger it might be facing, the city's defense committee still wanted black fatigue parties to work separately from whites. Black leaders James Forten, Absalom Jones, and Richard Allen organized 2,500 black men to labor in support services. Only when peace was declared did Philadelphia have a black battalion ready to march.

Not until October 1814 did a state, New York, authorize the creation of two black regiments, officered by whites. Roughly 2,000 enlisted men were recruited from among free blacks and slaves given permission by their owners; slaves were to be freed when discharged.[18] Gen. Andrew Jackson, in a proclamation of September 21, 1814, invited "freemen of color" to enlist, promising them the same compensation as whites. Four hundred blacks fought with Jackson in the battle of New Orleans in January 1815, earning his commendation for their valor.[19]

In the War of 1812, however, most of the action for blacks was in the navy, where they were already serving at the conflict's onset. Not only during the war but for several years after it, blacks constituted 10 to 20 percent of the crews.[20] In the navy, prejudice had given way to practicality; black and white seamen fought together, ate together, and shared quarters in the limited space available. Nonetheless, relations between black and white seamen varied from ship to ship, depending on the prejudices of the commanding officer.

Early on, aboard the *Governor Tompkins,* two black crew members, John Johnson and John Davis, were shot in a battle at sea. Johnson shouted encouragement to his mates as he lay dying, and Davis asked again and again to be thrown overboard to leave space for those still fighting. After the battle of Lake Erie in 1813, Commodore Oliver Perry praised the gallantry of the hundred blacks who constituted a quarter of his crews, saying that "they seem to be absolutely insensible to danger."[21]

In this war, as in the Revolution, the British invited slaves to seek refuge and eventual freedom with them. More than 3,500 responded to the Cochrane Proclamation issued by that vice admiral in April 1814. Of these, some 2,000 wound up in Nova Scotia.[22]

## The "Negro Fort"

During the War of 1812, a small British force under Lt. Col. Edward Nicholas allied itself with the Seminole Indians in Florida and rebuilt an old Spanish fort on the Apalachicola River. The Seminole had long provided refuge for runaway slaves, some of whom counseled the Indian nation, particularly in its dealings with the United States. When Nicholas departed after the war, he left the fort and a store of supplies, arms, and ammunition in the charge of the Seminole and blacks. Around this "Negro Fort," by then occupied mostly by some 3,000 blacks, settled a growing community of Indians and blacks, among them some 1,000 fugitives. From it, blacks allied with the neighboring Creek raided and terrorized slave owners across the border. When the Spanish authorities refused to intervene, the United States in the summer of 1816 sent gunboats to destroy the fort and return the fugitive slaves to their owners. Fire from the gunboats set off the fort's magazine, killing 270 people, mostly blacks. Other blacks were captured and reenslaved.

Nonetheless Indians and blacks kept up their resistance from new towns they founded on the Suwanee River. The continuing border wars finally led to Andrew Jackson's invasion of Florida. When the black commander Bowlegs got wind of an immense force of Americans and Indians friendly to them advancing on the fort, most Seminole fled, but the blacks fought a rearguard action to enable their families to escape to the swamps and eventually to the Bahamas. The United States annexed Florida in February 1819.[23]

## The Civil War: A White Man's War

At the outbreak of the Civil War in 1861, many free blacks attempted to enlist with the Union army, and black communities offered to organize combat regiments. These efforts were repulsed. To avoid antagonizing slave owners in the border states and in hopes of even picking up some support in the South, President Lincoln held that the war was being waged to preserve the Union, not to end slavery. In this white man's war, it was argued, blacks (free or slave) had no stake in the outcome.

Fugitive slaves from the South seeking freedom behind Federal lines often found themselves turned back or returned to their masters by Union officers. Field commanders marching into rebel territory sometimes felt obliged to reassure the local inhabitants that the sanctity of their property (slaves) would be respected. On occasion, Confederate slave owners and sheriffs were even allowed to enter Union territory and hunt for their runaway slaves.

Meanwhile antislavery commanders in the field, such as Gen. John C. Frémont, were freeing the slaves in the territories under their control—only to have their orders countermanded by Washington. But Gen. Benjamin Butler found a way to justify using the services of slaves who fled to the Union lines: he declared them contraband of war. In August 1861, Congress legitimated Butler's action with the First Confiscation Act, which made all property used to support the rebellion, including slaves, subject to prize and capture. Next, in December 1861, Congress prohibited the use of Federal forces to return fugitives to their masters.[24] Six months later, the Second Confiscation Act of July 17, 1862, authorized the president, at his discretion, to recruit blacks into the army. Every slave mustered into the army would be free, and his master (if loyal to the United States) would be compensated.[25] Lincoln, however, did not begin this recruitment for some time. Full-scale active recruitment got under way only in 1863.

Military necessity pushed toward abolition and the enlistment of blacks in the armed forces of the Union, for the South's huge slave labor force enabled it to send most of its white men of fighting age into the army—eventually some 75 percent. Meanwhile, the Union was using to advantage the services of the runaway slaves flooding behind Union lines wherever Federal troops appeared. These services ranged from housekeeping functions in army camps and hospitals to heavy labor on fortifications, roads, and bridges. "Contrabands" worked as wagon masters, teamsters, washerwomen, nurses, cooks, waiters, cleaners, carpenters, and blacksmiths; they served as scouts, spies, guides, and pilots.[26] Ineluctably, the war was becoming a battle to abolish slavery as well as to preserve the Union.

## *The Civil War: Arming of Contrabands and Recruitment of Black Troops*

In all theaters of the war, enterprising commanders in the field, faced with diminishing manpower reserves, began arming and drilling contrabands on their own authority. Washington wavered, censuring such an action of one general and endorsing that of another by ignoring it.

West of the Mississippi in late 1861, blacks associated with the Creek, Seminole, and Cherokee Indians fought their way north to Kansas to join Union regiments. Runaway slaves from the Kansas-Missouri-Arkansas frontier were being recruited—notably in Kansas by James H. Lane and James Montgomery—without official sanction of or even acknowledgment by Washington. As early as October 1862, black troops were fighting against Confederate irregulars on the Missouri border.[27]

In South Carolina, Gen. David Hunter's enlistment of black soldiers in May 1862 earned him official censure, and his black regiment was disbanded in August. The same month, the War Department authorized General Saxton, military governor of the South Carolina Sea Islands, to raise five regiments of black troops. On January 31, 1863, under the command of Col. Thomas W. Higginson, the 1st South Carolina Colored Volunteers became an official part of the Federal army—the first organization of black soldiers fully authorized by the War Department.[28] Higginson's men (and a second black regiment commanded by Col. James Montgomery) served with distinction in the interior of Georgia and Florida; in March 1863 they occupied Jacksonville.

When in May 1862 General Butler occupied New Orleans, he put to work many of the thousands of contrabands who fled there from plantations. At first, doubting the ability of blacks to fight, he refused to enlist them, rejecting the proposals of his subordinate Gen. John W. Phelps—who promptly resigned.[29] Shortly after, however, desperation for reenforcements forced General Butler to change his mind. He accepted the services of the Louisiana Native Guard, a black organization that had been formed to fight for the Confederacy. After the Confederate army retreated, the unit offered its services to General Butler. On May 27, 1863, those black soldiers fought valiantly under Butler's command at the battle of Port Hudson, sustaining great losses. They distinguished themselves once again in the battle of Milliken's Bend. Gradually field commanders, with no more sanction than the absence of an official reprimand, presented the Union government with the accomplished fact of trained and fighting black units.[30]

In the North, state governors short of manpower began to enlist blacks. In July 1862, Congress dropped the requirement that state militia members be white. In January 1863, the Union secretary of war authorized states to enlist black troops. Gov. John A. Andrew of Massachusetts sent agents around the country and soon more than filled the Massachusetts quota. The famous Massachusetts 54th Regiment included 287 former slaves.[31]

Other states soon followed suit. In June 1863, Rhode Island organized a black artillery regiment, later sent to New Orleans. Pennsylvania resisted the

General Thomas recruiting black troops in Louisiana during the Civil War (*Library of Congress*)

recruitment of blacks until Gen. Robert E. Lee's invasion of the state in 1863; in the early summer of that year, a group of public-spirited citizens recruited blacks, eventually enrolling ten full black regiments.[32] In November, in the face of the governor's resistance, black leaders and other prominent New Yorkers finally got permission from the secretary of war to organize black troops. On March 5, 1864, the 20th U.S. Colored Troops received their flag at a ceremony in which President Charles King of Columbia University said, "When you put on the uniform and swear allegiance to the standard of the Union, you stand emancipated, regenerated and disenthralled—the peer of the proudest soldier in the land."[33] The regiment then embarked for New Orleans.

Ohio, Connecticut, Michigan, Illinois, Indiana, Iowa, and Kansas each raised one or more black regiments, but recruitment was slowed because they simply were not enough blacks in their states. Congress then authorized northern governors to recruit blacks in Confederate territory occupied by Union troops. The Union commanders there resisted, lest they lose the labor of the contrabands. So the results were unimpressive until the federal government took over.

In May 1863, the war department established the Bureau for Colored Troops to control recruitment and training of blacks. Thereafter, the U.S. government began intensive recruiting of black soldiers directly into federal service. In some cases, the Union resorted to impressment, particularly of outlyers, but by and large blacks volunteered, often despite vigorous local white opposition. Federal agents also recruited significant numbers from the black settlements in Canada.[34] Gen. Lorenzo Thomas signed up many blacks in the Mississippi Valley. Special commissioners were appointed to recruit in the border states, where "white opposition to their recruitment was at times so fierce that black men and boys had to run and fight their way past armed posses and other white gauntlets on their way to the Union enlistment stations. Many blacks did not make it, and were left hanging on trees by the road, while others paid the price of a sheared-off ear or a bloodied head to join the federal forces." Despite these dangers, in Tennessee and Kentucky an astonishing 40 to 50 percent of the eligible black male population eventually served in the military.[35]

Recruitment of blacks ended soon after Lee's surrender. By then, the number of enlisted blacks had soared to 178,975, or approximately one-eighth of the entire Union army.[36]

## *The Civil War: Black Soldiers Fighting for the Union*

The Union seemed to have little to offer black soldiers but blood, sweat, tears, and inequities. They could hardly look forward to promotion above the noncommissioned ranks. Only a few blacks were commissioned; usually whites officered black units.

Black regiments were not always properly equipped. Obsolete arms were issued them. Sometimes the bayonets would not fit their muskets. More often than white troops, blacks were assigned fatigue duty like unloading ships, filling sandbags, and draining marshes. They could not avoid feeling singled out for menial labor.

Medical care was inadequate throughout the Civil War armies, North and South, partly because of the relatively primitive state of medicine, partly because no provisions had been made before the war for nurses. Too many of their surgeons

Black troops outside barracks, Civil War (*Library of Congress*)

were incompetent even by the standards of the day, and black units were likely to receive the worst of the lot—for few white doctors were willing to serve with them, and only eight black physicians were commissioned in the Union army.

Black soldiers did not at first receive equal pay, so that often their families were reduced to poverty. Racial prejudice all too often manifested itself in the assumption that blacks, no matter how gallantly they served, somehow deserved less than whites. This attitude so galled some black soldiers that month after month they refused to take any pay at all rather than take less than whites. Others came near to mutiny. For instance, Sgt. William Walker of the 3d South Carolina Volunteers was court-martialed and shot because he ordered his company to stack arms and resign from an army that broke its contract with them.[37] Not until June 15, 1864, did Congress authorize equal pay for black troops.

Finally, blacks had every reason to fear being taken prisoner, for the Confederacy thought of them not as soldiers but as rebelling slaves and therefore not prisoners of war. Blacks could never hope to be included in prisoner exchanges. At one point, the Confederate congress ruled that captured blacks or those who gave aid and comfort to the enemy should be dealt with according to the laws of the state in which they were captured—that is, they would probably be killed or enslaved. In an effort to retaliate and protect black troops, Lincoln in July 1863 announced that for every Union soldier enslaved a Rebel prisoner of war would be sentenced to hard labor; for every Union soldier killed in violation of the laws of war, a Rebel would be executed. Such records as exist indicate that captured black Union soldiers in fact were seldom enslaved, but in some cases they were killed rather than taken prisoner, as in the notorious massacre at Fort Pillow in April 1864.[38]

## *The Civil War: Black Sailors Fighting for the Union*

As in earlier wars, black sailors fared better than black soldiers. In September 1861, the navy adopted a policy of signing up former slaves. Contrabands fled to Union warships, where many saw active duty as cooks, coal heavers, firemen, and gunners. Their service as pilots was particularly critical, whatever their ratings, for their years of experience as boatmen in the winding channels of South Carolina, Georgia, and the Sea Islands had familiarized them with the coastal waters. In May 1862, the young Carolina slave Robert Smalls, a seaman on the Confederate gunboat *Planter,* with a black crew and white officers, managed a daring escape. In the absence of the officers, he smuggled aboard his family and that of his brother, then under the Confederate flag steamed out to open sea, where he hoisted a flag of truce and turned the gunboat over to the Union ships blockading the Charleston harbor. His skills and courage made his personal services as valuable as the gunboat he surrendered; eventually, he rose to the rank of captain in the Union navy.

On the Mississippi too, contrabands, both women and men, surged onto riverboats and were put to work. Women contraband nurses were the first women in history to serve aboard American naval vessels. They were rated as regular crew members.[39]

Eventually, blacks constituted about a quarter of the Union seamen; perhaps overall as many as 29,000 blacks served in the navy.[40] On some Union vessels, the crews were predominantly black: that of the gunboat *Glide,* for example, comprised 30 contrabands and only eight whites. Black casualties were estimated at eight hundred, about a quarter of the total, and another 2,000 black seamen died of disease. At least four black sailors won the Navy Medal of Honor.[41]

Bigoted naval captains on some ships tried to reduce blacks to Jim Crow status and to make their lives as miserable as possible.[42] Nonetheless, the prospects for a black sailor were better than for a black soldier.

## *The Civil War: The Confederacy*

Driven by loyalty to their home states, by hope for better treatment after the hostilities, or by the habit of identifying their own interests with those of the white community, some free blacks volunteered their services to the Confederacy, whether as laborers or as soldiers. In New Orleans, they actually organized two regiments of "Native Guards," which were joined with the state militia. The Louisiana Native Guards remained in New Orleans after the Confederates were driven out and fought for the Union under the command of General Butler.[43] Usually, though, Southern officials accepted offers of labor but rejected those to bear arms.

Confederates used both slaves and free blacks to construct defenses even before the war. They needed them, for the white southern ethos disdained physical labor. But as owners discovered that slaves working on fortifications might be killed, lost, or incapacitated or that they might escape, the owners lost their enthusiasm for sending them, sometimes demanding compensation for loss or injury to them, sometimes sending them only if forced. Even if owners were willing to hire out slaves, military demands for labor drove the market sky high. Beginning in 1862, Confederate states enacted legislation to impress slaves, with compensation to owners, mostly for work on fortifications but also on salt works, mines, railroads, and haulage. Its enforcement caused complaint all during the war.[44] The question of the use of slaves in the war effort divided Confederates one from another, pitting "state officials against national officials, national officials against army officers, army officers against slaveholders, and slaveholders against nonslaveholders."[45]

Many Confederate officers took slaves along as their personal servants in the army. But arming blacks, free or slave, raised hackles in most southern souls. All whites had grown up in fear of black insurrections. Slave owners had regularly searched slave cabins for weapons. Moreover, white Confederate soldiers thought that fighting alongside blacks would demean them.

As the war dragged on, however, the Confederacy grew desperate for manpower. It had drained the South of able-bodied white men; it had little choice but to arm blacks. Union victories and the desertions of white Confederate soldiers forced the Confederate Congress in February 1864 to declare "free black men between eighteen and fifty universally liable to impressment."[46] Despite the advocacy of General Lee and other Confederate officers, not until mid-March 1865, with the war already as good as lost, could the Confederate Congress bring itself to enact the Negro Soldier Law to enlist slaves as soldiers.

However, throughout the war the Confederacy had to learn and relearn that slaves differed from other property in having wills of their own. Although their discontent and rage never erupted into a major insurrection, they damaged the war effort at every turn. Confederate troops wasted untold time and energy trying to recapture escaping slaves.

The South, long dependent on slave labor, could no longer rely on it. Thousands upon thousands of slaves fled behind Union lines or followed in the wake of Union armies. When they did not flee, they often shirked or ignored or resisted orders. Soldiers fighting in the Confederate armies heard from their relatives at home of the problems thus created, and sometimes they deserted to attend to their farms and plantations. When they did, they might find no able-bodied laborers at all, or they might find themselves "betrayed" by their slaves, who guided Yankees to their hidden treasure-troves. They might lock up their slaves at night, they might redouble their patrols, but their harshest punishments only hastened the stampede of slaves northward. Sometimes the owners' inability even to feed their slaves caused a complete breakdown in discipline. From day to day, the masters' power declined, and the slaves' expectations of freedom heightened. Unable to work their wills as in the past by physical force, owners began to bargain with slaves to persuade them to work at all, offering them better conditions, a share of the crops, or even wages. Other whites simply abandoned their plantations and some of their slaves.

As Ira Berlin notes, "To prevent the transformation of plantations into federal recruiting stations, Confederate commanders ordered able-bodied black men removed deep into the interior of the South or to Texas. But attempts to tear black men from their families, rather than ending unrest, further stimulated flight."[47] The efforts of hard-pressed masters to "refugee," to move their most valuable slaves to the interior or even to Texas, motivated more slaves to escape, while those left behind on the abandoned plantations began to farm independently, establishing communities sympathetic to fugitives and to Union scouts.

By November 1864, the situation had grown so grave that Pres. Jefferson Davis proposed that the Confederate Congress consider emancipation.

## Chronicle of Events

**1656**
Massachusetts repeals the law of 1652 admitting blacks to military training.

**1704**
The South Carolina legislature passes an act "for raising and enlisting such slaves as shall be thought serviceable to this Province in times of Alarms." It is reenacted in 1708.

**1708**
In the colonial South, a law requires each militia captain "to enlist traine up and bring into the field for each white, one able Slave armed with gun or lance."

**1715**
Black slaves constitute part of the military force that in South Carolina meets and routs the Yamasee Indians.

**1755**
The Georgia legislature authorizes the enlistment of slaves in the militia under carefully controlled conditions.

**1760**
New Jersey prohibits the enlistment in the militia of "any slaves who are so for terms of life" without leave of their masters.

**1768**
British captain Wilson urges Boston slaves to rise, declaring that British troops have come to free them.

**1770**
*March 5:* In the "Boston Massacre," British soldiers shoot down several colonists, including Crispus Attucks, allegedly an escaped slave.

### *The American Revolution (1775–1783)*

**1775**
*April:* Blacks are among the minutemen battling the British at Lexington and Concord.

*May:* The Massachusetts Committee on Public Safety excludes slaves from the army being raised by the Continental Congress but permits the enlistment of free blacks.

*June 17:* Former slave Peter Salem is among the blacks who fight the British at the Battle of Bunker Hill; Peter Salem shoots British major Pitcairn.

*July 9:* Gen. George Washington announces a ban on further enlistment of blacks, slave or free, a policy endorsed by the Continental Congress in October.

*November 7:* Gov. Lord Dunmore of Virginia urges male slaves to desert their masters and join the British forces, promising good treatment and freedom.

*December 31:* General Washington rescinds the ban on the recruitment of free blacks, ordering their acceptance into the Continental Army.

**1777**
The states begin to admit nonwhite men into the army as draft substitutes and volunteers. Massachusetts leads the way early in the year by including blacks among those draft-eligible.

*July:* Prince, a black soldier with Colonel Barton captures British major general Prescott.

*October:* The Connecticut General Assembly authorizes the enlistment of slaves as substitutes for their masters, if the masters consent.

**1778**
*February:* The Rhode Island legislature votes to raise two battalions of slaves.

*August 29:* Black soldiers distinguish themselves at the battle of Rhode Island.

**1779**
*March 29:* The Continental Congress recommends to South Carolina and Georgia that they raise and train 3,000 slaves for service with the Continental Army, with the promise of emancipation at the end of the war. Neither state adopts the plan.

*June 30:* Gen. Sir Henry Clinton, British commander in chief, offers slaves freedom if they desert their masters, and he invites male slaves to join his forces.

**1781**
*March 20:* The New York General Assembly authorizes the raising of two regiments of black troops.

*May 14:* Black soldiers defend Colonel Greene at Points Bridge, New York.

**1783**
Virginia emancipates Virginia slaves who have served as soldiers in the Revolutionary War, effective at war's end.

**1785**
"Negroes, Indians and Mulattoes" are "exempted" from the army organized under the Articles of Confederation.

**1786**
*October:* The Virginia legislature votes to free James Armistead in recognition of his service as spy during the Revolutionary War, his master to be compensated from the state treasury.

**1792**
Congress excludes blacks from the U.S. military services.

## War of 1812 (1812–1815)

**1812**
The British transport many American slaves who seek refuge with them to the Bahamas, Bermuda, Nova Scotia, and New Brunswick.

**1813**
Black sailors contribute to Admiral Perry's victory against the British fleet in the Battle of Lake Erie.

**1814**
Blacks Richard Allen, James Forten, and Absalom Jones raise a force of 2,500 black men to protect Philadelphia against the British.

*April 4:* British Vice Adm. Sir Alexander Cochrane invites American slaves to take refuge with the British, promising an opportunity to become free British subjects and settlement in one of the British possessions in North America or the West Indies.

Integrated troops of the Battle of New Orleans, War of 1812 (*Library of Congress*)

*September 21:* Gen. Andrew Jackson invites the "Free Colored [male] inhabitants of Louisiana" to enlist in his forces.

*October 24:* The New York legislature authorizes the raising of two black regiments.

**1815**

*January 14:* The troops (including black soldiers) of Gen. Andrew Jackson defeat the British decisively at the Battle of New Orleans, two weeks after the treaty ending the war is signed in Ghent on December 24, 1814.

**1817**

The First Seminole War begins. Fugitive slaves support the Indians.

**1835**

The Second Seminole War begins. Black forces fight alongside the Indians against the U.S. Army.

**1857**

New Hampshire and Vermont repeal their laws against black enlistments in the state militia.

## *The Civil War (1861–1865)*

**1861**

*February:* In Montgomery, Alabama, the seceded states adopt the constitution of the Confederate States of America and elect Jefferson Davis provisional president.

*April 12:* The Civil War begins when Confederates fire upon Fort Sumter in Charleston, South Carolina. Free blacks respond to President Lincoln's call for 75,000 volunteers but are rejected.

*April 23:* Black men meeting in Boston offer to fight for the Union.

*May:* At Fortress Monroe in Virginia, Gen. Benjamin Butler declares fugitive slaves "contraband of war," refuses to surrender them, and frees them to be employed by the Union army.

*August 6:* Congress passes the First Confiscation Act, which provides that all property used in support of the rebellion, specifically including slaves, is subject to prize and capture.

*August 30:* Gen. John C. Frémont declares martial law in Missouri and frees slaves taken from disloyal owners. President Lincoln orders Frémont to modify his emancipation order to conform to existing law.

*September:* Secretary of the Navy Gideon Welles authorizes enlistment of fugitive slaves for naval service when that service is useful.

*October 14:* Secretary of War Simon Cameron authorizes Gen. Thomas W. Sherman to employ fugitive slaves as Union soldiers if needed in his campaign against the coast of South Carolina.

*December:* Secretary of War Simon Cameron recommends to Lincoln that slaves should be emancipated and armed. Lincoln disagrees.

**1862**

*March:* Gen. David Hunter begins to issue certificates of emancipation to all slaves who have been employed by the Confederacy.

*March 13:* An addition to the Articles of War prohibits Union forces to aid in the capture or return of runaway slaves of disloyal masters.

*April:* Gen. David Hunter, without authorization, raises a black regiment at Hilton Head, South Carolina. It is disbanded in August after the war

The gunboat *Planter,* run out of Charleston, South Carolina, and surrendered to the Union navy by Robert Smalls, May 1862 (*Engraving from* Harper's Weekly, *1862, courtesy of the U.S. Naval Historical Center*)

department refuses to pay or equip the regiment.

*April:* A black gunner at the Battle of New Orleans distinguishes himself and is awarded the Congressional Medal of Honor.

*May:* Slaves Robert and John Smalls seize the Confederate steamer Planter, run it out of Charleston harbor, and deliver it to the Union navy.

*May:* Gen. David Hunter declares free the slaves within the Department of the South. President Lincoln countermands this order, reserving to himself the power to free slaves.

*May:* Gen. David Hunter's efforts to recruit black men into the army provoke a national debate.

*July 17:* Passage of the Second Confiscation Act authorizes the president to employ "persons of African descent" in any capacity to suppress the rebellion. Slaves owned by disloyal masters are declared "forever free of their servitude" as soon as they cross Union lines. Slaves seeking refuge in Union army camps are to be protected against recapture and enslavement, welcomed, and put to work. The act also forbids military personnel to surrender fugitive slaves to disloyal owners.

Four fugitives who sailed the steamer *Planter* to the Union navy (*Library of Congress*)

*July 17:* Passage of the Militia Act authorizes the president "to receive into the service of the United States, for the purpose of constructing entrenchments, or performing camp service, or any other labor, or any military or naval service for which they may be found competent, persons of African descent." They will be paid $10 a month, of which three dollars will be deducted for clothing.

*August:* Gen. Benjamin Butler in New Orleans accepts into his command existing "Native Guard" regiments composed of free black soldiers and begins to recruit free blacks and former slaves for additional regiments.

*August 6:* President Lincoln agrees to the recruitment of black men as laborers with the army.

*August 25:* Congress authorizes recruitment of black soldiers in South Carolina.

*September:* Three regiments, constituting the "Black Brigade," are organized in Cincinnati to construct fortifications but are neither armed nor given uniforms. They are disbanded when the threat of Confederate attack ends.

*September 27:* The 1st Regiment of Louisiana Native Guards is mustered into Federal service, followed on October 12 by the 2d Regiment and on November 24 by the 3d Regiment.

*October:* The 1st Regiment of the Kansas Colored Volunteers, recruited by James Lane, engages in combat at Island Mount, Missouri.

*October 3:* Virginia authorizes the impressment of slaves to work on fortifications and for other military labor. Other Confederate states soon follow suit.

*October 11:* The Confederate Congress exempts from conscription one white man on each plantation with more than 20 slaves.

*November 15:* Company A, 1st South Carolina Volunteers, is organized—the first black regiment raised with full War Department authorization.

*December 23:* Confederate president Davis orders that captured black Union soldiers and their white officers not be treated as prisoners of war but remanded to state authorities for disposition according to state law.

**1863**

*January 1:* Pres. Lincoln issues the Emancipation Proclamation, freeing all slaves "in areas still in rebellion," and announces plans to recruit black soldiers and sailors throughout the North and in Union-occupied states of the Confederacy.

*January 13:* The 1st Regiment of the Kansas Colored Volunteers is mustered into Federal service.

*January 31:* The 1st South Carolina Colored Volunteers is mustered into Federal service.

*March 25:* Union general Lorenzo Thomas is sent to the Mississippi Valley to recruit as many black regiments as possible.

*March 26:* The Confederate Congress authorizes military commanders to impress private property, including slaves, for public service.

*April 30:* The Confederate Congress affirms that black soldiers captured by the Confederate army will be dealt with according to the laws of the state in which they are seized, not as prisoners of war.

*May:* Organization of the 54th Massachusetts Colored Infantry, the first black regiment in the free states, is completed.

*May 22:* The Federal War Department establishes the Bureau of Colored Troops to regulate and supervise the enlistment of black soldiers and the selection of white officers to command them.

*May 27:* The black soldiers of the 1st Louisiana Native Guards distinguish themselves in the battle of Port Hudson, the last Confederate fortification on the lower Mississippi. They fight valorously and sustain great losses.

*June:* Recruitment of black soldiers begins in Pennsylvania.

*June 7:* In the Battle of Milliken's Bend, a Union camp on the Mississippi, black soldiers repel a Confederate attack, defeating 2,000 Texans in hand-to-hand combat.

*June 14:* The black 14th Rhode Island Heavy Artillery Regiment is organized.

*July 18:* The 54th Massachusetts Colored Infantry leads the assault on Fort Wagner, South Carolina, losing half its men. In this battle Sgt. William H. Carney wins the Congressional Medal of Honor.

*July 30:* President Lincoln threatens retaliation if Confederates enslave or kill captured black soldiers.

*October 30:* The War Department orders recruitment of black soldiers in Maryland, Missouri, and Tennessee, owners loyal to the Union to be compensated for their slaves.

*November:* The Connecticut General Assembly authorizes the recruitment and training of black troops.

*November:* The regimental quota of the 5th U.S. Colored Regiment in Ohio is completed.

*December 25:* Former slave Robert Blake earns the Congressional Medal of Honor for his conduct as a powder-boy on the U.S.S. Marblehead on the Stono River, in South Carolina.

**1864**

Black Union soldiers at Vicksburg complain that their wives have been sent to an unknown destination.

By this time, ten full black regiments have been mustered in.

*January 2:* Confederate general Patrick R. Cleburne and a group of fellow officers in the Army of Tennessee propose "that we immediately commence training a large reserve of the most courageous of our slaves."

*February:* The Union failure to award black soldiers equal pay provokes near mutiny in the 54th Massachusetts and other black regiments.

*February 17:* The Confederate Congress authorizes the employment of 20,000 slaves at the same wages as privates and eventually enrolls one-fifth of all black males aged 18–45. By this act, the Confederate Congress intends "to increase the efficiency of the Army by employment of free negroes and slaves in certain capacities," also empowering the secretary of war to impress an additional 20,000 if need be.

*April:* Union army surgeon A. W. Kelly, on grounds of public health, tries to expel from Natchez all ex-slaves except those employed by and living with whites. Black soldiers swear revenge, some desert, and within a few weeks Kelly is relieved.

*April 12:* Confederate troops commanded by Gen. Nathan Bedford Forrest massacre captured black Union soldiers after the Battle of Fort Pillow, Tennessee.

*June 7:* The Union recruits male slaves in Kentucky into the army with or without the consent of their owners, but it compensates loyal owners.

*June 15:* Congress passes the Equalization Bill, granting black Union troops the same pay as white.

*July:* Black infantrymen and cavalry fight in the sieges of Petersburg and Richmond. Thirteen win the Medal of Honor for valor.

*December:* Two brigades of black troops contribute to the Union victory at the battle of Nashville.

**1865**

*January:* Gen. Robert E. Lee recommends the employment of blacks in the Confederate army.

*February 18:* Men of the 21st U.S. Colored Infantry are the first Union troops to enter Charleston after its evacuation by the Confederate army.

*March 13:* The Confederate Congress passes and President Davis signs the "Negro Soldier Bill," authorizing the enlistment of slaves as soldiers. Emancipation, however, requires the consent of the owners and of the states of their residence.

*April 9:* The Civil War effectively ends when General Lee surrenders his Army of Northern Virginia to Gen. Ulysses S. Grant at Appomattox Court House, Virginia. The last Confederate troops surrender May 10.

*May:* Union recruitment of black soldiers is terminated.

*July:* Congress creates six black regiments, with white officers, as part of the regular army.

## EYEWITNESS TESTIMONY

### *Colonial Period*

We account all generally from Sixteen to Sixty that are healthfull and strong bodys, both House-holders and Servants fit to beare Armes, *except Negroes* and slaves, whom wee arme not.

*Massachusetts governor Bradstreet, 1680, in Williams,* History *1:195.*

[Any slaves who] manfully Behave themselves in fight with the enemy . . . so as to deserve public Notice . . . shall be entitled to and receive from the public Tresury Yearly, and every Yr. A Livery Coat, and pair of Breeches, made of good red Negro Cloth turn'd up with Blue, and a Black Hat and pair of Black Shoes, and shall that Day in every Year (during their Lives) on which such Action Shall be perform'd be free'd and exempted from all personal Labour & Service to their owner or Manager.

*Georgia legislature, in Higginbotham,* In the Matter of Color, *260–61.*

### *The Revolutionary War*

Resolved, That it is the opinion of this committee, as the contest now between Great Britain and the colonies respects the liberties and privileges of the latter, which the colonies are determined to maintain, that the admission of any persons, as soldiers, into the army now raising, but such as are freeman, will be inconsistent with the principals [sic] that are supported, and reflect dishonor on this colony; and that no slaves be admitted into this army upon any consideration whatever.

*Committee of Safety of Massachusetts, May 29, 1775, in Williams,* History *1:334.*

*Resolved,* That the colonels of the several regiments of militia throughout the Colony have leave to enroll such a number of able male slaves, to be employed as pioneers and laborers, as public exigencies may require; and that a daily pay of seven shillings and sixpence be allowed for the service of each such slave while actually employed.

*South Carolina legislature, 1775, in Wilson,* Black Phalanx, *42.*

TO THE HONORABLE GENERAL COURT OF THE MASSACHUSETTS' BAY.

The subscribers beg leave to report to your Honorable House, (which we do in justice to the character of so brave a man), that under our own observation, we declare that a negro man named Salem Poor, of Col. Frye's regiment, Capt. Ame's company, in the late battle at Charleston, behaved like an experienced officer, as well as an excellent soldier. . . . [I]n the person of this said negro, centers a brave and gallant soldier. The reward due to so great and distinguished a character, we submit to Congress.
[14 signatures]
Cambridge, Dec. 5, 1775.

*Wilson,* Black Phalanx, *37.*

Your Lordship will observe by my letter, No. 34, that I have been endeavoring to raise two regiments here—one of white people, the other of black. The former goes on very slowly, but the latter very well, and would have been in great forwardness, had not a fever crept in amongst them, which carried off a great many very fine fellows.

*Lord Dunmore, royal governor of Virginia to the secretary of state in London, March 30, 1776, in Wilson,* Black Phalanx, *45.*

Whereas, for the preservation of the rights and liberties of the United States, it is necessary that the whole powers of government should be exerted in recruiting the Continental battalions; and whereas, His Excellency Gen. Washington hath enclosed to this state a proposal made to him by Brigadier General Varnum, to enlist into the two battalions, raising by this state, such slaves as should be willing to enter into the service; and whereas, history affords us frequent precedents of the wisest, the freest, and bravest nations having liberated their slaves, and enlisted them as soldiers to fight in defence of their country; and also whereas, the enemy, with a great force, have taken possession of the capital, and of a greater part of this state; and this state is obliged to raise a very considerable number of troops for its own immediate defence, where it is in a manner rendered impossible for this state to furnish recruits for the said two battalions, without adopting the said measure so recommended.

It is voted and resolved, that every able-bodied negro, mulatto, or Indian man slave, in this state, may enlist into either of the said two battalions, to serve during the continuance of the present war with Great Britain.

*It is further Voted and Resolved,* That every slave so enlisting shall, upon his passing muster before Col. Christopher Greene, be immediately discharged from the service of his master or mistress, and be absolutely free, as though he had never been encumbered with any kind of servitude or slavery.

*Rhode Island legislature, 1778, in Williams,* History *1:347–48.*

Whereas the enemy have adopted a practice of enrolling Negroes among their Troops, I do hereby give notice That all Negroes taken in arms, or upon any military Duty, shall be purchased for [the public service at] a stated Price; the money to be paid to the Captors.

But I do most strictly forbid any Person to sell or claim Right over any Negroe, the property of a Rebel, who may take Refuge with any part of this Army: And I do promise to every Negroe who shall desert the Rebel Standard, full security to follow within these Lines, any Occupation which he shall think proper.

*The Phillipsburg Proclamation, issued by the British commander in chief, June 30, 1779, in Williams,* History *1:357.*

[My slave] sometime in the month of July 1776, made his elopement and afterwards . . . entered the service of the United States in the 14th Virginia regiment, under the fictitious name of William Ferguson, and served until discharged from thence by Col. William Davies.

*Virginia slave owner asking compensation for his slave, October 22, 1789, in Johnston,* Race Relations, *14.*

I. *Whereas* . . . during the course of the war, many persons in this state had caused their slaves to enlist in certain regiments or corps raised within the same . . . as substitutes for free persons, whose lot or duty it was to serve in such regiments or corps, at the same time representing to such recruiting officers that the slaves so enlisted by their direction and concurrence were free; and . . . that on the expiration of the term of enlistment of such slaves that the former owners have attempted again to force them to return to a state of servitude, contrary to the principles, and to their own solemn promise.

II. And whereas it appears just and reasonable that all persons enlisted as aforesaid . . . have thereby of course contributed towards the establishment of American liberty and independence, should enjoy blessings of freedom as a reward for their toils and labours; *Be it therefore enacted,* that each and every slave, who by the appointment and direction of his owner hath enlisted in any regiment or corps raised within this state, either on continental or state establishment, . . . and hath served faithfully during the term of such enlistment, or hath been discharged from such service by some officer duly authorized to grant such discharge, shall . . . be fully and compleatly emancipated. . . .

*New York legislature, 1783, in Wilson,* Black Phalanx, *68–69.*

To The General Assembly of the State of North Carolina

The Petitioner of Ned Griffin a Man of mixed Blood Humbley Saieth that a Small space of Time before the battle of Gilford a certain William Kitchen then in the Service of his countrey as a Soldier Deserted from his line for which he was Turned in to the Continental Service to serve as the Law Directs—Your petitioner was then a Servant to William Griffin and was purchased by the said Kitchen for the purpose of Serving in His place, with a Solom Assurance that if he your Petitioner would faithfully serve the Term of Time that the said Kitchen was Returned for he should be a free man—Upon which said Promise and Assurance your Petitioner Consented to enter in to the Continental Service in said Kitchens Behalf and was Received by Colo: James Armstrong At Martinborough as a free Man[.] Your Petitioner further saieth that . . . at the Time that I was Received into Service by said Colo: Armstrong said Kitchen Openly Declared me to be free Man—The Faithfull purformance of the above agreement will appear from my Discharge,—some Time after your Petitioners Return he was Seized upon by said Kitchen and Sold to a Certain Abner Roberson who now holds me as a Servant—Your Petitioner therefore thinks that by Contract and merit he is Intitled to his Freedom. . . .

N Carolina his<br>
Edgecomb County Ned X Griffin<br>
April 4th 1784 mark

Documentary History of the Negro People *1: Doc. 4-b.*

In the beginning of the late war which gave America freedom, your petitioner shouldered his musket and repaired to the American standard, regardless of invitations trumpeted up by British proclamations for the slaves to emancipate themselves by becoming the assassins of their owners. Your petitioner avoided the rock that too many of his colour were shipwrecked on. He was taught that the war was levied on Americans not for the emancipation of the blacks, but for the subjugation of the whites, and he thought that the number of bondmen ought not to be augmented. Under these impressions he did actually campaign in both armies—in the American army as a soldier, in the British as a spy.

*Virginia petition, October 9, 1792, in Johnston,* Race Relations, *12.*

From an estimate I made at that time, on the best information I could collect, I supposed the State of Virginia lost [to the British], under Lord Cornwallis' hand, that year, about thirty thousand slaves; and that, of these twenty-seven thousand died of the small-pox and camp fever; the rest were partly sent to the West Indies, and exchanged for rum, sugar, coffee and fruit; and partly sent to New York, from whence they went, at the peace, either to Nova Scotia or to England.

*Thomas Jefferson, on the treatment of blacks who went with the British army, in Wilson,* Black Phalanx, *70.*

## Indian Wars

At fifteen, I was hired to Capt. George Smith, who volunteered to go to Tippecanoe [scene of an 1811 battle with Tecumseh]. I was a fifer in his company. The freedom of myself, Moses, and some others was promised us on our return. But the last time I saw Moses, he was bowed down in hellish slavery in Little Rock, Ark., and I had the misfortune to have to pay N. eighteen hundred dollars for my freedom.

*J. C. Brown, in* Four Fugitive Slave Narratives, *168.*

The [maroon] Negroes, from the commencement of the Florida [Second Seminole] war, have, for their numbers, been the most formidable foe, more bloodthirsty, active, and revengeful than the Indian. . . . Ten resolute negroes, with a knowledge of the country, are sufficient to desolate the frontier, from one extent to the other.

*U.S. Army officer, about 1840, in Blassingame,* Slave Community, *124.*

## War of 1812

Whereas it has been represented to me that many persons now resident in the United States have expressed a desire to withdraw therefrom with a view to entering His Majesty's service, or of being received as free settlers into some of His Majesty's colonies.

This is therefore to give notice that all persons who may be disposed to migrate from the United States, will with their families, be received on board of His Majesty's ship or vessels of War, or at the military posts that may be established upon or near the coast of the United States, when they will have their choice of either entering into His Majesty's sea or land force, or of being sent as free settlers to the British possessions in North America or the West Indies where they will meet with due encouragement.

Given under my hand at Bermuda this second day of April 1814, by command of Vice Admiral

Alex Cochrane

*In Grant, "Black Immigrants into Nova Scotia," 264–65.*

Our Negroes are flocking to the enemy from all quarters, which they convert into troops, vindictive and rapicious [*sic*]—with a minute knowledge of every byepath. They leave us as spies upon our strength, and they return upon us as guides and soldiers and incendiaries. . . . The example too which is held out in these bands of armed negroes and the weakness of the resistance which as yet has been made to oppose them, must have a strong effect upon those blacks which have not as yet been able to escape.

*Virginian J. P. Hungerford, August 3, 1814, in Grant, "Black Immigrants into Nova Scotia," 266.*

SECT. 6. *And be it further enacted,* That it shall be lawful for any able-bodied slave, with the written assent of his master or mistress, to enlist into the said corps; and the master or mistress of such slave shall be entitled to the pay and bounty allowed him for his service; and, further, that the said slave, at the time of receiving his discharge, shall be deemed and adjudged to have been legally manumitted from that time, and his said master or mistress shall not thenceforward be liable for his maintenance.

*New York law, October 24, 1814, in Wilson,* History *2: 23–25.*

## *Texas War of Independence*

Fourteen Negro slaves [from Texas] with their families came to me this day and I sent them free to Victoria.

*Mexican general Jose Urrea, April 3, 1836, in Campbell,* Empire, *44.*

## *The Civil War: The Confederacy*

Some of our people are fearful that when a large portion of our fighting men are taken from the country, that large numbers of our negroes aided by emissaries will ransack portions of the country, kill numbers of our inhabitants, and make their way to the black republicans. There is no doubt but that numbers of them believe that Lincoln's intention is to set them all free. Then, to counteract this idea, and make them assist in whipping the black republicans, which by the by would be the best thing that could be done, could they not be incorporated into our armies, say ten or twenty placed promiscuously in each company?

*John J. Cheatham, Confederate patriot, to the secretary of war, May 4, 1861, in* Freedom *2: Doc. 114.*

Genl Magruder directs that you will make a call upon the citizens of Gloucester, Middlesex and Mathews counties for one half of their male force of slaves to finish the works around Gloucester Point—They will be allowed fifty cents a day and a ration for each negro man during the time he is at work. . . . The free negroes will be impressed if they refuse to come and a force will be sent to bring them in. . . .

*Orders to the Confederate commander at Gloucester Point, Virginia, July 28, 1861, in* Freedom *1: Doc. 260A.*

According to instructions which you gave me by telegraph, I have detached militia men who are overseeing on plantations to do police and patrol duty upon the same. . . . [T]here is a great disposition among the Negroes to be insubordinate, and to run away and go to the federals. Within the last 12 months we have had to hang some 40 for plotting an insurrection, and there has been about that number put in irons.

*The provost marshal of Adams County to the governor of Mississippi, July 17, 1862, in Aptheker, "Notes on Slave Conspiracies in Confederate Mississippi," 76.*

Tyrone died this morning about four o'clock—another death from the sickness contracted on the batteries in Savannah last spring. Three out of the seven men [slaves sent to work on the fortifications] have died.

*Rev. Charles C. Jones, October 2, 1862, in* Children of Pride, *972.*

My name is John Parker. . . . [When] the excitement about the expected battle at Bull Run arose, [t]hey [the Confederates] said that all the colored people must then come and fight. I arrived at the Junction two days before the action commenced. They immediately placed me in one of the batteries. There were four colored men in our battery, I don't know how many there were in the others. We opened fire about ten o'clock on the morning of Sunday the 21st; couldn't see the Yankees at all and only fired at random. . . . My work was to hand the balls and swab out the cannon; in this we took turns. The officers aimed this gun; we fired grape shot. The balls from the Yankee guns fell thick all around. In one battery a shell burst and killed twenty, the rest ran. . . . We wish to our hearts that the Yankees would whip [the Confederates], and we would have run over to their side but our officers would have shot us if we had made the attempt.

Reading Journal, *quoted in* Douglass' Monthly *(March 1862), in McPherson,* Negro's Civil War, *25, 28.*

[S]lavery is a source of great strength to the enemy in a purely military point of view, by supplying him with an army from our granaries. . . . All along the lines slavery is comparatively valueless to us for labor, but of great and increasing worth to the enemy for information. It is an omnipresent spy system, pointing out our valuable men to the enemy, revealing our positions, purposes, and resources. . . .

Adequately to meet the causes which are now threatening ruin to our country, we propose . . . that we immediately commence training a large reserve of the most courageous of our slaves, and further that we guarantee freedom within a reasonable time to every slave in the South who shall remain true to the Confederacy in this war.

*Proposal of a group of Confederate officers, January 2, 1864, in McPherson,* Negro's Civil War, *245–46.*

The time has come to put into the army every able-bodied Negro as a soldier. . . . He must play an important part in the war. He caused the fight, he will have his portion of the burden to bear.

*Governor Allen of Louisiana to Confederate secretary of war, September 1864, in Du Bois,* Black Reconstruction, *117.*

Until our white population shall prove insufficient for the armies we require and can afford to keep the field, to employ as a soldier the Negro, who has merely been trained to labor, and as a laborer under the white man accustomed from his youth to the use of firearms, would scarcely be deemed wise or advantageous by any; and this is the question before us. But should the alternative ever be presented of subjugation or of the employment of the slave as a soldier, there seems no reason to doubt what should be our decision.

*President Jefferson Davis to the Confederate Congress, November 1864, in Du Bois,* Black Reconstruction, *117.*

For a year past I have seen that the period was fast approaching when we should be compelled to use every resource at our command for the defense of our liberties. . . . The negroes will certainly be made to fight against us if not armed for our defense. The drain of that source of our strength is steadily fatal, and irreversible by any other expedient than that of arming the slaves as an auxiliary force.

I further agree with you that if they are to fight for our freedom they are entitled to their own. . . .

General Lee . . . is strongly in favor of our using the negroes for defense, and emancipating them, if necessary, for that purpose. Can you not yourself write a series of articles in your papers, always urging this point as the true issue, viz, is it better for the negro to fight for us or against us?

*Letter from the Confederate secretary of war, December 21, 1864, in McPherson,* Negro's Civil War, *247–48.*

Slavery is lost or will be, & we had better as well emancipate if we can make anything by it now. . . . We can certainly live without negroes better than with yankees and without negroes both.

*James Branch O'Bryan, January 20, 1865, in McPherson,* For Cause, *231.*

Mother, I did not volunteer my services to fight for a free negroes country but to fight for a free white mans country & I do not think I love my country well enough to fight with [alongside] black soldiers.

*Confederate sergeant, February 18, 1865, reacting to the Confederate decision to recruit slaves as soldiers and offer them freedom at war's end, in McPherson,* For Cause, *172.*

## *The Civil War: The Union—Contrabands*

The [Union] guard on the bridge across the Anacostia arrested a negro who attempted to pass the sentries on the Maryland side. He seemed to feel confident that he was among friends, for he made no concealment of his character and purpose. He said he had walked sixty miles, and was going North. He was very much surprised and disappointed when he was taken into custody, and informed that he would be sent back to his master. He is now in the guard-house, and answers freely all questions relating to his weary march. Of course, such an arrest excites much comment among the men. Nearly all are restive under the thought of action as slave-catchers.

New York Herald, *1861(?), quoted in Brown,* American Rebellion, *57.*

In a loyal State I would put down a servile insurrection. In a state of rebellion I would confiscate that which was used to oppose my arms, and take all that property, which constituted the wealth of that State, and furnished the means by which the war is prosecuted, besides being the cause of the war; and if, in so doing, it should be objected that human beings were brought to the free enjoyment of life, liberty, and the pursuit of happiness, such objection might not require much consideration.

*Gen. Benjamin Butler, July 30, 1861, in Dumond,* Antislavery, *370.*

You will . . . avail yourself of the services of any persons, whether fugitives from labor or not, who may offer them to the National Government. You will employ such persons in such services as they may be fitted for—either as ordinary employees, or, if special circumstances seem to require it, in any other capacity, with such organization (in squads, companies, or otherwise) as you may deem most beneficial to the service[,] . . . this, however, not being a general arming of them for military service. . . . You will assure all loyal masters that

Congress will provide just compensation to them for the loss of the services of the persons so employed.

*Secretary of war to Gen. Thomas W. Sherman, October 14, 1861, in Cornish,* Sable Arm, *19.*

We had fifteen miles to go before we could get to the Federal blockade, and on the way we had to pass a rebel gunboat and a fort. I meant to wait till the tide fell, so that the gunboat would go back in the Cut where she lay at low water, but I did not see her till I got close upon her, and heard the men talking, and looked up and saw them on the deck. I kept close to the marsh, so they might not see me, and managed to get round the point. About a mile and a half above this point was the fort which I had to pass. I passed the fort in the same way as I passed the boat. After I got a little beyond, I crossed on to the same shore that she was, and after I got a little way along the shore, day broke as clear as could be. I looked back and could not see the fort, and I knew I was out of their reach.

About two hours and a half later we reached the Federal gunboats in Stono river. When I got in sight of the Union boats, I raised a white flag, and when I came near, they cheered me, and pointed to the flagship Pawnee. There I had the pleasure of a breakfast of hot coffee, ham, nice butter, and all under the American flag—all strange things in Charleston. There I gave the Almighty praise and glory for delivering me so far. On board the Pawnee I told the Captain about the Charleston harbor, and how the vessels run the blockade, and the next day but one they took two vessels from the information I gave them. Then we were put on board a transport vessel for Port Royal and reached there in safety. Capt. Elwell, Chief Quartermaster, gave me a piece of land, and I built me a little house. I waited on Capt. Elwell, and my wife washed for him and other officers. My

Contrabands building stockades, Civil War (*Library of Congress*)

wife used to sew for Gen. Hunter's wife, and about a week before we came North Gen. Hunter gave me a paper that made me forever free.

*William Summerson in the* National Anti-Slavery Standard, *December 27, 1862, quoted in Blassingame,* Slave Community, *701–2.*

A few days after the arrival of the contrabands, their services were needed in an important expedition in the interior. These negroes, upon being told what was wanted of them, although knowing that the enterprise would be attended with the greatest danger, and would require the utmost skill, volunteered their services. . . . [T]hey succeeded in penetrating the enemy's country, arresting three very important rebels, and conveying them to the fleet. In the return march, the rebels complained at their being made to walk so far and so fast; but Bob, the captain of the company, would occasionally be heard urging them along after this style: "March along dar, massa; no straggling to de rear: come, close up dar, close up dar! we're boss dis time."

*Brown,* American Rebellion, *213.*

There followed me back to Corinth, almost the entire Negro population of that valley. They came in every conceivable conveyance; from the master's private carriage to a wheelbarrow and they hitched to the conveyances, carts, haywagons, and sometimes a cow and a horse, and sometimes a fine team of horses, or a cow and an ox. Hundreds were on foot with their household goods packed on a mule, a horse, or a cow. They made a picturesque column, much larger than my command. At night our camp spread over a large territory. . . . We all arrived safely at Corinth, where I established the great contraband camp and guarded it by two companies of Negro soldiers that I uniformed, armed, and equipped without any authority to. . . .

*Union general Grenville Dodge, 1863, in Horton, "Submitting to the 'Shadow of Slavery,' " 130.*

Losing patience at the failure of all orders and exhortations to these poor people [slaves] to stay at home, General Davis . . . ordered the pontoon bridge at Ebenezer Creek to be taken up before the refugees who were following that corps had crossed, so as to leave them on the further bank of the unfordable stream and thus disembarrass the marching troops. . . . The poor refugees had their hearts so set on liberation, and the fear of falling into the hands of the Confederate cavalry was so great, that, with wild wailings and cries, the great crowd rushed, like a stampeded drove of cattle, into the water, those who could not swim as well as those who could, and many were drowned in spite of the earnest efforts of the soldiers to help them. . . . [T]here were many ignorant, simple souls to whom it was literally preferable to die freemen rather than to live slaves.

*Cox,* March, *37–38, in Bell,* Major Butler's Legacy, *382–83.*

## *The Civil War: The Union—Recruitment of Blacks*

The Department finds it necessary to adopt a regulation with respect to the large and increasing number of persons of color, commonly known as contraband, now subsisted at the navy yard and on board ships of war. . . . You are therefore authorized, when their services can be made useful to enlist them for the naval service, under the same forms and regulations as apply to other enlistments. They will be allowed, however, no higher rating than "boys" [apprentices, the lowest rank in the Navy], at a compensation of $10 per month and one ration a day.

*Secretary of the navy, September 20, 1861, in Aptheker, "The Negro in the Union Navy," 175–76.*

Recruiting poster, Civil War (*Library of Congress*)

The negroes are mistaken if they think white men can fight for them while they stay at home. We have opened the pathway. We don't want to threaten, but we have been saying that you would fight, and if you won't fight we will make you.

*Abolitionist state senator James Lane, recruiting speech in Leavenworth, Kansas, August 6, 1862, in Castel, "Civil War Kansas," 132–33.*

In these journeys through the country the recruiting officer often met with strange experiences. Recruits were taken wherever found, and as their earthly possessions usually consisted of but what they wore upon their backs, they required no time to settle their affairs. The laborer in the field would throw down his hoe or quit his plow and march away with the guard, leaving his late owner looking after him in speechless amazement. On one occasion the writer met a planter on the road, followed by two of his slaves, each driving a loaded wagon. The usual questions were asked and the whilom slaves joined the recruiting party, leaving their teams and late master standing in the highway.

*Historian of the 7th New York Regiment, in Wilson,* Black Phalanx, *130–31.*

If I could have carried a gun, I would have gone personally, but I thought it was my duty to talk to the people. I told them "that the young and able-bodied ought to go into the field like men, that they should stand up to the rack, and help the government." My oldest son, Tom, who was in California, enlisted on a man-of-war in San Francisco, and I suppose he must have been killed, as I have not heard from him since that time.

My son-in-law, Wheeler, enlisted in Detroit. I advised the people, in general terms, to do the same, and said that if any of them wished to go to enlist early, so as to secure the bounty offered, I would provide for their families till they could send the bounty-money to them. A number went, and some lost their bounty-money through "sharpers" lying in wait for them. . . .

Many in the States, both white and coloured, enlisted merely to receive the bounty, and then they "jumped the bounty," as it was termed—that is, they took the money and did not go into the army.

*Rev. Josiah Henson, an escaped slave, in* Four Fugitive Slave Narratives, *128–29, 133.*

## The Civil War: The Union—Black Soldiers

[T]he rebels drove our force towards the gunboats, taking colored men prisoners and murdering them. This so enraged them that they rallied, and charged the enemy more heroically and desperately than has been recorded during the war. It was a genuine bayonet-charge, a hand-to-hand fight. . . . One brave man took his former master prisoner, and brought him into camp with great gusto. A rebel prisoner made a particular request, that *his own* negroes should not be placed over him as a guard.

*Eyewitness account of a battle on June 7, 1863, in the Mississippi valley, in Brown,* American Rebellion, *137–38.*

The Battle of Olustee, or Ocean Pond, on the 20th of February, will be long remembered by the Eighth, which suffered terribly in the conflict. . . . It looked sad to see [black] men wounded coming into camp with their arms and equipments on, so great was their endurance and so determined were they to defend themselves till the death. . . . The order from the War Department, giving authority in this department to enroll and draft all male colored persons, is to be put into effect in a few days. It creates some excitement among those who prefer to be servants instead of soldiers. They are not very numerous here, as the Rebels have sent them far away.

*Sgt.-Maj. Rufus Jones, 8th U.S. Colored Infantry, April 16, 1864, in* Grand Army of Black Men, *41–42.*

On the march the Colored Soldiers as well as their white Officers were made the subject of much ridicule and many insulting remarks by the White Troops and in some instances petty outrages such as the pulling off the Caps of Colored Soldiers, stealing their horses etc was practiced by the White Soldiers. These insults as well as the jeers and taunts that they would not fight were borne by the Colored Soldiers patiently or punished with dignity by their Officers but in no instance did I hear Colored soldiers make any reply to insulting language used towards [them] by the White Troops.

On the 2d of October the forces reached the vicinity of the Salt Works and finding the enemy in force preparations were made for battle. . . . The point to be attacked was the side of a high mountain, the Rebels being posted about half way up behind rifle pits made of logs and stones to the height of three feet. All being in readiness the Brigade moved to the

Black troops liberating slaves in North Carolina, Civil War (*Library of Congress*)

attack. The Rebels opened upon them a terrific fire but the line pressed steadily forward up the steep side of the mountain until they found themselves within fifty yards of the Enemy. Here Col. Wade ordered his force to charge and the Negroes rushed upon the works with a yell and after a desperate struggle carried the entire line killing and wounding a large number of the enemy and capturing some prisoners. . . . Out of the four hundred engaged, one hundred and fourteen men and four officers fell killed or wounded. . . .

Such of the Colored Soldiers as fell into the hands of the Enemy during the battle were brutally murdered. The Negroes did not retaliate but treated the Rebel wounded with great kindness, carrying them water in their canteens and doing all they could to alleviate the sufferings of those whom the fortunes of war had placed in their hands. . . .

*James S. Brisbin, October 20, 1864, in* Freedom *2: Doc. 219.*

In battle's wild commotion
I won't at all object
If a nigger should stop a bullet
Coming for me direct.

*Marching ditty among some Union troops, in Burchard,* One Gallant Rush, *73.*

Sergt. William Walker, of Company A, Third South Carolina colored troops, was yesterday killed, in accordance with the sentence of a court-martial. He had declared he would no longer remain a soldier for seven dollars per month, and had brought his company to stack their arms before their captain's tent, refusing to do duty until they should be paid thirteen dollars a month, as had been agreed when they were enlisted by Col. Saxon. He was a smart soldier and an able man, dangerous as leader in a revolt. . . . He met his death unflinchingly. Out of eleven shots first fired, but one struck him. A reserve firing-party had been provided, and by these he was shot to death.

The mutiny for which this man suffered death arose entirely out of the inconsistent and contradictory orders of the Paymaster and the Treasury Department at Washington.

*Beaufort (S.C.)* Cor. Tribune, *1864(?), in Brown,* American Rebellion, *253.*

[M]y wife and children came with me [in October, 1864, to Camp Nelson, Kentucky], because my master said that if I enlisted he would not maintain them, and I knew they would be abused by him when I left. I had then four children, aged respectively ten, nine, seven, and four years. On my presenting myself as a recruit, I was told by the lieutenant in command to take my family into a tent within the limits of the camp. My wife and family occupied this tent by the express permission of the aforementioned officer, and never received any notice to leave until Tuesday, November 22, when a mounted guard gave my wife notice that she and her children must leave camp before early morning. This was about six o'clock at night. My little boy, about seven years of age, had been very sick. . . . My wife had no place to go. I told him that I was a soldier of the United States. He told me that it did not make any difference; he had orders to take all out of camp. He told my wife and family if they did not get up in the wagon he had, he would shoot the last one of them.

*Affidavit of Joseph Miller, in Gutman,* Black Family, *373. The little boy died.*

[I]n case of ultimate defeat, the Northern troops, black or white, would go home, while the First South Carolina must fight it out or be re-enslaved. This was one thing that made the St. John's River so attractive to them and even to me;—it was so much nearer the Everglades. I used seriously to ponder, during the darker periods of the war, whether I might not end my days as an outlaw,—a leader of Maroons.

*T. W. Higginson, white commander of a black regiment,* Army Life in a Black Regiment, *251.*

On the 29th of Oct., 1862, twenty-four men of the 1st Regiment of Kansas, Colored Volunteers, having advanced beyond the limits prescribed, were charged upon by one hundred and twenty of the Rebel cavalry. There was a desperate hand-to-hand encounter. . . . Out of the twenty-four men, only six escaped unhurt. The Rebels were armed with shot-guns, revolvers and sabres; our men with Austrian rifles and sabre bayonets. This last is a fearful weapon, and did terrible execution. Six Killer, the leader of the Cherokee negroes, shot two men, bayoneted a third, and laid the fourth with the butt of his gun. Another was attacked by three men. He discharged his rifle and had no time to load again. When asked to surrender, he replied by a stunning blow from the butt of his rifle, which knocked the Rebel off his horse.

So ended the battle of Island Mounds, which resulted in a complete victory to the. . . . negro regiment. . . . [Y]et four months passed and they were not mustered—still they adhered to their organization through every discouragement and disadvantage.

*Autobiography of James L. Smith, ex-slave, in* Five Black Lives, *222–23.*

Sir I have the honor to call your attention To the necesity of having a school for The benefit of our regement We have never Had an institution of that sort and we Stand deeply in need of instruction the majority of us having been slaves We wish to have some benefit of education To make of ourselves capable of business In the future . . . We wish to become a People capable of self support as we are Capable of being soldier. . . .

*First Sgt. John Sweeny to Tennessee Freedman's Bureau assistant commissioner, Nashville, Tennessee, October 8, 1865, in* Freedom *2: Doc. 248.*

After the war started, I ran off and joined the army. During the war I saw my mistress. She came to me and said, "Don't you remember how I nursed you when you were sick, and now you are fighting against me." I said, "No, Ma'am, I am not fighting against you. I am fighting for my freedom." . . . I was sent to Tullahoma for training. This was the biggest thing that ever happened in my life. I felt like a man, with a uniform on and a gun in my hand. . . .

*Ex-slave,* God Struck Me Dead, *102.*

## Civil War: The Union: Spies and Scouts

James Lawson . . . made his escape last December. . . . [He] shipped on board of "The Freeborn," flag-gunboat. . . . He furnished Capt. Magaw with much valuable intelligence concerning the rebel movements. . . .

On Thursday, week ago, it became necessary to obtain correct information of the enemy's movements. . . . "Jim," said the general [Sickles], "I want you to go over to-night and find out what forces they have at Aquia Creek and Fredericksburg. If you want any men to accompany you, pick them out." . . .

Away went Jim over to the contraband camp, and returning almost immediately, brought two very intelligent-looking darkies. . . .

"Well, here, Jim, you take my pistol, said Gen. Sickles, unbuckling it from his belt; "and, if you are successful, I will give you $100." . . .

Capt. Foster . . . landed them a short distance below the Potomac-Creek Batteries. They were to return early in the morning, but were unable, from the great distance they went in the interior. Long before daylight on Saturday morning, the gunboat was lying off at the appointed place. As the day dawned, Capt. Foster discovered a mounted picket-guard near the beach, and almost at the same instant saw Jim to the left of them, in the woods, sighting his gun at the rebel cavalry. He ordered the "gig" to be manned and rowed to the shore. The rebels moved along slowly, thinking to intercept the boat, when Foster gave them a shell, which scattered them. Jim, with only one of his original companions, and two fresh contrabands, came on board. Jim had *lost the other.* He [Cornelius] had been challenged by a picket when some distance in advance of Jim, and the negro, instead of answering the summons, fired the contents of Sickles's revolver at the picket. . . . [A]t that time the entire picket-guard rushed out of a small house near the spot, and fired the contents of their muskets at Jim's companion, killing him instantly. Jim and the other three hid themselves in a hollow, near a fence and, after the pickets gave up pursuit, crept through the woods to the shore. From the close proximity of the rebel pickets, Jim could not display a light, which was the signal for Capt. Foster to send a boat.

New York Times, *quoted in Brown,* American Rebellion, *62–64.*

This fearless woman [Harriet Tubman] was often sent into the rebel lines as a spy, and brought back valuable information as to the position of armies and batteries; she has been in battle when the shot was falling like hail, and the bodies of dead and wounded men were dropping around her like leaves in autumn; but the thought of fear never seems to have had place for a moment in her mind.

*Bradford,* Harriet, *102.*

# 12

# The End of Slavery 1861–1865

## THE HISTORICAL CONTEXT

### *The Union: The Rocky Road to Emancipation*

By the time the Civil War erupted, feeling for and against slavery ran high in the North as well as in the South. The newly inaugurated Abraham Lincoln believed it his prime duty to hold the Union together, with or without slavery. The United States had still to prove to the world that such a democracy could survive.

Although Lincoln personally thought slavery an evil, he doubted that blacks and whites could live peaceably together as equals. With reason, he worried about what was to become of blacks, once freed. Well into the war, he still saw colonization as the best possible solution. He edged toward emancipation hesitantly, basing his decisions about it on military and political advantage. Would proclaiming emancipation cause the border states to secede from the Union and join the Confederacy? Would it weaken the Union's military position by alienating soldiers who had enlisted to save the Union, not to free the slaves? Would it strengthen the Union's military position by depriving the South of its labor force and recruiting soldiers for the North? This last was a powerful argument, for the South's ability to consign almost all nonmilitary labor to blacks freed three-fourths of white men of military age to serve in the Confederate Army.[1]

Abolitionists urged upon the president the moral, political, and military advantages of emancipation. Abolitionist generals in the Union army repeatedly took matters into their own hands. Some of them insisted that slaves in territory they captured were contrabands of war, subject like any other enemy property to seizure. Others declared the slaves in captured territory free on their own authority. Repeatedly Lincoln voided such orders. But every one of them encouraged more slaves to think of freedom as near at hand or to try to seize it for themselves by following Union troops or fleeing to Union forts or ships.

Contrabands escaping to a Union ship (*Library of Congress*)

Up until the summer of 1862, Lincoln's actions discouraged abolitionists, particularly when he insisted that the government must as a matter of law and duty return fugitive slaves to their owners. When, for instance, in September of 1861 Lincoln countermanded General Frémont's emancipation order in Missouri, the editor of the *Anglo-African* wrote, "[T]he man who had reduced back to slavery the slaves of rebels in Missouri would order the army of the United States to put down a slave insurrection in Virginia or Georgia."[2] In fact, though, emancipation no longer depended on the will of one man, even the president of the United States. Willy-nilly, thousands of slaves claimed their own freedom, sometimes assisted by abolitionist Union soldiers. Independently of governmental action, they attained a kind of gradual emancipation. Slaves, wisely, did not rise up in a mass rebellion, but in their multitudes they left their owners' plantations and farms, either on their own or encouraged by Federal troops.

True enough, slaves could not count on assistance from these troops, for the more racist among them treated the blacks abominably. But some intended to free them as a matter of conscience; others wanted their services as drivers, cooks, or construction workers on fortifications. Slaves also brought to the aid of the Union an intimate familiarity with the countryside and waterways, as well as knowledge of where commodities had been hidden. "A big drove of soldiers comes into town," reminisced Mary Reynolds. "They say they's Federals. More'n half the niggers goes off with them soldiers, but I goes on back home 'cause of my old mammy. Next day them Yankees is swarming the place. Some the niggers wants to show them something. I follows to the woods. The niggers shows them soldiers a big pit in the ground, bigger'n a big house. It is got wooden doors that lifts up, but the top am sodded and grass growing on it, so you couldn't tell it. In that pit is stock, hosses and cows and mules and money and chinaware and silver and a mess of stuff them soldiers takes."[3] Slave owners looked at their slaves with new eyes, seeing them now not as beasts of burden or as devoted servants but as potential spies.

Lincoln twisted and turned, looking for alternatives to outright emancipation. In August 1861, he signed the First Confiscation Act, providing that when slaves were engaged in hostile military service, their owners forfeited claims to their labor, thus enabling the Union to accept the services of former slaves previously employed by the Confederacy. In March 1862, he got through the Congress provision for money to compensate slave owners of any state abolishing slavery, in the hope that border states would avail themselves of this face-saving possibility.

July 1862 saw a burst of similar presidential efforts. Lincoln proposed but failed to get through Congress a bill providing that "whenever the President of the United States shall be satisfied that any State shall have lawfully abolished slavery . . . [he] is to pay the State in 6% interest bearing bonds equal to the aggregate value, at X dollars per head." He appealed to congressmen from the border states to support gradual, compensated emancipation, with colonization of freed slaves outside the United States. The Second Confiscation Act freed the slaves of all traitors to and rebels against the Union. The Militia Act not only freed any enemy-owned slave who rendered military service to the Union but also his mother, wife, and children.

Only after all that did Lincoln, that same month, inform his cabinet that he intended to issue an emancipation proclamation—after a major military victory. Abolitionist lobbying, the pressure of events, and perhaps the successes of blacks in the Union army had gradually persuaded him that the advantages to

Slaves fleeing toward Union lines (*Library of Congress*)

the Union of emancipation exceeded its hazards. He announced his intention to the public in September in the Preliminary Emancipation Proclamation, after the Battle of Antietam, formally declaring his intention to free the slaves in the rebel states on January 1, 1863, and to offer financial assistance to loyal slave states if they would free their slaves.

The Emancipation Proclamation itself freed the slaves of all rebels against the Union—but, significantly and confusingly, not those of the loyal border states. The impact of the proclamation far outweighed that of specific terms. Many slaves, unsure of what freedom involved, with no access to accurate information, took the wish for the fact. Border state slaves understandably assumed that they were free—to the point that the Louisville *Journal* asked black leaders to explain to slaves that the proclamation did not affect slavery in Kentucky.[4] Annie Davis of Belair, Maryland, resorted to writing President Lincoln in August 1864: "Mr president It is my Desire to be free, to go to see my people on the eastern shore. My mistress wont let me you will please let me know if we are free, and what I can do. I write to you for advice. Please send me word this week, or as soon as possible and oblidge."[5]

## *The Union: Contrabands and Contraband Camps*

If emancipation lay only at the end of an uncharted road, so also no plan existed for a fresh start for freed slaves. They themselves could not see beyond attaining freedom, and those who dealt with them were operating catch as catch can. For 250 years, Americans had sown the wind of slavery. Now they were reaping the whirlwind.

Accustomed as Americans are today to pictures of refugees streaming through war-torn countries, it is hard for most to imagine such things in their own land. The Civil War overturned the southern economy and the southern way of life; ironically, no one suffered and endured as much in the process as the slaves whom it freed. Masters went off to fight in the Confederate army, leaving in charge of the slaves overseers or wives inexperienced in managing farms and plantations. Masters tried to move slaves out of the path of the advancing Union armies, sometimes upcountry, sometimes farther south, sometimes all the way to Texas. If slaves were too old, too sick, or too young to work, some masters abandoned them. Masters in retreat would shoot down their fleeing slaves rather than let them go free. Masters sent slaves to work for the very Confederate army that fought to keep them enslaved, or took them along as servants when they themselves joined up.

Amid all these uncertainties, slaves trained to obedience and passivity were suddenly confronted with the necessity of choice. Should they try to escape to the North or to follow Union troops? Escape was a difficult and dangerous effort. Many who tried did not make it. Consider those who tried to follow Sherman's army in its sweep through Georgia. Sherman, no abolitionist, saw the black men, women, and children in his wake as impediments to his military objective. He would not, perhaps could not, turn from that objective to provide for them, and hundreds suffered and died trying to keep up with his army.

In the words of Mary Livermore, an agent of the Union's Sanitary Commission traveling up the Mississippi on a riverboat laden with wounded soldiers and contrabands: "One afternoon, as the sunset was deepening into twilight, we made a bend in the river, when we received a momentary fright from a huge fire blazing red, straight before us, close at the water's edge. A great crowd was hovering about it, waving flags, gesticulating, and signalling us. As we came nearer, we found they were negroes, of all sizes, and had their little bundles in their hands or on their heads and backs.

"The captain dared not, or would not, stop. As the poor creatures saw us steaming directly by, they redoubled their exertions to attract our attention. Catching up blazing firebrands, they ran up the shore with them, waved them, threw them in air, and with the most frantic pantomime sought to convey to us a sense of their eagerness to be taken aboard. It seemed pitiful not to stop for them. . . . Doubtless they had signalled other boats ahead of us; and still they were left on the river banks, amid the gray moss-draped cottonwoods, as far from the land of freedom as ever."[6]

Or think of the bewilderment of a twelve-year-old slave. When the fighting came near one night, his mother sent a man to fetch him. "[W]e left for town about twelve o'clock. After we had gone some distance, the man showed me the way and left me. I went along half scared to death. All at once somebody said, "Halt! Who goes there?" I said, "Me." He asked me again who I was, and I just said, "Me." He told me to advance. I went up, and they got around me and asked me who I was and where I was going.

"I told them that I had been working, and that I was trying to find my mother. I was cold, so they made a big fire and told me to sit there by the fire until day, because it would be dangerous for me to go on that night.

"The next day they let me go on my way, and I found my mother. She hid me around until she got a chance to take me to a lady's house. All the slaves were running off about this time. I didn't know what the war was all about, but I used to hear the white people talking about the slaves getting ready to rise up against the white folks."[7]

Even if slaves escaped into free territory, where were they to go, and what were they to do? Many locations in the North, far from welcoming the contrabands—a term soon extended to former slaves generally—banned them. Hancock County, Illinois, for example, in February 1863 sold into service five blacks and a mulatto found guilty of remaining in the county for more than 10 days. The bidder who offered the shortest time of service won.[8] Race riots and violent labor demonstrations against blacks occurred in northern cities throughout the war.

More liberal communities often found themselves overwhelmed by the sheer numbers of contrabands. Levi Coffin wrote, "Many of the slaveholders fled farther South, taking their able-bodied slaves with them, and leaving the women and children, aged and sick ones, to take care of themselves. In many cases there was nothing for this helpless class to live upon. . . . Thousands gathered within the Union lines and were sent to various points up the river. Some were brought on boats to Cincinnati and left on the wharf without food and shelter or means of obtaining them. . . . The colored people here acted nobly, taking as many as they could and caring for them."[9]

The contrabands' best hope of succor lay in the camps operated by the Union military or by the semigovernmental, semiprivate freedmen's aid organizations. For the military, before the Emancipation Proclamation, uncertainty about the status of the contrabands complicated the problem. Were they free?

Contraband children entertaining Union troops, Louisiana (*Library of Congress*)

Who should pay for their support? Should those who worked for the military receive the same wages as others, or should those wages be applied to the support of other contrabands?

Moreover, the numbers of contrabands outran the available supplies. They had to live in deserted houses, in huts, in old army tents, in brush shelters, in the open fields. In the fall of 1862, Coffin visited a camp in Cairo, Illinois, where former slaves lived "in their crowded huts and sick rooms. . . . Many were sick from exposure and for want of sufficient clothing; they had no bedding nor cooking utensils. . . . The scanty rations issued by Government were their only subsistence. The weather being quite chilly, many of them were suffering with coughs and colds; that dreadful suffering—small-pox—was quite prevalent among them. . . ."[10] The hospitals hardly eased their suffering. As one superintendent reported, "Hospital not under charge of Superintendent. Its condition wretched in the extreme. Lack of medicines, of utensils, of vaccine matter. . . . No attention to sick in camp by surgeon. . . . *Diseases*—Pneumonia, fevers, small pox."[11] In a camp at Memphis where three large colonies of contrabands had set about cultivating the ground, it was necessary for the men to maintain a strong picket guard against Confederate raids.

Undoubtedly, many of the contrabands were physically worse off in these camps than they had been in slavery. They could not see into the uncertain future. Yet one of them preached, "We have been in the furnace of affliction, and are still, but God only means to separate the dross, and get us so that like the pure metal we may reflect the image of our Purifier, who is sitting by to watch the process. . . . We have need of faith, patience and perseverance, to realize the desired result. There must be no looking back to Egypt. Israel passed forty years in the wilderness, because of their unbelief. What if we cannot see right off the green fields of Canaan, Moses could not. . . . We must snap the chain of Satan, and educate ourselves and our children."[12]

Endless problems confronted the freed slaves. Years of dependence and enforced ignorance had ill fitted most of them for the responsibilities of liberty

Contrabands on their way to work (*Library of Congress*)

The naïve among them had expected money and an easy life as part of the freedom package. Few of them owned anything besides the clothes on their backs—certainly not means of production. Yet in a contraband camp near Washington, D.C., every morning they set off to work, the men for the government, the women to find what tasks they could as laundresses and housecleaners. In the camps, contrabands assisted by northern aid societies organized schools and churches. They reunited families. Former slave Susie King Taylor devoted herself to improving the lot of black soldiers: "I taught a great many of the comrades [of the South Carolina Volunteers] in Company E to read and write, when they were off duty. Nearly all were anxious to learn. . . . I was very happy to know my efforts were successful in camp, and also grateful for the appreciation of my services. I gave my services willingly for four years and three months without receiving a dollar. I was glad, however, to be allowed to go with the regiment, to care for the sick and afflicted comrades."[13]

## *The Freedmen's Bureau*

For most of the war, contrabands had to depend for help on volunteers, some of them in societies established for the purpose, others from long-existing abolitionist groups, and still others from associated organizations like the Sanitary Commission. Abolitionist Laura Haviland, for example, worked for a freedmen's aid commission: "In September [of 1864] I had a car-load of supplies ready, and

$400 in money. Of this amount, $298 was placed in my hands by friends at Adrian [Michigan], with the request of the donors that it should be retained in my own hands for disbursement on reaching the scene of suffering. At Chicago appeals were made to the Soldiers' Aid Society and Christian Commission for aid in the freedmen's department, and also to myself personally, on account of the great distress in Kansas after General Price's raid through Missouri, followed by Colonels Lane and Jennison, who drove thousands of poor whites and freedmen into that young State. I decided to hasten thither, with . . . an assistant.

"At Leavenworth we met J. R. Brown, . . . who had charge of both white refugees and freedmen and a sort of soldiers' home. . . . He kindly offered me headquarters in his establishment. . . . General Curtis . . . telegraphed for my supplies to be forwarded in preference to other army supplies, and gave me passes through the State to Fort Scott. . . . He also gave me liberty . . . to call upon quarter-masters for half, whole, or quarter rations, wherever suffering for food existed."[14]

Eventually in 1865, the federal government established the Bureau of Refugees, Freedmen, and Abandoned Lands (known as the Freedmen's Bureau) to assist blacks in building their new lives. The bureau understood its objectives to include "promotion of productive industry" and settling blacks "in homes of their own, with the guarantee of their absolute freedom and their right to justice before the law." Its pamphlets forbade compulsory, unpaid labor, encouraged sharecropping, and promised to try to settle blacks on confiscated or abandoned land.[15]

The agency had its work cut out for it. The freed blacks faced situations that would have daunted the most sophisticated and experienced citizens, and they faced them without the political, economic, and social power necessary to resolve them satisfactorily. Slaveholders could not restore slavery, but after the war they could and did put obstacles in the way of blacks trying to establish new lives. Southern legislatures enacted laws limiting the former slaves' legal rights. Under the black codes passed during Reconstruction, the Negro "could rent property or houses only in restricted areas; he must never be without his contract of labor or his license from the police; if he quit his work he could be arrested and sent to the house of correction for a year, or if he were captured and brought back, his captor would be paid a reward of five dollars, and ten cents a mile for travel. Over him his employer held a control as inflexible as the slave master's, while his children were reenslaved by apprenticeship laws. To restrict the movements of the freedmen were vagrancy laws, carrying penalties of hard labor or long imprisonment."[16]

Postwar vigilantes directed their wrath particularly against blacks who had fought for the Union and their families. In September 1866, Rhoda Ann Childs described a night of torture, in which eight men beat and raped her and beat her two daughters: "During the whipping one of the men ran his pistol into me, and Said he had a hell of a mind to pull the trigger, and Swore they ought to Shoot me, as my husband had been in the 'God damned Yankee Army,' and Swore they meant to kill every black Son-of-a-bitch they could find that had ever fought against them."[17]

One "Calvin. Holly, colered" wrote to the Mississippi branch of the Freedmen's Bureau in December of 1865 that "houses have been tourn down from over the heades of women and Children—and the old Negroes after they have worked there till they are 70 or 80 years of age drive them off in the cold to frieze and starve to death. . . . Some are being worked just as they ust to be when Slaves, without any compensation, Report came in town this morning that two colered women was found dead side the Jackson road with their throats cot lying side by side. . . . The Rebbles are going a bout in many places through the State and robbing the colered people of arms money and all they have and in many places killing."[18]

Indeed, despite the Emancipation Proclamation, the status of many blacks still was disputed. As late as the fall of 1865, blacks in Kentucky remained legally enslaved, according to that state's laws. So when the Freedmen's Bureau tried to help Wilson Hail collect the wages due him, H. Hale claimed that he owned the black man and thus was entitled to his wages.[19]

Bureau agents also acted as ombudsmen for blacks in such matters as negotiating contracts, resolving disputes, and protecting blacks against the rancor of whites. In August 1865, for instance, blacks who had supported themselves for two years on land abandoned by their owner, William Bonner, sought help from the bureau. Bonner had returned and persuaded them to work the property for him but had later reneged on his offer to reward them unless they would revert to their former condition of servitude.

The bureau did important work—not least in enabling blacks to regularize their marriages and put their families on a firmer basis, a matter that ranked high in the list of the blacks' concerns.

But the multiple problems of those newly freed also continued to require the services of hosts of volunteers. For example, during the war and immediately afterward, teachers for black schools were drawn largely from volunteers sponsored by such groups as church missionary societies. Many volunteers worked valiantly, enduring social ostracism from whites for their pains. Others condescended, particularly when they preached about the ways in which the newly freed ought to behave. The abolitionist Lydia Maria Child, for example, instructed them: "Be always respectful and polite toward your associates, and toward those who have been in the habit of considering you an inferior race. It is one of the best ways to prove that you are not inferior. Never allow yourselves to say or do anything in the presence of women of your own color which it would be improper for you to say or do in the presence of the most refined white ladies. Such a course will be an education for them as well as for yourselves. . . . [E]ven if you are as yet too poor to have a house and garden of your own, it is still in your power to be a credit and an example to your race."[20]

## *The Confederacy: Managing Chaos*

The southern states had not built strong, active prewar governments or communities. Southerners had devoted little effort and money to building schools, libraries, bridges, or roads. As John C. Calhoun remarked, "The Southern States are an aggregate . . . of communities, not of individuals. Every plantation is a little community, with the master at its head. . . . These small communities aggregated make the State in all."[21] Basing their economy on agriculture left most of the population, particularly the slaves, living on isolated farms and plantations. The patriarchal system had placed almost all the power in the hands not of governments but of individual men, who ruled their domains almost absolutely.

With the Civil War and the departure of many of these men, conditions deteriorated into anarchy. The aging minister and slave owner Charles C. Jones turned for advice on dealing with slaves who ran away to his attorney son, by then a lieutenant in the Confederate army. His son replied, "You ask me, my dear father, . . . whether Negroes deserting to the enemy can be summarily dealt with by the citizens themselves. . . . A trial by jury is accorded to everyone, whether white or black, where life is at stake. . . . Any punishment other than that involving a loss of life or limb could be legally inflicted without the intervention of judge or jury. If General Mercer refuses to take military cognizance of such cases, and they occur during the intervals of the sessions of the courts, I cannot see what can be done except to take the law in one's own hand. . . ."[22]

In July 1862, the provost marshal of Natchez, Mississippi, wrote in desperation to the governor: "I appeal to you for assistance, for I do assure you that if the overseers are taken off[,] this County will be left in a condition that will be by no means safe. I do not wish to except them from entire service [in the army], I only want to keep them until an emergency arises requiring their services, then let them go and do service, but don't let them be taken off as long as it can be helped—Also instructions as to the manner of proceeding against persons who will keep no overseer, and make but little provision for their Negroes, rendering it necessary for them to steal or starve and go naked. . . . [N]egroes seemingly are permitted to forage upon the Community—The owners will not look after them, will not provide for them, nor will they employ an overseer. The negroes have such large liberties, they are enabled to harbor runaways, who have fire arms, traverse the whole County, kill stock, and steal generally, supplying those who harbor them, and send to market by Negro market-men. The state of things in consequence to this in a few cases are a serious nuisance as well as dangerous to the Community. Complaints are made to me to remedy the evil. I am however at a loss how to proceed."[23]

The Confederacy simply did not possess the resources or the infrastructure to fight a war and protect the domestic peace as well. The task of coping with chaos fell mostly on individuals—particularly to the slaves and white women left behind on the plantations.

## *The Confederacy: Slaves' Experiences of the War*

Slaves and white women bore the brunt of the Yankee invasion of the South. Some slaves welcomed it, as an opportunity for freedom. Others tried to protect their mistresses from the Yankees. "That all changed after Massa go to war," reminisced former slave Pauline Grice. "First the 'Federate soldiers come and takes some mules and hosses, then some more come for the corn. After while, the Yankee soldiers comes and takes some more. When they gits through, they ain't much more tooking to be done. The year 'fore surrender, us am short of rations and sometime us hungry. Us sees no battling, but the cannon bang all day. Once they bang two whole days 'thout hardly stopping. That am when Missy got touch in the head, 'cause Massa and the boys in that battle. . . . Then word come Willie am kilt. . . . For her, it am trouble, trouble, and more trouble. . . . One day she tell us, 'The war am on us. The soldiers done took the rations. I can't sell the cotton, 'cause the blockade. . . . Now,' she say, 'all you colored folks born and raise here, and us always been good to you. I can't holp it 'cause rations am short, and I'll do all I can for you. Will you be patient with me?' All us stay there and holp Missy all us could."[24]

Ex-slave Mom Ryer Emanuel reacted differently, hailing the arrival of the Yankees. Her master had hidden all the supplies he could in pits dug under the slave cabins and then fled to the woods, leaving the women of the plantation to confront the Union soldiers: "No, child, they didn't bother nothing much, but some of the rations they got hold of. Often times, they would come through and kill chickens and butcher a cow up and cook it right there. Would eat all they wanted and then when they would go to leave, they would call all the plantation niggers to come there and would give them what was left. O Lord, us was glad to get them victuals, too. . . . Us been so glad, us say that us wish they would come back again. . . . Old Massa, he been stay in the swamp till he hear them Yankees been leave there, and then he come home and would keep sending to the colored people's houses to get a little bit of his rations to a time. Uncle Solomon and Sipp and Leve, they been et [as] much of Boss's rations [as] they wanted 'cause they been know the Yankees was coming back through to free them. . . . I tell you, honey, some of the colored people sure been speak praise to them Yankees."[25]

Perhaps a majority of slaves found their wartime experiences confusing and disorienting, swaying now toward exaggerated hopes of freedom and riches, now toward trying to defend themselves and their families as best they could against racist Union soldiers, vengeful slave owners, and starvation.

As noted above, when the Confederacy ran short of manpower, it turned to using slaves. From the beginning of the war, white officers had taken slaves into the army to act as servants. The Confederacy had also called on or forced owners to send a certain number of their slaves for such work as building ramparts and driving wagons. Owners typically were not happy at such demands, particularly as they learned that their slaves were mistreated, overworked, likely to take sick, and returned, if at all, in a weakened condition. "I fear that I have not acted for the best," Lizzie Neblett wrote her husband, "but I did not want to send any [of your slaves to work for the Confederate military] if I could help it, but if they come again Joe will have to go, & be put under any overseer they please, etc., but I can't help it."[26]

These short-term arrangements proved unsatisfactory to the military, too. No sooner would a slave gain skill in "encamping, marching, and packing trains" than he had to be returned to his owner. Maybe, officialdom came to think, the Confederacy needed "to acquire for the public service the entire property in the labor of the slave, and to pay therefor due compensation rather than to impress his labor for short terms. . . ."[27] Moreover, to keep the slave loyal, perhaps the Confederacy should promise him freedom and the right to live in his home state, once the war was over.

## *The Confederacy: White Women's Experiences of the War*

The departure of the slave owners to fight left the women of the Confederacy with the tasks of farm and plantation management, for which few of them were prepared. The men's ownership of all property together with the traditions of the southern lady meant that few women had management experience beyond the running of their households, though wives of small farmers were probably better off in this respect than their moneyed sisters. Almost all of the plantation mistresses were horrified by the necessity of doing the housework themselves, as they had grown up believing that it should be left to inferiors and had acquired no household skills.

They had to take over at the very moment that both their way of life and their value system were under attack. Of the difficulties they met, they talked most on the record about the problems of managing slaves. Certainly they faced a harder task than their menfolk had, as the repeated rumors of freedom made the slaves less inclined to obey and to work. The women's dependence on the slaves increased just as the slaves became more independent. "I tell you all this attention to farming is uphill work with me," Mrs. W. W. Boyce wrote her husband in the spring of 1862. "I can give orders first-rate, but when I am not obeyed, I can't keep my temper. . . . I am ever ready to give you a helping hand, but I must say I am heartily tired of trying to manage *free* negroes."[28] Frustrated mistresses suggested that they would be better off without the slaves than with them.

Besides, a good many of them feared their slaves. Stories of individual slave attacks on white women floated around—some true, some not. Ada Bacot was certain the fire in her neighbors' house was set by their slave Abel; Laura Lee was horrified when occupying troops released a Winchester slave convicted of murdering her mistress. In September 1862, the *Mobile Advertiser and Register* noted that a slave had succeeded in poisoning his master; the same month the *Richmond Enquirer* recorded the conviction of one Lavinia for torching her mistress's house. Abbie Brooks of Georgia described the terrible scars on the face of a woman neighbor who had been shoved into the fire by a slave. "All that saved her life was the negro taking fire and had to let go to her mistress to extinguish herself."[29]

Some women resorted to hiring overseers. But what with the shortage of manpower, it was difficult to find a good one. Women who had been insisting that what their blacks needed was a firm hand found themselves horrified by the cruelties of the overseers they hired.

Even older women who had firmly established their authority in their households could do little in the face of the destruction of the Southern economy. Mary Jones watched successive raids reduce resources until she could no longer operate her husband's plantations and needed to make other arrangements to support his slaves: "The lateness of the season makes it very difficult if not *impossible* to hire them [out to work for someone else]. *Jack* is the only one I have been able to hire as yet—for twenty-five dollars per month. Corn is now selling for twelve and twenty dollars per bushel, and I will have to purchase provisions for them at that price. . . . Your uncle has kindly offered the use of a place distant about five miles . . . that our people might plant; but as we are without mules, plows, or hoes, that would not be practicable. I must depend on hiring."[30] Such women as these, who had spent most of their adult lives supervising slaves and seeing to it that they were clothed, fed, sheltered, and nursed, experienced their departure as a betrayal.

## *The Aftermath*

Although technically the Civil War freed the slaves and held the Union together, a cold war was thereafter waged on both issues. Southern states continued

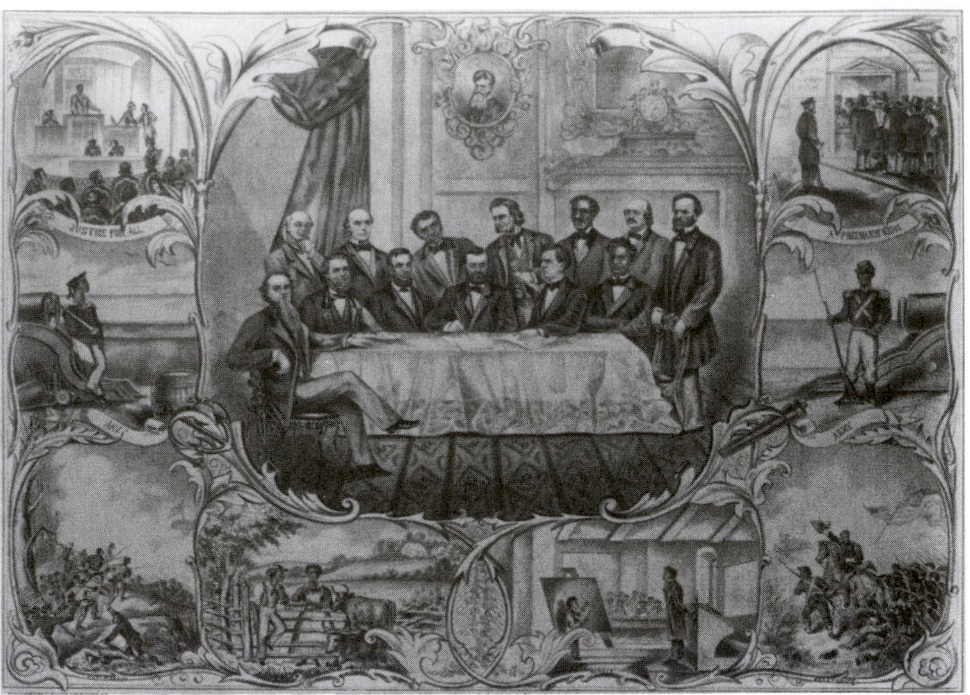

Poster celebrating the signing of the Fifteenth Amendment. Frederick Douglass is seated at the far right of the table. Robert Smalls stands behind Abraham Lincoln and U.S. Grant. Hiram Rhoades Revels, elected to the U.S. Senate in 1870, is the third black man. Note the celebration of black troops in the Union navy and army and at the battles of Port Hudson and Petersburg. *(Library of Congress)*

to insist on states' rights and to exclude blacks from full citizenship. The Confederate surrender was not accompanied with even a show of a change of heart among southern whites. Instead of cutting their losses and starting afresh, many of them resolved to rebuild their lives as closely as possible to what they had been. It was hard to know whom they resented more, abolitionists or freed blacks—but the blacks were within reach of their vengeance. Individually and as a society, working through their state legislatures, they limited the liberties of blacks socially, politically, and economically, insofar as they could.

Nationally too, the country defaulted on its obligations to blacks. Their hopes for grants of land faded. The lack of a master plan for their resettlement left aid for them up to a patchwork of volunteer agencies and their own efforts, individually and in organizations.

The federal government did act decisively, with the passage and ratification of the Thirteenth, Fourteenth, and Fifteenth Amendments to extend meaningful civil rights to blacks and protect them legally. In 1865, the Thirteenth Amendment prohibited slavery. In 1868, the Fourteenth Amendment defined U.S. citizenship so as to remove the political disabilities of former slaves and prohibited the states from violating due process or equal protection of the law. In 1870, the Fifteenth Amendment guaranteed the rights of citizens against national or state infringement based on race, color, or previous servitude.

Enforcement of any law, of course, depends in large part on the will of the populace. For a century after the end of the Civil War, the rights of blacks these amendments meant to guarantee were flagrantly violated, until the confrontations of the 1960s and 1970s caused another national convulsion. Even at the end of the 20th century, the nation still suffers the terrible consequences of slavery.

## Chronicle of Events

### 1861

Russia emancipates the serfs, who are to retain the land they have been working, though they do not gain complete freedom or equality.

A Georgia code specifies that jailors and constables shall be paid one dollar "for whipping a negro," and sets a limit of 39 lashes, not "inhumanly" done.

Texas, now a member of the Confederacy, absolutely prohibits manumission.

*March 2:* The U.S. Congress adopts and sends to the states a constitutional amendment (which fails of ratification) forbidding any subsequent amendment to "abolish or interfere . . . with the domestic institutions" of the states.

*May 24:* Fugitive slaves at Fortress Monroe, Virginia, are received and put to work by Union general Benjamin F. Butler, who declares them "contraband of war."

*August 6:* Congress passes (and Lincoln later signs) the First Confiscation Act, providing that when slaves are engaged in hostile military service, the owners' claims to their labor are forfeited. All property, including slaves, used in support of the rebellion is made subject to prize and capture. The Union can legally accept the services of any former slaves previously employed on behalf of the Confederacy. Fugitive slaves are thus transformed into contraband.

Contrabands arriving at Fortress Monroe, Virginia (*Library of Congress*)

*August 30:* Invoking martial law, Gen. John C. Frémont declares free the slaves of disloyal owners in Missouri; President Lincoln asks that he modify his order so as not to exceed congressional laws respecting emancipation.

*September 11:* General Frémont having refused to modify his emancipation order, President Lincoln orders him to do so.

*December 1:* Secretary of War Simon Cameron issues his annual report, from which President Lincoln has required the deletion of passages advocating emancipation and the employment of former slaves as military laborers and soldiers.

### 1862

Cuba ends the slave trade.

Utah abolishes slavery.

"Refugeeing"—taking slaves to Texas to keep them away from the advancing Union forces—becomes common.

In Corinth, Mississippi, blacks in a contraband camp organize a cohesive community for work, education, and worship, which the Federal government dismantles in 1863.

*March:* Lincoln proposes and Congress passes a resolution to provide pecuniary aid "to compensate for the inconveniences, public and private, produced by such change of system," to any state abolishing slavery.

*March 13:* Congress adopts an additional article of war forbidding members of the army and navy to return fugitive slaves to their owners.

*April 10:* A joint resolution of Congress offers monetary assistance to any state that will begin emancipation of its slaves.

*April 16:* Congress abolishes slavery in the District of Columbia, appropriating money to compensate owners up to three hundred dollars for each slave and providing for the removal and colonization of the freedmen to Haiti, Liberia, or other countries.

*May:* The Superior Court of the District of Columbia rules that the Fugitive Slave Law is as applicable to the District of Columbia as to any of the states.

*May 9:* General David Hunter declares free all slaves in South Carolina, Georgia, and Florida.

*May 19:* President Lincoln nullifies General Hunter's emancipation edict and urges the border states to embrace gradual, compensated emancipation.

*June 19:* Congress abolishes slavery in the territories.

*July:* Lincoln proposes, but Congress does not act on, a bill providing that "whenever the President of the United States shall be satisfied that any State shall have lawfully abolished slavery . . . [he] is to pay the State in 6% interest bearing bonds equal to the aggregate value, at X dollars per head."

*July 12:* Lincoln appeals to congressmen from the border states to support gradual, compensated emancipation, with colonization of freed slaves outside the United States.

*July 17:* Congress passes and Lincoln signs the Second Confiscation Act, providing that if anyone commits treason, his slaves are free and that slaves of all persons supporting rebellion are "forever free of their servitude, and not again held as slaves." Congress also passes a law saying that no slave escaping from one state into another will be delivered up except for a crime, unless he belongs to a loyal owner; the law also frees disloyal owners' slaves who come into the Union lines. Lincoln signs the Militia Act, freeing any enemy-owned slave who renders military service (for one ration and pay of $10 per month, less three dollars for clothing) and also freeing the slave's mother, wife, and children.

*July 22:* Lincoln tells his cabinet that he intends to free the slaves in the Confederate states.

*September 22:* In the Preliminary Emancipation Proclamation, Lincoln formally declares his intention to free the slaves in the rebel states on January 1, 1863, and to offer financial assistance to loyal slave states if they will free their slaves.

*December 31*: West Virginia is admitted into the Union as a free state.

**1863**

Slavery is abolished in all Dutch colonies.

The Women's Loyal National League is founded by militant feminists to ensure the complete elimination of slavery.

Poster celebrating the Emancipation Proclamation (*Library of Congress*)

*January 1:* Lincoln issues the Emancipation Proclamation.

*March 16:* Secretary of War Stanton appoints the American Freedmen's Inquiry Commission to investigate the condition of former slaves and recommend measures for their employment and welfare.

*June 18:* U.S. Commissioner Walter S. Coxe remands two fugitive slaves to claimants from Maryland (a Union state).

*July 13:* Draft rioters attack blacks in New York City and other northern cities.

*November:* Maryland abolishes slavery.

*December 8:* Lincoln issues the Proclamation of Amnesty and Reconstruction, offering pardon and restoration of property other than slaves to Confederates who swear allegiance to the Union and agree to accept emancipation, and proposing a plan by which loyal voters of a seceded state can begin to apply for readmission into the Union.

**1864**

Charles Sumner presents to the Senate a women's antislavery petition with thousands of signatures.

*January:* Missouri abolishes slavery.

*January 2*: Confederate major gen. Patrick R. Cleburne proposes freeing all the slaves and arming some of them to fight for the Confederacy.

*March:* John Eaton, superintendent of contrabands in the Department of the Tennessee and Arkansas, instructs Union army clergy to "solemnize the rite of marriage among Freedmen."

*March 16:* Pro-Union voters ratify a new Arkansas state constitution that abolishes slavery.

*June 28:* President Lincoln signs the repeal of the Fugitive Slave Law.

*September 3*: Pro-Union voters ratify a new Louisiana state constitution that abolishes slavery.

**1865**

Blacks in Vicksburg petition Congress not to seat Mississippi's delegates while blacks are denied the vote.

*January 12*: Twenty black leaders meet with Gen. William T. Sherman and Secretary of War Stanton to discuss the future of freedmen.

*January 16:* General Sherman sets aside part of coastal South Carolina, Georgia, and Florida for settlement exclusively by blacks, settlers to receive title to 40-acre plots.

*February 22:* An amendment to the Tennessee state constitution abolishes slavery.

*March 3:* Congress frees the wives and children of black soldiers.

*March 3:* Congress establishes the Bureau of Refugees, Freedmen, and Abandoned Lands (the Freedmen's Bureau) to oversee the transition from slavery to freedom.

*March 3:* Congress charters the Freedman's Bank, an interstate bank.

*December 18:* The Thirteenth Amendment, abolishing slavery throughout the United States, is ratified.

**1868**

*July 28:* The Fourteenth Amendment is ratified.

**1870**

*March 30:* The Fifteenth Amendment is ratified.

## Eyewitness Testimony

### *The Union: The Rocky Road to Emancipation*

Not only will we abstain from all interferences with your slaves, but we will, with an iron hand, crush any attempt at insurrection on their part.

*Union general George B. McClellan, "Proclamation to the People of Western Virginia," May 26, 1861.*

God's ahead ob Massa Linkum. God won't let Massa Linkum beat de South till he do the right thing. Massa Linkum he great man, and I'se poor nigger; but dis nigger can tell Massa Linkum how to save de money and de young men. He do it by setting de niggers free.

*Harriet Tubman, in Quarles, "Harriet Tubman's Unlikely Leadership," in* Black Women in American History *4:1145.*

[The Emancipation Proclamation] gave a new direction to the councils of the Cabinet, and to the conduct of the national arms. . . . [I took it] for a little more than it purported, and saw in its spirit a life and power far beyond its letter. Its meaning to me was the entire abolition of slavery, and I saw that its moral power would extend much further.

*Frederick Douglass, in Franklin,* The Emancipation Proclamation, *143.*

### *The Union: Contrabands and Contraband Camps*

I have worked by the month for six months . . . and the money is all my own; and I'll soon educate my children. But, brethren, don't be too free. . . . Don't lean on our master [the superintendent of the contraband camp]. . . . You must depend on yourselves.

*Virginia contraband in Washington, D.C., January 1, 1863, in Franklin,* Emancipation Proclamation, *106–7.*

Distribution of captured Confederate clothing to contrabands in North Carolina (*Library of Congress*)

Compared with white people at the North they [the contrabands] were not industrious, but they compared favorably with the humbler classes of whites at the South, and were even ahead of them in intellect and industry. Every morning the men of the camp went into the city to get work for the day. So did the women who had not young children to care for. Few of them failed to find employment. Government employed the men—and the women found chance jobs of house-cleaning, washing, etc., for which they asked and received moderate compensation. Many had thriven so well that they had commenced housekeeping by themselves. . . . The contraband camp at Washington was therefore very nearly a self-sustaining institution.

*Livermore,* My Story of the War, *258–59.*

As the half-imbruted contrabands came on board [the Mississippi riverboat], under military *surveillance,* clad in the tattered gray and black "nigger cloth," and shod with the clouted brogans of the plantation, my heart went out to them. Subdued, impassive, solemn, hope and courage now and then lighting up their sable faces, they were a most interesting study. Mothers carried their piquant-faced babies on one arm, and led little wooly-headed toddlers by the other. Old men and women, gray, nearly blind, some of them bent almost double, bore on their heads and backs the small "plunder" they had "toted" from their homes, on the plantation, or the "bread and meat" furnished them by some friendly authorities. They were all going forth, like the Israelites, "from the land of bondage to a land they knew not."

*Livermore,* My Story of the War, *242–43.*

While our army was at Grand Gulf, Miss., an intelligent contraband gave much valuable information as to the position of the enemy, and otherwise rendered himself useful to our forces. He finally fell into the hands of the rebels, who administered one hundred and fifty lashes, and placed an iron collar around his neck, riveting it on very strongly. Afterwards the negro was captured from the rebels at Baton Rouge, La., by Company F, Fourth Wisconsin, and was immediately released from the collar. This collar was a round rod of iron, two inches in circumference, riveted together before and behind with two iron prongs one inch wide, three fourths of an inch thick, and twelve inches long, rising from each side directly outside the ears.

*Livermore,* My Story of the War, *440.*

One day, a negro, who was believed trustworthy, was sent out of the enemy's [Confederate] lines with a six-mule team for a big load of wood. He had got beyond the pickets, and seemed to think it worth while to venture a little farther, and so kept on towards "Uncle Sam's boys." The rebel pickets saw him going, and rushed after him. Our men saw him coming, and rushed towards him. The ebony teamster whipped up his mules, shouted, hurrahed, and urged them on. Guns were fired on both sides, and the yelling and excitement were tremendous for a few minutes. But the negro gained the day, and ran out of slavery into freedom. He was taken to the quartermaster, who gave him several hundred dollars for his team, so he not only got his liberty but a good start.

*Livermore,* My Story of the War, *270–71.*

As the slaveholders fled before the advancing Union forces they took with them their able-bodied slaves, and when these tried to escape and reach the Union lines, they were pursued and fired upon by their masters who had rather shoot them down than let them go free.

*Coffin,* Reminiscences, *361.*

## *The Union: Freedmen's Aid Societies and The Freedmen's Bureau*

The Western Freedmen's Aid Commission was organized [in January, 1863]. . . . I was appointed general agent of this commission. . . .

General Grant . . . gave us free transportation for all supplies for the freedmen and for our agents and teachers. We sent efficient agents to attend to the proper and judicious distribution of the clothing and other articles, and a number of teachers, well supplied with books, to open schools among the colored people.

*Coffin,* Reminiscences, *359.*

[In 1864 in my work for a freedman's aid society I visited Fort Scott, Kansas.] Many of them [refugees and freedmen] had stopped here. . . . Here was a great number of the poor whites, called "Clay-eaters," who complained about government dealing rations to colored people. I heard one of them say that "if niggers would stay where they belonged, with their masters, they would have more white-bread and beef." I told

Union generals speaking to Freedmen (*Library of Congress*)

them, I had learned that many of their husbands were fighting against the [Union] government while the husbands of many of the colored women were fighting to sustain it, and I should favor those who were on the side of the government. . . .

On giving a description of the ignorance and filth of the poor whites I called on, Colonel Blair inquired, "What would you do with them?"

"I would keep body and soul together till Spring opens," I answered, "and then load up your great army wagons, and take them out upon the rich prairies and dump them out, giving them the homely adage, 'Root, pig, or die.'"

The greatest difficulty in managing this class was to get them to do any thing. Not so with colored people; they would do any thing they could find to do.

*Haviland,* A Woman's Life-Work, *370-71.*

## *The Confederacy: Managing Chaos*

A Southern planter wrote a friend in New York that four of his runaway slaves had returned voluntarily after a spell of "Yankee freedom." But several months later he complained bitterly that the same four had run away again—this time taking with them two hundred other slaves.

*1862 account, in Ottley and Weatherby,* Negro in New York, *iii.*

Cato [a slave] is taken; the other two, with others, are said to be on the Island [in Union hands]. Little Andrew, who married into the family, knew all about it and has told. . . . My determination is to turn them over to the proper authorities and let them be tried and dealt with as the public welfare may require. . . . They are traitors who may pilot an enemy into your *bedchamber!* They know every road and swamp and creek and plantation in the county, and are the worst of spies.

*Slaveholder Rev. Charles C. Jones, July 5, 1862, in* Children of Pride, *929–30.*

I have just returned from Middle Georgia, and have purchased Mr. Henry J. Schley's Buckhead plantation containing fourteen hundred and twelve acres at ten dollars per acre, and also his present corn crop. . . .

Mr. Schley tells me if at any time danger threatens, to send the Negroes up at once. . . . We can send the Negroes either by Central Railroad . . . or we can send them with wagons, etc. . . .

*Lt. Charles C. Jones Jr., October 8, 1862, in* Children of Pride, *974–75.*

[More than 10,000 slaves] flocked into Beaufort on the hegira of the whites, and held high carnival in the deserted mansions, smashing doors, mirrors and furniture, and appropriating all that took their fancy. After this sack, they remained at home upon the plantations and revelled in unwonted idleness and luxury, feasting upon the corn, cattle and turkeys of their fugitive masters.

*Gen. Isaac Ingalls Stevens, reporting events after whites fled their plantations, in Bell,* Major Butler's Legacy, *353.*

[Dr. Charles Carter was] obliged to go there [Louisiana & Mississippi] when the war broke out to prevent the confiscation of [his] property. . . . He says the privation & suffering around Natchez, which has not been devastated to any great extent by the armies, was chiefly among people of property, caused by the loss of articles supplied by commerce . . . and by the desertion of household servants. . . . In some cases, the stock & Negroes were carried off from plantations, by which the owners were prevented from planting a crop of cotton. He himself kept his Negroes & put in a crop last year, which, tho a small one, paid him, because of the high price as well as his average crop, 1,150 bales. He paid his Negroes wages, as other planters are glad to do. Wages are very high, $25 per month. Everyone considers slavery at an end & is preparing for the new state of things. Most of the planters in Miss. & Louisiana are Union men & have been from the first and are anxious to restore the Union.

*Sidney George Fisher, diary entry for March 4, 1864,* Philadelphia Perspectives, *467.*

When the war come along, Old Master just didn't know what to do. He always been taught not to raise his hand up and kill nobody—no matter how come—. . . and he wouldn't go and fight. He been taught that it was all right to have slaves and treat them like he want to, but he been taught it was sinful to go fight and kill to keep them. . . .

Old Master come down to the quarters and say, "Git everything bundled up and in the wagons for a long trip." The Negroes all come in, and everybody pitch in to help pack up the wagons. . . . Old Master had about five wagons on that trip down into Louisiana, but they was all full of stuff and only the old slaves and children could ride in them. I was big enough to walk most of the time, but one time I walked in the sun so long that I got sick, and they put me in the wagon for most the rest of the way.

We would come to places where the people said the Yankees had been and gone, but we didn't run into any Yankees. . . . We went on down to the south part of Mississippi and ferried across the big river at Baton Rouge. Then we went on to Lafayette, Louisiana, before we settled down anywhere. . . .

I seen lots of men in butternut clothes [Confederate soldiers] coming and going hither and yon, but they wasn't in bunches. They was mostly coming home to see their folks. Everybody was scared all the time, and two-three times when Old Master hired his negroes out to work, the man that hired them quit his place and went on west before they got the crop in. But Old Master got a place, and we put in a cotton crop, and I think he got some money by selling his place in Mississippi. Anyway, pretty soon after the cotton was all in, he moves again and goes to a place on Simonette Lake for the winter. . . .

The next spring Old Master loaded up again, and we struck out for Texas when the Yankees got too close again. But Master Bill didn't go to Texas, because the Confederates done come that winter and made him go to the army. . . . Old Master was hopping mad, but he couldn't do anything or they would make him go too, even if he was a preacher. . . . About that time it look like everybody in the world was going to Texas. When we would be going down the road, we would have to walk along the side all the time to let the wagons go past, all loaded with folks going to Texas.

Pretty soon Old Master say, "Git the wagons loaded again," and this time we start out with some other people, going north. We go north a while and then turn west, and cross the Sabine River and go to Nachedoches, Texas. Me and my brother Joe and my sister Adeline walked nearly all the way, but my little sister Harriet and my mammy rid in a wagon. Mammy was mighty poorly, and just when we got to the Sabine bottoms she had another baby. . . . Old Master went with a whole bunch of wagons on out to the prairie country in Coryell County and set up a farm where we just had to break the sod and didn't have to clear off much. . . .

We raised mostly cotton and just a little corn for feed. [Old Master] seemed like he changed a lot since we left Mississippi, and seem like he paid more attention to us and looked after us better. But most the people that already live there when we git there was mighty hard on their Negroes. . . .

One day Old Master come out from town and tell us that we all be set free, and we can go or stay just as we wish.

*Ex-slave Allen V. Manning, in* Lay My Burden Down, *94–97.*

## *The Confederacy: Slaves' Experiences of the War*

[The blacks' spontaneously singing "My country, 'tis of thee" was] so simple, so touching, so utterly unexpected and startling, that I can scarcely believe it on recalling. . . . I never saw anything so electric; it made all other words cheap; it seemed the choked voice of a race at last unloosed.

*Col. Thomas Wentworth Higginson, describing the Port Royal, South Carolina, celebration of the Emancipation Proclamation, in Franklin,* Emancipation Proclamation, *117–18.*

I was table waiter then, and after talking over the news at table, missus would say, "Now Tom, you mustn't repeat a word of this." I would look mighty obedient,—but, well—in less than half an hour, some way, every slave on the plantation would know what had been said up at massa's house. One would see sad faces when the Yankees got whipped. . . . By and by the rebels kept getting beaten, and then it was sing, sing, all through the slave quarters. Old missus asked what they were singing for, but they would only say, because we feel so happy. One night, the report of Lincoln's Proclamation came. Now, master had a son who was a young doctor. I always thought him the best man going: he used to give me money, and didn't believe much in slavery. Next morning I was sitting over in the slave quarters, waiting for breakfast, when the young doctor came along and spoke to my brother and sister, at the front door. . . . They jumped up and down, and shouted, and sang, and then told me I was free. I thought that very nice; for I supposed I should have everything like the doctor, and decided in a moment what kind of a horse I would ride.

*Ex-slave Thomas Rutling, 1872, in* Slave Testimony, *616–17.*

While Master Jim is out fighting the Yanks, the mistress is fiddling round with a neighbor man, Mr. Goldsmith. I is young then, but I knows enough that Master Jim's going be mighty mad when he hears about it.

The mistress didn't know I knows her secret, and I'm fixing to even up for some of them whippings she put off on me. That's why I tell Master Jim next time he come home.

"See that crack in the wall?" Master Jim says, "Yes," and I say, "It's just like the open door when the eyes are close to the wall." He peek and see into the bedroom. "That's how I find out about the mistress and Mr. Goldsmith," I tells him and I see he's getting mad.

"What do you mean?" And Master Jim grabs me hard by the arm like I was trying to get away.

"I see them in the bed."

That's all I say. The demon's got him, and Master Jim tears out of the room looking for the mistress.

Then I hears loud talking and pretty soon the mistress is screaming and calling for help, and if Old Master Ben hadn't drop in just then and stop the fight, why, I guess she be beat almost to death, that how mad the master was.

*Esther Easter, in* Lay My Burden Down, *195.*

[Visitor] number seven [at the office of the Sanitary Commission] was a colored woman, whose husband has been in the Fifty-fourth Massachusetts, under Col. Robert G. Shaw, from its organization. Not a cent has yet been paid by government to any colored soldier who has gone from Chicago. This woman was a slave when the war began,—is still, as far as any manumission by her master is concerned. Since her husband's absence, she has passed through hunger, cold, sickness, and bereavement. Her landlord, a rich man of the city, a German, put her out of her house on the sidewalk, in a cold rain storm, because she owed him five dollars for rent, and could not then earn it, as her child was sick unto death with scarlet fever. One of her colored neighbors, as poor as she, took her in; and the baby died on the next Sunday morning. She came to me to get the baby buried, without going to the poormaster. "It don't seem right for my child to be buried like a pauper," she said, "when her father is fighting for the country." And I agreed with her.

*Livermore,* My Story of the War, *599.*

There were several likely-looking negro-girls still in the cell [in a New Orleans jail], and three mothers. All of these mothers had sons in the Union army. . . . One of them had *three* sons in one regiment; the other had two sons, her only children; and the only child of the third, a boy of nineteen years, was a sergeant in a colored company. These mothers were all the *property* of rebels. . . . I asked them how they happened to be imprisoned, and was informed that their masters and mistresses had them "sent to prison for safe-keeping." One mother told me she was always treated well until her sons joined the negro regiment, since which time she had been whipped and otherwise sadly abused.

*Report to* The Boston Traveller, *quoted in Brown,* American Rebellion, *178–81.*

[M]istress called the colored people together and told them to pray—to pray mightily that the enemy may be driven back. So we prayed and prayed all over the plantation. But 'peared like de more de darkies prayed, de more nearer de Yankees come. Then the missus said, "stop all this praying for the enemies to come." So there was no more praying where mistress could hear it. . . . One day my mistress came out to me. "Maria, M'ria . . . what *does* you pray for?" "I prays, missus, that de Lord's will may be done." "But you mustn't pray that way. You must pray that our enemies may be driven back." "But missus, if it's de Lord's will to drive 'en back, den they will go back."

*Ex-slave Maria, in Raboteau,* Slave Religion, *309.*

The young mens in grey uniforms used to pass so gay and singing, in the big road. Their clothes was good, and we used to feed them the best we had on the place. Missy Angela would say, "Cato, they is our boys and given them the best this place 'fords." We taken out the hams and the wine and kilt chickens for them. That was at first.

Then the boys and mens in blue got to coming that way, and they was fine-looking men, too. Missy Angela would cry and say, "Cato, they is just mens and boys, and we got to feed them, too." We had a pavilion built in the yard, like they had at picnics, and we fed the Federals in that. Missy Angela set in to crying and says to the Yankees, "Don't take Cato. He is the only nigger man I got by me now. If you take Cato, I just don't know what I'll do." I tells them soldiers I got to stay by Missy Angela so long as I live. The Yankee mens say to her, "Don't 'sturb youself, we ain't gwine to take Cato or harm nothing of yours." The reason they's all right by us was 'cause we prepared for them, but with some folks they was rough something terrible.

*Ex-slave Cato, in* Lay My Burden Down, *87.*

[S]ince the issuing of the President's [emancipation] proclamation, Jonas H. French has stopped all of our night-meetings and has caused us to get permits to hold meetings on Sunday, and sends his police around to all of the colored churches every Sunday to examine all of the permits. He had all the slaves that were turned out of their former owners' yards re-arrested and sent back; those who belonged to rebels as well as those who belong to loyal persons. The slaves were mustered into the rebel army. He has them confined in jail to starve and die, and refuses their friends to see them. He is much worse than our rebel masters, he being the chief of police. Last night, after Gen. Banks left the city, Col. French issued a secret order to all the police-stations to arrest all the negroes who may be found in the streets, and at the places of amusement, and placed in jail. There were about five hundred, both free and slave, confined, without the least notice of cause,—persons who thought themselves free by the President's proclamation. . . .

*Letter from a black man in New Orleans to the* New York Tribune, *quoted in Brown,* American Rebellion, *181–82.*

Mother had lots of nice things, quilts and things, and kept 'em in a chest in her little old shack. One day a Yankee soldier climbed in the back window and took some of the quilts. He rolled 'em up and was walking out of the yard when Mother saw him and said,

"Why, you nasty, stinking rascal! You say you come down here to fight for the niggers, and now you're stealing from 'em." He said, "You're a goddam liar. I'm fighting for $14 a month and the Union."

*Ex-slave Sam Word, in* Lay My Burden Down, *206.*

My name is James Carter[.] I am about 44 years old[.] I was brought to Natchez Miss. . . . I belonged to George W. Fox a Druggist in Natchez. During the year I was arrested by the vigilance Committee here and tried for my life. . . . It was represented that certain colored men were in the habit of meeting in a Bayou called Mrs Boyds Bayou and drilling for the purpose of rising against the white. I was charged with getting dispatches from the enemy and reading them to these men. I was . . . tried for about three weeks almost each day. The final day they carried me out then they whipped me terribly. Several of them were whipping me at once. . . . The object in whipping me was to make me confess to something. . . . They would whip until I fainted and then stop and whip again. Dr Harper sat by and would feel my pulse and tell them when to stop and when to go on. . . . At the end of the trial they decided to hang me. . . . I was then taken to the gallows to be hung. . . . They then said to me that they had concluded not to hang me but would give me a whipping and send me home. I was told when I got back to town by Benjamin Pendleton a white man and a deacon in the Baptist Church that he had saved me from being hung. I belonged to his church and he had interfered and told them that I was a pious man and did not associate with these men who went to the Bayou.

*Ex-slave testifying before the Southern Claims Commission, March 31, 1874, in Jordan,* Tumult and Silence, *Document N, 328–29.*

## The Confederacy: White Women's Experiences of the War

[April 26, 1863] It has got to be such a disagreeable matter with me to whip, that I haven't even dressed Kate but once since you left, & then only a few cuts—I am too troubled in mind to get stirred up enough to whip. I made Thornton [another slave] whip Tom once.

[August 18, 1863] The negros are doing nothing. But ours are not doing that job alone[.] . . . [N]early all the negroes around here are at it, some of them are getting so high in anticipation of their glorious freedom by the Yankees I suppose, that they resist a whipping. I don't think we have one who will stay with us.

[August 28, 1863] I am so sick of trying to do a man's business when I am nothing but, a poor contemptible piece of multiplying human flesh tied to the house by a crying young one, looked upon as belonging to a race of inferior beings.

[November 17, 1863. The new part-time male overseer, Meyers,] will be right tight on the negroes I think, but they need it. . . .

[December 6, 1863 Meyers] don't treat [the slaves] as moral beings but manages by brute force.

[March 20, 1864. Please hire out your slaves or] give your negroes away and, I'll . . . work with my hands, as hard as I can, but my mind will rest.

*Lizzie Neblett, letters to her husband reporting her difficulties in managing his eleven slaves, in Faust,* Mothers of Invention, *65–70.*

At New Orleans, where we arrived April 6, 1864, . . . we visited ten colored schools in the city, filled with eager learners. One was taught by Mrs. Brice, who had in charge sixty scholars. She had been teaching here three years, under much persecution, and stemmed the torrent of opposition, sometimes in secret, before the war. Sister Brice and her husband had been struggling in this city nearly five years, through this bitter hate to the North, contending for Unionism everywhere, through civil, religious, and political life. We called on them, and spent two hours in eating oranges and listening to the fanaticisms and wild conceptions of this misguided people and terror-stricken multitude when the "Yankee" soldiers marched up the streets from the gun-boats. Schools were dismissed; the children cried as they ran home, telling those they met that the Yankees had come to kill them and their mothers. But there were those who cried for joy at the sight of the national flag.

*Haviland,* A Woman's Life-Work, *320.*

[Sue] had left. She is still at the Boro, and I am told has hired Elizabeth to work at Dr. Samuel Jones's. Flora is in a most unhappy and uncomfortable condition, doing very little, and that poorly. . . . I overheard an amusing conversation between Cook Kate and herself: they are looking forward to gold watches and chains, bracelets, and *blue veils* and silk dresses! Jack has entered a boarding house in Savannah, where I presume he will practice attitudes and act the Congo gentleman to perfection. Porter and Patience will provide for themselves. I shall cease my anxieties for the race. My life long . . . I have been laboring and caring for [the family slaves], and since the war labored with all my might to supply their wants, and expended everything I had upon their support, directly or indirectly; and this is their return.

*Mary Jones, in* Children of Pride, *1308.*

These [Yankee] men were so outrageous at the Negro houses that the Negro men were obliged to stay at their houses for the protection of their wives; and in some instances they rescued them from the hands of these infamous creatures.

*Mary Mallard, December 17, 1864, in* Children of Pride, *1229, 1230.*

[Moses] slept in the house, every night while at home, & protected everything in the house & yard & at these perilous times when deserters are committing depredations, on plantations every day, I am really so much frightened at night, that I am up nearly all night.

*Maria Hawkins, letter to Gov. Zebulon Vance of North Carolina, requesting release of her slave Moses from working for the Confederate army, in Faust,* Mothers of Invention, *62.*

The workings of Providence in reference to the African race are truly wonderful. The scourge [of the war] falls with peculiar weight upon them: with their emancipation must come their extermination. All history, from their first existence, proves them incapable of self-government; they perish when brought in conflict with the intellectual superiority of the Caucasian race. . . . I never heard such expressions of hatred and contempt as the Yankees heap upon our poor servants. One of them told me he did not know what God Almighty made Negroes for; all he wished was the power to blow their brains out.

*Plantation mistress Mary Jones, January 6, 1865, in* Children of Pride, *1244.*

## *The Aftermath*

When we all gits free, they's the long time letting us know.

*Isabella Boyd, in Campbell,* Empire, *249.*

I suppose you have learned even in the more secluded portions of the country that slavery is entirely abolished. . . . I know it is only intended for a greater humiliation and loss to *us*. . . . On our plantation everything is "at sixes and sevens." One day they work, and the next they come to town. Of course no management of them is allowed. Our Yankee masters think that *their* [the slaves'] term of slavery having expired, that the shackles they have abandoned . . . will do for us their former owners.

*Eva Jones, June 13, 1865, in* Children of Pride, *1274.*

After the war, Master Colonel Sims went to git the mail, and so he call Daniel Ivory, the overseer, and say to him, "Go round to all the quarters and tell all the niggers to come up, I got a paper to read to 'em. They're free now, so you can git you another job, 'cause I ain't got no more niggers which is my own." Niggers come up from the cabins nappy-headed, just like they gwine to the field. Master Colonel Sims, say, 'Caroline [that's my mammy], you is free as me. Pa said bring you back, and I's gwine do just that. So you go on and work and I'll pay you and your three oldest children $10 a month a head and $4 for Harriet"—that's me—and then he turned to the rest and say, "Now all you-uns will receive $10 a head till the crops is laid by." Don't you know before he got halfway through, over half them niggers was gone.

*Ex-slave Harriet Robinson, in* Lay My Burden Down, *229.*

Of the 108 slaves at these pits only four or five left Monday evening, but the next evening there was 30 or 40, the provisions were not entirely issued & some held back to get their weekly allowance of meat &c. The negroes were slow to realize the fact that they were free. Many disclaimed any disposition to be so, particularly Alfred, Philosophy &c. &c. But by Tuesday evening the fever was so high that every soul who had legs to walk was running to Richmond.

*Pit operator Christopher Q. Tompkins, April 1865, in Lewis,* Coal, Iron, and Slaves, *137.*

I charge you, men, to make your homes comfortable, and you, women, to make them happy. Work industriously. Be faithful to each other; be true and honest with all men. If you respect yourselves, others will respect you. There are Northerners who are prejudiced against you; but you can find the way to their hearts and consciences through their pockets. When they find that there are colored tradesmen who have money to spend, and colored farmers who want to buy goods of them, they will no longer call you Jack and Joe; they will begin to think that you are Mr. John Black and Mr. Joseph Brown.

*Speech by Judge Kelly to freedmen and freedwomen, Charleston, S.C., April, 1865, in Child,* Freedmen's Book, *263.*

It is not too late for the [federal] Government to adopt the correct policy in this matter [ownership of captured land]. Sooner or later, this division of property must come about; and the sooner, the better. The land tillers [the former slaves] are entitled by a paramount right to the possession of the soil they have so long cultivated. . . . If the Government will not give them the land, let it be rented to them. It is folly now to deny the Rebellion and not accept all its logical results.

New Orleans Tribune, *a black-owned newspaper, 1865, in Harding,* River, *256.*

The way we can best take care of ourselves is to have land, and turn it and till it by our own labor. . . . We want to be placed on land until we are able to buy it and make it our own. . . .

I would prefer to live by ourselves [rather than scattered among whites], as there is prejudice against us in the South that will take years to get over; but I do not know that I can answer for my brethren.

*Baptist minister Garrison Frazier speaking with Secretary of War Stanton and General Sherman, Savannah, 1865, in Harding,* River, *263.*

Some of us are soldiers and have had the privilege of fighting for our country in this war. . . . We want the privilege of voting. . . . [W]e cannot understand the justice of denying the elective franchise to men who have been fighting for the country, while it is freely given to men who have just returned from four years of fighting against it.

*Petition from the black community of North Carolina, 1865, in Harding,* River, *291.*

Many of the negroes . . . common plantation negroes, and day laborers in the towns and villages, were supporting little schools themselves. Everywhere, I found among them a disposition to get their children into schools, if possible. I had occasion very frequently to notice that porters in stores and laboring men about cotton warehouses, and cart drivers on the streets, had spelling books with them, and were studying them during the time they were not occupied with their work.

*Northern journalist Sidney Andrews, 1865, in Harding,* River, *308.*

From plantation to Senate. Left to right: Benjamin Turner of Alabama, H. R. Revels of Mississippi, Bishop Richard Allen of the A.M.E. Church, Frederick Douglass, Josiah T. Walls of Florida, Joseph H. Rainy of South Carolina, and Dr. William Wells Brown. (*Library of Congress*)

The laws which have made white men powerful have degraded us, because we were black and because we were reduced to the condition of chattels. But now that we are freemen—now that we are elevated, by the Providence of God, to manhood, we have resolved to stand up, and like men, speak and act for ourselves. We fully recognize the truth of the maxim, "The gods help those who help themselves. . . ."

We simply ask that we shall be recognized as *men;* that there be *no obstructions* placed in our way; that the same laws which govern *white men* shall govern *black men;* that we have the right of trial by jury of our peers; that schools be established for the education of *colored children* as well as white; and that the advantages of both colors shall, in this respect, be *equal;* that no impediments be put in the way of our acquiring homesteads for ourselves and our people; that, in short, we be dealt with as others are—in equity and justice.

*Black convention, "Address to the White Inhabitants of the State of South Carolina," 1865, in Harding,* River, *325.*

# APPENDIX A
## Documents

1. From a Virginia act of 1661
2. Virginia act of 1669 "About the Casuall Killings of Slaves"
3. From the charter of the Royal African Company, 1672
4. From a Virginia act of 1680
5. From a Virginia act of 1691 against miscegenation
6. From a British act to settle the trade to Africa, 1698
7. From the Virginia act of 1705 on the status of slaves
8. From a New York law of 1706
9. Circular letter from the [British] Board of Trade to the governors of the English colonies, relative to black slaves
10. Reply of Governor Cranston of Rhode Island
11. From a South Carolina law of 1740
12. From Lord Mansfield's decision in the *Sommersett Case,* 1773, in support of the doctrine that "As soon as a Negro comes into England he becomes free"
13. From Thomas Jefferson's early draft of the Declaration of Independence, a clause rejected by the Continental Congress
14. From the constitution of the Republic of Vermont, 1777
15. Massachusetts Chief Justice Cushing's charge to the jury in *Jennison* v. *Caldwell,* 1781
16. From the Northwest Ordinance of 1787
17. The Constitution of the United States, 1787
    *From Article I, Section 2*
    *From Article I, Section 9*
    *From Article IV, Section 2*
18. From the antislavery petition to the United States Congress of the Pennsylvania Antislavery Society, February 1790, signed by its president, Benjamin Franklin
19. From the Fugitive Slave Act of 1793
20. From an act of Congress, March 22, 1794, to prohibit the carrying on the slave trade from the United States to any foreign place or country
21. From an act of congress, March 2, 1807, to prohibit the importation of slaves into any port or place within the jurisdiction of the United States, from and after January 1, 1808
22. Black commentary on the speech of Mr. John Randolph, of Roanoke at the organizational meeting of the American Colonization Society, 1816
23. From an act of Congress, May 15, 1820
24. From *Walker's Appeal . . . to the Coloured Citizens of the World, But in Particular . . . to Those of the United States of America,* 1829

25. Excerpts from "Nero's" 1831 letter to the South received in Virginia soon after Nat Turner's insurrection
26. From Maria Stewart, "Religion and the Pure Principles of Morality: The Sure Foundation on Which We Must Build," October 1831
27. From Angelina Grimké's Appeal to the Christian Women of the South, 1836
28. From the constitution of the Republic of Texas, 1836: General Provisions
29. From the opinion of Chief Justice Shaw of Massachusetts in *Commonwealth* v. *Aves,* 1836
30. From the ruling of the U.S. Supreme Court in *Prigg* v. *Pennsylvania,* January 1842
31. From the Fugitive Slave Act of 1850
32. From Justice Roger Taney's opinion in the *Dred Scott* case, 1857
33. From an act of Congress, August 6, 1861, to confiscate property used for insurrectionary purpose
34. From the Constitution of the Confederate States of America, 1861
    *Article I, Section 9*
    *Article IV, Section 2*
35. From an act of Congress, April 16, 1862, for the release of certain persons held to service or labor in the District of Columbia
36. From an act of Congress, July 17, 1862, to suppress insurrection, to punish treason and rebellion, to seize and confiscate the property of rebels, and for other purposes
37. From Lincoln's proclamation of the act to suppress insurrection, July 25, 1862
38. The preliminary Emancipation Proclamation, September 22, 1862
39. The Emancipation Proclamation, January 1, 1863
40. Lincoln's order to protect black prisoners of war, 1863
41. From Act to Increase the Efficiency of the [Confederate] Army by the Employment of Free Negroes and Slaves in Certain Capacities, February 17, 1864
42. From an act to increase the military force of the Confederate states, March 23, 1865
43. The Thirteenth Amendment, ratified December 18, 1865
44. The Fourteenth Amendment, ratified July 28, 1868
45. The Fifteenth Amendment to the Constitution, ratified March 30, 1870.

## 1. From a Virginia Act of 1661

[I]n case any English servant shall run away in company of any negroes who are incapable of making satisfaction by addition of a time [because they are already in lifelong servitude]: . . . the English soe running away in the company with them shall at the time of service to their owne masters expired, serve the masters of the said negroes for their absence soe long as they should have done by this Act if they had not beene slaves, every christian in company serving his proportion; and if the negroes be lost or dye in such time of their being run away, the christian servants in company with them shall by proportion among them, either pay fewer [four?] thousand five hundred pounds of tobacco and caske or fewer yeares service for every negro so lost or dead.

## 2. Virginia Act of 1669 "About the Casuall Killings of Slaves"

Whereas the only law in force for the punishment of refractory servants resisting their master, mistress or overseer cannot be inflicted on negroes [because the punishment is extension of time, and the "negroes" are already enslaved for life], Nor the obstinacy of many of them by other than violent meanes suppress. *Be it enacted and declared by this grand assembly,* if any slave resist his master . . . and by the extremity of the correction should chance to die, that his death shall not be accompted Felony, but the master (or that other person appointed by the master to punish him) be acquit from molestation, since it cannot be presumed that propensed malice (which alone makes murther Felony) should induce any man to destroy his own estate.

## 3. From the Charter of the Royal African Company, 1672

Charles the Second by the Grace of God King of England Scotland France and Ireland, Defender of the Faith, etc., To all to whom these presents shall come, Greeting: Whereas all and singular the regions, countrys, dominions and territories, continents, coasts and places, now or at any time heretofore called or known by the name of names of Guinny, Buiny [Benin], Angola and South Barbary, or by any of them, or which are or have been reputed esteemed or taken to be parcel or member of any region country dominion territory or continent called Guinny or Binny, Angola or South Barbary and all and singular ports and havens, rivers, creeks, islands and places in the parts of Africa to them or any of them belonging, and the sole and onely trade and traffic thereof, are the undoubted right of Us our heirs and successors and are and have been enjoyed by Us and by our predecessors for many years past as in right of this our Crown of England.

And whereas the trade of the said regions, countries and places is of great advantage to our subjects of this Kingdom, . . .

Now know ye that We graciously tendering the encouragement and advancement of the said trade and to the end the new Company or Corporation hereafter erected and constituted may be the better enabled to maintain and enlarge the said trade and traffic . . . We have given and granted, and for Us our heirs and successors do hereby give and grant unto our dearest Brother James, Duke of York, Anthony, Earl of Shaftesbury, Mr. John Buckworth, Sir John Banks, John Bence, Esquire, William Earl of Craven, Mr. Jarvis Cartwright, Mr. Samuel Dashwood, Sir Richard Ford, Mr. Thomas Farrington, Captain Ferdinando Gorges, Mr. Edward Hoopegood, Mr. John Jeffries, Sir Andrew King, Charles Modyford, Esquire, Mr. Samuel Moyer, Mr. Peter Proby, Mr. Gabriel Roberts, Sir John Shaw, Mr. Benjamin Skutt, Sir Robert Vyner, Mr. Thomas Vernon, Mr. Nicholas Warren and Mr. Richard Young, their executors and assigns, all and singular the regions, countrys dominions, territories, continents, coasts and places lying and being within the limits and bounds hereafter mentioned (that is to say), beginning at the port of Sallee in South Barbary inclusive, and extending from thence to Cape De Bona Esperanza inclusive, with all the Islands near, adjoining to those Coasts and comprehended within the limits aforesaid, which regions, countrys, dominions, territories, continents, coasts, places and Islands have been heretofore called or known by the name of South Barbary, Guinny, Binny or Angola or by some or any other name or names, which are or have been reputed, esteemed or taken to be part, parcel or member of any Country, region, dominion, territory or continent within the limits aforesaid, and all and singular Ports, Harbours, Creeks, Islands, Lakes, and places in the parts of Africa, to them, or any of them, belonging or being under the obedience of any King, State, or Potentate of any Region, Dominion or Country within the limits aforesaid.

To have and To hold all and singular the said Regions, Countries, Dominions, Territories, Continents, Islands, Coasts and places aforesaid, and all and singular other the premises within the limits aforesaid, to the said James, Duke of York, Anthony, Earl of Shaftesbury, Mr. John Buckworth, Sir John Banks, John Bence, Esquire, William Earl of Craven, Mr. Jarvis Cartwright, Mr. Samuel Dashwood, Sir Richard Ford. Mr. Thomas Farrington, Captain Ferdinando Gorges, Mr. Edward Hoopegood, Mr. John Jeffries, Sir Andrew King, Charles Modyford, Esquire, Mr. Samuel Moyer, Mr. Peter Proby, Mr. Gabriel Roberts, Sir John Shaw, Mr. Benjamin Skutt, Sir Robert Vyner, Mr. Thomas Vernon, Mr. Nicholas Warren and Mr. Richard Young, their ex'ors and assigns, from the making of these, our Letters Pattent, for and during the term, and unto the full end and term of one thousand years, yielding and rendering therefore unto Us, our heirs and successors, two Elephants, whenever we, our heirs and successors, or any of them, shall arrive, land or come into the Dominions, Regions, Countrys, Territories, Plantations and places before mentioned, or any of them.

Nevertheless, our Will and pleasure is, And we do hereby declare the true intent and meaning of these presents to be, that this, our present grant and demise . . . and all the benefits, comodity, profits, and advantages made and to be made and gotten out of the same, or by reason of the term aforesaid, shall be and shall be interpreted to be in Trust and for the sole use, benefit and behoof of the Royal African Company of England hereafter mentioned, and their Successors, and after, in and by these presents Incorporated, or mentioned to be Incorporated, And, therefore, for the setting forward and furtherance of Trade intended, in the parts aforesaid, and the incouragement of the undertakers [entrepreneurs] in the discovering the Golden Mines and settling of Plantations, being an enterprise so laudable and conducing to so worthy an end as the increase of Traffic and Merchandize wherein this nation hath been famous; . . . We do will, ordain, constitute, appoint, give and grant unto our said dearest Brother James, Duke of York, His Highness, Prince Rupert, Anthony Earl of Shaftesbury, Henry, Earl of Arlington, [and 199 others] that they and all such others, as they shall from time to time think fit and convenient to receive into their Company and Society to be traders and adventurers with them to the said Countries, shall be one body Politick and Corporate of themselves, in deed and in name, by the name of the Royal African Company of England. . . .

And further, of Our more especial Grace, certain knowledge and mere motion, We do hereby, for us, our heirs and Successors, grant unto the said Royal African Company of England and their Successors, that it shall and may be lawful to and for the said Company and their Successors, and none others, from time to time to set to Sea such and so many shipps, pinnaces, and barks as shall be thought fitting . . . prepared and furnished with Ordnance, Artillery and Ammunition or any other habiliments in warlike manner fitt and necessary for their defence; And shall for ever hereafter have, use and enjoy all mines of Gold and Silver . . . which are or shall be found in all or any the places above mentioned, And the whole, entire and only Trade, liberty, use and privilege of Trade and Traffic into and from the said parts of Africa above mentioned. . . .

And likewise that it shall and may be lawful to and for the said Royal African Company of England and their Successors, and none others, from henceforth, at any time or times, from time to time, after the date of these presents, to use, prepare and set to Sea such and so many Ships, Barks and Pinnaces and such number of men to sail therein for the further discovery of the said Rivers and places before mentioned, and all Lands, Dominions and Territories within the compass of the same, paying always unto us, our heirs and Successors such customs, subsidies, imposts and other duties as shall be due and payable for and in respective of the exportation and importation of any goods, Wares and Merchandizes by them or any of them, to be exported or imported by virtue of these presents.

And of our further Royal Favour, . . . We do grant unto the said Royal African Company of England and their Successors that the said Regions, Countries, Dominions, Continents, Territories, Islands, Coasts, Rivers, places and passages within the limits and bounds aforesaid, or any of them, or the Lands, Seignories or Dominions thereunto adjoining shall not be visited, frequented or traded unto by any other of our subjects, or by any other of the subjects of our heirs and successors. . . .

We do hereby, for us, our heirs and Successors, grant and give full power and authority unto the said

Royal African Company of England and their successors for the time being, that they, by themselves, their factors, deputies and assigns, shall and may from time to time, and at all times hereafter, enter into any Ship, Vessel, house, shop, Cellar or work-house and attack, arrest, take and seize all and all manner of ships, vessels, Negroes, Slaves, goods, Wares and Merchandizes whatsoever which shall be brought from or carried to the places aforementioned, or any of them, contrary to our Will and pleasure, before in these presents expressed. . . .

And we do of our more especial grace and favour certain knowledge and mere motion for us our heirs and Successors give and grant unto the said Royal African Company of England, that the Governor, Sub-Governor, Deputy Governor and Assistants of the said Company for the time being . . . shall and may have the ordering rule and government of all such forts, factories and plantations as now are or shall be at any time hereafter settled by or under the said Company within the parts of Africa aforementioned, and also full power to make and declare peace and war with any of the heathen nations that are or shall be natives of any countries within the said territories in the said parts of Africa as there shall be occasion, as also that the said Governor, Sub-Governor and Deputy Governor and assistants, for the time being . . . shall have full power, license, and authority, to name and appoint Governors and Officers, from time to time, in the said factories and plantations, which said Governors shall have, and by these presents we do, for us, our heirs and Successors, give to them full power and authority to raise armies, train and muster such military forces as to them shall seem requisite and necessary and to execute and use within the said plantations the Laws called the Marshall [martial] Laws, for the defence of the said plantations against any foreign invasion or domestick insurrection or Rebellion. . . .

And for the more effectual encouragement of merchants that shall trade into the places aforesaid and for the attracting of trade to these parts We . . . erect constitute and establish a Court of Judicature to be held at such place or places, fort or forts, plantations or factories upon the said coasts as the said company shall from time to time direct and appoint, . . . [with] cognizance and power to hear and determine all cases of forfeiture and seizures of any ship or ships, goods and merchandizes trading and coming upon any of the said coasts or limits contrary to the true intent of these presents, and also all causes of mercantile or maritime bargains buying selling and bartering of wares whatsoever and all policies or acts of assurance all bills bonds or promises for payment of money on mercantile or trading contract all charter parties or covenants for afreighting of vessels and wages of mariners and all other mercantile and maritime cases whatsoever concerning any person or persons residing, coming or being in the places aforesaid, and all cases of tre[s]passes, injuries and wrongs done or committed upon the high sea or in any of the regions, territories, countries or places aforesaid concerning any person or persons residing coming or being in the parts of Africa within the bounds and limits aforesaid. . . .

In Witness etc. Witness the king at Westminster the seven and twentieth day of September [1672].

## 4. From a Virginia Act of 1680

Act X. Whereas the frequent meetings of considerable numbers of Negro slaves under pretense of feasts and burials is judged of dangerous consequence [it is] enacted that no Negro or slave may carry arms, such as any club, staff, gun, sword, or other weapon, nor go from his owner's plantation without a certificate and then only on necessary occasions; the punishment twenty lashes on the bare back, well laid on. And further, if any Negro lift up his hand against any Christian he shall receive thirty lashes, and if he absent himself or lie out from his master's service and resist lawful apprehension, he may be killed. . . .

## 5. From a Virginia Act of 1691 against Miscegenation

[Act XVI]. . . . whatsoever English or other white man or woman, bond or free, shall intermarry with a Negro, mulatto, or Indian man or woman, bond or free, he shall within three months be banished from this dominion forever.

And it is further enacted, that if any English woman being free shall have a bastard child by a Negro she shall pay fifteen pounds to the church wardens, and in default of such payment, she shall be taken into possession by the church wardens and disposed of for five years and the amount she brings shall be paid one-third to their majesties for the support of the government, one-third to . . . the parish where the offense is committed and the other third to the informer. The child shall be bound out by the church wardens until he is thirty years of age. In case the English woman that shall have a bastard is a servant she shall be sold by the church wardens (after her time is expired) for five years, and the child serve as aforesaid.

## 6. From a British Act to Settle the Trade to Africa, 1698

I. Whereas the Trade to Africa is highly beneficial and advantagious to this kingdom, and to the Plantations and Colonies thereunto belonging: and whereas Forts and Castles are undoubtedly necessary for the preservation and well carrying on the said Trade. . . . Be it therefore enacted by the King's most Excellent Majesty and by and with the Advice and Consent of the Lords Spiritual and Temporal and Commons in Parliament assembled and by the Authority of the same That from and after the Four and twentieth Day of June in the Year One thousand six hundred ninety and eight the said Royal African Company their Successors and Assigns by and with their Stock, and Duties herein after appointed to be paid, shall maintain, support and defend all such Forts and Castles as the said African Company now have in their Possession or shall hereafter purchase or erect . . . and at all times hereafter as occasion shall require shall supply with Men Artillery, Ammunition and Provision, and all other Necessaries and incident Charges whatsoever.

II. And the better to enable the said Royal African Company, their Successors and Assigns, to maintain the said Castles and Forts and for the Preservation and well carrying on the said Trade to and for the Advantage of England and the Plantations and Colonies thereunto belonging: Be it further enacted That it shall and may be lawfull to and for any of the Subjects of His Majesties Realm of England as well as for the said Company from and after the said Four and Twentieth Day of June to trade from England, and from and after the First of August One thousand six hundred ninety and eight from any of His Majesties Plantations and Colonies in America, to and for the Coast of Africa between Cape Mount and the Cape of Good Hope, the said Company and all other the said Subjects answering and paying for the Uses aforesaid a Duty of Ten Pounds per Centum ad Valorem for [of the value of] the Goods and Merchandize to be exported from England or from any of His Majesties Plantations or Colonies in America to and for the Coast of Africa between Cape Mount and the Cape of Good Hope and in proportion for a greater or lesser Value in Manner and Forme as herein after expressed. . . .

XIV. Provided always and be it enacted by the Authority aforesaid That all Persons being the natural born Subjects of England trading to the Coast of Africa as aforesaid and paying the Duties by this Act imposed, shall have the same Protection Security and Defence for their Persons Ships and Goods by from and in all the said Forts and Castles and the like Freedom and Security for their Negotiations and Trade to all Intents and Purposes whatsoever as the said Company their Agents Factors and Assigns and their Ships and Goods have, may or shall have, and that all and every person and Persons trading to Africa and paying the Duties as aforesaid may and are hereby impowered at their own Charge to Settle Factories [establishments for traders carrying on business in a foreign country] on any part of Africa within the Limits aforesaid according as they shall judge necessary and convenient for the carrying on their Trade without any Lett Hindrance or Molestation from the said Company, their Agents Factors or Assigns, and that all Persons not Members of the said Company so trading and paying the said Duties as aforesaid shall, together with their Shipps and Goods, be free from all Molestations Hindrances Restraints Arrests Seizures Penalties or other Impositions whatso[e]ver from the said Company, their Agents Factors or Assigns, for or by reason of their so trading, Any Charter Usage or Custom to the contrary in any wise notwithstanding. . . .

XX. And be it enacted by the Authority aforesaid, That no Governor or Deputy Governor of any of his Majesties Colonies or Plantations in America or His Majesties Judges in any Courts there for the time being nor any other Person or Persons for the use or on behalf of such Governor or Deputy Governor or Judges from and after the Nine and twentieth Day of September One thousand six hundred ninety eight shall be a Factor or Factors, Agent or Agents for the said Company, or any other Person or Persons for the Sale or disposal of any Negroes and that every Person offending herein shall Forfeit Five hundred pounds. . . .

Provided that this Act shall continue and be in Force Thirteen Years and thence to the end of the next Sessions of Parliament and no longer.

## 7. From the Virginia Act of 1705 on the Status of Slaves

XXIII. All Negro, mulatto, and Indian slaves within this dominion shall be held to be real estate and not chattels and shall descend unto heirs and widows according to the custom of land inheritance, and be held in "*fee simple*." . . .

Nothing is this act shall be construed to give the owner of a slave not seized of other real estate the right to vote as a freeholder. . . .

XXXIV. And if any slave resist his master, or owner, or other person, by his or her order, correcting such slave, and shall happen to be killed in such correction, it shall not be accounted felony; but the master, owner, and every such other person so giving correction, shall be free and acquit of all punishment and accusation for the same, as if such accident had never happened.

## 8. From a New York Law of 1706

All and every, Negro, Indian, Mulatto and Mestee Bastard child and children who is, are, and shall be born of any Negro, Indian, Mulatto or Mestee shall follow ye state and condition of the mother and shall be esteemed reputed taken & adjudged a Slave & slaves to all intents and purposes whatsoever.

## 9. Circular Letter from the [British] Board of Trade to the Governors of the English Colonies, Relative to Black Slaves

April 17, 1708

SIR: Some time since, the Queen was pleased to refer to us a petition relating to the trade of Africa, upon which we have heard what the Royal African Company, and the separate traders had to offer; and having otherwise informed ourselves, in the best manner we could, of the present state of that trade, we laid the same before Her Majesty. The consideration of that trade came afterwards into the house of commons, and a copy of our report was laid before the house; but the session being then too far spent to enter upon a matter of so great weight, and other business intervening, no progress was made therein. However, it being absolutely necessary that a trade so beneficial to the kingdom should be carried on to the greatest advantage, there is no doubt but the consideration thereof will come early before the Parliament at their next meeting; and as the well supplying of the plantations and colonies with sufficient number of negroes at reasonable prices, is in our opinion the chief point to be considered in regard to that trade, and as hitherto we have not been able to know how they have been supplied by the company, or by separate traders, otherwise than according to the respective accounts given by them, which for the most part are founded upon calculations made from their exports on one side and the other, and do differ so very much, that no certain judgment can be made upon those accounts.

Wherefore, that we may be able at the next meeting of the Parliament to lay before both houses when required, an exact and authentic state of that trade, particularly in regard to the several plantations and colonies; we do hereby desire and strictly require you, that upon the receipt hereof, you do inform yourself from the proper officers or otherwise, in the best manner you can, what number of negroes have been yearly imported directly from Africa into Jamaica, since the 24th of June, 1698, to the 25th of December, 1707, and at what rate per head they have been sold each year, one with another, distinguishing the numbers that have been imported on account of the Royal African Company, and those which have been imported by separate traders; as likewise the rates at which such negroes have been sold by the company and by separate traders. We must recommend it to your care to be as exact and diligent therein as possibly you can, and with the first opportunity to transmit to us such accounts as aforesaid, that they may arrive here in due time. . . .

Lastly, whatever accounts you shall from time to time send us touching these matters of the negro trade, we desire that the same may be distinct, and not intermixed with other matters; and that for the time to come, you do transmit to us the like half yearly accounts of negroes, by whom imported and at what rates sold; the first of such subsequent accounts, to begin from Christmas, 1707, to which time those now demanded, are to be given. . . .

P.S. We expect the best account you can give us, with that expedition which the shortness of the time requires.

Memorandum. This letter, mutatis mutandis, was writ to the Governors of Barbados, the Leeward Islands, Bermuda, New York, New Jersey, Maryland, the President of the Council of Virginia, the Governor of New Hampshire and the Massachusetts

Bay, the Deputy Governor of Pennsylvania, the Lords proprietors of Carolina, the Governors and Companies of Connecticut and Rhode Island.

## 10. Reply of Governor Cranston of Rhode Island

May it please your Lordships: In obedience to your Lordships' commands of the 15th of April last, to the trade of Africa.

We, having inspected into the books of Her Majesty's custom, and informed ourselves from the proper officers thereof, by strict inquiry, can lay before your Lordships no other account of that trade than the following, viz.:

1. That from the 24th of June, 1698, to the 25th of December, 1707, we have not had any negroes imported into this colony from the coast of Africa....

2. That on the 30th day of May, 1696, arrived at this port from the coast of Africa, the brigantine Seaflower, Thomas Windsor, master, having on board her forty-seven negroes, fourteen of which he disposed of in this colony, for betwixt £30 and £35 per head; the rest he transported by land for Boston, where his owners lived.

3. That on the 10th of August, the 19th and 28th of October, in the year 1700, sailed from this port three vessels, directly for the coast of Africa; the two former were sloops, the one commanded by Nicho's Hillgroue, the other by Jacob Bill; the last a ship, commanded by Edwin Caster, who was part owner of the said three vessels, in company with Thomas Bruster, and John Bates, merchants, of Barbadoes, and separate traders from thence to the coast of Africa; the said three vessels arriving safe to Barbadoes from the coast of Africa, where they made the disposition of their negroes.

4. That we have never had any vessels from the coast of Africa to this colony, nor any trade there, the brigantine above mentioned, excepted.

5. That the whole and only supply of negroes to this colony, is from the island of Barbadoes; from whence is imported one year with another, betwixt twenty and thirty; and if those arrive well and sound, the general price is from £30 to £40 per head.

According to your Lordships' desire, we have advised with the chiefest of our planters, and find but small encouragement for that trade to this colony; since by the best computation we can make, there would not be disposed in this colony above twenty or thirty at the most, annually; the reasons of which are chiefly to be attributed to the general dislike our planters have for them, by reason of their turbulent and unruly tempers.

And that most of our planters that are able and willing to purchase any of them, are supplied by the offspring of those they have already, which increase daily; and that the inclination of our people in general, is to employ white servants before Negroes....

Newport, on Rhode Island, December 5, 1708.

## 11. From a South Carolina Law of 1740

All Negroes, Indians (free Indians in amity with this government, and Negroes, mulattoes, and mestizoes, who are now free, excepted), mulattoes, and mestizoes, who are or shall hereafter be in this province and all their issue and offspring born or to be born, shall be and they are hereby declared to be and remain forever after absolute slaves, and shall follow the condition of their mother.

## 12. From Lord Mansfield's Decision in the *Sommersett Case,* 1772, in Support of the Doctrine That "As Soon as a Negro Comes into England He Becomes Free"

The state of slavery is of such a nature, that it is incapable of being introduced on any reasons, moral or political, but only by positive law, which preserves its force long after the reasons, occasion, and time itself from whence it was created, is erased from memory. It is so odious that nothing can be suffered to support it, but positive law [no such law existing in England]. Whatever inconveniences, therefore, may follow from the decision, I cannot say this case is allowed or approved by the law of England; and therefore the black must be discharged [freed].

## 13. From Thomas Jefferson's Early Draft of the Declaration of Independence, a Clause Rejected by the Continental Congress

[George III] has waged cruel war against human nature itself, violating its most sacred rights of life and liberty in the persons of a distant people who never offended him, captivating and carrying them into slavery in another hemisphere, or to incur miserable death in their transportation thither. This piratical warfare, the opprobrium of infidel powers, is the warfare of the Christian king of Great Britain. Determined to keep open a market where Men should be bought and sold, he has prostituted his negative veto for suppressing every legislative attempt to prohibit or to restrain this execrable commerce.

## 14. From the Constitution of the Republic of Vermont, 1777

No male person, born in this country, or brought from over sea, ought to be holden by law, to serve any person, as a servant, slave, or apprentice, after he arrives at the age of twenty-one years, nor female in like manner, after she arrives to the age of eighteen years, unless they are bound by their own consent, after they arrive at such age, or bound by law, for the payment of debts, damages, fines, costs, and the like.

## 15. Massachusetts Chief Justice Cushing's Charge to the Jury in *Jennison v. Caldwell*, 1781

The defense ... is founded on the assumed proposition that slavery had been by law established in this province: that rights to slaves, as property, acquired by law, ought not to be divested by any construction of the [1780] Constitution [of Massachusetts] by implication; and that slavery in that instrument is not expressly abolished. It is true ... that [slaves] had been considered by some of the Province laws as actually existing among us; but nowhere do we find it expressly established. It was a usage.... But whatever usages formerly prevailed . . ., they can no longer exist. Sentiments more favorable to the natural rights of mankind, and to that innate desire for liberty which heaven, without regard to complexion or shape, has planted in the human breast—have prevailed since the glorious struggle for our rights began. And these sentiments led the framers of our constitution of government—by which the people of this commonwealth have solemnly bound themselves to each other—to declare—*that all men are born free and equal; and that every subject is entitled to liberty,* and to have it guarded by the laws as well as his life and property.... [S]lavery is in my judgment as effectively abolished as it can be by the granting of rights and privileges wholly incompatible and repugnant to its existence. The court are therefore fully of the opinion that perpetual servitude can no longer be tolerated in our government....

## 16. From the Northwest Ordinance of 1787

Art. 2. The inhabitants of the said territory shall always be entitled to the benefits of the writ of *habeas corpus,* and of the trial of jury; of a proportionate representation of the people in the legislature; and of judicial proceedings according to the course of the common law. . . . No man shall be deprived of his liberty or property, but by the judgment of his peers or the law of the land; and, should the public exigencies make it necessary, for the common preservation, to take any person's property, or to demand his particular services, full compensation shall be made for the same. And, in the just preservation of rights and property, it is understood and declared, that no law ought ever to be made, or have force in the said territory, that shall, in any manner whatever, interfere with or affect private contracts or engagements, *bona fide* [in good faith], and without fraud, previously formed....

Art. 5. There shall be formed in the said territory, not less than three nor more than five States; . . . And, whenever any of the said States shall have sixty thousand free inhabitants therein, such State shall be admitted, by its delegates, into the Congress of the United States, on an equal footing with the original States in all respects whatever, . . . *Provided,* the constitution and government so to be formed, shall be republican, and in conformity to the principles contained in these articles....

Art. 6. There shall be neither slavery nor involuntary servitude in the said Territory, otherwise than in the punishment of crimes, whereof the party shall have been duly convicted; *provided,* always, that any person escaping into the same, from whom labor or service is lawfully claimed in any one of the original States, such fugitive may be lawfully reclaimed and conveyed to the person claiming his or her labor or service aforesaid.

## 17. The Constitution of the United States, 1787

### *From Article I, Section 2*

Representatives and direct Taxes shall be apportioned among the several States which may be included within this Union, according to their respective Numbers, which shall be determined by adding to the whole Number of free Persons, including those bound to Service for a Term of Years, and excluding Indians not taxed, three fifths of all other persons.

### *From Article I, Section 9*

The Migration or Importation of such Persons as any of the States now existing shall think proper to admit, shall not be prohibited by the Congress prior to the Year one thousand eight hundred and eight, but a Tax or duty may be imposed on such Importation, not exceeding ten dollars for each person.

### *From Article IV, Section 2*

No person held to Service or Labour in one State, under the Laws thereof, escaping into another, shall, in Consequence of any Law or Regulation therein, be discharged from such Service or Labour, but shall be delivered up on Claim of the Party to whom such Service or Labour may be due.

## 18. From the Antislavery Petition to the U.S. Congress of the Pennsylvania Antislavery Society February 1790, Signed by Its President Benjamin Franklin

From a persuasion that equal liberty was originally the portion, and is still the birthright of all men; and influenced by the strong ties of humanity, and the principles of their institution, your memorialists conceive themselves bound to use all justifiable endeavors to loosen the bonds of slavery, and promote a general enjoyment of the blessings of freedom. Under these impressions, they earnestly entreat your serious attention to the subject of slavery; that you will be pleased to countenance the restoration of liberty to those unhappy men, who alone, in this land of freedom are degraded into perpetual bondage, and who, amidst the general joy of surrounding freemen, are groaning in servile subjection; that you will devise means for removing this inconsistency from the character of the American people; that you will promote mercy and justice towards this distressed race, and that you will step to the very verge of the power vested in you for discouraging every species of traffic in the persons of our fellowmen.

## 19. From the Fugitive Slave Act of 1793

That when a person held to labor in any of the United States or in either of the Territories on the Northwest or South of the river Ohio, under the laws thereof, shall escape into any other of the said States or Territory, the person to whom such labor or service may be due, his agent or attorney, is hereby empowered to seize or arrest such fugitive from labor, and to take him or her before any Judge of the Circuit or District Courts of the United States, residing or being within the State, or before any magistrate of a county, city, or town corporate, wherein such seizure or arrest shall be made, and upon proof to the satisfaction of such judge or magistrate, either by oral testimony or affidavit taken before and certified by a magistrate of any such State or Territory, that the person so seized or arrested, doth, under the laws of the State or Territory from which he or she fled, owe service or labor to the person claiming him or her, it shall be the duty of such Judge or magistrate to give a certificate thereof to such claimant, his agent, or attorney, which shall be sufficient warrant for removing the said fugitive from labor to the State or Territory from which he or she fled.

## 20. From an Act of Congress, March 22, 1794, to Prohibit the Carrying on the Slave-trade from the United States to Any Foreign Place or Country

SECTION I. BE *it enacted by the Senate and House of Representatives of the United States of America, in Congress assembled,* That no citizen or citizens of the United States, or foreigner, or any other person coming into, or residing within the same, shall, for himself, or, any other person whatsoever, either as master, factor or owner, build, fit, equip, load or otherwise prepare any ship or vessel within any port or place of the said United States, nor shall cause any ship or vessel to sail from any port or place within the same, for the purpose of carrying on any trade or traffic in slaves, to any foreign country; or for the purpose of procuring, from any foreign kingdom, place or country, the inhabitants of such kingdom, place or country, to be transported to any foreign country, port or place whatever, to be sold or disposed of, as slaves: And if any ship or vessel shall be so fitted out, as aforesaid, for the said purposes, or shall be caused to sail, so as aforesaid, every such ship or vessel, her tackle, furniture, apparel and other appurtenances, shall be forfeited to the United Sates; and shall be liable to be seized, prosecuted and condemned, in any of the circuit courts or district court for the district, where the said ship or vessel may be found and seized.

SECTION II. *And be it further enacted,* That all and every person, so building, fitting out, equipping, loading, or otherwise preparing, or sending away, any ship or vessel, knowing, or intending, that the same shall be employed in such trade or business, contrary to the true intent and meaning of this act, or any ways aiding or abetting therein, shall severally forfeit and pay the sum of two thousand dollars, one moiety thereof, to the use of the United States, and the other moiety thereof, to the use of him or her, who shall sue for and prosecute the same.

SECTION III. *And be it further enacted,* That the owner, master or factor of each and every foreign ship or vessel, clearing out for any of the coasts or kingdoms of Africa, or suspected to be intended for the slave-trade, and the suspicion being declared to the officer of the customs, by any citizen, on oath or affirmation, and such information being to the satisfaction of the said officer, shall first give bond with sufficient sureties, to the Treasurer of the United States, that none of the natives of Africa, or any other foreign country or place, shall be taken on board the said ship or vessel, to be transported, or sold as slaves, in any other foreign port or place whatever, within nine months thereafter.

SECTION IV. *And be it further enacted,* That if any citizen or citizens of the United States shall, contrary to the true intent and meaning of this act, take on board, receive or transport any such persons, as above described in this act, for the purpose of selling them as slaves, as aforesaid, he or they shall forfeit and pay, for each and every person, so received on board, transported, or sold as aforesaid, the sum of two hundred dollars, to be recovered in any court of the United States proper to try the same; the one moiety thereof, to the use of the United States, and the other moiety to the use of such person or persons, who shall sue for and prosecute the same.

Frederick Augustus Muhlenberg,
*Speaker of the House of Representatives.*
John Adams,
*Vice-President of the United States, and President of the Senate.*

Approved—March the twenty-second, 1794.
Go: Washington, *President of the United States.*

## 21. From an Act of Congress, March 2, 1807, to Prohibit the Importation of Slaves into Any Port or Place within the Jurisdiction of the United States, from and after January 1, 1808

*Be it enacted* . . . That from and after the first day of January, one thousand eight hundred and eight, it shall not be lawful to import or bring into the United States or the territories thereof from any foreign kingdom, place or country, any negro, mulatto, or person of colour, with intent to hold, sell, or dispose of such negro, mulatto, or person of colour, as a slave, or to be held to service or labour.

SEC. 2. *And be it further enacted,* That no citizen or citizens of the United States, or any other person, shall, from and after the first day of January, in the year of our Lord one thousand eight hundred and eight, for himself, or themselves, or any other person whatsoever, either as master, factor, or owner build, fit, equip, load or otherwise prepare any ship or vessel to sail from any port or place within the same, for the purpose of procuring any negro, mulatto, or person of colour, from any foreign kingdom, place, or country, to be transported to any port or place whatsoever, within the jurisdiction of the United States, to be held, sold, or disposed of as slaves, or to be held to service or labour; and if any ship or vessel shall be so fitted out for the purpose aforesaid, or shall be caused to sail so as aforesaid, every such ship or vessel, her tackle, apparel, and furniture, shall be forfeited to the United States, and shall be liable to be seized, prosecuted, and condemned in any of the circuit courts or district courts, for the district where the said ship or vessel may be found or seized.

## 22. Black Commentary on the Speech of Mr. John Randolph, of Roanoke at the Organizational Meeting of the American Colonization Society, 1816

Said he:—

"There is no fear that this proposition would alarm the slave-holders; they had been accustomed to think seriously of the subject.—There was a popular work on agriculture, by John Taylor of Caroline, which was widely circulated, and much confided in, in Virginia. In that book, much read because coming from a practical man, this description of people were pointed out as a great evil. They had indeed been held up as the greater bug-bear to every man who feels an inclination to emancipate his slaves, not to create in the bosom of his country so great a nuisance. If a place could be provided for their reception, and a mode of sending them hence, there were hundreds, nay thousands of citizens who would, by manumitting their slaves, relieve themselves from the cares attendant on their possession. The great slave-holder . . . was frequently a mere sentry at his own door—bound to stay on his plantation to see that his slaves were properly treated, &c. (Mr. R. concluded by saying,) that he had thought it necessary to make these remarks being a slave-holder himself, to shew that, so far from being connected with abolition of slavery, the measure proposed would prove one of the greatest securities to enable the master to keep in possession of his own property."

Here is a demonstrative proof, of a plan got up, by a gang of slave-holders to select the free people of colour from among the slaves, that our more miserable brethren may be the better secured in ignorance and wretchedness, to work their farms and dig their mines, and thus go on enriching the Christians with their blood and groans.

If any of us see fit to go away, go to those who have been for many years, and are now our greatest earthly friends and benefactors—the English. If not so, go to our brethren, the Haytians, who, according to their word, are bound to protect and comfort us. . . .

And now brethren, . . . Should tyrants take it into their heads to emancipate any of you, remember that freedom is your natural right. You are men, as well as they, and instead of returning thanks to them for your freedom, return it to the Holy Ghost. . . . If they do not want to part with your labours, which have enriched them, let them keep you, and my word for it, that God Almighty, will break their strong brand. . . . Whether you believe it or not, I tell you that God will dash tyrants, in combination with devils, into atoms, and will bring you out from your wretchedness and miseries under these *Christian People!!!!!*

Those philanthropists and lovers of the human family, who have volunteered their services for our redemption from wretchedness, have a nigh claim on our gratitude, and we should always view them as our greatest earthly benefactors. . . .

In conclusion, I ask the candid and unprejudiced of the whole world, to search the pages of historians diligently, and see if the Antideluvians—the Sodomites—the Egyptians—the Babylonians—the Ninevites—the Carthagenians—the Persians—the Macedonians—the Greeks—the Romans—the Mahometans—the Jews—or devils, ever treated a set of human beings as the white Christians of America do us, the blacks, or Africans. I also ask the attention of the world of mankind to the declaration [of Independence] of these very American people, of the United States. . . .

See your Declaration Americans!!! Do you understand your own language? . . . Compare your own language . . . with your cruelties and murders inflicted by your cruel and unmerciful fathers and yourselves on our fathers and on us—men who have never given your fathers or you the least provocation!!!!!

The Americans may be as vigilant as they please, but they cannot be vigilant enough for the Lord, neither can they hide themselves, where he will not find and bring them out.

## 23. From an Act of Congress, May 15, 1820

If any citizen of the United States, being of the crew or ship's company of any foreign ship or vessel engaged in the slave trade, or any person whatever, being of the crew, or ship's company of any ship or vessel, owned in the whole or in part, or navigated for, or in behalf of, any citizen or citizens of the United States, shall . . . seize any negro or mulatto not held to service or labour by the laws of either of the states or territories of the United States, with intent to make such negro or mulatto a slave, or shall decoy, or . . . forcibly confine or detain, or aid and abet in forcibly confining or detaining, on board such ship or vessel, any negro . . ., such citizen or person shall be adjudged a pirate; and . . . shall suffer death.

## 24. From *Walker's Appeal . . . to the Coloured Citizens of the World, but in Particular . . . to Those of the United States of America*, 1829

[A]s the inhuman system of *slavery,* is the *source* from which most of our miseries proceed, I shall begin with that *curse* to *nations*. . . . [T]he labour of slaves comes too cheap to the avaricious usurpers, and is (as they think) of such great utility to the country where it exists, that those who are actuated by sordid avarice only, overlook the evils, which will as sure as the Lord lives, follow after the good. In fact, they are so happy to keep in ignorance and degradation, and to receive the homage and labour of the slaves, they forget that God rules in the armies of heaven and among the inhabitants of the earth, having his ears continually open to the cries, tears and groans of his oppressed people; and being a just and holy Being will at one day appear fully in behalf of the oppressed. . . .

I promised . . . to demonstrate . . . that we, (coloured people of these United States of America) are the *most wretched, degraded,* and *abject* set of beings that *ever lived* since the world began, and that the white Americans having reduced us to the wretched state of *slavery,* treat us in that condition *more cruel* (they being an enlight[en]ed and Christian people,) than any heathen nation did any people whom it had reduced to our condition. . . .

I saw a paragraph . . . in a South Carolina paper, which, speaking of the barbarity of the Turks, it said: "The Turks are the most barbarous people in the world—they treat the Greeks more like *brutes* than human beings." And in the same paper was an advertisement, which said, "Eight well built Virginia and Maryland *Negro fellows* and four *wenches* will positively be *sold* this day, *to the highest bidder!*" . . .

I have been for years troubling the pages of historians, to find out what our fathers have done to the *white Christians of America,* to merit such condign punishment as they have inflicted on them. . . . I have therefore, come to the immoveable conclusion, that they have, and do continue to punish as for nothing else, but for enriching them and their country. . . .

Ignorance, my brethren, is a mist, low down into the very dark and almost impenetrable abyss in which, our fathers for many centuries have been plunged. The Christians, and enlightened of Europe, and some of Asia, seeing the ignorance and consequent degradation of our fathers, instead of trying to enlighten them, by teaching them that religion and light with which God had blessed them, they have plunged them into wretchedness ten thousand times more intolerable, than if they had left them entirely to the Lord, and to add to their miseries, deep down into which they have plunged them tell, that they are an *inferior* and *distinct race* of beings, which they will be glad enough to recall and swallow by and by. . . .

[W]hen I view that mighty son of Africa, HANNIBAL, one of the greatest generals of antiquity, who defeated and cut off so many thousands of the white Romans or murderers, and who carried his victorious arms, to the very gate of Rome, and I give it as my candid opinion, that had Carthage been well united and had given him good support, he would have carried that cruel and barbarous city by storm. But they were dis-united, as the coloured people are now, in the United States of America, the reason our natural enemies are enabled to keep their feet on our throats. . . .

Beloved brethren—here let me tell you, and believe it, that the Lord our God . . . will give you a Hannibal. . . .

But what need have I to refer to antiquity, when Hayti, the glory of the blacks and terror of tyrants, is enough to convince the most avaricious and stupid of wretches. . . .

Ignorance and treachery one against the other—a grovelling service and abject submission to the lash of tyrants, we see plainly, my brethren, are not the natural elements of the blacks. . . .

[T]hey [whites] would die to a man, before they would suffer such things from men. Yes, how can our friends but be embarrassed, as Mr. Jefferson says, by the question, "What further is to be done with these people?" For while they are working for our emancipation, we are, by our treachery, wickedness and deceit, working against ourselves and our children—helping ours, and the enemies of God, to keep us and our dear little children in their infernal chains of slavery!!! . . .

Men of colour, who are also of sense, for you particularly is my APPEAL designed. Our more ignorant brethren are not able to penetrate its value. I call upon you therefore to cast your eyes upon the wretchedness of your brethren, and to do your utmost to enlighten them—*go to work and enlighten your brethren!*—Let the Lord see you doing what you can to rescue them and your selves from degradation. Do any of you say that you and your family are free and happy, and what have you to do with the wretched slaves and other people? So can I say, for I enjoy as much freedom as any of you, if I am not quite as well off as the best of you. Look into our freedom and happiness, and see of what kind they are composed!! They are of the very lowest kind—they are the very *dregs!*—they are the most servile and abject kind, that ever a people was in possession of. If any of you wish to know how FREE you are, let one of you start and go through the southern and western States of this country, and unless you travel as a slave to a white man . . . or have your free papers, . . . if they do not take you up and put you in jail, and if you cannot give good evidence of your freedom, sell you into eternal slavery, I am not a living man. . . .

I advance it therefore to you, not as a *problematical.* but as an unshaken and for ever immoveable *fact,* that your full glory and happiness, as well as all other coloured people under Heaven, shall never be fully consummated, but with the *entire emancipation of your enslaved brethren all over the world.*

There is great work for you to do. . . . You have to prove to the Americans and the world, that we are MEN, and not *brutes,* as we have been represented, and by millions treated. Remember, to let the aim of your labours among your brethren, and particularly the youths, be the dissemination of education and religion. . . .

I would crawl on my hands and knees through mud and mire, to the feet of a learned man, where I would sit and humbly supplicate him to instil [sic] into me, that which neither devils nor tyrants could remove, only with my life—for coloured people to acquire learning in this country, make tyrants quake and tremble on their sandy foundation? . . . Why, they know that their infernal deeds of cruelty will be made known to the world. Do you suppose one man of good sense and learning would submit himself, his father, mother, wife and children, to be slaves to a wretched man like himself, who, instead of compensating him for his labours, chains, hand-cuffs and beats him and family almost to death, leaving life enough in them, however, to work for, and call him master? No! no! he would cut his devilish throat from ear to ear, and well do slave-holders know it. . . .

It is a notorious fact, that the major part of the white Americans, have, ever since we have been among them, tried to keep us ignorant, and make us believe that God made us and our children to be slaves to them and theirs. *Oh! My God, have mercy on Christian Americans!!!* . . .

[Colonization is] a plan to get those of the coloured people, who are said to be free, away from among those of our brethren whom they unjustly hold in bondage, so that they [whites] may be enabled to keep them [slaves] the more secure in ignorance and wretchedness, to support them and their children, and consequently they would have the more obedient slave. For if the free are allowed to stay among the slave, they will have intercourse together, and, of course, the free will learn the slaves *bad habits,* by teaching them that they are MEN, as well as other people, and certainly *ought* and *must* be FREE. . . .

## 25. Excerpts from "Nero's" 1831 Letter to the South Received in Virginia Soon after Nat Turner's Insurrection

I have just been informed that my worthy friend has just arrived at N. York from his perilous and philanthropick enterprize at the South. Yes, he *has* arrived, and safe too, though he had many hair breadth escapes from the bullets of the modern Vandals of *Christian* Virginia. . . . He is a modern Leonidas, and the adored Chief of some *more* than three hundred men of colour (or *Negroes* if you please to denominate us) who have pledged ourselves with spartan fidelity to avenge the indignities offered to our race from the Slave holding Tyrant in the U. States. We have sworn in the most Solemn manner that we will not shrink from our holy and laudable purpose of vengeance, although we have to meet suffering and bear tortures that would have made the ghastly inquisitors of Spain and Portugal felt and *shown* pity. . . . [K]now ye coward race, that each of us . . . knows *how* to suffer and with a grace too. Our beloved Chief is a Native of Virginia; where he lived a slave till he was almost sixteen years old, when he found an opportunity to escape to St. Domingo, where his noble soul became warned by the spirit of freedom, and where he imbibed a righteous indignation, and an unqualified hatred for the oppressors of his race. His person is large and athletick; his deportment and manners dignified and urbane, his eye piercing, and at pleasure, can assume a fiendish malignity, which can wither any one in his presence, and which, I trust, will one day have its desired effect upon the coward hearts of many a Nabob, who now wields the sceptre of cruel domination. He is acquainted with, and speaks fluently most of the living European languages—he is a scholar and genius—he is acquainted with every avenue to the human heart—but more especially is he acquainted with all the feelings of a Slave; for he has himself been a slave. For more than three years he has been travelling, and has visited almost every Negro hut and quarters in the South States. Although he has travelled incog.[nito] both among you and your slaves, yet he knows all about the latter, and not a little of their masters. . . . O how would the boasted and bloated courage of some of your pompous great ones, have quailed had they known in whose presence they were, when in the garb and character of a mendicant negro he examined and scrutinized with an unerring ken their persons and characters. Notwithstanding *he* has returned; he has not left the field of our future enterprize unguarded—there are now among you souls of heroick daring who are reckless of their own fate can they but subserve our vindictive purpose. In addition to this band of worthies, who are among you, we have about thirty five chosen ones in Hayti, who are learning the French and Spanish languages and at the same time taking lessons from the venerable survivors of the Haytian Revolution[;] from this quarter the people of N. Orleans and Florida may expect some realities. . . . They will know how to use the knife, bludgeon, and the torch with effect—may the genius of Toussaint stimulate them to unremitting exertion. . . . We have no expectation of conquering the whites of the Southern States—our object is to seek revenge for indignities and abuses received—and to sell our live[s] at as high a price as possible . . . . Publick opinion at the North is in our favour—we have here the generous sympathies of White people—they wish us success—nay more; they contribute largely to our enterprize—true it is not publickly done, neither is there much effort to conceal it. . . . [L]ook at the Boston Patriot of the 20th Sept. and there you will see with zeal a college for people of colour is urged—such an Institution *will be established* in N. England. Already more than one hundred and sixty seven thousand dollars has been collected for that benevolent purpose in St. Domingo. We can obtain one hundred thousand doll[ars] from our own people in N. England and N. York. We have encouragement of assistance to a considerable amount from the White people in Pennsylvania and the States North[;] our spies and agents in Ohio and Upper Canada report favourably. We hope for much from the effort of agents lately sent to Europe. . . . Knowledge and information must move our machinery—our wrongs and sufferings will give sufficient excitement. We have already a printing press in agitation, indeed, we have one purchased, and are only waiting to ascertain *where* will be the most eligible situation for its location. From this engine we hope and most sanguinely expect to work wonders; by the assistance of the Mail, we shall be able to throw fire brands on your combustibles, that we trust, will not only make a blaze but scorch your very bones to a crisp. Of physical force we have no lack—when our plans are matured we shall be able to bring into the field three hundred thousand men who will be al[l] willing to hazard their lives in defence of our common rights—we have assurance of arms and ammunition from Non-Slaveholding States—I mean from individuals in those states, and Hayti offers an asylum for those who survive the approaching carnage.

Notwithstanding our agents are indispensably important to us, yet we put no confidence, or rather no dependence upon their help in the approaching day of carnage . . ., which will require all the sternness, cool determination, and ferocity that the human character, in its most savage state, is capable of—the white men (for they are white) we well know have not personal malignity sufficient to fit them for our use—a promiscuous slaughter of women and children would produce misgivings; and that would ruin us—we *have* men, *however,* to our liking; men that can perform deeds of death and destruction that would have made . . . a Tecumseh weep. Would to Heaven, we could enlist the Indians of Georgia in our common cause—and we are not without hopes that we shall. But you will say, are not such anticipations more than savage? I answer yes; yet the punishment will come far short of the demerit of your crimes—therefore bear it with fortitude[,] bear it as we have born[e] to see our race made more abject than the Helots of Greece. [A]nd is not Slavery a greater curse than any torture that terminates with death? . . . [W]e prefer to see every person of colour headless, and their "heads on poles" if you please than to see them servants to a debauched and effe[min]ate race of whites. O my bood boils when I think of the indignities we have suffered, and I long for the scene of retribution; and at that day let there be no more whining about cruelty and above all let there be no sympathy expressed for the "poor deluded blacks" who may fall in your battle. We defy you; do your best—we ask no favors—spare neither age nor sex, for we assure you that we shall not—that you shall destroy every vestage of a slave is what we desire. We laugh at your famous nuncios and bulls that "any more disturbance will terminate in the extermination of the black population." We know all about your "scare crows"; we know full well too, that you are not so fond of exterminating the "black population"—you are to [*sic*] inert to do without them—that is exactly what we want; and in case of "another disturbance" we will afford you every opportunity, and render you every necessary assistance in accomplishing so desirable an object—go on then, be men of stout hearts. I know that the southern[er]s like all tyrants are cowards; true when you get fuddled & whiskey makes you swell, and then you are bold enough to fire a pistol, and occasionally a miserable life is lost. But soon there will be an opportunity for you to retrieve your character; and should you be so fortunate as to get one of our leaders into your power, test his fortitude by every torture which your low and cowardly malignity can suggest, and while he is under the torture know and be assured that a band of us more than four years since pledged ourselves in a goblet made of the skull of a slaveholder, and that each of us signed our name to articles of confederation with our own life blood. From such a foe have you nothing to fear? Believe, if you please, that this is mere windy boasting—yet we know to the contrary—we know that there is a heavy charge that lies securely buried beneath you and though it may hereafter, as it has, frequently flash, yet be assured that the vindictive match of vengeance, will one day reach it, and tremendous will be the explosion—woe, to those who are within its influence—I should have been more explicit, were it not that I am fearful of communicating something that would lead to a discovery of some of our worthy agents among you. There are people in Boston, N. York, Philadelphia and Hartford who know more of the circumstances of the late insurrection than any Slave holder in Virginia or North Carolina. Our handbills and placards will soon be found in your streets, and there will be enough to read them; this you cannot prevent—the Post Office is free for anyone—any one has a right to receive communications through the medium of it—there is most surely machinery of vast power in the Press and Post Office. Believe or affect to believe that this long episle is all humbug—so much the better. . . . [M]y object in writing is hereafter to tantalize over you—for our revenge will be more sweet, if you know, that all the calamities you are to suffer, have been premeditated—I have just heard that the good work is going on in Delaware—You will make some allowance for my barbarous chirography and the incongruity of my composition, when you are informed that since the 1st of Sept. I have written twenty nine letters almost as long as this, and written too in cypher which is slow work, and requires great accuracy. . . .

Perhaps you would like to know something of the person that addresses you. I am not fond of speaking of myself; my history, therefore, shall be a brief and an "unvarnished tale." I am what is called a mulatto. What this refined appellation derived from I know not; possibly philologists might trace its origins to the honourable parentage of mule. I was born in the south of Virginia and a slave; though some of the proudest blood of the South cources [*sic*] in my veins—yet that profited me nothing; since my mother was a bond woman. In early boyhood I was permitted to learn to read—for I doubt not my father loved me, notwithstanding my Ishmael stamp. Nature gave me a thirst for knowledge, if not a genius for acquiring it. Every opportunity I had I read my *Father master's* newspaper. I read of happy N. England, where a *complexion* did not disfranchise a human being. I was fired with the thoughts of freedom. God only knows with what pain I looked upon my degraded situation. I saw with ineffable indignation the different treatment my *mother* received from my father's *wife*—my brothers and sisters looked at me with contempt, for no other reason than my colour being different from their own, and they were allowed to treat me with savage cruelty, althoug[h] I was their brother. I was singled out for the peculiar malignity of my *pious* mistress because I was the child of her husband—for this crime, however, I did not consider myself justly obnoxious to her spite. My father died, and then the full vials of vengeance were poured upon my own, and my poor mother's devoted head, from the amiable household of my mistress. After satiating their malice, I was selected to be sold to a Florida Trader. . . . I made a desperate struggle and fled; I came to N. England and was happy beyond expression in breathing the air of liberty. Soon after I learned that death had emancipated mother and set her to Heaven to enjoy the society of my father never more to be annoyed by the presence of my *infernal mistress.*

Since I have been here I have but one object in view, and that has been to avenge the wrongs and abuses the Slaves have received in the United States. I have followed every plan that possibility could suggest, or reveng[e] could prompt and have succeeded beyond my most sanguine expectations. I do not now fear to boast that our purpose in one way or another will be effected; prosperity has encouraged us to persevere, and hope has made us blind to all scruples. . . . We have now many a white agent in Florida, S. Carolina and Georgia. . . . Such are some of the fond prospects on which I dwell, and for which I live. I have a wife of my own colour, by whom I have seven children, and five of them boys—these I early brought to the altar of righteous retribution, and after invoking the shade of their sainted grandmother, . . . I made them pledge both soul and body that they would never spare neither wife, child nor property of a slaveholder—and that fire and sword should be their most merciful weapons—such are my deliberate sentiments, and I exult in them. . . . Do not flatter yourselves, that in consequence of our apparently *faux pas* [the unsuccessful Nat Turner insurrection] we shall be discouraged; that was expected by us—we did not calculate upon any thing of consequence—it was a mere feint—a squib to see if our piece was sure fire, or rather, a starting of the machinery to see if it was in order. I say machinery, for our operatives are little more than automatons that are moved at the will of another, or others. Fortunately not one or more than one of the men you caught in the late bustle, had any knowledge in the great enterprize, that is in agitation. Your Nat's and your Mark's were totally ignorant of the impulse by which they were moved. You seem to think that you will be perfectly safe for twenty years to come! My life for it, if thousands of Masters are not made, by their servants, to bite the dust with [in] twenty years or twenty *months!!!* Our plan is to operate upon the Sympathies, prejudices and superstitions of the miserable beings you at present lord it over; and above all to arrouse [sic] in their feelings a religious frenzy which is always effectual; only make them think that their leaders are inspired, or that they are doing God's service, and that will be enough to answer our purpose. We must make them believe that if they are killed in this crusade that heaven will be their reward, and that every person they kill, who countenances slavery, shall procure for them an additional jewel in their heavenly crown, and we shall have volunteers enough, and such too, as will fight. Of course you will debar them from religious meetings; that is exactly what we want. Our secret agents are among you, and it will be their business to inculcate a belief that they are persecuted for their religion, and of all the causes that ever operated upon human beings to produce a reaction, religious persecution is the most effectual—that is the grand fulcrum on which rest all our hopes. I repeat it our agents are among you, and they are too well paid with our gold to prove unfaithful—a Yankee, you know, will hazard his life for money.

[L]ittle do you know how many letters in cypher pass through your post office—and others, in the South States—though you would not be the wiser if you were to see them, for they are past your finding out—till you hear from us in characters of blood. . . . I remain *your* humble attentive watchful, and the *Publick's* obedient and faithful Servant.

Nero

## 26. From Maria Stewart, "Religion and the Pure Principles of Morality: The Sure Foundation on Which We Must Build," October 1831

I was born in Hartford, Connecticut, in 1803; was left an orphan at five years of age; was bound out in a clergyman's family; had the seeds of piety and virtue early sown in my mind, but was deprived of the advantages of education, though my soul thirsted for knowledge. Left them at fifteen years of age; attended Sabbath schools until I was twenty; in 1826 was married to James W. Stewart; was left a widow in 1829; was, as I humbly hope and trust, brought to the knowledge of the truth, as it is in Jesus, in 1830; in 1831 made a public profession of my faith in Jesus Christ.

From the moment I experienced the change, I felt a strong desire, with the help and assistance of God, to devote the remainder of my days to piety and virtue, and now possess that spirit of independence that, were I called upon, I would willingly sacrifice my life for the cause of God and my brethren.

All the nations of the earth are crying out for liberty and equality. Away, away with tyranny and oppression! And shall Afric's sons be silent any longer?

Far be it from me to recommend to you either to kill, burn, or destroy. But I would strongly recommend to you to improve your talents; let not one lie buried in the earth. Show forth your powers of mind. Prove to the world that

*Though black your skins as shades of night, your hearts are pure, your souls are white.*

This is the land of freedom. The press is at liberty. Every man has a right to express his opinion. Many think, because your skins are tinged with a sable hue, that you are an inferior race of beings; but God does not consider you as such. He hath formed and fashioned you in his own glorious image, and hath bestowed upon you reason and strong powers of intellect. He hath made you to have dominion over the beasts of the field, the fowls of the air, and the fish of the sea [Genesis 1:26]. He hath crowned you with glory and honor; hath made you but a little lower than the angels [Psalms 8:5] and according to the Constitution of these United States, he hath made all men free and equal. Then why should one worm say to another, "Keep you down there, while I sit up yonder; for I am better than thou?" It is not the color of the skin that makes the man, but it is the principles formed within the soul.

Many will suffer for pleading the cause of oppressed Africa, and I shall glory in being one of her martyrs; for I am firmly persuaded that the God in whom I trust is able to protect me from the rage and malice of mine enemies, and from them that will rise up against me, and if there is no other way for me to escape, he is able to take me to himself, as he did the most noble, fearless, and undaunted David Walker.

Never Will Virtue, Knowledge, And True Politeness Begin To Flow, Till The Pure Principles Of Religion and Morality Are Put Into Force. My Respected Friends, I feel almost unable to address you; almost incompetent to perform the task; and at times I have felt ready to exclaim, O that my head were waters, and mine eyes a fountain of tears, that I might weep day and night [Jeremiah 9:1], for the transgressions of the daughters of my people. Truly, my heart's desire and prayer is, that Ethiopia might stretch forth her hands unto God. But we have a great work to do. Never, no, never will the chains of slavery and ignorance burst, till we become united as one, and cultivate among ourselves the pure principles of piety, morality and virtue. I am sensible of my ignorance; but such knowledge as God has given to me, I impart to you. I am sensible of former prejudices; but it is high time for prejudices and animosities to cease from among us. I am sensible of exposing myself to calumny and reproach, but shall I, for fear of feeble man who shall die, hold my peace? Shall I for fear of scoffs and frowns, refrain my tongue? Ah, no! I speak as one that must give an account at the awful bar of God; I speak as a dying mortal to dying mortals. O, ye daughters of Africa, awake! Awake! Arise! No longer sleep nor slumber, but distinguish yourselves. Show forth to the world that ye are endowed with noble and exalted faculties. O, ye daughters of Africa! What have ye done to immortalize your names beyond the grave? What examples have ye set before the rising generation? What foundation have ye laid for generations yet unborn? Where are our union and love? And where is our sympathy, that weeps at another's woe, and hides the faults we see? And our daughters, where are they? Blushing in innocence and virtue? And our sons, do they bid fair to become crowns of glory to our hoary heads [Proverbs 16:31]? Where is the parent who is conscious of having faithfully discharged his duty, and at the last awful day of account, shall be able to say, here, Lord, is thy poor, unworthy servant, and the children thou hast given me? and where are the children that will arise and call them blessed? Alas, O God! Forgive me if I speak amiss; the minds of our tender babes are tainted as soon as they are born; they go astray, as it were, from the womb. Where is the maiden who will blush at vulgarity? And where is the youth who has written upon his manly brow a thirst for knowledge; whose ambitious mind soars above trifles, and longs for the time to come, when he shall redress the wrongs of his father and plead the cause of his brethren? Did the daughters of our land possess a delicacy of manners, combined with gentleness and dignity; did their pure minds hold vice in abhorrence and contempt, did they frown when their ears were polluted with its vile accents, would not their influence become powerful? Would not our brethren fall in love with their virtues? Their souls would become proud to display their talents. Able advocates would arise in our defence. Knowledge would begin to flow, and the chains of slavery and ignorance would melt like wax before the flames. I am but a feeble instrument. I am but as one particle of the small dust of the earth. You may frown or smile. After I am dead, perhaps before, God will surely rise up those who will more powerfully and eloquently plead the cause of virtue and the pure principles of morality than I am able to do. O virtue! How sacred is thy name! How pure are thy principles! Who can find a virtuous woman? For her price is far above rubies [Proverbs 31:10]. Blessed is the man who shall call her his wife; yea, happy is the child who shall call her mother. O woman, woman, would thou only strive to excel in merit and virtue; would thou only store thy mind with useful knowledge, great would be thine influence Do you say you are too far advanced in life now to begin? You are not too far advanced to instil these principles into the minds of your tender infants. Let them by no means be neglected. Discharge your duty faithfully, in every point of view: leave the event with God. So shall your skirts become clear of their blood [Jeremiah 2:34].

When I consider how little improvement has been made the last eight years; the apparent cold and indifferent state of the children of God; how few have been hopefully brought to the knowledge of the truth as it is in Jesus; that our young men and maidens are fainting and drooping, as it were, by the way-side, for the want of knowledge; when I see how few care to distinguish themselves either in religious or moral improvement, and when I see the greater part of our community following the vain bubbles of life with so much eagerness, which will only prove to them like the serpent's sting upon the bed of death, I really think we are in as wretched and miserable a state as was the house of Israel in the days of Jeremiah.

I suppose many of my friends will say, "Religion is all your theme." I hope my conduct will ever prove me to be what I profess, a true follower of Christ; and it is the religion of Jesus alone that will constitute your happiness here, and support you in a dying hour. O then, do not trifle with God and your own souls any longer. Do not presume to offer him the very dregs of your lives; but now, whilst you are blooming in health and vigor, consecrate the remnant or your days to him. . . .

I have been taking a survey of the American people in my own mind, and I see them thriving in arts and sciences, and in polite literature. Their highest aim is to excel in political, moral and religious improvement. They early consecrate their children to God, and their youth indeed are blushing in artless innocence. They wipe the tears from the orphan's eyes, and they cause the widow's heart to sing for joy [Job 29:13]! And their poorest ones, who have the least wish to excel, they promote! And those that have but one talent they encourage. But how very few are there among them that bestow one thought upon the benighted sons and daughters of Africa, who have enriched the soils of America with their tears and blood: few to promote their cause, none to encourage their talents. Under these circumstances, do not let our hearts be any longer discouraged; it is no use to murmur nor to repine; but let us promote ourselves and improve our own talents. And I am rejoiced to reflect that there are many able and talented ones among us, whose names might be recorded on the bright annals of fame. But "I can't," is a great barrier to the way. I hope it will soon be removed, and "I will," resume its place.

Righteousness exalteth a nation, but sin is a reproach to any people [Proverbs 14:34]. Why is it, my friends, that our minds have been blinded by ignorance, to the present moment? 'Tis on account of sin. Why is it that our church is involved in so much difficulty? It is on account of sin. Why is it that God has cut down, upon our right hand and upon our left, the most learned and intelligent of our men? O, shall I say, it is on account of sin! . . .

O, ye mothers, what a responsibility rests on you! You have souls committed to your charge, and God will require a strict account of you. It is you that must create in the minds of your little girls and boys a thirst for knowledge, the love of virtue, the abhorrence of vice, and the cultivation of a pure heart. . . .

Perhaps you will say that many parents have set pure examples at home, and they have not followed them. True, our expectations are often blasted; but let not this dishearten you. If they have faithfully discharged their duty, even after they are dead their works may live; their prodigal children may return to God and become heirs of salvation; if not, their children cannot rise and condemn them at the awful bar of God.

Perhaps you will say that you cannot send them to high schools and academies. You can have them taught in the first rudiments of useful knowledge; and then you can have private teachers who will instruct them in the higher branches; and their intelligence will become greater than ours, and their children will attain to higher advantages, and their children still higher; and then, though we are dead, our works shall live; though we are mouldering, our names shall not be forgotten. . . .

I am of a strong opinion that the day on which we unite, heart and soul, and turn our attention to knowledge and improvement, that day the hissing and reproach among the nations of the earth against us will cease. And even those who now point at us with the finger of scorn, will aid and befriend us. It is of no use for us to sit with our hands folded, hanging our heads like bulrushes, lamenting our wretched condition; but let us make a mighty effort, and arise; and if no one will promote or respect us, let us promote and respect ourselves.

The American ladies have the honor conferred on them, that by prudence and economy in their domestic concerns, and their unwearied attention in forming the minds and manners of their children, they laid the foundation of their becoming what they now are. The good women of Wethersfield, Conn., toiled in the blazing sun, year after year, weeding onions, then sold the seed and procured enough money to erect them a house of worship; and shall we not imitate their examples, as far as they are worthy of imitation? Why cannot we do something to distinguish ourselves, and contribute some of our hard earnings that would reflect honor upon our memories, and cause our children to arise and call us blessed? Shall it any longer be said of the daughters of Africa, they have no ambition, they have no force? By no means. Let every female heart become united, and let us raise a fund ourselves, and at the end of one year and a half, we might be able to lay the corner stone for the building of a High School, that the higher branches of knowledge might be enjoyed by us; and God would raise us up, and enough to aid us in our laudable designs. Let each one strive to excel in good housewifery, knowing that prudence and economy are the road to wealth. Let us not say we know this, or we know that, and practise nothing; but let us practise what we do know.

How long shall the fair daughters of Africa be compelled to bury their minds and talents beneath a load of iron pots and kettles? Until union, knowledge and love begin to flow among us. How long shall a mean set of men flatter us with their smiles, and enrich themselves with our hard earnings; their wives' fingers sparkling with rings, and they themselves laughing at our folly? Until we begin to promote and patronize each other. Shall we be a by-word among the nations any longer? Shall they laugh us to scorn forever? Do you ask, what can we do? Unite and build a store of your own, if you cannot procure a license. Fill one side with dry goods, and the other with groceries. Do you ask where is the money? We have spent more than enough for nonsense, to do what building we should want. We have never had an opportunity of displaying our talents; therefore the world thinks we know nothing. And we have been possessed by far too mean and cowardly a disposition, though I highly disapprove of an insolent or impertinent one. Do you ask the disposition I would have you possess? Possess the spirit of independence. The Americans do, and why should not you? Possess the spirit of men, bold and enterprising, fearless and undaunted. Sue for your rights and privileges. Know the reason that you cannot attain them. Weary them with your importunities. You can but die if you make the attempt; and we shall certainly die if you do not. The Americans have practised nothing but head-work these 200 years, and we have done their drudgery. And is it not high time for us to imitate their examples and practise head-work too, and keep what we have got, and get what we can? We need never to think that anybody is going to feel interested for us, if we do not feel interested for ourselves. That day we, as a people, hearken unto the voice of the Lord, our God, and walk in his ways and ordinances, and become distinguished for our ease, elegance and grace, combined with other virtues, that day the Lord will raise us up, and we shall begin to flourish.

Did every gentleman in America realize, as one, that they had got to become bondmen, and their wives, their sons, and their daughters, servants forever, to Great Britain, their very joints would become loosened, and tremblingly would smite one against another; their countenance would be filled with horror, every nerve and muscle would be forced into action, their souls would recoil at the very thought; their hearts would die within them, and death would be far more preferable. Then why have not Afric's sons the right to feel the same? Are not their wives, their sons, and their daughters, as dear to them as those of the white man's? Certainly God has not deprived them of the divine influences of his Holy Spirit, which is the greatest of all blessings, if they ask him. Then why should man any longer deprive his fellow-man of equal rights and privileges? Oh, America, America, foul and indelible is thy stain! Dark and dismal is the cloud which hangs over thee, for thy cruel wrongs and injuries to the fallen sons of Africa. The blood of her murdered ones cries to heaven for vengeance against thee. Thou art almost become drunken with the blood of her slain; thou hast enriched thyself through her toils and labors; and now thou refuseth to make even a small return. And thou hast caused the daughters of Africa to commit whoredoms and fornications, but upon thee be their curse.

O, ye great and mighty men of America, ye rich and powerful ones, many of you will call for the rocks and mountains to fall upon you, and to hide you from the wrath of the Lamb [Revelation 6:16], and from him that sitteth upon the throne; whilst many of the sable-skinned Africans you now despise will shine in the kingdom of heaven as the stars forever and ever. Charity begins at home, and those that provide not for their own are worse than infidels. We know that you are raising contributions to aid the gallant Poles, we know that you have befriended Greece and Ireland; and you have rejoiced with France, for her heroic deeds of valor. You have acknowledged all the nations of the earth, except Hayti, and you may publish, as far as the East is from the West, that you have two millions of negroes, who aspire no higher than to bow at your feet, and to court your smiles. You may kill, tyrannize, and oppress as much as you choose, until our cry shall come up before the throne of God; for I am firmly persuaded, that he will not suffer you to quell the proud, fearless, and undaunted spirits of the Africans forever; for in his own time, he is able to plead our cause against you, and to pour out upon you the ten plagues of Egypt. We will not come out against you with swords and staves, as against a thief [Matthew 26:55]; but we will tell you that our souls are fired with the same love of liberty and independence with which your souls are fired. We will tell you that too much of your blood flows in our veins, too much of your color in our skins, for us not to possess your spirits. We will tell you that it is our gold that clothes you in fine linen and purple, and causes you to fare sumptuously every day [Luke 16:19]; and it is the blood of our fathers, and the tears of our brethren that have enriched your soils, AND WE CLAIM OUR RIGHTS. We will tell you that we are not afraid of them that kill the body, and after that can do no more, but we will tell you whom we do fear. We fear Him who is able, after He hath killed, to destroy both soul and body in hell forever. Then, my brethren, sheath your swords, and calm your angry passions. Stand still and know that the Lord he is God. Vengeance is his, and he will repay. It is a long lane that has no turn. America has risen to her meridian. When you begin to thrive, she will begin to fall. God hath raised you up a Walker and a Garrison. Though Walker sleeps [has died], yet he lives, and his name shall be had in everlasting remembrance. I, even I, who am but a child, inexperienced to many of you, am a living witness to testify unto you this day, that I have seen the wicked in great power, spreading himself like a green bay tree, and lo, he passed away; yea, I diligently sought him, but he could not be found [Psalms 37:35]; and it is God alone that has inspired my heart to feel for Afric's woes. Then fret not yourselves because of evil doers. Fret not yourselves because of the men who bring wicked devices to pass; for they shall be cut down as the grass, and wither as the green herb. Trust in the Lord, and do good; so shalt thou dwell in the land, and verily thou shalt be fed. Encourage the noble-hearted Garrison. Prove to the world that you are neither ourang-outangs [*sic*], or a species of mere animals, but that you possess the same powers of intellect as the proudboasting American.

I am sensible, my brethren and friends, that many of you have been deprived of advantages, kept in utter ignorance, and that your minds are now darkened; and if any one of you have attempted to aspire after high and noble enterprises, you have met with so much opposition that your souls have become discouraged. For this very cause, a few of us have ventured to expose our lives in your behalf, to plead your cause against the great; and it will be of no use, unless you feel for yourselves and then your little ones, and exhibit the spirits of men. Oh then, turn your attention to knowledge and improvement; for knowledge is power. And God is able to fill you with wisdom and understanding, and to dispel your fears. Arm yourselves with the weapons of prayer. Put your trust in the living God. Persevere strictly in the paths of virtue. Let nothing be lacking on your part; and in God's own time, and his time is certainly the best, he will surely deliver you with a mighty hand and with an outstretched arm. . . .

## 27. From Angelina Grimké's Appeal to the Christian Women of the South, 1836

I have thus, I think, clearly proved to you seven propositions, viz.: First, that slavery is contrary to the declaration of our independence. Second, that it is contrary to the first charter of human rights, given to Adam, and renewed to Noah. Third, that the fact of slavery having been the subject of prophecy, furnishes *no* excuse whatever to slavedealers. Fourth, that no such system existed under the patriarchal dispensation. Fifth, that *slavery never* existed under the Jewish dispensation; but so far otherwise, that every servant was placed under the *protection of law,* and care taken not only to prevent all *involuntary servitude,* but all *voluntary perpetual* bondage. Sixth, that slavery in America reduces a *man* to a thing, a "chattel personal," *robs him* of *all* his rights as a *human being,* fetters both his mind and body, and protects the *master* in the most unnatural and unreasonable power, whilst it *throws him out* of the protection of law. Seventh, that slavery is contrary to the example and precepts of our holy and merciful Redeemer, and of his apostles. . . .

I know you [women] do not make the laws, but I also know that *you are the wives and mothers, the sisters and daughters of those who do;* and if you really suppose *you* can do nothing to overthrow slavery, you are greatly mistaken. You can do much in every way. . . .

1. Read . . . on the subject of slavery. Search the Scriptures daily. . . .

2. Pray over this subject.

3. Speak on this subject. . . . Speak then to your relatives, your friends, your acquaintances on the subject of slavery; be not afraid if you are conscientiously convinced it is *sinful,* to say so openly, but calmly, and to let your sentiments be known. If you are served by the slaves of others, try to ameliorate their condition as much as possible; never aggravate their faults . . . ; remember their extreme ignorance. . . . Discountenance *all* cruelty to them, all starvation, all corporal chastisement; these may brutalize and *break* their spirits, but will never bend them to willing, cheerful obedience. If possible, see that they are comfortably and *seasonably* fed, whether in the house or in the field; it is unreasonable and cruel to expect slaves to wait for their breakfast until eleven o'clock, when they rise at five or six. Do all you can, to induce their owners to clothe them well, and to allow them many little indulgences which would contribute to their comfort. Above all, try to persuade your husband, father, brothers and sons, that *slavery is a crime against God and man,* and that it is a great sin to keep *human beings* in such abject ignorance; to deny them the privilege of learning to read and write . . . And lastly, endeavour to inculcate submission on the part of the slaves, but whilst doing this be faithful in pleading the cause of the oppressed. . . .

4. Act on this subject. Some of you *own* slaves yourselves. *If* you believe slavery is *sinful,* set them at liberty, "undo the heavy burdens and let the oppressed go free." If they wish to remain with you, pay them wages, if not let them leave you. Should they remain, teach them, and have them taught the common branches of an English education. . . . [E]ncourage them to believe it is their *duty* to learn, if it were only that they might read the Bible.

But some of you will say, we can neither free our slaves nor teach them to read, for the laws of our state forbid it. Be not surprised when I say such wicked laws *ought to be no barrier* in the way of your duty, and I appeal to the Bible to prove this position. . . .

But some of you may say, if we do free our slaves, they will be taken up and sold, therefore there will be no use in doing it. . . . Duty is ours, and events are God's. If you think slavery is sinful, all *you* have to do is to set your slaves at liberty, do all you can to protect them, and in humble faith and fervent prayer, commend them to your common Father. . . .

But you will perhaps say, such a course of conduct would inevitably expose us to great suffering. Yes! my christian friends, I believe it would, but this will *not* excuse you or any one else for the neglect of *duty.* . . .

But you may say, we are *women,* how can our hearts endure persecution. And why not? Have not women stood up in all the dignity and strength of moral courage to be the leaders of the people, and to bear a faithful testimony for the truth whenever the providence of God has called them to do so. Are there no *women* in that noble army of martyrs. . . .?

The *women of the South can overthrow* this horrible system of oppression and cruelty, licentiousness and wrong. Such appeals to your legislatures would be irresistible, for there is something in the heart of man which *will bend under moral suasion.* There is a swift witness for truth in his bosom, which *will respond to truth* when it is uttered with calmness and dignity. If you could obtain but six signatures to such a petition in only one state, I would say, send up that petition, and be not in the least discouraged by the scoffs and jeers of the heartless, or the resolution of the house to lay it on the table. It will be a great thing if the subject can be introduced into your legislatures in any way, even by *women,* and *they* will be the most likely to introduce it there in the best possible manner, as a matter of *morals* and *religion,* not of expediency or politics. You may petition, too the different ecclesiastical bodies of the slave states. Slavery must be attacked with the whole power of truth and the sword of the spirit. You must take it up on *Christian* ground, and fight against it with Christian weapons, whilst your feet are shod with the preparation of the gospel of peace. And *you are now* loudly called upon by the cries of the widow and the orphan, to arise and gird yourselves for this great moral conflict, with the whole armour of righteousness upon the right hand and on the left.

## 28. From the Constitution of the Republic of Texas, 1836: General Provisions

Sec. 9: All persons of color who were slaves for life previous to their emigration to Texas, and who are now held in bondage, shall remain in the like state of servitude: *provided,* the said slave shall be the bona fide property of the person so holding said slave as aforesaid. Congress shall pass no laws to prohibit emigrants from bringing their slaves into the republic with them, and holding them by the same tenure by which such slaves were held in the United States; nor shall congress have power to emancipate slaves; nor shall any slave holder be allowed to emancipate his or her slave or slaves without the consent of congress, unless he or she shall send his or her slave or slaves without the limits of the republic. No free person of African descent, either in whole or in part, shall be permitted to reside permanently in the republic, without the consent of congress; and the importation or admission of Africans or negroes into this republic, excepting from the United States of America, is forever prohibited, and declared to be piracy.

## 29. From the Opinion of Chief Justice Shaw of Massachusetts in *Commonwealth v. Aves,* 1836

How, or by what act particularly, slavery was abolished in Massachusetts, whether by the adoption of the opinion in Sommersett's case, as a declaration and modification of the common law, or by the Declaration of Independence, or by the Constitution of 1780, it is not now very easy to determine, and it is rather a matter of curiosity than utility; being agreed on all hands, that if not abolished before, it was so by the declaration of rights.

## 30. From the Ruling of the U.S. Supreme Court in *Prigg v. Pennsylvania,* January 1842

[The power of legislation under the fugitive slave clause of the Constitution is] exclusive in the national government [and] not concurrent in the states. . . . [No state is bound to provide means to carry out the provisions of this clause] either by its courts or magistrates; but . . . the national government is bound, through its own proper departments, legislative, judicial, and executive, to enforce all the rights and duties growing out of this clause in the constitution. . . . [The object of this provision is] to secure to the citizens of the slaveholding states the complete right and title of ownership in their slaves, as property, in every state in the union into which they might escape. . . . We have not the slightest hesitation in holding, that . . . the owner of a slave is clothed with entire authority in every State in the Union, to seize and recapture his slave, whenever he can do it without any breach of the peace, or any illegal violence. . . .

## 31. From the Fugitive Slave Act of 1850

SEC. 5. *And be it further enacted,* That it shall be the duty of all marshals and deputy marshals to obey and execute all warrants and precepts issued under the provisions of this act, when to them directed; and should any marshal or deputy marshal refuse to receive such warrant, or other process, when tendered, or to use all proper means diligently to execute the same, he shall, on conviction thereof, be fined in the sum of one thousand dollars, to the use of such claimant . . .; and after arrest of such fugitive, by such marshal or his deputy, or whilst at any time in his custody under the provisions of this act, should such fugitive escape, whether with or without the assent of such marshal or his deputy, such marshal shall be liable, on his official bond, to be prosecuted for the benefit of such claimant, for the full value of the service or labor of said fugitive in the State, Territory, or District whence he escaped . . .; and all good citizens are hereby commanded to aid and assist in the prompt and efficient execution of this law, whenever their services may be required. . . .

SEC. 6. *And be it further enacted,* That when a person held to service or labor in any State or Territory of the United States, has heretofore or shall hereafter escape into another State or Territory of the United States, the person or persons to whom such service or labor may be due, or his, her, or their agent or attorney, duly authorized, by power of attorney, in writing, acknowledged and certified under the seal of some legal officer or court of the State or Territory in which the same may be executed, may pursue and reclaim such fugitive person, either by procuring a warrant from some one of the courts, judges, or commissioners aforesaid, of the proper circuit, district, or county, for the apprehension of such fugitive from service or labor, or by seizing and arresting such fugitive, where the same can be done without process, and by taking, or causing such person to be taken, forthwith before such court, judge, or commissioner, whose duty it shall be to hear and determine the case of such claimant in a summary manner; and upon satisfactory proof being made, by deposition or affidavit, in writing, to be taken and certified by such court, judge, or commissioner, or by other satisfactory testimony, duly taken and certified by some court, magistrate, justice of the peace, or other legal officer authorized to administer an oath and take depositions under the laws of the State or Territory from which such person owing service or labor may have escaped, with a certificate of such magistracy or other authority, as aforesaid, . . . and with proof, also by affidavit, of the identity of the person whose service or labor is claimed to be due as aforesaid, that the person so arrested does in fact owe service or labor to the person or persons claiming him or her, in the State or Territory from which such fugitive may have escaped as aforesaid, and that said person escaped, to make out and deliver to such claimant, his or her agent or attorney, a certificate setting forth the substantial facts as to the service or labor due from such fugitive to the claimant, and of his or her escape from the State or Territory in which such service or labor was due, to the State or Territory in which he or she was arrested, with authority to such claimant, or his or her agent or attorney, to use such reasonable force and restraint as may be necessary, under the circumstances of the case, to take and remove such fugitive person back to the State or Territory whence he or she may have escaped as aforesaid. In no trial or hearing under this act shall the testimony of such alleged fugitive be admitted in evidence; and the certificates in this . . . section mentioned, shall be conclusive of the right of the person or persons in whose favor granted, to remove such fugitive to the State or Territory from which he escaped, and shall prevent all molestation of such person or persons by any process issued by any court, judge, magistrate, or other person whomsoever.

SEC. 7. *And be it further enacted,* That any person who shall knowingly and willingly obstruct, hinder, or prevent such claimant, his agent or attorney, or any person or persons lawfully assisting him, her, or them, from arresting such a fugitive from service or labor, either with or without process as aforesaid, or shall rescue, or attempt to rescue, such fugitive from service or labor, from the custody of such claimant, his or her agent or attorney, or other person or persons lawfully assisting as aforesaid, when so arrested, pursuant to the authority herein given and declared; or shall aid, abet, or assist such person so owing service or labor as aforesaid, directly or indirectly, to escape from such claimant, his agent or attorney, or other person or persons legally authorized as aforesaid; or shall harbor or conceal such fugitive, so as to prevent the discovery and arrest of such person, after notice of knowledge of the fact that such person was a fugitive from service or labor as aforesaid, shall, for either of said offences, be subject to a fine not exceeding one thousand dollars, and imprisonment not exceeding six months, by indictment and conviction before the District Court of the United States for the district in which such offence may have been committed, or before the proper court of criminal jurisdiction . . .; and shall moreover forfeit and pay, by way of civil damages to the party injured by such illegal conduct, the sum of one thousand dollars, for each fugitive so lost as aforesaid, to be recovered by action of debt, in any of the District or Territorial Courts aforesaid, within whose jurisdiction the said offence may have been committed. . . .

SEC. 9. *And be it further enacted,* That, upon affidavit made by the claimant of such fugitive, his agent or attorney, after such certificate has been issued, that he has reason to apprehend that such fugitive will be rescued by force from his or their possession before he can be taken beyond the limits of the state in which the arrest is made, it shall be the duty of the officer making the arrest to retain such fugitive in his custody, and to remove him to the State whence he fled, and there to deliver him to said claimant, his agent, or attorney. . . .

## 32. From Justice Roger Taney's Opinion in the *Dred Scott* Case, 1857

*Note: In Missouri in 1833 the owner of Dred Scott sold him to Dr. John Emerson, a military surgeon, who in the pursuit of his career took Scott to the free state of Illinois and to the free Wisconsin Territory. In 1842 Scott and his wife Harriet returned to Missouri with Mrs. Emerson. In 1846, the Scotts instituted a suit for freedom against Mrs. Emerson, under Missouri law, where, according to precedent (especially* Rachael v. Walker, *1837), if a slave returned to Missouri after having sojourned in a free state or territory, that slave was entitled to freedom by virtue of residence in the free state or territory.*

The question is simply this: Can a negro, whose ancestors were imported into this country and sold as slaves, become a member of the political community formed and brought into existence by the Constitution of the United States, and as such become entitled to all the rights and privileges and immunities guaranteed by that instrument to the citizen? One of which rights is the privilege of suing in a court of the United States in the cases specified in the Constitution.

It will be observed that the plea applies to that class of persons only whose ancestors were negroes of the African race, and imported into this country, and sold and held as slaves. The only matter in issue before the court, therefore, is, whether the descendants of such slaves, when they shall be emancipated, or who are born of parents who had become free before their birth, are citizens of a State, in the sense in which the word citizen is used in the Constitution of the United States. And this being the only matter in dispute on the pleadings, the court must be understood as speaking in this opinion of that class only, that is, of those persons who are the descendants of Africans who were imported into this country and sold as slaves. . . .

We proceed to examine the case as presented by the pleadings.

The words "people of the United States" and "citizens" are synonymous terms, and mean the same thing. They both describe the political body who, according to our republican institutions, form the sovereignty, and who hold the power and conduct the government through their representatives. They are what we familiarly call the "sovereign people," and every citizen is one of this people, and a constituent member of this sovereignty. The question before us is, whether the class of persons described in the plea in abatement compose a portion of this people, and are constituent members of this sovereignty. We think they are not, and that they are not included, and were not intended to be included, under the word "citizen" in the Constitution, and can therefore claim none of the rights and privileges which that instrument provides for and secures to citizens of the United States. On the contrary, they were at that time considered as a subordinate and inferior class of beings, who had been subjugated by the dominant race, and, whether emancipated or not, yet remained subject to their authority, and had no rights or privileges but such as those who held the power and the government might choose to grant them.

It is not the province of the court to decide upon the justice or injustice, the policy or impolicy, of these laws. . . .

In discussing this question, we must not confound the rights of citizenship which a State may confer within its own limits, and the rights of citizenship as a member of the Union. It does not by any means follow, because he has all the rights and privileges of a State, that he must be a citizen of the United States. He may have all of the rights and privileges of the citizen of a State, and yet not be entitled to the rights and privileges of a citizen of any other State. For, previous to the adoption of the Constitution of the United States, every State had the undoubted right to confer on whomsoever it pleased the character of citizen, and to endow him with all its rights. But this character of course was confined to the boundaries of the State, and gave him no rights or privileges in other States beyond those secured to him by the laws of nations and the comity of States. Nor have the several States surrendered the power of conferring these rights and privileges by adopting the Constitution of the United States. Each State may still confer them upon an alien, or any one it thinks proper, or upon any class or description of persons; yet he would not be a citizen in the sense in which that word is used in the Constitution of the United States, nor entitled to sue as such in one of its courts, nor to the privileges and immunities of a citizen in the other States. The rights which he would acquire would be restricted to the State which gave them. The Constitution has conferred on Congress the right to establish an uniform rule of naturalization, and this right is evidently exclusive, and has always been held by this court to be so. Consequently no State, since the adoption of the

Constitution, can, by naturalizing an alien, invest him with the rights and privileges secured to a citizen of a State under the Federal Government, although, so far as the State alone was concerned, he would undoubtedly be entitled to the rights of a citizen, and clothed with all the rights and immunities which the Constitution and laws of the State attached to that character.

It is very clear, therefore, that no State can, by any act or law of its own, passed since the adoption of the Constitution, introduce a new member into the political community created by the Constitution of the United States. It cannot make him a member of this community by making him a member of its own. And, for the same reason, it cannot introduce any person or description of persons who were not intended to be embraced in this new political family, which the Constitution brought into existence, but were intended to be excluded from it.

The question then arises, whether the provisions of the Constitution, in relation to the personal rights and privileges to which the citizen of a State should be entitled, embraced the negro African race, at that time in this country, or who might afterwards be imported, who had then or should afterwards be made free in any State; and to put it in the power of a single State to make him a citizen of the United States, and indue him with the full rights of citizenship in every other State without their consent. Does the Constitution of the United States act upon him whenever he shall be made free under the laws of a State, and raised there to the rank of a citizen, and immediately clothe him with all the privileges of a citizen in every other State and in its own courts?

The court think the affirmative of these propositions cannot be maintained. And if it cannot, the plaintiff in error could not be a citizen of the State of Missouri, within the meaning of the Constitution of the United States, and, consequently, was not entitled to sue in its courts.

## 33. From an Act of Congress, August 6, 1861, to Confiscate Property Used for Insurrectionary Purpose

*Be it enacted* . . . That if, during the present or any future insurrection against the Government of the United States, after the President of the United States shall have declared by proclamation, that the laws of the United States are opposed, and the execution thereof obstructed by combinations too powerful to be suppressed by the ordinary course of judicial proceedings, or by the power vested in the marshals by law, any person or persons, his, her, or their agent, attorney, or employee, shall purchase or acquire, sell or give, any property of whatsoever kind or description, with intent to use or employ the same, or suffer the same to be used or employed, in aiding, abetting, or promoting such insurrection or resistance to the laws, or any person or persons engaged therein; or if any person or persons, being the owner or owners of any such property, shall knowingly use or employ, or consent to the use or employment of the same as aforesaid, all such property is hereby declared to be lawful subject of prize and capture wherever found; and it shall be the duty of the President of the United States to cause the same to be seized, confiscated, and condemned. . . .

SEC. 3 . *And be it further enacted,* That the Attorney-General, or any district attorney of the United States in which said property may at the time be, may institute the proceedings of condemnation, and in such case they shall be wholly for the benefit of the United States; or any person may file an information with such attorney, in which case the proceedings shall be for the use of such informer and the United States in equal parts.

SEC. 4. *And be it further enacted,* That whenever hereafter, during the present insurrection against the Government of the United States, any person claimed to be held to labor or service under the law of any State, shall be required or permitted by the person to whom such labor or service is claimed to be due, or by the lawful agent of such person, to take up arms against the United States, or shall be required or permitted by the person to whom such labor or service is claimed to be due, or his lawful agent, to work or to be employed in or upon any fort, navy yard, dock, armory, ship, entrenchment, or in any military or naval service whatsoever, against the Government and lawful authority of the United States, then, and in every such case, the person to whom such labor service is claimed to be due shall forfeit his claim to such labor, any law of the State or of the United States to the contrary notwithstanding. And whenever thereafter the person claiming such labor or service shall seek to enforce his claim, it shall be a full and sufficient answer to such claim that the person whose service or labor is claimed had been employed in hostile service against the Government of the United States contrary to the provisions of this act.

## 34. From the Constitution of the Confederate States of America, 1861

### *Article I, Section 9*

[The Confederate Congress is explicitly prohibited from passing any law] denying or impairing the right of property in negro slaves.

### *Article IV, Section 2*

The citizens of each State shall be entitled to all the privileges and immunities of citizens in the several States, and shall have the right of transit and sojourn in any Sate of this Confederacy, with their slaves and other property; and the right of property in said slaves shall not be thereby impaired. . . .

No slave or other person held to service or labor in any State or Territory of the Confederate States, under the laws thereof, escaping or lawfully carried into another, shall, in consequence of any law or regulation therein, be discharged from such service or labor; but shall be delivered up on claim of the party to whom such slave belongs, or to whom such service or labor may be due. . . .

The Confederate States may acquire new territory; and Congress shall have power to legislate and provide governments for the inhabitants of all territory belonging to the Confederate States, lying without the limits of the several States; and may permit them, at such times and in such manner as it may by law provide, to form States to be admitted into the Confederacy. In all such territory, the institution of negro slavery, as it now exists in the Confederate States, shall be recognized and protected by Congress and by the territorial government; and the inhabitants of the several Confederate States and Territories shall have the right to take to such Territory any slaves lawfully held by them in any of the States or Territories of the Confederate States. . . .

## 35. From an Act of Congress, April 16, 1862, for the Release of Certain Persons Held to Service or Labor in the District of Columbia

*Be it enacted* . . . That all persons held to service or labor within the District of Columbia by reason of African descent are hereby discharged and freed of and from all claim to such service or labor; and from and after the passage of this act neither slavery nor involuntary servitude, except for crime, whereof the party shall be duly convicted, shall hereafter exist in said District.

SEC. 2. *And be it further enacted,* That all persons loyal to the United States, holding claim to service or labor against persons discharged therefrom by this act, may, within ninety days from the passage thereof, but not thereafter, present to the commissioners hereinafter mentioned, their respective statements or petitions in writing, verified by oath or affirmation, setting forth the names, ages, and personal descriptions of such persons, the manner in which said petitioners acquired such claim, and any facts touching the value thereof, and declaring his allegiance to the Government of the United States during the present rebellion, nor in any way given aid or comfort thereto: *Provided,* That the oath of the party to the petition shall not be evidence of the facts therein stated.

SEC. 3. [Appointment of commissioners to investigate and determine validity of claims for compensation.] . . . *And provided, further,* That no claim shall be allowed for any slave or slaves brought into said District after the passage of this act, nor for any slave claimed by any person who has borne arms against the Government of the United States in the present rebellion, or in any way given aid and comfort thereto, or which originates in or by virtue of any transfer heretofore made, or which shall hereafter be made by any person who has in any manner aided or sustained the rebellion against the Government of the United States. . . .

SEC. 8. *And be it further enacted,* That any person or persons who shall kidnap, or in any manner transport or procure to be taken out of said District, any person or persons discharged and freed by the provisions of this act, or any free person or persons with intent to re-enslave or sell such person or persons into slavery, or shall re-enslave any of said freed persons, the person or persons so offending shall be deemed guilty of a felony, and on conviction thereof in any court of competent jurisdiction in said District, shall be imprisoned in the penitentiary not less that five nor more than twenty years. . . .

SEC. 10. *And be it further enacted,* That the said clerk [of the Circuit Court for the District of Columbia] shall, from time to time, on demand, and on receiving twenty-five cents therefor, prepare, sign, and deliver to each person made free or manumitted by this act, a certificate under the seal of said court, setting out the name, age, and description of such person, and stating that such person was duly manumitted and set free by this act.

SEC. 11. *And be it further enacted,* That the sum of one hundred thousand dollars, out of any money in the Treasury not otherwise appropriated, is hereby appropriated, to be expended under the direction of the President of the United States, to aid in the colonization and settlement of such free persons of African descent now residing in said District, including those to be liberated by this act, as may desire to emigrate to the Republics of Hayti or Liberia, or such other country beyond the limits of the United States as the President may determine: *Provided,* The expenditure for this purpose shall not exceed one hundred dollars for each emigrant.

SEC. 12. *And be it further enacted,* That all acts of Congress and all laws of the State of Maryland in force in said District, and all ordinances of the cities of Washington and Georgetown, inconsistent with the provisions of this act, are hereby repealed.

## 36. From an Act of Congress, July 17, 1862, to Suppress Insurrection, to Punish Treason and Rebellion, to Seize and Confiscate the Property of Rebels, and for Other Purposes

*Be it enacted* . . . That every person who shall hereafter commit the crime of treason against the United States, and shall be adjudged guilty thereof, shall suffer death, and all his slaves, if any, shall be declared and made free; or, at the discretion of the court, he shall be imprisoned for not less than five years and fined not less than ten thousand dollars, and all his slaves, if any, shall be declared and made free; said fine shall be levied and collected on any or all of the property, real and personal, excluding slaves, of which the said person so convicted was the owner at the time of committing the said crime, any sale or conveyance to the contrary notwithstanding.

SEC. 2. *And be it further enacted,* That if any person shall hereafter incite, set on foot, assist, or engage in any rebellion or insurrection against the authority of the United States, or the laws thereof, or shall give aid or comfort thereto, or shall engage in, or give aid and comfort to, any such existing rebellion or insurrection, and be convicted thereof, such person shall be punished by imprisonment for a period not exceeding ten years, or by a fine not exceeding ten thousand dollars, and by the liberation of all his slaves, if any he have; or by both of said punishments, at the discretion of the court.

SEC. 3. *And be it further enacted,* That every person guilty of either of the offences described in this act shall be forever incapable and disqualified to hold any office under the United States. . . .

SEC. 9. *And be it further enacted,* That all slaves of persons who shall hereafter be engaged in rebellion against the government of the United States, or who shall in any way give aid or comfort thereto, escaping from such persons and taking refuge within the lines of the army; and all slaves captured from such persons or deserted by them and coming under the control of the government of the United States; and all slaves of such persons found or being within any place occupied by rebel forces and afterwards occupied by the forces of the United States, shall be deemed captives of war, and shall be forever free of their servitude, and not again held as slaves.

SEC. 10. *And be it further enacted,* That no slave escaping into any State, Territory, or the District of Columbia, from any other State, shall be delivered up, or in any way impeded or hindered of his liberty, except for crime, or some offence against the laws, unless the person claiming said fugitive shall first make oath that the person to whom the labor or service of such fugitive is alleged to be due is his lawful owner, and has not borne arms against the United States in the present rebellion, nor in any way given aid and comfort thereto; and no person engaged in the military or naval service of the United States shall, under any pretence whatever, assume to decide on the validity of the claim of any person to the service or labor of any other person, or surrender up any such person to the claimant, on pain of being dismissed from the service.

SEC. 11. *And be it further enacted,* That the President of the United States is authorized to employ as many persons of African descent as he may deem necessary and proper for the suppression of this rebellion, and for this purpose he may organize and use them in such manner as he may judge best for the public welfare.

SEC. 12. *And be it further enacted,* That the President of the United States is hereby authorized to make provision for the transportation, colonization, and settlement, in some tropical country beyond the limits of the United States, of such persons of the African race, made free by the provisions of this act, as may be willing to emigrate, having first obtained the consent of the government of said country to their protection and settlement within the same, with all the rights and privileges of freemen.

## 37. From Lincoln's Proclamation of the Act to Suppress Insurrection, July 25, 1862

In pursuance of the sixth section of the act of Congress entitled "An act to suppress insurrection and to punish treason and rebellion, to seize and confiscate property of rebels, and for other purposes" Approved July 17, 1862, and which act, and the Joint Resolution explanatory thereof, are herewith published, I, Abraham Lincoln, President of the United States, do hereby proclaim to, and warn all persons within the contemplation of said sixth section to cease participating in, aiding, countenancing, or abetting the existing rebellion, or any rebellion against the government of the United States, and to return to their proper allegiance to the United States, on pain of the forfeitures and seizures, as within and by sixth section provided.

## 38. The Preliminary Emancipation Proclamation, September 22, 1862

I, Abraham Lincoln, President of the United States of America, and Commander-in-Chief of the Army and Navy thereof, do hereby proclaim and declare that hereafter, as heretofore, the war will be prosecuted for the object of practically restoring the constitutional relation between the United States, and each of the states, and the people thereof, in which states that relation is, or may be suspended, or disturbed.

That it is my purpose upon the next meeting of Congress to again recommend the adoption of a practical measure tendering pecuniary aid to the free acceptance or rejection of all slave states, so called, the people whereof may not then be in rebellion against the United States, and which states may then have voluntarily adopted, or thereafter may voluntarily adopt, immediate or gradual abolishment of slavery within their respective limits; and that the effort to colonize persons of African descent with their consent upon this continent, or elsewhere with the previously obtained consent of the Governments existing there will be continued.

That on the first day of January in the year of our Lord, one thousand eight hundred and sixty-three, all persons held as slaves within any state, or designated part of a state, the people whereof shall be in rebellion against the United States shall be then, thenceforward, and forever free; and the executive government of the United States including the military and naval authority thereof will recognize and maintain the freedom of such persons, and will do no act or acts to repress such persons, or any of them, in any efforts they may make for their actual freedom.

That the executive will, on the first day of January aforesaid, by proclamation, designate the States, and parts of states, if any, in which the people thereof respectively, shall then be in rebellion against the United States; and the fact that any state, or the people thereof shall, on that day be, in good faith represented in the Congress of the United States, by members chosen thereto, at elections wherein a majority of the qualified voters of such state shall have participated, shall, in the absence of strong countervailing testimony, be deemed conclusive evidence that such state and the people thereof, are not then in rebellion against the United States.

That attention is hereby called to an Act of Congress entitled "An act to make an additional Article of War" approved March 13, 1862, and which act is in the words and figure following:

*Be it enacted by the Senate and House of Representatives of the United States of America in Congress assembled,* That hereafter the following shall be promulgated as an additional article of war for the government of the army of the United States, and shall be obeyed and observed as such:

Article—All officers or persons in the military or naval service of the United States are prohibited from employing any of the forces under their respective commands for the purpose of returning fugitives from service or labor, who may have escaped from any persons to whom such service or labor is claimed to be due, and any officer who shall be found guilty by a court-martial of violating this article shall be dismissed from the service.

Sec. 2. *And be it further enacted,* That this act shall take effect from and after its passage.

Also to the ninth and tenth sections of an act entitled, "An Act to suppress Insurrection, to punish Treason and Rebellion, to seize and confiscate property of rebels, and for other purposes," approved July 17, 1862, and which sections are in the words and figures following:

Sec. 9. *And be it further enacted,* That all slaves of persons who shall hereafter be engaged in rebellion against the government of the United States, or who shall in any way give aid or comfort thereto, escaping from such persons and taking refuge within the lines of the army; and all slaves captured from such persons or deserted by them and coming under the control of the government of the United States; and all slaves of such persons found *on* or being within any place occupied by rebel forces and afterwards occupied by the forces of the United States, shall be deemed captives of war, and shall be forever free of their servitude and not again held as slaves.

Sec. 10. *And be it further enacted,* That no slave escaping into any State, territory, or the District of Columbia, from any other State, shall be delivered up, or in any way impeded or hindered of his liberty, except for crime, or some offence against the laws, unless the person claiming such fugitive shall first make oath that the person to whom the labor or service of such fugitive is alleged to be due is his lawful owner, and has not borne arms against the United States in the present rebellion, nor in any way given aid and comfort thereto; and no person engaged in the military or naval service of the United States shall, under any pretence whatever, assume to decide on the validity of the claim of any person to the service or labor of any other person, or surrender up any such person to the claimant, on pain of being dismissed from the service.

And I do hereby enjoin upon and order all persons engaged in the military and naval service of the United States to observe, obey, and enforce within their respective spheres of service, the act, and sections above recited.

And the executive will in due time recommend that all citizens of the United States who shall have remained loyal thereto throughout the rebellion shall (upon the restoration of the constitutional relation between the United States, and their respective states, and people, if that relation shall have been suspended or disturbed) be compensated for all losses by acts of the United States, including the loss of slaves.

In witness whereof, I have hereunto set my hand, and caused the seal of the United States to be affixed.

Done at the City of Washington, this twenty second day of September, in the year of our Lord, one thousand, eight hundred and sixty two, and of the Independence of the United States, the eighty seventh.

Abraham Lincoln
William H. Seward
Secretary of State

## 39. The Emancipation Proclamation, January 1, 1863

Whereas, on the twenty-second day of September, in the year of our Lord one thousand eight hundred and sixty two, a proclamation was issued by the President of the United States, containing, among other things, the following, to wit:

"That on the first day of January, in the year of our Lord one thousand eight hundred and sixty-three, all persons held as slaves within any State or designated part of a State, the people whereof shall then be in rebellion against the United States, shall be then, thenceforward, and forever free; and the Executive Government of the United States, including the military and naval authority thereof, will recognize and maintain the freedom of such persons, and will do no act or acts to repress such persons, or any of them, in any effort they may make for their actual freedom.

"That the Executive will, on the first day of January aforesaid, by proclamation, designate the States and parts of States, if any, in which the people thereof, shall on that day be, in good faith, represented in the Congress of the United States by members chosen thereto at elections wherein a majority of the qualified voters of such State shall have participated, shall in the absence of strong countervailing testimony, be deemed conclusive evidence that such State, and the people thereof, are not then in rebellion against the United States."

Now, therefore, I, Abraham Lincoln, President of the United States, by virtue of the power in me invested as Commander-in-Chief, of the Army and Navy of the United States in time of actual armed rebellion against authority and government of the United States, and as a fit and necessary war measure for suppressing said rebellion, do, on this first day of January, in the year of our Lord one thousand eight hundred and sixty three, and in accordance with my purpose so to do publicly proclaimed for the full period of one hundred days, from the day first above mentioned, order and designate as the States and parts of States wherein the people thereof respectively, are this day in rebellion against the United States, the following, to wit:

Arkansas, Texas, Louisiana, (except the Parishes of St. Bernard, Plaquemines, Jefferson, St. Johns, St. Charles, St. James Ascension, Assumption, Terrebonne, Lafourche, St. Mary, St. Martin, and Orleans, including the City of New-Orleans) Mississippi, Alabama, Florida, Georgia, South-Carolina, North-Carolina, and Virginia, (except the forty-eight counties designated as West Virginia, and also the counties of Berkley, Accomac, Northampton, Elizabeth-City, York, Princess Ann, and Norfolk, including the cities of Norfolk and Portsmouth; and which excepted parts are, for the present, left precisely as if this proclamation were not issued.)

And by virtue of the power, and for the purpose aforesaid, I do order and declare that all persons held as slaves within said designated States, and parts of States, are, and henceforward shall be free; and that the Executive government of the United States, including the military and naval authorities thereof, will recognize and maintain the freedom of said persons.

And I hereby enjoin upon the people so declared to be free to abstain from all violence, unless in necessary self-defence; and I recommend to them that, in all cases when allowed, they labor faithfully for reasonable wages.

And I further declare and make known that such persons of suitable condition, will be received into the armed service of the United States to garrison forts, positions, stations, and other places, and to man vessels of all sorts in said service.

And upon this act, sincerely believed to be an act of justice, warranted by the Constitution, upon military necessary, I invoke the considerate judgment of mankind, and the gracious favor of Almighty God.

In witness whereof, I have hereunto set my hand and caused the seal of the United States to be affixed.

Done at the City of Washington, this first day of January, in the year of our Lord one thousand eight hundred and sixty three, and of the Independence of the United States of America the eighty-seventh.

By the President: Abraham Lincoln
William H. Seward, Secretary of State

## 40. Lincoln's Order to Protect Black Prisoners of War, 1863

Executive Mansion, Washington, July 30, 1863

It is the duty of every government to give protection to its citizens of whatever class, color, or condition, and especially to those who are duly organized as soldiers in the public service. The law of nations and the usages and customs of war, as carried on by civilized powers, permit no distinction as to color in the treatment of prisoners of war as public enemies. To sell or enslave any captured person on account of his color, and for no offence against the laws of war, is a relapse into barbarism and a crime against the civilization of the age. The Government of the United States will give the same protection to all its soldiers; and if the enemy shall sell or enslave any one because of his color, the offence shall be punished by retaliation upon the enemy's prisoners in our hands.

It is therefore ordered that for every soldier of the United States killed in violation of the laws of war, a Rebel soldier shall be executed, and for every one enslaved by the enemy or sold into slavery, a Rebel soldier shall be placed at hard labor on the public works, and continue at such labor until the other shall be released and receive the treatment due a prisoner of war.

Abraham Lincoln

## 41. From an Act to Increase the Efficiency of the [Confederate] Army by the Employment of Free Negroes and Slaves in Certain Capacities, February 17, 1864

Whereas, the efficiency of the Army is greatly diminished by the withdrawal from the ranks of able-bodied soldiers to act as teamsters, and in various other capacities in which free negroes and slaves might be advantageously employed: Therefore,

*The Congress of the Confederate States of America do enact,* That all male free negroes and other free persons of color, not including those who are free under the treaty of Paris of eighteen hundred and three, or under the treaty with Spain of eighteen hundred and nineteen, resident in the Confederate States, between the ages of eighteen and fifty years, shall be held liable to perform such duties with the army, or in connection with the military defenses of the country, in the way of work upon fortifications or in Government works for the production or preparation of material of war, or in military hospitals, as the Secretary of War or the commanding general of the Trans-Mississippi Department may, from time to time, prescribe, and while engaged in the performance of such duties shall receive rations and clothing and compensation at the rate of eleven dollars a month. . . .

SEC. 2. That the Secretary of War is hereby authorized to employ for duties similar to those indicated in the preceding section of this act, as many male negro slaves, not to exceed twenty thousand, as in his judgment, the wants of the service may require, furnishing them, while so employed, with proper rations and clothing, under rules and regulations to be established by him, and paying to the owners of said slaves such wages as may be agreed upon with said owners for their use and service, and in the event of the loss of any slaves while so employed, by the act of the enemy, or by escape to the enemy, or by death inflicted by the enemy, or by disease contracted while in any service required of said slaves, then the owners of the same shall be entitled to receive the full value of such slaves. . . .

SEC. 3. That when the Secretary of War shall be unable to procure the service of slaves in any military department in sufficient numbers for the necessities of the Department, upon the terms and conditions set forth in the preceding section, then he is hereby authorized to impress the services of as many male slaves, not to exceed twenty thousand, as may be required, from time to time, to discharge the duties indicated in the first section of this act . . . *Provided,* That if the owner have but one male slave between the age of eighteen and fifty, he shall not be impressed against the will of said owner: *Provided further,* That free negroes shall be first impressed, and if there should be a deficiency, it shall be supplied by the impressment of slaves according to the foregoing provisions: *Provided further,* That in making the impressment, not more than one of every five male slaves between the ages of eighteen and forty-five shall be taken from any owner. . . .

## 42. From an Act to Increase the Military Force of the Confederate States, March 23, 1865

*The Congress of the Confederate States of America do enact,* That in order to provide additional forces to repel invasion, maintain the rightful possession of the Confederate States, secure their independence, and preserve their institutions, the President be, and he is hereby, authorized to ask for and accept from the owners of slaves, the services of such number of able-bodied negro men as he may deem expedient, for and during the war, to perform military service in whatever capacity he may direct. . . .

Sec. 3. That while employed in the service the said troops shall receive the same rations, clothing and compensation as are allowed to other troops in the same branch of the service. . . .

Sec. 5. That nothing in this act shall be construed to authorize a change in the relation which the said slaves shall bear toward their owners, except by consent of the owners and of the States in which they may reside, and in pursuance of the laws thereof.

## 43. The Thirteenth Amendment, Ratified December 18, 1865

*Section 1.* Neither slavery nor involuntary servitude, except as a punishment for a crime whereof the party shall have been duly convicted, shall exist within the United States, or any place subject to their jurisdiction.

*Section 2.* Congress shall have power to enforce this article by appropriate legislation.

## 44. The Fourteenth Amendment, Ratified July 28, 1868

*Section 1.* All persons born or naturalized in the United States, and subject to the jurisdiction thereof, are citizens of the United States and of the State wherein they reside. No state shall make or enforce any law which shall abridge the privileges or immunities of citizens of the United States; nor shall any State deprive any person of life, liberty, or property, without due process of law; nor deny to any person within its jurisdiction the equal protection of the laws.

*Section 2.* Representatives shall be apportioned among the several States according to their respective numbers, counting the whole number of persons in each State, excluding Indians not taxed. But when the right to vote at any election for the choice of electors for President and Vice President of the United States, Representatives in Congress, the Executive and Judicial officers of a State, or the members of the Legislature thereof, is denied to any of the male inhabitants of such State, being twenty-one years of age, and citizens of the United States, or in any way abridged, except for participation in rebellion, or other crime, the basis of representation therein shall be reduced in the proportion which the number of such male citizens shall bear to the whole number of male citizens twenty-one years of age in such State.

*Section 3.* No person shall be a Senator or Representative in Congress, or elector of President and Vice President, or hold any office, civil or military, under the United States, or under any State, who, having previously taken an oath, as a member of Congress, or as an officer of the United States, or as a member of any State legislature, or as an executive or judicial officer of any State, to support the Constitution of the United States, shall have engaged in insurrection or rebellion against the same, or given aid or comfort to the enemies thereof. But Congress may by a vote of two-thirds of each House, remove such disability.

*Section 4.* The validity of the public debt of the United States, authorized by law, including debts incurred for payment of pensions and bounties for services in suppressing insurrection or rebellion, shall not be questioned. But neither the United States nor any State shall assume or pay any debt or obligation incurred in aid of insurrection or rebellion against the United States, or any claim for the loss or emancipation of any slave, but all such debts, obligations and claims shall be held illegal and void.

*Section 5.* The Congress shall have power to enforce, by appropriate legislation, the provisions of this article.

## 45. The Fifteenth Amendment to the Constitution, Ratified March 30, 1870

*Section 1.* The right of citizens of the United States to vote shall not be denied or abridged by the United States or by any State on account of race, color, or previous condition of servitude.

*Section 2.* The Congress shall have power to enforce this article by appropriate legislation.

# APPENDIX B

# Biographies of Major Personalities

**Abraham** (ca. 1787–ca. 1871) *black leader, counselor to the Seminole*
Abraham fled from his master in Pensacola as a boy. He was possibly recruited by the British in the War of 1812 and landed on the Apalachicola River in Florida to help build the "Negro Fort." He eventually became the slave of the Seminole chief Mikonopi, whom in 1826 he accompanied as an interpreter in a delegation to Washington, for which service Mikonopi freed him. His emancipation was formally recorded on June 18, 1835. A shrewd and intelligent man, Abraham was Mikonopi's principal counselor and married the widow of the former chief of the Seminole nation. He fathered two or three sons and at least one daughter. A contemporary account described him as a "good soldier and intrepid leader," cunning and avaricious, with polished manners: "Abra'm, or Yobly, as the Indians call him, is the chief Interpreter, and latterly succeeded Jumper as 'sense carrier' to Miconope. This high chancellor and keeper of the king's conscience, also heads about five hundred negroes of whom he is legislator, judge, and executioner through his influence with the governor. . . . under an exterior of profound meekness [he] cloaks deep, dark, and bloody purposes. He has at once the crouch and spring of the panther. . . ."

Throughout the negotiations for the removal of the Seminole from Florida to Indian Territory (now Oklahoma) in the West, Abraham counseled resistance but kept open the lines of communication with the U.S. government. Meanwhile, he gathered arms and ammunition and rallied plantation slaves to join with the Indians. In the early years of the Second Seminole War, he fought ardently, retreating with the Indians to the swamps when the battles turned against them. His negotiating skills enabled the 1837 treaty by which the Seminole agreed to removal on the condition that their black allies accompany them. The bad faith of the American whites led to his imprisonment and that of his family; General Jesup threatened, "I have promised Abraham the freedom of his family if he be faithful to us, and I shall certainly hang him if he will not be faithful." Abraham then acted for the U.S. government in urging the Seminole and their black allies to surrender and accept transport to the West.

After his removal to the Indian Territory in 1839, he apparently lived there quietly raising cattle, though some authorities assert that in 1850 he went with Seminole into Mexico. In any case in 1852 he interpreted for an unsuccessful delegation sent to Florida to induce Seminole leader Billy Bowlegs to surrender with his people for transportation westward, a task that included a tour of the major eastern cities and a meeting with the president of the United States.

**Adams, John Quincy** (July 11, 1767–February 23, 1848) *public servant*
After his term as president of the United States (1824–28), Adams rounded out a distinguished career in government with eight terms in the House of Representatives (1831–48). Although not an abolitionist, he led the fight against the Gag Rule, which in 1836 had been passed by Congress to suppress the right of petition against slavery. In 1844 the rule was finally defeated, though not before Adams endured a move by southern congressmen to discipline him. In 1836, he argued that should civil war break out, the war powers of the Congress would enable it to interfere with slavery in every possible way. Later he extended this principle to say that in a state of war the military authority might order universal emancipation of the slaves.

Adams also fought against the annexation of Texas. In his memoirs he said, "This [opposition to the extension of slavery] is a cause upon which I am entering at the last stage of life, and with the certainty that I cannot advance in it far; my career must close, leaving the cause at the threshold. To open the way for others is all that I can do. The cause is good and great."

In 1841, Adams argued for the freedom of the slave ship *Amistad* mutineers before the Supreme Court of the United States, winning his case. Adams acted consistently as a man of principle, intensely devoted to the cause of freedom for all and his belief in the inalienable rights of human beings.

**Allen, Richard** (February 14, 1760–March 26, 1831) *founder and bishop of the African Methodist Episcopal church*
Born a slave, Allen preached his way into freedom by converting his master, who then enabled him and his family to obtain their liberty. He then supported himself through manual labor while continuing to preach to blacks and whites. In 1784, the Methodist Church in Baltimore recognized him as a minister. In the integrated St. George Methodist Church in Philadelphia, where he occasionally preached, whites angered blacks by ordering them to sit in the gallery. The blacks left in 1787, some to follow Absalom Jones in founding the African Protestant Episcopal Church, some to go with Richard Allen in organizing an independent Methodist church. In 1816, 16 similar black congregations formed the African Methodist Episcopal Church, electing Allen bishop. To this labor he devoted the rest of his life.

**Anthony, Susan B.** (February 15, 1820–March 13, 1906) *suffrage leader*
Known chiefly as a woman suffragist, Anthony worked also to abolish slavery. From 1856 to 1865 she served as the principal New York agent for William Lloyd Garrison's American Anti-Slavery Society. She and the group of abolitionist speakers she led encountered hostile mobs in upstate New York. In the Kansas-Nebraska controversy, she spent months trying to promote the entry of Kansas into the Union as a free state. During the Civil War, she and Elizabeth Cady Stanton organized the Women's Loyal National League, gathering hundreds of thousands of signatures on petitions for emancipation.

Woman suffragists, including Anthony, suffered defeat when the Fourteenth Amendment for the first time introduced the word "male" into the Constitution, demolishing suffragist hopes that women might be enfranchised along with black men. Ironically, their struggle against the exclusion of women as full citizens in the Fourteenth and Fifteenth Amendments forced Anthony and many other abolitionist women into competition against the black men whom they had long sought to liberate.

**Attucks, Crispus** (ca. 1723–March 5, 1770) *American patriot and martyr*
Attucks was apparently an escaped slave who had worked around the wharves in Boston, Massachusetts, and on whalers. A William Brown of Framingham, Massachusetts, advertised the loss of a slave named Crispus, whom he described as a mulatto six feet two inches tall, with short, curly hair, and about twenty-seven years old at the time he ran away; he also offered a reward of £10 for his capture and return. Attucks may have been of mixed Indian and black ancestry. When in March 1770 the frequent quarrels between Boston citizens and occupying British soldiers erupted into what came to be known as the Boston Massacre, Crispus Attucks was the first to fall to British fire. His body was placed in Fanueil Hall before burial with the three other victims in Boston's Middle Burying Ground.

**Bailey, Gamaliel** (December 3, 1807–June 5, 1859) *journalist, antislavery spokesperson*
During his adventurous life, Bailey worked as a teacher, editor, sailor, and physician. Converted to abolitionism in 1834 by the Lane Seminary debates, he served as an editor of the *Cincinnati Philanthropist,* the first antislavery paper in the West. His office there was mobbed three times, the last time evoking enough sympathy to enable him to begin a daily publication, the *Herald.* In 1847, he took over the editorship of the *National Era,* a weekly sponsored by the American and Foreign Anti-Slavery Society. The next year, when he was accused of helping fugitive slaves to escape, he faced down an angry mob. Ill health first interrupted and then ended his antislavery work and his life.

**Banneker, Benjamin** (November 9, 1731–October 26, 1806) *self-taught mathematician and astronomer*
Banneker, son and grandson of freed slaves, was born, grew up, and spent most of his life on a Maryland farm. His grandmother taught him to read and write, and the family sent him to a country school for several seasons. A man of great mathematical gifts, he

taught himself literature, history, mathematics, and astronomy. When he was almost sixty, he assisted in surveying the Federal Territory (now the District of Columbia). Soon after, with the support of abolition societies, he published *Benjamin Banneker's Pennsylvania, Delaware, Maryland and Virginia Almanack and Ephemeris, for the Year of Our Lord, 1792.* He sent the manuscript for this almanac to Thomas Jefferson, along with a letter urging the abolition of slavery; publication of the subsequent correspondence between Banneker and Jefferson helped sales. Banneker retired from tobacco farming to devote himself to his studies, publishing more almanacs that brought him an international reputation. It is said that when the French architect Pierre L'Enfant fled with the plans for Washington, D.C., Banneker was able to reconstruct them through his prodigious memory.

**Barrow, David** (1753–1819) *activist, antislavery Baptist minister*
Barrow preached in southern Virginia and northern North Carolina. In 1795, he founded the integrated Portsmouth-Norfolk church, installing the black Jacob Bishop as its pastor. Violent opposition to this action drove Barrow to Kentucky. There in 1805, the North District Association of Baptists expelled him for his views on slavery. For many years he presided over the Kentucky Abolition Society. He published a pamphlet, *Involuntary, Unlimited, Perpetual, Absolute, Hereditary Slavery Examined on the Principles of Nature, Reason, Justice, Policy, and Scripture.*

**Beecher, Catharine** (September 6, 1800–May 12, 1878) *author, educator*
Catharine Beecher was a member of the famous Beecher family of clergymen and a sister of Harriet Beecher Stowe. She benefited women of her day by pioneering teaching as a woman's profession, crusading against the exploitation of women factory workers and the indolence and subjection to fashion of wealthy women, and developing a pragmatic approach to housework and domestic architecture. At the same time, she preached that women should adopt a conventional social role, avoiding any activity that "throws woman into the attitude of a combatant, either for herself or others." Unlike most of her family, she did not embrace abolitionism. Accordingly, when the Grimké sisters defied tradition by speaking against slavery before audiences of both women and men, Beecher in 1837 took it upon herself to reproach them in *An Essay on Slavery and Abolitionism, with Reference to the Duty of American Females.* The next year, Angelina Grimké replied in the spirited *Letters to Catharine Beecher,* converting the exchange into more grist for the abolitionist mills.

**Bibb, Henry** (1815–after 1851) *fugitive slave, operator on the Underground Railroad, Canadian colonist*
After his flight from Kentucky slavery in 1837 and many recaptures and escapes in trying to rescue his wife, Bibb worked prominently in the mainline abolitionist movement. Despite his long opposition to colonization, the Fugitive Slave Law of 1850 drove him to Canada, where he at once organized blacks and whites to help the thousands of incoming fugitives form black communities, to which end he edited the *Voice of the Fugitive.* In 1851, he convoked the North American Convention of Colored Men in Toronto.

**Birney, James Gillespie** (February 4, 1792–November 25, 1857) *antislavery attorney*
Once a prominent citizen and a slaveholding planter in Alabama, Birney moved north to educate his sons in the free states. In 1832, he became an agent for the American Colonization Society in Tennessee, Alabama, Mississippi, Louisiana, and Arkansas. But in 1833 he resigned from the colonization society and from the Kentucky Society for the Gradual Relief of the State from Slavery, publicly freed his slaves, and in a *Letter on Colonization* renounced colonization as a failed effort that led to oppression. In October 1834, he became an agent for the American Anti-Slavery Society, soon thereafter organizing the Kentucky Anti-Slavery Society and announcing his intention of publishing an antislavery newspaper there—but local forces prevailed, driving him from the state and shutting down the Kentucky Anti-Slavery Society. In January 1836, Birney established his newspaper, the *Philanthropist,* in Cincinnati.

**Bourne, George** (June 13, 1780–November 20, 1845) *abolitionist clergyman*
An English-born pastor of a Virginia church, Bourne in 1816 advocated immediate emancipation in *The Book and Slavery Irreconcilable,* for which he was convicted of heresy by a Presbyterian council. Compelled to leave the South, he moved north, where he served

Presbyterian churches in New York and Quebec. In 1833, he switched to the more tolerant Dutch Reformed Church and continued to advocate abolitionism, helping to found the Anti-Slavery Society. That year he also published *An Address to the Presbyterian Church, Enforcing the Duty of Excluding All Slave-holders from the "Communion of Saints."* Four years later, he offered to its convention a resolution censuring clergymen who defended slavery. He protested to Garrison about the latter's advocacy of nonviolence, arguing that it ill served the antislavery cause. His many works included several other diatribes against slavery.

**Bowditch, Henry Ingersoll** (August 9, 1808–January 14, 1892) *abolitionist physician*
Beginning practice in Boston in 1834, Bowditch was converted by Garrison to the antislavery cause, joining a committee to assist the fugitive George Latimer. He ardently helped other slaves and encouraged antislavery sentiment in the North.

**Brown, John** (May 9, 1800–December 2, 1859) *militant abolitionist*
A tanner by trade, Brown envisioned himself as the slaves' savior, destined to lead them out of bondage into freedom in Appalachia. In 1855, he moved to Kansas during the struggle over whether that new state should be slave or free. On May 24, 1856, he led a small band (mostly his own sons) in massacring five non-slaveholding men from a proslavery Kansas community and mutilating their bodies. God had so decreed, he said. Then, in 1858, he proposed to coconspirators in Canada a "Provisional Constitution and Ordinances for the People of the United States"—a military dictatorship under Brown, to be established by an insurrection of armed slaves. For this unlikely project he attracted the support of certain highly respectable abolitionists (the Secret Six), who helped him buy guns, ammunition, and 950 pikes for the slaves he planned to rouse to rebellion. On October 16, 1859, with a handful of men, including just five blacks, he attempted to capture the U.S. arsenal at Harpers Ferry, Virginia, defended by marines under the command of Col. Robert E. Lee, U.S. Army. In the process, many were killed: a marine, a black freeman, three other civilians, and two of Brown's sons, along with eight others of his band. His efforts at rousing a black insurrection had failed, for most blacks recognized him as a man of words trying to be a man of deeds, and they knew better than to follow him. At his trial, while the public debated his sanity, Brown defended himself by saying that he had intended only a peaceful demonstration but that in any case slavery is an "unjustifiable War of one portion of its citizens upon another"—and in war anything goes. He was hanged on December 2, 1859. Although President Lincoln, Secretary of State Seward, and Senator Edward Everett condemned Brown's actions, such avowedly peace-loving citizens as Ralph Waldo Emerson and Henry Thoreau glorified him into martyrdom.

**Brown, William Wells** (ca. 1816–November 6, 1884) *writer, lecturer*
The son of a slave mother and a white slaveholder in Kentucky, Brown was hired out to a slave trader, sold to a merchant, and then sold to a riverboat captain. Escaping into Ohio, he worked on a lake steamer, in one year helping 60 fugitives to Canada, at the same time educating himself. In 1843, he became an agent for the New York Anti-Slavery Society. He published his *Narrative of William Wells Brown, a Fugitive Slave* in 1847. He lectured in Great Britain for five years, visited the Continent four times, and wrote three books. Back in the United States, he contributed both to the London *Daily News* and to American antislavery journals.

**Bruce, Blanche K.** (March 1, 1841–March 17, 1898) *first black to serve a full term in the U.S. Senate*
Born a slave in Virginia, Bruce was educated in Missouri and at Oberlin College. He settled in Mississippi, where he held several local offices, then became a state senator. He served in the U.S. Senate from 1874 to 1881, in his maiden speech protesting against the removal of federal troops from the South. In 1880 his name was proposed for vice president, but he was not nominated. Later he served in the federal treasury.

**Buffum, Arnold** (December 13, 1782–March 13, 1859) *inventor, antislavery lecturer*
Raised in an abolitionist Quaker family, his home a station on the Underground Railroad, as a boy Buffum learned the trade of hatter. In 1832, the New England Anti-Slavery Society, over which he presided, commissioned him as its lecturing agent. His accep-

tance of this position damaged him socially and economically, but he proved effective in it. In 1833, he helped found the American Anti-Slavery Society in Philadelphia, where he moved the next year. In 1840 he went to Ohio and Indiana, lecturing against slavery and editing the *Protectionist.* In later years, disagreeing with more radical abolitionists, Buffum championed the Liberty, Free-Soil, and Republican Parties as one succeeded the other.

**Burleigh, William Henry** (February 2, 1812–March 18, 1871) *journalist, reformer*
Apprenticed as a boy to a printer, Burleigh in 1833 with his brother Charles edited the *Unionist,* a paper founded to support Prudence Crandall's Connecticut school for young black women. Interested in a variety of reforms, in 1836 he undertook to lecture for the American Anti-Slavery Society while also editing various papers. In 1843, he took over the *Christian Freeman* (later the *Charter Oak*), published by the Connecticut Anti-Slavery Society. Several times he barely escaped mob violence, as when he protested against the Mexican War as a conflict fought for the "slave power."

**Burns, Anthony** (May 31, 1834–July 27, 1862) *fugitive slave*
Born a slave in Virginia, Burns learned to read and write as a boy. When his owner hired him out, he gained some degree of control over his own life, and in 1854 he stowed away on a ship bound for Boston. His owner learned his whereabouts from a letter Burns sent his brother and followed him to Boston. There he had Burns jailed on a false charge of theft. An antislavery mob stormed the jail, killing a policeman but failing to release Burns. Under the Fugitive Slave Law of 1850, federal troops were called out, along with state militia and the Boston police, all of whom confronted an angry crowd of some 50,000 antislavery agitators. Nonetheless, Burns was returned to Virginia, at an estimated cost to the government of $100,000.

This episode, at the height of the Kansas-Nebraska controversy, hardened northern sentiment against slavery. No other fugitive was ever removed from Boston. A group of Bostonians, mostly black, raised enough money to buy Burns's freedom. He went to the abolitionist town of Oberlin, Ohio, and then to Canada, where he became the minister of a small Baptist church.

**Campbell, Tunis G.** (1812–1891) *Reconstructionist and black separatist*
Commissioned by the military government as superintendent of islands for Georgia, Campbell established island colonies in which free blacks could learn to live independently. When his superiors ended that experiment in what whites termed "black nations" or "black kingdoms," he further aroused antagonism among whites by getting the vote for former slaves of McIntosh County, Georgia, and by winning a seat in the state senate, where he served until the legislature ousted him. He continued his struggle for black rights as a justice of the peace in Darien, Georgia, until white officers conspired to accuse and convict him of abuse of power. After his release from prison, he worked for black causes in Washington and Boston.

**Cary, Mary Ann Shadd** (October 9, 1823–June 5, 1893) *teacher, journalist, lawyer*
Born free, Cary early dedicated herself to elevating and freeing her race. Between 1839 and 1855, she founded or taught in schools for blacks in Delaware, Pennsylvania, and New York. In the 1850s, she led and spoke for black refugees from the Fugitive Slave Law of 1850 who had fled to Canada, where she opened a school for the American Missionary Society. However, she repudiated their Refugee Home Society, which "begged" funds to buy land and sell it to blacks: blacks could already, as Cary pointed out, buy government land at lower cost. In 1853, she helped found the *Provincial Freeman,* a nonsectarian, nonpartisan newspaper devoted to the interests of blacks in Canada, acting (in the nominal role of publishing agent) as its real editor. During the Civil War, she recruited black soldiers in the United States.

In 1869, widowed after a marriage of 13 years, Cary moved with her daughter to Washington, D.C., where she studied law and taught in the public schools. She retired from teaching in 1884.

**Chace, Elizabeth Buffum** (December 9, 1806–December 12, 1899) *antislavery and woman suffrage leader*
Born into an antislavery Quaker family and educated at Quaker schools, in 1828 Elizabeth Buffum married Samuel Buffington Chace, a textiles manufacturer. After their first five children died in childhood, in 1835 she turned to antislavery work, helping to organize and officiating in the Fall River (Massachusetts)

Female Anti-Slavery Society. In the 1840s and early 1850s, while bearing and rearing five more children, Chace arranged antislavery meetings, raised funds, circulated petitions, wrote letters, and entertained antislavery leaders—the nuts-and-bolts work of the movement. Her home was a station on the Underground Railroad. In 1843, she resigned from the Society of Friends because of its "proslavery position."

After the Civil War, she served as a vice president of the American Anti-Slavery Society. In 1877, she and her daughters resigned from the Rhode Island Woman's Club because it refused to admit a black member. In 1891, she published her *Anti-Slavery Reminiscences.*

**Chandler, Elizabeth Margaret** (December 24, 1807–November 2, 1834) *author, abolitionist*
Reared and educated a Quaker, Chandler began writing at 16, and at 18 she won a prize for her poem "The Slave-Ship." Benjamin Lundy then urged her to write in a similar vein for his newspaper, *The Genius of Universal Emancipation,* to which she regularly contributed for the rest of her short life, soon taking charge of its "Ladies Repository." Feeling strongly the moral duty of opposing slavery, she urged other women to fight against it, particularly by supporting the Free Produce movement. In 1836 she published two volumes of her writings. Antislavery meetings sang songs with her words.

In 1832, Chandler instigated the organization of the first antislavery society in Michigan.

**Chapman, Maria Weston** (July 25, 1806–July 12, 1885) *abolitionist*
At the cost of social ostracism and personal danger, in 1832 Chapman and twelve other women organized the Boston Female Anti-Slavery Society, which she led and for which she edited an annual report entitled *Right and Wrong in Boston.* The society labored to educate Boston's free blacks and to abolish slavery in the District of Columbia. Chapman helped to edit the *Liberator* and also the *Non-Resistant,* the publication of Garrison's New England Non-Resistance Society. In the disputes among abolitionists she sided with Garrison, in 1839 publishing a pamphlet *Right and Wrong in Massachusetts,* attributing the split in antislavery ranks to disagreement over woman's rights. She and her three sisters ran the Boston antislavery fairs that provided models for other cities, and she edited the fair's annual gift book, the *Liberty Bell.* In 1840, the American Anti-Slavery Society elected Chapman to its executive committee. She helped finance, found, and edit the *National Anti-Slavery Standard.* After the Emancipation Proclamation, she busied herself in her son's brokerage office, and in 1877 she edited a two-volume autobiography of her friend Harriet Martineau, to which she added lengthy memorial tributes and reminiscences.

**Child, Lydia Maria Francis** (February 11, 1802–October 20, 1880) *author, reformer*
Beginning her literary career at the age of 22, with the publication of a successful novel narrating the love of a white woman and a noble Indian, Francis continued it by publishing the bimonthly *Juvenile Miscellany,* the first American children's periodical. In 1828 she married the reformer David Lee Child. His earnings as a lawyer and editor dwindled even as hers increased, but he led the way into abolitionism, with Lydia Child following only after she met William Lloyd Garrison. In 1833, she published the important antislavery book *An Appeal in Favor of That Class of Americans Called Africans,* tracing the history of slavery, describing its evils, and rejecting colonization. The book converted to antislavery such important leaders as Wendell Phillips and Charles Sumner, and it provoked the ostracism of its author in Boston. Defiantly, and at the expense of sales of her books on other subjects, she went on to edit and write other antislavery books, including an *Anti-Slavery Catechism.*

In the mid-1830s, David Child tried to buoy up the Free Produce movement by raising beet sugar on a farm the couple bought in Massachusetts, an effort that predictably failed. In 1841, already a member of the executive committee of the American Anti-Slavery Society, Lydia Child began to edit its weekly, the *National Anti-Slavery Standard.* Her stormy tenure there ended in her resignation in 1843. Her husband succeeded her with equal lack of success, while she ventured into various kinds of journalism and books on a variety of subjects, constantly hampered by the unpopularity of her abolitionist convictions.

In 1850, the couple once again failed as farmers. By 1852, Lydia Child was once more writing, publishing the three-volume, *The Progress of Religious Ideas, through Successive Ages* in 1855, and a volume of inspirational selections, *Autumn's Leaves,* in 1857. Again her antislavery beliefs interrupted this work. In 1859, she offered to care for John Brown in prison, thereby evoking a harsh public scolding from the wife of the senator who had introduced the Fugitive Slave Act of 1850. Child responded by denouncing the slave system; she published the exchange as a pamphlet in 1860. She followed this with more abolitionist pamphlets and books, including a novel about two beautiful quadroons (that is, persons of one-quarter black ancestry).

**Christy, David** (1802–unknown) *geologist and antislavery writer*
In early life a newspaperman, in 1848 he became an agent of the American Colonization Society in Ohio, where he collected money to purchase land in Africa between Sierra Leone and Liberia for free American blacks, a colony he called "Ohio in Africa." He lectured on colonization before the Ohio legislature in 1849 and 1850, later publishing these lectures in a pamphlet *On the Present Relations of Free Labor to Slave in Tropical and Semi-Tropical Countries* and *The Republic of Liberia: Facts for Thinking Men.* His major work, *Cotton Is King: Or the Economical Relations of Slavery,* was intended to persuade abolitionists that their plans had completely failed.

**Clay, Cassius Marcellus** (October 19, 1810–July 22, 1903) *politician, abolitionist*
A belligerent, crusading Kentuckian, the pugnacious Clay pursued careers in the army and in politics. His already-established aversion to slavery was increased in his college days at Yale when he heard William Lloyd Garrison. Although he thrice served in the state legislature, his antislavery stance defeated him when he ran in 1841—an event that made him determined to abolish slavery in his state. To that end, in 1845 he started the *True American,* a newspaper, taking the precaution of arming his office with two cannons, lances, rifles, and a keg of powder ready to be set off—only to have his fellow Lexingtonians ship his armament to Cincinnati, where he moved his paper; later he published it as the *Examiner* from Louisville.

Opposing the annexation of Texas, Clay nonetheless served with honor in the Mexican War. When he returned to Kentucky after a period as a prisoner of war, for a time he supported his cousin Henry Clay, but in 1844 they quarreled over abolitionism. In 1849, he convened an emancipation party in Frankfort and ran on its ticket for governor. Joining the Republican Party at its inception, he accepted a diplomatic post in Russia, only to be recalled in 1862 to serve as a major general; he refused to fight unless the government abolished slavery in the rebel states. In 1863 he did fight briefly, then returned to Russia.

**Coffin, Levi B.** (October 28, 1789–September 16, 1877) *abolitionist*
Proudly known as "president of the Underground Railroad," a title first given him by slave hunters, Coffin with his wife Catherine helped more than 3,000 slaves escape over a period of more than 30 years. He earned his living as, successively, a schoolteacher, a merchant, a wholesaler, and a boardinghouse keeper. Throughout their lives, the Coffins devoted themselves to helping blacks, most famously through their daring work for the Underground Railroad, but also by laboring for the education of free blacks, assuming responsibility for individuals brought to them for assistance and raising money in the United States and England for the thousands of blacks in need. During the Civil War, Coffin headed the Western Freedmen's Aid Commission, which looked after newly freed slaves.

**Coles, Edward** (December 15, 1786–July 7, 1868) *abolitionist, governor of Illinois*
Born in Virginia of a slaveholding family, Coles early on, out of principle, embraced antislavery. In 1808, he inherited his father's plantation and slaves. In 1819, after considerable investigation of the Northwest, he moved to the new state of Illinois with his slaves; on the way, he told them that they were free. In their new home, he helped them make a fresh start.

In 1822, he ran for office against the proslavery forces in Illinois. As governor he urged the legislature to abolish the slavery that existed even though the state was nominally free. After a bitter fight, Coles triumphed, averting the possibility of a convention to amend the state constitution to allow slavery.

**Collins, John Anderson** (1810–1879) *abolitionist reformer*
A rather impractical idealist, Collins left Andover Theological Seminary before graduating, possibly because the seminary disapproved his helping abolitionists. He then took a post as general agent of the Massachusetts Anti-Slavery Society. In that capacity he traveled to England to raise funds for the cause. There,

and on his return, he was accused of plotting to destroy the U.S. government.

For a short time in 1840 and 1841, Collins edited the *Monthly Garland,* an antislavery magazine. He saw abolition as a part of a larger social reform to free mankind. In 1843, he formed a grandiose plan of multiple picnics and conventions to rally the country against slavery. His backers, however, were dismayed at his support of other causes, and he resigned to start a utopian community, fated soon to fail.

**Colman, Lucy Newhall** (July 26, 1817–January 18, 1906) *Abolitionist feminist lecturer*
Twice widowed by age 35, Colman with difficulty got a job at "the colored school" of Rochester, New York. The next year she managed to end racial discrimination in the schools there. She soon gave up teaching to lecture against slavery, in the face of vigorous and even dangerous opposition, for a time traveling with a young black woman.

During the Civil War as matron of the National Colored Orphan Asylum at Washington, she introduced sanitation, kindness, and organization into the previously mismanaged institution. She also superintended black schools, supported by the New York Aid Society, in the District of Columbia.

**Cowles, Betsey Mix** (February 9, 1810–July 25, 1876) *educator, reformer*
Cowles grew up in Ohio, where she began her teaching career in 1825. In the 1830s, she worked in the "infant school" movement (to teach very young children "right conduct" and the three Rs) while she continued her education at Oberlin College. After graduation she taught and worked as an administrator in grammar and high schools, in time involving herself in teacher training. In 1858, she became superintendent of schools in Painesville, Ohio. She finished her career in education in Delhi, New York, where she taught until about 1862.

Besides engaging in the peace and temperance movements, Cowles from 1835 on worked against slavery through women's groups, antislavery fairs, and perhaps the Underground Railroad. She raised money for the cause and wrote against slavery. She, her sister Cornelia, and her brother Lewis sang antislavery ballads and hymns at abolition meetings. She fought against prejudice in the schools. Her advocacy of woman's rights and her friendship with Abby Kelley Foster made her a Garrisonian.

**Cox, Hannah Peirce** (November 12, 1797–April 15, 1876) *Quaker antislavery worker*
Cox and her second husband, Quaker farmer John Cox, were attracted to the antislavery cause by Garrison's *The Liberator* and John Greenleaf Whittier's poems. After the burning of Pennsylvania Hall in 1838 during a women's antislavery convention, she dedicated herself to emancipation. The Coxes operated a station on the Underground Railroad and generously entertained antislavery advocates, including Garrison, Whittier, and Lucretia Mott.

**Craft, William** (1827–1900) **and Ellen Craft** (ca. 1826–ca. 1897) *fugitive slaves*
Born into slavery in Georgia, the two met and married when their respective masters settled near Macon. They are known particularly because of their escape from slavery during the Christmas holidays in 1848, in which the light-skinned Ellen, daughter of her master, disguised herself as a sickly, deaf young white man traveling north with his servant for medical treatment. They settled in Boston, where Ellen worked as a seamstress and William as a carpenter. After the passage of the Fugitive Slave Act of 1850, two agents of their owners pursued them to Boston, thwarted only by the Boston Vigilance Committee and the local black community.

The Crafts were then persuaded to leave the country for their safety. Along with fugitive William Wells Brown, they toured England and Scotland, delivering lectures against slavery and for temperance. During the mid-1850s, the Crafts attended Ockham Agricultural College in Surrey, their tuition paid by British abolitionists. They studied academic subjects and taught carpentry and sewing. In 1860 they published their autobiography, *Running a Thousand Miles for Freedom.* From 1862 to 1867, William made several extended visits to Africa to promote cotton production and trade with Britain. After their return to the United States in 1869, they founded a cooperative farm and school in Bryan County, Georgia.

**Crandall, Prudence** (September 3, 1803–January 28, 1890) *Abolitionist educator*
When in 1833 Crandall's Canterbury Female Boarding School in Connecticut failed because she had admitted a black student, she established a teacher-training boarding school for black girls. The citizens of Canterbury, particularly those who belonged

to the American Colonization Society, reacted in outrage. Stores refused to sell her food. The Congregational church barred her pupils, and the town threatened to prosecute them as paupers. The state outlawed any school that accepted out-of-state blacks without the town's consent. Civil authorities put Crandall in jail. Although abolitionists, including William Lloyd Garrison and Arthur Tappan, rallied to her rescue, the court convicted Crandall, ruling that blacks were not citizens; the conviction was reversed on appeal.

Frustrated in their attempts to stop Crandall legally, the townspeople turned to vigilantism, breaking school windows, poisoning the school well, even resorting to arson. In the fall of 1834 Crandall was forced to close the school. Eventually she and her new husband, abolitionist Calvin Philleo, moved to Illinois, where Crandall turned to other reforms.

**Cuffe, Paul** (January 17, 1759–September 9, 1817) *shipowner, navigator, pioneer in the colonization movement*
The son of a free black father and an Indian mother, Cuffe went to sea on a whaling vessel at 16. Despite setbacks, including pirate attacks, he established his own shipping business. By 1806 he owned several vessels and a good bit of property on land.

Throughout his career Cuffe worked actively for the rights of blacks. In 1780, he and his brother John unsuccessfully sued Massachusetts for denying suffrage to taxpaying citizens. In 1783 they helped lead a movement that obtained legal rights and privileges for blacks in that state. In 1797 he built a public school and hired a teacher.

He long advocated black emigration to Africa, using his own money to assist it. In 1811 he sailed to Sierra Leone and there formed the Friendly Society to encourage immigration from the United States. In 1815, at his own expense, he moved 38 blacks to Sierra Leone.

**Davis, Paulina Wright** (August 7, 1813–August 24, 1876) *feminist, reformer, suffragist*
Known primarily for her work for woman's rights and woman's health, Davis also worked against slavery. The home she shared with her husband, merchant Francis Wright, was attacked by a mob after they helped arrange the Utica, New York, antislavery convention of October 1835. After her husband's death, she married the antislavery Democrat Thomas Davis, who in 1852 was elected to Congress. In May 1850, at a Boston antislavery meeting, Davis and other suffragists planned the first national woman's rights convention, and she took charge of the arrangements.

**Deitzler, George Washington** (November 30, 1826–April 10, 1884) *Kansas antislavery leader*
In 1855, Deitzler engaged in organizing a free-state government to oppose the proslavery government of the territory of Kansas, collecting arms given by Bostonians and forming military companies among free-state advocates. In the "Wakarusa War" that November, he served as aide-de-camp to the commander of these companies, sometimes assuming command himself. Consequently, he was indicted with other leaders on a charge of treason, but after he spent a few months under arrest, the charge was dropped. Deitzler continued his free-state activities, including writing for the press and serving as a member of the free-state territorial legislature of 1857–58, speaker of the House of Representatives, and a senator under the Topeka constitution.

During the Civil War he organized the first regiment of Kansas volunteer infantry, eventually attaining the rank of general.

**Delany, Martin R.** (May 6, 1812–January 24, 1885) *abolitionist, critic, first black major in the U.S. Army*
Born free in what is now West Virginia, Delany learned pride in his African heritage from his family. Something of a Renaissance man, during his lifetime Delany engaged in a variety of occupations while continuing to work for the rights of blacks.

In 1831, he entered a school established by Pittsburgh's African Educational Society. In 1843 he founded the paper the *Mystery,* and from 1847 to 1849 he worked with Frederick Douglass on the *North Star,* during which period he was mobbed. In 1852 Delany published *The Condition, Elevation, Emigration and Destiny of the Colored People of the United States Politically Considered.* Educated in medicine at Harvard, he served in the Pittsburgh cholera epidemic of 1854.

In the disputes as to the best course for black people, Delany was something of a radical. Believing that blacks would never be fully accepted as free citizens in this country, Delany early argued for emigration. In 1854 he issued a call for a national emigration convention, of which he became an important officer. Another such convention commissioned him to explore the Valley of the Niger "for the purpose," the official record states, "of science and for general information and without any reference to, and with the Board being entirely opposed to, any Emigration there as such." He sailed on this mission in 1859.

Back in the United States, Delany recruited black soldiers and acted as an examining surgeon in Chicago. In 1865 he was commissioned a major. After the war, among other positions, he served on the Freedmen's Bureau. In 1879, his *Principia of Ethnology: The Origin of Races and Color* appeared.

Frederick Douglass once observed that he thanked "God for making me a man simply; but Delany always thanks him for making him a *black man*."

**De Wolf, James** (March 18, 1764–December 21, 1837) *slave trader, manufacturer, senator*
As a boy, DeWolf adventured on pirate-ridden seas and fought in the American Revolution. By age 20 he was a ship's master, and by 25 he had made a fortune. Backed by wealthy Rhode Island merchants, he traded in African slaves, often personally supervising their sale in southern ports of the United States, though he landed most of them in the West Indies. Apparently without a qualm, he stayed in the slave trade at least until 1808. By 1812 he was investing in cotton mills, and his ventures there shifted his interest away from slaves to white millworkers. In the Senate, where he advocated protection for cotton manufacture, he opposed extending slavery to the West.

**Dickinson, Anna** (October 28, 1842–October 22, 1932) *orator*
Daughter of an abolitionist father, Dickinson grew up in poverty after he died but was educated at a Quaker school for five years. At 14 she wrote an article for William Lloyd Garrison's *Liberator.* She was, successively, a copyist, a schoolteacher, and a worker in the U.S. Mint. And at 18 she made her first speech before the Pennsylvania Anti-Slavery Society. Her success there led to further lecturing, which turned into a full-time career. Her speeches for the Republicans contributed to the reelection of Abraham Lincoln.

In peacetime, Dickinson became one of the stars of the lyceum lecture circuit.

**Douglas, Stephen Arnold** (April 23, 1813–June 3, 1861) *statesman, orator*
This Democratic congressman (1843–47) and U.S. senator (1847–61) from Illinois argued that the question of whether a territory or state should be slave or free ought to be left to its settlers—to "squatter sovereignty." This idea underlay the Compromise of 1850 and the Kansas-Nebraska Act (1854). Douglas opposed Abraham Lincoln in 1858 in the Lincoln-Douglas debates and in the 1860 presidential race.

**Douglass, Frederick (born Frederick Augustus Bailey)** (ca. February 1817–February 20, 1895) *prominent abolitionist, orator, journalist*
The son of a white father and Harriet Bailey, a slave of mixed African and American Indian descent, from whom he was early separated, Douglass was born and raised in harsh slavery, against which he fought determinedly. He spent time in jail for conspiring to escape.

He taught himself secretly to read and studied oratory. He learned shipbuilding, hired his own time, and in 1838 managed to escape. With his wife, a free black woman, he settled in New Bedford, Massachusetts, and for a time he supported himself as a common laborer.

In 1841 an abolitionist friend asked him to speak at the convention of the Massachusetts Anti-Slavery Society, which at once offered him a job as its agent. He became a prominent abolitionist, a brave and moving lecturer whose activities provoked attacks on his person. To answer doubts that a man of his stature, bearing, and ability could ever have been a slave, in 1845 he published his autobiography, *Narrative of the Life of Frederick Douglass*—a daring move that might easily have led to his recapture. He then visited Great Britain and Ireland for two years; in 1847, to protect him against reenslavement, British friends enabled him to buy his freedom.

They also made it possible for him to establish his abolitionist paper *North Star* in Rochester, New York. All this set him at odds with Garrison and other white abolitionists, who did not see the necessity for the *North Star,* disapproved of anyone's buying freedom, and disagreed with the tactics Douglass endorsed.

Nonetheless, Douglass edited the *North Star* for 17 years, during which he also lectured, supported woman suffrage, and participated in politics. When John Brown was arrested, Douglass was one of several abolitionists who had to flee to Canada lest they be indicted for conspiracy; he then returned to England for six months of lecturing.

During the Civil War he recruited blacks, including two of his own sons, for the Union military. Lincoln consulted him. Reconstruction, during which he agitated for civil rights and suffrage for black men, brought him several posts of honor in the government and in private business.

**Douglass, Sarah Mapps Douglass** (September 9, 1806–September 8, 1882) *teacher and abolitionist*
The daughter of a well-off black family of Philadelphia, Douglass was privately educated. In the 1820s she founded a school for black children, later supported by the Philadelphia Female Anti-Slavery Society, of which she was a member—as were Lucretia Mott and the Grimké sisters. Her interracial relationships enabled her to teach her white friends the cruel effects of racial prejudice—including that of the Philadelphia Society of Friends, to which she belonged.

In 1853, Douglass took a position at the Quaker-supported Institute for Colored Youth, where she stayed until she retired in 1877. In 1855 she married an Episcopalian priest. After the Civil War, she served as vice chair of the Women's Pennsylvania Branch of the American Freedmen's Aid Commission.

**Edgerton, Sidney** (August 17, 1818–July 19, 1900) *abolitionist congressman, governor of Montana*
Two years after graduating from law school in 1846, Edgerton served as a delegate to the Free-Soil Convention. In 1856, he participated in the first Republican National Convention. As a congressman, he worked to abolish slavery in the territories, in the District of Columbia, and on U.S. public property.

**Embree, Elihu** (November 11, 1782–December 4, 1820) *Quaker abolitionist*
Living in eastern Tennessee, amid widespread opposition to slavery, Embree freed his slaves shortly before 1815 and joined the Society of Friends. He became a leader of the Manumission Society of Tennessee, in 1819 beginning publication of the weekly *Manumission Intelligencer* (later the *Emancipator*), perhaps the first American periodical completely devoted to antislavery. In it he advocated not only universal freedom, calling upon masters to free their slaves, but also racial equality. He sent a memorial for abolition to the state legislature, excoriated states that excluded free blacks, and vigorously opposed the admission of Missouri as a slave state.

**Fairbank, Calvin** (November 3, 1816–October 12, 1898) *abolitionist Methodist clergyman*
As a boy in rural New York, Fairbank became acquainted with two escaped slaves, an experience that taught him to detest slavery. As an adult he worked ardently and fearlessly to free blacks, venturing into slave states as far south as Arkansas to abduct them, learning the tricks of disguise and deception. As an agent for the Underground Railroad, he smuggled some 47 runaways into freedom. In 1842 he was sentenced to 15 years for assisting in the escape of the Lewis Hayden family; he served four before the governor pardoned him.

When Fairbank again took up his work, he was kidnapped from Indiana into Kentucky and again sentenced to 15 years, serving under miserable conditions from 1851 until 1864, when he was again pardoned. In later life, as an employee of missionary, benevolent, and educational institutions, he lectured or preached on the cruelty of slaveholders, relating his own adventures.

**Fee, John Gregg** (September 9, 1816–January 11, 1901) *abolitionist, educator*
Kentuckian Fee's conversion to abolitionism at Lane Seminary prompted his slaveholding family to disinherit him. Fee founded and served three antislavery Presbyterian churches in Kentucky, the best known of these being the Berea Union Church. Though his synod censured him and mobs shot at, clubbed, and stoned him, he went on to establish and run an abolitionist school, now Berea College. False reports of his involvement in John Brown's raid on Harpers Ferry drove him from his native state, to which he returned only in 1863, to work with black soldiers. He devoted his postwar life to the Berea church and college.

**Fessenden, Samuel** (July 16, 1784–March 19, 1869) *abolitionist lawyer*
Fessenden officiated in the Anti-Slavery Society and served in the Maine state legislature. Disagreeing with both major political parties, he ran for Congress and the governorship on the Liberty Party ticket, a stratagem to demonstrate and strengthen antislavery sentiment. Throughout his career he insisted on the necessity of preserving the Union.

**Follen, Charles** (September 4, 1796–January 13, 1840) *abolitionist professor and Unitarian minister*
Emigrating to the United States as a political refugee from Germany in 1824, he was appointed to teach German at Harvard, where he later taught in the divinity school. By 1830, Follen was speaking against slavery. When he became active in the New England Anti-Slavery Society, Harvard refused to renew his contract. He then took a Unitarian pastorate in New York City but lost it within a year because of his abolitionism. Nonetheless he continued his abolitionist work and supported other causes that he believed would strengthen democracy in this country.

**Follen, Eliza Lee Cabot** (August 15, 1787–January 26, 1860) *author and antislavery advocate*
A member of a prominent Boston family, Cabot was well educated and deeply religious. In 1828, she married Charles Follen. After his death in 1840, she wrote and edited to support her son and herself, mostly in the fields of juvenalia and religion. Throughout her life she was dedicated to antislavery. Her tracts included *A Letter to Mothers in the Free States* and *Anti-Slavery Hymns and Songs.* She officiated in both the Massachusetts and the American antislavery societies.

**Forten, Charlotte (Charlotte Grimké)** (August 17, 1837–July 23, 1914) *teacher, author*
Forten was born free into a wealthy black abolitionist family in Philadelphia. In 1856, she began teaching in a white school while continuing her studies on her own and working against slavery. Problems with her health kept her at home from 1858 until 1861. Late in 1862, however, she went to the sea islands off South Carolina and Georgia, where Union forces were trying to demonstrate that with the proper help blacks could function as free citizens. As a volunteer teacher for former slaves, Forten found her task frustrating, partly because of the suspicions of local blacks but also because of the climate and her own bad health. She wrote about her experiences for the *Atlantic Monthly* in "Life on the Sea Islands." She returned to Philadelphia in 1864 and spent several years reading and occasionally writing and teaching. In 1873, she was appointed to a federal clerkship.

In 1878, at 41, Forten married black minister Francis Grimké, nephew of Sarah and Angelina Grimké.

**Forten, James** (September 2, 1766–March 4, 1842) *wealthy, free black sailmaker; advocate of abolition, temperance, peace, woman's rights*
Forten enlisted in the colonial navy at 14 as a drummer boy, was captured by the English, and exchanged. After another voyage to London, he was apprenticed to a sailmaker in Philadelphia. In time, he set up in business for himself, eventually hiring 40 whites and blacks. In 1814, with Richard Allen and Absalom Jones, he raised a force of 2,500 black volunteers to protect the city against the British.

Forten consistently worked for the welfare of blacks, opposing colonization. He always refused to sell rigging to the owners of slavers. He also furnished William Lloyd Garrison with critical support for the *Liberator.*

**Foster, Abigail Kelley** (January 15, 1810–January 14, 1887) *abolitionist, women's rights lecturer*
Born a Quaker and educated by Quakers, Kelley began her career by teaching in a Friends school. Garrison's *Liberator* inspired her to work in antislavery societies. In September 1838, she helped Garrison found the New England Non-Resistant Society.

Following the example of the Grimké sisters, whom she met at an antislavery convention, she first addressed a mixed audience of women and men at the second women's antislavery convention in May 1838 in Philadelphia. Impressed with her ability, Theodore Weld and other abolitionists urged Kelley to devote all her time to lecturing against slavery. Her family objected, presumably because of the stigma against women who spoke in public. Nonetheless, in May 1839 she started on that course, announcing, "Whatever ways and means are right for men to adopt in reforming the world, are right also for women to adopt in pursuing the same object." In 1840, opposition to her appointment to the business committee of the American Anti-Slavery Society led to a protest that split that organization, with Garrisonians insisting on woman's rights.

For more than 15 years Kelley traveled as an agent, lecturing and organizing antislavery societies and fairs, and setting an example for Paulina Wright Davis, Jane Elizabeth Hitchcock Jones, Lucy Stone, Betsey Mix Cowles, Sallie Holley, and Susan B. Anthony. She withstood numerous attacks on her reputation, as well as the many hardships of traveling in the mid-19th century on a limited budget. In 1845, she married fellow agent Stephen Symonds Foster, who eventually assumed most of the care of their only child so that she might continue lecturing against slavery and for temperance and women's rights. The farm they purchased became a station of the Underground Railroad. In the late 1850s, the Fosters parted company with Garrison over their demands for an abolitionist political party.

In 1870, poor health and a fading voice curtailed Abby Foster's lectures, though she continued her advocacy of women's rights.

**Foster, Stephen Symonds** (November 17, 1809–September 8, 1881) *abolitionist reformer, farmer*
Converted to the antislavery cause in his student days, Foster broke off his theological training when he came to doubt that churches upheld Christian principles. He scrounged a living lecturing against slavery. A Garrisonian, he advocated disunion. He always insisted that the political, religious, and business establishments all over the United States, not just in the South, bore the responsibility for supporting slavery. About 1841 he began interrupting church services to ask the congregations to listen to him; most congregations did not respond favorably. He again attacked the stance of the churches on slavery in his 1843 pamphlet *The Brotherhood of Thieves; or a True Picture of the American Church and Clergy.* In 1845, he married abolitionist lecturer Abigail Kelley.

**Free Frank** (1771–1857) *entrepreneurial slave*
His master, George McWhorter, took Frank at age 24 to the frontier in Pulaski County, Kentucky, between the Appalachian highlands and the Cumberland River. Frank helped his master clear and run two farm homesteads, becoming skilled in animal husbandry, dairying, land improvement, the use and maintenance of equipment and machinery, and the construction of buildings. He also established a reputation for honesty and industry. When the second farm was operating well enough not to need his full-time labor, some time between 1801 and 1808, McWhorter allowed Frank to hire his own time, although technically that was illegal.

Pulaski County at that time was a land of opportunity for an enterprising slave. A labor shortage created a need for his services, and the relatively low proportion of blacks in the population lulled white fears and allowed blacks to carry guns and move about. Some time before 1810, McWhorter moved on, leaving Frank in charge of his farm. Frank made the most of his opportunities. He not only managed the farm but also appropriated land to raise crops of his own and began to manufacture saltpeter, a component of gunpowder.

In 1815, McWhorter died. The heirs not only left Frank in charge of the farm but promised him that he could buy his freedom for $500. First, though, in 1817 he bought for $800 his wife Lucy, whom he had married in 1799. Once she was free, she added to the family income through household crafts (like making cloth, candles, and soap), so that in just two years they were able to buy his freedom—after which he registered himself in the census as "Free Frank."

At once they set themselves another goal—liberating their four children born in slavery. (Three younger children, born after their mother was freed, never knew slavery.) In the 1820s, the couple invested in land and expanded their farming operation. In 1829 they bought Frank, their eldest son, who had run away to Canada and returned only after manumission, by trading away their saltpeter factory. The next year Frank, Lucy, young Frank, and their three youngest children moved to Illinois, where they established a new farm. In 1836 Frank founded the town of New Philadelphia, investing in real estate there. In the 1840s and 1850s, Frank and Lucy succeeded in buying the freedom of their three other children *and* their descendants. Even the money from Frank's estate was used for this purpose. Altogether, in the four decades from 1817 to 1857 Frank and Lucy bought 16 family members, for about $15,000.

**Gage, Frances Dana Barker** (October 12, 1808–November 10, 1884) *reformer, lecturer, author*
During her Ohio girlhood, with her family's encouragement, Barker helped fugitive slaves. In 1829 she married James L. Gage, a lawyer and iron founder. While she bore and raised their eight children, she read widely, published poems, and developed strong views on slavery, women's rights, and temperance, a "triune cause" in which she involved herself for the rest of her life. By 1850, she had begun to establish herself as a speaker and writer, primarily of advice to women.

In St. Louis, where the Gages moved in 1853, she provoked hostility by her radicalism. The family lived through three fires, perhaps set because of her antislavery views. In 1860, homeless and without a business, they moved back to Ohio, where Gage had to support the family because of her husband's poor health.

In 1861, with four sons in the Union army, Gage and her daughter Mary joined in the effort in the Sea Islands off the coasts of Georgia and South Carolina to demonstrate that with education and economic aid freed slaves could support themselves and live independently. There, Gen. Rufus Saxton put her and her daughter to work, without pay. Called home by her husband's fatal illness, Gage lectured to raise money for her work and then returned to Parris Island. But in November 1863 she took to the road, speaking before soldiers' aid societies about the condition of the freed slaves and raising money for the freedmen's association and soldier relief. To the end of her life, she continued her reform activities in her "triune cause."

**Garnet, Henry Highland** (1815–February 13, 1882) *prominent black antislavery leader, missionary to Jamaica*
Born a slave, Garnet escaped to New York when his father led his whole family to freedom; he spent his boyhood pursued by agents of their former owner. Noyes Academy in Canaan, New Hampshire, admitted him and 11 other blacks, but local farmers soon drove them out. Garnet later graduated from the Oneida Theological Institute and became pastor of a black Presbyterian church in Troy, New York, an educator of black children, and a forthright spokesman for equal rights and antislavery. He and Frederick Douglass opposed one another on the means of achieving abolition, Garnet advocating militancy and Douglass persuasion. But both supported political action, the Liberty Party, and the federal government during the Civil War. Garnet preached the sermon before the House of Representatives celebrating passage of the Thirteenth Amendment, the first black to speak in public in the nation's capital. He died in Monrovia, Liberia, where he was the minister (ambassador) of the United States.

**Garrett, Thomas** (August 21, 1789–January 25, 1871) *abolitionist hardware merchant, toolmaker*
An outspoken red-headed Quaker, Garrett committed himself as a youth to help "God's poor escaping from the prison house of slavery." At age 24, he rescued a free black woman who had been kidnapped from his father's house. Settling in Wilmington, Delaware, in 1822, he made his home a station on the Underground Railroad, on a much-traveled escape route. Because it was only eight miles from free territory in Pennsylvania, Wilmington was haunted by sheriffs' and slave owners' representatives.

Garrett developed a network of helpers, both black and white, and informed himself about the legal protections for fugitive slaves. He contemptuously waved away slave hunters' guns and knives, saying, "On with thee. Anyone who stoops to such low methods is a coward and I will have no dealings with him." Knowing the hazards of escape attempts, Garrett never encouraged slaves to flee, but he protected all who approached him.

In 1848, two Maryland slave owners sued Garrett, claiming that he and John Hunn had harbored a family of eight slaves and helped them to escape. The evidence showed that Garrett and Hunn had scrupulously followed the law, having had no indication that the fugitives they assisted were slaves. An allegedly packed jury and Chief Justice Roger Taney of the U.S. Supreme Court (later to issue the notorious *Dred Scott* decision) found them guilty notwithstanding and fined Garrett $5,400—wiping him out financially. He responded in an hour-long speech: "I have assisted fourteen hundred slaves in the past twenty-five years on their way to the North. I now consider this penalty imposed upon me as a license for the remainder of my life. I am now past sixty and have not a dollar to my name, but . . . if anyone knows of a poor slave who needs shelter and a breakfast, send him to me. . . ."

By 1863, 2,700 slaves had passed through his hands—not counting those he helped before he began to keep records.

**Garrison, William Lloyd** (December 10, 1805–May 4, 1879) *reformer, Christian anarchist*
Garrison, who emigrated to the United States from Nova Scotia, had little formal education, but he was apprenticed to a printer and newspaper editor. The first newspaper he edited, the *Free Press* of Newburyport, Massachusetts, failed. He then joined the staff of the *National Philanthropist,* a temperance paper. About 1828, Quaker Benjamin Lundy talked to him about the evils of slavery, and soon thereafter he delivered his first lecture against it. By the summer of 1829 he was working in Baltimore on the weekly *Genius of Universal Emancipation,* and for the next 30 years he devoted himself to abolitionism.

As a young man he favored colonization and gradual emancipation. As he matured, he grew more radical, building a significant following but eventually angering many antislavery workers by his extreme views. He attacked those who disagreed with him in strong language; he denounced the churches; eventually, he rejected the idea of government itself, repudiating the Constitution as a proslavery document. But he never advocated violence, insisting on the power of moral suasion. He advanced no plan for abolition but uncompromisingly demanded it.

In 1830, he launched the influential antislavery weekly *The Liberator,* which gave opportunity for black leaders to express their views, although circulation never exceeded 3,000. In 1831 he helped to draft the constitution for the New England Anti-Slavery Society, and the next year became its paid agent. He went on to assist in organizing such societies in New York and Philadelphia. In 1835, he was seized at an abolitionist meeting and dragged through the streets with a rope around his neck.

Garrison alienated many of his fellow abolitionists, particularly by trying to link abolitionism with other reforms, such as woman's rights. In 1840, the American Anti-Slavery Society split over this issue and Garrison's opposition to political action, leaving him firmly in charge of the remnants of that organization, over which he presided for the next 22 terms. At the World's Anti-Slavery Convention in London in 1840, he refused to participate because women were excluded, although he had long been prominent in British abolitionism. He began to call upon the *North* to secede from the Union, arguing that the U.S. Constitution was "a covenant with death and an agreement with hell" that "should be annulled." In 1854, he publicly burned a copy of the Constitution.

When the South seceded, Garrison rejoiced, and in 1862 he praised Lincoln's Emancipation Proclamation. In 1863, the two factions of abolitionists were reconciled. With the passage of the Thirteenth Amendment he closed the *Liberator,* turning his attention to prohibition, women's suffrage, justice for American Indians, and the elimination of prostitution.

**Gibbons, Abigail Hopper** (December 7, 1801–January 16, 1893) *reformer, welfare worker*
Hopper grew up the daughter of a Quaker minister mother and a father who spent much of his time and money in helping blacks, whether free or fugitive slave. She adopted her parents' values, interesting herself particularly in prison reform and antislavery. As a young woman, she founded and for a decade ran a school for Quaker children. In 1833 she married James Sloan Gibbons, a Quaker merchant and banker; she spent most of her life with him in New York City. They had six children.

Gibbons worked effectively in the Manhattan Anti-Slavery Society, running fairs to raise money. When in 1842 the Yearly Meeting of the Society of Friends disowned her father and husband for their abolitionism, she resigned.

During the Civil War, she and her daughter Sarah served as nurses for more than three years. In this work she clashed with army officers, in part because she insisted on generous treatment for contrabands. During the New York draft riots of 1863, a mob vandalized her home. Gibbons spent the end of her life as she had the beginning, trying to remedy social problems.

**Giddings, Joshua Reed** (October 6, 1795–May 27, 1864) *abolitionist attorney, congressman*
In Congress, the stiffnecked, aggressive Giddings supported John Quincy Adams in his efforts to protect the petition rights of antislavery citizens. He denied the power of the federal government to tax in order to support slavery, and he saw the annexation of Texas and the Mexican War as power plays by proslavery forces. When the House of Representatives censured him for his opposition to any federal measure to defend the slave trade along the coast, Giddings resigned, appealed to the voters, and was reelected. In 1848 he left the Whig Party to join the Free Soil Party, and in 1854, when the Missouri Compromise was repealed, he joined the Republicans. Opposing disunion, he argued for the president's wartime powers to emancipate slaves in rebellious states. Although bad health prevented his reelection after 1858, he remained politically active and in 1861 became consul-general to Canada.

**Greenfield, Elizabeth Taylor** (ca. 1817–March 31, 1876) *singer known as "the Black Swan"*
Greenfield was born a slave in Natchez, Mississippi. When she was a small child, her mistress took all her slaves to Philadelphia, freed them, and sent most of them to Liberia. Elizabeth remained with her and adopted her last name. Her former owner sought a

musical education for her, but the teacher to whom she applied refused to accept her, for fear of offending his white pupils. She then taught herself, with the help of a neighbor.

In 1851 her singing impressed a number of influential people, who sponsored concerts for her. That winter she went on tour throughout the Northeast, after which her sponsors sent her to tour in England, under the aegis of such prominent figures as the duchess of Sutherland. But her manager defaulted, defeating her plans for study there. She returned to Philadelphia, where she taught and gave concerts for several years. She was the first black American musician to win a wide international reputation.

**Grew, Mary** (September 1, 1813–October 10, 1896) *abolitionist, suffragist*
As a girl in Hartford, Connecticut, the daughter of a minister, Grew taught a Sunday school class of black children. After moving to Philadelphia, she joined the Female Anti-Slavery Society, to which Lucretia Mott and Sarah Pugh also belonged and in which she soon was elected to office. A supporter and personal friend of William Lloyd Garrison, Grew served as an officer of the state branch of the American Anti-Slavery Society and as coeditor of the *Pennsylvania Freeman.* She also worked in the Free Produce Association.

A lecturer and writer, Grew appeared prominently at the Anti-Slavery Convention of American Women of 1838, when a proslavery mob heckled the speakers and attacked Pennsylvania Hall, site of the meeting. At the World's Anti-Slavery Convention of 1840, she and the other women elected as delegates were excluded from the floor. Henceforth she added women's rights to her reform work.

**Griffing, Josephine Sophia White** (December 18, 1814–February 18, 1872) *reformer, welfare worker among freedmen*
Born and raised in Connecticut, White married Charles Stockman Spooner Griffing, a machinist, and in 1842 they moved to Ohio. A Garrisonian, she repudiated the Union because it permitted slaveholding. She made her home a station on the Underground Railroad. She served prominently in the Western Anti-Slavery Society both as a volunteer and, from 1851–1855, as a paid agent who lectured against slavery and sang abolitionist songs. She also wrote for the *Anti-Slavery Bugle.* During the Civil War she joined the Women's Loyal National League, founded to ensure the complete elimination of slavery, lecturing for it and in 1864 collecting signatures for a women's antislavery petition.

Like many another woman, through her abolitionist activities Griffing evolved into a supporter of women's rights. But she also continued to work for blacks after the Civil War. She lobbied unsuccessfully for a federally sponsored welfare program for blacks to settle them throughout the North, and successfully for the Freedmen's Bureau—only to become its frequent and vigorous critic when it came into being. She did, however, serve in the bureau on and off until it disbanded in 1869. In 1865, she became the general agent of the National Freedmen's Relief Association of the District of Columbia. In that capacity she ran a settlement program for freed blacks, helped many to find jobs and homes in the North, and founded an industrial school to train women to sew.

**Grimké, Archibald** (August 17, 1849–February 25, 1930) *lawyer, writer, activist*
Born a slave in South Carolina, Archibald was one of three sons of slave nurse Nancy Weston and her master, Henry Grimké. In his childhood, he was taught to read and write. Cruelly treated by his white half-brother who inherited him from Henry, Archibald ran away, hiding in the home of sympathetic whites until the end of the Civil War. Toward the end of the war, he and his brother Francis, who had served as a valet to a Confederate officer, volunteered as officers' boys in the Union army. At war's end they studied in a freedman's school in Charleston, whose headmistress arranged opportunities for them in the North; they were soon enrolled in Lincoln University in Pennsylvania. In 1868, their aunts, abolitionists Sarah and Angelina Grimké, discovered their existence and identity, sponsored their continuing studies—for Archibald at Harvard Law School and for Francis at Princeton Theological Seminary—and introduced them to many influential friends, both black and white. Later as pastor of a church in Washington, D.C., Francis gained a national reputation as a preacher and defender of blacks.

Archibald distinguished himself as a writer on racial affairs and as an activist. In 1883 he undertook the editorship of the black newspaper the *Hub,* published in Boston; in it he supported Republican candidates and the causes of racial equality and woman's suffrage. In 1886, however, accusing Republicans of deserting blacks, he left the party, eventually turning to the Democrats. In 1894, President Cleveland appointed him consul to the Dominican Republic. In the early 20th century, he helped to found the National Association for the Advancement of Colored People and for some years presided over its District of Columbia branch.

**Grimké, Sarah** (November 26, 1792–December 23, 1873) and **Angelina Grimké** (February 20, 1805–October 26, 1879) *Abolitionists, women's rights pioneers*

Daughters of a wealthy slaveholding family of Charleston, South Carolina, Sarah and Angelina were raised as proper southern young ladies and educated by private tutors. Sarah protested early on at being denied the opportunity to study serious academic subjects. On a trip north as nurse for her ailing father, this deeply religious woman was impressed by the Quakers she met, especially because of their opposition to slavery. She left the Anglican Church and in 1821 moved to Philadelphia.

Angelina shared Sarah's views on slavery, horrified particularly by the beatings inflicted on slaves. In 1829 she followed Sarah north, where both of them devoted themselves to charity. Their convictions about slavery strengthened, and in 1835 Angelina felt called to oppose it actively. After William Lloyd Garrison published a letter from her in the *Liberator,* she wrote *An Appeal to the Christian Women of the South* and signed it—defying the convention that ladies' names should appear in public only when they were born, when they were married, and when they died. She also accepted an appointment as agent of the American Anti-Slavery Society, undertaking to hold meetings for small groups of women. As these meetings grew, drawing men as well as women, Angelina again broke with tradition by addressing "promiscuous" audiences—that is, of both genders. In 1836, Sarah, disturbed by discrimination against blacks in Friends' meetings, left the Society and published an *Epistle to the Clergy of the Southern States,* refuting the idea that the Bible justifies slavery.

The Grimké sisters by this time were devoting themselves to the abolitionist cause. Angelina wrote another pamphlet, *Appeal to the Women of the Nominally Free States,* and testified before a committee of the Massachusetts legislature on antislavery petitions. Though Angelina starred on their lecture tours, Sarah too spoke on occasion.

When in 1837 the Massachusetts Congregational ministerial association issued a "Pastoral Letter" condemning them for unwomanly behavior, the Grimkés had to confront their own covert feminism. What they might not have sought in their own behalf—the right of free speech—they demanded for the sake of abolitionism. Sarah wrote on the subject in *Letters on the Equality of the Sexes, and the Condition of Woman,* and Angelina defended herself in a series of letters to the *Liberator.* Many abolitionists criticized them for their stand—including the daring Theodore Weld.

The Grimkés had met Weld in 1836 at an abolitionist training course that he taught; he and Angelina had at once been drawn to each other. They married on May 14, 1838, in Philadelphia, in a simple ceremony attended by black and white abolitionist friends. On May 16, Angelina spoke before the woman's antislavery convention there, heckled by an angry mob—the last lecture she ever gave. The Welds and Sarah henceforth lived and worked together. Most notably, they compiled *American Slavery as It Is: Testimony of a Thousand Witnesses* (1839), an effort to undermine slavery by showing its horrors in reports from southern newspapers and slave owners. Their disapproval of political action separated them from many other abolitionists, and ill health and their own poverty forced them into other activities, mostly educational.

In 1868, the Grimké sisters discovered the existence of two nephews, Archibald and Francis, sons of a Grimké brother and a slave mother. The sisters immediately took them into the family and assumed responsibility for their education, at considerable personal sacrifice.

**Grinnell, Josiah Bushnell** (December 22, 1821–March 31, 1891) *abolitionist clergyman*

Grinnell, a Vermont Congregationalist, may have preached the first antislavery sermon ever heard in Washington, D.C., in about 1851. At any rate, his views forced his departure for New York City, where he served another church until his voice faltered. He then pioneered as an Iowa farmer and was influential in the founding of the town of Grinnell, a church, and what is now Grinnell College. In 1856, he was elected to the state senate on a Republican ticket and a platform of no liquor, free schools, and "No Nationalizing of Slavery." Developing a reputation as a leading abolitionist, he received into his home escaped slaves rescued by John Brown. As a U.S. congressman from 1863 to 1867, he supported Lincoln, urging the enlistment of black soldiers. After the war, he fought to make black suffrage a requirement for the readmission of rebel states to the Union.

**Hallowell, Richard Price** (December 16, 1835–January 5, 1904) *abolitionist merchant*
Educated as a Quaker, Hallowell early embraced the antislavery cause, refusing to work with a company that sold the products of slave labor. An activist, on occasion he helped to guard William Lloyd Garrison and Wendell Phillips. In 1859, he went with an antislavery group to receive John Brown's body. During the Civil War, he recruited black soldiers and struggled to get them equal pay. When peace came he worked to help blacks, particularly by starting and financing schools for them in the South.

**Harper, Frances Ellen Watkins** (September 24, 1825–February 22, 1911) *abolitionist poet, lecturer*
Born free, Watkins was educated at the school of her uncle, Rev. William Watkins, after which she learned to sew in a Baltimore household in which she worked to support herself. In 1850, she began to teach sewing.

Under the influence of William Still and Boston abolitionists, Harper began to lecture against slavery in August 1854. The Maine Anti-Slavery Society hired her as its agent. She interspersed her talks with readings from her own book of 1854, *Poems on Miscellaneous Subjects.* She also wrote poems, stories, and articles for abolitionist papers.

In 1860 she married Fenton Harper. After his death in 1864, she resumed her lectures, speaking on blacks' need for education, temperance, and domestic morality but also against white racial violence. In later life she also tried to help curb delinquency among black youth, and in 1896 she helped to organize the National Association of Colored Women.

**Haven, Gilbert** (September 19, 1821–January 3, 1880) *abolitionist Methodist bishop.*
Even as a student, Haven held antislavery views. As a clergyman he preached and wrote on the immorality of slavery. During the Civil War he served as an army chaplain and worked to secure both civil rights and social equality for blacks, insisting on the necessity of complete integration of the races. After the war he kept on practicing what he preached, at the cost of ostracism and threats of violence. Not only did he support black schools in the South with his own money and funds that he raised, but he recruited teachers for them. Moreover, in articles, sermons, and lectures he exposed the ways in which southern whites repressed blacks in the postwar years.

**Haviland, Laura Smith** (December 20, 1808–April 20, 1898) *abolitionist, worker for freedmen's welfare*
In 1829, Haviland and her husband, the Quaker farmer Charles Haviland Jr., with Elizabeth M. Chandler organized the first antislavery society in Michigan. They resigned from the Society of Friends when that group disapproved their abolitionist activity. In 1837, the couple founded a school for poor children, later making it into a manual-labor preparatory school open to all regardless of gender or race.

After the tragic death of her husband, parents, sister, and youngest child in an 1845 epidemic, Haviland devoted herself to the antislavery cause, doing missionary work among blacks both in the North and in the slave states. She also lectured for antislavery societies and escorted fugitives on the Underground Railroad, even venturing into the South. During the Civil War she visited hospitals and prison camps to work with contrabands, in 1864 signing on as an agent of the Freedmen's Aid Commission, for which she traveled through the South. In 1879, she helped to resettle blacks in Kansas.

**Hazard, Thomas** (September 15, 1720–August 26, 1798) *abolitionist*
In the early 1740s, a church deacon told Hazard that Quakers who held slaves were not Christians—as did he, his family (some of whom were slave traders), and almost everyone he knew. Hazard decided that the deacon was right; he began to use free labor on his farm and to convert others to antislavery. In 1774, he worked on a Quaker committee that submitted a bill to the Rhode Island legislature prohibiting the importation of blacks. In 1783, another Quaker committee on which he sat successfully petitioned the legislature to abolish slavery. In 1787, the Providence Society for Abolishing the Slave Trade, which Hazard had helped to found, persuaded the legislature to act again.

**Henson, Josiah** (June 15, 1789–1883) *fugitive slave, autobiographer, colonizer, allegedly the model for Harriet Beecher Stowe's Uncle Tom*
As a youth Henson endured the tyrannies of slavery, seeing his mother assaulted and his father mutilated. He was maimed for life by an enemy of one of his three successive owners. Nonetheless, he was converted to Christianity at age 18 and later became a preacher in the Methodist Episcopal Church. He married at 22 and fathered 12 children. During the many years that he toiled faithfully for his owners, he bore responsibility for the work of other slaves. Even one master's bad faith in a "contract" to allow Henson to purchase his freedom with money he had earned by preaching did not prompt him to escape. But when in 1830 he learned that he was to be sold, he decided to escape to Canada. He fled with his wife and four of his children, assisted by Indians and a Scots steamer captain on Lake Erie.

In Canada, Henson worked for pay and shares, farmed, preached, and helped slaves escape and succeed in a new life. In 1834, he led a group of blacks to invest in land near Colchester. With the intention of instilling "the Yankee spirit . . . into my fellow slaves," he cooperated with white abolitionists in establishing the British-American Institute, a manual-labor school around which the town of Dawn grew. Several times he went to England on the community's behalf. In 1849, Henson published a well-received narrative, *The Life of Josiah Henson*. In the divisions among the abolitionist forces, he sided with those who opposed violence.

**Higginson, Thomas Wentworth** (December 22, 1823–May 9, 1911) *abolitionist, woman suffragist, soldier, author*
Higginson took both his undergraduate and his divinity degrees at Harvard, after which he became first a Unitarian minister and then pastor of a "free church." During his pastorates, he devoted much of his time and energy to community activities, temperance, women's suffrage, and abolitionism.

In the abolitionist movement, he joined with those who wished to dissolve the Union because it allowed and enforced slavery. A daring and adventurous activist, he served on vigilance committees to rescue fugitive slaves, including Anthony Burns. In 1856 he not only worked in the East for a free Kansas but traveled west for this cause, meeting John Brown, whom he ardently supported.

With the outbreak of the Civil War, Higginson abandoned his pulpit to recruit and train soldiers. In November 1862, he accepted the colonelcy of the First South Carolina Volunteers, a black regiment, holding it until he was invalided out because of a wound. He described his experiences in *Army Life in a Black Regiment*. He devoted his postwar life to writing sketches, a novel, memoirs, and biographies, and to working for reforms, especially women's suffrage.

**Holley, Myron** (April 29, 1779–March 4, 1841) *lawyer, merchant, politician, abolitionist*
In 1837, Holley began to interest himself in antislavery political action. In 1839, he failed to persuade the Cleveland antislavery convention to present a slate in the national election; he succeeded, however, at a larger convention in getting James G. Birney nominated as an antislavery candidate. His advocacy led to the formation of the Liberty Party in 1840. From 1839 almost until his death, Holley edited the *Rochester Freeman*.

**Holley, Sallie** (February 17, 1818–January 12, 1893) *abolitionist lecturer, teacher of freed slaves*
Daughter of Myron Holley, the principal founder of the Liberty Party, Sallie Holley was brought up on antislavery talk. In her girlhood, she refused a proposal of marriage on the grounds that her suitor had voted for Henry Clay. In 1847, she went to Oberlin College, though her brother begged her not to expose herself to insult by going to the "nigger school"—that is, a college that had begun to admit blacks in 1834. While there she responded to the call of Abby Kelley Foster for more women to speak on behalf of slave women. She soon accepted an invitation from the blacks of Sandusky, Ohio, to address a celebration of West Indian emancipation. When Oberlin's president's wife warned her against staying in a black's house, Holley responded, "Mrs. Mahan, I should certainly feel it my duty to accept any such invitation as a testimony to my principles, and, really, to those professed by this Institution." After graduation in 1851, she became an agent for the Anti-Slavery Society, a course that she vigorously pursued until emancipation, reporting on her tours with letters to Garrison's *Liberator.*

During the Civil War, Holley lectured for black suffrage and collected clothing for freed slaves. When the

American Anti-Slavery Society dissolved in 1870, she joined her friend Carolina Putnam, who had founded a school for blacks. For the next 20 years they worked together, dependent on northern contributions and black labor, ostracized by the whites around them. They instructed not only in reading and writing but also in politics, housekeeping, and gardening.

**Hopper, Isaac Tatem** (December 3, 1771–May 7, 1852) *Quaker abolitionist, Underground Railroad operator, prison reformer*
Early sympathetic to slaves, as a member of the Pennsylvania Abolition Society Hopper began before 1800 to help blacks escape. For their protection, he educated himself in laws that affected them and pleaded for them before Philadelphia courts. When he moved to New York City in 1829, he carried on his antislavery activities there, often shipping fugitives to Providence and Boston by water. In 1841, he joined forces with Lydia Maria Child in editing the *National Anti-Slavery Standard*. He and his son were both mobbed, and with other members of his family Hopper was disowned by the New York Monthly Meeting of the Society of Friends.

**Howland, Emily** (November 20, 1827–June 29, 1929) *educator, reformer, philanthropist*
Bored with housekeeping for her Quaker family, whose home was a station on the Underground Railroad, Howland began in her late teens to read widely about slavery and to attend abolitionist conventions. In 1856 she volunteered to take over Myrtilla Miner's Washington school for free black girls, which she conducted for two years with a black assistant. The experience transformed her, introducing her to influential people and helping her gain confidence, even to the point of facing down a hostile mob.

In 1863, she began to teach in contraband camps in and around Washington. In 1867 she experimented with settling former slave families on 400 acres her father bought in Virginia, founding a school there. Soon called back to family responsibilities by her mother's death, Howland devoted much time and effort to women's education and women's rights generally, as well as to the temperance and peace movements, but still focused on black education. For more than 50 years, she continued to support the Virginia school she had established. She also contributed to many other black schools, regularly visiting them.

**Hutchinson, Abigail Jemima** (August 29, 1829–November 24, 1892) *singer, feminist, reformer*
Hutchinson is best remembered as a member of a professional singing group, known successively as the Aeolian Vocalists and the Hutchinson Family. Beginning in 1843, the family contributed its services to antislavery, at some personal risk, singing "The Slave's Lament" and other songs at abolitionist rallies.

**Jackson, James Caleb** (March 28, 1811–July 11, 1895) *abolitionist physician reformer*
As a young man, under the guidance of Gerrit Smith, Jackson became in 1838 an agent of the Massachusetts Anti-Slavery Society and in 1840 secretary of the American Anti-Slavery Society. For a period he helped to edit the *National Anti-Slavery Standard*. Funded by Smith, in 1841 Jackson founded the *Madison County abolitionist* in upstate New York and went on to edit other papers. In 1847 he sponsored the fourth-party Liberty League, a descendant of the Liberty Party.

**Johnson, Oliver** (December 27, 1809–December 10, 1889) *antislavery leader, editor, reformer*
An admirer and associate of William Lloyd Garrison, Johnson stood with him through the disagreements and divisions among the antislavery forces. Periodically he substituted for Garrison in editing *The Liberator*. In 1832 he helped to found the New England Anti-Slavery Society, for which four years later he became an agent. Up until the Civil War he lectured, wrote, and edited papers against slavery—including the *Anti-Slavery Bugle*, the *Pennsylvania Freeman*, and the *National Anti-Slavery Standard*.

**Jones, Absalom** (1746–unknown) *first African-American Episcopalian priest*
Born a slave, Jones taught himself to read. When at age 16 he was sold to a Philadelphia owner, he attended a Quaker night school for blacks. With his earnings he bought first his wife's freedom, then in 1784 his own. As a lay minister in St. George's Methodist Episcopal church, he shared the outrage of his friend Richard Allen when the white members decided to relegate the blacks to the balcony. The blacks left and in 1787 founded the Free African Society, with Allen and Jones as leaders. This society used its monthly dues to help the needy. In 1794 the church built by the society became a member of the Episcopal Diocese of Pennsylvania, retaining control over its parochial affairs.

Jones was ordained as a priest on September 21, 1802. He participated actively in the civic affairs of the black community and of the city, consistently denouncing slavery.

**Jones, Charles Colcock** (1804–unknown) *"Apostle to the Blacks"*
A Presbyterian minister as well as a plantation and slave owner, in 1832 Jones resigned his position at the First Presbyterian Church of Savannah to become a missionary to slaves. He upheld the institution of slavery and prided himself on being a kind and just master. In Liberty County, Georgia, he helped build three churches for slaves and then rode from one church to another, preaching and teaching, stressing the slaves' "duty" of obedience to their masters. He wrote two books, *Catechism of Scripture Doctrine and Practice* and *The Religious Instruction of the Negroes in the United States.* From 1837 to 1838 and again from 1848 to 1850, he served as professor of ecclesiastical history and church polity at the Presbyterian Theological Seminary in Columbia, South Carolina. From 1850 to 1853, he worked in Philadelphia as corresponding secretary of the Board of Domestic Missions of the Presbyterian Church, where he reinvigorated the board and aroused the denomination to the plight of the blacks. In 1853 he collapsed into semi-invalidism, and retreated to his Georgia plantations, teaching and preaching as his strength permitted.

**Jones, Jane Elizabeth Hitchcock** (March 13, 1813–January 13, 1896) *antislavery and feminist lecturer*
In the early 1840s, Hitchcock toured with Abby Kelley Foster, lecturing against slavery. In 1845 she joined with several fellow lecturers in organizing antislavery societies around Salem, Ohio. There she and the Quaker Benjamin Smith Jones, whom she married the next year, coedited the *Anti-Slavery Bugle.* She also ran an antislavery book agency and in 1848 wrote a tract for children, *The Young abolitionists.*

After attending the first convention of Ohio women in 1850, Jones worked ardently for women's rights. She turned to lecturing on women's legal and customary disabilities and, after studying medicine, on good health and hygiene for women. But in 1856 she again picked up antislavery work, combining it with her labors for women.

**Julian, George Washington** (May 5, 1817–July 7, 1899) *abolitionist attorney, reformer-politician*
About 1845, already in the Indiana state legislature, Julian began to write against slavery. A few years later, he shifted from the Whig to the Free Soil party, on whose ticket he was elected to Congress in 1848. There he fought against such measures as the Fugitive Slave Law of 1850. In 1852 he ran for the vice presidency as the Free Soil candidate. A founder of the Republican Party in 1856, he was five times elected to Congress. During the Civil War he supported Lincoln and urged him to emancipate the slaves. After the war he worked for black suffrage.

**Keckley, Elizabeth** (ca. 1818–May 26, 1907) *freed slave, dressmaker*
Keckley as a slave helped to support her mistress's family by her work as seamstress and dressmaker. She married the ne'er-do-well James Keckley under the impression that he was a free black but later separated from him. In 1855, borrowing from her patrons, she purchased her own freedom and that of her son, later repaying the loan in full. In 1860, she moved from St. Louis to Washington, D.C.

After Lincoln's inauguration as president she sewed for Mary Todd Lincoln, becoming her friend, confidante, and traveling companion. During the Civil War she founded and headed a Contraband Relief Association to assist fugitive slaves coming to Washington, D.C.

In 1868 a ghost-written book, *Behind the Scenes,* appeared in Keckley's name. It embarrassed Mrs. Lincoln by revealing her private opinions of people, details of the Lincolns' family life, and Mrs. Lincoln's efforts in 1867 to sell her personal effects to settle debts. Although Keckley protested that she had intended to improve Mrs. Lincoln's image, the book ended their friendship and ruined Keckley's standing in the black community.

**Kemble, Frances Anne (Fanny)** (November 27, 1809–January 15, 1893) *British actress, author*
Born into an illustrious theatrical family, Kemble achieved fame as a brilliant actress in England. Her marriage in 1834 to Pierce Butler, whom she knew as a charming young Philadelphian, resulted from a successful American tour that she undertook with her father in 1832. Publication in 1835 of her flippant *Journal of a Residence in America* damaged her marriage,

which later ended, in large part over slavery. The Butlers separated in 1845 when she discovered his infidelity; she resumed her career as author and actress and later as theatrical reader. In 1849 Butler divorced Kemble for desertion, "tho'," wrote her friend Rebecca Gratz, "it is well known he drove her out from her privileges of Mother & wife long before she attempted to earn a maintenance for herself in a profession she loathes [acting]."

During the Civil War she published her *Journal of a Residence on a Georgian Plantation in 1838–1839.* This book reveals her horror at discovering the realities of slavery and the knowledge that from it her husband derived his wealth. Her inability to abate the cruelties inflicted on the slaves frustrated her and made her question her husband's character. By its publication she hoped to win friends among the British for the Union. Later in her life she published autobiographical memoirs and *Notes upon Some of Shakespeare's Plays.*

**Lane, Lunsford** (unknown–unknown) *black abolitionist*
Born a slave in Raleigh, North Carolina, Lunsford freed himself by hiring out and manufacturing tobacco, but he had to leave the state before he could purchase his wife and children. Returning for them, he was savaged by a mob. He lectured for the American Anti-Slavery Society and served as an army nurse in the Civil War.

**Leavitt, Joshua** (September 8, 1794–January 16, 1873) *clergyman, reformer, abolitionist, editor*
In 1831, Leavitt began editing the *Evangelist,* which among other causes advocated abolition—the first of several newspapers he edited in opposition to slavery. For a time, he belonged to the American Colonization Society. A cofounder of the New York Anti-Slavery Society, Leavitt helped to merge it into the National Anti-Slavery Society.

**Lee, Luther** (November 30, 1800–December 13, 1889) *abolitionist Methodist clergyman*
Already opposed to slavery early in his career, Lee declared himself an abolitionist when Elijah Lovejoy was assassinated in 1837. Within his denomination, he worked to stimulate the growth of Wesleyan antislavery societies. He also defended other abolitionist clergy in church trials brought by Methodist conservatives. In 1843 with other abolitionists, Lee split from his denomination to found the antislavery Wesleyan Methodist Connection of America, over which he soon presided.

As an agent of the American Anti-Slavery Society, Lee spoke so expressively and effectively that he was the target of a good deal of violence from proslavery forces. Committed to political action against slavery, in 1840 he helped to found the Liberty Party.

**LeMoyne, Francis Julius** (September 4, 1798–October 14, 1879) *abolitionist physician*
In the 1830s, LeMoyne debated against slavery and against colonization, a movement that he thought was promoted by proslavery forces. In 1840 he ran for the vice presidency on the Liberty Party ticket, and in 1841, 1844, and 1847 for the Pennsylvania Abolitionist ticket—always unsuccessfully. He made his house a station on the Underground Railroad. He also financially supported the American Missionary Association's LeMoyne Normal Institute for blacks.

**Liele, George** (ca. 1750–1820) *slave minister*
Born in Virginia, Liele was converted by a Baptist minister. He began preaching by exhorting his fellow slaves on his home plantation and the surrounding plantations. He went on to establish a church for blacks in Savannah, winning support of their owners by baptizing only with their permission. After he left for Jamaica in the early 1780s, Andrew Bryan, one of his converts, succeeded him as pastor of the Savannah church. Liele founded churches in the West Indies as well as in the British colonies in North America, often teaching his parishioners to read.

**Loguen, Jermain Wesley** (ca. 1813–September 30, 1872) *bishop of the African Methodist Episcopal Zion church, writer, lecturer*
Born in Tennessee of a slaveholding father and a black mother kidnapped from Ohio, Loguen escaped to Canada when he was about 21. There he learned to read, and after two years of hard work and thrift was able to study at the Oneida Institute in upstate New York. He became successively an elder, a pastor, and a bishop in the African Methodist Episcopal Zion Church, with pastorates in upstate New York. He opened schools for black children in Utica and Syracuse, spoke against slavery, and officiated in the Underground Railroad. Liberty Party men sought his

support for their presidential candidate. He aided hundreds of fugitives, finally fleeing to Canada when he was indicted in the rescue of the fugitive slave Jerry in 1851. He published his *Narrative* in 1859.

**Loring, Ellis Gray** (April 14, 1803–May 24, 1858) *antislavery lawyer*
In 1831 Loring helped to organize the New England Anti-Slavery Society, although he favored gradual emancipation rather than immediate abolition. The social censure and economic losses his antislavery stance brought did not deter him. He was a moderate in his views and his choices of antislavery strategies. In his 1838 *Address to the abolitionists of Massachusetts on the Subject of Political Action,* he advocated petitions to legislatures, public interrogation of candidates, and the use of the ballot. Yet he supported Garrison's *Liberator* financially. He and his wife Louisa turned their home into an antislavery center and a shelter for fugitive slaves. In his office Loring oversaw the law studies of a young black man. As a lawyer he fought against Massachusetts efforts to silence abolitionists. He also used his skills as an attorney for blacks, notably in the case of the slave Med, for whom he won a judgment that a slave brought by his owner into the state could not be removed from it against the slave's will.

**Lovejoy, Elijah Parish** (November 9, 1802–November 7, 1837) *the "martyr abolitionist"*
A Presbyterian minister and editor of the Presbyterian weekly *St. Louis Observer,* Lovejoy propagandized against slavery, intemperance, and "popery." When the paper aroused protests, he moved it to Alton, Illinois, a prosperous community that favored gradual emancipation. But as Lovejoy's increasingly radical views turned his paper toward immediate abolitionism, some citizens began to have doubts about him. When his press arrived from St. Louis on a Sunday, Lovejoy's piety forbade him to move it, so he left it on the wharf, where someone dumped it in the river. Alton citizens raised money for a new one, even while proclaiming their disapproval of abolitionism, and Lovejoy promised to avoid the subject in his columns. He not only failed to keep that promise but also helped to organize a state auxiliary of the American Anti-Slavery Society.

Mobs destroyed his presses repeatedly. In November 1837, when the most recent replacement press arrived, armed abolitionists gathered to defend it, as moderates begged Lovejoy to leave. He announced his readiness for martyrdom and found it on November 7, when during a battle around the warehouse where the press was stored he was shot dead.

**Lovejoy, Owen** (January 6, 1811–March 25, 1864) *abolitionist Congregational clergyman, statesman*
From the beginning of his brother Elijah's antislavery activities, Owen Lovejoy supported him and the cause. In his ministry he always spoke out against slavery, even when Illinois prohibited abolitionist meetings, and even under threat of violence. In 1854 he ran successfully for the Illinois state legislature on the Republican ticket, early on opting for Abraham Lincoln as a man who could hold the party together. Elected to Congress in 1856, he functioned there as an impassioned radical and in Illinois as a supporter of the conservative Lincoln, whom Lovejoy continued to support after Lincoln's election to the presidency. Lovejoy introduced the bill by which slavery was abolished in all U.S. territories.

**Lundy, Benjamin** (January 4, 1789–August 22, 1839) *Quaker antislavery activist*
A self-educated, prickly, restless man, a saddler by trade, in his lifetime Lundy roamed the American countryside and traveled abroad to Haiti, Canada, and Mexico. In 1815, in Ohio, he began his known activist career by organizing the Union Humane Society to combat racial prejudice, remove legal restrictions on blacks, help blacks illegally held in bondage, protect and aid free blacks, and work for the abolition of slavery. His early recognition of the importance of cooperation among antislavery societies foreshadowed the national antislavery organizations. For a time in 1817 and 1818, he assisted Charles Osborn in publishing *The Philanthropist,* and in 1821 he began publication of *The Genius of Universal Emancipation*.

About 1825 and for ten years thereafter, he investigated the possibilities of colonization. He endorsed Frances Wright's scheme of permitting slaves to purchase their freedom by cooperative labor on the land, followed by compulsory colonization. He traveled widely in search of possible sites for colonies.

In 1827, his antislavery activities provoked a beating from slave trader Austin Woolfolk, who claimed that

Lundy had libeled him. In 1828, on a lecture tour through the northern states, Lundy converted William Lloyd Garrison to abolitionism and persuaded him to help edit *The Genius.* They soon parted company, however, and in 1835 *The Genius* ceased publication, giving way to *The National Enquirer and Constitutional Advocate of Universal Liberty,* in which Lundy vociferously opposed what he thought of as slaveholders' plots to wrest Texas from Mexico.

When in 1838 a proslavery mob burned Pennsylvania Hall in Philadelphia, Lundy lost all his papers. Once again he moved, this time to Illinois, where he resurrected *The Genius.*

**McKim, James Miller** (November 14, 1810–June 13, 1874) *antislavery Presbyterian clergyman*
An advocate of immediate abolition, McKim at the age of 23 represented Carlisle, Pennsylvania, blacks in founding the American Anti-Slavery Society. When this action, together with his conversion of his entire congregation to antislavery, brought denominational wrath down on him, he left the ministry and became an antislavery speaker under the tutelage of Theodore Weld. Later he served as publishing agent and corresponding secretary of the Pennsylvania Anti-Slavery Society and editor of the *Pennsylvania Freeman.* He and his wife Sarah protected fugitive slaves from slave hunters. They also accompanied the group that received John Brown's body.

During the Civil War, McKim enlisted black soldiers and established the Philadelphia Port Royal Relief Committee to aid contrabands. In 1863, under the aegis of the Pennsylvania Freedmen's Relief Association, he founded schools for blacks in the South. At war's end he shifted to work for the American Freedman's Union Commission to promote black education.

**Mercer, Margaret** (July 1, 1791–September 17, 1846) *antislavery worker, reformer, educator*
For many years, Mercer dedicated most of her time and energy to the American Colonization Society, hoping to encourage manumission and gradually eliminate slavery. She freed the slaves she inherited on her Maryland father's death and sent those who wished it to Liberia. She also raised funds to buy the freedom of other slaves and to educate blacks in Liberia.

**Miller, Jonathan Peckham** (February 24, 1796–February 17, 1847) *soldier, Greek sympathizer, lawyer, antislavery advocate*
After fighting and raising money for Greek freedom from the Ottoman Empire, Miller studied law and served in the Vermont legislature. There he introduced a resolution urging Vermont congressional representatives to work for the abolition of slavery and of the slave trade in the District of Columbia. He continued to devote time and energy to the antislavery cause, lecturing, and in 1840 acting as delegate to the World's Anti-Slavery Convention in London.

**Mott, James** (June 20, 1788–January 26, 1868) *abolitionist manufacturer, merchant, reformer*
A birthright Quaker, Mott sacrificed a flourishing cotton business to his principles, refusing to go on dealing in the product of slave labor. He and his wife Lucretia endured many attacks for their antislavery activities, which they continued until emancipation. Both helped to organize the American Anti-Slavery Society, and both were elected delegates to the 1840 World's Anti-Slavery Convention. After 1850 they sheltered fugitive slaves in their home.

**Mott, Lucretia Coffin** (January 3, 1793–November 11, 1880) *Quaker minister, abolitionist, women's rights pioneer*
Both Lucretia Mott and her husband James were prominent figures in the Quaker and abolitionist communities. In the 1827 split within the Society of Friends, they took the side of Elias Hicks, whose denunciations of slavery persuaded them not to use any slave products, at least knowingly. Not only did they speak out for the free produce movement, but James Mott at considerable risk and cost shifted from the cotton to the wool business.

Lucretia Mott met William Lloyd Garrison about 1831. In 1833 she attended the Philadelphia convention that he had called to organize the American Anti-Slavery Society (AASS). Because that society did not admit women, she helped to establish the Philadelphia Female Anti-Slavery Society. Later, when the AASS opened its membership to women, she joined and held office in it. She stood with Garrison in demanding immediate emancipation.

Mott repeatedly showed her courage in the abolitionist cause. Because of her "radical" stand on slavery she endured the criticism of her fellow Quakers—but not passively. When Quaker minister Rachel Barker preached against her at the Philadelphia Yearly Meeting for more than an hour, Mott preached back for another. Because of her antislavery activities, on one of her lecture and visitation tours someone tampered with her carriage, and inns refused her service. But she continued to speak against slavery both at Quaker meetings and before the state legislatures of Delaware, New Jersey, and Pennsylvania. She participated in setting up the Anti-Slavery Convention of American Women, which met in 1838 in Philadelphia in the brand-new Pennsylvania Hall. When mobs disturbed its sessions, Mott set an example of calm for the other participants. On May 17, proslavery advocates fired the building and started toward the Motts' home, where the family quietly awaited them; fortunately, they never reached the house. Again in 1840, when she was traveling through Delaware visiting Friends' meetings and speaking against slavery, Mott pleaded with a mob to take her rather than her male companion, whom they were intent on tarring and feathering. In 1843, she preached in a Unitarian church to an audience that included 40 congressmen.

When in 1840 the World's Anti-Slavery Convention in London refused to seat Mott and the other officially elected women delegates of the American Anti-Slavery Society, her reaction won her the title of "the *Lioness* of the Convention." This experience and Mott's meeting there with Elizabeth Cady Stanton led to the first women's rights convention, in 1848, in Seneca Falls, New York. In both these causes Mott was fighting for emancipation.

After the Civil War and the passage of the Thirteenth Amendment, Mott propagandized for black suffrage, working through the Friends Association of Philadelphia for the Aid and Elevation of the Freedmen, which provided both educational and economic aid to blacks. She labored for the rest of her life for the causes to which she had dedicated herself. At 77 she undertook to speak in all the black churches of Philadelphia.

**Nelson, David** (September 24, 1793–October 17, 1844) *abolitionist Presbyterian physician, clergyman, educator*
Before 1831, Nelson freed his slaves. In 1835, Theodore Weld's oratory persuaded him to dedicate himself to the antislavery cause, accepting an appointment as agent from the American Anti-Slavery Society (AASS). Nelson preached manumission to his congregation, calling upon slaveholders to free their slaves. Marion College thereupon ended his presidency, the state of Missouri expelled him, and mobs attacked him. Nonetheless, he continued his work for the AASS in Illinois until bad health forced him to stop in 1840.

**Osborn, Charles** (August 21, 1775–December 29, 1850) *Quaker abolitionist preacher*
During his residences in Tennessee, Ohio, Indiana, and Michigan, and in his travels all over the country in his ministry, Osborn preached against slavery. In 1815 he organized the Tennessee Manumission Society, and in 1816 he founded other such societies in North Carolina. He edited briefly the antislavery *Philanthropist,* denouncing colonization as a plot of slaveholders to protect slavery and rid the country of free blacks. In 1842, he helped to found the Free Produce Association of Wayne County, Indiana, and to establish the *Free Labor Advocate and Anti-Slavery Chronicle.* That year conservative Quakers ousted Osborn and other abolitionists from the governing committee of the Indiana Yearly Meeting, on which he had long sat, causing him to break away in 1843 to help found the Indiana Yearly Meeting of Anti-Slavery Friends.

**Pennington, James W. C.** (1809–October, 1870) *Presbyterian pastor, author of the first history of blacks by a black man in the New World*
Born a slave, Pennington was trained as a stonemason and blacksmith. Outraged by his master's cruel treatment of his family and himself, about 1828 with the help of Quakers he escaped to the North, where Quakers taught him reading, writing, and the elements of Christianity. He continued studying on his own, supporting himself as a farmer, a teacher, and finally a minister. For many years he served a Presbyterian church in New York City.

Pennington tried vainly to purchase his parents' freedom and his own. Eventually he helped his father and two brothers escape to Canada. Some of his sisters married free men, who bought their freedom, and three of his brothers were bought by "conscience slaveholders," who held them only for a term of years.

Pennington intended his *Text Book of the Origin and History of the Colored People* (1841) primarily for school children. In 1849 he published his memoirs, as *The Fugitive Blacksmith.* While he was still legally a slave, the University of Heidelberg conferred upon him the degree of doctor of divinity. He served five terms as a member of the General Convention for the Improvement of the Free Colored People. As late as 1859 he was still writing for the *Anglo-American* magazine.

**Phillips, Wendell** (November 29, 1811–February 2, 1884) *wealthy abolitionist reformer, lawyer, orator*
Early in 1837, Phillips publicly announced his belief in abolition, and later that year he denounced the assassination of Elijah Lovejoy in a speech so stirring as to place him in the forefront of the movement. Encouraged by his wife, he began lecturing against slavery. On most issues he sided with William Lloyd Garrison, avoiding association with a political party and condemning the U.S. Constitution for its compromises on slavery. Unlike Garrison, he did not eschew the use of violence in the cause. At the World's Anti-Slavery Society Convention of 1840, he supported Garrison in insisting (vainly) that women delegates be seated.

The passion of Phillips's oratory often aroused hostile responses and physical threats. Doubtless, however, it deepened his own convictions, which with time grew more extreme. He opposed the annexation of Texas and then the Mexican War, and ultimately he advocated disunion. During the Civil War he harshly criticized Lincoln, until the issuance of the Emancipation Proclamation. After the war, over Garrison's opposition, Phillips kept the American Anti-Slavery Society going, with Phillips himself its president.

**Pugh, Sarah** (October 6, 1800–August 1, 1884) *teacher, abolitionist, feminist*
Educated by Quakers, in 1821 Pugh began teaching at a Friends' school in Philadelphia. In 1829 she started her own elementary school, where she taught for more than 10 years. In 1835, the British abolitionist George Thompson converted her to abolitionism. She launched into antislavery activities in the Philadelphia Female Anti-Slavery Society, over which she later presided; in the Pennsylvania Anti-Slavery Society, which for many years met in her home; and in the American Anti-Slavery Society, in which she remained loyal to Garrison and the cause of immediate emancipation. One of the group of women delegates denied seats at the World's Anti-Slavery Convention in 1840, Pugh wrote the formal protest of the Pennsylvanians among them. On that trip she made friends with many British abolitionists, and in 1851 at their invitation joined their antislavery work. Back in Philadelphia 17 months later, she resumed her work for the local movement, presiding over meetings and working on fund-raising fairs.

After the Civil War, Pugh devoted herself to working for the freedmen and the rights of women.

**Purvis, Robert, Sr.** (1810–unknown) *the richest black man in America*
A fair man who could have passed for white, Purvis chose to identify with the blacks of Philadelphia, marrying James Forten's daughter Harriet. He helped to organize both the American and the Philadelphia Anti-Slavery Societies. He headed Philadelphia's Vigilance Committee, which protected fugitive slaves, and spent endless hours in the work of the Underground Railroad

**Rankin, John** (1793–unknown) *activist antislavery minister*
Born in Tennessee, Rankin began his ministry in 1817 in Kentucky. In 1821, he moved to the Presbyterian church of Ripley, Ohio, which he served for 44 years. His home was a station on the Underground Railroad; for his assistance to fugitive slaves he was more than once mobbed by Kentuckians. In 1823, he published *Letters on American Slavery, Addressed to Mr. Thomas Rankin, Merchant at Middlebrook, Augusta County, Virginia.* He also lectured for the American Antislavery Society and led the fight against slavery in the Presbyterian General Assemblies.

**Realf, Richard** (June 14, 1834–October 28, 1878) *abolitionist poet*
An 1854 emigrant from Britain to the United States, in 1856 Realf went west as a newspaper correspondent, where he associated until 1858 with John Brown. Returning the next year, he was arrested after Brown's attack on Harpers Ferry. A commissioned officer during the Civil War, he served for a time on Reconstruction duty with a black regiment.

**Remond, Charles Lenox** (February 1, 1810–December 22, 1873) *black antislavery leader*
The son of a wealthy Boston merchant, Remond became a lecturer for the American Anti-Slavery Society in 1838. In 1840, he went to the World's Anti-Slavery Society Convention in England. Later,

he lectured for 18 months in the British Isles. He returned to the United States with a petition signed by 60,000 Irish asking Irish-Americans to support the antislavery cause. Then he resumed his American tours, this time with Frederick Douglass.

**Remond, Sarah Parker** (June 6, 1826–after 1887) *abolitionist lecturer, physician*
Remond was the daughter of a wealthy black abolitionist merchant of Salem, Massachusetts, and the sister of Charles Remond. She supplemented her public school education with extensive reading.

As an adult she participated actively in antislavery societies. Often insulted because of her race, Sarah Remond in 1853 won a suit against the New York Athenaeum for refusing her a seat. In 1856, she began lecturing as an agent for the American Anti-Slavery Society, touring New England with her brother Charles. In 1858 she appeared on the platform of the National Woman's Rights Convention.

That summer she went to England, where for the first time, she said, she was cordially received by white women as a sister. Quite different was her reception at the American legation, which refused her a visa for France on the grounds that her passport was invalid: she could not be a U.S. citizen, the diplomats ruled. For some time she continued her education at Bedford College for Ladies in London, lecturing against slavery during the vacations. She was part of an important group of American blacks who swayed British public opinion toward the Union during the Civil War.

After the war she returned briefly to the United States, working for equal rights for all Americans, blacks and women included, in the integrated American Equal Rights Association, established in 1866. Then she went back to Europe. In Italy, she became a physician and apparently married.

**Ross, Alexander Milton** (December 13, 1832–October 27, 1897) *physician, abolitionist, naturalist, reformer*
A Canadian, Ross studied medicine in New York state from 1851 to 1855 but was apparently not licensed until 1875. After his medical studies he interested himself in abolition. Harriet Beecher Stowe's *Uncle Tom's Cabin* confirmed his determination to devote himself to abolition. "To me," Ross later wrote, "it was a command. A deep and settled conviction impressed me that it was my duty to let the oppressed go free." In 1856, he visited Gerrit Smith, who agreed to introduce him to other abolitionists involved in the Underground Railroad, people who could teach him their strategies. Together Ross and Smith traveled to Boston, New York, Philadelphia, Ohio, and Indiana. On this trip, Ross said, "I was initiated into a knowledge of the relief societies and the methods adopted to circulate information among the slaves of the South; the routes to be taken by the slaves, after leaving the so-called free states; and the relief posts where shelter and aid for transportation could be obtained." The abolitionists Theodore Parker and Lewis Tappan, as well as Smith, backed Ross in his new undertakings.

Ross daringly roamed through Maryland, Tennessee, Kentucky, and Virginia, and later penetrated into the Deep South. He went to New Orleans, and thence to Selma and Huntsville in Alabama; Columbus and Vicksburg in Mississippi; Augusta, Georgia; and Charleston, South Carolina. He found that many slaves had heard of Canada from blacks brought south from the border states and from their masters' warnings against going there, but that most thought it too far away to reach.

Ross developed his own methods, adopting different pretenses for his travels. Often he stayed in one place for several weeks, sizing up slaves and inviting those he thought most intelligent and trustworthy to a meeting, perhaps at the home of a black preacher. There he might tell the 30 or 40 he had selected about the possibility of escape to Canada and ask them to pass the news along to others whom they trusted. If by the next day some of them had decided to act, he would give them more information and equip them with gear (such as a compass) and food, or he himself might lead them to an Underground Railroad station or even to Canada. Of the first group of nine that he so conducted, all reached Canada safely; in 1863, he enlisted three of these into a black regiment. Ross continued this work through the Civil War, often in danger of his life, but never captured. During the war, he also acted as Lincoln's secret agent to uncover Confederate activities in Canada.

For several years after the war, Ross turned to collecting and classifying Canadian flora and fauna. His work brought him fame among scholars, and several European princes decorated him for it. Later still he focused on public health, trying to improve sanitation and battling against compulsory vaccination for smallpox.

**Ruggles, David** (1810–1849) *abolitionist*
The son of free black parents and born in Norwich, Connecticut, Ruggles moved as a young man to New York City, where he ran a temperance grocery and a printing business, distributing antislavery tracts in his bookshop and reading room. In 1833, he became a traveling agent for the *Emancipator* to boost the newspaper's circulation and to raise funds for the American Anti-Slavery Society. Ruggles, who considered a free press the primary bulwark against slavery, devoted his editorial career to promoting abolitionism, racial pride, and black uplift.

As a leader of the New York Committee of Vigilance (1835–1839), he searched the city for slaves illegally detained by southern masters, and he used the courts to protect fugitives, despite official connivance in the kidnapping of free blacks, and uncooperative white judges. He personally assisted in the escape of over six hundred fugitives, directing them to the Underground Railroad. He thereby attracted the enmity of kidnappers and the part of officialdom that wanted to destroy the vigilance committee. In 1839 these elements succeeded in jailing him, endangering his health. He resigned from the committee that year.

Thereafter, with the support of other blacks and Lydia Maria Child, Ruggles founded and successfully ran the country's first hydropathic treatment center, where he also offered a "cutaneous electricity" treatment.

**Russwurm, John B.** (October 1, 1799–June 17, 1851) *antislavery writer*
Educated in Canada and at Bowdoin College, Russwurm established in 1827 the first black newspaper, *Freedom's Journal* (later the *Rights of All*), in New York. He advocated immediate emancipation, but his support of colonization alienated many other blacks. Later, he moved to Liberia to superintend its schools.

**Salem, Peter (Salem Middlesex, Salem Poor)** (ca. 1750–1816) *soldier*
Salem was born into slavery in Framingham, Massachusetts. He was owned first by Capt. Jeremiah Belknap and then by Maj. Lawson Buckminister. He was given his freedom so that he could join the army. He volunteered for the Framingham militia. With his company, he fought in the battles of Lexington and Concord. He is best known for his deeds in the battle of Bunker Hill. Legend says it was he who shot the British Commander, Major Pitcairn, killing him instantly and thus checking, temporarily, the advance of the Redcoats. He served unharmed in the Continental Army for seven years. He married Katie Benson at the end of the war.

**Scott, Orange** (February 13, 1800–July 31, 1847) *antislavery Methodist clergyman*
Scott's activity in the antislavery movement began in 1833, when he introduced a discussion of slavery into the Boston Methodist paper, *Zion's Herald*. In 1836, when an antislavery speech at the General Conference caused his bishop to refuse to reappoint him, Scott accepted a position as an agent for the American Anti-Slavery Society, even as he continued to encourage consideration of the topic in Methodist publications and conferences. A Lowell, Massachusetts, church called him to its pastorate in defiance of episcopal authority. The fight that followed involved Scott in a split from the denomination and the establishment of the antislavery Wesleyan Methodist Connection of America. For this new denomination he edited the *True Wesleyan*. His 1846 book, *The Grounds of Secession from the M. E. Church: Being an Examination of her Connection with Slavery, and Also of her Form of Government*, explained why he had withdrawn.

**Shaw, Robert Gould** (1837–1863) *commander of a black Civil War regiment*
Born into a well-to-do, antislavery family, Shaw studied abroad and at Harvard, then entered an uncle's mercantile firm in New York City. Although for some time he had favored disunion, he supported Lincoln's candidacy. As soon as the Civil War started he went south with the New York state militia, which he had already joined, and in May 1861, he was commissioned a second lieutenant in the 2d Massachusetts Regiment. After a year of service behind the lines, with such distasteful duties as apprehending runaway slaves and returning them to their masters, Shaw fought his first battle in May 1862, at Winchester in the Shenandoah Valley. Other battles, including Antietam, turned him into a seasoned veteran.

On January 30, 1863, at age 25, he was offered the command of the Massachusetts 54th Infantry

Regiment, Colored, by Gov. John Andrew. In the face of his youth, his engagement to Annie Haggerty, and the near-certainty that the Confederacy would retaliate against the Union's use of black soldiers by declaring their white officers criminals guilty of inciting insurrection, Shaw hesitated, refused, and then accepted. His mother wrote: "God rewards a hundred-fold every good aspiration of his children, and this is my reward for asking [for] my children not earthly honors, but souls to see the right and courage to follow it. Now I feel ready to die, for I see you willing to give your support to the cause of truth that is lying crushed and bleeding."

On May 28, 1863, a few weeks after his marriage, Shaw and his regiment left by sea for St. Simons Island, Georgia. There they were put under the command of Col. James Montgomery, whose brutality and hatred of the enemy horrified Shaw. Montgomery involved the 54th on June 10, 1863, in an unopposed raid on the town of Darien, Georgia; Shaw refused to allow his men to loot or to order them to burn the town. In July, for the first time, members of the regiment came under fire, fighting bravely on James Island, near Charleston. Days later, the regiment led an assault on Fort Wagner, advancing under murderous fire, with Colonel Shaw on foot at their head. Shaw was poised on the ramparts when he was killed and fell into the fort. After hand-to-hand fighting, the remnants of the regiment retreated down the slope before the fort and fired from there. Shaw's parents later requested that his body remain where the Confederates had contemptuously buried it—with his soldiers. In his memory, the Shaw family contributed large sums to the rebuilding of Darien.

**Smalls, Robert** (April 5, 1839–February 22, 1915) *Civil War hero, congressman*
A man of many skills, as a slave Smalls worked as a hotel waiter, a hack driver, and a rigger. In 1861, the Confederates forced him to serve on the crew of the gunboat *Planter.* The next year, in the absence of the ship's white officers, he stowed away his family and his brother's family, sailed the ship out of Charleston harbor under the Confederate flag, and surrendered it to the blockading federal squadron. He then served aboard the *Planter* in the Union navy, saving the steamer when its commander deserted under fire. This heroic action earned him the rank of captain.

During Reconstruction, Smalls served as delegate to the National Union Convention and the South Carolina constitutional convention. In 1875, after terms in the state legislature, he was elected to Congress.

**Smith, Gerrit** (March 6, 1797–December 28, 1874) *antislavery philanthropist, reformer*
Smith wanted to use his vast wealth, partly inherited and partly of his own making, to benefit the human race. Sometimes he succeeded; sometimes he failed, as when he tried to colonize blacks in the Adirondack forest. In the antislavery movement, which he joined in 1835, he favored compensated emancipation of slaves. Though more moderate than his friend William Lloyd Garrison, Smith nonetheless helped fugitive slaves, even after authorities had arrested them. An important contributor to the New England Emigrant Aid Company of Massachusetts, set up to enable antislavery emigrants to settle in Kansas, Smith upheld the use of violence there, on the grounds that the federal government was supporting the proslavery forces. He also funded John Brown, though the failure of the raid on Harpers Ferry and fear of exposure as Brown's supporter sent Smith temporarily insane.

Smith believed in political action against slavery. He helped to establish the Liberty Party, running as its candidate for governor of New York. He served briefly in Congress as an independent in 1853 and 1854. During the Civil War he wrote and spoke for the Union, joining the Republicans in time to campaign for Lincoln's reelection. After the war, he favored black suffrage and moderation toward southern whites.

**Stewart, Alvan** (September 1, 1790–May 1, 1849) *abolitionist lawyer*
Something of an eccentric, Stewart began his career as an antislavery activist in 1834 by joining the American Anti-Slavery Society (AASS) and founding several local antislavery societies, including the New York State Anti-Slavery Society, over which he presided. He tried unsuccessfully to revise the creed of the AASS, arguing that slavery violated the Constitution in that it deprived the slaves of their freedom without due process of law. He also disturbed the national organization by his efforts to run the New York society independently, even excluding agents of the AASS from it.

An advocate of political action, Stewart in 1840 helped organize the Liberty Party but was soon discouraged by the lack of support for its ticket. Thereafter he devoted his antislavery activities mainly to legal efforts for slaves, as when he challenged the constitutionality of slavery before the New Jersey supreme court.

**Stewart, Maria W. Miller** (1803–December 17, 1879) *teacher, public speaker*
Stewart was the first American-born woman and the first black to speak from a public platform. Mentored by James Walker and William Lloyd Garrison, Stewart wrote for the *Liberator.* Garrison also published some of her work in tract form, notably "Religion and the Pure Principles of Morality." In 1832 and 1833, Stewart composed and delivered four addresses in Boston: one to the First African Baptist Church of Boston, one to the Afric-American Female Intelligence Society, one at Franklin Hall, and one at the African Masonic Hall—all reprinted in the *Liberator.* Her final speech announced her decision to move to New York: she could not help her cause in Boston, she felt, because her own community had condemned her for daring to speak publicly.

Stewart saw knowledge as potential salvation. Deploring the ignorance and degradation imposed upon blacks, and despairing of help from whites, she exhorted free blacks to educate themselves and sue for their rights. She vigorously opposed the efforts of colonizationists to send them back to Africa, declaring, "I am a true born American; your blood flows in my veins, and your spirit fires my breast."

She taught in New York public schools until 1852, then moved to Baltimore, where she set up a private school for black children. In 1861 she moved again, this time to Washington, D.C., where she taught for a while and then worked as a matron in the Freedmen's Hospital. In 1871 she opened a Sunday school for children in the area around the hospital. She used her pension as a widow of a soldier in the War of 1812 to publish a second edition of her speeches and writing.

**Still, Peter** (ca. 1800–after 1854) *driver, later freedman*
Kidnapped with his brother Levin from their Pennsylvania home as a boy, Peter Still served for 40 years as a slave, at first in Lexington, Kentucky. At nine, he was put to work in his master's brickyard; four years later he was sold, along with Levin. In 1817, Levin was sent to Alabama with a nephew of their owner, who in 1818 on the death of his uncle inherited Peter as well.

In Alabama, Peter and Levin raised cotton on the land of their master, Levi Gist, and with his brother ran a store. Gist flourished, acquiring more land, and he made Peter, now almost 21, his personal servant. In time, Peter married a young slave, Vina, on a neighboring plantation and started a family. Their lives together were marked by losses: Levin died, Vina's mother was taken South, and Gist died. Six years later the executors of the estate sold it and hired out the slaves. For a year, in 1846, Peter hired his own time. By his own request he was hired out in 1847 to sympathetic German Jews Joseph and Isaac Friedman. About 1849 Peter asked the Friedmans to buy him, so that he might later buy himself. In April of 1850, when he was almost 50, Peter completed his payments, freed himself, and went North. An emissary sent to lead his wife and children out of slavery succeeded in getting them to Ohio, where they were recaptured. The owner demanded $5,000 for Peter's wife and children. Undaunted, Peter traveled through the North, telling his story and collecting money as he went from antislavery sympathizers. By late 1854 he had the sum in hand. His wife and children were brought North—though their former master refused to let a widowed son take his child without payment.

**Still, William** (October 7, 1821–July 14, 1902) *abolitionist*
Still was born to a father who had bought his own freedom and a mother who had twice escaped. In 1847, he began work as a clerk for the Pennsylvania Society for the Abolition of Slavery, personally sheltering most of the fugitives who escaped as far as Philadelphia. He recorded their names and in 1855 toured Canada to see how they were faring. His *The Underground Railroad,* published in 1872, would relate many of their experiences. His historical sense also manifested itself in 1861, when he helped to start an association to collect data about black people.

Unlike most white abolitionists, Still recognized the necessity of improving the quality of life for free blacks. For eight years, in the face of criticism from other blacks, he campaigned against segregation on Philadelphia street cars until the Pennsylvania legislature finally ended it in 1867. Against popular opposition he supported the Democratic candidate for mayor in 1874 and argued against the establishment of a black bank. Until the end of his life he imaginatively and energetically worked for the well-being of blacks, serving on the Freedmen's Aid Commission, in 1880 founding the first black YMCA, and managing homes for aged blacks, needy black children, and the orphans of black soldiers and sailors.

**Stone, Lucy** (August 13, 1818–October 18, 1893) *feminist, abolitionist*
Best known as an advocate of woman's rights, Stone, inspired by Abby Kelley Foster, began her public career in 1847 lecturing for the American Anti-Slavery Society, which tried to limit her feminist work. They compromised by allowing her to lecture on women's rights at her own expense during the week and to speak against slavery on weekends. Frequently threatened, she faced hostile audiences without flinching.

In 1855 Stone abandoned her resolution never to marry, accepting the proposal of Henry Blackwell, with whom she had one child, a daughter. With her moral and financial support, he experimented extensively, though unsuccessfully, with growing sugar beets, as part of the free produce movement.

She supported the Women's Loyal National League, founded by Elizabeth Cady Stanton and Susan B. Anthony to encourage the passage of the Thirteenth Amendment. After the Civil War, Stone helped to found and officiated in the American Equal Rights Association in the cause of both black and woman suffrage. Stone supported the Fifteenth Amendment, unlike Stanton and Anthony, who would support it only if it included women's suffrage.

**Stowe, Harriet Beecher** (June 14, 1811–July 1, 1896) *author*
Stowe was born into the gifted Beecher family. Her father, Lyman Beecher, was a clergyman, a profession into which his sons followed him. Her older sister Catharine Beecher, whom in her girlhood Harriet assisted in her school, pioneered teaching as a profession for women.

In 1836 Harriet married Calvin Ellis Stowe, who taught in the Cincinnati theological seminary over which Lyman Beecher presided. Even during the years in which she was bearing seven children, she augmented his salary by writing and keeping schools.

In 1850, the year of the most severe Fugitive Slave Law, the family moved to Maine. All her life Harriet had heard debates over slavery, had read abolitionist literature, had even opened her home to fugitive slaves. For Harriet the 1850 law was a crisis of conscience, giving her at last a theme that aroused her passions. How, she asked, could a just and loving God permit the cruelties of slavery? How could a "Christian" nation permit them within its boundaries?

In response, she wrote *Uncle Tom's Cabin,* an epic of 19th-century life that forced Americans to look hard at themselves and their country. It was sentimental, and its vision of slave life was often both stereotypical and condescending, but Stowe empathized with slave women's anguish over the separation of families. Through her own grief over the death of one of her babies, she identified with their dread of losing their children. Her courageous black women overcome despair to save themselves and their families—Cassie by "haunting" the devilish overseer Simon Legree, and Eliza by her frantic crossing of the ice-filled river. Stowe understood, too—and demonstrated in her novel—the corruption that slavery inflicted upon both slaves and slaveholders. Her book, a runaway bestseller, moved the nation one step closer to civil war.

**Stuart, Charles** (1783–1865) *British godfather of the American antislavery movement*
After 13 years as an officer in the forces of the British East India Company, Stuart immigrated to Canada in 1796. In 1824, as principal of a school in upper New York state, he met the young Theodore Weld, whom he mentored and adopted as his protégé, imbuing him with antislavery principles.

In 1828, Stuart returned to England to campaign for the abolition of slavery in the British West Indies. There he successfully propagandized against the American Colonization Society. His pamphlet *The West India Question* provided the basis for the creed of the American Anti-Slavery Society when it was organized in 1831, with Weld's active participation. In such ways he infused the incipient American abolitionism with the energy of the British movement. From 1834 to 1838 Stuart directly served the American cause by lecturing as its agent in Ohio, Vermont, and New York, even in the face of mob violence. From 1840 to 1842 he raised funds in England for anti-Garrisonian abolitionists.

**Sumner, Charles** (January 6, 1811–March 11, 1874) *abolitionist U.S. senator*
The son of a man who not only condemned slavery but also opposed the exclusion of black children from schools and the prohibition of interracial marriages, Sumner in 1845 established a reputation as an orator and a man of principle. In 1848, he ran successfully for the U.S. Senate on a ticket formed by a coalition of Free Soilers and Democrats, being seated after a prolonged election dispute in 1851.

Throughout his Senate career, Sumner excited anger and hatred among proslavery forces within his own constituency and in the South. Time and again he roused their fury, as when he tried valiantly but vainly to nullify the effect of the notorious Fugitive Slave Law of 1850 by persuading the Senate not to appropriate funds for its enforcement, but instead to repeal it. He kindled a firestorm by not only presenting petition after petition against the Kansas-Nebraska bill but attacking it in one of the most vituperative speeches ever heard in the Senate—a speech that directly and personally insulted other senators. In retaliation, Rep. Preston S. Brooks, a relative of one of the offended senators, beat Sumner on the Senate floor, so badly that Sumner could not resume his duties for three and a half years. Nonetheless, on his return he continued to indict slavery as passionately as ever, and in 1861 at the Massachusetts Republican convention he called for emancipation as a means to end the war—the first prominent statesman to do so.

During the Civil War, as chairman of the committee on foreign relations, Sumner protected the Union by opposing resolutions that might have provoked war between the United States and France or England. Looking beyond emancipation, he recognized the need of blacks for civil rights. In February 1862, he began to argue that the seceded states had lost all rights under the Constitution. After the war he continued to focus on black rights, succeeding in forcing states that wished readmission to the Union to grant black suffrage, though he failed to guarantee the freed slaves free schools and free farmsteads, as he had hoped to do.

**Sunderland, La Roy** (April 22, 1804–May 15, 1885) *abolitionist*
As a young Methodist minister, Sunderland enlisted other clergy in the antislavery cause, organizing the first antislavery society in that church—even after he withdrew from its ministry in 1833. In 1836, he began to edit the new Methodist antislavery paper, *Zion's Watchman,* enduring repeated attacks from the denomination's bishops. In 1842, with other dissidents, he withdrew to found the antislavery Wesleyan Connection of America, but ultimately religious doubts prevented his joining it.

**Tappan, Arthur** (May 22, 1786–July 23, 1865) *silk merchant, abolitionist philanthropist*
Seeing himself as God's steward, Tappan decided to use the fortune he and his brother Lewis Tappan had earned to promote Christianity and suppress vice. When in 1835 Theodore Weld and most of the other students withdrew from the Lane Theological Seminary because it tried to restrict their discussion of slavery, Arthur Tappan privately pledged his entire income to secure the establishment of Oberlin College, in whose seminary the former Lane students enrolled.

Once a supporter of colonization as a means of gradual emancipation of slaves, Tappan soon turned to abolitionism. He funded many efforts to attain that goal and to help blacks in other ways: he supported publication of the *Liberator,* the *Emancipator,* the *American and Foreign Anti-Slavery Reporter,* and the *National Era;* he backed a failed attempt to found a black college in New Haven; and he funded Prudence Crandall's school for young black women in Connecticut. After the 1840 division in the American Anti-Slavery Society, Tappan presided over the new anti-Garrisonian American and Foreign Anti-Slavery Society. Committed to political action, he enlisted in the Liberty Party. In 1850 he publicly announced that he would defy the new Fugitive Slave Law, continuing to help escaping blacks, and repeatedly ignoring threats of kidnapping and assassination.

**Tappan, Lewis** (May 23, 1788–June 21, 1873) *abolitionist merchant*
As a founder of the New York Anti-Slavery Society and the American Anti-Slavery Society, Lewis shared the opinions of his brother Arthur. In retaliation for his antislavery activities, an 1834 mob wrecked his house and burned his furniture. He served prominently on the committee to free the slave ship *Amistad* captives. Like Arthur, he believed that the antislavery movement should confine itself to a single cause: accordingly, in 1840 he helped to orga-

nize the American and Foreign Anti-Slavery Society (AFASS), for which he acted as treasurer. Recognizing the importance to the movement of allies, he kept in close touch with English abolitionists and used his religious connections to win the cooperation of the churches and missionary societies. When the American Board, which he had financially supported, refused its cooperation, he helped to found the antislavery American Missionary Association (AMA). He also financed the daring Canadian Alexander M. Ross in his work to help slaves escape.

In time choosing a more radical course and holding that the federal government had the constitutional power to abolish slavery in all the states, Tappan in 1855 resigned his position as treasurer with the AFASS to officiate in the new Abolition Society. He also turned his energies toward supporting the constructive work for blacks of the AMA.

**Taylor, John W.** (March 26, 1784–September 18, 1854) *New York antislavery congressman*
In the House of Representatives, where he served from 1813 to 1833, Taylor won prominence through his antislavery arguments, particularly on the questions of admitting new states and prohibiting slavery in the territories. He based his arguments on the theory that from its power to admit new states, Congress derived the power to *refuse* to admit and to set conditions on which it would admit. The constitutional power given Congress to prohibit the importation or migration of slaves after 1808, he said, meant that that body could prohibit the passage of slaves from one commonwealth to another. What was more, Congress had the duty to limit slavery as inconsistent with the republican form of government.

Taylor believed that his antislavery stance cost him reelection as Speaker of the House in 1821 and 1825, and reelection to Congress in 1833.

**Taylor, Susie King** (1848–1912) *Civil War nurse*
Taylor learned to read and write while still a slave. In 1863, she volunteered as a nurse in Beaufort, South Carolina, and served with the 1st Regiment of South Carolina Volunteers. After the war she worked as a maid.

**Torrey, Charles Turner** (November 21, 1813–May 9, 1846) *abolitionist*
The bristly Torrey failed in all professions he undertook—the ministry, editing, reporting, and lecturing. He began his antislavery career as a theological student at Andover, where he organized a student antislavery society. Within the movement he opposed William Lloyd Garrison, leading Massachusetts conservative abolitionists out of the American Anti-Slavery Society in 1838 to found the *Massachusetts Abolitionist* and the Massachusetts Abolition Society, for which he briefly and unsuccessfully served as agent.

As an abolitionist, Torrey was the central figure in two trials. In 1842 he was arrested while reporting as a freelance reporter on the 1842 "Convention of Slaveholders" in Maryland, but he was not convicted. In 1844 he was again arrested in Baltimore for helping slaves escape. This time he was convicted and sentenced to six years' hard labor. He died in prison.

**Towne, Laura Matilda** (May 3, 1825–February 22, 1901) *educator*
Born free to well-off black parents, Towne early became an abolitionist. In her Pennsylvania girlhood, she studied homeopathic medicine and later taught at various "charity schools."

In 1861, she responded to a call for doctors and teachers to join the "Port Royal Experiment," a Union project in the Sea Islands off the coast of Georgia and South Carolina to educate former slaves and set up a viable black economy. There she distributed clothing, practiced medicine, and taught school. With her friend Ellen Murray, she founded and taught at the highly successful Penn School for blacks on St. Helena Island. After 1870 she trained teachers there.

Towne stayed with Penn School for the rest of her life, while also serving as a public health officer and an unofficial legal adviser in blacks' struggle to gain ownership of land. Most of the time she worked as a volunteer, with the school's expenses paid successively by the Pennsylvania Relief Association, the Benezet Society of Germantown, Pennsylvania, and the Towne family.

**Truth, Sojourner (Isabella)** (ca.1797–November 26, 1883) *preacher, abolitionist, suffragist, reformer*
Truth, born Isabella, lived the first part of her life as a slave, enduring cruel treatment, forced to watch her father die neglected, and having two of her daughters sold away from her. In 1827 she fled and, with the

help of Quaker friends, successfully sued for the freedom of her son Peter, who had been illegally sold.

In about 1829 she moved to New York City, taking employment as a domestic. After misadventures with religious fanatics, in 1843 she obeyed the command of voices she heard to rename herself and travel the countryside, preaching and singing. She walked through Long Island and Connecticut, proclaiming her faith at camp meetings, on the streets, and in churches. She spent that winter in a commune in Northampton, Massachusetts, where she first learned about the abolitionist movement. Abolitionist leaders promoted her travels and speeches.

About 1850, Truth moved to Salem, Ohio, using the office of the *Anti-Slavery Bugle* as headquarters for her travels in Indiana, Missouri, and Kansas, and supporting herself by selling her autobiography. Slavery advocates clubbed her in Kansas and mobbed her in Missouri. In the mid 1850s she moved to Battle Creek, Michigan. During the Civil War she solicited food and clothing throughout Michigan for black soldiers. In late 1864, as "counselor to the freed people" for the National Freedmen's Relief Association, she began collecting signatures on a petition for a "Negro State," urging that blacks be settled on western public lands—a movement that failed but encouraged the migration to Kansas and Missouri of many blacks. There Truth preached to them on cleanliness and godliness. Long into her old age, she continued to lecture on religion, black rights, and women's suffrage.

**Tubman, Harriet** (ca. 1820–March 10, 1913)
*rescuer of slaves, Civil War scout, nurse*
Enslaved from birth, threatened in 1849 with being sold out of Maryland, Tubman escaped to Philadelphia. In December 1850 she began guiding other slaves to freedom, beginning with her sister and her two children. In the decade before the Civil War she made some nineteen trips into Maryland, delivering slaves to the North, often to Canada, where she lived for several years. According to Sarah Bradford, Tubman's first biographer, this "Moses of her people" delivered some 300 fugitives into the promised land of freedom—not one of whom was ever recaptured. Sometimes she worked alone, sometimes with antislavery activists in the Underground Railroad. Her daring, courage, and ingenuity at one point raised the price on her head to $40,000. In the North, she defied the fugitive slave law, once leading a crowd to release a slave from custody. She was an adviser of John Brown.

Early in 1862, Tubman volunteered her services to Maj. Gen. David Hunter, commander of the Department of the South. She served throughout the Civil War as a spy and scout, getting information from blacks behind Confederate lines. She also nursed and helped freedmen who had fled north. After the war, in her Auburn, New York, home, she cared not only for her own aged parents, whom she had earlier rescued, but for other old people and black orphans. She found time also to support southern freedmen's schools and to work for woman suffrage. Not until 1897 did Congress finally award her a pension—$20 a month—for her wartime service.

**Turner, Nat** (October 2, 1800–November 11, 1831) *slave, revolutionary*
Brought up by a religious family that treated him as one created for a special purpose, Turner believed himself divinely appointed to free American slaves. His family and community alleged that he had learned to read without a teacher. Rumor bruited his powers as a healer. God, Turner believed, spoke to him in visions: at age 25, he said, "I saw white spirits and black spirits engaged in battle, and the sun was darkened—the thunder rolled in the Heavens, and blood flowed in streams—and I heard a voice saying, 'Such is your luck, such you are called to see, and let it come rough or smooth, you must surely bear it.'" He interpreted drops on a field of corn as "the blood of Christ . . . shed on this earth . . . and now . . . returning to earth. . . . It was plain to me that . . . the great day of judgment was at hand." In 1831, seeing an eclipse of the sun as a sign to rebel, he led about 60 slaves in a revolt, the Southampton Insurrection, in which 55 whites were killed. The revolt failed, and Turner was hanged.

**Vesey, Denmark** (ca. 1767–July 2, 1822)
*revolutionary*
In 1781, a slave trader, Captain Vesey of Charleston, took this young slave aboard as part of his cargo at St. Thomas. Struck by the boy's attractiveness and intelligence, the ship's officers indulged him, dubbing him "Telemaque" (later corrupted into Denmark) Vesey sold him at San Domingo but on his next voyage received him back from his buyer, who complained that he had epilepsy. He served the captain faithfully

until 1800, when he bought his freedom with lottery winnings. As a free man, he supported himself as a carpenter in Charleston. His great strength and activity, and perhaps his allegedly despotic temperament, aroused awe in the slave community. In 1822, he was accused of incitement to insurrection and hanged.

**Walker, David** (September 28, 1785–June 28, 1830) *free black leader*
Born in North Carolina of a slave father and a free mother, as a youth Walker wandered through the South, directly observing the horrors of slavery. "If I remain in this bloody land," he said, "I will not live long. As true as God reigns, I will be avenged for the sorrow which my people have suffered. This is not the place for me—no, no. I must leave this part of the country. It will be a great trial for me to live on the same soil where so many men are in slavery; certainly I cannot remain where I must hear their chains continually, and where I must encounter the insults of their hypocritical enslavers. Go, I must!" In the 1820s, he settled in Boston, where he set himself up as a dealer in second-hand clothing. There he contributed time and money to help Boston's blacks—as an agent of the Underground Railroad, an organizer and lecturer for the General Colored Association of Massachusetts, and an agent for the black newspaper *Freedom's Journal*. In 1829 he wrote *Walker's Appeal, in Four Articles: Together with a Preamble to the Colored Citizens of the World, But in Particular, and Very Expressly to Those of the United States of America*. It deeply agitated southerners. The governor of Georgia asked the mayor of Boston to suppress the *Appeal*. When the mayor refused, a group of Georgians put a price on Walker's head. He died suddenly and mysteriously.

**Ward, Samuel Ringgold** (October 17, 1817–ca. 1866) *"the Black Daniel Webster"*
Born a slave in Maryland, Ward escaped with his parents when he was three. His oratorical gifts led to his working from 1839 as an agent of the American Anti-Slavery Society and later of the New York State Anti-Slavery Society. For several years he served as a pastor, in one case with an entirely white congregation. In 1846 he signed up with the Liberty Party, speaking throughout the North. After he helped a fugitive to escape, he fled to Canada, where as an agent of the Anti-Slavery Society of Canada he organized new branches, lectured, and worked among fugitives from American slavery. He raised money for them in Great Britain; a British Quaker whom he met there gave him 50 acres in Jamaica, where he spent the rest of his life.

**Weld, Theodore Dwight** (November 23, 1803–February 3, 1895) *abolitionist*
Beginning his life's work in 1825, Weld evangelized for two years in the "holy band" of Charles Finney. A gifted and charismatic young man, he attracted the attention of Lewis and Arthur Tappan and, most influentially, Charles Stuart. Stuart paid for his education, mentored him, and above all instilled in him a zeal for abolition, for which Weld labored from 1830 on.

Weld converted to this cause many who later led the American antislavery movement, including Lewis and Arthur Tappan, politicians Joshua R. Giddings and Edwin M. Stanton, the preacher Henry Ward Beecher, Harriett Beecher Stowe, the faculty of Western Reserve College, many Presbyterian clergy, and almost the entire student body of Lane Seminary, to which Weld himself belonged. When the seminary tried to repress their debates on slavery, Weld led an exodus of sympathetic students to Oberlin College. These students then, under Weld's tutelage, acted as agents for the newly founded American Anti-Slavery Society (AASS), bravely and effectively preaching emancipation as an act of benevolence in the face of mob violence. To this group of 30-odd the AASS in 1836 added another 40 agents, including Angelina and Sarah Grimké—all of whom Weld trained. After he strained his voice in speaking, Weld wrote pamphlet after pamphlet for the AASS and conducted a national campaign for antislavery petitions addressed to Congress. He and Angelina Grimké married in 1838.

He went on to advise Whig congressmen who were breaking with their party over the slavery issue. In 1843, Weld retired from public life. With the Grimkés, he put together *American Slavery as It Is,* an effort to condemn slavery through the words of slaveholders and other proslavery advocates.

Weld stood out among abolitionists in many ways—notably for his widespread influence and his genuine desire for equality among blacks and whites.

**Wheatley, Phillis** (ca. 1753–December 5, 1784) *black poet*
Kidnapped as a child in Senegal and brought to Boston in 1761, Wheatley was bought by merchant-

tailor John Wheatley and his wife. Impressed by her intelligence and bearing, the Wheatleys assigned her only light tasks and treated her almost as a daughter. The Wheatley's twin daughters, some ten years older, taught her to read and write English, which she quickly mastered. In her early teens she began writing poetry, celebrating the themes of learning, virtue, and redemption through Christ. In 1770 she became a member of the Old South Meeting House and started publishing poetry.

In 1773 the Wheatleys sent her abroad for her health, accompanied by their son. For five weeks she enjoyed a triumphal tour, during which a patron arranged for the publication of her only book, *Poems on Various Subjects, Religious and Moral.* Mrs. Wheatley's illness called her home.

After the deaths of both Mr. and Mrs. Wheatley, the family disintegrated, and Phyllis dropped from fame, except for a brief period in 1776 when her poem to George Washington was published. In 1778 she married a free black, John Peters. He failed in his duties as husband and father to the three children she bore him, two of whom soon died. She was forced to work in a cheap lodging house to support herself and the other child, but soon her health gave way. Mother and child died on December 5, 1784.

**Whittier, John Greenleaf** (December 17, 1807–September 7, 1892) *abolitionist poet*
Under the influence of William Lloyd Garrison, Whittier became an abolitionist in 1833. He immediately attended an antislavery convention in Philadelphia, and for the next 30 years devoted himself to writing poems on slavery. Despite the ostracism and physical attacks that his views evoked, he was elected to the Massachusetts legislature in 1835. His antislavery activities ranged from lecturing to lobbying to employment as an agent of the American Anti-Slavery Society (AASS). In 1838 a mob burned down the new Pennsylvania Hall during a woman's antislavery convention and destroyed the office of the paper that he was editing, the *Pennsylvania Freeman.*

Despite his friendship with Garrison, when the AASS split in 1840 he went with the dissidents who formed the American and Foreign Anti-Slavery Society. In 1842, the Liberty Party ran Whittier as its candidate for Congress, and in 1844 and 1845 it made him editor of its paper, in which he opposed the annexation of Texas. He continued his political activism into the 1870s, being influential in Charles Sumner's election to the Senate and helping to found the Republican Party. Nonetheless, today much of his reputation rests on his abolition poems.

**Woolman, John** (October 19, 1720–October 7, 1772) *Quaker minister, pioneer abolitionist, tailor*
Woolman focused his Quaker ministry against slavery, which he believed inconsistent with Christianity. Wherever he went, even in the centers of the slave trade in New Jersey and Rhode Island, he denounced it. Although he lived to see few fruits of these labors, his influence lingered among abolitionists, particularly through his 1774 *Journal* and his 1754 *Some Considerations on the Keeping of Negroes.*

**Wright, Frances** (September 6, 1795–December 13, 1852) *writer, reformer*
A Scot by birth, Wright attracted controversy in the United States through her appearances on the lecture platform. She devoted considerable passion and energy to black rights, in 1825 publishing *A Plan for the Gradual Abolition of Slavery in the United States without Danger of Loss to the Citizens of the South,* in which she urged that blacks be permitted to labor on public land to earn money to buy their freedom. Putting her money where her ideals were, she founded a model settlement based on this principle, purchasing 640 acres in Tennessee for the purpose. She named her plantation Nashoba and put in charge her sister, a Scottish overseer, and a mulatto New Orleans schoolteacher. Only one slaveholder accepted her invitation to cooperate, leaving there a pregnant slave and her five children. Wright bought other slaves, whom she settled there. Everything went wrong, from bad health on account of the climate, through the slaves' reluctance to work, to a scandal through which the colony got a reputation as a bastion of free love. By 1828, the colony was dilapidated and unworkable.

Undaunted, Wright transported the slaves to Haiti, freed them, and arranged for housing and jobs for them. She again published her proposal and launched an attack on racially segregated schools, organized religion, taboos on interracial sexual relations, and marriage. Despite the widespread condemnation she thus earned, she continued to promote her ideas, particularly on religion and education, becoming an important figure in the emerging labor movement.

**York** (ca. 1770–ca. 1832) *slave who accompanied the Lewis and Clark expedition*
The son of two slaves, Rose and Old York, in 1799 York was inherited by William Clark, who employed him as his own body servant. On the Lewis and Clark expedition of 1804 to 1806, York accompanied his master as a body servant but also acted as a member of the expedition. In the Lewis and Clark diaries he is mentioned as hunting and trading with the Indians for food. Legend has it that he also interpreted, but the evidence is shaky.

Perhaps his most important contribution to the expedition was the novelty he presented to the Indians, many of whom had never seen a black man before. They thought him something inexplicable, and therefore perhaps sacred or possessed of superhuman powers. The Flathead thought him a notable warrior, because their own victorious warriors proclaimed their triumphs by blackening themselves with charcoal. Frequently, the Indians tried to rub or wash off the black from his skin, a familiarity that York usually bore patiently.

After the expedition York remained in slavery for at least another five years, but in 1811 he and Clark fell out, and he was hired out to a master who treated him badly. Eventually he was freed. Things went awry for him, and he lost the little property he had been given.

# Appendix C
## Glossary

**asiento** The privilege to supply slaves to Spain's American colonies.

**barracoon** An enclosure in which slaves are temporarily detained in Africa.

**black trade** Trade in Africa with the native people rather than with the European factors.

**bound person** One who is indentured.

**cat** Cat-o'-nine-tails—a whip made of nine knotted cords attached to a handle.

**coffle,** or **kaffle** A train of slaves driven along together.

**colonization** Settling liberated slaves and other free blacks in communities, usually in places remote from their former American homes.

**comey,** or **coomey** Duty paid to an African king for the privilege of trading.

**commission merchant** Agent who disposed of a planter's crop and bought supplies not available near home. He sometimes also bought or sold slaves for the planter.

**contraband** A slave who sought refuge with or was impressed by the Union forces. The term came into use because the Union argued that in wartime it had a right to free or enroll the property of its enemies.

**dash** Present or bribe given to African authorities for their cooperation in slave trading.

***donatio causa mortis*** A gift made in contemplation of death, which the donor may revoke if he does not die as he expects.

**driver** *Slave driver* was used variously for a slave trader, a white overseer, or a black supervisor of field labor. A slave who supervised or policed field hands was also called by such terms as *foreman, overlooker, leading man, headman, boss, whipping boss, crew leader, overdriver, underdriver,* and *straw boss.*

**factor** Commission agent.

**fancy girls** Slave women, usually light skinned, used as concubines or prostitutes.

**free produce movement** An effort to avoid the use of the products of slave labor.

**gag rule** A congressional rule of 1836 that prevented abolitionist petitions from being introduced, read, or discussed in Congress.

**griffe** Offspring of a black person and a mulatto. *Griffe* was used especially in the Deep South, where the term *mulatto* was sometimes limited to the offspring of one white and one black person.

**hiring out** The practice by which a master either permitted his slave to work for someone else for a set sum of money or allowed a slave to negotiate an agreement to work for pay for someone else. In the latter case, far more common in cities than in the countryside, the slave usually paid the master a fixed sum each week and assumed responsibility for his or her own support.

**hushharbor** Secret slave church in the woods, the sounds from which were muffled by walls made of trees, brush, and wet blankets hung from branches.

**indenture** Contract by which an apprentice is bound to a master for a limited time period, sometimes with the promise of payment at the end of the term. Many Europeans indentured themselves for passage money to North America. Although they suffered some of the disadvantages of slaves, the law protected them against the worst abuses of slavery.

**insurrection** A rising up against established authority; an incipient or limited rebellion.

**intelligence** Often used, especially in defenses of slavery, to denote not inborn ability to learn and think but that ability as improved by education: thus whites were said to have superior intelligence because they had the leisure and the means to acquire education.

**intendant** A foreign official who supervises a certain district.

**jackson whites** Term for a racially mixed (black, white, and Indian) group along the New Jersey–New York state line, possibly descended from Algonquin Indians, Dutch and British settlers, and free blacks. *Jacks* was an 18th-century term for freed slaves.

**jump the broomstick** The most common irregular slave marriage ritual, in which the couple joined hands and steped or jumped over a broomstick. Another such ritual was *marriage by the blanket,* in which the woman laid her blanket alongside the man's.

**manumission** An exercise of the property holder's right to renounce ownership of his property—thus, a slaveholder's freeing of his slave.

**maroon** An escaped slave who joins with others to establish a colony where they can defend themselves and sometimes prey upon the surrounding countryside; or the colony itself. Synonymous with *outlyer.* Authorities variously ascribe the term as coming from a mountaintop, runaway slave, and hog hunter.

**mestizo** A person of mixed parentage, especially in the western United States, the offspring of a Spanish or Portuguese person and an American Indian.

**mulatto** Any person of mixed black and white ancestry.

**mustee** Any person of mixed black and American Indian blood.

**negro seamen laws** Laws enacted in several southern states providing that black crew members of any ship coming into port must be arrested and held in jail until their vessel left. The constitutionality of these laws was much debated.

**nullification** An extremist doctrine of states rights holding that a state could declare null and void any federal law it deems unconstitutional.

**outlyer** See **maroon.**

**outside children** Children born outside of wedlock; also *stolen children* or *children by the way.*

**patting or clapping juba** A slave creation, complex clapping patterns such as striking the hands on the knees, then striking the hands together, then striking the right shoulder with one hand, the left with the other, while keeping time with the feet and singing.

**pani (pawnee)** So many members of the Pawnee Indian tribe were enslaved that *pani* became a term for "Indian slave."

**perpetuanas** Coarse wool serges for trade with Africa.

**personal liberty laws** Laws enacted by many northern states to prevent kidnapping, in an effort to strike a balance between the rights of slaveholders and the rights of free blacks threatened by the Fugitive Slave Law of 1793.

**popular sovereignty** See SQUATTER SOVEREIGNTY.

**preemption** The act or right of buying land, etc., before, or in preference to, others; especially such a right granted to a settler on public land.

**refugeeing** Taking slaves to Texas to keep them out of the way of the advancing Union forces. The practice became common in late 1862 and continued through much of 1864.

**secret six** This group of respectable citizens—philanthropist Gerrit Smith; teacher of the blind Dr. Samuel Gridley Howe; wealthy manufacturer George L. Stearns; liberal clergyman and commanding officer of a Civil War black regiment, Rev. Thomas Wentworth Higginson; Franklin B. Sanborn, secretary of the Massachusetts Kansas Committee; and Unitarian clergyman Rev. Theodore Parker, reputedly the most learned man of his time—helped finance John Brown's insurrection, for that purpose diverting money and arms contributed to the Massachusetts-Kansas Aid Committee for peaceable purposes. Brown left behind at his Maryland farmhouse papers implicating many people, causing all of the Secret Six but Higginson to panic; some fled.

**sell a slave running** Sell a slave who has run away, usually for a low price, the buyer speculating that he may be able to capture the slave and make a profit.

**serf** A person tied to land and who owed labor service to a lord of that estate. Unlike a slave, a serf had rights to marry, establish a household, and hold property; the lord could not kill the serf with impunity.

**shake the lion's paw** Enter British territory; thus, for a slave, be freed.

**shout** A subdued form of dance, sometimes incorporated into worship; also called *dancing before the Lord*.

**soul driver** Slave trader.

**Southampton Insurrection** Nat Turner's rebellion of 1831.

**squatter sovereignty** The idea, first proposed in 1847, that the settlers of a territory, not the federal government, should decide whether a new state should be slave or free. Also known as *popular sovereignty.*

**statu liberi** A legal term used in Louisiana, applying to slaves legally promised freedom in the future.

**supercargo** Ship's officer in charge of cargo.

**ten percent men** Private English traders in Africa obliged to pay that duty to maintain the trading forts.

# NOTES

## 1. The West Coast of Africa: 1441–1866

1. 1854, quoted in Reynolds, *African Slavery,* 9.
2. Klein and Lovejoy, "Slavery in West Africa," 207.
3. See Miller, *Way of Death,* 39–51.
4. Bontemps, *Great Slave Narratives,* 12.
5. Miller, *Way of Death,* 94.
6. "As Jean Bazin has argued, a large percentage of those moved into trade at any time were probably already in slavery, that is to say, they were simply being reinslaved." Klein and Lovejoy, "Slavery in West Africa," 210.
7. *New York Times,* Connecticut section, September 20, 1998. See also the introduction in Reynolds, *Stand the Storm.*
8. Buckmaster, *Let My People Go,* 3.
9. Coughtry, *Notorious Triangle,* 18.
10. See, for instance, slave trader Capt. William Snelgrave, *A New Account of Some Parts of Guinea and the Slave Trade* (1734) in Dow, *Slave Ships,* xix–xxi.
11. Quoted in Dow, *Slave Ships,* 136–37.
12. Ibid., 9.
13. Donnan, *Slave Trade Documents* 1:284–85.
14. Pope-Hennessy, *Sins of the Fathers,* 264.
15. Quoted in Reynolds, *African Slavery,* 44–45.
16. Agent at Cape Coast, ca. 1700, in Davies, *Royal African Company,* 239.
17. 1704, quoted in Pope-Hennessy, *Sins of the Fathers,* 77.
18. Davies, *Royal African Company,* 217–18.
19. Pope-Hennessy, *Sins of the Fathers,* 234.
20. Donnan, *Slave Trade Documents* 2:213.
21. Coughtry, *Notorious Triangle,* 116.
22. A State of the Trade to Africa presented to the House of Commons by the Council of Trade, 1709, in Donnan, *Slave Trade Documents* 2:57.
23. Quoted in Wax, "Negro Resistance," 4.
24. Quoted in Rawley, *Transatlantic Slave Trade,* 294.
25. Miller, *Way of Death,* 661.
26. Quoted in Pope-Hennessy, *Sins of the Fathers,* 45.
27. Rawley, *Transatlantic Slave Trade,* 261.
28. *Revelations of a Slave Smuggler,* 1860, in Dow, *Slave Ships,* 212.
29. Howard, *American Slavers,* Appendix B, 224.
30. Introduction to Canot, *African Slaver,* ix–x.
31. Pope-Hennessy, *Sins of the Fathers,* 274.
32. Reynolds, *African Slavery,* 57; and Rawley, *Transatlantic Slave Trade,* 18.

## 2. The Middle Passage: 1500–1866

1. Donnan, *Slave Trade Documents* 1:141–42.
2. Quoted in Anstey, *Atlantic Slave Trade,* 13.
3. Rawley, *Transatlantic Slave Trade,* 293.
4. Bontemps, *Great Slave Narratives,* 28–29.
5. Donnan, *Slave Trade Documents* 1:459.
6. Bontemps, *Great Slave Narratives,* 27.
7. Quoted in Dow, *Slave Ships,* 144.
8. Quoted in Reynolds, *African Slavery,* 50–51.
9. Miller, *Way of Death,* 438.
10. Quoted in Dow, *Slave Ships,* 148.
11. John Weskett, *A Compete Digest of the Laws, Theory and Practice of Insurance* (1781), quoted in Reynolds, *African Slavery,* 50.
12. William Vernon to Capt. Grey, August 27, 1786, in Coughtry, *Notorious Triangle,* 147.
13. Miller, *Way of Death,* 409–10.
14. Harding, *River,* 22–23.
15. Quoted in Donnan, *Slave Trade Documents* 2:281–82.
16. Harding, *River,* 12.
17. Ibid., 20.
18. Wax, "Negro Resistance," 7.
19. Harding, *River,* 14.
20. Ibid., 20.
21. Donnan, *Slave Trade Documents* 1:406–10.
22. Blassingame, *Slave Community,* 8, and *Hartford Courant,* September 21, 1998.
23. Donnan, *Slave Trade Documents* 1:206–8.
24. Miller, *Way of Death,* 437–38.
25. Rawley, *Transatlantic Slave Trade,* 300–31.
26. Donnan, *Slave Trade Documents* 1:141–45 passim.
27. Quoted in Miller, *Way of Death,* 426.
28. Donnan, *Slave Trade Documents* 1:459.
29. Coughtry, *Notorious Triangle,* 98–99.
30. Rawley, *Transatlantic Slave Trade,* 294.
31. *Hartford Courant,* September 21, 1998.

## 3. Americans in the Slave Trade: 1526–1865

1. Higginbotham, *In the Matter of Color,* 20f.; and Buckmaster, *Let My People Go,* 3.
2. Owens, *Property,* 7–9.
3. Bancroft, *Slave Trading,* 2; and Owens, *Property,* 7–9.
4. Alford, *Prince among Slaves,* 131.
5. Quoted in Wax, "Preferences for Slaves," 377.
6. Coffin, *Reminiscences,* x–xi.
7. Mannix, *Black Cargoes,* 202, 203.
8. Oakes, *Ruling Race,* 230f.
9. Littlefield, *Rice and Slaves,* 65.
10. Higginbotham, *In the Matter of Color,* 5, 45, 120–21.
11. Quoted in Bancroft, *Slave Trading,* 69.
12. Quoted in Catterell, *Judicial Cases* 1:215.
13. Quoted in Rawick, *The American Slave* 1:173.
14. Quoted in Bancroft, *Slave Trading,* 81, n. 36.
15. Quoted in Oakes, *Ruling Race,* 61–62.
16. Olmstead, *Cotton Kingdom* 1:14.
17. Quoted in Tadman, *Speculators and Slaves,* 106.
18. Quoted in Bancroft, *Slave Trading,* 363–64.
19. Quoted in Tadman, *Speculators and Slaves,* 85.
20. Ibid., 88.
21. Higginbotham, *In the Matter of Color,* 53.
22. Higginbotham, *In the Matter of Color,* 211–12.
23. *Appeal to the Christian Women of the South* (1836), in Dumond, *Antislavery,* 192.
24. Higginbotham, *In the Matter of Color,* 113–17, passim.
25. Quoted in Tadman, *Speculators and Slaves,* 75.
26. Quoted in *Slave Testimony,* 704–6.
27. Bancroft, *Slave Trading,* 204.
28. Phillips, *American Negro Slavery,* 189, 191.
29. Quoted in Goodell, *Slave Code,* 54.
30. Phillips, *American Negro Slavery,* 381–82.
31. Quoted in Bracey, *American Slavery,* 17.
32. Blassingame, *Slave Testimony,* 403.
33. Murray, *Proud Shoes,* 97.
34. Quoted in Bancroft, *Slave Trading,* 322.
35. Ibid, 217.
36. Tadman, *Speculators and Slaves,* 101.
37. Ibid., 167.
38. Kay and Cary, *Slavery in North Carolina,* 204.
39. Botkin, *Lay My Burden Down,* 184–85.
40. Aptheker, *Documentary History of the Negro People in the United States,* 126.
41. Oakes, *Ruling Race,* 118.
42. Torrey, *American Slave Trade,* 43–44, n.
43. Wheeler, *Law of Slavery,* 385–86, 306.
44. Crowe, *With Thackeray in America,* 105.
45. Clinton, *Plantation Mistress,* 213.
46. Fehrenbacher, *Dred Scott Case,* 30.
47. Ibid., 31.

## 4. Slave Life: 1619–1865

1. Owens, *Property,* 7–9.
2. Tadman, *Speculators and Slaves,* 159; Fox-Genovese, *Plantation Mistress,* 295.
3. Thomas, *Secret Eye,* 3, n. 6.
4. *Narrative,* 50.
5. Olmsted, *Cotton Kingdom,* 480.
6. Ibid., 80–81.
7. White, *Ar'n't I a Woman?* 83, 84.
8. Kemble, *Journal,* 67–68.
9. Olmsted, *Cotton Kingdom,* 95.
10. Bell, *Major Butler's Legacy,* 156.
11. Allen Brown, letter of December 7, 1834, in Owens, *Property,* 46.
12. Mattie Fannen, in Fox-Genovese, *Plantation Household,* 147.
13. *Narrative,* 13.
14. Dumond, *Antislavery,* 347–48.
15. Gutman, *Black Family,* 275, 276.
16. Ibid., 137.
17. Johnson, *God Struck Me Dead,* 156–57.
18. Kemble, *Journal,* 247–48.
19. Ibid., 245–46.
20. Gutman, *Black Family,* 66–73 passim.
21. Phillips, *American Negro Slavery,* 264–65.
22. Fox-Genovese, *Plantation Households,* 324.
23. Kemble, *Journal,* 240–41.
24. Angelina Grimké, in Goodell, *Slave Code,* 117.
25. Blassingname, *Slave Testimony,* 594.
26. White, *Ar'n't I a Woman?* 89.
27. *Excursion,* 204.
28. Fox-Genovese, *Plantation Household,* 9.
29. Kemble, *Journal,* 10–11.
30. Olmstead, *Cotton Kingdom,* 475, n. 1.
31. Johnston, *Race Relations,* 255.
32. Olmstead, *Cotton Kingdom,* 329.
33. Williams, *History of the Negro Race,* 35–36.
34. Fox-Genovese, *Plantation Household,* 134.
35. Kemble, *Journal,* 159.
36. Fox-Genovese, Johnston, *Race Relations,* 244–45.
37. *Plantation Household,* 315.
38. Berlin, *Freedom* 1, 3:7.
39. Kemble, *Journal,* 314.
40. Blassingame, *Slave Community,* 63.
41. Lambert, "I Saw the Book Talk," 195.
42. Johnson, *God Struck Me Dead,* ix.
43. Raboteau, *Slave Religion,* 8.
44. Ibid., 311–12.
45. Ibid., 67.
46. Botkin, *Lay My Burden Down,* 36–37.
47. Owens, *Property,* 142.
47. Botkin, *Lay My Burden Down,* 22–23.

## 5. Slave Work: 1619–1865

1. Fox-Genovese, *Plantation Household,* 165.
2. Rawick, *American Slave,* Alabama.
3. Kemble, *Journal,* 279.
4. Fox-Genovese, *Plantation Household,* 137.
5. Owens, *Property,* 118.
6. Ibid., 109.
7. Olmstead, *Cotton Kingdom,* 187.
8. Bell, *Major Butler's Legacy,* 116.
9. Owens, *Property,* 181.
10. Yancy, "The Stuart Double Plow," 48.
11. Kemble, *Journal,* 188.
12. Fox-Genovese, *Plantation Households,* 176.
13. Jordan, *Tumult and Silence,* 193.
14. Bell, *Major Butler's Legacy,* 146.
15. Olmsted, *Cotton Kingdom,* 192–94.
16. Bell, *Major Butler's Legacy,* 154.
17. Fogel and Engerman say that "only 30 percent of plantations with one hundred or more slaves employed white overseers." *Time on the Cross,* 211.
18. Blassingame, *Slave Community,* 173, 176.
19. Douglas, *Narrative,* 39–40.
20. Blassingame, *Slave Community,* 177.
21. Olmstead, *Cotton Kingdom,* 187, 188.
22. Fox-Genovese, *Plantation Households,* 186.
23. Gutman, *Black Family,* 77–78.
24. Murray, *Proud Shoes,* 39.
25. Campbell, *Empire,* 125.
26. Redpath, *Roving Editor,* 124–26.
27. Starobin, *Industrial Slavery,* 200–1.
28. Olmsted, *Cotton Kingdom,* 426–27.
29. Douglas, *Narrative,* 70.
30. Bontemps, *Great Slave Narratives,* 208–9.
31. Owens, *Property,* 168.
32. Miller, *Dictionary of Afro-American Slavery,* 322.
33. Olmsted, *Cotton Kingdom,* 40.
34. Starobin, *Industrial Slavery,* 53.
35. Olmsted, *Cotton Kingdom,* 114–15.
36. Kay and Cary, *Slavery in North Carolina,* 49.
37. Wheeler, *Law of Slavery,* 447–48.
38. Olmstead, *Cotton Kingdom,* 75.
39. Trexler, *Slavery in Missouri,* 178.
40. Myers, *Children of Pride,* 241.
41. Starobin, *Industrial Slavery,* 209–10.
42. Lewis, *Coal, Iron, and Slaves,* 227.
43. Bancroft, *Slave Trading,* 146.
44. Miller, *Dictionary of Afro-American Slavery,* 321, 323.
45. Casterby, *South Carolina Rice Plantation,* 350.
46. Fogel and Engerman, *Time on the Cross,* 149.
47. *Four Fugitive Slave Narratives,* 62.

## 6. Runaways: 1619–1865

1. Botkin, *Lay My Burden Down,* 179–80.
2. Redpath, *Roving Editor,* 40–41.
3. Letter, Anne Winchester Penniman collection.
4. Phillips, *American Negro Slavery,* 286.
5. Kemble, *Journal,* 344.
6. Siebert, *Underground Railroad,* 237, 340–42.
7. Gutman, *Black Family,* 267.
8. Siebert, *Underground Railroad,* 161–62.
9. *Four Fugitive Slave Narratives,* 190.
10. Botkin, *Lay My Burden Down,* 186–89.
11. Siebert, *Underground Railroad,* 90.
12. Ibid., 105–6.
13. *Troy Whig,* April 28, 1859, quoted in Bradford, *Harriet,* 143–49.

## 7. Canada, Other Refuges, and the Colonization/Emigration Movement: 1501–1865

1. Winks, *Blacks in Canada,* 9, 10. Professor Winks's excellent and readable book is the standard work on the subject; we draw on it for the figures cited herein.
2. Walker, *Black Loyalists,* 18ff.
3. Winks, *Blacks in Canada,* 33.
4. Grant, "Black Immigrants into Nova Scotia," 255.
5. Winks, *Blacks in Canada,* 115.
6. Howe, *Refugee,* 69–70.
7. No reliable estimate of the total number of blacks who emigrated to Canada exists or can be made. Dumond, *Anti-Slavery,* 336, surveys a number of estimates: The American Anti-Slavery Society investigation of 1837 showed 10,000 blacks in Upper Canada. Missionaries Isaac Rice and Hiram Wilson placed the number in Upper Canada (essentially Ontario, so-called until 1841) in 1850 at 20,000. Samuel J. May agreed, but William Wells Brown claimed 25,000. Rev. William Mitchell, a Canadian black missionary, estimated that at least 1,200 fugitives reached Toronto and its area every year. Levi Coffin estimated 40,000 in the whole of Canada in 1844. Within three months after the Fugitive Slave Act of 1850 passed, at least 3,000 reached Canada. By 1860 there were 60,000 blacks in Upper Canada alone, of whom 45,000 were fugitive slaves. Winks, *Blacks in Canada,* 176 and 240.
8. Blassingame, *Slave Testimony,* 164.
9. Delany, *Condition,* 178, 181.
10. Of its first 18 expeditions after its start in 1820, the American Colonization Society reported in 1832 that it transported 1,487 emigrants, of whom 230 died. For the year 1853 it had worked up to only 782. Fox, *American Colonization Society,* 56, and Williams, *History of the Negro Race,* 98.

## 8. Rebels: 1526–1865

1. Carroll, *Slave Insurrections,* 103–4.
2. Campbell, *Empire,* 225–26.
3. Roger B. Taney, quoted in Desmond, *Antislavery,* 144.
4. Wheeler, *Law of Slavery,* 212–13.
5. Finkelman, *Law of Freedom,* 200.
6. White, *Ar'n't I a Woman?* 152.
7. Finkelman, *Law of Freedom,* 195.
8. Ibid., 199.
9. Ibid., 261.
10. Charlotte Foster, in Fox-Genovese, *Plantation Households,* 329.
11. Bracey, *American Slavery,* 55.
12. Douglas, *Narrative,* 81–83.
13. Mullin, *Flight and Rebellion,* 58–59.
14. Harding, *River,* 198–99.
15. Fox-Genovese, *Plantation Households,* 314.
16. Johnston, *Race Relations,* 21–22.
17. McLaurin, *Celia,* 86.
18. Owens, *Property,* 5.
19. Hine, *Black Women in American History* 3:989.
20. Coffin, *Reminiscences,* 95.
21. Faust, *Mothers of Invention,* 59–60.
22. Kemble, *Journal,* 39.
23. Tise, *Proslavery,* 319–20.
24. Williams, *History of the Negro Race,* 227.
25. Fox-Genovese, *Plantation Households,* 303.
26. Newspaper account quoted in Aptheker, *One Continual Cry,* 86–87.
27. Starobin, *Industrial Slavery,* 90.
28. Porter, *Negro on the American Frontier,* 381.
29. Carroll, *Slave Insurrections,* 90.
30. "The Vesey Plot: A Reconsideration," in Bracey, *American Slavery,* 131.
31. Nat Turner's statement while a prisoner, in Aptheker, *A Documentary History of the Negro People in the United States,* 120, 123–24.
32. Starobin, *Industrial Slavery,* 115.
33. Aptheker, *American Negro Slave Revolts,* 163.
34. Aptheker, "Additional Data on American Maroons," 452.
35. Dumond, *Antislavery,* 368.

## 9. Indians as Slaves, as Friends and Enemies of Black Slaves, and as Slaveholders: 1529–1865

1. Lauber, *Indian Slavery,* 311.
2. Olexer, *Enslavement of the American Indian,* 172.
3. Morris, *Southern Slavery,* 19.
4. Catterall, *Judicial Cases concerning Slavery* 4:455.
5. Phillips, *American Negro Slavery,* 102.
6. Olexer, *Enslavement of the American Indian,* 199–200.
7. Morgan, *American Slavery, American Freedom,* 328–29.
8. Olexer, *Enslavement of the American Indian,* 116.
9. Lauber, *Indian Slavery,* 121.
10. Olexer, *Enslavement of the American Indian,* 109.
11. Ibid., 195–96.
12. Blassingame, *Slave Testimony,* 698.
13. Ibid., 238.
14. Webre, "The Problem of Indian Slavery," in *Louisiana History* 25: 119.
15. Porter, *Negro on the American Frontier,* 13.
16. Peter Kalm, *Travels into North America,* quoted in Porter, *Negro on the American Frontier,* 21.
17. Porter, *Negro on the American Frontier,* 34–35.
18. Johnston, *Race Relations,* 285.
19. Porter, *Negro on the American Frontier,* 70–71.
20. Strother, *Underground Railroad in Connecticut,* 19.
21. Porter, *Negro on the American Frontier,* 377–78.
22. Blassingame, *Slave Testimony,* 321–23.
23. Porter, *Negro on the American Frontier,* 172.
24. Ibid., 105.
25. Miller, *Dictionary of Afro-American Slavery* 1:435.
26. Perdue, *Slavery and Cherokee Society,* 40.
27. Ibid., 78.
28. Oakes, *Ruling Race,* 45ff.
29. Blassingame, *Slave Community,* 121.
30. Genovese, *From Rebellion to Revolution,* 74.
31. Botkin, *Lay My Burden Down,* 130.
32. Perdue, *Slavery and Cherokee Society,* 81.
33. Porter, *Negro on the American Frontier,* 117.
34. Botkin, *Lay My Burden Down,* 130–35.

## 10. The Argument over Slavery: 1637–1865

1. Coffin, *Reminiscences,* xi.
2. *New Travels in the United States of America,* quoted in Kates, "Abolition, Deportation, Integration," 38.
3. *Democracy in America,* 360.
4. *Philadelphia Perspective,* 210–11.
5. Owens, *Property,* 3.
6. Bancroft, *Slave Trading,* 7.
7. Campbell, *Empire,* 3.
8. Buckmaster, *Let My People Go,* 64.
9. Oakes, *Ruling Race,* 134.
10. Bontemps, *Great Slave Narratives,* 323.
11. Locke, *Anti-Slavery,* 59–60.
12. Ibid, 172–73.
13. Redpath, *Roving Editor,* 96–97.
14. Williams, *History of the Negro Race* 1:211–12.
15. Letter in the Anne Winchester Penniman collection.
16. Berwanger, *Frontier against Slavery,* 125–26.
17. Kraditor, *American Abolitionism,* 197.
18. Harding, *River,* 127.
19. Ibid., 139.
20. Ibid., 203.
21. Ibid., 152.

22. Quarles, *Negro in the American Revolution,* 38.
23. Ibid., 44.
24. *Philadelphia Perspective,* 306–7.
25. Dumond, *Antislavery,* 206.
26. Williams, *History of the Negro Race* 1:432.
27. Blake, *Slavery and the Slave Trade,* 526.
28. Kraditor, *American Abolitionism,* 233, n. 91.
29. Ibid., 233, n. 95.
30. Blake, *Slavery and the Slave Trade,* 669.
31. Ibid., 678.
32. Ira Berlin, New Forum chat room, April 1999.

## 11. Black Soldiers in America's Wars: 1635-1865

1. Kay and Cary, *Slavery in North Carolina,* 60.
2. Wilson, *Black Phalanx,* 26; Williams, *History* 1:194–95.
3. Quarles, *Negro in the American Revolution,* 8.
4. Higginbotham, *In the Matter of Color,* 222.
5. Porter, *Negro on the American Frontier,* 158.
6. Quarles, *Negro in the American Revolution,* 12.
7. Ibid., 9.
8. Dumond, *Antislavery,* 111, and Quarles, *Negro in the American Revolution,* 52.
9. Quarles, *Negro in the American Revolution,* 86–88. See also Aptheker, "Negro in the Union Navy," 170. On the creation of American navies, see Richard Buel Jr., *In Irons,* ch. 4.
10. Quarles, *Negro in the American Revolution,* 95.
11. Ibid., 27–29.
12. Ball, *Slaves in the Family,* 229–30.
13. Walker, *Black Loyalists,* 8.
14. Ibid., 3–4.
15. *Revolution Remembered,* 26. Ironically, Grant's master was a Tory.
16. Wesley, *In Freedom's Footsteps,* 146.
17. Wilson, *Black Phalanx,* 80.
18. Ibid., 83.
19. Williams, *History* 2:23, and Wesley, *In Freedom's Footsteps,* 148.
20. Aptheker, "The Negro in the Union Navy," 171.
21. Wesley, *In Freedom's Footsteps,* 149–50.
22. Walker, *Black Loyalists,* 389.
23. Porter, *Negro on the American Frontier,* 223–62.
24. Wilson, *Black Phalanx,* 104.
25. Ibid., 112.
26. Herbert Aptheker estimates that some 500,000 slaves escaped or came into the Union lines during the war. McPherson, *Negro's Civil War,* 56.
27. Porter, *The Negro on the American Frontier,* 467; Cornish, *Sable Arm,* ch. 4.
28. Cornish, *Sable Arm,* 92.
29. Hollandsworth, *Louisiana Native Guards,* 13–14.
30. No one knows how many of these early black soldiers were contrabands. General Butler's claim that his black troops were all free avoided political problems, but Wilson, *Black Phalanx,* 95, estimates that more than half were fugitives. In other cases a policy of "don't ask, don't tell" obscures the record. Cornish, *Sable Arm,* 66.
31. Quarles, *Negro in the Civil War,* 184–85.
32. Ibid., 186–88.
33. Ibid., 191.
34. Winks, *Blacks in Canada,* 152.
35. Harding, *River,* 249–50.
36. Quarles, *Negro in the Civil War,* 199.
37. McPherson, *Negro's Civil War,* 205.
38. Ibid., 335–36, n. 7; and Cornish, *Sable Arm,* ch. 9.
39. Roca, "Presence and Precedents," 94–95, 105–7.
40. McPherson, *Negro's Civil War,* 160.
41. Quarles, *Negro in the Civil War,* 230–32.
42. Aptheker, "The Negro in the Union Navy," 188.
43. Quarles, *Negro in the Civil War,* 38. See above: The Louisiana Native Guards had remained in New Orleans after the Confederates were driven out and fought for the Union under the command of General Benjamin Butler.
44. Nelson, "Confederate Slave Impressment, 392–410.
45. Berlin, *Freedom* 1:664.
46. Ibid. 1:679.
47. Berlin, *Freedom,* 1:675.

## 12. The End of Slavery: 1863–1865

1. Faust, *Mothers of Invention,* 30.
2. Thomas Hamilton, quoted in Harding, *River,* 225.
3. Botkin, *Lay My Burden Down,* 124.
4. Franklin, *Emancipation Proclamation,* 82.
5. Berlin, *Free at Last,* 349.
6. *My Story of the War,* 350.
7. Johnson, *God Struck Me Dead,* 117.
8. Brown, *American Rebellion,* 144–45.
9. *Reminiscences,* 355.
10. Ibid., 356–57.
11. Berlin, *Free at Last,* 189.
12. Raboteau, *Slave Religion,* 320.
13. *Civil War Memoirs,* 52.
14. *A Woman's Life-Work,* 360–61.
15. Berlin, *Free at Last,* 331, n.
16. Buckmaster, *Let My People Go,* xvii.
17. Berlin, *Free at Last,* 537.
18. Ibid., 523.
19. Ibid., 417–18.
20. *Freedmen's Book,* 270–72.
21. Faust, *Mothers of Invention,* 32.
22. Myers, *Children of Pride,* 939–40.
23. Jordan, *Tumult and Silence,* Document K, 324.
24. Botkin, *Lay My Burden Down,* 238–39.
25. Ibid., 218.
26. Campbell, *Empire,* 238.

27. Confederate president Jefferson Davis, November 7, 1864, message to the Confederate Congress, in Durden, *Gray and the Black,* 102–3.
28. Faust, *Mothers of Invention,* 73–74.
29. Ibid., 58.
30. Myers, *Children of Pride,* 1267.

# BIBLIOGRAPHY


Abel, Annie Heloise. *The Slaveholding Indians.* 3 vols. Cleveland, Ohio: A. H. Clark, 1915–25.

———. *The American Indian as Slaveholder and Secessionist.* Lincoln: University of Nebraska Press, 1992 [1915].

Achates. *Reflections Occasioned by the Late Disturbances in Charleston.* 1822. In *Slave Insurrections: Selected Documents.* Westport, Conn.: Negro Universities Press, 1970 [1822, 1860].

Adams, John Quincy. *Memoirs.* Ed. Charles Francis Adams. 12 vols. Freeport, N.Y.: Books for Libraries Press, 1959 [1874–77].

Alford, Terry. *Prince among Slaves.* New York: Harcourt Brace Jovanovich, 1977.

Andrews, Ethan Allen. *Slavery and the Domestic Slave Trade in the United States.* Freeport, N.Y.: Books for Libraries Press, 1971 [1836].

Andrews, William L., ed. *Sisters of the Spirit: Three Black Women's Autobiographies of the Nineteenth Century.* Bloomington: Indiana University Press, 1986.

Anstey, Roger T. *The Atlantic Slave Trade and British Abolition, 1760–1810.* Atlantic Highlands, N.J.: Humanities Press, 1975.

Aptheker, Herbert. "Additional Data on American Maroons." *Journal of Negro History* 32 (1947): 452–60.

———. *"One Continual Cry": David Walker's Appeal to the Colored Citizens of the World (1829–1830).* New York: Humanities Press, 1965.

———. *A Documentary History of the Negro People in the United States.* New York: Citadel, 1994 [1951].

———. "The Negro in the Union Navy." *Journal of Negro History* 32 (1947): 171ff.

———. *American Negro Slave Revolts.* New York: International, 1943.

———. "Maroons within the Present Limits of the United States." *Journal of Negro History* 24 (1939): 167–84.

Aptheker, Herbert, ed. *A Documentary History of the Negro People in the United States.* 2 vols. New York: Citadel, 1990 [1951].

Bacon, Thomas. *Sermons Addressed to Masters and Servants, Published in the Year 1734.* Winchester, Va., 1813.

Baily, Marilyn. "From Cincinnati, Ohio to Wilberforce, Canada: A Note on Antebellum Colonization." *Journal of Negro History* 58 (1973): 427–40.

Ball, Edward. *Slaves in the Family.* New York: Farrar, Straus & Giroux, 1998.

Ballenger, Seale. *Hell's Bells: A Tribute to the Spitfires, Bad Seeds, & Steel Magnolias of the New and Old South.* Berkeley, Calif.: Conari, 1997.

Bancroft, Frederic. *Slave Trading in the Old South.* New York: Frederick Ungar, 1931.

Bauer, Raymond A., and Alice H. Bauer. "Day to Day Resistance to Slavery." *Journal of Negro History* 27 (1942): 388–419.

Beale, Jane Howison. *The Journal of Jane Howison Beale of Fredericksburg, Virginia, 1850–1862.* Fredericksburg, Va.: Historic Fredericksburg Foundation, 1979.

Bell, Howard H. "Negro Nationalism: A Factor in Emigration Projects, 1858–1861." *Journal of Negro History* 28 (1962): 42–53.

Bell, Malcolm, Jr. *Major Butler's Legacy: Five Generations of a Slaveholding Family.* Athens: University of Georgia Press, 1987.

Bellamy, Donnie D. "The Legal Status of Black Georgians during the Colonial and Revolutionary Eras." *Journal of Negro History* 74 (1989): 1–10.

Berlin, Ira. "After Nat Turner: A Letter from the North." *Journal of Negro History* 55, (1970): 144–50.

———. *Many Thousands Gone: The First Two Centuries of Slavery in North America.* Cambridge, Mass.: Harvard University Press, 1998.

———. *Slaves without Masters: The Free Negro in the Antebellum South.* New York: Random House, 1974.

Berlin, Ira, et al., eds. *Freedom: A Documentary History of Emancipation, 1861–67,* Series 1 and 2. New York: Cambridge University Press, 1985.

———. *Free at Last: A Documentary History of Slavery, Freedom, and the Civil War.* New York: New Press, 1992.

Berwanger, Eugene. *The Frontier against Slavery: Western Anti-Negro Prejudice and the Slavery Extension Controversy.* Urbana: University of Illinois Press, 1967.

Betts, Robert B. *In Search of York: The Slave Who Went to the Pacific with Lewis and Clark.* Boulder: Colorado Associated University Press, 1985.

Beverly, Robert. *The History of Virginia in Four Parts.* 2nd ed. London, 1722.

Bibb, Henry. *Narrative of the Life and Adventures of Henry Bibb.* In *Puttin' on Ole Massa.* Edited by Gilbert Osofsky. New York: Harper and Row, 1969.

Billington, Monroe Lee, and Roger D. Hardaway. *African Americans on the Western Frontier.* Boulder: University Press of Colorado, 1998.

Black, Frederick R. "Benjamin Drew's Refugee and the Black Family." *Journal of Negro History* 57 (1972): 284–89.

Blackett, R. J. M. *Building an Antislavery Wall: Black Americans in the Atlantic Abolitionist Movement, 1830–1860.* Baton Rouge: Louisiana State University Press, 1983.

Blake, W. O. *The History of Slavery and the Slave Trade.* Columbus, Ohio: J. H. Miller, 1858.

Blane, William N. *An Excursion through the United States and Canada during the Years 1822–1823.* New York: Negro University Press, 1969 [1824].

Blassingame, John W. "The Planter on the Couch: Earle Thrope and the Psychodynamics of Slavery." *Journal of Negro History* 60 (1975), 320–31.

———. *The Slave Community: Plantation Life in the Antebellum South.* New York: Oxford University Press, 1972.

Blassingame, John W., ed. *Slave Testimony: Two Centuries of Letters, Speeches, Interviews, and Autobiographies.* Baton Rouge: Louisiana State University Press, 1977.

Bogin, Ruth. "Sarah Parker Remond: Black Abolitionist from Salem." In *Black Women in American History,* edited by Darlene Clark Hine. Vol. 1, 135–66. Brooklyn, N.Y.: Carlson, 1990.

Bontemps, Arna. *Five Black Lives,* ed. Middletown, Conn.: Wesleyan University Press 1971.

———. *Great Slave Narratives.* Boston: Beacon, 1969.

Botkin, B. A., ed. *Lay My Burden Down: A Folk History of Slavery.* Chicago: University of Chicago Press, 1945.

Boxer, Charles R. *The Portuguese Seaborne Empire, 1415–1825.* New York: Knopf, 1969.

———. *The Golden Age of Brazil, 1695–1750.* Berkeley: University of California Press, 1962.

Bracey, John, August Meirer, and Elliott Rudwick, eds. *American Slavery: The Question of Resistance.* Belmont, Calif.: Wadsworth, 1971.

Bradford, Sarah H. *Harriet Tubman: The Moses of Her People.* 2nd ed. New York: Corinth, 1994 [1886].

Brown, William Wells. *Narrative of William W. Brown, a Fugitive Slave.* In *Four Fugitive Slave Narratives.* Reading, Mass.: Addison Wesley, 1969.

———. *The Negro in the American Rebellion: His Heroism and His Fidelity.* New York: Citadel, 1971 [1867].

Bruce, Dickson D., Jr. *Archibald Grimke: Portrait of a Black Independent.* Baton Rouge: Louisiana State University Press, 1993.

Buckingham, J. S. *The Slave States of America.* 2 vols. New York, 1968 [1842].

Buckmaster, Henrietta. *Let My People Go: The Story of the Underground Railroad and the Growth of the Abolition Movement.* Columbia: University of South Carolina Press, 1992 [1941].

Burchard, Peter. *One Gallant Rush: Robert Gould Shaw and His Brave Black Regiment.* New York: St. Martin's, 1965.

Campbell, Randolph B. *An Empire for Slavery: The Peculiar Institution in Texas, 1821–1865.* Baton Rouge: Louisiana State University Press, 1989.

Campbell, Stanley W. *The Slave Catchers: Enforcement of the Fugitive Slave Law, 1850–1860.* New York: W. W. Norton, 1972 [1968].

Canot, Theodore. *Adventures of an African Slaver.* New York: Dover, 1969 [1854].

Carroll, John M., ed. *The Black Military Experience in the American Midwest.* New York: Liveright, 1971.

Carroll, Joseph Cephas. *Slave Insurrections in the United States, 1800–1865.* New York: New American Library, 1938.

Cassell, Frank A. "Slaves of the Chesapeake Bay Area and the War of 1812." *Journal of Negro History* 57 (1972): 144–55.

Castel, Albert. "Civil War Kansas and the Negro." *Journal of Negro History* 51 (1966): 125–38.

Caswall, Henry. "The Western World Revisited, 1854." In "Documents," *Journal of Negro History* 2 (1917): 184–85.

Catterall, Helen T., ed. *Judicial Cases concerning American Slavery and the Negro.* 5 vols. New York: Octagon, 1968.

Chesnut, Mary. *Mary Chesnut's Civil War.* Edited by C. Vann Woodward. New Haven, Conn.: Yale University Press, 1981.

———. *The Private Mary Chesnut: The Unpublished Civil War Diaries.* Edited by C. Vann Woodward and Elisabeth Muhlenfeld. New York: Oxford University Press, 1984.

Child, Lydia Maria. *An Appeal in Favor of That Class of Americans Called Africans.* New York: Arno and the *New York Times,* 1968 [1836].

———. *The Freedmen's Book.* New York: Arno and the *New York Times,* 1968 [1865].

Clinton, Catherine. "Caught in the Web of the Big House: Women and Slavery." In *The Web of Southern Relations: Women, Family and Education,* edited by Walter J. Fraser Jr., R. Frank Saunders Jr., and Jon L. Wakelyn, Athens: University of Georgia Press, 1985.

———. *The Plantation Mistress: Woman's World in the Old South.* New York: Pantheon, 1982.

Cobb, Thomas R. R. *An Inquiry into the Law of Negro Slavery in the United States of America to Which Is Prefixed an Historical Sketch of Slavery.* New York: Negro University Press, 1968 [1858].

Coffin, Joshua, ed. *An Account of the Principal Slave Insurrections.* In *Slave Insurrections, Selected Documents.* New York: Westport, Conn.: Negro Universities Press, 1970 [1822, 1860].

Coffin, Levi. *Reminiscences of Levi Coffin: The Reputed President of the Underground Railroad.* Edited by Ben Richmond. Richmond, Ind.: Friends United Press, 1991 [1876].

Cole, Johnetta. "Militant Black Women in Early United States History." In *Black Women in American History,* edited by Darlene Clark Hine, Vol. 1, 261–67. Brooklyn, N.Y.: Carlson, 1990.

Connor, Sam. "Cleburne and the Unthinkable," *Civil War Times* (February 1998): 45–47.

Cornish, Dudley T. *The Sable Arm: Black Troops in the Union Army, 1861–1865.* Lawrence: University Press of Kansas, 1987.

Cott, Nancy F., ed. *Roots of Bitterness: Documents of the Social History of American Women.* New York: Dutton, 1972.

Coughtry, Jay. *The Notorious Triangle: Rhode Island and the African Slave Trade, 1700–1807.* Philadelphia: Temple University Press, 1981.

Craft, William and Ellen. *Running a Thousand Miles for Freedom, or, The Escape of William and Ellen Craft from Slavery.* In *Great Slave Narratives,* edited by Arna Bontemps. Boston: Beacon, 1969 [1860].

Crowe, Eyre. *With Thackeray in America.* New York: Scribner's, 1893.

Crow, Jeffrey J., and Larry E. Tise, eds. *The Southern Experience in the American Revolution.* Chapel Hill: University of North Carolina Press, 1978.

Culpepper, Marilyn M. *Trials & Triumphs: Women of the American Civil War.* East Lansing: Michigan State University Press, 1991.

Cunningham, Constance A. "Sin of Omission: Black Women in 19th Century American History." In *Black Women in American History,* edited by Darlene Clark Hine, Vol. 1. Brooklyn, N.Y.: Carlson, 1990, 275–86.

Curtin, Phillip. *The Atlantic Slave Trade: A Census.* Madison: University of Wisconsin Press, 1969.

Curtin, Phillip D., ed. *Africa Remembered: Narratives by West Africans from the Era of the Slave Trade.* Madison: University of Wisconsin Press, 1967.

Dann, John C., ed. *The Revolution Remembered: Eyewitness Accounts of the War for Independence.* Chicago: University of Chicago Press, 1980.

Davidson, Basil. *The African Slave Trade: Precolonial.* Boston: Little, Brown, 1961.

Davies, K. G. *The Royal African Company.* New York: Octagon, 1975.

Davis, Charles T., and Henry Louis Gates Jr., ed. *The Slave's Narrative.* New York: Oxford University Press, 1985.

Davis, Edwin Adams. *Plantation Life in the Florida Parishes of Louisiana, 1836–1846, as Reflected in the Diary of Bennet H. Barrow.* New York: Columbia University Press, 1943.

Davis, Thomas J. "The New York Slave Conspiracy of 1741 as Black Protest." *Journal of Negro History* 56 (1971): 17–30.

de Crevecoeur, J. Hector St. John. *Letters from an American Farmer and Sketches of Eighteenth-Century America.* Edited by Albert E. Stone. New York: Penguin, 1981.

de Graef, Lawrence B. "Race, Sex, and Region: Black Women in the American West, 1850–1920." In *Black Women in American History,* edited by Darlene Clark Hine. Vol. 1. Brooklyn, N.Y.: Carlson, 1990, 303–13.

Deutrich, Mabel E., and Virginia C. Purdy, eds. *Clio Was a Woman: Studies in the History of American Women.* Washington, D.C.: Howard University Press, 1980.

Donnan, Elizabeth, ed. *Documents Illustrative of the History of the Slave Trade to America.* 2 vols. New York: Octagon, 1965 [1930].

Douglass, Frederick. *Narrative of the Life of Frederick Douglass, an American Slave.* New York: Signet, 1968 [1845].

Dow, George Francis. *Slave Ships and Slaving.* Salem, Mass.: Marine Research Society, 1927.

Drake, Frederick C., ed. "Secret History of the Slave Trade to Cuba Written by an American Naval Officer, Robert Wilson Schufeldt." *Journal of Negro History* 55 (1970): 220–30.

Drew, Benjamin, ed. *A North-Side View of Slavery; The Refugee, Or the Narratives of Fugitive Slaves in Canada.* Boston: John P. Jewett, 1856.

Du Bois, W. E. B. *Black Reconstruction: An Essay toward a History of the Part Which Black Folk Played in the Attempt to Reconstruct Democracy in America, 1860–1880.* New York: Harcourt Brace, 1935.

Dumond, Dwight Lowell. *Antislavery: The Crusade for Freedom to America.* New York: Norton, 1966 [1961].

Durden, Robert F. *The Gray and the Black: The Confederate Debate on Emancipation.* Baton Rouge: Louisiana State University Press, 1972.

Easterby, J. H., ed. *The South Carolina Rice Plantation as Revealed in the Papers of Robert F. W. Allston.* Chicago: University of Chicago Press, 1945.

Edelstein, Tilden G. *Strange Enthusiasm: A Life of Thomas Wentworth Higginson.* New Haven, Conn.: Yale University Press, 1968.

Egypt, Ophelia S., J. Masuoka, and Charles S. Johnson, eds. *Unwritten History of Slavery: Autobiographical Accounts of Negro Ex-Slaves.* Nashville, Tenn.: Fisk University Press, 1945.

Ehrlich, Walter. "The Origins of the Dred Scott Case." *Journal of Negro History* 59 (1974): 132–42.

Elkins, Stanley M. *Slavery: A Problem in American Institutional and Intellectual Life,* 2nd ed. Chicago: University of Chicago Press, 1968 [1959].

Elliott, E. N. ed. *Cotton Is King and Pro-Slavery Arguments.* New York: Johnson Reprint, 1968 [1860].

Eppes, Susan Bradford. *The Negro of the Old South: A Bit of Period History.* Macon, Ga.: J. W. Burke, 1941.

Farr, James. "A Slow Boat to Nowhere: The Multi-Racial Crews of the American Whaling Industry." *Journal of Negro History* 68 (1983): 159–70.

Faust, Drew Gilpin. *Mothers of Invention: Women of the Slaveholding South in the American Civil War.* Chapel Hill: University of North Carolina Press, 1996.

Faust, Drew Gilpin, ed. *Ideology of Slavery: Proslavery Thought in the Antebellum South, 1830–1860.* Baton Rouge: University of Louisiana Press, 1981.

Fehrenbacher, Don E. *Slavery, Law, and Politics: The Dred Scott Case in Historical Perspective.* New York: Oxford University Press, 1981.

Fishel, L. H., and B. Quarles, eds. *The Negro American: A Documentary History.* Glenview, Ill.: Scott, Foresman, 1967.

Finkelman, Paul. *The Law of Freedom and Bondage: A Casebook.* New York: Oceana, 1986.

———. *Slavery and the Law.* New York: Madison House, 1997.

———. *Slavery in the Courtroom: An Annotated Bibliography of American Cases.* Washington, D.C.: Library of Congress 1985.

Finkelman, Paul, ed. *African-Americans and the Law.* New York: Garland, 1992.

Fisher, Sidney George. *A Philadelphia Perspective: The Diary of Sidney George Fisher Covering the Years 1834–1871.* Edited by Nicholas B. Wainwright. Philadelphia: Historical Society of Pennsylvania, 1967.

Fitzhugh, George. *Cannibals All! Or, Slaves without Masters.* Cambridge: Harvard University Press, 1960 [1857].

Fogel, Robert William, and Stanley L. Engerman. *Time on the Cross: The Economics of American Negro Slavery.* Boston: Little, Brown, 1974.

Foner, Philip S. *Business and Slavery: The New York Merchants and the Irrepressible Conflict.* Chapel Hill: University of North Carolina Press, 1941.

Forten, Charlotte. *The Journal of Charlotte Forten.* Edited by Ray A. Billington. New York: Norton, 1981 [1953].

*Four Fugitive Slave Narratives,* introduction by Robin W. Winks. Reading, Mass.: Addison Wesley, 1969.

Fox, Early Lee. *The American Colonization Society, 1817–1840.* Baltimore: Johns Hopkins University Press, 1919.

Fox-Genovese, Elizabeth. "Strategies and Forms of Resistance: Focus on Slave Women in the United States." In *Black Women in American History,* edited by Darlene Clark Hine. Vol. 2. Brooklyn, N.Y.: Carlson, 1990, 409–31.

———. *Within the Plantation Household: Black and White Women of the Old South.* Chapel Hill: University of North Carolina Press, 1988.

Franklin, John Hope. *The Emancipation Proclamation.* Garden City, N.Y.: Doubleday, 1963.

———. "The Enslavement of Free Negroes in North Carolina." *Journal of Negro History* 29 (1944): 401–28.

———. *From Slavery to Freedom: A History of American Negroes.* New York: Knopf, 1994 [1956].

———. *George Washington Williams: A Biography.* Durham, N.C.: Duke University Press, 1998 [1985].

Fraser, Walter J., Jr., R. Frank Saunders Jr., and Jon L. Wakelyn, eds. *The Web of Southern Social Relations: Women, Family, & Education.* Athens: University of Georgia Press, 1985.

Garrett, Raneo B. *Famous First Facts about Negroes.* New York: Arno, 1972.

Gemery, Henry A., and Jan S. Hogendorn, eds. *The Uncommon Market: Essays in the Economic History of the Atlantic Slave Trade.* New York: Academic Press, 1979.

Genovese, Eugene D. *From Rebellion to Revolution: Afro-American Slave Revolts in the Making of the Modern World.* Baton Rouge: Louisiana State University Press, 1979.

———. *Roll, Jordan, Roll: The World the Slaves Made.* New York: Vintage Books, 1974.

Gilbert, Olive. *Narrative of Sojourner Truth, a Northern Slave, Emancipated from Bodily Servitude by the State of New York in 1828, including a Book of Life.* Edited by Frances Titus. Salem, N. H.: Ayer, 1987 [1878].

Glatthaar, Joseph T. *Forged in Battle: The Civil War Alliance of Black Soldiers and White Officers.* New York: Free Press, 1990.

Godson, Martha Graham. "Medical-Botanical Contribution of African Slave Women to American Medicine." In *Black Women in American History,* edited by Darlene Clark Hine. Vol. 2. Brooklyn, N.Y.: Carlson, 1990, 473–84.

Goodell, William. *The American Slave Code in Theory and Practice.* New York: Negro Universities Press, 1968 [1853].

Grant, Anne. *Memoirs of an American Lady, with Sketches of the Manners and Customs in America as They Existed Previous to the Revolution.* London: Printed for Longman, Hurst, Rees and Orme, 1808.

Grant, John N. "Black Immigrants into Nova Scotia, 1776–1815," *Journal of Negro History* 58 (1973): 253–70.

Gregory, Chester W. "Black Women in Pre-Federal America." In *Clio Was a Woman: Studies in the History of American Women,* edited by Mabel E. Deutrich and Virginia C. Purdy, Washington, D.C.: Howard University Press, 1980.

Grimes, William. *Life of William Grimes, the Runaway Slave.* In *Five Black Lives,* introduction by Arna Bontemps. Middletown, Conn.: Wesleyan University Press, 1971 [1855].

Grimké, Angelina. "An Appeal to the Christian Women of the South." 1836. In *The Feminist Papers,* edited by Alice S. Rossi, New York: Bantam, 1978, 296–304.

Gutman, Herbert. *The Black Family in Slavery and Freedom, 1750–1925.* New York: Vintage Books, 1976.

Hakluyt, Richard. *Hakluyt's Voyages; Principal Navigations, Voyages, Traffiques, and Discoveries of the English Nation.* New York: Viking, 1965 [1903–05].

Halliburton, R., Jr. *Red over Black: Black Slavery among the Cherokee Indians.* Westport, Conn.: Greenwood, 1977.

Hamilton, J. "An Account of the Late Intended Insurrection among a Portion of the Blacks of This City, Charleston, S.C." In *Slave Insurrections: Selected Document.* Westport, Conn.: Negro Universities Press, 1970.

Hamilton, Jeff. *My Master: The Inside Story of Sam Houston and His Times.* Edited by Lenoir Hunt. Dallas, Tex.: State House Press, 1992 [1940].

Harding, Vincent. *There Is a River: The Black Struggle for Freedom in America.* New York: Harcourt Brace, 1981.

Harper, Ida Husted. *The Life and Works of Susan B. Anthony.* 3 vols. Indianapolis, Ind.: Hollenbeck, 1898.

Harper, William, "Harper on Slavery." In *Cotton Is King and Pro-Slavery Arguments,* edited by E. N. Elliott. New York: Johnson Reprint, 1968 [1860].

Harris, Sheldon H. "An American's Impressions of Sierra Leone in 1811." *Journal of Negro History* 47 (1962): 35–41.

Hartgrove, W. B. "The Story of Maria Louise Moore and Fannie M. Richards." *Journal of Negro History* 1 (1916).

Haven, R. "John Brown and Heman Humphrey: An Unpublished Letter." *Journal of Negro History* 52 (1967): 220–24.

Haviland, Laura S. *A Woman's Life-Work: Labors and Experiences of Laura S. Haviland.* New York: Arno, 1969 [1889].

Hawks, Esther Hill. *A Woman Doctor's Civil War: Esther Hill Hawks' Diary.* Edited by Gerald Schwartz. Columbia: University of South Carolina Press, 1984.

Henson, Josiah. *Life of Josiah Henson, Formerly a Slave, Now an Inhabitant of Canada, as Narrated by Himself.* In *Four Fugitive Slave Narratives.* Reading, Mass.: Addison Wesley, 1969.

Higginbotham, A. Leon, Jr. *In the Matter of Color: Race and the American Legal Process: The Colonial Period.* New York: Oxford University Press, 1978.

Higginson, Thomas Wentworth. *Army Life in a Black Regiment.* Williamstown, Mass.: Corner House, 1971 [1870].

Hine, Darlene Clark, ed. *Black Women in American History.* 4 vols. Brooklyn, N.Y.: Carlson, 1990.

Hine, Darlene Clark, and Kathleen Thompson. *A Shining Thread of Hope: The History of Black Women in America.* New York: Broadway Books, 1997.

Hodes, Martha. *White Women, Black Men: Illicit Sex in the Nineteenth-Century South.* New Haven, Conn.: Yale University Press, 1997.

Hollandsworth, James G. *The Louisiana Native Guards.* Baton Rouge: Louisiana State University Press, 1995.

Holley, Sallie. *A Life for Liberty: Anti-Slavery and Other Letters of Sallie Holley.* Edited by John White Chadwick. New York: G. P. Putnam's Sons, 1899.

Holmes, Jack D. L. "The Abortive Slave Revolt at Pointe Coupe, Louisiana, 1795." *Louisiana History* 11 (1970): 341–62.

Horton, Paul. "Submitting to the 'Shadow of Slavery': The Secession Crisis and Civil War in Alabama's Lawrence County." *Civil War History* 44 (1988): 130ff.

Howard, Warren S. *American Slavers and the Federal Law, 1837–1862.* Berkeley: University of California Press, 1963.

Howe, Samuel Gridley. *Report to the Freedmen's Inquiry Committee; The Refugees from Slavery in Canada West.* New York: Arno, 1969 [1864].

Hudson, Charles M., ed. *Red, White and Black: Symposium on Indians in the Old South.* Athens: University of Georgia Press, 1971.

Hunter, Tera W. *To 'Joy My Freedom: Southern Black Women's Lives and Labors after the Civil War.* Cambridge, Mass.: Harvard University Press, 1997.

Hymowitz, Carol, and Michaele Weissman. *A History of Women in America.* New York: Bantam, 1978.

Jacobs, Harriet. *Incidents in the Life of a Slave Girl.* Edited by Lydia Maria Child; introduction by Valerie Smith. New York: Oxford University Press, 1988 [1861].

Jefferson, Thomas. *The Portable Thomas Jefferson.* Edited by Merrill D. Peterson. New York: Penguin, 1975.

Johnson, Charles S., ed. *God Struck Me Dead: Religious Conversion Experiences and Autobiographies of Negro Ex-Slaves.* Philadelphia: United Church Press, 1969 [1945].

Johnson, Michael P. "Runaway Slaves and the Slave Communities in South Carolina, 1799 to 1830." *William and Mary Quarterly:* 38 (1981): 418–41.

———. "Smothered Slave Infants: Were Slave Mothers at Fault?" *Journal of Southern History* 47 (1981): 493–520.

Johnson, Michael P., and James L. Roark. *Black Masters: A Free Family of Color in the Old South.* New York: W. W. Norton, 1984.

Johnston, James H. *Race Relations in Virginia and Miscegenation in the South, 1776–1860.* Amherst: University of Massachusetts Press, 1970.

Jones, Charles C. *A Catechism of Scripture, Doctrine and Practice for Families and Sabbath Schools. Designed Also for the Oral Instruction of Colored Persons.* 3rd ed. Savannah, Ga., 1844 [1837].

———. *The Religious Instruction of the Negroes in the United States.* Savannah, Ga: Thomas Purse, 1842.

Jones, George Fenwick. "The Black Hessians: Negroes Recruited by the Hessians in South Carolina and Other Colonies." *South Carolina Historical Magazine* 83 (1982).

Jones, Howard. *Mutiny on the Amistad.* New York: Oxford University Press, 1987.

Jones, Jacqueline. *Labor of Love, Labor of Sorrow: Black Women, Work, and the Family from Slavery to the Present.* New York: Basic Books, 1985.

Jones, Thomas. *The Experience of Thomas Jones, Who Was a Slave for Forty-Three Years.* Boston, 1850.

Jordan, Winthrop D. *Tumult and Silence at Second Creek: An Inquiry into a Civil War Slave Conspiracy.* Baton Rouge: Louisiana State University Press, 1993.

———. *White over Black: American Attitudes toward the Negro, 1550–1812.* Chapel Hill: University of North Carolina Press, 1968.

Josephy, Alvin M. *The Civil War in the American West.* New York: Vintage Books, 1993.

Kates, Don B., Jr. "Abolition, Deportation, Integration: Attitudes toward Slavery in the Early Republic." *Journal of Negro History* 53 (1968): 33–47.

Kay, Marvin L. Michael, and Lorin Lee Cary. *Slavery in North Carolina, 1748–1775.* Chapel Hill: University of North Carolina Press, 1995.

Keckley, Elizabeth. *Behind the Scenes: Thirty Years a Slave, and Four Years in the White House.* New York: Ayer, 1968 [1868].

Kemble, Frances Anne. *Further Records.* New York, 1891.

———. *Journal of a Residence on a Georgian Plantation in 1838–1839.* Edited by John A. Scott. New York: Alfred A. Knopf, 1961.

Klein, Martin, and Paul E. Lovejoy, "Slavery in West Africa." In *The Uncommon Market: Essays in the Economic History of the Atlantic Slave Trade,* edited by Henry A. Gemery and Jan S. Hogendorn. New York: Academic Press, 1979.

Kraditor, Aileen S. *Means and Ends in American Abolitionism: Garrison and His Critics on Strategy and Tactics, 1834–1850.* Chicago: Elephant Paperbacks, 1989 [1967].

Lambert, Frank. "'I Saw the Book Talk': Slave Readings of the First Great Awakening." *Journal of Negro History* 77 (1992): 184–98.

Landon, Fred. "The Negro Migration to Canada after the Passing of the Fugitive Slave Act." *Journal of Negro History* 5 (1920): 22.

Langley, Harold D. "The Negro in the Navy and Merchant Service, 1798–1860." *Journal of Negro History* 52 (1967): 273–86.

Lapp, Rudolph M. "The Negro in Gold Rush California." *Journal of Negro History* 49 (1964): 81–98.

Lauber, Almon Wheeler. *Indian Slavery in Colonial Times within the Present Limits of the United States.* New York: Columbia University Press, 1913.

Leigh, Frances Butler. *Ten Years on a Georgia Plantation since the War.* New York: Negro Universities Press, 1969 [1883].

Lepore, Jill. *The Name of War: King Philip's War and the Origins of American Identity.* New York: Knopf, 1998.

Lerner, Gerda. *The Grimké Sisters from South Carolina: Pioneers for Women's Rights and Abolition.* New York: Schocken, 1967.

Lerner, Gerda, ed. *Black Women in White America: A Documentary History.* New York: Vintage, 1973.

"Letters Largely Personal or Private." *Journal of Negro History* 11 (1926): 63–64.

*Letters of Theodore Dwight Weld, Angelina Grimke Weld and Sarah Grimke, 1822–1844.* Gloucester, Mass.: Peter Smith/American Historical Association, 1965.

Lewis, Ronald L. *Coal, Iron, and Slaves: Industrial Slavery in Maryland and Virginia, 1715–1865.* Westport, Conn.: Greenwood, 1979.

———. "Slavery on Chesapeake Iron Plantations before the American Revolution." *Journal of Negro History* 59 (1974): 242–54.

———. *Rice and Slaves, Ethnicity and the Slave Trade in Colonial South Carolina.* Baton Rouge: Louisiana State University Press, 1981.

Littlefield, Daniel F. *Africans and Seminoles: From Removal to Emancipation.* Westport, Conn.: Greenwood, 1977.

Litwak, Leon F. *Been in the Storm So Long: The Aftermath of Slavery.* New York: Knopf, 1979.

Livermore, Mary Ashton Rice. *My Story of the War: A Woman's Narrative of Four Years Personal Experience as Nurse in the Union Army, and in Relief Work at Home, in Hospitals, Camps, and at the Front during the War of Rebellion.* Introduction by Nina Silber. New York: Da Capo, 1995 [1887].

Locke, Mary S. *Anti-Slavery in America, from the Introduction of African Slaves to the Prohibition of the Slave Trade.* New York: Johnson Reprints, 1968 [1901].

Logan, Raymond W., and Michael R. Winston, eds. *Dictionary of American Negro Biography.* New York: Norton, 1982.

Lovejoy, Paul E. *Transformations in Slavery: A History of Slavery in Africa.* New York: Cambridge University Press, 1983.

Lovejoy, Paul E., ed. *The Ideology of Slavery in Africa.* Beverly Hills, Calif.: Sage, 1981.

Lovejoy, Paul E., and Jan S. Hogendorn. "Slave Marketing in West Africa." In *The Uncommon Market: Essays in the Economic History of the Atlantic Slave Trade,* edited by Henry A. Gemery and Jan S. Hogendorn. New York: Academic Press, 1979.

Lundy, Benjamin. *The Life, Travels and Opinions of Benjamin Lundy.* Edited by Thomas Earle. New York: Negro Universities Press, 1969 [1847].

Lunsford, Lane. *The Narrative of Lunsford Lane.* Boston, 1848.

McCord, Louisa Susannah. "Uncle Tom's Cabin." *Southern Quarterly Review* 23 (1853): 81–120.

McCurry, Stephanie. *Masters of Small Worlds: Yeoman Households, Gender Relations, and the Political Culture in the Antebellum South Carolina Low Country.* New York: Oxford University Press, 1995.

McDonogh, John. "A Letter of John McDonogh on African Colonization." *African Repository* (February 19, 1843): 48–62.

McFeely, William S. *Frederick Douglass.* New York: Norton, 1991.

McLaurin, Melton A. *Celia: A Slave.* Athens: University of Georgia Press, 1991.

McLoughlin, William G. *The Cherokee Ghost Dance: Essays on the Southeastern Indians, 1789–1861.* Macon, Ga.: Mercer University Press, 1994.

———. *Tongue of Flame: The Life of Lydia Maria Child.* New York: Thomas Y. Crowell, 1965.

McPherson, James M. *For Cause and Comrades: Why Men Fought in the Civil War.* New York: Oxford University Press, 1997.

———. *Marching toward Freedom: Blacks in the Civil War.* New York: Facts on File, 1991.

———. *The Negro's Civil War: How American Blacks Felt and Acted during the War for the Union.* New York: Ballantine, 1991.

Maginnes, David R. "The Case of the Court House Rioters in the Rendition of the Fugitive Slave Anthony Burns, 1854." *Journal of Negro History* 56 (1971): 31–43.

Mannix, Daniel Pratt. *Black Cargoes: A History of the Atlantic Slave Trade, 1518–1865.* New York: Viking, 1962.

Martineau, Harriet. *The Martyr Age of the United States of America.* New York: Arno, 1969 [1839].

———. *Society in America.* 3 vols. London: Saunders and Otley, 1837.

Massey, Mary E. *Refugee Life in the Confederacy.* Baton Rouge: Louisiana State University Press, 1964.

Maury, Ann. *Memoirs of a Huguenot Family.* New York: G. P. Putnam, 1907 [1872].

May, Samuel. *Some Recollections of our Anti-Slavery Conflict.* New York: Arno, 1968 [1869].

Merrell, James H. "'Our Bond of Peace': Patterns of Intercultural Exchange in the Carolina Piedmont, 1650–1750." In *The Uncommon Market: Essays in the Economic History of the Atlantic Slave Trade,* edited by Henry A. Gemery and Jan S. Hogendorn. New York: Academic Press, 1979.

Miller, Edward A., Jr. *The Black Civil War Soldiers of Illinois: The Story of the Twenty-Ninth U.S. Colored Infantry.* Columbus: University of South Carolina Press, 1998.

Miller, Joseph C. "Some Aspects of the Commercial Organization of Slaving at Luanda, Angola—1760–1830." In *The Uncommon Market: Essays in the Economic History of the Atlantic Slave Trade,* ed. Henry A. Gemery and Jan S. Hagedorn. New York: Academic Press, 1979.

———. *Way of Death: Merchant Capitalism and the Angolan Slave Trade, 1730–1830.* Madison: University of Wisconsin Press, 1988.

Miller, Randall M., and John David Smith, eds. *Dictionary of Afro-American Slavery.* Westport, Conn.: Greenwood, 1997.

Miller, William Lee. *Arguing about Slavery: John Quincy Adams and the Great Battle in the United States Congress.* New York: Vintage Books, 1998.

Moore, George H. *Notes on the History of Slavery in Massachusetts.* New York: Negro Universities Press, 1968.

Morgan, Edmund S. *American Slavery, American Freedom: The Ordeal of Colonial Virginia.* New York: W. W. Norton, 1975.

Morgan, Philip D. *Slave Counterpoint: Black Culture in the Eighteenth-Century Chesapeake and Lowcountry.* Chapel Hill: University of North Carolina Press, 1998.

Morris, Thomas D. *Southern Slavery and the Law, 1619–1860.* Chapel Hill: University of North Carolina Press, 1996.

Morrison, Michael A. *Slavery and the American West: The Eclipse of Manifest Destiny and the Coming of the Civil War.* Chapel Hill: University of North Carolina Press, 1997.

Morse, Jedidiah. *A Report to the Secretary of War on Indian Affairs.* New Haven, Conn., 1822.

Motley, Constance Baker. *Equal Justice under Law.* New York: Farrar, Straus and Giroux, 1998.

Mullin, Gerald W. *Flight and Rebellion: Slave Resistance in Eighteenth-Century Virginia.* New York: Oxford University Press, 1972.

Munford, Clarence J., and Michael Zeuske. "Black Slavery, Class Struggle, Fear and Revolution in St. Domingue and Cuba, 1785–1795." *Journal of Negro History* 73 (1988): 12–32.

Murray, Pauli. *Proud Shoes.* New York: Harper and Row, 1978.

Myers, Robert Manson, ed. *The Children of Pride: A True Story of Georgia and the Civil War.* New Haven, Conn.: Yale University Press, 1972.

Nelson, Bernard H. "Confederate Slave Impressment Legislation, 1861–1865." *Journal of Negro History* 31 (1946): 392–410.

Newman, Debra L. "Black Women in the Era of the American Revolution in Pennsylvania." *Journal of Negro History* 61 (1976): 276–89.

Nichols, Roger L. *Indians in the United States and Canada: A Comparative History.* Lincoln: University of Nebraska Press, 1998.

Noble, Jeanne. *Beautiful, Also, Are the Souls of My Black Sisters: A History of the Black Woman in America.* Englewood Cliffs, N.J.: Prentice Hall, 1978.

Oakes, James. *The Ruling Race: A History of American Slaveholders.* New York: Knopf, 1982.

———. *The Whirlwind of War: Voices of the Storm, 1861–1865.* New York: HarperCollins, 1998.

Oates, Stephen B. *The Approaching Fury: Voices of the Storm, 1820–1861.* New York: HarperCollins, 1997.

———. *The Fires of Jubilee: Nat Turner's Fierce Rebellion.* New York: HarperCollins, 1975.

———. *To Purge This Land with Blood: A Biography of John Brown.* Amherst, Mass.: University of Massachusetts Press, 1984.

Obitko, Mary Ellen. "Custodians of a House of Resistance: Black Women Respond to Slavery." In *Black Women in American History* edited by Darlene Clark Hine, Vol. 3. Brooklyn, N.Y.: Carlson, 1990, 983–98.

*Official Records of the Union and Confederate Armies.* Washington, D.C., 1880–1901.

*Official Records of the Union and Confederate Navies.* Washington, D.C., 1894–1927.

Olexer, Barbara. *The Enslavement of the American Indian.* Monroe, N.Y.: Library Research Associates, 1982.

Olmsted, Frederick Law. *The Cotton Kingdom: A Traveller's Observations on Cotton and Slavery in the American Slave States.* Edited by Arthur M. Schlesinger. New York: Alfred A. Knopf, 1966.

Osofsky, Gilbert, ed. *Puttin' on Ole Massa.* New York: Harper and Row, 1969.

Owens, Leslie Howard. *This Species of Property: Slave Life and Culture in the Old South.* New York: Oxford University Press, 1976.

Parkhurst, Jessie W. "The Role of the Black Mammy in the Plantation Household." *Journal of Negro History* 23 (1938): 349–69.

Parrish, Lydia. *Slave Songs of the Georgia Sea Islands.* Athens: University of Georgia Press, 1942.

Pearson, Henry G. *James S. Wadsworth of Genesco.* New York: C. Scribner's Sons, 1913.

Pease, Jane H., and William H. Pease. *The Fugitive Slave Law and Anthony Burns: A Problem in Law Enforcement.* Philadelphia: J. B. Lippincott, 1975.

———. "Walker's Appeal Comes to Charleston: A Note and Documents." *Journal of Negro History* 59 (1965): 287–92.

———. "Organized Negro Communities: A North American Experiment." *Journal of Negro History* 47 (1962): 19–34.

Pennington, James W. C. *The Fugitive Blacksmith: Or, Events in the History of James W. C. Pennington, Pastor of a Presbyterian Church, New York, Formerly a Slave in the State of Maryland.* In *Great Slave Narratives.* Edited by Arna Bontemps. Boston: Beacon, 1969.

Pennington, Patience. *A Woman Rice Planter.* Edited by Cornelius O. Cathey. Cambridge, Mass.: Harvard University Press, 1961 [1913].

Perdue, Theda. *Slavery and the Evolution of Cherokee Society, 1540–1866.* Knoxville: University of Tennessee Press, 1979.

Pettit, Eber M. *Sketches in the History of the Underground Railroad.* Freeport, N.Y.: Books for Libraries Press, 1971 [1879].

Phillips, Ulrich B. *American Negro Slavery: A Survey of the Supply, Employment and Control of Negro Labor as Determined by the Plantation Regime.* Baton Rouge: Louisiana State University Press, 1969 [1918].

———. *Plantation and Frontier Documents, 1649–1863.* 2 vols. Cleveland: Arthur H. Clarke, 1909.

Pickard, Kate E. R. *The Kidnapped and the Ransomed, Being the Personal Recollections of Peter Still and His Wife "Vina," after Forty Years of Slavery.* New York: Negro Universities Press, 1968 [1856].

Pinckney, Thomas. "Reflections, Occasioned by the Late Disturbances in Charleston." In *Slave Insurrections: Selected Documents.* Westport, Conn.: Negro Universities Press, 1970 [1822, 1860].

Pope-Hennessy, James. *Sins of the Fathers: A Study of the Atlantic Slave Traders, 1441–1807.* New York: Capricorn, 1969.

Porter, Dorothy B. "Sarah Parker Remond, Abolitionist and Physician." In *Black Women in American History,* edited by Darlene Clark Hine. Vol. 4. Brooklyn, N.Y.: Carlson, 1990. 1125–31

Porter, Kenneth Wiggins. *The Negro on the American Frontier.* New York: Arno, 1971.

———. "Relations between Negroes and Indians within the Present Limits of the United States." *Journal of Negro History* 17 (1932): 287–367.

Price, Richard. *Maroon Societies: Rebel Slave Communities in the Americas.* Baltimore: Johns Hopkins University Press, 1973.

Putney, Martha S. "Black Merchant Seamen of Newport, 1803–1865: A Case Study in Foreign Commerce." *Journal of Negro History* 57 (1972): 56–68.

Quarles, Benjamin. *Black Abolitionists.* New York: Da Capo, 1991 [1969].

———. "Harriet Tubman's Unlikely Leadership." In *Black Women in American History,* edited by Darlene Clark Hine. Vol. 4. Brooklyn, N.Y.: Carlson, 1990, 1133–47

———. *The Negro in the American Revolution.* New York: W. W. Norton, 1973.

———. *The Negro in the Civil War.* Boston: Little, Brown, 1969.

Raboteau, Albert J. *Slave Religion: The "Invisible Institution" in the Antebellum South.* New York: Oxford University Press, 1978.

Rankin, John. *Letters on American Slavery.* New York: Arno, 1969 [1838].

Rawick, George, ed. *The American Slave: A Composite Autobiography.* 19 vols. and supplements. Westport, Conn.: Greenwood, 1972.

Rawley, James A. *The Transatlantic Slave Trade: A History.* New York: W. W. Norton, 1981.

Redford, Dorothy Spruill, with Michael D'Orso. *Somerset Homecoming: Recovering a Lost Heritage.* New York: Doubleday, 1988.

Redkey, Edwin S., ed. *A Grand Army of Black Men: Letters from African-American Soldiers in the Union Army, 1861–1865.* New York: Cambridge University Press, 1992.

Redpath, James. *The Roving Editor, or, Talks with Slaves in Southern States.* Edited by John R. McKivigan. University Park: Pennsylvania State University Press, 1996 [1859].

*The Refugee: A North-Side View of Slavery* [1856]. In *Four Fugitive Slave Narratives.* Reading, Mass.: Addison Wesley, 1969.

Reynolds, Edward. *Stand the Storm: A History of the Atlantic Slave Trade.* New York: Allison and Busby, 1985.

Ripley, C. Peter, ed. *The Black Abolitionist Papers.* 5 vols. Chapel Hill: University of North Carolina Press, 1987–1992.

Robinson, Armstead. "Day of Jubilo: Civil War and the Demise of Slavery in the Mississippi Valley, 1861–1865." Ph.D. diss. University of Rochester, 1976.

Roca, Steven Louis. "Presence and Precedents: The USS *Red Rover* during the American Civil War, 1861–1865." *Civil War History* 44 (1998): 91–110.

Roethler, Michael Donald. *Negro Slavery among the Cherokee Indians, 1540–1866.* New York, 1964.

Rosengarten, Theodore. *Tombee: Portrait of a Cotton Planter, with the Plantation Journal of Thomas B. Chaplin (1822–1890).* New York: William Morrow, 1986.

Ross, Alexander Milton. *Recollections and Experiences of an Abolitionist from 1855 to 1865.* Northbrook, Ill.: Metro Books, 1972 [1876].

Rossi, Alice, ed. *The Feminist Papers.* Chicago: Northwest University Press, 1973.

———. *Slavery and the Law.* New York: Madison House, 1997.

Savage, W. Sherman. "The Negro in the History of the Pacific Northwest." *Journal of Negro History* 13 (1928): 255–64.

———. "The Negro in the Westward Movement." *Journal of Negro History* 25 (1940): 533–34.

Scarborough, William K. *The Overseer: Plantation Management in the Old South.* Baton Rouge: Louisiana State University Press, 1988.

Schultz, Jane E. "Between Scylla and Charybdis: Clara Barton's Wartime Odyssey." *Minerva: Quarterly Report on Women and the Military* 14 (1996): 45–68.

———. "Women at the Front: Gender and Genre in Literature of the American Civil War." Ph.D. diss., University of Michigan, 1988.

Sherman, William T. *Memoirs.* 2 vols. New York: Da Capo Press, 1984 [1875].

Siebert, Wilbur H. *The Underground Railroad from Slavery to Freedom.* New York: Macmillan, 1898.

*Six Women's Slave Narratives.* New York: Oxford University Press, 1988.

*Slave Insurrections: Selected Documents.* Westport, Conn.: Negro Universities Press, 1970 [1822, 1860].

Smedley, R. C. *History of the Underground Railroad in Chester and the Neighboring Counties of Pennsylvania.* Lancaster, Pa., 1883.

Smith, Abbott E. *Colonists in Bondage.* Chapel Hill: University of North Carolina Press, 1947.

Smith, Amanda. *An Autobiography: The Story of the Lord's Dealings with Mrs. Amanda Smith, the Colored Evangelist.* New York: Oxford University Press, 1988 [1893].

Smith, James L. *Autobiography of James L. Smith.* In *Five Black Lives,* introduced by Arna Bontemps. Middletown, Conn.: Wesleyan University Press, 1971.

Smith, Venture. *A Narrative of the Life and Adventures of Venture, a Native of Africa.* New London, Conn., 1798.

*The South Vindicated from the Treason and Fanaticism of the Northern Abolitionists.* New York: Negro Universities Press, 1969 [1836].

Spector, Robert M. "The Quock Walker Cases (1781–83): The Abolition of Slavery and Negro Citizenship in Early Massachusetts." *Journal of Negro History* 53 (1968): 12–32.

Stampp, Kenneth M. *The Peculiar Institution: Slavery in the Ante-Bellum South.* New York: Vintage Books, 1956.

Stanton, Elizabeth Cady. *Eighty Years and More: Reminiscences 1815–1897.* New York: Schocken, 1971 [1898].

Stanton, Theodore, and Harriot Stanton Blatch, eds. *Elizabeth Cady Stanton: As Revealed in Her Letters, Diary and Reminiscences.* 2 vols. New York: Arno and the *New York Times,* 1969 [1922].

Staples, Brent. Editorial, *New York Times,* November 15, 1998.

Starobin, Robert. "Disciplining Industrial Slaves in the Old South." *Journal of Negro History* 53 (1968): 111–28.

———. *Industrial Slavery in the Old South*. New York: Oxford University Press, 1970.

Starobin, Robert S., ed. *Blacks in Bondage: Letters from American Slaves.* Princeton, N.J.: Markus Wiener, 1974.

Stavisky, Leonard. "Negro Craftsmanship in Colonial America." *Journal of Negro History* 32 (1947): 421.

Stealey, John Edmund, III. "Slavery and the West Virginia Salt Industry." *Journal of Negro History* 59 (1974): 105–31.

Stepto, Robert B. *From behind the Veil: A Study of Afro-American Narrative.* Urbana: University of Illinois Press, 1979.

———. *The Making of an Afro-American: Martin Robison Delany, 1812–1885.* Garden City, N.Y.: Doubleday, 1971.

Sterling, Dorothy. *Captain of the* Planter: *The Story of Robert Smalls.* Garden City, N.Y.: Doubleday, 1958.

Sterling, Dorothy, ed. *We Are Your Sisters: Black Women in the Nineteenth Century.* New York: W. W. Norton, 1984.

Steward, Austin. *Twenty-Two Years a Slave and Forty Years a Freeman* [1857]. In *Four Fugitive Slave Narratives,* introdution by Robin W. Winks. Reading, Mass.: Addison Wesley, 1969.

[Stewart, Maria W.] *Maria W. Stewart: America's First Black Woman Political Writer, Essays and Speeches.* Edited by Marilyn Richardson. Bloomington: Indiana University Press, 1987.

Still, Peter, and Vina Still. *The Kidnapped and the Ransomed.* New York: Negro Universities Press, 1968 [1856].

Still, William. *The Underground Railroad: A Record of Facts, Authentic Narratives, Letters, etc.* Philadelphia: Porter and Coates, 1872.

[Stone, Kate.] *Brokenburn: The Journal of Kate Stone, 1861–1868.* Edited by John Q. Anderson. Baton Rouge: Louisiana State University Press, 1955.

Straubing, Harold Elk, comp. *In Hospital and Camp: The Civil War through the Eyes of Its Doctors and Nurses.* Harrisburg, Pa.: Stackpole Books, 1993.

Strother, Horatio T. *The Underground Railroad in Connecticut.* Middletown, Conn.: Wesleyan University Press, 1962.

Styron, William. *The Confessions of Nat Turner.* New York: Random House, 1967.

Tadman, Michael. *Speculators and Slaves: Masters, Traders, and Slaves in the Old South.* Madison: University of Wisconsin Press, 1989.

Takaki, Ronald T. *A Pro-Slavery Crusade: The Agitation to Reopen the African Slave Trade.* New York: Free Press, 1971.

Taylor, Frances Cloud. *The Trackless Trail Leads On.* Kennett Square, Pa.: KNA, 1995.

Taylor, Susie King. *A Black Woman's Civil War Memoirs.* Edited by Patricia W. Romero and Willie Lee Rose. Princeton, N.J.: Markus Wiener, 1997.

[Thomas, Ella Gertrude Clanton.] *The Secret Eye: The Journal of Ella Gertrude Clanton Thomas, 1848–1889.* Edited by Virginia Ingraham Burr. Chapel Hill: University of North Carolina Press, 1990.

Thomas, Hugh. *The Slave Trade: The Story of the Atlantic Slave Trade, 1440–1870.* New York: Simon and Schuster, 1997.

Thomas, Velma Maia. *Lest We Forget.* New York: Crown, 1997.

*Three Negro Classics.* New York: Avon, 1965 [1901].

Tise, Larry E. *Proslavery: A History of the Defense of Slavery in America, 1701–1840.* Athens: University of Georgia Press, 1987.

de Tocqueville, Alexis. *Democracy in America,* trans. George Lawrence, edited by J. P. Mayer. Garden City, N.Y.: Anchor, 1969.

Torrey, Jesse. *American Slave Trade.* New York: Negro Universities Press, 1971 [1822].

[Towne, Laura M.] *Letters and Diary of Laura M. Towne Written from the Sea Islands of South Carolina, 1862–1884.* Edited by Rupert Sargent Holland. New York: Negro Universities Press, 1969 [1912].

Trexler, Harrison Anthony. *Slavery in Missouri, 1804–1865.* Baltimore: Johns Hopkins University Press, 1914.

[Truth, Sojourner.] *Narrative of Sojourner Truth.* Edited by Margaret Washington. New York: Vintage, 1993 [1850].

Tushnet, Mark V. *The American Law of Slavery, 1810–1860: Considerations of Humanity and Interest.* Princeton, N.J.: Princeton University Press, 1981.

Tyler, Ronnie C. "Fugitive Slaves in Mexico." *Journal of Negro History* 57 (1972): 1–12.

U.S. Bureau of the Census. *Historical Statistics of the United States: Colonial Times to 1957.* Washington, D.C.: 1960.

Usner, Daniel H., Jr. "American Indians in Colonial New Orleans." In *Powhatan's Mantle: Indians in the Colonial Southwest,* edited by Peter H. Wood, Gregory A. Wasselkov, and M. Thomas Hatley. Lincoln: University of Nebraska Press, 1989.

Van Deburg, William L. *The Slave Drivers: Black Agricultural Labor Supervisors in the Antebellum South.* Westport, Conn.: Greenwood, 1979.

Vassa, Gustavus. *The Life of Olaudah Equiano, or Gustavus Vassa, the African* [1794]. In *Great Slave Narratives,* edited by Arna Bontemps. Boston: Beacon, 1969.

Venture. *A Narrative of the Life and Adventures of Venture* [1798]. In *Five Black Lives,* introduced by Arna Bontemps. Middletown, Conn.: Wesleyan University Press, 1971.

Wakeman, Sarah Rosetta. *An Uncommon Soldier: The Civil War Letters of Sarah Rosetta Wakeman, alias Private Lyons Wakeman.* Edited by Lauren Cook Burgess. Pasadena, Md.: Minerva Center, 1994.

Walker, James W. St. G. *The Black Loyalists: The Search for a Promised Land in Nova Scotia and Sierra Leone, 1783–1870.* Toronto: University of Toronto Press, 1992 [1976].

Walker, Juliet E. K. "Pioneer Slave Entrepreneurship—Patterns, Processes, and Perspectives: The Case of the Slave Free Frank on the Kentucky Pennyroyal, 1795–1819." *Journal of Negro History* 68 (1983): 289–308.

Washington, Booker T. *Up from Slavery* [1901]. In *Three Negro Classics.* New York: Avon, 1965 [1901].

Wax, Donald D. "The Great Risque We Run": The Aftermath of Slave Rebellion at Stono, South Carolina, 1739–1745." *Journal of Negro History* 67 (1982): 136–47.

———. "Preferences for Slaves in Colonial America." *Journal of Negro History* 58 (1973): 371–401.

———. "Negro Resistance to the Early American Slave Trade." *Journal of Negro History* 51 (1966): 1–15.

Webber, Thomas L. *Deep Like the Rivers: Education in the Slave Quarter Community, 1831–1865.* New York: Norton, 1978.

Webre, Stephen. "The Problem of Indian Slavery in Spanish Louisiana, 1769–1803." *Louisiana History* 25 (1984): 117–35.

Weiner, Marli Frances. *Mistresses and Slaves: Plantation Women in South Carolina, 1830–80.* Urbana: University of Illinois Press, 1997.

———. "Plantation Mistress and Female Slaves: Gender, Race, and South Carolina Women, 1830–1880." Ph.D. diss., University of Rochester, 1985.

Weisenburger, Steven. *Modern Medea: A Family Story of Slavery and Child-Murder from the Old South.* New York: Hill and Wang, 1998.

Weld, Theodore Dwight. *American Slavery as It Is: The Testimony of a Thousand Witnesses.* New York, 1839.

Wells, Tom Henderson. "Charles Augustus Lafayette Lamar: Gentleman Slave Trader." *Georgia Historical Quarterly* 47 (1963).

Wesley, Charles H. *In Freedom's Footsteps: From the African Background to the Civil War.* Cornwells Heights, Pa.: Publishers Company, 1978.

Weston, G. M. *The Progress of Slavery in the United States.* Washington, D.C.: Negro Universities Press, 1969 [1858].

Wheeler, Jacob D. *A Practical Treatise on the Law of Slavery.* New York: Negro Universities Press, 1968 [1837].

Wheeler, Leslie, ed. *Loving Warriors: Selected Letters of Lucy Stone and Henry B. Blackwell, 1853 to 1893.* New York: Dial, 1981.

White, Deborah Gray. *Ar'n't I a Woman? Female Slaves in the Plantation South.* New York: W. W. Norton, 1985.

Whitten, David O. *Andrew Durnford: A Black Sugar Planter in Antebellum Louisiana.* Natchitoches, La.: Northwestern State University Press, 1981.

Williams, George W. *A History of the Negro Race in America from 1619 to 1880.* 2 vols. New York: Bergman, 1968 [1883].

———. *History of the Negro Troops in the War of the Rebellion.* New York: Harper, 1888.

Williamson, Hugh P. "Document: The State of Missouri against Celia, A Slave." *Midwest Journal* 8 (1956): 408–20.

Williamson, Joel. *New People: Miscegenation and Mulattoes in the United States.* New York: Free Press, 1980.

Wilson, Joseph T. *The Black Phalanx: African-American Soldiers in the War of Independence, the War of 1812, and the Civil War.* New York: Da Capo, 1994 [1887].

Winks, Robin W. *The Blacks in Canada: A History.* Montreal: McGill-Queen's University Press, 1971.

Winston, Sanford. "Indian Slavery in the Carolina Region." *Journal of Negro History* 19 (1934): 431–38.

Winther, Oscar Osburn, ed. *Theodore Upson: With Sherman to the Sea.* Baton Rouge: University of Louisiana Press, 1943.

Wish, Harvey. "American Slave Insurrections before 1861." *Journal of Negro History* 22 (1937): 299–320.

Wittenmyer, Annie Turner. *Under the Guns: A Woman's Reminiscences of the Civil War.* Boston: E. B. Stillings, 1895.

Wood, Betty. *The Origins of American Slavery.* New York: Hill and Wang, 1997.

Wood, Peter H. *Black Majority: Negroes in Colonial South Carolina from 1670 through the Stono Rebellion.* New York: Knopf, 1974.

Wood, Peter H., Gregory A. Wasselkov, and M. Thomas Hatley, eds. *Powhatan's Mantle: Indians in the Colonial Southwest.* Lincoln: University of Nebraska Press, 1989.

Woodward, C. Vann. *The Burden of Southern History.* Baton Rouge: Louisiana State University Press, 1960.

Yancy, Dorothy Cowser. "The Stuart Double Plow and Double Scraper: The Invention of a Slave." *Journal of Negro History* 69 (1984): 48–52.

Yellin, Jean Fagan. "The Text and Contexts of Harriet Jacobs' *Incidents in the Life of a Slave Girl: Written by Herself.*" In *The Slave's Narrative,* edited by Charles T. Davis and Henry Louis Gates, Jr. New York: Oxford University Press, 1985.

Yellin, Jean Fagan, and John C. Van Horne, eds. *The Abolitionist Sisterhood: Women's Political Culture in Antebellum America.* Ithaca, N.Y.: Cornell University Press, 1994.

Yetman, Norman R., ed. *Life under the "Peculiar Institution": Selections from the Slave Narrative Collection.* New York: Holt, Rinehart, and Winston, 1970.

# INDEX

Page locators in **boldface** indicate main entries.
Page locators in *italic* indicate illustrations. Page locators followed by *g* indicate glossary entries.

## D

## M

## Q



## R

## Y



## Z